THE ARDEN SHAKESPEARE

THIRD SERIES

General Editors: Richard Proudfoot, Ann Thompson,
David Scott Kastan and H.R. Woudhuysen

Associate General Editor for this volume:
George Walton Williams

KING
HENRY IV
PART 2

THE ARDEN SHAKESPEARE

ALL'S WELL THAT ENDS WELL	edited by G.K. Hunter*
ANTONY AND CLEOPATRA	edited by John Wilders
AS YOU LIKE IT	edited by Juliet Dusinberre
THE COMEDY OF ERRORS	edited by R.A. Foakes*
CORIOLANUS	edited by Peter Holland
CYMBELINE	edited by J.M. Nosworthy*
DOUBLE FALSEHOOD	edited by Brean Hammond
HAMLET	edited by Ann Thompson and Neil Taylor
JULIUS CAESAR	edited by David Daniell
KING HENRY IV PART 1	edited by David Scott Kastan
KING HENRY IV PART 2	edited by James C. Bulman
KING HENRY V	edited by T.W. Craik
KING HENRY VI PART 1	edited by Edward Burns
KING HENRY VI PART 2	edited by Ronald Knowles
KING HENRY VI PART 3	edited by John D. Cox and Eric Rasmussen
KING HENRY VIII	edited by Gordon McMullan
KING JOHN	edited by E.A.J. Honigmann*
KING LEAR	edited by R.A. Foakes
KING RICHARD II	edited by Charles Forker
KING RICHARD III	edited by James R. Siemon
LOVE'S LABOUR'S LOST	edited by H.R. Woudhuysen
MACBETH	edited by Sandra Clark and Pamela Mason
MEASURE FOR MEASURE	edited by J.W. Lever*
THE MERCHANT OF VENICE	edited by John Drakakis
THE MERRY WIVES OF WINDSOR	edited by Giorgio Melchiori
A MIDSUMMER NIGHT'S DREAM	edited by Harold F. Brooks*
MUCH ADO ABOUT NOTHING	edited by Claire McEachern
OTHELLO	edited by E.A.J. Honigmann
PERICLES	edited by Suzanne Gossett
SHAKESPEARE'S POEMS	edited by Katherine Duncan-Jones and H.R. Woudhuysen
ROMEO AND JULIET	edited by René Weis
SHAKESPEARE'S SONNETS	edited by Katherine Duncan-Jones
THE TAMING OF THE SHREW	edited by Barbara Hodgdon
THE TEMPEST, Revised	edited by Virginia Mason Vaughan and Alden T. Vaughan
TIMON OF ATHENS	edited by Anthony B. Dawson and Gretchen E. Minton
TITUS ANDRONICUS	edited by Jonathan Bate
TROILUS AND CRESSIDA, Revised	edited by David Bevington
TWELFTH NIGHT	edited by Keir Elam
THE TWO GENTLEMEN OF VERONA	edited by William C. Carroll
THE TWO NOBLE KINSMEN, Revised	edited by Lois Potter
THE WINTER'S TALE	edited by John Pitcher

* Second series

THE ARDEN SHAKESPEARE

KING HENRY IV PART 2

Edited by

JAMES C. BULMAN

THE ARDEN SHAKESPEARE
LONDON · NEW YORK · OXFORD · NEW DELHI · SYDNEY

THE ARDEN SHAKESPEARE
Bloomsbury Publishing Plc
50 Bedford Square, London, WC1B 3DP, UK
1385 Broadway, New York, NY 10018, USA
29 Earlsfort Terrace, Dublin 2, Ireland

BLOOMSBURY, THE ARDEN SHAKESPEARE and the Arden Shakespeare logo
are trademarks of Bloomsbury Publishing Plc

First published 2016
Reprinted 2017 (twice), 2018, 2019 (twice), 2020, 2021, 2022, 2024

The general editors of the Arden Shakespeare have been W.J. Craig and
R.H. Case (first series 1899–1944)
Una Ellis-Fermor, Harold F. Brooks, Harold Jenkins and Brian Morris
(second series 1946–82)

Present general editors (third series) Richard Proudfoot, Ann Thompson,
David Scott Kastan and H.R. Woudhuysen

James C. Bulman has asserted his right under the Copyright, Designs and
Patents Act, 1988, to be identified as author of this work.

Cover design by Newell and Sorrell
Cover image © David Hiscock

A catalogue record for this book is available from the British Library.

A catalog record for this book is available from the Library of Congress.

ISBN: HB: 978-1-9042-7136-9
PB: 978-1-9042-7137-6
ePDF: 978-1-4081-5183-9
ePub: 978-1-4081-5184-6

Series: The Arden Shakespeare Third Series

Typeset by Graphicraft Limited, Hong Kong
Printed and bound in Great Britain

To find out more about our authors and books visit www.bloomsbury.com
and sign up for our newsletters.

The Editor

James C. Bulman holds the Henry B. and Patricia Bush Tippie Chair in English at Allegheny College. A general editor of the *Shakespeare in Performance* series for Manchester University Press, he has written a stage history of *Merchant of Venice* (1991) and edited anthologies on *Shakespeare on Television* (1988), *Shakespeare, Theory, and Performance* (1996) and *Shakespeare Re-Dressed: Cross-Gender Casting in Contemporary Performance* (2007). His other books include *The Heroic Idiom of Shakespearean Tragedy* (1985), *Comedy from Shakespeare to Sheridan* (with A.R. Braunmuller, 1986) and the forthcoming *Oxford Handbook of Shakespeare and Performance*. He is a former President of the Shakespeare Association of America.

For Beth

CONTENTS

Contents

LIST OF ILLUSTRATIONS

GENERAL EDITORS' PREFACE

The earliest volume in the first Arden series, Edward Dowden's *Hamlet*, was published in 1899. Since then the Arden Shakespeare has been widely acknowledged as the pre-eminent Shakespeare edition, valued by scholars, students, actors and 'the great variety of readers' alike for its clearly presented and reliable texts, its full annotation and its richly informative introductions.

In the third Arden series we seek to maintain these well-established qualities and general characteristics, preserving our predecessors' commitment to presenting the play as it has been shaped in history. Each volume necessarily has its own particular emphasis which reflects the unique possibilities and problems posed by the work in question, and the series as a whole seeks to maintain the highest standards of scholarship, combined with attractive and accessible presentation.

Newly edited from the original documents, texts are presented in fully modernized form, with a textual apparatus that records all substantial divergences from those early printings. The notes and introductions focus on the conditions and possibilities of meaning that editors, critics and performers (on stage and screen) have discovered in the play. While building upon the rich history of scholarly activity that has long shaped our understanding of Shakespeare's works, this third series of the Arden Shakespeare is enlivened by a new generation's encounter with Shakespeare.

THE TEXT

On each page of the play itself, readers will find a passage of text supported by commentary and textual notes. Act and scene divisions (seldom present in the early editions and often the product of eighteenth-century or later scholarship) have been retained for ease of reference, but have been given less prominence than in previous series. Editorial indications of location of the action have been removed to the textual notes or commentary.

In the text itself, elided forms in the early texts are spelt out in full in verse lines wherever they indicate a usual late twentieth-century pronunciation that requires no special indication and wherever they occur in prose (except where they indicate non-standard pronunciation). In verse speeches, marks of elision are retained where they are necessary guides to the scansion and pronunciation of the line. Final -ed in past tense and participial forms of verbs is always printed as -ed, without accent, never as -'d, but wherever the required pronunciation diverges from modern usage a note in the commentary draws attention to the fact. Where the final -ed should be given syllabic value contrary to modern usage, e.g.

Doth Silvia know that I am banished?

(*TGV* 3.1.214)

the note will take the form

214 **banished** banishèd

Conventional lineation of divided verse lines shared by two or more speakers has been reconsidered and sometimes rearranged. Except for the familiar *Exit* and *Exeunt*, Latin forms in stage directions and speech prefixes have been translated into English and the original Latin forms recorded in the textual notes.

COMMENTARY AND TEXTUAL NOTES

Notes in the commentary, for which a major source will be the *Oxford English Dictionary*, offer glossarial and other explication of verbal difficulties; they may also include discussion of points of interpretation and, in relevant cases, substantial extracts from Shakespeare's source material. Editors will not usually offer glossarial notes for words adequately defined in the latest edition of *The Concise Oxford Dictionary* or *Merriam-Webster's Collegiate Dictionary*, but in cases of doubt they will include notes. Attention, however, will be drawn to places where more than one likely interpretation can be proposed and to significant verbal and syntactic complexity. Notes preceded by *discuss editorial emendations or variant readings.

Headnotes to acts or scenes discuss, where appropriate, questions of scene location, the play's treatment of source materials, and major difficulties of staging. The list of roles (so headed to emphasize the play's status as a text for performance) is also considered in the commentary notes. These may include comment on plausible patterns of casting with the resources of an Elizabethan or Jacobean acting company and also on any variation in the description of roles in their speech prefixes in the early editions.

The textual notes are designed to let readers know when the edited text diverges from the early edition(s) or manuscript sources on which it is based. Wherever this happens the note will record the rejected reading of the early edition(s) or manuscript, in original spelling, and the source of the reading adopted in this edition. Other forms from the early edition(s) or manuscript recorded in these notes will include some spellings of particular interest or significance and original forms of translated stage directions. Where two or more early editions are involved, for instance with *Othello*, the notes also record all important differences between them. The textual notes take a form that has been in use since the nineteenth century. This comprises, first: line reference, reading adopted in the text and closing square bracket; then: abbreviated reference, in italic, to the earliest edition to adopt the accepted reading, italic semicolon and noteworthy alternative reading(s), each with abbreviated italic reference to its source.

Conventions used in these textual notes include the following. The solidus / is used, in notes quoting verse or discussing verse lining, to indicate line endings. Distinctive spellings of the base text follow the square bracket without indication of source and are enclosed in italic brackets. Names enclosed in italic brackets indicate originators of conjectural emendations when these did not originate in an edition of the text, or when the named edition records a conjecture not accepted into its text. Stage directions (SDs) are referred to by the number of the line within or immediately after which they are placed. Line numbers with a decimal point relate to centred entry SDs not falling within a verse line and to SDs more than one line long, with the number after the point indicating the line within the SD: e.g. 78.4 refers to the fourth line of the SD following line 78. Lines of SDs at the start of a scene are numbered 0.1, 0.2, etc. Where only a line number precedes a square bracket, e.g. 128], the note relates to the whole line; where SD is added to the number, it relates to the whole of a SD within or immediately following the line. Speech prefixes (SPs) follow similar conventions, 203 SP] referring to the speaker's name for line 203. Where a SP reference takes the form, e.g. 38+ SP, it relates to all subsequent speeches assigned to that speaker in the scene in question.

Where, as with *King Henry V*, one of the early editions is a so-called 'bad quarto' (that is, a text either heavily adapted, or reconstructed from memory, or both), the divergences from the present edition are too great to be recorded in full in the notes. In these cases, with the exception of *Hamlet*, which prints an edited text of the Quarto of 1603, the editions will include a reduced photographic facsimile of the 'bad quarto' in an appendix.

INTRODUCTION

Both the introduction and the commentary are designed to present the plays as texts for performance, and make appropriate reference to stage, film and television versions, as well as introducing the reader to the range of critical approaches to the plays. They discuss the history of the reception of the texts within the theatre and scholarship and beyond, investigating the interdependency of the literary text and the surrounding 'cultural text' both at the time of the original production of Shakespeare's works and during their long and rich afterlife.

PREFACE

Like Falstaff, I have heard the chimes at midnight. Anyone who has edited *Henry IV, Part Two* has undoubtedly heard them repeatedly, for the play's textual problems are complicated enough to keep an editor up all night. Yet my editorial tribulations have been lightened by the generosity of many colleagues and friends whose mention here cannot begin to relieve my indebtedness to them. I want first to remember two mentors who will hear the chimes no more, but whose thoughtful guidance taught me to take nothing for granted in preparing a text for publication, and whose exemplary standards served as a model of intellectual rigour: James Nosworthy, my tutor at the University of Wales; and Eugene Waith, my doctoral supervisor at Yale University.

More recently, I have benefited from the wisdom of Arden editors whose advice was neither shallow nor silent. Richard Proudfoot, who asked me to undertake this project longer ago than I wish to remember, wryly warned me that I might find editing the play a bit difficult. I've often marvelled at his understatement. George Walton Williams, a punctilious textual scholar with particular expertise in the problems of *Part Two*, let no glib assumption go unchallenged and thus saved me from making countless errors. In fairness, this play should have been his to edit. And David Kastan, my general editor, proved to be a most discerning reader and stylist whose keen eye, encouragement and unfailing good sense kept my editing on track long after his patience should have run out. All three of these editors share a passion for Shakespeare's histories that I have found inspiring.

In my first year of editing the play, the late Charles Forker, who prepared the magisterial edition of *Richard II* for Arden 3, gave me expert advice on how to approach collation; and the work of previous editors of *Part Two* – especially

A.R. Humphreys, Giorgio Melchiori and René Weis – influenced my own work on the play at every turn, setting out the terms of scholarly debate with incisive clarity. My notes in the commentary cannot begin to acknowledge my indebtedness to them.

My gratitude to the Arden publisher, Margaret Bartley, is boundless. Queen of tact and diplomacy, she clothed threats in a velvet glove, extended a helping hand – or a deadline – when I had no right to expect that she would, and eventually gave her assent to a volume that had grown to a Falstaffian girth. I consider myself extraordinarily fortunate to have had her as my publisher. And Jane Armstrong's guidance through the final phases of readying the manuscript for publication has proved invaluable. When told that she was the best copy editor in Shakespeare publishing today, I had no idea how meticulous her editing would be, how keen her eye for detail or how discerning her judgement. It has been a pleasure to work with her; and if errors remain, they are all mine, not hers.

One benefit of taking so long to complete this edition is that I have had the time to discover complex patterns in the history of scholarship about the play, its texts and its performance history. Procrastination, therefore (or so I try to persuade myself), has deepened my account of the play in the critical introduction and the appendices. Some of my discoveries have already appeared in print, and I am grateful to the following editors for having invited me to contribute essays to their volumes: Mick Hattaway (*The Cambridge Companion to Shakespeare's History Plays*), Peter Holland (*Shakespeare Survey 63*), Randall Martin and Katherine Scheil (*Shakespeare / Adaptation / Modern Drama*) and Barbara Mujica (*Shakespeare and the Spanish Comedia*). I have also presented work in progress at a number of conferences. I am grateful to the late Reg Foakes for allowing me to audition material at his seminar on editing at the International Shakespeare Congress; to Ann Thompson for organizing a Shakespeare Association of

America (SAA) seminar for which I wrote a paper on the play's textual transmission; to Rob Ormsby and Don Weingust for asking me to present my work on conflated texts of the two *Henry IV* plays at a meeting of the American Society for Theater Research; to Suzanne Gossett and Jeff Masten for their astute criticism of a paper I wrote for Timothy Billings's SAA seminar on glossing; to the members of my own SAA seminar on *2H4*, in particular Jonathan Baldo and Will Sharpe, whose insightful work is cited in the Introduction; and to the members of the Columbia University Shakespeare Seminar for inviting me to share a history of the (mis)fortunes of Falstaff in performance with them.

Over the years I have had the privilege to do research in libraries and archives whose staffs have made my work both pleasurable and efficient. At the Folger Shakespeare Library, which has become a second home to me, I owe a great debt to Georgianna Ziegler, Head of Reference, and to Betsy Walsh and her staff in the Reading Room, whose courtesy and expertise are unparalleled: Rosalind Larry, LuEllen DeHaven, Harold Batie, Camille Seerattan and Alan Katz. I am grateful as well to the staff at the Shakespeare Centre Library in Stratford-upon-Avon, where I cut my teeth on promptbooks and performance materials forty years ago – particularly to Marian Pringle, Sylvia Morris, and the late Mary White. At the Shakespeare Institute of the University of Birmingham, where I spent a semester as a Senior Research Fellow, my work was facilitated by the many kindnesses of Director Kate McLuskie, Librarian Karin Brown and Administrative Assistants Juliet Creese and Rebecca White. I am grateful, too, to the staffs of the British Library and the New York Public Library for the Performing Arts; and, for their help in securing photos for this edition, I thank Helen Hargest at the Shakespeare Birthplace Trust, Gavin Clark and Georgia Butler at the National Theatre Archives, Ruth Frendo and Cordelia Morrison at Shakespeare's Globe, and Emily Hockley at Bloomsbury Publishing.

My work on the play has been aided by numerous scholars and friends who read portions of the manuscript, offered unpublished material of their own, or provided other types of assistance. I am deeply indebted to Juliet Dusinberre for reading the critical introduction and offering the kind of trenchant critique that only a friend will; to John Jowett and Paul Werstine for combing through my work on 'The Text' (Appendix 1) and strengthening it with their scholarly prowess; and to Jim Siemon for offering helpful advice on my analysis of the Gloucestershire scenes. I am grateful, too, to Judith Anderson, Barbara Mowat and Gail Paster for sharing material with me that proved most timely for my research; to James Gibson for sending me a draft of his essay on Oldcastle before its publication and to Susan Cerasano for putting me in touch with him; to Ginger and Alden Vaughan for lending me research materials from their Arden edition of *The Tempest*; to David Lindley, Andrew Hope and Bob King for additions to the commentary; and to Ayanna Thompson and Harry Lennix for arranging a director's cut of the then still unreleased film *H4* to be sent to me. For years of stimulating conversation and insights which have improved the edition in less tangible ways, I thank my friends and fellow Shakespeareans Bill Carroll, Sam Crowl, Bob Miola, Jim Ogden, Carol Rutter, and Herb and Judy Weil. With a generosity that cannot be repaid, Miriam Gilbert shared with me her notes on the play, her encyclopedic knowledge of performance and her house in Stratford for a glorious semester in 2009; and Barbara Hodgdon, in her pioneering work on the play's performance history, taught me to think about the fortunes of *Part Two* in an entirely new way.

Other debts, equally profound but of a different sort, have been accruing for just as long. To Pat and Henry Tippie, who endowed the research chair I have held for nearly two decades, I owe an incalculable debt of gratitude. Their largesse has enabled me to spend extended periods of time at research libraries and to attend performances of the play by theatre companies in North America and abroad. Allegheny College Presidents Richard Cook and James Mullen, and Provost Linda DeMeritt, have given me unstinting support, granting me sabbatic leaves to further my research; and no request has been too trivial for the wonderful staff at the Allegheny College library, especially Linda Bills, Don Vrabel, Cynthia Burton, Jane Westenfeld, Rita Manning and Linda Ernst. I have profited from stimulating conversations with my colleagues in the Medieval and Renaissance Studies program – Amelia Carr, Jennifer Hellwarth and Glenn Holland – and from the encouragement of other colleagues, Diane D'Amico, Ben Slote and the late Fred Frank.

My oldest colleagues and treasured friends Lloyd Michaels and Bruce Smith have, over many a lingering lunch, endured hours of lamentation about my editorial travails. Still have they borne it with a patient shrug, and with genial prodding have admonished me to get on with the task at hand. Kristin Goss and Grant Williams have offered me congenial company, good food and drink and generous moral support during my many visits to the Folger Library. Sally and Doug Caraganis years ago surprised me with an original playbill for Macready's 1821 coronation production of *King Henry the Fourth – Part the Second*, which ever since has hung over my office desk as a reminder of how much work yet remained to be done. And what can I say of Beth Watkins? My debt to her is infinite. Long accustomed to hearing the chimes at midnight with me, she has borne so much and been fubbed off so often that it is a shame to be thought on. In a bold ploy to put my passion for this project in perspective, she alternated between assuring me that the world wasn't waiting with bated breath for another edition of *Part Two* and threatening me with divorce if I didn't finish the damned thing. I dedicate this volume to her, with love.

James C. Bulman

INTRODUCTION

THE PROBLEM OF BEING SECOND-BORN

Like a younger sibling, *Henry IV, Part Two* has long lived in the shadow of the more popular *Part One*. Often viewed as an uninspired sequel, it lacks the earlier play's exuberantly festive spirit and political urgency: its mixing of kings and clowns seems less purposeful; its plot, more digressive; its conclusion, less satisfying. And while it may have brilliant moments on which to stake a claim to greatness, these often fall outside the parameters of the play's historical narrative and can be dismissed as irrelevant to the story of Prince Harry's reformation.[1] Audiences expecting a sequel that builds upon the royal victory at Shrewsbury are invariably disappointed, for *Part Two* instead duplicates the narrative arc of the earlier play for little apparent reason: another northern rebellion threatens King Henry's tenuous hold on power, and the prodigal Prince of Wales again has to prove himself worthy of his father's trust, as if he has never redeemed his indignities on Percy's head in *Part One*. Furthermore, the play is larded with comic scenes featuring Falstaff and his followers which compete for attention with the play's chronicle history, the two elements cobbled together seemingly without regard to narrative coherence or artful plotting. Such apparent disregard of conventional dramaturgy has led generations of critics to dismiss *Part Two* as a pale

---

1   I call the Prince 'Harry' rather than the more commonly used 'Hal' because he is referred to as Harry 21 times in the play but only four times as Hal. When discussing the Prince in *Part One*, I revert to calling him Hal because that is the familiar name by which Falstaff refers to him 35 times: with the exception of Poins's use of 'Hal' twice, the name occurs 'only on Falstaff's lips' (A. Barton, 110). Falstaff calls the Prince by the more formal 'Harry' only when impersonating the King at the tavern (*1H4* 2.4.388–404). In *Part One*, 'Harry' is a name shared by the Prince and his rival Hotspur; in *Part Two*, it is used for the King and for Hotspur, but only three times each. The name, in effect, belongs to the Prince alone in *Part Two*.

imitation of a glittering original, 'a diminished shadow of its predecessor . . . that has always presented itself as *1 Henry IV* gone sour' (Booth, 270), a 'rambling and episodic' sequel whose concern with 'political events [has] run down' (Worsley & Wilson, 72), a 'ramshackle grab-bag of a piece' (David, 'History', 137), or an artless 'patchwork' of a play (Smidt, 109) in which nothing of note happens until the King dies, the Prince is crowned and the misleader of his youth is banished.[1]

Yet these complaints ignore the peculiar merits of *Part Two* as Shakespeare's most radical experiment in dramatizing English history. Though an integral part of the tetralogy on whose sweep of events it depends to be fully understood, *Part Two* nevertheless breaks the mould of previous history plays by including relatively little political history – events foregrounding power struggles among the nobility in Henry IV's reign – and offering in its place a panorama of an England unrecorded by chroniclers. Unlike sequels that simply strive to repeat the successful formula of an original, *Part Two* has a darker tone and more ambitious aims than *Part One*. Its originality resides in the casual way it casts a wide net over England, gathering in groups of people whose unwritten histories rival in importance, and at times surpass, the chronicle history which concludes with Prince Harry's succession. The fact that Shakespeare chose to dramatize comparatively little material about Henry IV's reign following the royal victory at Shrewsbury in *Part One* liberated him to improvise, to explore and to envision

---

1   Stephen Booth's indictment of the play as a 'still-born [and] exhausted point-for-point echo of Part 1' is especially searing. The play's preoccupation with frustrated expectations, he argues, becomes the governing principle of the play's aesthetic as well; but Shakespeare's 'perverse rhetorical purpose . . . whereby one treats of ennui by engendering it in one's audience' is 'misconceived' and has never succeeded 'in making his audience like it'; for 'one cannot reasonably ask artists and audiences to submit to a disappointing play on the grounds that it succeeds in being disappointing'. Booth thus favours 'abandoning *2 Henry IV* to print and bardolatrous festivals' (270).

history with a creative licence that his previous history plays, more deeply bound to their chronicle sources, did not.

Part Two conceives of the final years of King Henry's reign in terms of contemporary social history, with marginalized characters providing a gloss not only on events dramatized in the political plot but also, anachronistically, on English society in the 1590s. Drawing on oral traditions and popular nostalgia as a counterweight to the authority of chronicle narratives, the play creates a world rich in the quotidian life of Elizabethan subcultures and populated by characters more authentically realized than many of those drawn from chronicles – tavern hostess and whore, swaggering ensign and impecunious knight, menials and hangers-on, country justices and rag-tag recruits – who collectively paint a picture of contemporary English society more inclusive than one finds in any other Shakespeare history play. To this end, far from being a liability, an episodic structure serves the play well by taking socially and geographically diverse and unrelated characters into its generous embrace. My goal in this introduction is, in part, to unfetter the idiosyncratic brilliance of *Part Two* from the assumption that the play simply and unsuccessfully imitates *Part One*, and to recognize it as an imaginatively autonomous work which, more than any other of Shakespeare's chronicle plays, broadens one's sense of what history can be.

A two-part play?

It is not customary to regard *Part Two* as an independent play. For reasons I shall discuss later, a critical movement that reached its pinnacle in the mid-twentieth century, intent on linking Shakespeare's English histories together as a cycle, relegated *Part Two* to a status subordinate not only to *Part One* but to the other plays in the second tetralogy as well. The peculiar merits of *Part Two* as an anomalous history of diverse social groups were subjugated to the demands of an overarching royal narrative.

The nature of the relationship between the two parts of *Henry IV* has always vexed scholars. There has been no agreement about whether the two parts were originally planned as one play and then divided during composition, or as two integrated plays about one king's reign; or whether instead *Part One* was written as an independent play and *Part Two* conceived later as 'an unpremeditated sequel'.[1] Critics have often noted that episodes in *Part Two* echo those in *Part One* to an unprecedented degree, with a similar alternation of court and tavern scenes, the distribution of high seriousness and low comedy within them so nearly identical that structurally, according to M.A. Shaaber, *Part Two* 'is almost a carbon copy of the first play'.[2] G.K. Hunter likewise regards the plays as a 'diptych . . . in which the repetition of shape and design focuses attention on what is common in the two parts' (237).[3] Rather than follow the proportions of *Part One*, however, Shakespeare relegates most of the royal history in *Part Two* to the final two acts – the King makes a brief first appearance in Act 3 and is not seen again until his deathbed scene in Act 4 – and grants a far larger portion of the play to Falstaff's comic interactions with those low-life characters who frequent the tavern and, later, with the country justices and recruits in Gloucestershire. The number of lines spoken by the major characters in each play reveals this shift in emphasis. In the 1598 Quarto of *Part One*, Falstaff speaks 542 of the play's 2,857 lines; Hotspur, 538; the

---

1 C.F. Tucker Brooke speculates that the play may have been 'an unpremeditated addition caused by the enormous effectiveness of the byfigure of Falstaff' (333); and Shaaber borrows Brooke's term to interpret the play as 'an unpremeditated sequel' ('Unity', 223).

2 Shaaber painstakingly diagrams the number of scenes in the two plays, finding in the disposition of those involving chronicle history and those involving Falstaff evidence that Shakespeare simply copied the successful formula of the first play in the second ('Unity', 221). To a degree, however, Shaaber ignores differences in the structures of the two plays to make his point.

3 Sherman H. Hawkins elaborates on Hunter's argument in 'The structural problem revisited'.

Prince, 514; and the King, 338 – a parity which demonstrates an artful balance between scenes of comedy and chronicle history. In the 1600 Quarto (second issue) of *Part Two*, however, Falstaff speaks 525 of the play's 2,861 lines; the Prince, only 293; and the King, 291 – a disparity which indicates the prominence of Falstaff relative to the King and Prince (King, 85–6, 188–93).

Falstaff's scenes in *Part Two*, moreover, unlike his scenes in *Part One* which thematically echo the preoccupations of its royal history, often bear a tenuous or even oppositional relationship to the political plot. Indeed, the chicanery and dishonesty that characterize Falstaff's behaviour serve as a moral gloss on the play's chronicle history, which dramatizes how the rebels, whose common cause is subverted by individual self-interest, are ultimately tricked by Westmorland and Prince John into a false amnesty – a substitution of machiavellian policy for the more honourable chivalric combat that concludes *Part One* at Shrewsbury, and a fitting climax to a play which throughout echoes the structure and situations of *Part One* only to re-view them with an eye towards human frailties, self-deception and cynical *Realpolitik*. If *Part Two* replicates the structure of *Part One* in a way that calls attention to their parallels, therefore, it does so with subversive intent; for at every turn, *Part Two* thwarts the expectations raised by such parallels. It offers policy in place of honour, substitutes disease and death for the celebration of living, and calls into question the official version of history to which *Part One* more resolutely adheres. *Part Two* is, as P.H. Davison argues, as much the 'obverse' of *Part One* as its sequel (9).

Sequels do not demand consistency of character or continuity of plot to be effective; and indeed, *Part Two* quickly establishes its own distinct dramatic parameters. A new rebellion only tangential to that in *Part One* now threatens the King and must be suppressed; Prince Harry, whose chivalric honours won at Shrewsbury go unmentioned, again consorts with his tavern companions and once more must stage a convincing reformation; and old evidence of the Prince's flouting of royal authority – the legend that he once boxed the Lord Chief Justice on the ear – is resurrected to create a new source of conflict. If the Lord Chief Justice is introduced as a voice of authority and judicial integrity to compensate for the reduced role played by the ailing King, other new characters are introduced to create a comedy more acerbic and less genial than that in *Part One*. The tart-tongued whore Doll Tearsheet, the hair-triggered Ancient Pistol, the aptly named Justices Shallow and Silence, the amorally pragmatic Davy and the yeomen and labourers who are recruited to serve in Falstaff's charge of foot – delightfully plain-spoken characters with names such as Mouldy, Bullcalf and Feeble – all populate a world entirely independent of the court.

Furthermore, characters from *Part One* are reintroduced in different circumstances. The Hostess, for example, who was simply a tavern-keeper and claimed to be 'an honest man's wife' (3.3.119) in the earlier play, is now a brothel-keeper and a widow who seeks to marry Falstaff in order to gentle her condition. She is a much more fully-fleshed character in *Part Two*, her idiosyncratic use of malapropisms and bawdy innuendo cunningly developed from hints in *Part One*. Bardolph, too, more obviously a man-servant to Falstaff – 'I bought him in Paul's' (1.2.53) where masterless men went to seek employment – than he was in *Part One*, is given a new and larger role to play as Falstaff's corrupt corporal. He also is said to be the man on whose behalf the Prince once struck the Lord Chief Justice (56–7), suggesting that his behaviour has been 'countenanced' by the Prince's royal favour.[1] Above all, Sir John Falstaff is reconceived as older, more hobbled

---

1 On the convergence of service and friendship as a form of paternalistic protection, 'a legacy of feudal obligations' which helps to explain Bardolph's role in the play, see Weil, 81–4.

6

by disease and more cynical than his festive counterpart in the earlier play. He now operates as a free agent, no longer in the company of the Prince: until the final scene, they appear together just once, and then, only briefly. Rather than living by thievery and by the good graces of the Prince, he uses his reputation for valour falsely won at Shrewsbury to cut a fashionable figure in the world, and he tries to borrow a thousand pounds – unsuccessfully from the Lord Chief Justice, successfully from Justice Shallow – to finance his indulgences. Thus the core relationship in *Part One* between the Prince and Falstaff is moved to the margins in *Part Two*, and Falstaff is allowed to dominate much of the play with grand social and political aspirations which require a calculated exploitation of others. While differences such as these would be inexplicable if *Parts One* and *Two* had been conceived together as a single history, unpremeditated sequels afford authors the freedom to refashion characters in this way, for consistency must inevitably give way to good storytelling.

Most critically, Shakespeare had to decide what to do with the Prince after his victory over Hotspur at Shrewsbury. The answer, apparently, was to pretend that his reformation as a chivalric hero had never happened. For most who come to *Part Two* after *Part One*, Harry appears unaccountably to have relapsed. Although he has just returned victorious from a military campaign, nothing is made of the honours he accrued in battle, and the promises he made to his father are seemingly forgotten. Instead, he again consorts with his lowborn friends; and although he declares that he feels 'much to blame / So idly to profane the precious time' (2.4.366–7), when the King inquires after him on his deathbed, he is told that the Prince is dining in London 'With Poins and other his continual followers' (4.3.53). This report prompts the King to lament anew his son's 'headstrong riot' (62) and to predict that when he inherits the throne, England will suffer 'th'unguided days / And rotten times' he has long feared (59–60).

Shakespeare thus resuscitates Harry's reputation as a scape-grace from *Part One* and resets the hurdle over which the prodigal son must leap once again to convince his father of his fidelity and the world of his worth.

Of course, it is possible to regard this duplication of Harry's reformation as a 'symbolic arrangement' in which the Prince learns chivalric honour in *Part One* and civil justice in *Part Two*[1] – an argument which reinforces the belief that the two plays were planned together as one; or as 'parallel and complementary phases of a process which is to be understood emblematically rather than chronologically' (Smidt, 109) – a scheme which satisfies the neatness of formalist criticism more easily than it reconciles inconsistencies between the plays. Alternatively, one might agree with Geoffrey Bullough that 'a pattern of repetition in political matters was essential to Shakespeare's historical and moral purpose', and that because 'Shakespeare was not as yet interested in stages of growth in character', he could conform to chronicle accounts 'that the Prince's behaviour was inconsistent and declined after Shrewsbury' (Bullough, 4.159); or agree with Harold Jenkins that it is in the nature of legendary heroes such as the future Henry V to trace the same narrative arc in every story told about them, for folklore always requires such heroes to 'be at the same point twice' – and thus the *Henry IV* plays dramatize 'not two princely reformations but two versions of a single reformation' (Jenkins, 20–1). But the fact that Harry's apparent

---

1   Wilson, *First Part*, x–xii. He had introduced this idea three years earlier in *Fortunes*, 64; E.M.W. Tillyard expanded it in his study of how Morality traditions influenced the development of the Prince (264–304); and Humphreys (*1H4*, xxviii), embraced the idea that 'the moral events' of the two plays, 'Hal's redemption in chivalry and justice', run thematically 'in parallel'. Irving Ribner viewed the Prince's twin reformations similarly as 'a ritual process to be taken more sym- bolically than literally', each one 'necessary to the creation of the perfect king' (171). Wilson's 'symbolic arrangement' persisted even as late as 1982, when Hawkins explored how the two *Henry IV* plays portray the 'moral testing' of the Prince in 'valor' and 'justice' (296–8).

lapse has invited such diverse explanations suggests that none of them is fully convincing. Disputing that the Prince's reformation in the two plays is a 'single process', Paul Yachnin adopts the perspective of an audience member viewing *Part Two* for the first time: 'neither the King nor Worcester seems to think that Hal's delinquency in the second play is anything other than a continuous and uninterrupted state of lawlessness', he observes; 'they do not seem to think Hal has relapsed after having been converted because neither seems able to remember that Hal has already redeemed himself in the first play' (Yachnin, 119). The Prince's conversion, in other words, is a self-contained narrative in *Part Two*; and with an amnesia facilitated by their being caught up in the immediacy of a compelling dramatic action, audiences can accept the logic of his reformation without having to recall his similar trajectory in *Part One*.

Part Two, then, is arguably a sequel that need not rely on *Part One* to be understood. As early as 1746, John Upton insisted that 'these plays are independent each of the other. . . . To call [them], *first and second parts*, is as injurious to the author-character of Shakespeare as it would be to Sophocles, to call his two plays on Oedipus, *first and second parts of King Oedipus*'.[1] Certainly the earliest editions of *Part One* made no mention of an anticipated sequel: they billed the play simply as *The History of Henrie the Fourth*, a title which it retained up to the publication of the Folio in 1623, when it was called *The First Part*, and which would be used in reversion in the 1639 Quarto.[2] Leah Marcus argues that the 'unifying'

1 John Upton, *Critical Observations on Shakespeare*, 2nd edn, 1748, rpt. in Vickers, *Shakespeare*, 3.294–5.

2 See Kastan, *1H4*, 18. Kastan records an early reference to the play as 'the firste part' in the Stationers' Register for 25 June 1603, but this reference, he suggests, was intended to distinguish the play from *Part Two*, which had also been published in quarto, and confirms that the two plays 'were understood to be independent and self-sufficient'.

terms *Part One* and *Part Two* used in the Folio, just as with the three parts of *Henry VI*, mark the beginning of an attempt to transform 'the playtexts from records of performance to a form of literature in its own right' (Marcus, 26). In other words, the impulse to view the two plays as one was literary in origin but had little bearing on how they might have been viewed by early audiences. As an instructive counter-example, David Kastan cites the way in which the two parts of *Tamburlaine* were marketed and published in the 1590 Quarto as one work 'divided into Two Tragicall Discourses' (*1H4*, 21–2). Quarto publications of the two *Henry IV* plays, on the contrary, remained entirely discrete enterprises, suggesting that they were not seen as one work divided into two parts. There is no evidence that they were ever printed together prior to publication of the Folio.

Nonetheless, *Part Two* bears so strong a resemblance to *Part One* that it could never have been written without it, leading Samuel Johnson in his 1765 edition to object,

> Mr *Upton* thinks these two plays improperly called the *first* and *second parts* of *Henry* the *fourth* . . . [yet they] will appear to every reader, who shall peruse them without ambition of critical discoveries, to be so connected that the second is merely a sequel to the first; to be two only because they are too long to be one.[1]

Nine years later, Edward Capell ventured further that 'both these plays appear to have been plan'd at the same time, and with great judgement'.[2] Granted, the historical events chronicled in the two plays are sequential, and some of the episodes and characters in *Part Two* are undoubtedly enriched by knowledge of those in *Part One*. Any justification for the new King's

---

1   Johnson, 4.235; rpt. in Vickers, *Shakespeare*, 5.121.
2   Capell, *Notes*, vol. 1, cited in Humphreys, Ard[2], xxii.

rejection of Falstaff, for example, looks back most searchingly to their relationship in *Part One*, in which the Prince's close bond with Falstaff formed the emotional core of the play. Without a knowledge of that relationship, audiences at *Part Two* find Falstaff's rejection less explicably motivated and less poignant. Furthermore, why would *Part One* have included an otherwise extraneous scene of the Archbishop's attempt to reinforce his 'confederacy' late in the play (4.4) had Shakespeare not been planning a sequel featuring continued rebellion in the kingdom? And why would the King, in his final speech (5.5.35–8), determine to send Prince John and Westmorland to York to thwart that rebellion?

In 1943, John Dover Wilson, citing Dr Johnson, speculated that the two plays must have been planned together with 'unity and continuity' in mind, since *Part Two*, clearly 'a continuation of the same play . . . is itself unintelligible without Part I'.[1] Just a year later, E.M.W. Tillyard, advancing a providential reading of English history which he termed the Tudor Myth, contended in a highly influential study of Shakespeare's English histories as a cycle of plays that the two *Henry IV* plays are so intertwined, and their significance so dependent on events dramatized in the two plays that bookend them (*Richard II* and *Henry V*), that they cannot be properly understood unless read together as one history (Tillyard, 234–44, 264).[2] The work of Dover Wilson and Tillyard has been enormously influential on subsequent criticism, so much so that since the mid-twentieth century, *Part Two* has almost never been written about or performed without *Part One*.

---

1 Wilson, *Fortunes*, 4. Just two years later, in 1945, Wilson altered his view to allow that Shakespeare may originally have planned a single play, then revised his plan when 'Falstaff, grown "out of all compass", needed a double drama to contain him': 'Origins', 15.

2 The anticipation of Tillyard's work by the German critics August Schlegel and Hermann Ulrici is discussed on pp. 32–33.

A theory of composition advanced by Harold Jenkins in 1955 comes close to effecting a reconciliation between the opposing views of Upton and Johnson. He proposes that Shakespeare set out to write one *Henry IV* play and was quite far along in drafting it – into Act 3 of what is now *Part One* – when, realizing that he had too much material for one play, he decided to divide the material into two plays, allowing the Battle of Shrewsbury to conclude the first and thereby saving the consequences of Prince Harry's reformation – his deathbed reconciliation with his father, his coronation as Henry V and the repudiation of his tavern companions – for the second. Such a division would allow Shakespeare to increase the scope of the comic scenes in both plays and to foreground the exploits of Falstaff, who had grown 'out of all compass' in his early draft (*1H4* 3.3.20; cf. Wilson, 'Origins', 15). The merit of Jenkins's theory is that it helps to explain inconsistencies between the two plays that otherwise remain inexplicable. It explains, for instance, why there is so little chronicle history dramatized in *Part Two*, where, if Shakespeare had planned two plays from the outset, he surely would not have envisioned a history play in which so little of political significance happens and in which more than half the lines are taken up with unhistorical and episodic comedy.

It also helps to account for the anomalous setting of Justice Shallow's farm in Gloucestershire. Falstaff would presumably recruit soldiers along the Great North Road, a coaching route between London and York that today is followed by the A1, if he were marching to meet Prince John in Yorkshire; and a reference to Stamford fair at 3.2.38 suggests that Shakespeare might once have had Lincolnshire in mind as the location of Shallow's farm. But repeated references to people and places in the West Midlands – to Will Squele, a Cotsole (i.e. Cotswold) man (3.2.21); Thomas Wart (137); Hinckley Fair (5.1.23); and two litigants with Gloucestershire roots, William Visor of Woncote and Clement Perkes a'th' hill

(5.1.36–7) – confirm that Falstaff's request to return to London from York via Gloucestershire at 4.2.79–80, however incongruous, is not an error: he has indeed marched through Gloucestershire to recruit soldiers for wars in the north. If scenes at Shallow's farm had originally been intended for inclusion in the play now known as *Part One*, however, this apparent inconsistency becomes suddenly explicable, for Falstaff's stopping to recruit a charge of foot in the West Midlands on his march to Shrewsbury would have made perfect sense. Furthermore, three of the men he enlists in *Part Two* – Shadow, Wart, Feeble – are humorous incarnations of the 'scarecrows' and 'slaves as ragged as Lazarus' whom Falstaff admits to recruiting in *Part One* after he has allowed the more able, affluent, but cowardly 'yeomen's sons' and 'contracted bachelors' to bribe their way out of military service (4.2.13–37). In other words, as Kristian Smidt suggests (111–12), by transferring Gloucestershire scenes from the original draft of a single *Henry IV* play to a second part less driven by chronicle sources, Shakespeare gained the space to develop Falstaff's recruitment of soldiers and exploitation of Justice Shallow as an independent plot, even if he failed to adjust the location of Shallow's farm northward; and he replaced the recruiting scene he had written to precede the Battle of Shrewsbury with a much shorter soliloquy in which Falstaff cynically confesses to having 'misused the King's press damnably' (*Part One* 4.2.12–13).

In his 1966 Arden edition of the play, A.R. Humphreys counters Jenkins's theory by arguing that, given the parallels between Prince Hal and Hotspur upon which *Part One* is structured, Shakespeare must have planned Hal's victory over Hotspur at Shrewsbury as the climax of the play (xxiv). Humphreys argues less persuasively that Shakespeare intended from the outset that the Prince's coronation and his rejection of Falstaff should conclude a second play: in other words, that the two parts were planned together as distinct but co-ordinated plays. It is possible to reconcile Jenkins's and Humphreys's positions, however, by examining the possibility, as Samuel Johnson was the first to do,[1] that while the first *Henry IV* play was always planned as the play that came to be called *The First Part* in the Folio, the second play Shakespeare originally envisioned would have begun with the King's death, the Prince's coronation and the rejection of Falstaff (at that point called Oldcastle), and then proceeded to dramatize events in the reign of Henry V, as is done in Shakespeare's chief dramatic source, a hybrid-history called *The Famous Victories of Henry the Fifth* (see pp. 128–33).

Entered in the Stationers' Register in 1594 and printed by Thomas Creede in 1598 but performed by the Queen's Men as much as ten years earlier, *Famous Victories*, even in the corrupted state in which it has survived, reveals a sure sense of how to animate the scattered materials of the wild Prince legend 'through the medium of comic drama' (Bevington, 20) which proved enormously influential on Shakespeare's *Henry IV* plays. The first half of the play depicts the Prince as a wastrel who, with his boon companions Oldcastle, Ned and Tom, takes part in a robbery, visits his father with possibly parricidal intent, but eventually – and unexpectedly – repents. The Prince's repentance is followed by a brief episode in which he takes the crown from his sleeping father and, pleading his innocence in doing so, earns the dying King's blessing. Though this story of reformation is uncomplicated by any history of rebellion against the King (Corbin & Sedge, 22), it clearly provided the comic core for *Part One* and modelled tensions in the royal family for *Part Two*.

---

1 In his endnote to *Part Two*, Johnson allows that 'As this play was not, to our know-ledge, divided into acts by the authour, I could be content to conclude it with the death of *Henry* the Fourth. . . . These scenes which now make up the fifth act of *Henry the Fourth* might then be the first of *Henry the Fifth*; but the truth is that they do unite very commodiously to either play' (4.255; rpt. in Vickers, *Shakespeare*, 5.123).

The second half of *Famous Victories* dramatizes the reign of Henry V from his accession to the throne, rejection of his erstwhile companions and humorous response to the provocative gift of tennis balls from the 'Lord Prince Dolphin' (all in one scene), through his victory at Agincourt, to a peace accord with the French and the promise of Katherine's hand in marriage. The play thus falls quite neatly into two discrete sections, one depicting the Prince's madcap youth and reformation, the other his victory over the French; and given the apparently truncated nature of the text, it is conceivable that *Famous Victories* was itself originally performed as a two-part play, with the first part corresponding roughly to Shakespeare's *Part One* with some overlap with *Part Two*; the second, in compressed form, to the final act and one-half of *Part Two* and to *Henry V*.[1] Its most significant influence on Shakespeare seems to have been structural – on his decision to write an indecorous hybrid-history unlike the histories he had written before, mixing scenes of chronicle material with low comedy, and on his conception of a bipartite play in which to dramatize the evolution of Harry from prodigal prince to legendary king.

My own view is that the original *Henry IV* play was always planned to end with the Battle of Shrewsbury, and that its sequel – perhaps to be called *Henry V* – was to have begun with events now dramatized in the last act and one-half of *Part Two* and continued through the reign of Henry V;[2] but that the second play Shakespeare wrote took shape only when he realized that he had too much comic material to include in the first play, excised some of it, and then, when *Henry IV* proved hugely successful in performance, decided to write

---

1 Wilson, 'Origins', 2–16, conjectures that the text of *Famous Victories* represents 'a much abridged and debased version of two plays belonging to the Queen's company', which performed them in the 1580s as a vehicle for Richard Tarlton.

2 My view is anticipated by, and indebted to, Shaaber ('Unity', 221) and Kastan (*1H4*, 21).

a sequel which would foreground the exploits of Falstaff and his followers, recuperate some of the excised material and conclude with the death of the King, the Prince's accession to the throne and his rejection of Falstaff, leaving the reign of Henry V for a third play. Only at this point, I believe, did he mine Holinshed for another rebellion from which to fashion a political plot for *Part Two* and insert in *Part One* the anticipatory references to the Prelate's Rebellion mentioned earlier (see pp. 99–100). This theory explains what is otherwise nearly inexplicable: why, if *Henry IV* was originally conceived as a two-part play, Shakespeare saved so little chronicle history for the second part, deprived it of the narrative coherence of the first part, opted for a more discursive structure and echoed so many of the comic scenes and situations from *Part One* in a much darker and more cynical vein. It would be odd indeed for Shakespeare to have planned the two parts to be so different from one another in tone if he intended them to tell one story.

Moreover, an unforeseen decision to write an opportunistic sequel focusing on Falstaff – a decision that caused him to abandon, or at least defer, the play about Henry V he had initially contemplated – would explain why, suddenly unencumbered by the prescribed history of the Prince's reformation, Shakespeare chose to dramatize a minor rebellion in Holinshed whose quashing would illustrate an unsavoury political calculation alien to the chivalric ethos on display at Shrewsbury; why he found himself free to explore a wider spectrum of society than any chronicle source examined and to flesh out the play with characters and situations of his own devising; in sum, why he was at liberty to construct a truly original history play which foregrounds those marginalized groups that comprised the vast majority of Elizabethan society and whose actions could comically counterpoint events depicted in the play's more sober scenes of chronicle history.

THE PLAY IN PERFORMANCE

Part Two *as an autonomous play*

The history of *Part Two* in performance is bound up with the debate over its origins: whether one perceives *Henry IV* as two distinct plays, as one ten-act play in two parts or as two chapters in a larger cycle of plays. Can *Part Two* survive in the theatre as an autonomous work with its own special character, or must it be played as part of a longer historical narrative, a cog in the wheel of the Plantagenet family saga? There is no evidence that the two parts were performed consecutively – that is, on successive days – during Shakespeare's lifetime (Crane, 291–5; Yachnin, 163–79); and the one piece of documented evidence that they were performed in proximity to one another, to celebrate the marriage of Princess Elizabeth to the Elector Palatine during the festival season at Whitehall in 1612/13, refers to them not as *Henry IV* plays but by the names of characters who had no doubt proved most popular in each one, *The Hotspur* and *Sir Iohn Falstaffe*,[1] suggesting that the focus had been not so much on the plays' historical continuity as on those flamboyant figures who had captured theatregoers' imaginations. Tellingly, the title-page of the Quarto edition of *Part Two* (1600) provides evidence of the popularity of the play's 'humourists' by advertising 'the humours of sir Iohn Fal-*staffe, and swaggering* Pistoll'.

While many in Shakespeare's audience might already have seen *Part One* and thus been able to bring to *Part Two* the knowledge of a larger historical frame – a knowledge which of

---

1 Corroborative evidence that this *Falstaffe* play refers to *Part Two* has been found on a fragment of paper in records of the King's Office of the Revels, inserted in a MS of the *History of Richard III*, which lists plays being considered for court performances in 1619/20 and on which is written 'nd [presumably '2nd'] part of Falstaff not plaid theis 7. yeres' – that is, since 1612/13. This is the last record of a performance of *Part Two* before the closing of the theatres by Parliament in 1642. See Marcham, 33, and Melchiori, 37.

course can deepen one's appreciation of both plays – *Part Two* in the late sixteenth and early seventeenth centuries probably held the stage as an autonomous play. For although *Part Two* is essentially parasitic and, like any sequel, would not have been written without an original to serve as a template, it is not required that the two be played together for the sequel to be understood. Even a superficial knowledge of the history of Henry IV's reign – his usurpation of Richard's throne, his defeat of the northern rebels and his fraught relationship with the Prince of Wales – would have been sufficient to draw an audience into the action of *Part Two*; and while much has been made of the play's beginning *in medias res*, with contradictory reports being brought to Northumberland about what has happened to Hotspur and the rebel forces at the Battle of Shrewsbury, Rumour's abbreviated history of events would have sufficed to inform audiences what had occurred before the play, if such were necessary. Thus the opening scene would have proved no more confusing than the opening scene of *Richard II*, in which Mowbray's complicity in the murder of Richard's uncle Thomas of Woodstock, if not known beforehand, could be figured out by accusations levelled against him by Bolingbroke; or the opening scene of *Part One*, in which the causes of the conflict between Henry, his northern supporters and those who remained loyal to Richard may be gleaned from the dialogue between the King and Westmorland. The opening of *Part Two* should have proved no less penetrable: those spectators who had seen *Part One* would have recognized the ironies of the false reports brought to Northumberland; those who had not would have been in the same situation as Northumberland himself and learned with him to distinguish true from false report.

All this suggests that *Part Two* could have been acted effectively without being paired with *Part One*, just as *Part One* often was performed on its own. There is no evidence that the two were ever performed together in a public theatre, on the

same or on consecutive days, until the eighteenth century.[1]
Indeed, to the degree that *Part Two* held the stage at all until
the twentieth century, it did so for the most part independently
of *Part One*. When it was first revived after the Restoration, by
Thomas Betterton in 1704, Falstaff had already assumed a life
beyond the confines of his role in the histories. His evolution
had begun early, with Shakespeare's writing of *The Merry
Wives of Windsor* to capitalize on Falstaff's popularity by
depicting him as an Elizabethan roué. During the closure of
the theatres in the mid-seventeenth century, a short droll called
The Bouncing Knight, excerpted from scenes in *Part One*,
kept Falstaff before the public eye (Potter, 287, and Kastan,
1H4, 80–1); and when theatres reopened after the Restoration,
both *Part One* and *Merry Wives* proved immediately popular.
Falstaff was becoming a legend in his own right. Betterton's
success in exploiting the humorous potential of the fat knight
in *Part One* (he had earlier played Hotspur) no doubt inspired
him to increase his profits by offering another star vehicle –
Part Two – featuring 'the Humours of Sir *John Falstaffe*, and
Justice *Shallow*' (*The Sequel*, title-page).

Betterton altered *The Sequel of Henry the Fourth* in various
ways, most notably by making Falstaff the only character of
any consequence in the first three of its five acts. All references
to Hotspur and to the rebellion in the north so central to *Part
One* were expunged: the Induction and the opening scene in
which Northumberland receives word of his son's death were
cut entirely, as was the scene in which Northumberland is urged
by his wife and daughter-in-law to flee to Scotland. With these

1 Charles Beecher Hogan (1.144–94 and 2.238–77) records all performances, by
theatre, of *Part One* and *Part Two* during the eighteenth century in London. Though
Part One was frequently performed on its own and was clearly more popular than
Part Two, theatres would regularly stage the two plays during the same season; but
performances of them were often separated by weeks or months, so that audiences
could see the two in proximity only occasionally. The same trend continued
throughout the nineteenth century: see Norwood, 348–415.

scenes removed, connections between *Part Two* and the climactic Battle of Shrewsbury in *Part One* were severed. The political action of Betterton's first three acts involved only an abbreviated scene to introduce the Prelate's Rebellion in Act 1 and a conflation of the Gaultree scenes to conclude it in Act 3. Furthermore, the scene that introduces the King (3.1) was omitted, as it had been in the first issue of the Quarto, and instead the insomniac King's soliloquy concluding 'Uneasy lies the head that wears a crown' (3.1.4–31) was transposed to the scene of his death. The result of such alterations was to create, for the first three acts, a prose comedy in which Falstaff holds the stage for all but a minor and quickly quelled political rebellion; and notably, his great tavern scene (2.4) and his recruiting scene at Justice Shallow's farm (3.2) were juxtaposed, as they had been in the first issue of the Quarto, yielding 658 lines of Falstaffian comedy uninterrupted by any chronicle history.

Betterton's compression into one act (Act 4) of the climactic scenes at court – the King's illness and death and the new King's confrontation of the Lord Chief Justice – may have been prompted by the same neo-classical impulse to avoid unnecessary changes of locale that caused Dryden to reduce the number of scenes in his adaptation of *Troilus and Cressida*. Arguably, though, Betterton was more concerned with the decorum of genre and intended to segregate the 'tragick part', as Samuel Johnson called it,[1] from the rest of the play as a discrete dramatic unit, tonally distinct from the prose comedy that had preceded it. The practice of segregating the chronicle plot from the comic scenes continued throughout the eighteenth and into the nineteenth century, as John Bell's acting edition of 1773 and John Philip Kemble's of 1804 attest.[2] Indeed, even the most celebrated production of the play as royal history –

---

1 End-note to *Part Two* in *Plays*, 4.235; rpt. in Vickers, *Shakespeare*, 5.124.
2 See Odell, 1.41–2, 54.

mounted by William Macready in 1821 to commemorate the accession of George IV – which embellished Harry's coronation with four scenes of ceremonial spectacle and music added at the end, drew on a text that rearranged the play in the same way as Betterton, allowing Falstaff to dominate the stage until the scene of the King's death.[1]

While Betterton's alterations permitted *Part Two* to be performed as an autonomous Falstaff play, it is worth noting that he enhanced its autonomy not by revising the text, as so many Restoration and eighteenth-century producers did with other Shakespeare plays, but by less intrusive cuts, transpositions and scenic rearrangement. The independence of *Part Two* as a Falstaff play was always already implicit in Shakespeare's text, and this version was revived repeatedly – without *Part One* – until 1744, with James Quin replacing Betterton as Falstaff for thirty years, joined by Colley Cibber as a celebrated Justice Shallow in 1720 and later by Cibber's son Theophilus as the Ancient Pistol.[2]

It was not necessary, however, for the text to be so altered in order to stand on its own as a performable play. As early as 1736, Shakespeare's original text was revived, and it played in rivalry with Betterton's *Sequel* for nearly a decade in

---

1 The text for this production, which starred Macready as the King, Charles Kemble as the Prince and John Fawcett as Falstaff, was basically the same as that used by J.P. Kemble for his 1804 production, published by Mrs Inchbald in 1808. It has been published in facsimile as *Henry IV, Part 2: Coronation Production 1821*. Opening at Covent Garden on 25 June and running for twenty-seven consecutive performances, this was the most successful production of the play in the nineteenth century (Norwood, 362). See also Odell's description of the staging, 1.166–9.

2 Of Cibber's performance in 1738–9, Thomas Davies wrote, 'His manner was so perfectly simple, his looks so vacant . . . that it will be impossible for any surviving spectator not to smile at the remembrance of it. . . . Cibber's transition from asking the price of bullocks, to trite, but grave, reflections on mortality, was so natural, and attended with such an unmeaning roll of his small pig's-eyes . . . that I question if any actor was ever superior in the conception or expression of such solemn insignificancy' (1.306–7, rpt. in Wells, 19–20).

1 Playbill for Macready's *King Henry the Fourth – Part the Second*, featuring an elaborate coronation scene, performed at the Theatre Royal, Covent Garden, 1821

roughly equal numbers of performances. By the 1750s, only Shakespeare's text of *Part Two* was regularly performed, and in 1758 David Garrick managed by the brilliance of his playing the King to restore something of the balance between Falstaffian comedy and chronicle history that had been forsaken during the previous half-century. Garrick's version was acted sixty times up to 1784, the last recorded performance of the play in London in the eighteenth century (Hogan, 2.276–7); and its popularity demonstrates that *Part Two* as Shakespeare had written it proved stageworthy and accessible to audiences nearly two

2   Stephen Kemble (1758–1822) as Falstaff. Drawn by G. Harlowe; engraved by J. Rogers; published by G. Virtue, 1825

3   Samuel Phelps (1804–78) as Henry IV: 'How many thousand of my poorest subjects / Are at this hour asleep!' [3.1.4–5]; photograph *c.* 1864

hundred years after its first performance, without having to be revised, rearranged or, above all, performed only as the second part of a two-part play. The same alternation of versions of *Part Two* – as a Falstaff play that benefits from cuts and transpositions, or as a history play that can stand without alteration – was played out in England and America for the next century and a half.[1]

1   On the sparse stage history of *Part Two* in America up to the early twentieth century, with 'at least five revivals' of note, see Winter, 373–6. The most notable of these was mounted in 1841 by James Hackett, a popular American Falstaff who, in a reversal of the usual flow of high culture, played the role in England as well.

Although the history plays lost some of their allure for prudish Victorian audiences who took offence at the mixing of regal kings and vulgar clowns, Falstaff continued to be a role coveted by actors ambitious to achieve the summit of Shakespearean comedy: Stephen Kemble, John Fawcett and an American who won audiences on both sides of the Atlantic, James Henry Hackett. Samuel Phelps made a name for himself as a great Falstaff in 1846 and held the stage for nearly thirty years. In 1864, to celebrate the tercentenary of Shakespeare's birth, Drury Lane staged both parts of *Henry IV*, with Phelps playing Falstaff in *Part One* and doubling the King and Shallow in *Part Two* – the first attempt to offer the play as a two-part epic to commemorate Shakespeare as a national hero (Odell, 1.299–300). But if Phelps's intention was to combine the plays as one integrated royal history, he missed the mark. Switching actors in key roles of course impeded a sense of continuity. Furthermore, *Part One* opened on Easter Monday, but *Part Two* was not staged until the autumn in a version cut and rearranged much like Bell's, with the chronicle material heavily curtailed in order to foreground the comedy of Falstaff and his companions.

The two parts of *Henry IV* were thus, as they had been for more than two centuries, performed independently; and so they would be, with few exceptions, well into the twentieth century. A survey of productions by Frank Benson's Stratford-upon-Avon company, for example, reveals that *Part Two* was performed frequently – in eleven of thirty-three seasons between 1894 and 1923 – but that only once, in 1905, was *Part One* performed during the same season. Clearly, the success of *Part Two* on the stage had never been dependent on *Part One*, which was not performed at all in Stratford between 1909 and 1923; and, acted in versions that were for the most part faithful to Shakespeare's text, *Part Two* had established itself by 1932 – the year in which the two parts were performed together to mark the opening of the Shakespeare Memorial Theatre – as a history play that could flourish on the Stratford stage quite independent of its by then less-often-performed first part.

The rise of the two-part play

'The superbly generous girth of Shakespeare's *Henry IV* plays', wrote Dominic Cavendish in his review of the productions at Shakespeare's Globe in 2010, gives them the breadth of 'a warts-and-all national epic about the England he loved, ranging from nobility to riff-raff, from battlefields to brothels, from the city to the countryside, and from high politics to low humour' (*Telegraph*, 15 July 2010); and they have indeed been embraced by generations of English as a celebration of their manifold identities. Both parts of *Henry IV* are enriched when they are performed together. Staging them as one play in ten acts benefits the chronicle history by bringing the story of the northern rebellion to a conclusion, by fleshing out the decline of the King from a vital participant in the war against the rebels to an anguished, dying monarch, and by tracing more fully the arc of Harry's growth to kingship. But the real beneficiary is Falstaff; for the complex and often emotionally ambivalent relationship between him and Hal in *Part One* helps to justify the new King's banishment of him in *Part Two* which otherwise, in a play that permits them only one brief meeting before it, can seem insufficiently motivated.

When the two plays are performed together, *Henry IV* almost inevitably becomes the story of Falstaff. As Peter Orford writes, Falstaff is the character whose role bookends these two plays: the plot traces his rise and fall, and therefore, structurally, 'the hero of this two-part story [is] the fat knight' (93). The movement to stage *Henry IV* as one ten-act play in two parts began early in the twentieth century, and by all accounts these productions foregrounded the fortunes of Falstaff, not the maturation of the prodigal Prince. When the Old Vic staged the plays together in 1920, for example, the allocation of parts by the two directors, Russell Thorndike and Charles Warburton, revealed their conviction that Falstaff, not Harry, was the pivotal role. Warburton played Hal in *Part One* but the Lord Chief Justice in *Part Two*, with the actor who played Hotspur being promoted to Hal, thus robbing the Prince of any credible continuity for audiences who saw the plays in successive weeks. Thorndike, however, played Falstaff in both parts and thus provided the thread to stitch the two parts together: the ten-act play was about him, not about the Prince.[1] The same was true when William Bridges-Adams staged the plays in Stratford in 1932. Conceived as a grand national epic for that occasion, *Henry IV* was in fact received, as it had been in earlier two-part productions, as the history of Falstaff, with the King and Prince playing lesser roles.[2] Despite the novelty of presenting the plays in sequence as a continuous historical narrative, therefore, early two-part productions such as these attested to the abiding importance of the actor playing Falstaff to their overall success.

In what was widely praised as the best production of the plays in the first half of the twentieth century, John Burrell's staging of *Henry IV* for the Old Vic in 1945 showcased two performances which have become the stuff of theatrical legend: that of Ralph Richardson, who played Falstaff with a gentlemanly dignity (*Observer*, 30 September 1945) and 'a greatness of spirit that transcended the mere hulk of flesh' (Williamson, 158); and that of Laurence Olivier, who played both a stuttering Hotspur and a humorously fastidious and

---

1 Orford, 90–1, discusses the Old Vic directors' apparent ambivalence about staging the two parts of *Henry IV* as 'offering one unified vision' while disregarding continuity of casting. Other productions of the two parts together include Barry Jackson's for the Birmingham Rep in 1921 and Robert Atkins's for the Old Vic in 1923, both of which more successfully offered them as one unified play (Orford, 92–4).

2 Witness, for example, the *Sheffield Telegraph* review of 25 April 1932 emphasizing Falstaff's emergence as a fully-fleshed 'conscious' character, and the *Evening News* review of the same date describing the scene in which Falstaff is 'cruelly spurned by the newly-crowned king' as unforgettable.

lecherous Justice Shallow.[1] The comic genius of Olivier's portrayal of Shallow suggests how centrally the Gloucestershire scenes figured as nostalgic representations of a merry Elizabethan past which, in the aftermath of the Second World War, reminded audiences of all that was worth preserving about an England that had nearly fallen to an enemy whose bombs had destroyed too much of its cultural heritage. In contrast, the maturation of Harry seemed to matter little. Nicholas Hannen's King Henry was so 'well-meaning, kind, sincere, and decent' a father that the Prince had 'nothing to rebel against' (McMillin, 28); and scant critical attention was paid to Michael Warre, an actor whose Prince Harry lacked psychological depth and who, 'prompted to play the Prince in such society as [Richardson and Olivier], inevitably remains in the junior school. How otherwise?' (*Observer*, 30 September 1945). This *Part Two* was primarily, as it had been for centuries, a play about Falstaff, with the King, the Prince and Plantagenet history reduced to subordinate roles.

In these and countless subsequent productions of *Henry IV* as a two-part play, in both Britain and North America, the audience's attention has continued to be drawn to those idiosyncratic characters who give the greatest theatrical pleasure: Hotspur, Pistol, Shallow and, above all, Falstaff. As recently as 2005, by which time performing the two parts together had become *de rigueur*, Nicholas Hytner, whose staging for the National Theatre drew acclaim for Michael Gambon's Falstaff, confirmed that 'it all started off with Michael. Though I suspect that every production of *Henry IV* should start there, because if you don't know who's going to

1   The key to Olivier's performance of Shallow as a 'crapulous, paltering scarecrow of a man', according to Kenneth Tynan's memorable account, 'is old-maidishness': he 'has quick, commiserating eyes and the kind of delight in dispensing food and drink that one associates with a favourite aunt'; indeed, one might mistake him for 'a crone-like pantomime dame . . . were it not for the beady delectation that steals into his eyes at the mention of sex' (48–53).

4   Laurence Olivier as Justice Shallow in a production directed by John Burrell for the Old Vic Theatre Company, at the New Theatre London, 1945

play Falstaff there's no point in doing them' (in Merlin, 2). The impulse to stage the two plays as one with Falstaff as the centre of attention has inevitably led producers on occasion to conflate the texts with sufficient abridgement to allow them to be performed in only three hours. As I detail in Appendix 2, such conflations have a long history, beginning with a text prepared for private performance by Sir Edward Dering, *c.* 1622; but they have become more common in the past half-century, first with Orson Welles's enormously influential 1965 film then called *Falstaff*,[1] in which the text was shaped to foreground the exploits and repeated rejections of Welles's hugely fat and

---

1   The title was changed to *Chimes at Midnight* for its US release. For the screenplay, Welles adapted conflations he had staged in the US (1938) and Ireland (1960). See pp. 482–95.

5   Orson Welles as Falstaff in his film *Falstaff* (American title, *Chimes at Midnight*) made in Spain in 1965

dangerously compelling Falstaff, and later in such productions as the popular *Henry IV* at Lincoln Center in 2003, which, by combining Falstaff scenes and curtailing the plays' chronicle material, provided a vehicle for the comic talents of Kevin Kline. Such conflations have achieved what many assume Shakespeare initially set out to do: create a single play about the reign of Henry IV, erasing any awkward duplications and inconsistencies inherent in the two-part play.

The play as part of a cycle

In contrast to the centuries-long tradition of performing *Part Two* as a Falstaff play, either on its own or paired with *Part One*, a critical movement in the mid-twentieth century intent on linking Shakespeare's English histories together as a cycle relegated *Part Two* to a status subordinate not only to *Part One*, but to the other plays in the second tetralogy as well. Despite the fact that these four plays, unlike those in the first tetralogy, are formally and stylistically different from one another and probably were not intended for serial performance (Grene, 28–9), the insistence on prioritizing their chronicle history resulted in the subjugation of the peculiar merits of *Part Two* as an anomalous history of marginalized social groups to the demands of an overarching royal narrative.

In 1944, as the war in Europe was entering its final phase and Burrell was preparing his *Henry IV* for the Old Vic, a scholarly work was published that would profoundly influence subsequent productions of the two *Henry IV* plays. In *Shakespeare's History Plays*, Tillyard advanced the idea that the eight plays spanning the period from Richard II's reign to the end of the Wars of the Roses had been written as a cycle to endorse the providential reading of English history he termed the Tudor Myth, and that in the *Henry IV* plays, Shakespeare emphasized the Prince's evolution from prodigal son to chivalric hero as the culmination of England's moral progress: Harry became the great hero king towards whose redemptive figure everything in the earlier plays pointed.[1] In a book published the following year, Una Ellis-Fermor likewise found in the cycle of eight plays an insistent exploration of 'the statesman-king, the leader and the public man' (36) which would culminate in 'the complete figure' of Henry V (45). Such a view required that the two parts of *Henry IV* be treated 'as a single play' (Tillyard, 264); thus *Part Two* must always have been premeditated, and indeed none of the plays could be viewed as an independent work written without the goals of the whole cycle in mind. This argument, which

---

1   Tillyard, 269. He interprets the Prince as 'a man of large powers, Olympian loftiness, and high sophistication' who throughout the two plays embodies 'the abstract Renaissance conception of the perfect ruler' defined by Castiglione, Lyly and Elyot (275–80). Three years later, Lily Bess Campbell, in another ground-breaking book, viewed the plays somewhat differently, though still as a cycle, by reading them in the light of contemporary historical writing and Tudor political propaganda.

rapidly gained acceptance as dogma, would have important consequences for the staging of the *Henry IV* plays and would forever alter the fortunes of *Part Two*.

The belief that Shakespeare had written his histories as a cycle was not new to German scholars who had regarded them as such more than a century before Tillyard. In his 1808 lectures, August Schlegel had interpreted them as 'an historical poem in the dramatic form, of which the separate plays constitute the rhapsodies'; in its totality, a 'mirror of kings' which, he urges, 'should be the manual of young princes' (419–20); and in 1839, the philosopher Hermann Ulrici confirmed Schlegel's romantic idea that the eight plays together constitute a national epic, discussing them as treatises on the reign of each of the five kings and therefore drawing no distinction between the two parts of *Henry IV* or the three parts of *Henry VI* (368–78, 385–97, 403–16).

In 1864, to celebrate the tercentenary of Shakespeare's birth and dramatize the concept of national identity in advance of Germany's unification in 1871, Franz Dingelstedt put Ulrici's design into practice by staging the eight history plays as a unified cycle at the Weimar Theatre. Dingelstedt's cycle, whose historical arc drew heavily on the classical five-act structure, privileged those plays that he saw as exposition (*Richard II*), climax (*Henry V*) and resolution (*Richard III*). The plays in the middle – the two parts of *Henry IV* and three parts of *Henry VI* – provided the connective tissue to hold together those plays that focused on individual monarchs, and thus in themselves were deemed less important.[1] Tillyard, in contrast, regarded the

---

1   Robert K. Sarlos (117–31) discusses Dingelstedt as a pioneer in the staging of Shakespeare's histories as a unified cycle and in cutting or revising significant portions of plays, especially the three parts of *Henry VI*, to ensure narrative coherence; Grene (31–5) explores Dingelstedt's indebtedness to 'the ever greater canonization of Shakespeare' as the German national poet. Decades later, in Stratford-upon-Avon, Frank Benson was credited with originating the history cycle when he staged six history plays together in what was dubbed 'The Week of Kings'

education of the Prince as fundamental to the meaning of the cycle; for him, the two parts of *Henry IV*, integrally planned and masterful in their cohesion, foregrounded an element indispensable to the four plays he referred to as the second tetralogy: Harry's *Bildungsroman*.

The decision by Anthony Quayle and Michael Redgrave to stage a history cycle at Stratford in 1951, in celebration of the Festival of Britain, marked a shift in the fortunes of the *Henry IV* plays. Inspired both by Tillyard's view of the history 'sequence' as 'an organic whole' (236) and by Dover Wilson's argument that the two parts of *Henry IV* dramatize one of history's great conversion stories in which 'the technical centre of the play is not the fat knight but the lean prince' (*Fortunes*, 17), this cycle placed the royal *Bildungsroman* front and centre. *Part Two* invariably diminishes in singularity when it is performed as a middle play dependent on those that surround it for context. With emphasis falling on the royal family rather than on the fortunes of Falstaff, what matters most in *Part Two* occurs in the last two acts. According to T.C. Worsley, critic for the *New Statesman*, 'the great scenes of Henry IV's death gain immeasurably from our having traced the relationship of father and son from its beginning', and 'Falstaff is brought into a proper proportion'.[1] In this design, Falstaff represents a crucial obstacle to the Prince's moral reformation, 'typifying Vanity in every sense of the word' (Wilson, *Fortunes*, 17), and thus his rejection can be regarded as 'not a "priggish" repudiation . . . but

in 1901; but unlike Dingelstedt's, his cycle was not a coherent dramatization of Plantagenet history. Rather, his selection of plays was opportunistic, drawing on productions he had mounted in previous years, each focused on an individual king. *Henry IV, Part Two* was chosen because of the accession of the Prince as Henry V, but *Part One* was not, Benson instead opting to revive *King John*. Grene (35–8) and Orford (83–8) provide illuminating accounts of Benson's cycle and its revival in 1905 and 1906. See also Sally Beauman on Benson's resistance to Charles Flower's suggestion that he present a cycle of history plays (32–3).

1   This and the following quotations from newspaper reviews of the 1951 productions are cited by Worsley in Worsley & Wilson, 48–76.

6   Mistress Quickly (Rosalind Atkinson), Falstaff (Anthony Quayle) and Doll
    Tearsheet (Heather Stannard) in a production directed by Michael Redgrave
    at the Shakespeare Memorial Theatre, Stratford-upon-Avon, 1951

a necessary step, indeed the sacrifice which we see Royalty
exacting relentlessly from those worthy to assume it' (Philip
Hope-Wallace, *Time and Tide*). *Part Two*, therefore, began to
be performed regularly with *Part One* as a history play whose
comic digressions and carnivalesque subversions served only
to justify the political imperatives of what had come to be
known as the second tetralogy.

Quayle himself played a Falstaff who, while larger than life
in the tradition of his predecessors, was less benign and more
flagrantly licentious: his was not a comic performance, but that
of a straight man playing comedy – a thin man in a fat suit – his
bonhomie, like his girth, seeming more prosthetic than real
(Shaughnessy, 65–7). Made up like a 'gargoyle' (Cecil Wilson,
Daily Mail), he looked 'rather grotesque than laughable . . . and

his smile when it appears is a painted smile' (Ivor Brown, *The Times*). To the critic of the *Manchester Guardian*, Falstaff seemed 'supremely conscious of his own depravity'; 'beneath the padded belly, the swollen legs and the slightly too clownish pink and white paint on the face' hides 'a pathological Fat Knight' who does not 'believe in his own bluster'; and the *Times* critic concurred that Falstaff was 'never for a moment sentimentalised. . . . He is superbly funny but openly contemptible.'

Quayle's flamboyant style of acting stood in sharp contrast to the more naturalistic acting of newcomer Richard Burton, whose performance as the Prince was most notable for its watchful calculation and intense introspection: 'deep, reserved, assured but essentially complex', this Harry 'knows where, in the long run, he is going' (Worsley & Wilson, 51). He 'maintains [his] detachment with a hard smiling grace' (Ivor Brown, *The Times*), and 'never seems to laugh *with* Falstaff, but always at him'. Almost as an allegory for the direction the play would take in the next half-century, this Prince was torn between two fathers – the King of 'surging command' and dignity (David, *Shakespeare*, 199), played by Harry Andrews, who 'carried the epic story, fiery into grey, with unbroken power' (*Manchester Guardian*), and the roguish knight whose company Harry could enjoy but whom he knew from the outset he would one day banish. Burton thus delivered his 'I know you all' soliloquy (*Part One* 1.2.185–207) not as a rationalization for his past behaviour but with a strong 'sense of destiny' (Ivor Brown, *Times*); his emotional distance from Falstaff allowed him to act the play-extempore with such seriousness of purpose that his 'I do; I will' (2.4.468) registered as a threat or even a decision already made; and the rejection scene, when it came, was played dispassionately, not sentimentally, as it had been for more than two centuries. Young Burton thus 'out-manoeuvred . . . the established actor' who played Falstaff: next to Quayle, whose performance was 'visibly and conspicuously a product of theatrical artifice', Burton's Prince seemed 'authentic and

7 *King Henry IV [part 2] Act IV sc. IV* [4.3]. Painted by Henry E. Corbould; engraved by John Parker Davis (1832–1910); published by London Printing and Publishing, mid-nineteenth century

real' (Bragg, 71–2) – a clash of acting styles in which Burton's pointed to the future as surely has Quayle's harked back to the past (Shaughnessy, 66).

The conception of the plays as a unified cycle whose 'true hero' is the Prince has had consequences for the way *Henry IV* has been staged ever since; for if the plays are viewed as a coherent history culminating in the legendary reign of Henry V, then inevitably one may read the end in the beginning, and retrospectively, the outcome of *Part Two* informs the tone and colouration of *Part One*. One's gaze is trained from the first on the use to which the Prince puts his tavern days as he grows in

8 Prince Henry (Richard Burton) addressing the crown over his sleeping
father (Harry Andrews) in a production directed by Michael Redgrave at
the Shakespeare Memorial Theatre, Stratford-upon-Avon, 1951

political acumen, and one's delight in the comic triumph of
Falstaff in *Part One* is tempered by a knowledge that the older,
more corrupt knight in *Part Two* will be banished from the
court. Productions of the history cycle for the past sixty years
have typically foregrounded the story of the Prince of Wales as
the king in waiting, and political and domestic conflicts have
often trumped comedy.

Indeed, directors have used history cycles to address issues
of contemporary relevance and to serve overtly ideological
agendas. French director Roger Planchon, for instance, adapting
the *Henry IV* plays for the opening of his Théâtre de la Cité in

a working-class suburb of Lyon in 1957, employed alienation techniques practised by Bertolt Brecht's Berliner Ensemble to expose 'the cruel realities of the French colonial war in Algeria, then entering its final phase' (*Guardian*, 20 May 2009). The plays were pared back to their 'bare social bones', according to Kenneth Tynan, 'and each scene was prefaced by a caption, projected onto a screen, that summed up the import of what we were about to see' (*New York Magazine*, 8 January 1959).[1] The old king was played as a 'political adventurer', the Prince as 'utterly ruthless' and Falstaff as a cynical opportunist who embodied 'the hard materialism of the new age' (Daoust). Yet Planchon's didactic Marxism led him to subject individual characterization 'to the larger image of declining feudalism', and he interpolated mimed scenes 'suggesting the sufferings of the common man or the harshness of the ruling classes' (Jean Jacquot, 'International notes: France', *SS 13*, 1960). His 'political intention was readily acceptable to the industrial audience of Villeurbanne' (Robert Speaight, 73); and the productions' success led to their revival in Paris in 1959.

Five years later, in 1963–4, Peter Hall and John Barton of the recently formed Royal Shakespeare Company (RSC) also embraced the Berliner Ensemble's epic style to advance the idea that the plays of both tetralogies dramatize a 'Grand Mechanism' of history in which 'the drama played out between [kings] is always the same' (Kott, 9) and individual will is always overborne by the inexorable crush of political events.[2]

---

1 Tynan's and the critical citations that follow are quoted in an account of the production in Leiter, 186–7.

2 Underlying Hall and Barton's concept of Shakespeare's entire cycle of histories – they had staged the first tetralogy in 1963 – was Jan Kott's *Shakespeare Our Contemporary*, first published in Poland in 1961, which viewed the plays through the lens of Eastern European Marxism tinged with French Existentialism and even Absurdism, as if they had fused the politics of Brecht with the nihilism of Sartre or Beckett. Kott regarded the cycle as 'a constant procession of kings' in which history itself is the protagonist (9, 30). For his discussion of the 'Grand Mechanism' of history, see his chapter 1, 'Kings'.

In Hall's words, the plays expose 'the corrupting seductions experienced by anyone who wields power', and he believed that their depiction of 'one of the bloodiest and most hypocritical periods of history would teach many lessons about the present' (Addenbrooke, 127). In Hall's staging of the two parts of *Henry IV*, performed on the same monolithic set of steel that had reinforced the brutality of the first tetralogy, the Prince (Ian Holm) was motivated by a 'cold-blooded' machiavellianism; he was 'unpredictable, given to bouts of withdrawn and uncongenial behaviour' (McMillin, 62), at times betraying an almost modern sense of alienation; he used his companions for political advantage, and his relationship with Falstaff (Hugh Griffith) was far from warm. Falstaff, for his part, was less genial than menacingly opportunistic; and the 'remote and unapproachable' King (Eric Porter) was a man who now lived with the consequences of having given in to the seductions of power which, in Hall's view, undergird the plays' portrayal of history (McMillin, 63).

Performances of the history cycle by the English Shakespeare Company (ESC) two decades later, 1986–9, had a more contemporary ideological agenda. Seeking to offer a counter-cultural alternative to the hegemony of the RSC, founders Michael Bogdanov and Michael Pennington saw in the histories a gloss on the abuses of the Conservative government which would appeal to audiences whose view of politics and 'official history' had grown increasingly sceptical in the wake of Thatcherism's opportunistic grasp of the social contract and its promotion of predatory forms of privatization. 'We are in the era of New Brutalism', Bogdanov asserted, 'where a supposed return to Victorian values under the guise of initiative and incentive [has] masked the true goal of greed, avarice, exploitation and self.' He made the connection to the *Henry*s even more explicit: 'Boardrooms may have replaced the Palace at Westminster, Chairpersons (mainly men) replaced monarchs, but the rules [are] the same' (Bogdanov & Pennington, 24–5).

In this context, the two parts of *Henry IV* seemed to reflect the *Realpolitik* of government with clinical precision – a study, as Stephen Greenblatt put it a year before the plays were staged, in how power 'is based on predation and betrayal'; and 'what appeared as clarity' to Tillyard, who saw in the histories a reinforcement of providential order and degree, may turn out to be no more than 'a conjurer's trick concealing confusion in order to buy time and stave off the collapse of an illusion' (34).[1]

In the ESC productions, a mixture of styles and periods immediately signalled that this would not be the kind of history audiences had come to expect. By eschewing historical verisimilitude, the productions' eclectic costuming – a jarring juxtaposition of modern, 1930s and 1940s, Victorian, Elizabethan and medieval – would 'free the audiences' imagination' to make associations among different cultures and periods and to deny 'the pastness of the past' (Hodgdon, *Part Two*, 127; see also Bogdanov & Pennington, 28–32). The Prince's costuming was revelatory. In *Part One*, he dressed in torn jeans and looked like a social drop-out at odds with his efficiently bureaucratic father. For Shrewsbury, he donned medieval armour. And when he first appeared in *Part Two*, drinking a beer with Poins, he wore cricketing trousers, an open-neck red shirt and plimsolls, the image of a bored public-school type. At forty-three, however, Pennington was too old to play the Prince as a young man uncertain of his future. His sardonic wit and superior attitude branded him as a closet Conservative of a Thatcherite stripe, waiting for his moment to

---

1 The political criticism introduced by Greenblatt, called the new historicism in North America, coincided with the rise of an even more ideologically inflected criticism called cultural materialism in the UK. Works such as Jonathan Dollimore's *Radical Tragedy* (1984), John Drakakis's *Alternative Shakespeares* (1985), Graham Holderness's *Shakespeare's History* (1985) and Jonathan Dollimore and Alan Sinfield's *Political Shakespeare* (1985), in which Greenblatt's essay first appeared, analysed the plays in terms of class conflict, economic relations and the nature of power – the very things that were of interest to Bogdanov.

come; a 'nasty young man who has little capacity to care about anybody' (Ray Conlogue, *Globe and Mail*, 25 May 1987), 'darker, craftier [and] altogether more sinister' than Princes past (Thomas M. Disch, *The Nation*, 25 June 1988). Opposite him, John Woodvine's 'huge, charming George Formby of a Falstaff', sporting a 1930s 'deckchair-striped blazer' (Conlogue; Michael Ratcliffe, *Observer*, 28 December 1986), was a dapper gentleman whose excesses were those of the indolent, pleasure-loving upper classes. By rejecting him, Harry was in effect killing off the 'old England' of class privilege and moral lassitude and replacing it with an amoral political efficiency that British audiences would easily recognize.

In these productions, furthermore, the discursive structure of *Part Two*, which offers a welter of alternative histories to rival the 'official' history of men in power – those of the women, menials, peasants, unemployed and hangers-on who populate Falstaff's world – was seen to promote a Marxist understanding of history from the bottom up, as a depiction of class struggle and hegemonic oppression, rather than from the top down.[1] Those characters who offered so much of the production's amusement – Mistress Quickly as a savvy businesswoman determined to collect her due from Sir John; a feistily vulgar, leather-mini-skirted Doll Tearsheet who carries a knife in her belt with which she threatens Pistol's groin; a Punk Pistol who wraps himself in a Union Jack to celebrate Harry's coronation; and a doddering Justice Shallow, steeped in sack, who cagily intends to use Falstaff for his own advancement – now appeared not simply as comic diversions, but as parodic reflections of the self-interest and political hypocrisy of those in power. In the words of Barbara Hodgdon, 'Falstaff's comic world . . . was revealed not as history's amusingly playful carnival alternative, but as its dangerous double' (*Part Two*, 132).

---

1 For particularly astute cultural materialist analyses of the two *Henry IV* plays, see Howard & Rackin, 160–85, and Rackin, *passim*.

Other productions, however, eschewed political ideology. In 1975 Terry Hands staged a *Henriad* (as the second tetralogy without *Richard II* came to be called) for the RSC which instead focused on the domestic drama of Harry's dysfunctional relationship with his father. Brewster Mason's Falstaff posed little threat to the Prince: he was beguilingly gentlemanly, 'softer-centred than he might be' (Robert Cushman, *Observer*, 29 June 1975); and while his behaviour may have been immoral, he lacked his predecessors' pleasure in licentiousness and hovered only 'at the margins of family dynamics' where the true centre of the play lay (Hodgdon, *Part Two*, 82). The Prince faced a more serious threat in his father. Emrys James's King was a 'devious, self-pitying politician, a temperamental exhibitionist' (David, *Shakespeare*, 199) who projected his own self-loathing onto his son, while Alan Howard played the Prince as a moody introvert – keenly intelligent, caustically ironic and emotionally estranged from the father who has given up on him. The strained relationship between them dominated the two plays. In taking the crown from his father's pillow, Harry enacted a parricidal fantasy that drew on the Oedipal myth, eliciting from his father a scalding denunciation which exposed the raw nerves of their discord – the King's guilt for his sins and disgust with his son; the Prince's craving a love and approval his father has too long withheld. As the emotional climax of the play, this scene served to motivate Harry's reformation and to explain his behaviour in the production of *Henry V* that had opened the cycle: it dramatized his learning to improvise, to play expedient roles and to manipulate others to gain what he desires, but always uncertain of himself, never confident of the outcome. This staging of the two parts of *Henry IV* as plays in which national politics are thrashed out in the intimate arena of domestic conflict has had a deep influence on subsequent productions.

For the past several decades, directors have often allowed the family psychodrama of unrequited royals to take centre stage. The Prince has become a role coveted by young actors. He has been played by Gerard Murphy (RSC, 1982) as an immature 'high-class lout' (Jim Hiley, in Trussler, 58) with no interest in kingship and no instinct for majesty, frustrated by the disapproval of an ascetic, penitent father who feels only disdain for him; by Will Houston (RSC, 2000) as an enigmatic young man with 'a propensity for paranoia' who 'betray[s] . . . a suppressed craving to be loved' (Charles Spencer, *Daily Telegraph*, 21 April 2000) but who, when confronted by his father, may have been 'merely playing for emotional advantage' (Michael Dobson, *SS 54* (2001), 279); by Matthew Macfadyen (NT, 2005) 'as a brooding solitary who hangs out in taverns as a way of gaining his father's attention' (Michael Billington, *Guardian*, 4 May 2005); and by Geoffrey Streatfield (RSC, 2008) as an unseasoned actor who 'hadn't worked out the plot' (Carol Rutter, *SS 62* (2009), 355) and whose apparently 'cold, time-filling indifference' disguised a 'solitary . . . quest for surrogate fathers' (Billington, *Guardian*, 17 April 2008). Unsurprisingly, given this psychoanalytic approach to the tension between father and son, the King has gained new prominence as well, so much so that in Michael Attenborough's staging of the *Henry IV* plays in 2000, David Troughton's 'remarkably forceful portrayal' (John Peter, *Sunday Times*, 30 April 2000) of the King as 'a psychotic thug who suddenly finds himself troubled by a remorselessly gnawing conscience' (Spencer, *Telegraph*) became the 'pivotal performance' and 'defining presence' of the play (Billington, *Guardian*, 20 April 2000; John Peter, *Sunday Times*), his 'power and authority . . . establish[ing] a new centre of gravity' (Robert Hole, *whatsonstage.com*, 20 February 2001).

In the shift to regarding the two parts of *Henry IV* as primarily an investigation of domestic dysfunction, Falstaff has moved perceptibly to the margins. In many productions he has shrunk from a huge bombard of sack from whose size sprang much humour to a man who is simply and impressively large. Fat, after all, is no longer a laughing matter. This change is consistent with a more realistic and psychologically nuanced conception of Falstaff as a knight fallen on hard times, a down-at-heel aristocrat desperate to preserve a shred of dignity. Actors now play Falstaff with an introspection of a Stanislavskian stripe, eschewing, as Robert Shaughnessy notes, 'the representational conventions of Shakespeare's text' that once gave definition to the fat knight's performances (68). Together with *Part One*, *Part Two* traces the dramatic career of a melancholic knight who often betrays a sense of tragic inevitability that edges his performance with a dispiriting darkness.

As played by Robert Stephens (RSC, 1991), Falstaff has become a ruined and bitter man who 'veer[s] melancholically between bouts of hedonistic indulgence and darkly scathing fits of insecurity' (Michael Coveney, *Observer*, 21 April 1991) 'a solitary hedonist yearning for a son' (Billington, *Guardian*, 18 April 1991), who, 'desperately pained by his isolation and the self-awareness that went with it . . . search[ed] for an embrace' that the Prince 'found it so difficult to give him' (Peter Holland, *SS 45* (1992), 143); as played by Desmond Barrit (RSC, 2000), 'a complex, rather sad figure for whom the tragedy of disappointment and rejection is clearly just around the corner' (Hole, *whatonstage.com*, 20 February 2001), a man 'with a haunted horror of mortality and a desperate need to be loved' whose jokes betray 'a terrible loneliness' (Spencer, *Telegraph*); as played by Michael Gambon (NT, 2005), a 'deeply melancholic' old man, (Paul Taylor, *Independent*, 6 May 2005), 'darkly afraid of death' (Matt Wolf, *New York Times*, 11 May 2005), who 'vainly reach[es] out to [the Prince] for a gesture of affection that never quite comes' (Taylor, *Independent*, 6 May 2005); and at the extreme, as played by David Warner (RSC, 2008) a 'morose' opportunist (Rutter, *SS 62* (2009), 355) with a world-weary ennui and 'a leonine melancholy' that infect the whole production. A Falstaff such as these, conceived as 'only one part of the fabric of the play, not its centre' (Billington,

Guardian, 4 May 2005), can embody the comic spirit of the *Henry IV* plays only fitfully. Instead he has acquired a disturbing pathology which has transformed his character into something quite different from what it once seemed to be.

Falstaff versus history

Playing *Part Two* as one of a cycle of history plays, therefore, has come at the expense of the sublimely resilient Falstaff for whom the play was once prized. Falstaff's role is subsumed in a larger story of royal family politics which focuses on a tortured Prince whose emergence as Henry V must be prepared for by a seriousness of purpose which, even in *Part One*, creates a palpable tension between him and Falstaff. This tension is amply evident in *The Hollow Crown*, the four-play cycle filmed by the BBC, first broadcast in 2012, and distributed worldwide. Directed by Richard Eyre, the two *Henry IV* plays vividly dramatize this tension between the political play and the Falstaff play. Eyre's film of *Part Two* focuses most intently on the relationship between the King and the Prince. In a reversal of what Betterton did three centuries earlier, Eyre manipulates the text to introduce the King early in order to foreground his concerns about the Prince, which in the text are not mentioned until 4.3. Here, the first 80 lines of that scene are moved to a position very early, in Act 1; the King, played by Jeremy Irons as a 'paranoid and mercurial' older man 'given to bursts of rage at any hint of waking up the past' (Kelly Newman O'Connor, *Shakespeare Newsletter*, Spring 2013, 100), sits at a table in Westminster inquiring of his sons the whereabouts of the Prince of Wales, and, hearing that he dines with his usual companions in Eastcheap, gives vent to powerful anger. The King's soliloquy on sleep is also moved forward from Act 3 to a position prior to the tavern scene in Act 2, where it stands alone, a tragic meditation in which the King registers despair over his own spiritual ills: 'the correlation between the health of the body politic and the health of the king has rarely been more eloquently portrayed' (Matthew Lyons, *wordpress. com*, 16 July 2012).

Eyre's rearrangement of these scenes prepares more forcefully for the confrontation of father and son. When the Prince enters to find his father seemingly dead, he removes the crown lying on the pillow and takes it to the adjacent throne room, where he sits on the throne and, tears streaming down his cheeks, crowns himself – an act of auto-genesis which looks deeply incriminating to the King when he bursts into the throne room. Crucially, the King does not berate Harry in private, as he does in the text. Rather, he does so in front of Warwick, Westmorland, guards and his other three sons who, alarmed by his fury, have followed him. Eyre thus films the scene as a public humiliation of the Prince; and when Harry launches into his speech of self-exculpation, he speaks not just to his father, but to the audience of his brothers and nobles to whom his eyes keep returning. Harry's declaration of loyalty thus becomes a public performance. His father recognizes the value of that performance when, having crumpled on the dais, he acknowledges that God must have put it in Harry's mind to steal the crown so that he could acquit himself 'so wisely in excuse of it' (4.3.309), a tacit recognition of the rhetorical and political skill which, in Henry's eyes, will qualify his son for kingship.

The casting of Simon Russell Beale as Falstaff is symptomatic of the sobering effect that playing the *Henry IV* plays as part of a cycle has had. A stocky man with an unkempt white beard and a face that grows increasingly red with drink, Falstaff resembles a gnome more than a traditional Lord of Misrule. Considerably shorter than other characters and particularly so alongside the lanky, matinée-idol Prince of Tom Hiddleston, he looks like a man who is constantly trying to measure up to others, but failing. His vulnerability is emphasized by his limp, his being perpetually out of breath and his impotence with Doll, for which he apologizes with a self-deprecatory 'I am old' (2.4.274).

Even in his reminiscences with Justice Shallow, 'We have heard the chimes at midnight' (3.2.214), Falstaff in close-up looks haunted by the idea of death, his 'lack of levity', as one critic observes, tinged 'with a rueful awareness of his own mortality' (O'Connor, 201). In the opinion of another, Beale charts a 'slow descent into the desperate melancholy of age and failure' but shows too little of the 'beguiling, quixotic charm' that has historically been the hallmark of great Falstaffs (Lyons).

Beale, an actor noted more for wit than for warmth, offers a keenly intelligent performance whose naturalism is ideally modulated for the medium of television. The camera's focus on his expressive face, and particularly his eyes, which throw 'baleful looks of recognition of the frailty of his position' (*oughttobeclowns.blogspot.com*, 15 July 2012), frequently captures a kind of pleading for acceptance which registers as early as his first scene with the Prince in *Part One* when he

9   Falstaff (Simon Russell Beale) and Mistress Quickly (Julie Walters) in *Henry IV, Part Two* (2.1) for the BBC2 tetralogy, *The Hollow Crown*, 2012

begs, 'When thou art king . . . do not hang a thief' – and more forcefully in 'Banish not him thy Harry's company'. In their one tavern scene together in *Part Two*, caught having made derogatory comments about the Prince and Poins, Falstaff repeatedly utters 'No abuse, Hal' (2.4.317–27) with increasing anxiety in a voice that turns treble with fear, like a child afraid of chastisement. This exchange has little of the buoyancy that used to characterize their relationship: Falstaff responds with desperation to the Prince's censure, and Hiddleston conveys no sense of fun in having caught Falstaff in a lie one last time. He has already banished him, as Falstaff clearly apprehends.

The relationship between Falstaff and the Prince is never one of equals in Eyre's *Henry IV*, and their scenes together have little of the geniality traditionally associated with them. One always detects an anticipation of future division between the two men, always in the Prince a 'coldness' and an 'emotional distance' towards his old companion (*civiliantheatre.com*, 15 July 2012), always in Falstaff a fear of losing Harry's protection. As one critic observes, Falstaff 'is never far away from panic', and, objecting to such vulnerability in a character traditionally played as brashly resilient, adds, 'Falstaff should have more confidence and lust for life' (O'Connor, 102). Thus, when the rejection scene comes, his pleading eyes and his suppliant posture are things the audience has seen before; the inevitability of this moment has been telescoped in scenes as early as *Part One*, and his tears of disbelief allow him no time to regain the composure, as more confident Falstaffs do, to assure his followers convincingly that he will be sent for soon at night.

The last image of the film, of soldiers thrusting Falstaff out of the doors of Westminster, the camera lingering over his distraught face in close-up, puts emphasis on Falstaff's tragedy and on the ruthlessness of state policy under the new King. Just as Prince John's soldiers have done at Gaultree – and the film shows them on horseback slaughtering rebel soldiers who flee on foot – the King's soldiers here round up the scattered stray in London: first Doll and the Hostess; now Falstaff and his followers. The sombre tone of this conclusion is of a piece with the rest of the production. It marks the ultimate capitulation of Shakespeare's most exuberantly comic character to the demands of playing *Henry IV* as part of a cycle; it seals the defeat of the plays' festive spirit by the inexorable force of chronicle history. The tragedy of Falstaff serves the purposes of state. Eyre's production is the culmination of decades of suppressing comedy in the interest of dramatizing how power is gained and preserved. For a new generation of audiences, Eyre foregrounds the politics of repression and expulsion. The film thus requires a Falstaff whose interiority is as compelling as that of the Prince or the King. It also denies Falstaff his comic heart.

This is not to say that all recent productions of *Henry IV* have been this dark. Occasionally, especially if there is no *Henry V* to which they must build, productions have preserved a better balance between the play's scenes of comedy and chronicle history. With great comic actors such as Kevin Kline in a performance of the conflated *Henry IV* plays at Lincoln Center in 2003 (see pp. 490–5), or Roger Allam in a rousing performance of both parts at Shakespeare's Globe in 2010, or Anthony Sher in a robust staging of them for the RSC in 2014–15, the play has achieved a satisfying tonal unity between the royal family saga and those scenes of festive merriment which offer an alternative to it. Indeed, Sher's Falstaff, padded so grossly that he moves at a snail's pace, is a throwback to Falstaffs of previous generations in his overweening self-confidence and his ability to out-manoeuvre others with wit and wordplay. His command of every situation is evident in the pace of his delivery: Sher's 'pukka-accented Falstaff delivers his witty speeches with an imperturbably unhurried, self-relishing deliberation' and with a comic 'refusal to change gear' even when, unaware that the Prince has moved on, his situation changes (Paul Taylor, *Independent*, 18 April 2014). Thus marked by an arrogant 'inability to . . . adapt' (Dominic Cavendish, *Telegraph*, 17 April

2014), he is floored – and speechless – when the new King banishes him.

If Sher's performance eschewed the pathology of Falstaffian self-doubt and unrequited longing that had evolved during the latter half of the twentieth century, Dominic Dromgoole's rehabilitation of Falstaff as a comic hero was even more theatrically compelling. His staging for Shakespeare's Globe, in which the entire theatre served as a playing space, allowed a fluidity of performance and a level of audience involvement such as might have been common when the *Henry IV* plays were performed at the Curtain more than four hundred years ago. Dromgoole began *Part Two*, as he had *Part One*, with a mummers' play. A group of actors mounted a scaffold at the rear of the yard and began a broadly pantomimic enactment of the Battle of Shrewsbury, 'involving plenty of knock-about, daggers of lath, exaggerated death and miraculous resurrection' and above all, Falstaff, celebrated killer of Hostpur, sporting a huge erect phallus, 'metamorphosed in the popular imagination into St. George killing the dragon' (Carol Rutter, *SS 64* (2011), 345). Audience members were cast as medieval spectators receiving news as a form of entertainment. As Will Sharpe observes, 'the Globe frequently employs similar tactics' to encourage 'actor/audience relationships', thereby validating 'the perception that Renaissance playgoing was a boisterous, interactive affair'. But Dromgoole had more in mind, for spectators were being alerted to the ways in which history is framed and disseminated for popular consumption. The mummers' play thus anticipated the speech of Rumour, which was divided among several actors who spoke from different points in the theatre to recount as tragic narrative the history they had just enacted as comedy, using the 'locale and dislocation from events' to insist upon 'the impossibility of meaningful historiography' and to expose how 'fragmentary chaos' ultimately yields to 'the communal shaping of historical record' (Sharpe).

In a space such as the new Globe, Falstaff has the opportunity, as the first Falstaff no doubt had at the Curtain,[1] of directly addressing the audience, appealing to their sympathies and making them complicit in his strategies. Roger Allam took full advantage of that opportunity. A dashing actor with an impressive bearing, impeccable comic timing and a baritone voice 'so fruity you want to bottle it' (Cavendish, *Telegraph*, 16 July 2010), he restored the sense, too often forgotten in recent productions, 'that this wonderfully reprehensible character is also a life force' (Spencer, *Telegraph* 15 July 2010). Though padded, he had 'the stature to realize a larger-than-life character' and to earn the Prince's accusation that he is a stuffed cloak-bag of guts even without being corpulent (Peter Brown, *London Theatre Guide*, 14 July 2010); and his quick wit, clever asides and 'ripe, roguish charisma' (Spencer) earned him the audience's allegiance from the start. Allam's entrance is anticipated by street vendors who throng the stage, setting up their stalls and singing a ballad about the brave deeds of Falstaff at Shrewsbury. When he enters to their applause, 'fully the swaggering showman', he slyly motions for the audience to applaud as well and to join him in another jubilant chorus of ''Twas Falstaff that carried the day'.

---

1   Who first played Falstaff is unclear, and evidence is slender. David Wiles makes a good case for Will Kemp (116–35), the famous comedian who played clown roles for the Chamberlain's Men in the 1590s and was noted for his dancing, which may suggest that he spoke the Epilogue as well. King, however, suggests that principal actors in Elizabethan theatre companies played the major roles and were not necessarily typecast (62–3). Thus John Heminge has been proposed as a likely candidate to play Falstaff (Winter, 330–1). But Kastan makes a stronger case for Thomas Pope (*1H4*, 78–9), who also played clown roles for the company and quite possibly acted Buffone in Jonson's *Every Man Out of His Humour*, a role not unlike that of Falstaff, a 'prophane Iester' addicted to sack (Jonson, 3.423–4). Kastan argues that even if Kemp originated the role of Falstaff, Pope is likely to have taken it over when Kemp left the company in 1599, with John Lowin, who joined the company in 1603, assuming the role from Pope.

10   Roger Allam as Falstaff in Dominic Dromgoole's production of the two
      Henry IV plays at Shakespeare's Globe, London, 2010

Allam's Falstaff traces a remarkable dramatic arc from the
jovial knight in *Part One* to the cynically self-promoting
arriviste of *Part Two*, now decked out in fine clothing and
dining out on his reputation for valour at Shrewsbury. He delights
in his own verbal dexterity as he spars with the Lord Chief
Justice, knowing that his reputation for valour at Shrewsbury
will buy him a reprieve; and he manages to keep up the pace of
verbal sparring even as he thrusts and parries with the officers
who try to arrest him at the Hostess's suit. Aware of how
charismatic he is, this formidable Falstaff plays shamelessly to
the crowd; but he is also dangerously manipulative. So confident
is he of his command over others, including the Prince, that it

never occurs to him to doubt that he will eventually play a prominent role in Henry V's court. Thus the public repudiation by his 'sweet boy', when it comes, is the more powerful for taking him by surprise. His 'limbs shaking uncontrollably', he hears his rejection as a death sentence (Cavendish).

This unabashedly extrovert Falstaff, so different from the melancholic Falstaffs of decades past whose humour thinly disguised their mortal fears, was matched in exuberance by the affable Prince of Jamie Parker. Far from the emotionally distant Harry who is tortured by self-doubt and yearns for his father's love, Parker joins the exploits of his tavern companions in *Part One* with relish, and there is little sense that his pleasure in Falstaff's company has diminished in the tavern scene of *Part Two*. Yet 'stiff bristles' are visible beneath his 'boyish exterior' and 'childish pleasure in pranks', according to one critic; 'he isn't so much sewing his wild oats as harvesting them all in one go, as if already well aware that he hasn't got a lot of time left' (Lyn Gardner, *Guardian*, 15 July 2010); and to another, his 'affability is only skin deep and barely masks the steely calculation that lies beneath' (Spencer). Ultimately, Parker's Prince is 'far shrewder than Falstaff, a man who . . . is so busy putting on a performance that he fails to notice that the script is changing' (Gardner). Thus the audience does not share Falstaff's surprise when the young King condemns in tones of 'rapier steeliness' Falstaff's ill-judged interruption of the coronation procession (Gardner). This is a Harry whose star has risen, even as Falstaff's has fallen without his knowing it; and although Falstaff holds centre stage with his richly theatrical performance, the threads of festive comedy and chronicle history are woven together with a seamlessness rarely achieved in productions of these two plays.

Over the centuries, larger-than-life Falstaffs such as this have been allowed to dominate the play even if they have ultimately been contained by a power structure that spits them out. But such productions are increasingly rare. The *Henry IV* plays, particularly *Part Two*, have in recent decades come to be regarded as serious explorations of the performance of power; and in them, Falstaff is often reduced to a marginal figure tinged with anxiety and fatalistic melancholy, at odds not only with the Prince but with the buoyant Sir John – 'the best of Comical Characters', according to John Dryden in 1668[1] – whose popularity once prompted theatre companies to call the play *Falstaff*.

FALSTAFF AND HIS FRIENDS

Falstaff and the decline of festivity

Neither wit nor honesty ought to think themselves safe with such a companion when they see Henry seduced by Falstaff.

(Samuel Johnson, 1765)

Falstaff has been seducing audiences for more than four hundred years. Fat, old, dissipated and given to lying, Falstaff is a knight – *Sir* John – who, like many on the margins of the Elizabethan court, is impecunious and preys on others. He cheats, he whores and he eats and drinks to excess; but he does so with such joyful abandon and defends himself with such shameless brio that he has acquired a stature beyond that of any other comic character in Shakespeare.[2] He embodies the

---

1 See 'An Essay of Dramatick Poesie' in Dryden, 62.

2 Winter puts the paradox of Falstaff's attractiveness as follows: he 'is a hardened reprobate, an inveterate sinner, a selfish worldling, an insensate, gross old man, who lives – and thrives! – in our unmitigated and continuous censure. . . . But he possesses such force of character, such power of mind, such humor, experience, worldly wisdom, shrewd sagacity, illimitable animal spirits, keen discernment, trenchant wit, and personal fascination that we like him, almost love him, in open and conscious defiance of instinct, knowledge, judgment, morals, and taste' (325).

spirit of hedonism, and although his days are numbered by pleasures of the flesh, he has managed to strike a responsive chord in all but the most moralistic of critics. As William Hazlitt wrote in excuse of his moral depravity, 'Falstaff's wit is an emanation of a fine constitution; an exuberance of good humour and good-nature; an overflowing of his love of laughter and good-fellowship; a giving vent to his heart's ease, and over-contentment with himself and others . . . The unrestrained indulgence of his own ease, appetites, and convenience, has neither malice nor hypocrisy in it . . . and we no more object to the character of Falstaff in a moral point of view than we should think of bringing an excellent comedian, who should represent him to the life, before one of the police offices' (*Characters*, 152).

Above all, Falstaff has perfected the art of survival. If in *Part One* he invents a preposterous fiction to excuse his cowardice at the Gad's Hill robbery and, even more boldly, claims to have killed Hotspur, in *Part Two*, bolstered by his reputation as a war hero, he engages in a battle of wits with the Lord Chief Justice and adroitly talks his way out of derogatory remarks he has made about Prince Harry and Poins. To create a figure this resourceful, Shakespeare rifled various stock characters from earlier drama. The *miles gloriosus* of Roman comedy served as a model for Falstaff's inflated lies about his exploits at Gad's Hill; the Vice of medieval Morality plays underlies his gregarious promotion of lewd behaviours in the Prince; and the tradition of electing a Lord of Misrule to displace legitimate authority during the Christmas revels in London allowed Shakespeare's audience to link Falstaff to native holiday customs. Like a Lord of Misrule, Falstaff represents freedom from restraint – he becomes a site of social transgression who appeals to the anarchic instincts in viewers of every stripe. None of these sources, however, can account for the comic resourcefulness of a character who has the privilege of addressing the audience directly and offering commentary that often subverts the pretences which inform the behaviour of the play's political figures.

The Falstaff of *Part Two* in some ways differs markedly from the Falstaff of *Part One*. In the earlier play, he serves as a surrogate father for the Prince: their relationship is the driving force of the play.[1] In *Part Two*, however, Falstaff and the Prince cross paths only twice – briefly at the tavern, and again at the end of the play, when the new King banishes Falstaff in earnest. For the rest of the play, Shakespeare's most daring strategy was to give Falstaff his own scenes to bustle in, unimpeded by the burden of the Prince's protection or the demands of chronicle history. He created a world rich in the quotidian life of Elizabethan subcultures. Falstaff dominates this world; and since his role is significantly larger than anyone else's, it isn't surprising that performances of *Part Two* have sometimes been billed as *Falstaff*.[2] In so far as the play has achieved popularity, it is because audiences have paid to see *him*.

Despite the plays' ostensible temporal continuity, Falstaff in *Part Two* is an older, more diseased and more corrupt figure than he was in *Part One*. He thrives on the reputation for valour falsely won at Shrewsbury and therefore is determined to cut a figure in the world. He refuses to succumb to the economic hardship endured by many veterans in the final decades of the sixteenth century: instead, he will indulge his taste for fashion to appear a complete courtier by buying rich

---

1 In her psychoanalytic study of the *Henry IV* plays, Valerie Traub argues that Falstaff takes the place of an absent mother, his swollen belly figuring 'the female reproductive body' upon which the Prince's development as 'a "prototypical" male subject' depends (456–62).

2 It is not unusual for directors to call the play *Falstaff* in order to distinguish it from *Henry IV, Part One*, as Stuart Burge did with his production for the Stratford Festival in Ontario, 1965, and Joseph Anthony did the following year when staging *Part Two* for the American Shakespeare Festival in Stratford, Connecticut. For Burge's production, see Leiter, 195–7; for Anthony's, see Cooper, 110–12.

clothing on credit.[1] To pay for these material markers of his social status, he relies on a military pension which, he slyly avouches, will be increased by the limp (''Tis no matter if I do halt') which he will claim is a war injury (1.2.244–5) instead of a symptom of gout or the pox brought on by leading a life of dissipation. Indeed, his opening speech wryly acknowledges the reputation he has earned among theatre audiences as well his contemporaries: 'The brain of this foolish compounded clay-man is not able to invent anything that intends to laughter more than I invent or is invented on me; I am not only witty in myself, but the cause that wit is in other men' (6–11).

Falstaff's complaints about his gout, his tailor and his purse establish key motifs for the play's chronicle history as well: age, disease and consumption, both moral and physical, plague the King and Northumberland alike. The thread connecting Falstaff most securely to the royal narrative, however, is his pairing with the Lord Chief Justice, a scrupulously virtuous man who, according to legend, once had the Prince jailed for boxing him in the ear (see pp. 129–30). In a sense, these two old men offer competing centres of authority for England and for the Prince. Perhaps because they both recognize this, the animosity between them is palpable. Falstaff makes audacious witticisms about the Chief Justice's age – 'You that are old consider not the capacities of us that are young' (174–6) – which the Chief Justice is able to parry tap for tap, a stand-off that should alert Falstaff that his exploitation of others cannot last indefinitely:

1   Falstaff's wardrobe may also be financed by his corrupt practices as a captain, such as accepting bribes and collecting 'dead pay'; see p. 85. Paul A. Jorgensen discusses the crown's apparent lack of concern with the plight of returning veterans (*World*, 210–13). Although Falstaff cynically predicts in *Part One* that the few survivors among his regiment 'are for the town's end to beg during life' (5.3.39), in fact there were 'occasional . . . hospitals for the maimed, and pensions for a few deserving veterans', Falstaff presumably one of the deserving few. On the failure of the military profession to thrive under the Tudors, and the consequent estrangement of the 'bluff' professional soldier from the Tudor court, see A. Ferguson, 101–5.

Do you set down your name in the scroll of youth,
that are written down old with all the characters
of age? Have you not a moist eye, a dry hand, a
yellow cheek, a white beard, a decreasing leg, an
increasing belly?

(179–83)

Though audiences may anticipate that Harry, when he is King,
will embrace the Lord Chief Justice as his chief adviser as
surely as he will reject Falstaff, their joy lies in watching
Falstaff attempt to outwit him – 'My lord, I was born about
three of the clock in the afternoon, with a white head and
something a round belly' (187–9)[1] – and presumptuously beg
him for a thousand pounds to furnish his next expedition.

Puns announce Falstaff's strategy for survival early in the
play, when, in cursing his big toe – 'A pox of this gout, or a gout
of this pox' (243) – he vows to turn his diseases to commodity.[2]
Attempting to work his way around the Lord Chief Justice, he
confesses that he suffers from 'the disease of not listening'
(122) and repeatedly puns about his own girth. When the Chief
Justice tells him that he lives 'in great infamy', Falstaff replies,
'He that buckles himself in my belt cannot live in less' (137–40);
and here begins a string of puns about wishing his 'waste'
(waist) slenderer (143–4), burning as long as a wassail candle
whose 'wax' (growth) proves his worth (159–60), and following
the Prince not as his 'ill angel' but as genuine currency, for an
'ill angel [counterfeit gold coin] is light, but I hope he that
looks upon me will take me without weighing' (166–8). Such
wordplay, intended to disarm the opposition, demonstrates
Falstaff's virtuosity in turning ironic self-deprecation to

---

1 This line can be interpreted as a metadramatic reference to Falstaff's birth as a
   fully-fleshed theatrical character, three o'clock being the time of an afternoon
   performance at an outdoor Elizabethan theatre.
2 The best study of Falstaff's prose idiom remains Vickers, *Artistry*, 118–41.

advantage and colours his rapaciousness with apparently benign humour.

If Falstaff in *Part One* embodied carnivalesque energy, the cynical opportunism of Falstaff in *Part Two* marks how far he has declined from such energy. This decline involves both a recognition – on the part of the characters as well as the audience – that festivity is a thing of the past, and a consequent nostalgia for it. Falstaff is at the centre of the play's nostalgia for the merry England dramatized in *Part One*. The play's only tavern scene illustrates how nostalgia functions by invoking the memory of an equivalent scene in *Part One* – both of them occurring late in Act 2 – in which merriment, generosity and a festive spirit reigned. The scene in *Part Two* is suffused with a longing for such merriment but darkened by a recognition that festivity may be irrecoverable. Where, in the earlier play, the scene focused on the Prince and Poins's exposure of Falstaff's increasingly inflated lies about his bravery at Gad's Hill, the exposure of Falstaff in *Part Two* is thinly plotted and almost incidental. It has made generations of playgoers nostalgic for the vibrant comedy of the tavern scene in *Part One*. Recollections of the earlier play are explicit when the Prince and Poins briefly mock Francis the drawer with 'Anon, anon, sir!' (2.4.285), an echo of their more elaborate joke at his expense in *Part One*; and when, after Falstaff protests that he has recognized them through their disguises and the Prince responds, 'Yea, and you knew me as you did when you ran away by Gad's Hill' (310–11), their exchange bids an audience recall the comic vitality of the earlier scene and, in so doing, recognize the diminished pleasure, and even pointlessness, of goading Falstaff in this play.

In place of festive merriment, the tavern scene in *Part Two* offers a tonally more complex confrontation between Falstaff and the Ancient Pistol. A scurrilous rogue whose mock-heroics parody the chivalric ethos embodied so memorably in Hotspur (who often, in stagings of the two plays together, is played by the same actor), Pistol is a braggart soldier of Jonsonian proportions. He purports to hold military rank – 'ancient' being a corrupt form of 'ensign' – and is appropriately named for a weapon new in sixteenth-century England, dangerously temperamental and likely to go off without warning (see Garber, 349). Pistol is also a 'swaggerer', or quarreller, a term that is used to characterize him fourteen times in the course of the play. Swaggering denoted a behaviour of aggressive bravado marked onstage by an eccentrically flamboyant style of acting which made Pistol second only to Falstaff in popularity with Elizabethan audiences, as evidenced by his name appearing on the title-page of the Quarto: 'with the exploits of Falstaff and the Swaggering Pistol'.[1] A coward whose most serious threat is 'tearing a poor whore's ruff in a bawdy house' (2.4.144–5), an action which signified sexual assault in drama of the period, he stands as the *reductio ad absurdum* of bygone theatrical heroism and marks the decline of English chivalry in an age of political self-interest.

Pistol's soldiership amounts to no more than theatrical imposture. He derives his language from the outmoded fustian of a previous generation of stage heroes, and his bravery runs no deeper than an absurd hodgepodge of misremembered tags and scraps from old plays by Robert Greene, George Peele, Thomas Kyd and Christopher Marlowe.[2] His butchering of heroic verse recalls those hyperbolic sentiments which once invoked a world of greatness not unlike that imagined by Hotspur, but which now sound ludicrously out of date. 'Shall

---

1 Hattaway, 'Falstaff', notes that the recurrence of the term in *Henry V*, when Williams characterizes Pistol as 'a rascal that swaggered with me last night' (4.7.123–4), attests to the enduring association of the term with Pistol's performance.

2 In addition to the obvious parody of heroic diction in Marlowe and others, Lever ('French') argues that some of Pistol's lines closely resemble the Braggart's bungling of classical allusions in John Eliot's *Ortho-epia Gallica*.

11   *Theophilus Cibber* [1703–58] *in the character of Ancient Pistol*, after a
print by John Laguerre (*c.* 1733)

pack-horses, and hollow pampered jades of Asia, which cannot
go but thirty mile a day, compare with Caesars and with
Cannibals and Troyant Greeks?' he rants (164–7), nonsensically
echoing great speeches of *Tamburlaine*, the play whose two-
part structure underlies that of *Henry IV*. And his misquotation
of Peele's *Battle of Alcazar* inflates his rage against Doll
Tearsheet with classical bombast: 'I'll see her damned first! To
Pluto's damned lake – by this hand – to th'infernal deep, with
Erebus and tortures vile also!' (157–9).

61

Falstaff's rescuing Doll from Pistol's attack on her honour – or at least on her ruff – leads to a poignantly nostalgic scene which is tonally at odds with the festive tone of the tavern scene in *Part One*. There, the clever way in which Falstaff refashioned his cowardice at Gad's Hill as bravery led to laughter and merriment. Here, Doll's attempt to recapture a heroic past for Falstaff that may never have existed leads to a frank appraisal of his decline. 'Thou art as valorous as Hector of Troy, worth five of Agamemnon', she assures him; but in the next breath, she bids him to be mindful of his own mortality: 'when wilt thou leave fighting a'days, and foining a'nights and begin to patch up thine old body for heaven?' (220–1, 233–5). Falstaff acknowledges that his days are numbered: 'Peace, good Doll. Do not speak like a death's-head: do not bid me remember mind end' (236–7). The tenderness of this exchange tempers Doll's far less sympathetic appraisal of Falstaff's situation earlier in the scene: 'Come, I'll be friends with thee, Jack: thou art going to the wars, and whether I shall ever see thee again or no there is nobody cares' (66–8). The dialogue Doll and Falstaff share in this scene is delicately poised between loving nostalgia and brutal candour, between longing for a bygone heroism, always more imagined than actual, and present awareness of the impotence and ravages of age.

Tonally, this scene depicts the season of Lent after Shrovetide: its echoes of an earlier festive world give rise to a longing for the past akin to what was felt by many in England for whom the Protestant Reformation had meant 'the collapse . . . of festivity' (Hutton, 89).[1] Patrick Collinson notes that by the time of Elizabeth's reign, 'Merry England' had become a phrase

---

1   C.L. Barber equates Falstaff with the festive spirit of Bacchus and Shrove Tuesday (67–73): the mood of *Part One* with carnival, and of *Part Two* with Lenten restraint, a 'trial of carnival' (213–14). For other discussions of Falstaff as a site of carnivalesque resistance to the authority and power of state, see Holderness, 'Carnival'; Grady; and Laroque. Cressy, 13–33, discusses how the rhythm of the liturgical year in Elizabethan England affected national memory.

12   *Doll Tearsheet, Falstaff, Henry & Poins* (2.4). Painted by Henry Fuseli;
      engraved by William Leney; published by J. & J. Boydell in 1795

signifying 'almost the same thing as Catholic England' (135).
Indeed, as early as 1552 Dr John Caius complained that the
Reformation, with its suppression of festivity as a form of
social disorder, had destroyed 'the old world, when this country
was called merry England' (in Hutton, 89). The scuttling of
those 'merrie and sportful' pastimes of a bygone (and Catholic)
world nostalgically celebrated in John Stow's *Survey of London*
(1.91) – a work published within a year of the first performance
of *Henry IV, Part Two* – gathered momentum as the sixteenth
century drew to a close. Francis the Drawer remembers the
pleasure of that festive world: his remark anticipating the
arrival of the Prince and Poins pointedly uses the archaic word

'utas' for such merriment: 'By the mass, here will be old utas!' (2.4.19). Furthermore, by invoking the Mass in his oath, Francis 'links Roman Catholic ritual, by now long outlawed in England, to the nearly ritualistic pranks at the expense of Falstaff' (Baldo, 81). Paradoxically, as Jonathan Baldo observes, the figure who stands as the vestigial embodiment of that merry world was originally named for a proto-Puritan martyr who was put to death by Henry V: 'Shakespeare installs a representative of the forces that many Elizabethans held responsible for the demise of England's merry past as a synecdoche for that very past. . . . By fusing, or confusing, the wildly distorted figure of a Reformation martyr with the merry world the Reformation was thought to have swept aside, Shakespeare outrageously constructs a figure of forgetfulness and historical revisionism as the object of a powerful, irresistible nostalgia' (83).

Falstaff as Oldcastle

Falstaff was originally called Sir John Oldcastle, the name of a Lollard leader who ran afoul of authorities for his radical beliefs, may have been involved in a plot to assassinate his friend Henry V, and was ultimately hanged in chains and burned at the stake 'for the doctrine of wiclyffe and for treason (as that age supposed)', according to Francis Thynne (in McKeen, 1.22). He was known by the name Oldcastle in early performances of *Part One* and may have been so designated during the composition of the first act of *Part Two* as well.[1] Censorship by the Lord Chamberlain, William Brooke, a collateral descendant of Oldcastle, apparently forced Shakespeare to change the name in late 1596 or early 1597, for reasons I assess on pp. 134–42. Obliged to find a substitution,

---

1 A speech prefix in the 1600 Quarto reads '*Old.*' (1.2.121) but may have resulted from a memory lapse. The second Epilogue issues an explicit corrective: 'Oldcastle died martyr, and this is not the man' (Epil.32). For the Oxford editors' justification of their reversion to the name Oldcastle, see Taylor, 'Fortunes', 95–100, and Kastan's judicious rebuttal in 'Oldcastle'.

Shakespeare adapted the name of another knight, Sir John Fastolf, who was also a contemporary of Henry V and had already played a role in *Henry VI, Part One*.[1]

What Shakespeare may have had in mind by naming his fat knight after a Lollard martyr is unclear. The most innocuous explanation is that he borrowed the name without further thought from his source play, *The Famous Victories of Henry the Fifth*, in which Oldcastle is one of the Prince's three boon companions with whom he commits robbery, though this Oldcastle has neither the humour nor the girth of Falstaff, and the thieving exploits of these 'knights' in the source play served as only a skeleton on which Shakespeare fleshed out his comic scenes of the Gad's Hill robbery. Drawing inspiration from *Famous Victories* does not imply, of course, that Shakespeare was unaware of the true identity of the historical Oldcastle. Indeed, he could not have been ignorant of the implications of naming his debauched knight after a figure whose reputation had been rehabilitated in the sixteenth century by John Bale in *A brefe Chronycle concernynge the Examinacyon and death of the blessed Martyr of Christ Syr Johan Oldecastell the Lorde Cobham* (1544) and most adamantly by John Foxe in *Actes and Monuments* (1563), works which sought to create for a newly reformed England a history of Protestant struggle and martyrdom which found in Oldcastle's 'life and death the pattern of virtuous opposition to a corrupt clergy that underpinned the godly nation itself'.[2]

---

1 G.W. Williams cogently argues that Shakespeare decided against replacing the name of one historical personage, Oldcastle, with that of another, Sir John Fastolf, a knight much honoured for his service in the French Wars. Although the speech prefix '*Fast.*' occurs twice in Q0 of *1H4*, Shakespeare clearly changed his mind during the course of composition and, rather than simply recycle a name he had already used, altered the spelling to Falstaff 'to avoid having it resemble "Fastolf" or any common variant of the name' ('Second', 82).

2 Kastan, *1H4*, 58. Alice-Lyle Scoufos surveys sixteenth-century accounts of Oldcastle's martyrdom in works by More, Bale, Foxe, Stow, Hall and Holinshed (44–69).

Why, then, would Shakespeare have risked lampooning a Protestant martyr for an audience whose sympathies may have lain with the very principles of religious reform for which Oldcastle gave his life? Though recent speculation that Shakespeare was a Catholic has led Gary Taylor to argue that in ridiculing Oldcastle's excesses, Shakespeare was exploiting 'a point of view that many of his contemporaries would have regarded as "papist"' ('Fortunes', 99), by the end of the sixteenth century Lollards were regarded as 'precursors [not] of the national church', as Foxe had urged, but 'of the nonconforming sectaries who threatened to undermine it' – that is, Puritans, that 'godly brotherhood' who had sought a more radical reformation of the Church than the crown was willing to permit (Kastan, *1H4*, 60), whose influence had grown alarmingly in the last decades of the century and who were increasingly opposed to all forms of pleasurable entertainment, especially theatre. 'Whatever Shakespeare's own religious leanings,' Kastan concludes, 'certainly most members of his audience in 1596 would . . . have viewed the travesty of a Lollard martyr' as 'an entirely orthodox commitment, designed to reflect upon the nonconformity that the Queen herself had termed "prejudicial to the religion established, to her crown, to her government, and to her subjects"'.[1]

By naming his debauched knight for a Lollard martyr, therefore, Shakespeare appears to have been contributing to contemporary political satire against non-conformists 'as grotesque individuals living in carnivalesque communities',[2] glancing wryly at the hypocrisies of which Puritans were often accused – gluttony, lust, covetousness and deceit. Kristen Poole

---

1   Kastan, *1H4*, 60–1, quoting Neale, 2.163.
2   Poole, 'Saints', 54. Holderness applies Bakhtin's theory of the carnivalesque, with its central image of the gargantuan body and its dominant discourse of the grotesque, to the Rabelaisian figure of Falstaff (*History*, 79–101). On the radical potential of the Elizabethan clown to alter playgoers' perspectives, see Weimann; Bristol; and Helgerson, 215–28.

traces the history of the carnivalesque Puritan figure to the Marprelate controversy, in which Anglican bishops, responding to witty anti-ecclesiastic pamphlets written by young nonconformists under the pseudonym Martin Marprelate, hired writers such as Greene, John Lyly, Anthony Munday and Thomas Nashe to 'challenge Martin on his own ground' (Poole, 'Saints', 58) by turning the satirical figure of the bishop-as-voluptuary into a satire of the Puritan himself. Nashe, for example, vows to attack Puritan 'Hipocrites' by 'imitating . . . that merry man Rablays'; and 'throughout the anti-Martinist literature, Martin becomes "the ape, the dronke, and the madde": he copulates, vomits, drinks, [and] gorges himself'[1] – those same behaviours in which Falstaff indulges.

In the two *Henry IV* plays Falstaff attempts to cloak such behaviour in a layer of pious cant common among Puritans. He quotes the Bible more liberally than any other character in Shakespeare, 26 times in *Part One* and 15 in *Part Two* (Shaheen, *History*, 153). The Prince, he assures the Lord Chief Justice in *Part Two*, 'repents', though 'not in ashes and sackcloth' (1.2.197–8; cf. Matthew, 11.21); in a borrowing from Ephesians, 5.18–19, which recommends 'making melodie to the Lord in your hearts', he claims to be an enthusiastic singer of spiritual songs: 'For my voice, I have lost it with hallowing and singing of anthems' (1.2.189–90), a behaviour that firmly linked Puritans with Lollards (Ainger, 1.145); and he repeatedly refers to himself as a 'saint' (that is, one of God's elect) and to salvation by faith alone. Just as tellingly, Falstaff mimics 'the scriptural style of the sanctimonious Puritan' (Hemingway, 37–8) in the letter he writes to the Prince when he signs himself, *'Thine by yea and no . . . Jack Falstaff with my family, John*

---

1 Nashe, 3.342, 374, cited in Poole, 'Saints', 59; see also Kaul. The most searching study of Nashe's formative influence on Falstaff's comic prose style, especially on his absurd parodies of rhetorical tropes and his delight in grotesque physical imagery, is Rhodes. For Nashe's possible influence on Falstaff's Calvinist speech, see Tobin.

with my brothers and sisters' (2.2.128–30) – 'yea and no' being a common Puritan oath derived from Matthew,[1] and 'brothers and sisters' being terms by which nonconformists addressed one another.

Yet motivation must be considered here, for Falstaff mimics the 'conventicler style' not unselfconsciously, as naturalized discourse, but ironically, for comic effect. Can Falstaff be deliberately parodying Calvinist cant if he is himself a parodic embodiment of the Rabelaisian Puritan akin to those circulated in contemporary pamphlets and stage lampoons? Although Poole asserts that he does not 'parody the self-styled saints in a determined, willful way' (*Religion*, 37), Falstaff in *Part Two* is certainly a knowing parodist, a strategic mocker of nonconformists who uses their cant wittily to excuse his gratuitous insults of the Prince. 'I dispraised [thee] before the wicked, that the wicked might not fall in love with thee' (2.4.323–4), he explains, using a term – 'the wicked' – that Puritans adopted from the book of Proverbs to apply to non-believers (Shaheen, *History*, 165); to which the Prince responds in kind: 'Is thine hostess here of the wicked? Or is thy boy of the wicked? Or honest Bardolph, whose zeal burns in his nose, of the wicked?' (331–4). The mention of Bardolph's 'zeal', a favourite Puritan term for religious fervour, prompts Falstaff to respond with another Calvinist affront: 'The fiend hath pricked down Bardolph irrecoverable' (336–7). Others in the play apply sectarian terminology to Falstaff with equal irony: the Prince calls him a 'withered elder', punning on the term used for an officer in the Presbyterian church (261), and the Page refers to Falstaff and his dining companions, Doll and the Hostess, as 'Ephesians . . . of the old church' (2.2.146) – a possible reference to 'the prime church of the Ephesians . . . which was the Puritan court of appeal for purity of life' (Ard[2], 2.2.142n.).

---

1 'Let your communication be, Yea, yea: Nay, nay. For whatsoeuer is more then these, commeth of euil' (Matthew, 5.37).

Falstaff derides Puritanism most explicitly when he condemns those smug city tradesmen to whom he owes so much on credit. 'Let him be damned like the glutton!' he curses the silk merchant who won't take his bond (1.2.35), alluding to the parable of Dives, the rich glutton who goes to hell and asks that Lazarus 'dippe the tip of his finger in water, and coole my tongue: for I am tormented in this flame' (Luke, 16.19–31):

> Pray God his tongue be hotter! A whoreson Achitophel, a rascal – yea forsooth knave – to bear a gentleman in hand and then stand upon 'security'. The whoreson smoothy-pates do now wear nothing but high shoes and bunches of keys at their girdles
>
> (1.2.35–40)

Falstaff's biblically inflected invective runs through the catalogue of anti-Puritan slurs. He calls the merchant a 'whoreson Achitophel', alluding to the counsellor who was treacherous to King David (2 Samuel, 15.12), and 'a rascal', a 'yea forsooth knave', belittling the merchant's use of the citizens' oath 'yea forsooth' as a sign of tradesmen's fawning respectability. He then mocks these grasping tradesmen as 'whoreson smoothy-pates' – smooth because they eschewed fashionably long hair and cropped their hair short, thus becoming known as Roundheads; their 'high [cork-soled] shoes', a sign of pride which revealed their social aspirations; and their 'bunches of keys', suggestive of the prosperity such nonconformists had achieved in the burgeoning market economy of London. References such as these contribute to the topicality of the play and its immersion in Elizabethan material and political culture. As a comment on those religious reformers whose influence within the Anglican Church was growing stronger as the century drew to a close, Shakespeare's choice

69

of Oldcastle as the name for his fat knight had undeniable satiric point.

The tavern world: wordplay as social critique

The figures who frequent the tavern represent Shakespeare's most imaginative foray into the material world of Elizabethan 'low' culture. Mistress Quickly's role, in particular, is different from what it was in *Part One*, more deeply embedded in the social matrix of Elizabethan London. Managing a tavern was one of the few avenues by which lower-class women could achieve economic independence and social recognition, and Mistress Quickly is acutely aware of her position.[1] A widow past her prime, she has lived in hope for the past twenty years that Falstaff would marry her and thus, as a knight, offer her social advancement by making her 'my lady' (2.1.91); and although she attempts to have him arrested for non-payment of his tavern debt – a debt which substitutes for his failure to honour his promise of marriage – her affection for him eventually prompts her, in a comic about-face, to yield to his asking to borrow yet another ten pounds, evidence of her prosperity as a businesswoman.

No one is better at recounting the past or has a keener memory for domestic detail than the Hostess. Her recollection of Falstaff's marriage proposal years earlier has the digressive anecdotal structure, redundancy and unsophisticated paratactic syntax characteristic of oral storytelling (Thorne, 58): 'Thou didst swear to me upon a parcel-gilt goblet,' she reminds him, 'sitting in my Dolphin chamber at the round table by a seacoal fire upon Wednesday in Wheeson week, when the Prince broke thy head for liking his father to a singing man of Windsor' (85–9). The momentous event that spurs her memory is

---

1   Jean E. Howard and Phyllis Rackin discuss the entrepreneurial Mistress Quickly as an anarchic figure, the sexualizing and criminalizing of whom coincide with her economic prosperity (176–85).

overwhelmed by a wealth of detail about her material surroundings which reveals a great deal about her commercial success and her standing as a member of the mercantile class. Her reminiscence continues with a seemingly random narrative which, through its piling up 'superfluous circumstantial detail' and its 'compulsive repetition of the past', seeks 'to halt time's advance' and even 'to deny temporality itself' (Thorne, 58–9): 'goodwife Keech the butcher's wife', she recalls, came upstairs 'to borrow a mess of vinegar, telling us she had a good dish of prawns, whereby thou didst desire to eat some, whereby I told thee they were ill for a green wound'; but 'when she was gone downstairs,' the Hostess recalls, Falstaff told her 'to be no more so familiarity with such poor people, saying that ere long they should call me madam' (2.1.92–100). Falstaff's promise to gentle the Hostess's condition by marrying her is given shape and substance by the mundane details of its retelling, a rambling account of past events brought vividly to life by the selective memory of a woman for whom they have become the only history that matters.

Furthermore, to a much greater degree than in *Part One*, Mistress Quickly has a riotously original way of speaking through which she unwittingly reveals her sexual history with Falstaff and punctures her pretence to respectability. Unlike Falstaff's devious and self-serving wordplay, the Hostess's involves the use of malapropisms and unintentional *double entendres*. Her comic attempt to use a vocabulary beyond her ken betrays her bourgeois social aspirations, just as her bawdy puns betray her profession as a brothel-keeper. Her conversation with the two officers whom she has enlisted to arrest Falstaff for non-payment of debt is riddled with humorous sexual innuendo. The Hostess admits that Falstaff has 'stabbed' her 'most beastly' in her 'house' (13–14), conjuring an image of his mounting her from the rear in the manner of beasts; and further, she claims that if his weapon is out, he will 'foin like any devil' (16), foin being a fencing term meaning to pierce with a pointed

13   *Sir John, I arrest you at the suit of Mrs. Quickly* (2.1). Painted by Henry
     Singleton; engraved by Gilbert Stuart; published by Longman in 1807

weapon.[1] And to his face, she decries him as 'a honeyseed,
a man queller, and a woman queller' (51–2), malapropisms for
'homicide' and man- or woman-'killer' which suggest that he
will stab either sex indiscriminately.

At the opening of her next speech, the Hostess inadvertently
reveals two sources of frustration with Falstaff rather than one:
his refusal to repay the money he owes her and his unwillingness
to compensate her with marriage for his use of her body. Her

---

1   As a gloss on this line, Partridge cites the undictionaried proverb
    'A standing prick hath no conscience' (114–15).

being 'undone' by his 'going' (22) most obviously refers to her being financially ruined by his leaving for the wars, either because he owes her a vast sum which he presumably will never repay or because she will be losing her best customer. But 'go' was also a slang term for having sex, and her being 'undone' by Falstaff's 'going' thus glances ironically at the use he has presumably made of her virtue and the consequent damage to her reputation. She further accuses him of spending his money on indulgences elsewhere, such as at 'Pie Corner' (25).

Adjacent to the centre of horse-trading in Smithfield and so named for the cooks' shops there, Pie Corner was a familiar resort of prostitutes. Known for its brothels since at least 1393, it was still being mentioned in court records two centuries later: in 1586 a parson 'most shamfully committed carnall copulacon . . . twise in one Treales house a cook by Pye Corner', and in 1608 a woman was seen 'occupied in a stable at Pye Corner'.[1] Unsurprisingly, the phrase itself had become slang for the female pudendum. Therefore, by complaining that Falstaff comes 'continuantly' (a humorous malapropism which conflates 'continually' and 'continently') to Pie Corner 'to buy a saddle' (25–6), the Hostess unwittingly intimates that he frequents her own tavern for sex as well, especially since buying a saddle (as in a saddle of mutton; hence, a piece of flesh) was a popular euphemism for whoring. Her *double entendres* thus sound like what today might be called unconscious slips by which she reveals what she would fain deny.

She continues her inadvertent self-exposure by mispronouncing the legal phrase for filing a lawsuit, 'enter the action', when she begins her plea with 'since my exion is entered and my case so openly known to the world' (28–30). Entering her 'exion' plays on sexual penetration, and her phonetic rendering of 'action' suggests that she may be imitating the way her betters

---

1 Gowing, *Dangers*, 73, and 'Gender', 16. See also Williams, *Revolution*, 259. For a fuller examination of the function of sexual wordplay as social critique in *Part Two*, see Bulman, 'Bawdy'.

pronounce it. Furthermore, 'case', defined as a receptacle or seed-vessel, was a common slang term for vagina, so the fact that her case is 'openly known to the world' becomes a richly humorous confession. As the offending party in her 'case', Falstaff, she insists, must be 'brought in to his answer' (30): that is, either brought to court to answer the charges, or made to marry her.

The Hostess's lust for bourgeois respectability is palpable here. She wants Sir John to make her a lady and thereby to cleanse the unsavoury reputation (the 'ill name' she complains of in 2.4.90) that she fears she has gained by running a tavern which, she later protests, is not a bawdy house.[1] Although in *Part One* she identifies herself as 'an honest man's wife' (3.3.119), in this scene she calls herself a 'poor widow' (2.1.68), a status that grants her the independence of an entrepreneurial business-owner and at the same time allows her to claim the vulnerability of a 'poor lone woman' whose business could be ruined by a customer's non-payment of debt. As Jean Howard and Phyllis Rackin remark (176–85), the Hostess is both empowered by her economic independence and yet threatened by a man who has the power to undo her. This threat explains the urgency behind her desire to arrest Falstaff: the only way she can preserve her status will be either through immediate payment, thus secur-ing her economic independence, or through marriage, which, although it would forfeit her legal independence, will 'gentle' her condition and allow her not to be bothered by others' censure. That her unwitting sexual wordplay and malapropisms implicate her in the very behaviours that she is trying to disavow is the

---

1   Peter Clark discusses the tavern as a permissive site where all classes could con-verge for public drinking as a 'family of vagrancy' (111–15). Shakespeare collapses under one roof an alehouse, a tavern (which offered wine) and a brothel. Usually identified as the Boar's Head, Mistress Quickly's tavern may allude to a historical tavern – there were six by that name in London – which served as a playing space for actors long before there were public theatres. Andrew Gurr notes that a Boar's Head in Whitechapel was converted from an innyard to a playhouse in 1599 (117).

major source of humour in this passage; and her final image of herself in this speech as 'an ass and a beast to bear every knave's wrong' (36–7) rounds out her self-exposure by recalling the image of bestial copulation with which she began her list of grievances against Falstaff.

The bawdy wordplay in *Part Two* keeps the play finely poised between chronicle history and contemporary social critique. Prostitution, for example, is of central importance to *Part Two*, both as a social issue that would resonate with Elizabethan audiences aware of the growing number of prostitutes – and the increasing incidence of sexually transmitted disease – in a burgeoning London,[1] and as a metaphor for the behaviour of those historical figures in the play for whom selling themselves, or screwing others, had become a political fact of life. Doll Tearsheet, one of the 'parish heifers' (2.2.153), whom Mistress Quickly brings to Falstaff for a last night of merriment before he goes off to war, operates on the lowest rung of a decidedly contemporary social ladder. As a prostitute, she is a woman of independent if meagre means, as she reveals when she accosts Pistol for 'tearing a poor whore's ruff in a bawdy house' (2.4.144–5), the large ruff being an item commonly worn by Elizabethan prostitutes (Rackin, 138–9).

Swaggerers such as Pistol were expected to be found in brothels. Indeed, as a brothel 'captain' with an anachronistically

---

1   Since the accession of Elizabeth, brothels had reopened and prospered not only in the suburbs beyond the jurisdiction of London's conservative city fathers, but within the city itself, as Mistress Quickly's establishment anachronistically confirms. Brothels, however, bred crime and disease, problems featured more prominently in *Measure for Measure* (1604), in which the pimp Pompey Bum reports that by proclamation, 'All houses [brothels] in the suburbs of Vienna must be plucked down' (1.2.88–9). Lever relates this to a proclamation by King James on 16 September 1603 which called for the pulling down of houses in London's suburbs to prevent the spread of the plague by 'dissolute and idle persons', a measure which 'bore heavily upon the numerous brothels and gaming houses which proliferated on the outskirts of the city' (*Measure*, xxxii–xxxiii).

phallic name whose bawdy potential the Hostess reveals when she pronounces it as 'Peesel', or Pizzle (2.4.162), Pistol may be directly involved in Doll's trade, for she intimates that he 'lives upon mouldy stewed prunes' (146–7), food associated with brothels because they were thought to be 'part of the cure for venereal disease' (Clowes, 161). Pistol's punning exchange with Falstaff about toasting ('charging') the Hostess with a cup of sack (111–17) reinforces the sexual underpinnings of their alliance by humorously yoking Pistol's ostensible military prowess (pistol, discharging, bullets) to his penchant for drinking (charging, proofs) and, finally, to his using the Hostess for sexual gratification ('I will discharge upon her . . . with two bullets', 114–15). This bond between Pistol and the tavern women grows firmer late in the play when the Beadle who is arresting the Hostess and Doll tells them that 'the man is dead that you and Pistol beat amongst you' (5.4.16–17) – testimony to the violence that commonly erupted in brothels, and evidence that despite her protestations, the Hostess does indeed run a bawdy house.

The insistent references in 2.4 to the world of prostitution in contemporary London invest the scene's subsequent wordplay with a surprising cultural urgency. The Hostess, for example, reveals her profession when Falstaff accuses her of having 'another indictment upon thee, for suffering flesh to be eaten in thy house contrary to the law' (2.4.347–9) – flesh being a *double entendre* equating meat with women, both of which are consumed on her premises. She unwittingly proves his accusation true by protesting, 'All vict'lers do so. What's a joint of mutton or two in a whole Lent?' (351–2), wherein she uses common terms for whores (cf. her use of 'saddle' at 2.1.26) and their purveyors (victuallers). By confessing a minor infringement of the proclamation passed by the Privy Council in 1588 forbidding the consumption of meat during Lent, she also, in a wonderful if inadvertent expression of moral laxity, pleads guilty to the crime of running a brothel. The Hostess's riotous misuse of language, then, serves as a site of carnivalesque resistance to the laws of the land by which enterprising women such as herself and Doll are criminalized.[1]

Like many in the 1590s, Falstaff demonizes prostitutes as threats to the physical health of men and to the moral health of society. He accuses Doll of being a vector of disease who infects her clients: presuming to speak for all men, he says, 'you help to make the diseases, Doll. We catch of you' (45–6). When she retorts that the only thing her clients 'catch' – that is, steal – from her are her 'chains' and her 'jewels' (49), Falstaff with characteristic dexterity turns her words into their scatological equivalents – 'Your brooches, pearls and ouches!' (50) – all of which are euphemisms for the carbuncles, pimples and pustules caused by venereal diseases.

Falstaff then issues a brilliant barrage of military *double entendres* which equate the sickness that results from sexual 'combat' with the wounds of war and, in so doing, recalls his own service at Shrewsbury. He argues that 'To serve bravely' – in bed or in battle – 'is to come halting off' (51) – that is, to limp owing to a wound or to sexual exertion that leaves one unable to stand. His wordplay grows more pointed when, as one destined for the war in the north, he figures 'the rake's passage from quean to quack . . . as a move from field of battle to field dressing station' (Williams, *Revolution*, 211); for the wounded soldier, he announces, goes 'to surgery bravely' (53), an association of the dressing of war wounds with treatment for the pox which continues his demonization of Doll.

Ultimately, Falstaff asserts, whores lead men to damnation. Doll, he tells the Prince, is 'in hell already and burns poor souls' (342–3) – wordplay which condemns the effect of her trade on clients, for burning means infecting with venereal diseases, just

---

1 Hodgdon observes that by the end of the play, 'the potential threats Carnival represents are displaced onto the play's women' who are 'demonized as corrupt, set aside and excluded from the commonwealth' (*End*, 172).

as it does in Sonnet 144: 'Till my bad angel fire my good one out' (14). Falstaff's stream of misogynist *double entendres* in this scene thus potently demeans women as agents of the spiritual and physical corruption of men, a displacement of responsibility that was common among Elizabethan writers. By analogy, too, Falstaff's wordplay about the pox provides a gloss on the anarchy that has plagued the kingdom since the usurpation of King Richard's throne – 'we are all diseased, / And with our surfeiting and wanton hours / Have brought ourselves into a burning fever, / And we must bleed for it' (4.1.54–7) – and on those diseases that fester in the King and Northumberland, men whose ills, both physical and moral, inform the scenes that flank 2.4 (2.3, 3.1) and are of greater consequence to the state – if not to the play – than Falstaff's.

The diverse idioms in *Part Two* through which socially marginalized characters reveal differences in region, class and occupation dramatize an expansion of the cultural boundaries of nationhood to a greater degree than Shakespeare's earlier history plays do.[1] In *Part One* the Prince, who boasts that he 'can drink with any tinker in his own language' (2.4.18–19), implies that learning the vernacular will be essential if he intends to govern an emerging English nation, though he does not show much linguistic virtuosity beyond thieves' cant.[2] In *Part Two*, the importance of a vernacular education is made explicit: 'The Prince but studies his companions / Like a strange tongue,' Warwick assures the King, 'wherein, to gain the language, / 'Tis needful that the most immodest word / Be

---

1 Of the early histories, only *Henry VI, Part Two* attempts to dramatize an expansion of such boundaries, by including Jack Cade's rebellion, which echoes the Puritan Hacket's 1591 London uprising and anachronistically reflects the cultural anxieties of that decade.

2 Hodgdon, *First Part*, 210–11 and 250–7, cites Thomas Dekker's *Lantern and Candlelight* as a guide to the hierarchy of London's vagrant population and reprints his first chapter, 'Of Canting', as a context in which to read the colloquialisms, 'strange tongues' and 'gross terms' used by the low-lifes in *Part One*.

looked upon and learnt' (4.3.68–71).[1] In the distinctive idioms of the Prince's companions – Bardolph, Doll, Pistol, the Hostess and, above all, Falstaff – Shakespeare provides alternatives to the official speech of the court for him to study. As Howard and Rackin put it, 'the distance of various characters from the culture's center of power and importance is marked by their linguistic distance from perfect command of the King's English' (182).

Falstaff in Gloucestershire

Half-way through the play, just after Shakespeare has brought on the ill King for the first time (3.1), the action shifts unexpectedly from the city to the country, where life moves to the rhythms of the agricultural year. The back-biting worlds of court and tavern yield to a world of rural foison and good fellowship; political self-interest, to hospitality and community. This depiction of rural values deepens the play's investigation of English society at a moment of radical social and economic change, the 1590s, when agrarian culture was falling victim to bad crops, enclosures and the prospect of employment in towns and cities. To this world Falstaff comes, stopping at the estate of Robert Shallow, Esquire, to recruit soldiers for the war. The play never returns to the tavern: Shakespeare's inspiration was to replace it with what looks, at first glance, to be a more Edenic way of life – with characters whose apparent innocence sets them apart from their more dissolute London counterparts, and

---

1 Steven Mullaney discusses the Prince's language lesson in terms of the evolution of an English vernacular in the sixteenth century, a time when 'an imaginative sympathy' allowed 'alien voices and ideologies not merely to be recorded or studied, but entered into and enacted quite fully' (76–85). This process is imitated when the Prince's study of a 'strange tongue' involves his developing 'an appetite for the unfamiliar details of popular culture, for the manners and morals, the ways of speech and material conditions of life on the margins of society, among the masterless men, bawds, bankrupts, wayward apprentices, and refugees from country reforms' to which his father so strenuously objects (79–80).

through whom he reinforces themes of remembrance, self-deception and human folly, but in a new key. It is as if, having allowed Falstaff to play out the comedy of the tavern world even without the catalyst of the Prince in the first two acts, Shakespeare decided to move him to a world where his eminence ('now Sir John', says Shallow, 3.2.25) will be honoured and allow him to exploit his wit and greed without fear of retribution, as was the risk in a London where the Lord Chief Justice held sway.

At the centre of this world are two country justices, Shallow and his cousin Silence, who, with their appropriate charactonyms, provincial speech patterns and idiosyncratic memories are among the most indelible portraits Shakespeare ever painted. Shallow is an old man who vainly reminisces about his days as a student at Clement's Inn, one of London's Inns of Chancery, where, he imagines, 'they will talk of mad Shallow yet' (14–15). He names his friends there as if they were present, 'swinge-bucklers' all (22); he recounts their rowdy escapades and visits to the 'bona robas' (23); and with a memory for detail as keen as the Hostess's, he brags about 'a merry night' he spent 'in the Windmill in Saint George's Field' (195–7) and about an epic fight he once had with one 'Samson Stockfish, a fruiterer, behind Gray's Inn' (32–3). He also recalls that 'Jack Falstaff' was then just 'a boy, and page to Thomas Mowbray' (25–6), a detail which fixes the age of Falstaff, who in *Part One* admits to being already 'threescore' (2.4.413), at seventy or near, since Shallow was at Clement's Inn 'fifty-five year ago' (*Part Two*, 3.2.210).[1] Shallow's anecdotal self-invention reveals a longing for a past that is irrecoverable because it is not the stuff of history, but a 'private or collective

---

1 Shallow's establishing a link between Falstaff and Thomas Mowbray, Duke of Norfolk, makes Falstaff by association an adversary of the King, who, as Henry Bolingbroke in *Richard II*, accused Mowbray of treason. Though this association is not made explicit here, and Falstaff fights on behalf of the King, it nevertheless provides a history for any antagonism the two men may feel towards one another.

mythology' (Boym, xv) born of imagination and shared only with others of a sympathetic mind. Shallow's 'Ha, cousin Silence, that thou hadst seen that that this knight and I have seen' is indulgently confirmed by Falstaff's 'We have heard the chimes at midnight, Master Shallow' (3.2.211–15), yet Falstaff consents to this mythology with an eye to his own advantage: he recognizes it for what it is, an old man's foolish fantasy.[1]

Shallow's yokefellow of equity, Justice Silence, is, unlike Shallow, a man of few words. He is presumably meant to be somewhat younger than Shallow, since he speaks of still having a son at Oxford 'to [his] cost' (12), though he is often played for comic effect as a man in extreme dotage, even older than Shallow. Nevertheless, Silence is familiar with Shallow's history at Clement's Inn, no doubt from having been regaled with his exploits repeatedly: 'You were called lusty Shallow then, cousin' (16) he comments, feeding him the line like a straight man to a comic. What characterizes their conversation most vividly, however, is the fine equipoise of Shallow's memory of a past he has embellished and his blunt acknowledgement of the present reality –'Jesu, Jesu, the mad days that I have spent! And to see how many of my old acquaintance are dead' (33–4) – and, in the next breath, the juxtaposition of that acknowledgement with his vital interest in animal husbandry: 'Death, as the psalmist saith, is certain to all; all shall die. How a good yoke of bullocks at Stamford fair?' (37–8). The delicate humour and pathos with which an old man's recognition of mortality is poised against his undimmed will to live are unmatched in Shakespeare's canon.

In soliloquy, however, Falstaff casts a cold eye on the vanity of Shallow's reminiscences – 'Lord, how subject we old men

---

1 When Shallow asks, 'O Sir John, do you remember since we lay all night in the Windmill . . . ?' (194–5), Falstaff obviously humours him with his reply – 'No more of that, Master Shallow' (196) – since, as a mere boy, Falstaff would not have accompanied Shallow to a brothel. By confirming Shallow's memorial delusion, Falstaff is priming him for his request of a thousand pounds.

are to this vice of lying!' (301–2) – witheringly exposing the self-delusion of a man who remembers himself as a lothario but who, in Falstaff's scathing corrective, 'was the very genius of famine, yet lecherous as a monkey, and the whores called him mandrake' (312–14). A mandrake was an herb whose root, according to Gerard's *Herball*, resembled 'the legs of a man, with other parts of his body, adioining thereto as the priuie parts', and was thought since ancient times to be an aphrodisiac (Gerard, 2.280). If the whores thus mocked Shallow's insatiable lust, Falstaff's wordplay calls his taste into question as well: ''A came ever in the rearward of the fashion' (314–15), he asserts, suggesting that Shallow was rustic in his habits and dress but also implying that he may have practised buggery – a common prejudice about sexual preferences in the country (Partridge, 145).

Having thoroughly exposed Shallow as a fantasist, Falstaff vows to 'make him a philosopher's two stones to me' (328). Alchemists believed that one of these stones would confer eternal youth and the other would transmute base metals into gold. Since Falstaff intends to grow rich by Shallow and is presumably interested in only *one* of the stones, his mention of *two* stones increases the likelihood that he is playing on stones as slang for a man's testicles. In other words, Falstaff swears to have Shallow by the balls – a situation in which Shallow, eager to buy a friend at court, is a willing accomplice.

Yet Falstaff's cynical appraisal does not erase the fact that through characters such as Shallow, Silence and the Hostess, Shakespeare gives greater prominence than in any other history play to the idiosyncratic accounts of 'old folk, Time's doting chronicles' (4.3.126), whose nostalgic ramblings preserve a popular history that has nothing to do with weighty concerns of state. Personal anecdotes and reminiscences such as theirs were kept alive by an oral tradition that made their stories more ephemeral and less regulated than the stories recorded by chroniclers. As Adam Fox observes, 'In many of the reminiscences of elder inhabitants is a nostalgia for the old days [when] . . . hospitality was greater and life was simpler. . . . To this extent there could be something inherently subversive about popular perceptions of the past' (221–2).[1] Though perhaps not subversive, the oral memory-histories of older characters in *Part Two*, in their disorderly accumulation of details and local topological references, nevertheless resist incorporation into the play's dramatization of dynastic struggle in England's Plantagenet past. 'What might be construed as an irrelevant detour from the linear syntax of political history,' writes Alison Thorne, 'reveals itself, from a different standpoint, as a door opening briefly to areas of social history that were largely occluded by the state-centred focus of most Tudor historiography' (58–9). In doing so, it allows the histories of commoners to stand independent of, and rival in importance, the chronicle history by which the Tudors tried to forge a coherent narrative of English identity.[2]

To the idyllic prosperity of Shallow's farm Falstaff brings the predatory ethos of an 'old pike' (3.2.329). Where in *Part One* he admits in soliloquy to having recruited 'slaves as ragged as Lazarus in the painted cloth' (4.2.21–2) because other more able-bodied recruits have 'bought out their services' (28), in

---

1 Keith Thomas concurs that 'in a semi-literate society, still much dependent on oral tradition, it was the old who controlled access to the past. They were the repositories of history and custom, of pedigree and descent' (233–4).

2 Thorne's observation (58–9) of course applies as well to the scenes in Eastcheap as to those in Gloucestershire. Naomi Conn Liebler perceptively reads 4.3 as a scene that narrows 'the play of history to selective frames of personal memory', and therefore as 'the foil to [King] Henry's opportunism', for it 'casts a shadow over the reliability of memory and nostalgia as justification for his present aggression' (87). For a discussion of how communal memory led to distortion, how oral testimony as a way of preserving the past persisted in local communities well into the sixteenth century, and how the printed word eventually displaced oral testimony in its 'creation . . . of a national master narrative that largely excluded both the remembered and the local', see Woolf, *Social*, 276–99.

Part Two Shakespeare dramatizes that process.[1] Falstaff carries the values of greed and self-interest with him from London to the country. His recruitment of foot soldiers is tainted by a scheme to make money in which he seeks to conscript men who will be able to bribe their way out of service; and it is unsurprising that they should wish to do so, because, as Will Sharpe observes ('Geography'), these men live far from the centres of power, are ignorant of what is going on in Westminster, have no investment in ideological conflict, and thus are mere pawns in a war waged by selfish nobles. When the ablest among them – the yeomen farmers Bullcalf and Mouldy, who have no appetite for fighting – bribe Bardolph to let them go, Falstaff proves guilty of the same corrupt practices that brought shame to Elizabethan commanders whose abuses were catalogued in military conduct books.[2]

Indeed, a letter written by Justices of the Peace in Gloucestershire, recorded on 25 May 1593, inveighed against frauds in recruitment perpetrated by 'inferior officers . . . who for their own private gain have . . . sold, freed and exchaunged the most part of al such as were men of anie sufficienye and habillitie before suxh time as they were delivered over to their

---

1   Patricia A. Cahill explains that 'recruitment' – reinforcing an army with fresh troops – is an anachronistic term first used in 1645, when the New Model Army was organized by Parliament. Instead, this scene depicts a 'muster', 'the practice of gathering men in a country for inspection of numbers or for training', the responsibility for which, after the 1570s, fell to local officials such as Justice Shallow, who 'were required to report in their returns on all men eligible to serve' and 'chosen for service'. The term is first used in the Induction (12), when Rumour 'grandly takes responsibility for the "fearful musters" [12] that have uprooted the men of the country' (*Breach*, 73–4).

2   See de Somogyi, 42–51, and Fortescue, 1.112–26. Among contemporary observers, Barnaby Riche asserts in *Path-Way* (1587) that captains are often incompetent and corrupt, negligent of their men and provisions, cowardly and undisciplined, and, at worst, thieving murderers; and Nashe, in *Pierce Pennilesse* (1592), ranks captains among those who devote themselves to corrupt pleasures such as gaming, drinking and whoring.

captaines to be imbarqued and sent over [to Normandy and Brittany]'.[1] Although levying men for service had become so difficult by the late sixteenth century that soldiers were being recruited from prisons or by means of the press-gang, corruption among recruiters was never condoned, and Falstaff's behaviour, however comic, is morally censurable. Even worse than taking bribes, Falstaff is guilty of taking 'dead pay', that is, entering in his muster book the names of dead or non-existent men (called 'shadows') whose earnings he would then pocket for himself. His punning confession at the expense of the recruit named Shadow – 'Shadow will serve for summer. Prick him, for we have a number of shadows fill up the muster book' (3.2.134–6) – reveals just how brazenly he abuses the King's press. As a result of such fraudulence, Falstaff winds up selecting, over Shallow's protest, only the least physically able recruits for service: the emaciated Wart, the 'half-faced fellow' Shadow (265–6), and the women's tailor Feeble. Although his justification for doing so – 'Care I for the limb, the thews, the stature, bulk and big assemblance of a man? Give me the spirit, Master Shallow!' (259–61) – draws perversely on an argument made by Elizabethan theorists that 'courage & minde is as much to bee respected as the bodye',[2] Falstaff's recruitment practices are nonetheless reprehensible; for in effect, he betrays a lack of concern for the war effort and is willing to sacrifice anyone to it but himself.

The tissue of bawdy wordplay that served as social critique in the tavern world also underscores the immorality of the

---

1 Located by RP in *Acts of Privy Council of England*, 237, Item 3.
2 Thomas Proctor, fols 21–2, cited in Jorgensen, 'Rank', 34. Jorgensen also quotes Matthew Sutcliffe, *The Practice, Proceedings, and Lawes of Armes* (1593) as offering an argument that Falstaff uses to justify recruiting Feeble: 'Men of meane stature are for the most part more vigorous and couragious . . . and commonly excell great bodied men in swiftness end running' (65). Compare Falstaff: 'And for a retreat, how swiftly will this Feeble . . . run off!' (3.2.268–70).

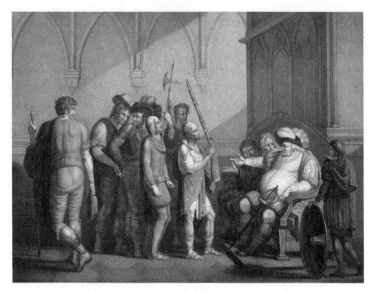

14 *Second part of King Henry the Fourth,* ACT III, SCENE II. *Justice Shallow's seat in Gloucestershire.* Falstaff to Wart: 'Come, manage me your caliver' [3.2.273]. Painted by J. Durno; engraved by T. Ryder; published by J. & J. Boydell in 1798

recruiting scene. The most common verb for recruiting was 'prick', and Falstaff's repeated command for Bardolph to 'Prick him' – that is, to mark down a recruit's name in the impressment log – fills yeomen and householders such as Mouldy and Bullcalf with dread. But 'prick' is also a word on whose bawdy potential Shakespeare plays relentlessly. Mouldy, for example, employs it in the interest of self-preservation: 'I was pricked well enough before, and you could have let me alone,' he protests (112–13); and while 'pricked' here could simply mean henpecked, it more suggestively refers to his sexual endowment. As a ribald pun, it alerts the listener to continued wordplay in the next line, when he complains that his 'old dame will be undone now for one to do her husbandry and her drudgery' (113–14). For a yeoman, husbandry and drudgery signify farm work; but they had bawdy double meanings as well. Husbandry referred to fulfilling a man's conjugal role, and drudgery was a comic term for the sexual labour involved in cuckolding another man, as Shakespeare would use it in *All's Well*: 'He that ears my land spares my team, and gives me leave to in the crop. If I be his cuckold, he's my drudge' (1.3.44–6). Without such labour, Mouldy argues, his 'old lady' will be, like the Hostess at 2.1.22, 'undone,' the now-unearthed pun on 'do' intimating that she will go without sex in his absence.[1] Although Mouldy's second mention of his 'old dame' later in the scene indicates that he is referring to his mother (3.2.229–32), his first use of it encourages the listener to infer that he means his wife, making his wordplay on husbandry and drudgery, in retrospect, look deceptively opportunistic. Despite the apparent innocence of the rural society on view, then, Mouldy betrays the same selfishness and duplicity as his counterparts in the city. Indeed, the vein of wordplay that runs through the recruitment scene creates a subtext of cultural debasement at odds with the nostalgic ideals of a virtuous country life – hard work, honesty and loyalty – which the scene ostensibly depicts.

For his part, Falstaff employs wordplay with a 'callous and unimaginative cratylism' (A. Barton, 109) to deride the recruits as mercilessly as he has done the Hostess and Doll: Wart is of 'ragged appearance' (262); Shadow is likely to be 'a cold soldier' (124); and it is time for Mouldy to be 'used' (107). His mockery of Feeble the women's tailor is particularly demeaning. The term 'tailor' itself was a sexual pun signifying a fornicator, a man who used his *tail* or penis to penetrate a customer. Falstaff thus makes Feeble the butt of an easy sexual joke when he warns Shallow about the danger of pricking him, for 'if he had

---

1   R.W. Dent quotes an early modern source: 'To dig anothers garden' meant 'to Cuckold one, to do his work and drudgery, as they say for him' (L57).

been a man's tailor, he'd a' pricked you' (153–4). Yet Feeble is the one recruit to express a sense of patriotic duty as he rejects the option to buy out his service: 'We owe God a death. I'll ne'er bear a base mind . . . No man's too good to serve 's prince' (236–8), a proverbial sentiment that echoes the Prince's admonition to Falstaff at Shrewsbury, 'Why, thou owest God a death' (*Part One* 5.1.126). With a fine Shakespearean irony, Feeble, the least likely of the recruits, embodies the moral integrity which one is hard pressed to find among characters elsewhere in the play.

Yet the sublime comedy of the final two Gloucestershire scenes, in which Falstaff has returned to 'fetch off' (3.2.300) the two country justices, offsets to a degree the cynicism of the recruitment scene with a celebration of rural plenty and unfeigned friendship. They offer an autumnal depiction of an after-supper gathering to enjoy pippins of Shallow's 'own graffing' (5.3.2–3), to mellow in the effects of drinking too much sack, and to listen to Silence, a man of few words until now, sing irrepressibly about the joys of wine and women. In these scenes, *Part Two* recaptures to a degree the festive energy that characterized the tavern scenes in *Part One*. Insisting that Falstaff stay to dinner, Shallow sputters a welcome with repetitions characteristic of old people's speech: 'I will not excuse you. You shall not be excused. Excuses shall not be admitted. There is no excuse shall serve. You shall not be excused' (5.1.4–6). He tempts Falstaff with the abundance of a prosperous farm, instructing his man Davy to have the cook prepare his choicest viands – 'Some pigeons, Davy, a couple of short-legged hens, a joint of mutton and any pretty little tiny kickshaws' (24–6).

Life's pleasures are celebrated most unexpectedly by Silence, however, who in performance often steals the limelight from the other comic characters, his loquaciousness all the funnier because so unexpected. Happily drunk, he sings snatches of old songs that recall a time of festive indulgence:

15   Silence (Adrian Scarborough), Falstaff (Michael Gambon), Davy (Ian
      Gelder) and Shallow (John Wood) at table enjoying a rural repast (5.3)
      in a production directed by Nicholas Hytner on the Olivier stage at the
      National Theatre, 2005

> Do nothing but eat and make good cheer,
> And praise God for the merry year,
> When flesh is cheap and females dear,
> And lusty lads roam here and there
> So merrily,
> And ever among so merrily.

(5.3.17–22)

Silence is a man at peace with himself and the world. 'I have
been merry twice and once ere now' (39–40), he reminisces
before being carried to bed, and that reminiscence – for once,
probably unembellished – is both sad and endearing. In
Silence's inebriation the play's nostalgia for a bygone England
is most humorously portrayed: he repeatedly sings the refrain
'Be merry, be merry' (36), and the merriment of the scene

attests that festive practices associated with Catholicism persisted most strongly among the rural laity, those 'merry reprobates' who, in *Part Two*, 'are more precisely associated with calendrical celebrations' of 'the old church' than any characters in *Part One*.[1] The longing for holiday unfettered by the restraints associated with the Reformation was a subversive feature of England's religious landscape in the late sixteenth century, and such longing is most palpable in the Gloucestershire scenes when the guests at the feast not only recall a merrier time, but anticipate that England may once again be merry when Harry is crowned king.

Even these mellow scenes of festivity, however, are not without complication. Shallow does not exercise the authority over his servants that he should, and, as a minor official of the crown, his dispensation of justice is far from unimpeachable. His man Davy, who undertakes the proper management of the farm and alone has the perspicacity to recognize the lousy condition of Falstaff's men, solicits Shallow to fix a lawsuit on behalf of his friend Visor. Although Davy grants that Visor is a 'knave' (5.1.39) whose cause is unjust, he assumes that his loyal service to Shallow entitles him to request a legal favour 'once or twice in a quarter' (42–6); and Shallow assures him that Visor shall 'have no wrong' (50). This evidence of moral laxity and judicial corruption may seem incongruous in an idyllic England whose values seem to contrast those of the court, but as Falstaff points out in his soliloquy, proportion and degree are not kept in Shallow's household: servants bear themselves with authority and justice obliges *them* (63–6). This topsy-turvy world stands ironically at odds with the myth of England's golden age and

---

1 Jensen, 157. In an illuminating review of the complaints made 'by Puritan controversialists' about 'residual rural Catholicism' (Walsham, 103), Baldo (85–8, following Wallace, 27–49) quotes a preacher who 'numbered among the persistent errors of what he termed "country divinitie" a nostalgia for the old days and an attachment to the customs of one's forefathers'.

with the court of King Henry, where, by the end of the play, hierarchy will be affirmed, legitimate succession upheld and the Lord Chief Justice asked to maintain the rule of law. Moreover, when Falstaff bilks Shallow of a thousand pounds, one need not view Shallow as an innocent victim, for with that money he hopes to ensure favour at court when Falstaff's minion comes to power. Indeed, Shallow's determination to 'use [Falstaff] well', for 'A friend i'th' court is better than a penny in purse' (28–9), attests to an ulterior motive for Shallow's hospitality, as does his flattery of Bardolph by calling him 'Master' (5.3.58, 63) in anticipation of his preferment under the new King.[1] Shallow's aspirations are as self-serving as Falstaff's, his bribery as bald as Mouldy's or Bullcalf's. The dishonour of the country justice stands in marked contrast to the integrity of the Lord Chief Justice, who acts on his belief that true justice is blind to self-interest, bribes and threats.

No matter how comically poignant these Gloucestershire scenes are, therefore, they depict an unweeded garden whose nature is often as rank as that of the London streets. Despite the traditional view of Shallow's farm as Shakespeare's paean to a passing world of innocence and communal trust, corruption flourishes as much among the gentry and yeomen in the country as among the prostitutes, swaggerers and old soldiers in the city, or, indeed, among the lords who are vying for power in the play's chronicle history. To a degree, rural England turns out to be not so much an idyllic alternative to the tavern world as an extension of it.

---

1   Judith Weil discusses the 'probing examination of ambitious retainers and their hopes' in *Part Two*, illustrating how the tradition of 'countenancing' – that is, supporting or protecting – a 'friend' is crucial to an understanding of Falstaff's relationship not only to the Prince, but to those in service to him such as Bardolph and the Page, and to those who, like Shallow, hope to benefit from his friendship (80–91). Even Davy has applied the principle to Visor: 'The knave is mine honest friend, sir; therefore I beseech you let him be countenanced' (5.1.48–9).

The rejection of Falstaff

The scenes leading up to the rejection of Falstaff proceed with a keen sense of tragic irony. Both of the scenes on Shallow's farm in Act 5 are preceded by scenes of the royal family newly come into focus – that is, with the confirmation of Harry as his father's son and worthy heir. The emotional reconciliation of the dying King with the repentant Prince in 4.3 immediately precedes Falstaff's return to Gloucestershire to cheat Shallow out of a thousand pounds: Falstaff's delighted boast that he will 'devise matter enough out of this Shallow to keep Prince Harry in continual laughter the wearing out of six fashions' (5.1.76–8) is naively ironic, because we have just had proof that the reformed Harry will no longer be be amused by such matter. Even more pointedly, the new King's reassurance that he has cast aside his former self (5.2.121–32) and will embrace the Lord Chief Justice to be the tutor to his youth sets in bold relief Falstaff's claim in the following scene, upon hearing news that the old King is dead, that 'I know the young King is sick for me' (5.3.135). His delighted assumption of royal privilege, therefore, sounds ominously premature:

> Master Shallow – my Lord Shallow – be what thou wilt: I am Fortune's steward. . . . Let us take any man's horses: the laws of England are at my commandment. Blessed are they that have been my friends, and woe to my Lord Chief Justice!
>
> (129–38)

Shortly thereafter, the new regime's determination to clean up the stews by arresting the Hostess and Doll Tearsheet (5.4) demonstrates that Falstaff's friends will have no protection under King Harry. Shakespeare thus prepares his audiences, as surely as Sophocles prepared audiences in *Oedipus*, for the final tragic irony: Falstaff's fall from grace at the very moment he thinks that riot will be enthroned.

Falstaff's interruption of the King's coronation procession presumes on a privilege that the audience knows is no longer his. Aware that he is inappropriately dressed for the occasion, his clothes 'stained with travel' (5.5.24), he convinces himself that 'This poor show doth better' because it 'doth infer the zeal [he] had to see' his minion crowned (13–14). More audaciously, his calling out to 'King Hal' as 'my sweet boy' (39, 42) stops the royal procession. It is offensive not just because he claims too much familiarity, but because by yoking his private nickname for Henry to the title King, he is guilty of an egregious breach of decorum.[1] Morally, the audience knows that Falstaff should not be permitted to come within the compass of Henry V's court. The King of course must banish plump Jack – as he has promised to do in *Part One* – and retain the Lord Chief Justice if he is to gain credibility among his subjects. 'Make less thy body hence' (51), he commands, asserting 'a new regime of trim reckonings . . . mobilized against decaying aristocratic corpulence' (Goldberg, 172). His rejection of Falstaff, while harsh, is a political necessity; and it begins with an ironic echo of his 'I know you all' soliloquy in *Part One* (1.2.185): 'I know thee not, old man. Fall to thy prayers' (46).

But as centuries of audiences would attest, such necessity is dramatically unsavoury, for the Prince appears in his coronation as the impersonal manifestation of state will, and Falstaff, the all-too-human victim of a callous political system. It was Falstaff, after all, who in soliloquy aptly characterized Prince John as cold-blooded but held out some hope that Harry, because he drinks 'good store of fertile sherris' (4.2.119–20), might put a more humane face on government. As King, however, Harry becomes as 'sober-blooded' (85–6) as his

---

1   A. Barton notes that Falstaff's 'attempt to signal intimacy is not only a little too insistent, but glaringly one-sided', for the Prince never 'reciprocate[s] in kind' (110).

16 The rejection of Falstaff (Brewster Mason) by King Henry V (Alan Howard), in a Royal Shakespeare Company production directed by Terry Hands at the Royal Shakespeare Theatre, Stratford-upon-Avon, 1975

brother. When he warns Falstaff that 'the grave doth gape / For thee thrice wider than for other men' (5.5.52–3), he recalls the feigned death of Falstaff at Shrewsbury, over whose corpse he delivered an affectionate epitaph: 'Death hath not struck so fat a deer today' (*Part One* 5.4.106). Here, he speaks no epitaph and his allusion to Falstaff's size is cruel. As Warburton shrewdly observed in a note to Theobald's edition (3.539), however, the King risks 'falling back into *Hal*' with this mocking reference to his old friend's 'Bulk'; 'but He perceives it at once, is afraid Sir *John* should take the Advantage of it, so checks both himself and the Knight with "*Reply not to me with a Fool-born jest*"' (Vickers, *Shakespeare*, 2.534). This observation hints at the depth of the young King's struggle to maintain an emotional detachment in the face of a man who once appealed, and may still appeal, to his need for paternal acceptance and his desire for a release from royal obligation.

Falstaff, of course, must be removed as an impediment to Harry's exercising the law of the land, and the public nature of the rejection may be advantageous to the new King's authority being seen as legitimate. Falstaff's public indiscretion merits a public rebuke, and critics who view the play as being primarily about the education of a Prince are quick to condone it. Drawing on the King's promise that Falstaff will be given 'advancement' according to how he 'reform[s]' (5.567–9), Samuel Johnson reasons that 'if it be considered that the fat knight has never uttered one sentiment of generosity, and with all his power of exciting mirth has nothing in him that can be esteemed, no great pain will be suffered from the reflection that he is compelled to live honestly' (*Plays*; in Vickers, *Shakespeare*, 5.122–3). Such moral justification for Falstaff's banishment fed Dover Wilson's judgement that the young King's 'choice between Justice and Vanity' had made Falstaff's rejection 'inevitable' and his committal to the Fleet – 'a prison of a special and superior kind' reserved for the 'temporary custody' of important notables – neither 'a hardship [nor] a disgrace', but rather 'a compliment' (*Fortunes*, 117–20); and Wilson in turn influenced A.R. Humphreys's assertion that 'the opposed evolutions of Falstaff and Hal' should 'dispel any notion that Falstaff is scurvily treated. . . . Falstaff's hubris positively demands a public scene; he flaunts his way of life for all to see, and boasts that it will be the King's, too. The public disgrace is the appropriate nemesis, and the punishment is lenient' (lix).

Such rationales for Falstaff's rejection have been adapted more recently by anthropological critics who have viewed him unsympathetically as a site of carnivalesque misrule which must be overborne by the forces of order, for 'the antihierarchical chaos he embodies, conceived according to the satiric anti-Puritan model, has rendered him too dangerous a voice for inclusion in the serious business of governance' (Tiffany, 278);[1] and by new historicist critics such as Greenblatt, who, while suspending moral judgement, nevertheless argues that the power of state in *Part Two* is preserved by a series of 'squalid betrayals', of which the King's rejection of Falstaff is the 'final, definitive betrayal' out of which his 'formal majesty' is secured (40). In other words Falstaff, who has appeared throughout the two plays to have undermined royal authority, turns out paradoxically to have been its prop; or, in Barbara Hodgdon's succinct phrasing, 'while Hal and Henry IV *are* history, Falstaff *serves* it' (*Part Two*, 15).

Critics concede that Falstaff's punishment could have been worse: after all, he is not to be detained long at the Fleet, and the King grants him an allowance sufficient to live on, holding out the possibility of advancement if he reforms. But clemency is not the dramatic impression one is left with. An Elizabethan audience would have been acutely aware that Queen Elizabeth habitually imprisoned favourites simply for incurring her displeasure. Furthermore, the vast humanity of Falstaff's role militates against the 'historical' reading of the rejection scene in which what Falstaff *represents*, rather than who he *is*, becomes the justification for his banishment: it accounts for the displeasure of audiences and readers who, unwilling to view dramatic character reductively as merely having a schematic moral or political function, find his rejection unpalatable. As Moody E. Prior argues, Falstaff's rejection 'amounts . . . to the crushing of a comic figure whose natural fate is not to go down in defeat but in triumph'. A 'magnificent' comic hero such as this was

---

1   'Hal's project', according to Michael D. Bristol's Bakhtinian reading, 'is eventually to break the rhythmic alternation between the abundance of the material principle embodied in carnival and the abstemious social discipline embodied in Lent by establishing a permanent sovereignty of Lenten civil policy' (206). Jensen writes that 'since the second Henriad . . . participates in the secularizing process by which traditional celebrations were redirected towards a celebration of English nationhood, Falstaff must be banished from that world' (192).

17 The rejection of Falstaff (Desmond Barrit) by King Henry V (William Houston), in a Royal Shakespeare Company production directed by Michael Attenborough at the Swan Theatre, Stratford-upon-Avon, 2000

'not created for such ends. No matter by what critical avenues the rejection of Falstaff is approached, the unpleasantness of which so many have complained cannot be argued away' (166–7).

An objection to the King's treatment of Falstaff was first recorded by Nicholas Rowe, who, in the essay prefixed to his 1709 edition of the plays, protests that since Shakespeare 'has given [Falstaff] so much Wit as to make him almost too agreeable . . . I don't know whether some People have not, in remembrance of the Diversion he had formerly afforded 'em, been sorry to see his Friend *Hal* use him so scurvily when he comes to the Crown in the End' (Vickers, *Shakespeare*, 2.195). Corbin Morris, who regarded Falstaff as 'entirely an amiable Character', explained in 1744 that his 'Imprisonment and Death', far from being merited, were 'written by *Shakespeare* in Compliance with the *Austerity* of the Times, and in order to avoid the Imputation of encouraging *Idleness* and mirthful *Riot* by too amiable and happy an Example' (Vickers, *Shakespeare*, 3.122). This sentimental appreciation of Falstaff's humanity was shared by Maurice Morgann, who lamented in his famous *Essay on the dramatic character of Sir John Falstaff* (1777), 'we can scarcely forgive the ingratitude of the Prince in the new-born virtue of the King, and we curse the severity of the poetic justice which consigns our old good-natured delightful companion to the . . . dishonours of the *Fleet*' (*Falstaff*, 149).

A half-century later, William Hazlitt speculated with keen psychological insight that the reason 'we never could forgive the Prince's treatment of Falstaff' (*Characters*, 155) is that 'the imperfect and even deformed characters in Shakespeare's plays, as done to the life, by forming a part of our personal consciousness, claim our personal forgiveness, and suspend or evade our moral judgement, by bribing our self-love to side with them' (*Lectures*, 40). Such sentiments reached their apogee in an essay by A.C. Bradley in 1902, which argued in opposition to moralizing critics that 'Falstaff's dismissal to the Fleet, and his subsequent death, prove beyond doubt that his rejection was meant by Shakespeare to be taken as a catastrophe which not even his humour could enable him to surmount' (253).[1]

The final humiliation of Falstaff is his loss of the most potent weapon in his arsenal, the pun. Always the rapier he wields to talk his way out of awkward situations, here the pun

---

1 Similar views have continued to be expressed, as by Jonas A. Barish who, in regarding the rejection of Falstaff as a litmus test for audiences, discusses the loss of humanity incurred by the Prince when he elects morality over holiday.

is wrested from him and turned against him by Shallow, who realizes that he has been robbed of a thousand pounds. When Falstaff seeks to convince Shallow that 'I will be the man yet that shall make you great' (5.5.78–9), Shallow counters with a disparaging rebuttal – 'I cannot perceive how, unless you give me your doublet and stuff me out with straw' (80–1) – turning a pun that Falstaff once applied to himself with ironic self-deprecation (1.2.137–44) into a sour joke which insists that Falstaff is 'great' only in being fat. And when, in an attempt to recover, Falstaff reassures Shallow that the King's banishment of him 'was but a colour' (5.5.85), Shallow's retort shades 'colour' into a pun on 'collar' that signifies hanging – 'A colour that I fear you will die in, Sir John' (86) – to which Falstaff has no ready reply. Denied control of the pun, Falstaff is defenceless.

The corralling of Falstaff and his followers, along with the arrest of Doll and the Hostess, effectively silences those voices that have provided socially diverse narrative histories ungoverned by the chronically sanctioned history of state. But if the play ends with a repressive assertion of hegemonic order, nevertheless those voices have been heard, and heard memorably, in some of the most idiosyncratically delightful scenes Shakespeare ever wrote. At the centre of these scenes is neither the King nor the Prince, but a fat knight who embodies a moral licence and an irrepressible vitality that are crushed by the apparatus of state – an apparatus which, if a force of historical inevitability, nevertheless is at odds with both human compassion and theatrical pleasure. In all but the most militant productions, the state does not win the audience's sympathy. Falstaff does.

THE PLAY AS CHRONICLE HISTORY

Shakespeare took risks in *Part Two*. Faced with constructing a sequel to *Part One* which had no obvious source of political tension following the defeat of the rebels at Shrewsbury, he searched the chronicles for a continuing threat to the monarchy which would serve *Part Two* as crucially as the Percy rebellion had served *Part One*. In doing so, he 'omitted or pushed to the periphery ... most of the political and military incidents' given prominence in chroniclers' accounts of the last decade of Henry's reign (Thorne, 53): Glendower's persistent marauding along the Welsh borders, French incursions into England's territorial possessions, and an uprising led by Northumberland, whose defeat at the Battle of Bramham Moor would have allowed Shakespeare, had he so chosen, to dramatize the suppression of rebellion with a victory as heroic as that at Shrewsbury. Instead, he elevated the Prelate's Rebellion to a greater significance than it achieves in Holinshed.

Shakespeare may not have anticipated using this rebellion at all when planning *Henry IV*. His original idea may have been to follow *Part One* with a play about Henry V that begins with the death of the old king. When he decided to write a second *Henry IV* play, however, his choice to make theatrical capital of so relatively minor a conspiracy allowed him to foreground themes of time and chance, mistrust and self-interest which distinguish his portrayal of history in *Part Two*. Unlike *Part One*, whose king is firmly in command from the start and in which the royal narrative provides a firm scaffold on which to hang the historical events chronicled in the play, chronicle history in *Part Two* is introduced by scenes with the rebels, who are uncertain of their course and, in the case of Northumberland, quickly dismissed from the play. Thus the most powerful rebel in *Part One*, father of Hotspur, disappears from view in Act 2; his death is only briefly reported to the King late in the play; and the Prelate's Rebellion, plotted in Act 1, does not resume until Act 4.[1]

---

1   Shakespeare's decision to dramatize the Prelate's Rebellion may account for his taking from Holinshed (3.529) the name of a noble who had participated in it, Lord

The Prelate's Rebellion

The allegorical figure of Rumour casts doubt on the reliability of chronicle reportage at the opening of the play. Dressed in a robe *'painted full of tongues'* (Ind.0.1–2), Rumour may have cut a strikingly theatrical figure as 'a vast, fearful monster', like Virgil's goddess Fama, 'with a watchful eye miraculously set under every feather which grows on her, and for every one of them a tongue in a mouth which is loud of speech, and an ear ever alert'.[1] Rumour's slanderous tongues function to promote disorder 'in every language', 'Stuffing the ears of men with false reports', thus introducing the unreliability of speech as one of the primary concerns in the play (7–8). 'Rumour is a pipe / Blown by surmises, Jealousy's conjectures' (15–16), who warns that no news should be trusted; and this is borne out in the ensuing scene when Northumberland hears contradictory reports that his son Hotspur has won the field at Shrewsbury or has died there. False expectation among the rebels works its mischief further when Hastings and Lord Bardolph miscalculate the size of the opposing forces (1.3.63–80) and assume that Northumberland will bring reinforcements, despite their acknowledgement that 'in a theme so bloody-faced as this, / Conjecture, expectation and surmise / Of aids incertain should not be admitted' (22–4). The danger of such expectation is dramatized shortly thereafter when Northumberland is persuaded by his wife and Lady Percy to fly to Scotland rather than bring reinforcements to the rebel army. Though Northumberland protests that his 'honour is at pawn' (2.3.7),

'Berdolfe', or Bardolph, and risking confusion with the name of the low-life Bardolph who had already proved popular as a companion of Falstaff in *Part One* (where his name is spelled 'Bardoll' in early quartos) and who reappears as Falstaff's man-servant and corporal in *Part Two*.

1 Virgil, *Aen.*, 4.180–3, cited in Garber, who draws a provocative analogy between Rumour and the Rainbow Portrait of Queen Elizabeth (*c.* 1600), who is 'depicted wearing a cloak adorned with eyes and ears, implying that she sees and hears everything' (345).

he capitulates to Lady Percy's impassioned plea that he should not 'hold [his] honour more precise and nice / With others' (40–1) than with Hotspur, whom he failed to support with troops at Shrewsbury. This brief scene, Shakespeare's invention, defies chronicle tradition by empowering aristocratic women – rare in the histories – and by exposing the precariousness of the rebel position. There is little faith among the rebels in this play, no pretence to honourable behaviour, and none of the nobility embodied in Hotspur. They live in a world of mocked expectations.

The rebellion comes to an ignominious end in Act 4, when Prince John and Westmorland outsmart the rebels with a ruse at Gaultree Forest. They succeed because the rebel leaders – particularly the Archbishop, who tries to put a moral gloss on political action – momentarily lower their guard and choose to believe the Prince's promise that their grievances will be redressed. Once they are tricked into discharging their army, John is free to arrest them for capital treason without fear of reprisal. This way of quashing the rebellion is dramatically risky: it denies audiences the thrill of an onstage battle such as Shrewsbury and frustrates their desire to witness individual heroism in a noble cause. Here, the victors are those who employ machiavellian policy with greatest skill. The Gaultree episode thus offers a view of history as radically contingent and amoral. It is devoid of the chivalric ethos which, albeit compromised, informed the military conflict in *Part One*.

Politically, it is the play's climactic scene. But dramatically, like so much else in *Part Two*, it is not the climax that the play seems to have prepared for.[1] It undercuts the audience's expectations and thus makes a fascinating contrast with the way in which the rebels are defeated at Shrewsbury. There, the focus

---

1 In opposition to the totalizing discourse of critics 'who claim that everything [in *2H4*] is answerable to the Great Idea of a tetralogy', Edward Pechter astutely analyses the Gaultree episode as an exposure of the rebels' futile attempts to find origins for their cause in an indeterminate past (39–45).

was on battle; here, on negotiation. There, Prince Harry scaled chivalric heights to defeat the charismatic Hotspur in one-on-one combat; here, Prince John, a minor figure in the play, wins by double-crossing the rebels. The world of chivalry thus gives way to a world of policy: Prince John, even though his strategy might be defensible as a means of saving the kingdom from protracted civil wars, nevertheless appears cold and perfidious – a student of Machiavelli, as some in Shakespeare's audience would have recognized – and his political subterfuge is rewarded.

Elizabethan audiences, however, may have condoned such subterfuge as necessary and even godly. On the one hand, as Jorgensen details in his analysis of sixteenth-century treatises on the morality of military conduct, perfidy was usually condemned in dealing with one's enemies, with whom, as Thomas Elyot in *The Boke Named the Gouernour* urged, 'consideration aught to be had of iustyce and honestie' (3.5).[1] Yet 'the growing stress and wearisomeness of military campaigns' in the 1590s, particularly against the Irish, were 'reducing the English government to desperation and unscrupulousness' (Humphreys, 238), and honour was rapidly being supplanted by expedience in the conduct of war. Apologists for the government were quick to enlist God on their side. One anonymous commentator in 1591 praised the English general Sir John Norris for his victory over rebels in Brittany, '[w]hereby we may see how God rebateth the edge of rebel harts, daunteth their courages and ranverseth their actions with his byblows or unlooked-for countrebluffs'.[2] The Church unsurprisingly spoke out powerfully against rebellion as a sacrilege. Archbishop Sandys, for example, exhorted hearers to obey those in office, for 'God . . . hateth iniquity, and will not suffer conspiracy, rebellion, or treason against

1 Jorgensen's 'Dastardly' is the basis of Humphreys's consideration of the moral ambiguity of the Gaultree episode in his edition of *Part Two* (Ard[2], 237–40).
2 *The True Reporte of the Service in Britanie Performed lately by the Honourable Knight Sir Iohn Norreys . . . before Guignand* (1591), sig. A3.

lawful magistrates either unrevealed or unrevenged.'[1] While Elizabethan audiences may have balked at Prince John's boast that 'God, and not we, hath safely fought today' (4.1.349) and been sceptical of his promise to redress the rebels' grievances 'with a most Christian care' (343), they nevertheless may have understood his perfidy as a necessary expedient born of political desperation (Humphreys, 238). Indeed, they may have found greater fault with the Archbishop for sacrilegiously enlisting the authority of the Church to incite rebellion – 'the Bishop / Turns insurrection to religion' (1.1.200–1) – and, according to Holinshed (3.529), for abusing his spiritual office by 'promising forgiueness of sinnes to all them, whose hap it was to die in the quarrel' (Humphreys, 238, 240).[2]

Ultimately, of course, one can only speculate how Elizabethan audiences would have responded to the Gaultree episode, for there is no hard evidence. That is not true for later audiences, however, whose distaste for the scene has been vividly documented. Dr Johnson spoke eloquently for generations of readers and playgoers who, on hearing Prince John sentence 'these traitors to the block of death' (4.1.350), have felt 'indignation to find this horrible violation of faith passed over thus slightly by the poet, without any note of censure or detestation' (*Plays*; rpt. in Vickers, *Shakespeare*, 5.122). Elizabeth Montagu, feeling a similar moral revulsion, concurred with Johnson four years later in wishing that Shakespeare 'had employed his eloquence too in arraigning the baseness and treachery of John of Lancaster's conduct in breaking his covenant with the rebels' (ch. 4; rpt. in Vickers, *Shakespeare*, 5.334). Benjamin Heath addressed the ambiguities of the scene more circumspectly than either Johnson or Montagu,

---

1   This sermon was delivered *c*. 1580–5 and published in 1585. See Sandys, 200.

2   Tiffany (281) suggests that Shakespeare may be 'appropriating the antiprelatical feeling of the Elizabethan Puritans . . . for the monarchy or royal family itself' when Prince John 'chastises the Archbishop of York, "th'imagined voice of God himself," for "misus[ing] the reverence of [his] place" ' (4.1.247, 251).

104

acknowledging that although the Gaultree double-cross 'is founded in strict historical truth' and Shakespeare 'is undoubtedly justifiable in giving it us as he found it', it nevertheless has 'a very unhappy and disagreeable effect on the reader or spectator, as instead of acquiescence at least in the punishment of the rebels it cannot fail of exciting in him compassion toward them when so treacherously ensnared, as well as a very high degree of indignation against Prince John . . . for prostituting his character by so deliberate and odious a piece of perfidy' (260–1; rpt. in Vickers, *Shakespeare*, 4.557). Shakespeare was not the moralist some would have him be; nor was his goal to revise history as poetic justice.[1]

For viewers today, the Gaultree episode is often regarded as an exposé of the cynical abuse of power on both sides. Among the rebels, Northumberland, who has saved his skin by fleeing to Scotland, sends a patently false excuse for failing to assist his brothers in arms (4.1.6–16); the Archbishop uses his ecclesiastical authority to sanction a rebellion which may be motivated as much by private revenge as by common grievances, as he intimates when he yokes his 'brother general' (94) – that is, the 'commonwealth' – with his 'brother born' (95) – William Scroop, who was beheaded by Bolingbroke – as justification for his quarrel;[2] and Mowbray, distrustful of the King, wants war at any price in payment for allegations of treason made by Bolingbroke against his father, which led to his banishment

---

1 Among eighteenth-century commentators, only Capell defended Shakespeare's decision to dramatize the episode as he did. While admitting that Prince John would seem '[b]lameable' to readers such as Johnson, Montagu and Heath, Capell reminded them that John's actions are shown 'no disapprobation' by the chroniclers from whom Shakespeare drew his material, 'the passive-obedience doctrine running so high with them that all proceedings with the rebels were reckon'd justifiable' (*Notes*, 179; rpt. in Vickers, *Shakespeare*, 5.559).

2 William Scroop (or le Scrope), Earl of Wiltshire, was actually the Archbishop's cousin, beheaded by Bolingbroke for treason in 1399 (see *R2* 3.2.138–42). Shakespeare, following Holinshed (3.522), erroneously believed him to be brother to the Archbishop (*1H4* 1.3.265–6). See List of Roles, 9n.

from England (*R2* 1.1.35–46, 87–108). Motives among the royal party are scarcely less self-serving. The capture of the rebel leaders succeeds in ridding the King of the most potent threat to his rule and paves the way for his son's succession; and the plan for doing so was devised by Westmorland, who attached his star to Bolingbroke's when seeking to redress wrongs done by King Richard, yet now arrogantly claims a King's authority to determine whether wrongs alleged by others need to be redressed at all. No one's hands are clean; no one's motives honourable. Shakespeare seldom depicted politics more astutely.

Gaultree is the moral counter to Shrewsbury: it is about peace ignobly won, and it needs no Falstaff to add an ironic gloss on the proceedings. Without his capture of the rebel knight Collevile, however, the longest act in the play would be a relentless succession of political scenes unleavened by Falstaffian wit. Collevile's capture, however, is but a thin counterpart to Falstaff's bogus killing of Hotspur at the Battle of Shrewsbury (*Part One* 5.4.120–8), and its humour depends on the audience's recalling the reputation for valour he gained thereby: cf. 1.2.149–52. Falstaff at Gaultree lacks the dramatic purpose he had at Shrewsbury. There, his self-serving behaviour and pragmatic commentary provided an ironic counterpoint to the chivalrous deeds and heroic hyperbole of the warring factions. Here, his capture of Collevile simply echoes the taking of the rebel leaders by a trick; and with no acts of valour in need of counterpointing, Falstaff's role is superfluous. His appearance at Gaultree provides comic relief, but no ideological alternative to the main action.

The royal family saga

In a radical departure from *Part One*, Shakespeare displaces the royal narrative of *Part Two* by banishing the King and Prince to the outskirts of the play for much of its first four acts. Harry's first scene, which does not occur until Act 2, affords him little to do other than languish in idleness and entertain himself by making a scabrous attack on Poins's character, and his late arrival at the tavern in 2.4 to trick Falstaff is of little consequence. The King makes his first appearance only in Act 3, in a scene which does not so much advance the plot as establish that he, like the kingdom, suffers from unrest: 'Uneasy lies the head that wears a crown' (3.1.31). This scene, furthermore, was omitted for some unknown reason from the first issue of the Quarto (see pp. 440–7): clearly it was written not to advance the plot but because without it, Henry would not appear until his deathbed scene in Act 4.

The opening scene of Act 3 thus introduces a much-needed royal presence to weigh against the Prelate's Rebellion. It depicts the ailing King – now at his palace in Westminster (2.4.360) – and his nobles as political strategists who are trying to cope with the uncertainties of war and the 'revolution of the times' (3.1.46) which defeat even the best-laid plans. 'How chances, mocks / And changes fill the cup of alteration / With divers liquors!' laments the King (51–3), who lives in constant fear that his usurpation of Richard will be punished by the rebellion of those who once helped him to the throne. This scene reinforces the themes of sickness, betrayal, guilt and political necessity which, as embodied in Henry, lend the play a tragic resonance to balance the comedy of the Falstaff plot.

Rumour plays a significant role in exacerbating the King's distress. In discussing the unhealthy state of the nation with his nobles in terms similar to those used by the Archbishop –

> Then you perceive the body of our kingdom,
> How foul it is, what rank diseases grow,
> And with what danger, near the heart of it

(38–40)

– he falls victim to unreliable reportage as readily as the rebels do. Calculating the number of enemy troops, he worries that 'They say the Bishop and Northumberland / Are fifty thousand strong' (95–6), a figure Warwick disputes by invoking the danger of listening to the false reports that Rumour warned against in the Induction: 'It cannot be, my lord. / Rumour doth double, like the voice and echo, / The number of the feared' (96–8). Yet just a few lines later, in an attempt to bring comfort to the King, Warwick himself appears to have fallen victim to rumour by reporting that he has received 'A certain instance that Glendower is dead' (103), when in fact Glendower was still very much alive. No news, it seems, is to be trusted.

Furthermore, the King indulges in a revisionist history in which rumour and memory become faulty allies. In recounting Richard's prophecy that civil war will be the wages of usurpation, a prophetic theory of history to which he here seems to subscribe, he looks to the Earl of Warwick for confirmation:

> But which of you was by –
> [*to Warwick*] You, cousin Neville, as I may
>   remember –
> When Richard, with his eye brimful of tears,
> Then checked and rated by Northumberland,
> Did speak these words, now proved a prophecy?
> 'Northumberland, thou ladder by the which
> My cousin Bolinbroke ascends my throne' –
> Though then, God knows, I had no such intent . . .
> 'The time will come that foul sin, gathering head,
> Shall break into corruption' – so went on,
> Foretelling this same time's condition
> And the division of our amity.

> (65–79)

Henry's calling on Warwick as witness, however, is a fiction, for no Earl of Warwick appears in *Richard II*, and the family name of Warwick in *Part Two* was Beauchamp, not Neville. Yet Warwick apparently does not dare to contradict the King. On the other hand, Shakespeare himself may have been misremembering. Since the Earl of Westmorland was named Rafe Neuill in both Holinshed (3.529) and Stow (*Annales*, 529), it is conceivable that Shakespeare meant to include Westmorland in this scene, not Warwick.

Yet there is more to Henry's sleight-of-memory. In *Richard II*, Richard is 'checked and rated' in the deposition scene (4.1.222–52) when Northumberland attempts to get him to confess his crimes against the state. The lines Henry quotes, however, are from 5.1.55–65, a confrontation scene from which he was absent. Furthermore, the lines themselves are misquoted: Richard's reference to 'The mounting Bolingbroke' (5.1.56), with its accusation of predatory ambition, here becomes the familiar 'My cousin Bolingbroke'; and Richard's poetic 'The time shall not be many hours of age / More than it is' (57–8) becomes a more prosaic 'The time shall come'. Various explanations for these misquotations are possible, from the exculpatory (Henry was not present and therefore is simply reporting hearsay) to the machiavellian (Henry calculatedly revises Richard's words to play down his own role as usurper). In any case, the effect of these snatches of misremembered quotation is of thought-in-process, so that Henry's speech, with its self-interruptions akin to those in Hamlet's first soliloquy, has a veneer of authenticity.

This misrecollection of events in *Richard II* also contributes to the network of reports by which *Part Two* interrogates the nature of historical truth and invention. While one might assume that the King is knowingly revising events in order to exculpate himself, his refashioning of history is similar to that indulged in by the Hostess and Justice Shallow: anecdotal, self-serving and based on faulty memorial reconstruction. In the middle of the play, then, in 3.1 and 3.2, Shakespeare dramatizes the unreliability of historical narration in both the court and the country, and in this way he subjects the stories of those in power to public scrutiny. Beginning with Rumour's false report of what happened at Shrewsbury and ending with the King's reporting the prophecy that he would die in Jerusalem (see pp. 127–8), a bit of lore which suggests that he is not committed to obliterating all vestiges of popular belief when it can serve his purpose, *Part Two* uses oral testimony to complicate chronicle history with the dramatic immediacy of history as personal reminiscence.

The climax of chronicle history in *Part Two* involves not the quashing of rebellion, as in *Part One*, but the question of succession – the fitness of Harry to rule after the King's death. The royal plot comes into focus only in the final quarter of the play. Shakespeare carefully keeps the King and Prince Harry, who have remained in London following the Welsh campaign, out of the Gaultree episode. Although they may be tainted as the beneficiaries of Prince John's policy, they are neither its instruments nor its authors: the King has appeared only once before news of Gaultree is brought to him, and the Prince has been kept in the wings, appearing briefly in two scenes of little political import, though he does admit to 'bleed[ing] inwardly that [his] father is so sick' and laments that his 'keeping such vile company' as Poins makes that admission sound hypocritical (2.2.46–8). Now, the dying King asks for his son; but, told that he is dining in London 'With Poins and other his continual followers' (4.3.53), the King grieves to imagine the 'rotten times' England is destined to have when he is succeeded by his son, 'when his headstrong riot hath no curb' and 'rage and hot blood are his counsellors' (60–3). When they meet, therefore, their interaction is politically and emotionally charged.

Attending on his sleeping father, Harry thinks him dead and takes the crown into the next chamber. The King, who wakes to find the crown missing, summons his son to scold him for his impatience. Where, during their confrontation in *Part One*, the Prince was able to redeem himself by appropriating the chivalric diction of Hotspur, here the stakes are higher: the King is on his deathbed, Harry has in his hands evidence of a parricidal wish, and this will be their final interview. The King's accusations sting:

Harry the Fifth is crowned! Up, vanity!
Down, royal state! All you sage counsellors, hence,
And to the English court assemble now
From every region apes of idleness!

(249–52)

Harry, who has been found 'in the next room / Washing with kindly tears his gentle cheeks' (212–13), responds to his father's rebuke with seemingly unfeigned emotion and seeks to prove his loyalty and love; but as he does so, he recounts a speech which bears little resemblance to what he actually has spoken just moments earlier. Then, the words he spoke to his apparently dead father were sober and politically aware: 'My due from thee is this imperial crown, / Which, as immediate from thy place and blood, / Derives itself to me' (172–4). Now, his remembered apostrophe to the crown is far more histrionic and self-justifying: 'I spake unto this crown as having sense / And thus upbraided it: "The care on thee depending / Hath fed upon the body of my father; / Therefore thou best of gold art worse than gold"' (287–90). The Prince's recollection of what he said, which continues for several more lines, amounts to a theatrical fiction intended to exonerate him from the disloyalty of which he stands accused – the sort of revisionism at which Harry repeatedly proves himself skilled. It is sufficient, however, to win his father's trust:

God put in thy mind to take [the crown] hence,
That thou might'st win the more thy father's love,
Pleading so wisely in excuse of it.

(307–9)

What the King seems to admire most, and what gives him hope for England's future, is Harry's speaking so eloquently in his own defence, a talent which reassures the King that his son has mastered the art of political rhetoric sufficiently to rule the land. In performance, though, their reconciliation can prove to be far more emotionally moving than I have here allowed. Often, in an uncharacteristic show of paternal affection, the King embraces the Prince, beginning his speech with a passionate 'O my son!' borrowed from the Folio;[1] and a repentant Harry, drying his tears, sits on the bed – the King instructs him to sit 'by my bed' (310), but actors invariably elect to make the scene more intimate by having the father and son in closer proximity – while the King offers him 'the very latest counsel / That ever [he] shall breathe' (311–12).

In his dying speech, the King gives the Prince instruction in policy, rehearsing the devious methods by which he came to power – thereby calling into question his earlier protest that 'God knows, I had no such intent' (3.1.72) – and urging him, as a means of diverting rebellion after his accession, 'to busy giddy minds / With foreign quarrels' (4.3.342–3). The father and son are more honest with each other in this scene than in its counterpart in *Part One* (3.2), yet they share a sense of political calculation which allows the upshot of their conversation – Harry's determination to keep the crown – to sidestep the question of legitimacy: 'You won it, wore it, kept it, gave it me; / Then plain and right must my possession be' (349–50). This couplet occludes the sins of usurpation and regicide by which Henry secured the throne and thus permits his son to substitute linear succession for divine right.[2]

The scene following the King's death provides the first public evidence of Harry's ability to reform from a wild youth

---

1 On the likelihood that his hypermetrical vocative was an actor's interpolation which helped to convey more forcefully the King's sudden change of heart, see 4.3.307n.

2 *Henry V*, however, offers evidence that this issue is not resolved in Harry's mind. His prayer before the Battle of Agincourt itemizing what he has done to atone for his father's sins (4.1.289–302) suggests that he is not entirely convinced of his right to the throne and that, to a degree, he believes in superstitious forms of atonement – a frame of mind at odds with the pragmatism he demonstrates here.

18   *The Palace at Westminster. King Henry & the Prince of Wales*: 'O
pardon me, my liege!' [4.3.268]. Painted by Josiah Boydell; engraved by
Robert Thew; published by J. & J. Boydell in 1798

to a sober king, for the promise of reformation he made privately
in *Part One* (1.2.198–207) is here reaffirmed to his brothers
and other nobles, who fear that 'all will be overturned' (5.2.19)
and riot enthroned. Harry moves quickly to allay their fears,
reassuring them that 'This is the English, not the Turkish, court:
/ Not Amurath an Amurath succeeds, / But Harry, Harry' (47–
9). To convince them further, he draws from a biblical passage
about shedding the old Adam and rising anew clad in 'the whole
armour of God' (Ephesians, 6.13–16), vowing that he has
become a new man, his youthful misrule buried with his father:

19 Prince Henry (Matthew Macfadyen) at the bedside of the King (David
    Bradley) in 4.3, in a production directed by Nicholas Hytner on the
    Olivier stage at the National Theatre, 2005

> My father is gone wild into his grave,
> For in his tomb lie my affections;
> And with his spirits sadly I survive
> To mock the expectation of the world,
> To frustrate prophecies and to raze out
> Rotten opinion, who hath writ me down
> After my seeming.

> (122–8)

Here the mocking of expectation that has characterized so
much of the play's chronicle history comes full circle: Harry
apparently believes in a consensual transfer of wildness from
the prodigal son to the usurping father which permits the
'instantly reformed son to become the legitimate heir' (Crewe,

'Reforming', 236). Harry and his father have exchanged personae: King Henry has assumed his son's transgressions in death, and in Harry, his father's sobriety lives on.

The fate of the Lord Chief Justice becomes the litmus test for the sincerity of Harry's conversion: whether, as King, he will be willing to overlook the Justice's imprisoning him for a box on the ear or instead will exact revenge on him and elevate Falstaff as his chief counsellor. Having witnessed the Prince's confession to his father in the deathbed scene, audiences should not be surprised by his about-face; but the fact that the others were *not* witness to that confession heightens the irony of their fears of him and makes his new humility all the more satisfying. Yet the old Harry who likes to toy with others and make them squirm resurfaces here, for although one may assume that a reformed Prince will deal magnanimously with the Justice, he in fact berates him, accuses him of disrespect and leaves everyone present doubting his capacity to be impartial. To the Justice's claim that if he 'be measured rightly, / Your majesty hath no just cause to hate me' (5.2.65–6), the King replies,

> No? How might a prince of my great hopes forget
> So great indignities you laid upon me?
> What – rate, rebuke and roughly send to prison
> Th'immediate heir of England?

> (67–70)

Whether Harry is simply playing a sadistic game with the Justice or genuinely entertains thoughts of retaliation is uncertain, but his accusation motivates a great speech in which the Justice insists on the inviolable rule of law – in contrast to the easy justice which holds sway in Gloucestershire – and ostensibly convinces the new King of his fitness for the job: 'Therefore still bear the balance and the sword' (102). By retaining the Lord Chief Justice as a surrogate 'father to [his] youth' (117), Harry in effect displaces forever the anarchy of Falstaff, an assurance that lends even deeper irony to Falstaff's bravado in the following scene, when he boasts that 'the laws of England are at [his] commandment' (5.3.136–7).

The shaping of history: chronicles as sources

By the late sixteenth century, folio chronicles, far too expensive for most buyers, had lost much of their appeal and were not being as widely read as they once had been.[1] But history itself remained a popular subject in cheap abridgements; and another way in which it was disseminated was through history plays which drew on chronicles, of which at least 70 were written between 1588 and 1603, ten of them by Shakespeare. For the historical plot of *Part Two*, Shakespeare drew heavily from the revised 1587 edition of Holinshed's *Chronicles*, a work to which he turned for material in at least thirteen plays. The *Chronicles* are not, like the work of modern historians, narrated from a single authorial perspective; rather, they are a compendium of historical narratives written by earlier chroniclers who freely borrowed from one another – particularly, for the period covered in this play, Thomas of Walsingham, Abraham Fleming, Edward Hall, Robert Fabyan and John Stow – which Holinshed assembled and which sometimes offer differing, even contradictory accounts of the same event. Explaining the poly-vocality of his approach, Holinshed writes in his Preface that he has 'rather chosen to shew the diversitie' of opinion among his sources than 'by over-ruling them . . . to frame them to agree to my liking'.[2] Study of how

1 In *Reading*, D.R. Woolf discusses 'the death of the chronicle' (21–36), detailing how, as a 'vendible genre, designed for public consumption rather than for institutional or corporate record-keeping, the Tudor chronicle was at the whim of a market that was to prove both soft and short-lived' (21). The Bishops' Ban of 1599, which included histories, may also have depressed the sale of folio chronicles.

2 Cited by Patterson, 15. In chs 2–4, Patterson explains the methods used by Holinshed to compile the chronicles of earlier authors, and the methods used by revisers of the 1587 edition (Holinshed having died in 1582). For a broader discussion of 'both the popular chronicle and the more learned historical writing', see Kastan, 'English', esp. 167–73.

Shakespeare used elements of these different accounts to shape his historical plot reveals a great deal about his attitude towards the reign of Henry IV, and his own biases and preoccupations.

In his first recounting of what happened at Gaultree, for example, Holinshed draws explicitly on Walsingham – 'Thus saith *Walsingham*' (3.530) – whose *Historia Anglicana* was published in 1418, just a few years after the events it narrates. In Walsingham's account, when the Archbishop of York and the Earl Marshal had assembled an army in York and posted articles of grievance against the King, the King cut short his campaign in Wales and sped north, joined by the Earl of Westmorland and Prince John of Lancaster, who with his army had been appointed to defend the Scottish border. Westmorland, perceiving the great strength of the rebel army, 'subtille deuised how to quaile their purpose' (3.529) and dispatched messengers to the Archbishop to learn the cause of his uprising. When the Archbishop offered his articles of grievance, Westmorland sent word that he '*lik*ed of the archbishops holie and vertuous intent and purpose' and offered to meet with him. The Archbishop, 'reioising thereat', persuaded the Earl Marshal to go with him to 'commune togither' with Westmorland, who duly offered to do his best to effect a 'reformation'. Westmorland, however, 'vsing more policie' than honesty, proposed that they '*drinke togither* in signe of agreement' so that soldiers on both sides would witness their new league of amity, and he then urged that they dismiss their armies to 'depart home to their woonted trades and occupations'. The Archbishop accordingly sent word to his troops, who laid down their arms and 'brake vp their field and returned homewards'. Secretly, however, Westmorland had commanded an increase in his own numbers and, certain of the rebels' vulnerability, proceeded to arrest the unsuspecting Archbishop, the Earl Marshal and 'diuerse other' for treason (3.530).

Holinshed then reports that 'others write somewhat otherwise of this matter' and offers a rival account based on different sources. In it, briefly, Westmorland and the lord Rafe Eeuers persuaded the Archbishop and Earl Marshal to meet them 'vpon a ground *iust* in the midwaie betwixt both the *armies*', where Westmorland derided them for embarking on so 'perilous an enterprise' and instructed them to 'submit themselues . . . vnto the kings mercie', failing which John of Lancaster, whose army was present 'with banners spread', 'was ready to trie the matter by dint of sword'. Cowed by this threat, the Archbishop and Earl Marshal surrendered to the King (in the person of Westmorland) and to Prince John (who was only sixteen at the time) 'and returned not to their armie', at which point their troops fled; 'but, being pursued, manie were taken, manie slaine, and manie spoiled of that that they had about them'. The conclusion of both narratives is the same: the rebels were brought to the King at Pomfret and subsequently beheaded at York; and though 'indemnitie were promised' to some of the leaders, 'yet was the same to none of them at anie hand performed' (3.530).

By adhering more closely to Walsingham's account, Shakespeare puts a sinister gloss on the events at Gaultree. He thereby emphasizes first, the political cunning of Westmorland in pretending to accept the articles of grievance in order to manipulate the Archbishop; second, the naive political idealism of the Archbishop in trusting him; third, the skilful ploy by which Westmorland arranges a show of amity among the leaders in order to prompt the rebel army to disband; and finally, the duplicity with which Westmorland draws a dubious distinction between the grievances and the aggrieved when he agrees to redress the causes for rebellion but then arrests the rebels. Westmorland in the second account is far less treacherous; yet to heighten the drama, Shakespeare alters details in the first account by borrowing from the second. Most notably, he increases the prominence of Prince John, who plays an insignificant role in the first but stands at the ready with his army in the second, and makes him the ultimate royal authority for the ruse. Westmorland may have manipulated events behind the scenes, but in the play John appears as a calculating Machiavel, a 'sober-blooded boy' who, according to Falstaff, 'drinks no wine' (4.2.85–8), though he pledges his faith to the rebels by making a show of drinking in front of the troops. Furthermore, by choosing the second version's account of how the rebels meet with Prince John and Westmorland midway between both armies, Shakespeare not only creates a more theatrical confrontation, but foregrounds the treacherous ploy, reported by Walsingham, by which the armies are instructed to disband. The royal army will not move until Prince John himself gives the order, whereas the rebel army scatters in disarray, as described in the second version. In the alarums and skirmishes that follow, Shakespeare dramatizes the mayhem reported in the second version. Finally, where Walsingham reveals the duplicity of Westmorland's strategy before the rebels succumb to it, Shakespeare does not, so that the outcome of Gaultree takes the audience unawares. The double-crossing of the rebels is designed to have maximum theatrical impact: the audience finds itself in the same position as – and thus may be inclined to sympathize with – the unsuspecting Archbishop and Earl Marshal.

Throughout *Part Two*, Shakespeare conflates the history narrated in Holinshed, compressing time and anticipating events with such slick causality that, as Bullough observes, ten years of Henry's reign are telescoped into only a few weeks (4.253). Using Hall's *Vnion of the Two Noble and Illustre Families of Lancastre and Yorke* (1548) as his source, Holinshed reports that following the defeat of the rebels at Shrewsbury on 21 July 1403, the King moved his army against the Earl of Northumberland (3.524), who was conspiring 'with Richard Scrope Archbishop of York, Thomas Mowbraie Earl Marshal . . . and diuerse others' (3.529). He summoned Northumberland to York and 'dissembled' to make peace with him because he apparently did not dare to punish him, Northumberland having armies to support him in his castles at 'Berwike . . . Alnewike, Warkewoorth' and elsewhere. The King and Prince Harry then returned to the Welsh border to pursue Owen Glendower, who 'caessed not to doo much mischeefe' (3.529). Meanwhile Northumberland, who was to have provided the military might for the Archbishop's uprising, was thwarted in his intent because the Archbishop moved too speedily and precipitously for Northumberland to muster his forces; and 'hearing that . . . his confederats [were] brought to confusion through too much hast of the archbishop', he 'with three hundred horse got him to Berwicke', then 'fled with the lord Berdolfe in Scotland' (3.530). Shakespeare alters this account to reverse the chronology, turning a consequence of the defeat of the rebels by Prince John in 1405 – Northumberland's fleeing to Scotland – into an ignominious cause of that defeat. Thereafter, according to Holinshed, Northumberland and Lord Bardolph joined forces with the Welsh; and when Glendower was eventually routed by the King's forces in 1406, they fled to France to seek aid. Returning to Scotland, Northumberland recruited a considerable army to wage war against the King anew, retook several of his own castles in the north, but was finally defeated and 'slaine outright' at the Battle of Bramham Moor in 1408 (3.534).

Shakespeare's recasting of historical events insists on a tight organization of cause and effect. All the events which in Holinshed occur up to Northumberland's death play out in Shakespeare as a direct and immediate result of the death of Hotspur at Shrewsbury. In the opening scene, as Northumberland hears conflicting rumours of what transpired there, Morton reports that the king has sent a 'speedy power' (1.1.133) led by Westmorland and Prince John to encounter him – a shrewd conflation of two accounts in Holinshed, the King's pursuit of Northumberland following the Battle of Shrewsbury and his march north to quell the Prelate's Rebellion two years later. In that same scene, Northumberland receives word that the Archbishop is already up in arms in York (189–90): the Prelate's Rebellion in 1405 is thereby made simultaneous with the Battle of Shrewsbury in 1403, as had been anticipated in *Part One* (5.5.34–8).

While the Archbishop clearly counts on reinforcements from Northumberland, who is not far away at Warkworth, the Earl, still smarting over the loss of his son at Shrewsbury, bows to the wishes of his wife and daughter-in-law who, shaming him with the memory of Hotspur, urge him to forsake his honour and flee to Scotland, not to muster forces, as in Holinshed, but to await the outcome of the Archbishop's revolt. Shakespeare thus attributes more complicated motives to Northumberland than Holinshed does, with the death of Hotspur becoming a direct cause of Northumberland's failure to support the Archbishop at Gaultree. Only passing reference is made to the death of Northumberland late in the play, and no mention is made of the protracted warfare which, in Holinshed's account, occurred between 1405 and 1408. In this way Shakespeare causally and sequentially links the episodes of *Part Two* with those in *Part One*, forging a historical unity between the two plays that conceals a much more fragmented chronology.

Episodes within the court of Henry IV, particularly those involving the King's illness and his relationship with Prince Harry, are similarly compressed and reshaped. The second and final appearance of King Henry in this play is, in effect, a deathbed scene. Its compression of history hastens a process that in fact took years. Here, on the day of his death, 20 March 1413, Henry receives reports of Prince John's capture of the rebels at Gaultree (1405) and the defeat of Northumberland and Lord Bardolph at Bramham Moor (1408), in both of which events, historically, the King himself was involved. Such compression pays off dramatically. The King's confronting Prince Harry immediately following Prince John's victory at Gaultree highlights the problem of royal succession: Henry is not at all sure that Harry will have the support of his brothers, two of whom are introduced for the first time. Furthermore, the imminence of the King's death adds a radical political instability to a confrontation that otherwise parallels a similar scene in *Part One* (3.2) wherein the King chastises his son for bad behaviour and Harry promises his father to reform. In this play, as so often, that promise is undercut with irony.

Holinshed reports that the King's deteriorating health was first noticed in 1411, whereas in the play, both the Prince (2.2.38–9) and the Earl of Warwick (3.1.104–6) allude to the King's illness prior to the defeat of the rebels at Gaultree, which, as indicated above, follows hard on the heels of the Battle of Shrewsbury; and the King's death, which occurred two years later in 1413, is dramatized shortly after Prince John brings him word of that defeat – therefore, in the play's logic, moving his death forward by eight years to 1405, although Henry himself has earlier lamented that 'It is but eight years since / This Percy was the man nearest my soul' (3.1.60–1) – i.e. in 1399, the year in which Northumberland helped Henry to usurp the throne – suggesting that the scene of his death occurs in 1407. Thus Shakespeare employs a kind of double time scheme, dramatizing an onward rush of events that drives the historical narrative and confines it to a matter of weeks, yet at times allowing the course of history to seem more protracted, even if not fully in accordance with Holinshed's chronology.

Holinshed also provides the narrative frame for the play's great scene of confrontation between father and son (4.3). In Holinshed, the King asks for his crown to be set beside him on a pillow and then suddenly falls into a coma so death-like that those about him 'covered his face with a linnen cloth'. Being told of his father's death, the Prince enters the chamber and takes the crown. The King awakes, calls for his son, and demands an explanation. What follows is brief and unemotional: Harry excuses himself by claiming that since to 'all mens iudgements you seemed dead in this world', he took the crown as heir apparent, 'as mine owne, and not as yours'. In response, the King expresses a passing doubt about the legitimacy of his own possession of the crown ('what right I had to it, God knoweth'), but Harry vows to keep it 'with the sword against all mine enimies', at which point the King dies, committing all to God (3.541). If this account provided a framework for the scene in the play, Shakespeare also drew on an earlier exchange between the King and Prince in Holinshed that had served as the source for 3.2 in *Part One*. In it the Prince, alarmed that his political enemies were slandering him for his riotous life and causing the King to suspect that he might try to usurp the throne, comes to court with 'a great traine' of followers to kneel before his bedridden father, swear true allegiance, and offer a dagger so that the King might dispatch him and thus rid himself of suspicion, 'adding . . . that his life was not so deare to him, that he wished to liue one daie with his displeasure'. The King, overcome by this show of filial piety, embraces his son and 'restore[s him] to his fauour' (3.538).

Episodes in the King's vexed relationship with his son are telescoped and reshaped throughout the play. Historically, the King was ill as early as 1405 and thus brought Prince Henry into public life as the head of the Privy Council. By 1411, however, at the urging of his uncle the Chancellor Thomas Beaufort, the Prince attempted to force his sick father's abdication, as a result of which the King dismissed him from the Council and replaced him with his second son, Thomas, Duke of Clarence. Twice, in efforts to prevent the new Council from forging an alliance with the Armagnacs, the Prince led a band of armed followers to try to assert his political will, in effect presuming on his father's weakness to stage a *coup*.[1] Holinshed neglects to record this darkly sinister intrigue of the ambitious young Prince, preferring instead to promulgate stories of his youthful impetuosity. Indeed, the story recounted

1 Many chroniclers – Stow, Camden, Speed, Holinshed – invented tales of Harry's madcap youth to mask evidence of a strong political antagonism between father and son which led the Privy Council, staunch supporter of the Prince, to seek the King's abdication, and as a consequence led the King, fearing armed rebellion, to dismiss the Prince and his friends from all state offices. See McFarlane, 92–3, 121–3.

above of the Prince's appearing at court with a group of his followers – which the King understandably fears is a threat – revises as a legend of filial piety the Prince's attempt to wrest power from the King by a show of force. A father's disappointment in his son's prodigal ways, after all, was safer subject-matter than a king's fear of a prince's political ambition.

Thomas of Clarence thus had a potentially adversarial relationship with his older brother; and as if to acknowledge that there may be more to the story than he relates, Holinshed adds that the King admonished Harry to be good to his brothers when he accedes to the throne. Other chroniclers address the situation more directly. In Stow's *Annales*, for example, the dying King tells the Prince that he fears Clarence might oppose his succession, but the Prince's sober and generous reply – 'I shall honor & loue my brethren aboue all men, as long as they be to me true, faithfull and obedient' (545) – prompts the King to praise his magnanimity. This passage in Stow probably inspired the speech in *Part Two* in which the King admonishes Clarence not to neglect his brother:

> He loves thee, and thou dost neglect him, Thomas.
> Thou hast a better place in his affection
> Than all thy brothers. Cherish it, my boy,
> And noble offices thou mayst effect
> Of mediation, after I am dead,
> Between his greatness and thy other brethren. . . .
> For he is gracious, if he be observed:
> He hath a tear for pity and a hand
> Open as day for meting charity.

> (4.3.21–32)

The effect of this speech is to reveal the King's sanguine view of the Prince's potential for leadership without complicating the audience's view of the Prince with a history of his attempt to wrest power from his father by force. The King's speech to the Prince in Stow's *Annales*, furthermore, reinforces themes of Godliness, justice and good government which may also have influenced Shakespeare's shaping of their final conversation.

If Holinshed provided material chiefly for the play's political plot, Shakespeare was especially indebted to Samuel Daniel's *Civil Wars* in fleshing out the deathbed conversation between father and son.[1] Daniel provides a poetic account of chronicle history which moves directly from the Battle of Shrewsbury (3.114) to the King's apoplexy and his final advice to the Prince, omitting everything else that happened between these events.[2] The King, diseased, despondent and wracked by a guilty conscience, suffers 'intricate turmoils and sorrowes deepe'. Addressing the crown with grave doubt about its future – 'And now how do I leave thee unto mine, / Which it is dread to keepe, death to resigne' (120) – he falls into a trance, his 'soule rapt wholly with . . . present horror' (121). The Prince enters and takes the crown; but the King revives, intent on redressing his 'wrong' by returning the crown 'to whom it seem'd to apperteine' (122) – presumably the 5th Earl of March, whom Richard II designated his heir – and when he discovers that the Prince has removed it, he remonstrates with him in words that closely resemble Shakespeare's: 'O Sonne what needes thee make such speed / Unto that care, where feare exceeds thy right?' (124). The Prince offers a brazenly

---

1   In addition to Daniel's influence on the shaping of the domestic conflict in *Part Two*, the paralleling of Hal and Hotspur as young men in *Part One*, even though the historical Hotspur was three years older than the King, came directly from *CW*. See Moorman, esp. 77–83, and Wilson, 'Origins', 4–6.

2   King Henry's illness, a paralysis whose symptoms and causes Falstaff aptly catalogues at 1.2.108–18, was chronicled by Thomas Otterbourne in 1408. Some writers identified the disease as leprosy inflicted on Henry as divine punishment for his murder of Richard II or execution of Archbishop Scrope, but Hall dismisses this as falsehood, as does Holinshed, who argues that the King suffered 'a sore sicknesse, which was not a leprosie, striken by the hand of God (saith master *Hall*) as foolish friers imagined; but a verie apoplexie, of the which he languished till his appointed hour' (Holinshed, 3.541).

unembarrassed reply, calculated to assure his father that lineal succession can trump the crime by which the crown was initially gained: 'Time will appease them well that now complaine, / And ratefie our interest in the end; / What wrong hath not continuance quite outworne? / Yeares makes that right which never was so borne' (125). Still repentant, the King admonishes the Prince to add virtue to his policy, for 'vertuous deeds . . . well may prove our wrong to be our right: / And let the goodnes of the managing / Race out the blot of foule attayning quite' (126). At issue here are matters undeveloped by Holinshed but prominent in Shakespeare: the King's unquiet soul and contrition over an ill-gotten crown, a vexed debate over whether the Prince has a lineal right to the throne and, as in Stow, an emphasis on the importance of good governance to justify his keeping it. In a telling adjustment to his source material, however, Shakespeare's King is less penitent and more politically circumspect about his own acquisition of the crown than Daniel's; the Prince, more penitent and apologetic for having taken it, and less calculating in his vow to maintain it.

Daniel's King is not entirely devoid of policy on his deathbed, however, for he concludes his advice to the Prince with a rather unethical expedient: 'To thee is left to finish my intent', he tells his son, 'Who to be safe must never idly stand; / But some great actions entertaine thou still / To hold their mindes who else will practise ill' (127). The great action the King has in mind is the 'sacred warre' (127) that he himself was never able to wage; and here, he recommends it to the Prince as a tactic to divert the energies of those nobles who 'are inur'd to mutinie' (129). This cynical strategy, whose self-serving motive undermines the ostensibly religious purpose – atonement – for which the King would have undertaken his crusade, directly influenced Shakespeare's wily King who, on his deathbed, admits to having had an ulterior motive for planning to 'lead out many to the Holy Land, / Lest rest and lying still might make them look / Too near unto my state' (4.3.339–41). His subsequent advice to the Prince 'to busy giddy minds / With foreign quarrels' (342–3) thus sounds unabashedly machiavellian. Holinshed, in contrast, attributes a more earnest religious zeal to the King's preparations to embark on a voyage to the Holy Land. In his account, the King shortly before his death ordered ships and galleys to be built for his trip 'to recover the citie of Jerusalem from the Infidels. For it greeved him to consider the great malice of christian princes, that were bent upon a mischeefous purpose to destroie one another, to the perill of their owne soules, rather than to make war against the enimies of the christian faith' (3.540). Shakespeare's Henry for the most part seems to have a similar faith and purpose. He initially plans a crusade against the infidels to atone for the murder of King Richard – 'I'll make a voyage to the Holy Land / To wash this blood from off my guilty hand' (*R2* 5.6.49–50) – and while it is postponed by civil unrest in *Part One* (1.1.47–8), in *Part Two* he reiterates his penitential desire to go to the Holy Land (3.1.107–8) and later indicates that the necessary preparations have been made (4.3.1–7). In his advice to the Prince shortly thereafter, however, undertaking a crusade has become a political strategy that casts suspicion on his earlier protestations of penitence.

In this cynical light, his dying wish to be carried to the Jerusalem Chamber, too, can be seen as a politically contrived substitution for the holy war he never undertook. Indeed, his crediting the prophecy that he was to die in Jerusalem, as Shakespeare has him profess (4.3.364–8), is something that even Holinshed doubts: 'Whether this was true that so he spake, as one that gave too much credit to foolish prohesies & vaine tales, or whether it was fained . . . we leave it to the advised reader to judge' (3.540). There is a tradition of such ironic prophecies (see 4.3.360–8n.), and Shakespeare's Henry, ever the realist, no doubt appreciates the irony of his situation. Yet even on his deathbed, the anguished King is not beyond using prophecy to political advantage in a last attempt to fashion his own legacy as a divinely sanctioned ruler. One's final response to the King, then, is appropriately mixed. He is a complicated figure, politically skilled, personally remote, morally compromised and, in death, not entirely sympathetic.

The shaping of history: Famous Victories
as source

The scene of the King's confrontation with his son may have come to Shakespeare most directly from *The Famous Victories of Henry the Fifth*. It is difficult to overestimate the importance of this source; for crude as it is dramaturgically (see pp. 14–15), its portrayal of events in Prince Henry's life seems to have directly inspired Shakespeare, offering a shape and even a language for scenes in his *Henry IV* and *Henry V* plays. Two such scenes in *Famous Victories* – the first likely to have been fashioned from material in Holinshed's *Chronicles*, the second from Hall's *Union* – involve tense meetings between father and son. In the first, the Prince is summoned to the court but has scant concern for his father's illness: 'the breath shall be no sooner out of his mouth but I will clap the crown on my head' (5.34–5), he tartly tells his companions. When the Prince enters his father's presence '*with a dagger in his hand*' (6.0), the sick King thinks that he intends to kill him; but suddenly stricken with compunction, the Prince assures him, ''Tis not the crown that I come for, sweet father, because I am unworthy' (20–1), and, lamenting his sinful life, he exits; but his father calls him back, pardons him and pleads with him to become God's servant, at which the Prince, relieved, pledges conversion in a line adapted from Holinshed, 'I am born new again' (37–8).

Shortly thereafter, the Prince returns to visit his sleeping father for a second time and, thinking him dead, chastises himself for dereliction, vows to 'weep day and night' (8.20), and exits with the crown. The scene that ensues when the King awakes is echoed distinctly and repeatedly by Shakespeare in *Part Two*. The King reproaches the Prince for not having the patience to wait for him to die – 'dost thou think the time so long that thou wouldst have it before the breath be out of my mouth?' (37–8); and in response the Prince falls to his knees to excuse himself with words similar to those spoken by Shakespeare's Prince: 'finding you . . . past all recovery, and dead, to my thinking . . . what should I do, but with weeping tears lament the death of you, my father?' (40–3). The King, pleased with this answer, commands his son to stand up and puts him in possession of the crown, 'that none deprive thee of it after my death' (51–2), after which, following Holinshed, he confesses, 'God knows, my son, how hardly I came by it, and how hardly I have maintained it' (56–7), lines which Shakespeare develops at length. The Prince in turn reassures his father, 'he that seeks to take the crown from my head, let him look that his armour be thicker then mine, or I will pierce him to the heart' (59–61).

Famous Victories also dramatizes the legendary episode in which the Prince is imprisoned for boxing the Lord Chief Justice on the ear. Shakespeare alludes to this episode twice in *Part Two*: first as reported by Falstaff's Page – 'Sir, here comes the nobleman that committed the Prince for striking him about Bardolph' (1.2.56–7) – and later as confirmed by the Lord Chief Justice, who reminds the new King,

> Your highness pleased to forget my place, . . .
> And struck me in my very seat of judgement,
> Whereon, as an offender to your father,
> I gave bold way to my authority
> And did commit you [to a term in prison].

> (5.2.76–82)

This is the reason the Justice fears for his life once the Prince inherits the throne from his father. As the new King asks, 'How might a prince of my great hopes forget / So great indignities you laid upon me?' (67–8). The legend itself was widely recorded, most notably by Elyot in *The Boke Named the*

Gouernour in 1531 (2.6) and later by Stow in *Annales* (547–8), who follows Elyot nearly verbatim. In this account, the Prince appears before the bar furious that one of the 'servantes whom he well favoured' – only Shakespeare identifies him as Bardolph – has been arraigned for felony.[1] The Prince commands that his servant be set at liberty; but when the Lord Chief Justice refuses, the Prince, 'all in a fury', approaches the bench and physically threatens the judge. Unmoved, the Lord Chief Justice reminds the Prince that he represents the person of the King, reprimands him for his 'contempte and disobedience' of that office, and commits him to 'the prison of the kings bench'. When told of this judgement, the King expresses gratitude to have not only so impartial a judge as the Lord Chief Justice, but 'also a sonne who can suffre semblably and obey justice'. Holinshed, who recalls this episode only briefly, borrows from an alternate version written by Robert Redmayne *c*. 1540 (Wilson, 'Origins', 7) in which the Prince commits physical assault – 'how once to hie offense of the king his father, [the Prince] had with his fist striken the cheefe justice' (3.543) – for which the King expels him from his Privy Council and replaces him with his brother, Thomas of Clarence. *Famous Victories* borrows from Holinshed the detail of Harry's assaulting the Chief Justice – '*He giveth him a box on the ear*' (4.69) – and Shakespeare follows suit.

More strikingly, however, *Famous Victories* expands the role of the Lord Chief Justice. After the coronation, the new King summons the Lord Chief Justice, who fears the worst, and, 'for revengement' of being committed to the Fleet, chooses him 'to be my Protector over my realm' while he is in France, explaining that he values the impartiality of his judgement: 'for you, that would not spare me, I think will not spare

---

1 In *Famous Victories*, the Prince identifies the person he attempts to rescue as 'my man', a thief appropriately named Cutbert Cutter who robbed a carrier at Gad's Hill (4.1–86).

another' (9.144–50). Shakespeare moves this scene prior to the coronation and alters it so that Harry first challenges the Chief Justice to defend his decision to 'rate, rebuke and roughly send to prison / Th'immediate heir of England' (5.2.69–70) and then, as if persuaded by the Justice's argument, rewards him by retaining him in office. This is a typically Shakespearean transformation of source material. By making the Justice squirm in fear of retaliation, Harry enjoys a kind of revenge for past injuries even though he has apparently already decided to keep him in office. He has staged the scene to disorient those present by surprising them with his magnanimity, evidence that the madcap Prince still finds refuge in the reformed King. Furthermore, Shakespeare transfers to Harry sentiments that in Elyot and Stow are spoken by his father, allowing the new King to moralize for the Justice his own response to being committed to prison and thereby to fashion a role for himself that insists on the fundamental honour of the Prince he used to be:

> I do wish your honours may increase
> Till you do live to see a son of mine
> Offend you and obey you as I did;
> So shall I live to speak my father's words:
> 'Happy am I that have a man so bold
> That dares do justice on my proper son,
> And not less happy having such a son
> That would deliver up his greatness so.'

(5.2.103–10)

The young King thus determines how his own history will be glossed: he is, as ever, the master of self-fashioning. His embrace of the Justice as his chief counsellor and 'father to [his] youth' (117), however, is unhistorical. Although Stow (*Annales*, 547–8) makes much of the Prince's submission to the Lord Chief Justice at the time of his arrest, he reports no further meeting between the two; and Holinshed, who observes that Henry V 'elected the best learned men in the lawes of the

131

realme, to the offices of iustice' (3.543), makes no specific mention of the Lord Chief Justice. Shakespeare's only source for their meeting is *Famous Victories*.

The new King's rejection of Falstaff and his tavern companions also had its seeds in the brief scene in *Famous Victories* in which Oldcastle and Ned, prototypes for Falstaff and Ned Poins, interrupt the coronation procession by reminding the King of his promises to them. They note with alarm that he looks 'very much changed' (9.34), and he, pausing soberly, concurs: 'so I am indeed, and so must thou be . . . or else I must cause thee to be changed' (39–41). The King admonishes them, 'mend thy manners, and be more modester in thy terms; for my unfeigned grief is not to be ruled by thy flattering and dissembling talk' (37–9). Declaring that he will 'abandon and abolish [their] company for ever', he commands them 'not upon pain of death to approach my presence by ten miles' space. Then, if I hear well of you, it may be I will do somewhat for you' (45–8).[1] The details of the King's judicious dealing with his erstwhile companions are recorded in Hall, Holinshed and Stow, but only *Famous Victories* offers a scene in which the King confronts those old familiars who have dared to interrupt his coronation procession, advertises his own reformation, and publicly banishes them. Without this model, Shakespeare might never have written the great scene in which the King rejects Falstaff.

Famous Victories, then, provided the most immediate source for Shakespeare's shaping of chronicle history. Primarily, its alternation of low comic scenes involving the Prince and his companions with scenes of royal history offered a hybrid structural model for both parts of *Henry IV*. Stories of the Prince's riotous youth had become the stuff of folklore and

---

1 Holinshed, a likely source for this scene, adds the telling detail that the King refused to allow his former companions to come within 'ten miles of his court or presence' (3.543).

were promulgated early in sources such as Tito Livio's *Vita Henrici Quinti* (1437), William Caxton's revision of the *Brut Chronicle* (1482) and Robert Fabyan's *The New Chronicles of England and France* (1516). As revealed in the permutations of the dagger episode discussed above, these stories domesticated the Prince's serious political offences against his father as something more forgivably jejune – a young man's rebelling against the expectations of his place, the actual danger of his actions to the realm occluded by a more benign focus on his youthful impetuosity. The early scenes in *Famous Victories*, in which officials from the King's treasury are robbed by the Prince, Ned, Tom and Sir John Oldcastle, are more pertinent to *Part One*, although Oldcastle is but a sketch of the fat knight he would become in Shakespeare. Nevertheless, when word of the King's death is received, Oldcastle rejoices that 'we shall all be kings', and Ned proclaims, 'I shall be Lord Chief Justice of England' (9.7–8) – a clear anticipation of Falstaff's boast in *Part Two*, 'Blessed are they that have been my friends, and woe to my Lord Chief Justice!' (5.3.137–8). Falstaff's recruitment of soldiers in Gloucestershire may owe a debt to a brief episode in *Famous Victories*, sc. 10, in which a captain conscripts two clowns for the wars in France, one of whom, John Cobbler, like Mouldy in *Part Two*, begs to be allowed to stay at home to do his husbandry, while the other, Derick, like Feeble, is willing to do his patriotic duty. But Shakespeare's recruitment scene really has no identifiable source, just as Falstaff himself ultimately transcends all attempts to discover sources for his greatness. He is an original.

DATING THE PLAY

The evidence: Oldcastle revisited

Henry IV, Part Two was entered in the Stationers' Register on 23 August 1600. It was written and performed considerably earlier than that, but establishing probable dates requires a return to the matter of Sir John Oldcastle as a cause of controversy in *Part One*. What is undisputed is that when Shakespeare wrote the first *Henry IV* play Falstaff was called Oldcastle, and the character was played by that name during early performances. There is little agreement, however, about whether the change in name was forced by the Cobham family, who were collateral descendants of Oldcastle, and specifically by the 10th Lord Cobham, William Brooke, who became Lord Chamberlain and therefore would have been in a position to instruct the Master of the Revels, Edmund Tilney, to censor the play; or was necessitated by an outpouring of sentiment by reformers against parodying as a figure of Rabelaisian excess a Lollard who, thanks to writers such as Bale and Foxe (see p. 65), was now seen as a martyr to the Protestant cause; or was made by Shakespeare himself, in anticipation of objections likely to be forthcoming after Brooke was named Lord Chamberlain.[1]

Evidence suggests that Oldcastle's name was changed to Falstaff at some point in late 1596 or early 1597. William Brooke had been appointed Lord Chamberlain on 8 August 1596 following the death of the previous holder of that office, Henry Carey, on 23 July. Since it is unlikely that Shakespeare, as a practical man of the theatre, would have deliberately set out to offend the Lord Chamberlain by parodying his illustrious ancestor as a comic degenerate, *Part One* had probably been licensed by Edmund Tilney prior to Henry Carey's death and possibly performed at The Theatre in Shoreditch before the London Privy Council closed the playhouses on 22 July, since 'by drawing of much people together increase of sicknes [was]

---

1 Kastan warns against uncritically assuming political censorship, for Shakespeare himself, understanding the political climate, may have made the change in Oldcastle's name himself to avoid intervention by the authorities (*1H4*, 54).

feared'.[1] In early summer, it could not have been anticipated that Henry Carey, Lord Hunsdon, would die, nor that Lord Cobham would succeed him; therefore, offending the Lord Chamberlain would not have been an issue. Even if Tilney licensed the play after Brooke's appointment, he might not have anticipated objection; for while he was probably aware that the Cobhams were collateral descendants of Oldcastle, in 1594 he had licensed *Famous Victories*, in which Oldcastle was a drinking companion of the Prince, without protest from the Brooke family. Thus he could reasonably have assumed that *Henry IV* would give no more offence than the earlier play (Dutton, *Mastering*, 104, cited by Gibson, 102).

In fact, however, a letter written by Richard James in 1633–4 and attached to the manuscript edition of Thomas Hoccleve's 'The legend and defence of ye Noble knight and Martyr Sir Jhon [*sic*] Oldcastel' confirms that the Cobham family did indeed take umbrage at Shakespeare's mockery of their ancestor:

That in Shakespeares first shewe of Harry ye fift, ye person with which he vntertook to play a buffone was not Falstaffe, but Sr Jhon Oldcastle, and that offence

---

1 E.K. Chambers quotes the Privy Council prohibition in *Elizabethan*, 4.319. E.A.J. Honigmann makes a strong case for the composition of *Part One* in early 1596; for, he argues, a later date would require us 'to believe in a Shakespeare so dim-witted that he did not foresee what is obvious to us – the Cobhams would take offence, and the Lord Chamberlain could compel the players to back down. These difficulties disappear, however, if *Henry IV* was written – or at least begun – before Lord Cobham became Lord Chamberlain. Move back *1 Henry IV* a few months, to the first half of 1596, and a very different picture emerges' (122). Gibson agrees that dating the composition and licensing of the play 'during the first half of 1596 . . . well before Lord Hunsdon's death, well before the appointment of Lord Cobham as his successor, simply removed William Brooke from the equation, in one stroke of Ockham's razor cutting through the critical thicket of invented quarrels, logical inconsistencies, and improbable circumstances otherwise generated by a date during the second half of 1596 or early 1597' (102).

beinge worthily taken by personages descended from
his title . . . the poet was putt to make an ignorant shifte
of abusing Sr Jhon Falstaffe or Fastolphe, a man not
inferior of virtue though not so famous in pietie as
the other.[1]

Such evidence has led some to argue that Lord Cobham shared
the London Privy Council's Puritan antipathy to theatre and
therefore demanded that the name be changed;[2] others to argue
that Shakespeare had misgauged the degree to which his
'identification of a hypocritical fat "misleader of youth" with a
revered Lollard martyr [had] deeply offended many Protestants',
an offence that William Brooke in his position as Lord
Chamberlain, forced by public opinion, could hardly ignore;[3]
and still others to argue that Brooke, far from being antipathetic
to players, was in fact their advocate and censored the use of
Oldcastle's name only to protect them from an anti-theatrical
prejudice which might have jeopardized their freedom to
perform.[4] While a case can be made for each of these positions,
the evidence – apart from the letter by Richard James – is slim
to nonexistent. Recently James M. Gibson has sifted through
other evidence which, while circumstantial, cumulatively suggests when and why Oldcastle's name may have been changed
and, coincidentally, offers credible dates for performances of
both *Henry IV* plays.

---

1 The full text of the letter appears in James, 137–8. It is cited in Taylor, 'Cobham',
   334–42, and Gibson, 97–8.
2 Gibson cites, for example, Chambers, *Elizabethan*, 1.297; Hotson, 15; Wilson,
   'Origins', 13; and Bevington, *Tudor*, 257.
3 Taylor, 'Cobham', 349; see also Pendleton, 65–70.
4 Gibson identifies Green, 113–14, as the first proponent of this theory, which finds
   its most articulate expression in Corbin & Sedge: 'If the complaint were [Brooke's],
   it is plausible that it was designed as much to cool the temper of the "Puritan city
   authorities" campaign against the theatres which, in 1596/97, was vociferous and
   proving to be effective, as to protect his own reputation' (11).

If William Brooke took offence at the unflattering portrayal of his ancestor and instructed Tilney to order Shakespeare's company to change Oldcastle's name, he must have done so between 8 August, when he became Lord Chamberlain, and his death on 6 March 1597, and probably before 24 January, the day on which he withdrew from the court to mourn the death of his daughter Elizabeth at his Blackfriars house, after which he would not have attended theatrical performances.[1] He is unlikely to have seen a public performance of *Part One* when the company returned to London in October for a short season at the Swan, for no evidence survives that he had any interest in attending plays and, at the age of seventy, he had accepted the position of Lord Chamberlain only reluctantly. It is possible, then, to narrow the dates of his seeing *Part One* to four court performances during the Christmas festivities, when the Lord Chamberlain's Men (now known as Lord Hunsdon's Men, in honour of the late Lord Chamberlain), the only company invited to play at court, performed on 26 and 27 December 1596 and on 1 and 6 January 1597.[2]

Gibson introduces two additional pieces of evidence that help to fix the date of a court performance of *Part One* as 26 December. The first is an undated letter to Brooke from Edward Jones, the Queen's secretary for the French language, which refers to a court performance of an unnamed 'play on Sunday night' at which Brooke presided as Lord Chamberlain: the only one on a Sunday at which he could have presided was on 26 December. At that performance, Jones describes an incident in which Lord Cobham severely rebuked him, unjustly in his opinion, for having moved through the hall to where his pregnant wife was sitting 'to aske her how she did & not to stay there'. Jones protests to Lord Cobham, 'lifting up your staffe

---

1 McKeen, 666–8; Fehrenbach, 96; and P.W. White, 67.
2 Brooke was in mourning when the two Shrovetide performances occurred on 6 and 8 February and thus would not have attended them.

at me, [you] called me sirra and bide me get me lower saucy fellowe besides other wordes of disgrace'. Jones's keen humiliation is reflected in his repeated use of the word 'disgrace' along with 'wronge', 'displeasure' and 'skorne'.[1] Other factors may have contributed to the strength of Jones's indignation: he was allied with the Essex and Southampton faction against the Cobhams, and William Brooke had recently been awarded the lucrative wardship of Jones's stepson (McKeen, 652–3, and P.W. White, 67). But apparently Cobham overreacted to a trivial breach of decorum – if there was any breach at all – so egregiously that he disrupted the performance of the play. Paul Whitfield White speculates that the performance itself, more than Jones's *faux pas*, may have incited Cobham's anger: 'we cannot be sure of the play in question that night, but it is noteworthy that the one Shakespearean work repeatedly assigned to this winter season, *The First Part of Henry IV*, depicted in its earliest productions Cobham's Lollard ancestor, Sir John Oldcastle, second Lord Cobham, as a degenerate buffoon. If indeed *1 Henry IV* was performed that eventful Sunday evening, then the Lord Chamberlain clearly had another reason to be indignant' (71).

The second piece of evidence that Brooke may have been angered more by the performance than by Edward Jones comes from a letter by Master of the Revels Edmund Tilney, dated 25 January (probably 1599 or 1600),[2] in which he recounts that a couple of years earlier, 'I receuid diuerss braue letters fro*m* *ye* last L*ord* Chamberlayn When he & I were att odds. In w*h*ich letter he peromptoryly Chardgeth me y*at* I dealt badly & malliciusly w*ith* hyme'. Though the cause of Cobham's having

---

1 The letter was first printed by Chambers in 'Gleanings', 76–7, and reprinted with a photograph of the original in P.W. White, 66–71.

2 The letter, written by Tilney to Sir William More of Loseley in Surrey, is published in Streitberger. Fehrenbach disputes an earlier dating of the letter at 1594/95, when Carey was Lord Chamberlain, and persuasively argues that it was written in 1599 or 1600 and refers to the period when Brooke held that office (88–90).

written such letters is unclear, it seems to Tilney unwarranted; and thus Robert J. Fehrenbach reasonably asks, 'What could more offend, more embarrass this Lord Chamberlain – who feared both family shame and being thought "unapt" by his Queen – than for one of his ancestors to be caricatured before the Court and the Queen by those he was to regulate? Such an event would have been considered by Cobham as the cruelest of jokes, with him the butt' (95).

None of this, of course, is proof that a court performance of *Part One* during the Christmas festivities in 1596 caused offence to Lord Cobham, but the circumstantial evidence for his intervention is strong. Only the Lord Chamberlain's Men performed at court during the Christmas and Shrovetide festivities of 1596–7; Edward Jones affirms that Lord Cobham presided over a Sunday performance, and that performance could only have been on 26 December; something during that performance provoked Cobham to be uncharacteristically angry with Jones; and something happened around that same time to put Cobham at odds with his Master of the Revels, Edmund Tilney, resulting in a barrage of angry letters. White, in his analysis of Jones's letter, and Fehrenbach, in his analysis of Tilney's, reach similar conclusions about the probable cause, and Gibson makes their coincidence explicit, arguing that a plausible – perhaps the most plausible – 'explanation of the evidence here at the epicentre of the Cobham controversy is the perceived, albeit unintentional, personal insult to William Brooke and his family on 26 December 1596 during a performance at Court of the uncensored *1 Henry IV* featuring the comic hero Sir John Oldcastle, a performance presided over by a humiliated, angry, and powerful old man, who lashed out at Edward Jones with his white rod and lashed out at Edmund Tilney with "diuerss braue letters" ' (106).

If in fact Cobham was irate that Tilney had neglected to remove the offensive material from the play before licensing it, he would presumably have demanded that the name Oldcastle be changed; and Tilney would have responded quickly, perhaps in January 1597, requiring the Lord Chamberlain's Men to make suitable revisions not only to *Part One* but also to *Part Two*, which by that time – six months or more after *Part One* had been licensed – was certainly well under way, and which, upon completion, he would be asked to license. The survival of '*Old.*' as a vestigial speech prefix at 1.2.121 in the Quarto of *Part Two* seems to confirm that work on the play was already in progress before censorship occurred, as does a stage direction for *sir Iohn Russel* to enter at the top of 2.2, a name changed to *Bardolfe* in the Folio and in subsequent editions but which appeared regularly (though spelled 'Rossill') in quartos of *Part One* – 'strong presumptive evidence', according to Humphreys, 'that Shakespeare had got at least into Act II of Part 2 before rechristening his characters' (xv–xvi).[1] It is also likely that Shakespeare, while purging the name Oldcastle from *Part Two*, slyly included two implicit references to the enforced change: first, in the Lord Chief Justice's withering reply to Falstaff, 'Do you set down your name in the scroll of youth, that are written down *old* with all the characters of age?' (1.2.179–81; italics added); and second, in Poins's ridicule of Falstaff's beginning a letter by proclaiming his title, '*John Falstaff, Knight*': 'Every man must know that,' mocks Poins, 'as oft as he has occasion to name himself' (2.2.107–9). Such lines gain satiric point if they are read as allusions to the censoring of a name.[2]

Further to 'assuage the anger of William Brooke' (Gibson, 112), Tilney may also have required a transcript to be made of *Part One* to demonstrate that changes had been carried out and

1 Russell was the family name of the Earls of Bedford, as Harvey, whose name appears in *1H4* 1.2.154, was that of the third husband of the Earl of Southampton's mother: these names were changed to Bardolph and Peto probably at the same time Oldcastle was changed to Falstaff, and for a similar reason, to avoid giving offence to noble families. See 2.2.0.1n.

2 See Taylor, 'Fortunes', 96, repeated in Taylor, 'Cobham', 353. Shakespeare continued to make ironic allusions to the censorship of Oldcastle's name in *MW* and *HV*.

all offensive references to the Cobhams' ancestor eliminated. This transcript would have served as the basis for the Quarto edition entered in the Stationers' Register on 25 February 1597/8 and published later that year.[1] There is evidence, too, that whoever prepared the fair copy for *Part One* also prepared a transcript of *Part Two*; for while the idiosyncratic 1600 Quarto of *Part Two* appears to have been printed from a theatrical playbook based on Shakespeare's untidy holograph (see pp. 432–40), the text underlying the Folio edition, in which speech prefixes and stage directions have been regularized, corrections made and the whole given 'a certain degree of literary finish' (Shaaber, Variorum, 513), has marked affinities with the Quarto text of *Part One*. Alice Walker was the first to claim their kinship. 'The text with which this Folio play appears to me to have most in common is the *1 Henry IV* Quarto, which similarly seems to preserve a full score of the play . . . and suffers noticeably from the same pedantry in language as the Folio *2 Henry IV*' she writes. 'The manuscript which was collated with a copy of the *2 Henry IV* quarto to serve as Folio copy was a companion piece to the manuscript from which the *1 Henry IV* quarto was printed, the work of the same hand and roughly of the same date'.[2] John Jowett agrees with Walker that 'a single scribe prepared literary transcripts of the two *Henry IV* plays' (*TxC*, 331). What occasioned these transcripts has remained a mystery for many scholars, but Gibson's conjecture has a persuasive logic: Tilney's requirement that all offending Oldcastle references be removed from both parts of *Henry IV* would have been sufficient cause for anomalous 'literary' copies of the two plays to have been made. George Walton

---

1   Chambers, *Shakespeare*, 1.382, suggests that 'Possibly a desire to advertise the purging of the offence led to the publication of *1 Henry IV* unusually soon after its production'; cited by Gibson, 112.
2   Walker, *Textual*, 109, 111; cited by Gibson, 111. For discussion of the provenance of the Folio text, see pp. 457–70.

Williams provides a succinct answer to the critical question, 'Why should there have been fair copies of two sets of foul papers that were made neither for the Folio nor for a prompt book? Fortunately, an answer for the two *Henry IV* plays and for them only is available: the fair copy of both parts might have been prepared to prove to Oldcastle's angry posterity that their ancestor had been removed from both plays' ('Text', 179).

What conclusion, then, can be drawn about the dates of the composition and first performance of *Part Two*? One may speculate with reasonable confidence that the play was completed within a year of *Part One*, and perhaps as early as January or February 1597, when, before licensing, it would have been subject to the same censorship that caused Oldcastle to be renamed in *Part One*. One may speculate with a bit less confidence that *Part Two* was one of the two Shrovetide plays scheduled for presentation at court on 6 or 8 February,[1] and further, that following William Brooke's angry response to a court performance of *Part One* at Christmas, Tilney 'required the addition of a disclaimer to the Epilogue' of *Part Two* (Gibson, 112), to be spoken after every performance, to the effect that Falstaff is in no way meant to represent the famous Protestant martyr Sir John Oldcastle.

The Epilogue(s)

The effect of the Oldcastle controversy on *Part Two* is attested to by the vexed state of the play's Epilogue, which, as printed in Q and F, is unusually long and in some ways incoherent. If the Epilogue is in fact a compilation of two different epilogues, one written for a court performance, the other for public performances, and each addressing the uproar caused by a court

---

1   Green argues that *Part Two* was 'at least completed if not performed' between January and April 1597, and he speculates that it may have been one of the plays performed by the Lord Chamberlain's Men during the Christmas and Shrovetide festivities at court (192–4).

performance of *Part One*, then the Epilogue as printed makes much more sense and adds to the hypothesis that *Part Two* was performed not long after Tilney censored the plays.

The Epilogue is unusual because it is written in prose and is uncommonly long. Its length may be explained, however, by the fact that it has two discrete parts that were probably composed at different times and in response to different circumstances, and these parts are uncomfortably merged in Q and F. The first part (Epil.1–17) is unconventional for an epilogue. It may have been written for a performance at court, possibly during Shrovetide 1597, and, unusually, seems to have been spoken not by an actor in the play but by Shakespeare in his own person, who confesses that the speech 'is of my own making' (5), apologizes for an unidentified play that was 'displeasing' to the audience (9), and hopes that this one, featuring the newly rechristened Falstaff, will make amends. The unprecedented decision for the playwright himself to speak the Epilogue would have made little sense unless the apology for a previous offence was deemed sufficiently important, as the use of Oldcastle's name clearly was.

As James Shapiro notes, however, the initial social deference of the speaker – the curtsy, the begging of pardon (1–3) – gives way to a novel idea that playwright and audience are participants in a business transaction, a 'venture' (7, 11) in which he is the debtor (15), they his 'creditors' (12) and the play itself an investment (Shapiro, 34–5). These mercantile images recall not only those used by the rebel leaders in the opening scene and by Falstaff throughout the play, but also the venture capitalism dramatized in *The Merchant of Venice*, which was probably performed in the same season.[1] If this sequel to the offending *Henry IV, Part One* fails to please, the Epilogue warns, the playwright will 'break' – go bankrupt – and the playgoers

---

1 The Epilogue's conception of theatre as a 'credit economy' – a site of both holiday pleasure and commercial exchange – is discussed by Levine, 428–31.

therefore will 'lose' (Epil.12). The business of playgoing thus unites Shakespeare and the audience in a joint-stock company wherein, he advises them, their duty is to remit and his, to 'promise . . . infinitely' (15–16) – no servitude for him. He maintains this self-assurance even when kneeling before them at the end, a traditional way for an actor to submit to the audience's judgement; for, he says, he kneels only 'to pray for the Queen' (17), not to beg for their applause.[1] His deference to royalty brings this unusual authorial apologia to a fitting conclusion.[2]

It is unlikely that the second and third sections of the Epilogue (18–34) would have followed the first. Together forming a coherent unit, they were probably written for public performances and spoken by Falstaff, who, having managed to evade the authorities who were carrying him to the Fleet, rushes back onto the stage to beg the audience for acquittal. As Shapiro notes, Shakespeare's epilogues 'tend to straddle fictional and real worlds' (34), and Falstaff's return would ingeniously have raised the question of whether the actor was still speaking in character. That question would have been answered in part by the actor's clever revelation of his own identity when he asks to be commanded 'to use [his] legs' (Epil.19), for Will Kemp – the likeliest candidate to have played Falstaff (see p. 57n.1) – was a dancer whose jigs were popular with Elizabethan audiences. Kemp's subsequent reference to dancing 'out of your debt' as

---

1   Prayers for the Queen at the end of plays were 'as common at court and private performances as terminal jigs were in the amphitheatre playhouses', according to Hattaway ('Dating', 154); but Stern counters that such prayers assumed the *absence* of an authority figure and thus were more typical of touring or public performances (123–4, 127).

2   F's transposition of the prayer for the Queen from the end of the 'court' epilogue to the end of the 'public' epilogue has little justification other than to tie the two parts together as if they were originally meant to be one, which patently they were not. The confusion of a scribe or compositor about how the parts of the Epilogue are related, however, is understandable.

but 'light payment' (20) puns in typical fashion on Falstaff's failure to repay the thousand pounds he has borrowed from Shallow – actor and role once again conflated; and he proceeds to appeal for the playgoers' forgiveness with a *captatio beneuolentiae* which, much like the epilogue in *As You Like It*, plays humorously on the battle between the sexes. The dance Kemp has promised occurs at the end, for he indicates that when his legs are weary, he will bid the audience good night (33–4), having given them 'satisfaction' (21) with a jig.

If indeed the actor playing Falstaff performed this Epilogue at the Curtain, the final section would have acquired special potency, for its subject is the identity of Falstaff himself and the offence given by that character when he was named Oldcastle, an association which Shakespeare's company was forced to disavow. Kemp himself is assigned the task of reassuring playgoers that 'Oldcastle died martyr, and this is not the man' (32). In Fehrenbach's view, this disavowal must have been dictated by 'Tilney's campaign to launder the plays of any lingering offence to the Brooke family. The famous Oldcastle line in that final speech, so unsubtle, so unfunny, so overtly pointed, and so unrelated to the rest of the play, comes off more like an official announcement made by a stern Master of the Revels than a witty quip . . . written by a clever playwright' (97).

As if for proof that the name Oldcastle is not at issue here, the speaker tells the audience that Shakespeare is contemplating another Falstaff play in which the fat knight will follow the King to France where he 'shall die of a sweat' (Epil.30), a term often used for a cure for syphilis.[1] But this in itself is problematic, because it recalls numerous sweating references which directly link Falstaff to the historical Oldcastle who, refusing to recant,

---

1 Humphreys (Ard[2]), citing Thomas Cogan (265), notes that 'the English sweat', or sweating-sickness, typically referred either to the plague or, more pertinent to the sybaritic Falstaff, to venereal disease brought on by 'excesse and superfluitie, especially in eating and drinking . . . and women'.

was burned at the stake – references which intimate that this indeed *was* 'the man'.[1] In *Part One*, for example, the Prince says, 'Away, good Ned. Falstaff sweats to death' (2.2.105); and in *Part Two*, Falstaff lards his own speech with references to sweating. 'I mean not to sweat extraordinarily' in the wars, he tells the Lord Chief Justice (1.2.208–9). 'Do ye yield, sir, or shall I sweat for you?' he asked Colleville; for 'If I do sweat, they are the drops of thy lovers and they weep for thy death' (4.2.11–14). And he reassures Shallow that the new King will be moved to see them 'stained with travel and sweating with desire to see him' (5.5.24–5). In a play where references to Falstaff's sweating are so insistent, the memory of Oldcastle's death by fire hovers just beneath the surface. Despite its denial of Falstaff's identity as the historical Oldcastle, then, the Epilogue forges a strong link between them. Furthermore, it is the only epilogue in which Shakespeare reveals his plans for a future play. It is ironic that in the play he eventually wrote, Falstaff indeed is martyred, not by the audience's 'hard opinions' (Epil.31), but by the King's. Obviously, then, although Shakespeare was contemplating *Henry V* at this time, he had not yet decided to exclude Falstaff from it.

EDITORIAL CHOICES

There are two, arguably three, different versions of *Henry IV, Part Two*, but for various reasons none of them provides a fully authoritative basis for an edition. For reasons explained in Appendix 1, I deem it prudent to use the text with the least apparent intervention, the first issue of the Quarto in 1600 (Qa), and to add to it those passages from the other texts which seem authoritative: 3.1 from the second issue of the Quarto (Qb,

---

1   Kastan records that Oldcastle was 'hanged in chains and burned at St Giles Fields, the spectacular martyrdom grimly memorialized in one of the woodcuts in Foxe's *Acts and Monuments*' (*1H4*, 53–4).

1600) and eight passages which appear for the first time in the 1623 Folio (F) – but otherwise to alter only what, in Qa, is obviously in error by seeking alternative readings in F. In cases where a reading in Qa is defensible, even though another reading may seem preferable, I typically choose it, explaining the merits of each reading in the commentary.

All passages found in F but not in Q, and all alternative readings of single words or phrases adopted from F, are enclosed by superscript Fs. Speech prefixes have been silently regularized, with names and titles spelled out in full, not abbreviated. As is customary in Arden editions, I have modernized spelling and punctuation; I have, however, retained archaic spellings if they indicate idiomatic pronunciations or regionalisms that are important in defining a character's social class or geographic origin. Where there are differences in punctuation between Q and F that could lead to discrepant readings of a speech or passage, I follow the lead of Q, though I do so fully aware that a scribe's or compositor's habits of punctuation have inevitably contaminated the punctuation they found in their copy-text. In cases where F has printed as verse what in Q is prose, I elect to follow Q for reasons explained in my account of how F compositors encountered problems in casting-off (see pp. 470–7). When differences between Q and F spelling or punctuation are significant enough to affect meaning, those differences are discussed in the commentary notes.

Finally, I have kept stage directions to a minimum, reprinting those in Q and only occasionally adding to them directions from F (within superscript Fs) or fleshing them out with information (in brackets) such as entrances and exits that may be necessary to a basic understanding of the action. Although it is tempting for modern editors to provide fuller stage directions to help readers visualize what may be occurring on stage, such directions violate the spirit of original Elizabethan theatrical practice, in which actors figured out what to do from cues given in their individual 'part' copies without explicit direction. They

147

also limit the imaginative interplay between text and reader, wherein one combs the text for clues to piece together a picture of what may be transpiring, then imagines alternatives to that picture in which the most obvious clues are rejected, and new possibilities for staging replace them. For the most part, required stage business is implicit in the text. An editor need not make it explicit.

KING HENRY IV
PART TWO

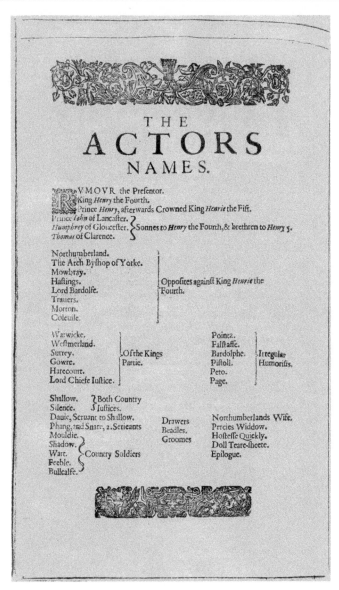

THE
ACTORS
NAMES.

RVMOVR the Prefentor.
King *Henry* the Fourth.
Prince *Henry*, afterwards Crowned King *Henrie* the Fift.
Prince Iohn of Lancafter.
Humphrey of Gloucefter. } Sonnes to *Henry* the Fourth, & brethren to *Henry* 5.
Thomas of Clarence.

Northumberland.
The Arch Byfhop of Yorke.
Mowbray.
Haftings. } Oppofites againft King *Henrie* the
Lord Bardolfe. Fourth.
Trauers.
Morton.
Coleuile.

Warwicke.
Weftmerland.
Surrey. } Of the Kings
Gowre. Partie.
Harecourt.
Lord Chiefe Iuftice.

Pointz.
Falftaffe.
Bardolphe. } Irregular
Piftoll. Humorifts.
Peto.
Page.

Shallow. } Both Country
Silence. } Iuftices.
Dauie, Seruant to Shallow.
Phang, and Snare, 2. Serieants
Mouldie.
Shadow. } Country Soldiers
Wart.
Feeble.
Bullcalfe.

Drawers
Beadles.
Groomes

Northumberlands Wife.
Percies Widdow.
Hofteffe Quickly.
Doll Teare-fheete.
Epilogue.

20 'The Actors Names', from the 1623 Folio (sig. gg8ᵛ)

RUMOUR, the Presenter
KING Henry the Fourth
PRINCE Henry [Harry],
afterwards crowned KING Henry the Fifth

Prince JOHN of Lancaster ⎫	*sons to Henry the*	5
Humphrey[, Duke] of GLOUCESTER ⎬	*Fourth, and brethren*	
Thomas[, Duke] of CLARENCE ⎭	*to Henry the Fifth*	

[Henry Percy, Earl of] NORTHUMBERLAND ⎫		
ARCHBISHOP of York		
[Lord] MOWBRAY[, Earl Marshal]		10
[Lord] HASTINGS ⎬	*opposites against*	
LORD BARDOLPH	*King Henry the*	
TRAVERS	*Fourth*	
MORTON		
[Sir John] COLLEVILE ⎭		15

[Earl of] WARWICK ⎫		
[Earl of] WESTMORLAND		
[Earl of] Surrey		
[Sir John Blunt] ⎬	*of the King's party*	
GOWER		20
HARCOURT		
Lord Chief JUSTICE		
[SERVANT *to the Lord Chief Justice*] ⎭		

[Ned] POINS ⎫		
[Sir John] FALSTAFF		25
BARDOLPH ⎬	*irregular humorists*	
[Ancient] PISTOL		
PETO		
[PAGE *to Falstaff*] ⎭		

[Robert] SHALLOW ⎫	*both country justices*	30
SILENCE ⎭		

DAVY, *servant to Shallow*

FANG
SNARE } *two sergeants*

[Ralph] MOULDY   35
[Simon] SHADOW
[Thomas] WART } *country soldiers*
[Francis] FEEBLE
[Peter] BULLCALF

[LADY NORTHUMBERLAND,]   *Northumberland's wife* 40
[LADY PERCY,] *Percy's widow*
HOSTESS[, Mistress] Quickly
DOLL Tearsheet
[Speaker of the] EPILOGUE

[FRANCIS, *a drawer*]   45
DRAWER
[Two] BEADLES
[Three] STREWERS *of rushes*
[PORTER]
[MESSENGER]   50
[Page to the King]

[Soldiers, Captain, Musicians, Servants, Attendants]

LIST OF ROLES not in Q; adapted from 'THE ACTORS NAMES' in F (sig. gg8ᵛ). Speaking roles are designated by names in upper case. Names and titles not in F are in brackets. F omits three speaking roles – those of the Porter (1.1), the Lord Chief Justice's Servant (1.2) and the Messenger (4.1) – which were added by Capell. Only three other plays in F have similar lists: *Tem*, *MM* and *Oth*.

1   **RUMOUR** an allegorical figure whose appearance draws on that of Fame, a mythic creature whose multiple tongues and eyes are indicative of the unreliability of historical reportage. Rumour is therefore an appropriate 'presenter' of what transpires in the play. For sources and analogues, see Ind.0.1–2n.

2   **KING Henry the Fourth** (1367–1413), called Bolingbroke for the Lincolnshire castle in which he was born, was the eldest son of John of Gaunt – Duke of Lancaster and the most powerful noble in the realm – and usurper of Richard II's throne in

1399. His reign was fraught with civil unrest, particularly rebellions led by the powerful Percy family who had helped him to the crown (1403–8), the Welsh chieftain Owen Glendower (1400–12) and Richard Scrope, Archbishop of York (1405). Though Henry succeeded in suppressing these threats to his government, familial discord proved equally threatening when the Prince of Wales joined his father's ruling Council in 1407, made powerful political alliances and, during a period of the King's ill health, challenged his father's authority. In 1411 the King retaliated by dismissing the Prince from the Council and replacing him with his second son, Thomas of Clarence. Throughout his reign, Henry was plagued by doubts of his legitimacy on account of his having deposed Richard, God's anointed king, and, it is alleged, having had him put to death.

3   **PRINCE Henry** (1386–1422), eldest son of Henry IV and his first wife Mary Bohun, born at Monmouth and therefore called Harry Monmouth, was made Prince of Wales in 1399 at the age of 12 and acceded to the throne on his father's death in 1413, becoming the legendary king and warrior Henry V. Stories of his madcap youth that circulated during his lifetime were embellished by later chroniclers; however, they are contradicted by his participation as early as 1400 in attempts to suppress the Welsh insurrection led by Owen Glendower, by his fighting in his father's cause – and sustaining a facial wound – at the Battle of Shrewsbury in 1403, and by his taking full command of English forces against the Welsh from 1406–8. Legends of his riotous misdeeds and his miraculous reformation may, however, have served to counterbalance the reported discord that arose between the Prince and his father over his role in the Council and possibly his ambition to supplant him as king. See pp. 121–6.

5   **Prince JOHN of Lancaster** (1389–1435), third son of Henry IV, was only 16 at the time of his encountering the rebels at Gaultree in 1405. He was knighted at his father's coronation in 1399, made Constable of England in 1403, and between 1403 and 1405 given lands forfeited by the Percy family, which ensured him a considerable income. Holinshed refers to him as John of Lancaster after the place of his birth, but in the play he is mistakenly called Duke of Lancaster, a title rightly belonging to his brother Thomas of Clarence, as Stow reports: 'Then the king rose and made his eldest sonne prince of Wales . . . his second sonne was there made Duke of Lancast[er]' (*Annales*, 513). John was in fact created Duke of Bedford by his brother Henry V in 1414, and by that title he plays a role in *1H6*.

6   **Humphrey, Duke of GLOUCESTER** (1390–1447), fourth and youngest son of Henry IV, was knighted by his father in 1399, but unlike his older brothers was given no significant military command during his father's reign. He was created Duke of Gloucester by Henry V in 1414, and in that capacity he fought in the French wars, suffering a wound at Agincourt, where he was rescued by Henry himself. He figures prominently in the *H6* plays as Protector of England during Henry VI's minority.

7   **Thomas, Duke of CLARENCE** (1387–1421), second and ostensibly favourite son of Henry IV, was at a young age appointed the King's lieutenant in Ireland, where he served intermittently from 1401 to 1409 until his father's illness gave him reason to return to London. According to chroniclers, he frequently indulged in unseemly behaviour at taverns and brothels in the company of his brother John. Stow reports that on St John's Eve 1410 the two princes were the principal instigators of a riot in Eastcheap (*Annales*, 550). Nevertheless, after Thomas's marriage to the rich widow of the Earl of Somerset in 1410, the King in 1411 bestowed upon him the titles Earl of Albemarle and Duke of Clarence, and appointed him president of his Council when Prince Henry fell from favour. With titles and wealth to support him, he was given a major military command, and led the King's expedition against the Duke of Burgundy in 1412 – a snub to Prince Henry, who worried that his succession to the throne might be in jeopardy. The

brothers apparently resolved their differences when Henry acceded to the throne, however, and Clarence played a major role in the French wars.

8 **NORTHUMBERLAND** Henry Percy (1341–1408), 1st Earl of Northumberland, provided the military backing for Henry Bolingbroke when the latter usurped Richard II's throne in 1399, and was rewarded when he became the leading member of the new King's royal Council. He subsequently turned against Henry for apparent ingratitude and, in an attempt to maintain his authority as the most powerful lord in the north of England, joined his son Henry Percy (Hotspur) and his brother, the Earl of Worcester, in a protracted insurrection. Though Northumberland submitted to the King and was briefly imprisoned after the rebel defeat at Shrewsbury – a battle in which he did not participate – there was insufficient evidence to charge him with treason, so he secured a royal pardon. Nevertheless, he was forced to forfeit some of his lands and revenues, and in 1405 he led another rebellion against the King, joining Lord Bardolph, Thomas Mowbray and Richard Scrope, Archbishop of York. When his attempt to remove the Earl of Westmorland at Durham failed, he abandoned Mowbray and Scrope and fled to Scotland in the company of Lord Bardolph. Three years later, the two fugitive lords launched an ill-starred invasion of England, but they did not get far. At the Battle of Bramham Moor in Yorkshire, in February 1408, Northumberland was killed. His body, as befitted a traitor, was decapitated and quartered, and his head sent to London for display on London Bridge.

9 **ARCHBISHOP of York**, Richard Scrope (or Scroope, as spelled in Q and F; *c.* 1350–1405), third son of Baron Scrope of Masham in the north and a distinguished canon lawyer, was appointed to head the commission receiving Richard II's 'voluntary' abdication in 1399. Though at first a loyal subject of Henry IV, he may have quietly supported the Percy rebellion in 1403. His manifesto of 1405, which incited the people of York to rise up against

the King, brought his sympathy with the Percys into the open: in it, he complained of the King's abuse of the Church and clergy, excessive taxation, misappropriation of revenue and unfair treatment of members of the nobility. Shakespeare seems also to imply a private motive for Scrope's insurgency by erroneously reporting him to be the brother of William Scrope, Earl of Wiltshire, whom Bolingbroke had beheaded for treason in 1399 (see *1H4* 1.3.265–6); in fact the Earl was only the Archbishop's cousin. Whatever his motivation, as leader of the Prelate's Rebellion, Scrope was presumably relying on the military backing of Northumberland: without it, the eight or nine thousand followers who rallied behind him scarcely constituted a credible army. Thus incapable of resisting the forces led by Westmorland and Prince John, Scrope may have surrendered unconditionally at Gaultree Forest on 29 May, or else been deceived, as chroniclers report, into thinking that his grievances would be addressed. But the King was intent on making an example of the treasonous archbishop, so Scrope, like his fellow insurgents, was beheaded – the first English prelate to be condemned to death by due process of law.

10 **MOWBRAY**, Thomas (1385–1405), 2nd Earl of Nottingham, was the eldest son of Thomas Mowbray, 1st Duke of Norfolk and Henry Bolingbroke's antagonist who died in exile in 1399 and whom, according to Shallow (3.2.24–6), young Falstaff served as page. He did not succeed to his father's dukedom; nor, although the Mowbrays claimed to be hereditary Marshals of England, did he succeed his father as Marshal. Instead, Henry IV appointed the Earl of Westmorland to that office for life, though young Mowbray was allowed to style himself 'Earl Marshal' as a courtesy. Why he joined the Prelate's Rebellion is uncertain. Though he petitioned the King to recover his father's estates, Henry was slow to grant him his inheritance, having earlier dispersed some of those lands to his own followers. A more likely cause of Mowbray's decision to join

the northern rebels was resentment that the King had withheld the marshalcy from him. When the rebellion failed, Mowbray was imprisoned with Archbishop Scrope at Pontefract and put to death as a traitor.

11 **HASTINGS** The person who joined the Prelate's Rebellion was not Lord Hastings, as Holinshed reports (3.529), but Sir Ralph Hastings. It is unclear whether his life was spared when the rebels dispersed, or whether, like the others, he was beheaded.

12 **LORD BARDOLPH** Thomas, 5th Baron Bardolf, Lord of Wormegay and elsewhere, was first summoned to parliament in 1390 and presumably remained loyal to the crown until 1405, when he joined Northumberland in his rebellion against Henry IV. He fled with Northumberland to Scotland, thereafter to Wales and then to France. He and Northumberland led troops in an invasion of England from Scotland in 1408 and suffered defeat in the Battle of Bramham Moor, where Northumberland was slain. Holinshed reports that Lord Bardolph 'was taken, but sore wounded, so that he shortlie after died of the hurts' (3. 534). His body, subjected to the traitor's fate, was quartered and decapitated.

13 **TRAVERS** There is no mention of such a character in Holinshed or other chroniclers. Shakespeare seems to have invented him for this play.

14 **MORTON** like Travers, a character apparently invented by Shakespeare

15 **Sir John COLLEVILE** A knight by the name of Collevile (also spelled 'Colevile' in QF) is not mentioned in Holinshed's account of the rebels' defeat at Gaultree Forest, but is included in a list of conspirators beheaded at Durham. If, however, that list was not Shakespeare's source for this character, he may have borrowed the name from a 'Sir John Colvyl, Knight' who joined Henry V on his French expedition in 1415, or from 'Sir John Colvill' – perhaps the same person – who was Governor of Wisbech Castle in 1416.

16 **WARWICK** Richard Beauchamp (1382– 1439), 13th Earl of Warwick, was a godson of Richard II and Richard Scrope (see 9n.). His family suffered in the last years of Richard's reign, when the Mowbrays were

given disputed land claimed by the earls of Warwick, and was saved by the accession of Henry IV, who knighted young Beauchamp at his coronation in 1399. Beauchamp served ably in the Welsh campaign against Owen Glendower before receiving his father's title and lands in 1403, and fought for the King at the Battle of Shrewsbury. Despite his relationship with Archbishop Scrope, he assisted with his arrest and trial in 1405. During the Welsh campaigns he became a strong ally of the Prince of Wales, and his appointment to the royal Council in 1410 coincided with the Prince's rise to power on the Council. When the King recovered power for himself in 1411, Warwick was removed from the Council along with the Prince. Shakespeare mistakenly has the King refer to Warwick as 'cousin Neville' at 3.1.66, perhaps confusing Warwick's family name with that of the Earl of Westmorland (see 17n.), or possibly taking the name from his son-in-law Richard Nevill, who became Earl of Warwick, in his wife's right, during the reign of Henry VI.

17 **WESTMORLAND** Ralph Neville (*c.* 1364–1425), 1st Earl of Westmorland and scion of a northern family as powerful as the Percys, was the first lord to offer support to the banished Henry Bolingbroke, his brother-in-law, when he returned from France to claim his patrimony. As a reward, on his coronation day Henry created him Marshal of England for life. Henry's grant of land in southern Scotland to Northumberland, however, limited Westmorland's influence in the north and may have fed a growing rivalry between them. Warwick used the Percys' rebellion in 1403 as an opportunity to break that family's hold on the north. After the Battle of Shrewsbury, Westmorland intercepted Northumberland's march south with reinforcements, forced him back to Warkworth and urged the King to take the Percy castles by force. Though the King pardoned Northumberland in 1404 and affected a reconciliation between the two rival lords, it was shortlived. In 1405, Northumberland led a raid on a castle where he knew Westmorland to be staying, with the

intention of capturing him; but Westmorland was forewarned of the raid and escaped. Northumberland fled to Scotland, and Westmorland was left to quash the Prelate's Rebellion, first by defeating retainers of Percy and Mowbray near Thirsk, and then by marching towards York, where he intercepted the Archbishop's forces and used guile to get the rebel leaders to lay down their arms (see pp. 117–19). Westmorland was rewarded for his loyalty to the King with vast swaths of Percy lands. The QF spelling 'Westmerland' no doubt indicates its pronunciation, with emphasis falling on the first syllable.

18 **Surrey** Thomas Fitzalan (1381–1415), 5th Earl of Arundel and 10th Earl of Surrey, joined Bolingbroke in exile in Paris and accompanied him on his return to England. Knighted by Henry IV in 1399 and restored to the title and estates of his father, who had been executed by Richard II in 1397, he for years fought to maintain the King's authority in the Welsh marches, where he was allied with the Prince of Wales, the Earl of Warwick, and others. In 1405 he was sent north to suppress the Prelate's Rebellion, where he and Thomas Beaufort were invested with authority to pass a judgement of execution on the Archbishop of York. His subsequent fortunes were increasingly attached to those of Prince Harry. After the Prince was dismissed from the royal Council, Surrey held no further office, military or political, until Henry V acceded to the throne. Holinshed erroneously records the death of 'Thomas Beauford earle of Surrie' in 1410 (3.536). On Surrey's status as a mute character in the play, see 3.1.31.1n.

19 **Sir John Blunt** A mute character in the retinue of Prince John at Gaultree, Blunt may have been the son of Sir Walter Blount, a loyal Lancastrian who was killed fighting for the King at Shrewsbury. John was made a Knight of the Garter and lost his life at the siege of Rouen in 1418. See 3.1.31.1n.

20 **GOWER** a name Shakespeare uses for a captain in *H5* and again for the Chorus in *Per.* Gower here figures as a messenger for the Lord Chief Justice. Holinshed, in his

account of the reign of Henry IV, devotes a paragraph to the poet John Gower (3.541), possibly inspiring Shakespeare to use the name.

21 **HARCOURT** perhaps a name Shakespeare chose at random. The Harcourt (de Harcourt) family had been prominent gentry in the central midlands since the Norman invasion. A Sir Thomas Harcourt was Sheriff of Berkshire in 1407.

22 **Lord Chief JUSTICE** Sir William Gascoigne (*c.* 1350–1419), said to have studied at Cambridge and the Inner Temple, was one of Richard II's sergeants-at-law during the 1380s, and in the 1390s was retained by Bolingbroke, served as chief justice of the Lancaster palatinate, and became attorney to Bolingbroke during his banishment. Henry IV named Gascoigne Chief Justice of the King's Bench in 1400; in 1403 he was commissioned to raise forces against the Earl of Northumberland and was made justice of assize for the northern circuit, including Northumberland and Yorkshire where the Percys were plotting rebellion; in 1405 he was assigned to receive the submission of, and to fine, the Earl's confederates. Some chronicles report, though without substantiation, that Henry assigned Gascoigne to try Archbishop Scrope for treason, but that when Henry insisted that a death sentence be passed, Gascoigne refused, arguing that the laws of the kingdom gave no secular court the right to adjudge a bishop to death. Whether true or not, the story attests to Gascoigne's reputation for moral probity and judicial independence. The most famous story circulated about him involved his imprisoning the Prince of Wales for attempting to rescue one of his favourites from the bar of the King's Bench: see pp. 129–30 for an account of variations in the legend. Shakespeare employs this story to dramatize the reformation of the Prince, who, now wearing the crown, praises the Chief Justice for committing him into the hands of justice and asks him to remain in office to wield *Th'unstained sword* and to 'be as a father to my youth' (5.2.113, 117). In fact, however, Henry V did not renew Gascoigne's appointment as Chief Justice,

but replaced him with William Hankeford only a week after his accession.

24 **POINS** A bosom friend of Prince Harry in both parts of *H4*, Ned Poins vows that the 'worst that they can say of me is that I am a second brother' (2.2.63–4), suggesting that he is a gentleman who, as a younger son, will inherit little money and no estate, but is nonetheless worthy to keep company with the Prince. Shakespeare may have derived his name from a noble Gloucestershire family named Poyntz dating back to the Norman conquest (when the name was Fitzpons), whose barons played an influential role in the court of Edward I and of subsequent kings, including Henry VIII.

25 **FALSTAFF** An impecunious knight whose situation to a degree mirrors that of other veterans in the reign of Elizabeth, but whose 'brave deeds' at Shrewsbury have earned him a crown pension, Sir John Falstaff in *1H4* was originally named Sir John Oldcastle, after a Protestant martyr who was burned in 1417 by order of his friend Henry V. The name was changed prior to the printing of quarto editions following a protest made after the play was performed, probably by the 10th Lord Cobham, the Lord Chamberlain and a collateral descendant of Oldcastle. See pp. 134–42 for an account of this controversy and residual references to Oldcastle in *2H4*. The name Shakespeare substituted, Falstaff, may have derived from Sir John Fastolf, a nobleman who appears in *1H6* as a cowardly foil to Sir John Talbot, though in life he was honoured for his service in the French wars: the SP *'Fast.'* occurs twice in Q0 of *1H4*. However, in keeping with other charactonyms in *2H4* such as Shallow and Silence, Falstaff's name may have been intended to suggest his traits of cowardice and deception in battle (falsestaff) or his ultimate rejection by Henry V (fall-staff).

26 **BARDOLPH** A droll, red-faced alcoholic, and manservant to Falstaff, whom as his corrupt 'corporal' he helps to recruit soldiers in Gloucestershire, Bardolph is identified by Shakespeare as the man over whose arraignment for felony the Prince once struck the Lord Chief Justice (1.2.56– 7). Called Bardoll or Bardol in quarto editions of *1H4*, his name in *2H4* may have shifted to a variant form owing to the proximate appearance of Lord Bardolph as Northumberland's chief confederate. This form of his name remained consistent in *2H4*, *H5* and *MW*, as well as F *1H4*. Shakespeare had originally designated the character as Russell (the family name of the Earls of Bedford), apparently changing it when he changed Oldcastle to Falstaff, and for the same reason, to avoid giving offence to a noble family (see p. 140). Nevertheless, it is curious that the new name Shakespeare chose was that of Sir Reginald Cobham's wife, Bardolf (Chambers, *Shakespeare*, 1.25).

27 **PISTOL** A scurrilous braggart and a familiar of Doll Tearsheet, the ancient Pistol – ancient being military rank equivalent to ensign, though Falstaff later addresses him as his lieutenant (5.5.88) – is repeatedly called a 'swaggerer', someone who quarrels, boasts, bullies, and is especially violent towards women. His idiom of mock-heroics identifies him as a fraud, and as such he holds a privileged place in Falstaff's entourage. Most obviously identified with a temperamental new 16th-century weapon likely to go off without warning, Pistol's name may also derive from the Italian *pistolfo*, translated by Florio in 1611 as 'a roguing beggar, a cantler, an vpright man that liueth by cosenage' (see 2.4.69n).

28 **PETO** A companion of the Prince who plays a significant role in *1H4* but appears in this play only to bring a message to him in the tavern, Peto, like Poins, seems to be well born. Peto was the name of a Warwickshire family, and William Peto, a clergyman in the reigns of Henry VIII and Mary, was elected Cardinal in 1557. In *1H4* the character seems originally to have been called Harvey, the family name of the third husband of the Earl of Southampton's mother, but Shakespeare changed the name to Peto, probably at the time he altered Falstaff's and Bardolph's original names.

29 **PAGE** *to Falstaff* A page in the middle ages was a young male servant in service to

a nobleman, often acting as his messenger, or as an apprentice squire to a knight. Falstaff is reported by Justice Shallow to have been page to Thomas Mowbray, Duke of Norfolk (3.2.24–6). Typically well born himself, the boy at about age seven would join a noble household as a personal servant, and for the next seven years would receive training in military conduct, dress and protocols. Falstaff's Page, of course, would have learned very different manners of conduct and dress, as the Prince observes at 2.2.67–9. It is likely that Shakespeare's company at this time had a small boy actor with considerable comic talent.

30 **SHALLOW** A gentleman some years older than Falstaff, whom he remembers as a page when he himself was a student at Clement's Inn, and therefore in his 70s, Robert Shallow serves as a justice of the peace in Gloucestershire. As such, he is responsible for mustering local men for service in the King's wars. Though Shallow claims to be poor, his farm, as Falstaff observes, is rich in *land and beefs* (3.2.326). His name, of course, reveals his lack of depth and his gullibility in relation to others who wish to use him for their own purposes.

31 **SILENCE** Shallow's yoke-fellow of equity, Silence is another justice of the peace in Gloucestershire, a *cousin* to Shallow (3.2.4–5), and, as his name suggests, a man of few words. Though often played to comic effect as old and decrepit, Silence has a son at Oxford (*to my cost*, 12) and thus is probably younger than Shallow.

32 **DAVY** In Falstaff's words, Davy is Shallow's *serving-man and . . . husband* (5.3.11), i.e. the person who manages the farm and its resources. A pragmatist, Davy is not above manipulating Justice Shallow for his own ends, as when he gets him to fix a case for an *arrant knave* who is his friend (5.1.39).

33 **FANG** an officer of the law, or constable, whose name is indicative of his function: to seize or apprehend offenders

34 **SNARE** A *yeoman* (2.1.3), traditional second to a constable, whose name means to capture or catch by entangling, Snare may have been played by a cadaverously

thin actor in Shakespeare's company, John Sincklo, who doubled as the Beadle and possibly as Simon Shadow.

35 **MOULDY** One of the two ablest recruits from whom Falstaff is to choose, Ralph Mouldy is a farmer prosperous enough to bribe his way out of service. His name, suggestive of his occupation, refers to soft, crumbly earth suitable for growing plants.

36 **SHADOW** a recruit whose name suggests emaciation, and therefore a role possibly played by John Sincklo. Simon Shadow's name also invokes, in Falstaff's punning confession, the corrupt practice by some captains of filling their muster books with the names of dead or fictitious men, called 'shadows', whose earnings they would pocket for themselves as 'dead pay'.

37 **WART** Possibly named for a Thomas Warter of Gloucestershire (see 3.2.137n.), Thomas Wart is ridiculed for his ragged appearance, lice-infested clothing, small stature and unsuitability for military service. Yet Falstaff uses these characteristics to justify selecting him as someone who could handle a light musket (caliver) more dexterously than the more obviously fit recruits.

38 **FEEBLE** As a women's tailor, Francis Feeble is mocked with the stereotype of effeminacy and sexual deviance, yet he proves to be the most courageously patriotic of all the recruits.

39 **BULLCALF** As his name suggests, Peter Bullcalf is a young man of considerable physical prowess, and therefore the most likely recruit; but ironically, as a coward who would rather be hanged than serve, he is the first to offer Bardolph a bribe.

40 **LADY NORTHUMBERLAND** Not Hotspur's mother, Lady Northumberland was the Earl's second wife, Maud Lucy, the widow of Gilbert Umfraville, Earl of Angus, and daughter of Lord Thomas Lucy. Her inheritance of the Lucy family estates made Northumberland the largest landowner in Cumberland. After Maud died in 1398, Northumberland did not marry again. Shakespeare thus takes poetic licence by resurrecting her for a scene (2.3) which occurs just prior to the Prelate's Rebellion in 1405.

41 **LADY PERCY** Widow of Hotspur, Elizabethan Mortimer (1371–1444?) was the older sister of Sir Edmund Mortimer, whom Shakespeare mistakenly identifies as the man Richard II had designated heir presumptive to the throne, when in fact the designated heir was Mortimer's nephew, 5th Earl of March. She plays a larger and more comic role in *1H4*, where she is called Kate, than in this play, where her stinging denunciation of Northumberland for his abandonment of Hotspur at Shrewsbury persuades him to flee to Scotland.

42 **HOSTESS Quickly** proprietress of the Eastcheap tavern commonly called the Boar's Head (see 2.2.142–3n.). In *1H4* Mistress Quickly is the wife of *an honest man* (3.3.93), but in *2H4* she claims to be a widow (2.1.68) whom Falstaff has sworn for the past 20 years to marry. A middle-aged woman whose tavern runs the risk of becoming known as a brothel, she yearns for the respectability that marriage to a knight – Sir John – would bring her; yet her idiosyncratic speech, full of comic malapropisms and inadvertent double entendres, reveals much of what she tries to keep hidden, including her moral laxity as a business woman and her sexual history with Falstaff.

43 **DOLL Tearsheet** Falstaff's favourite whore and apparently an employee of Mistress Quickly, Doll has a tempestuous relationship with Pistol which culminates in their allegedly beating a man to death at the tavern (5.4.15–17), for which she and the Hostess are arrested. With Falstaff, however, Doll is indulgently affectionate: their unsentimental farewell as he goes off to war (2.4) is one of the most indelible scenes in the play. Doll's name reveals her occupation, variations having appeared in earlier works such as the *Playe of Robyn Hode* (*c.* 1560): 'She is a trul of trust, to serve a frier at his lust, / A prycker, a prauncer, a terer of shetes' (116–17; Ritson, 2.199. Steevens[4] noted the parallel).

44 **EPILOGUE** The epilogue may in fact be two discrete epilogues fused together for the publication of Q in 1600. The speaker of the first may have been Shakespeare himself; of the second, the actor who played Falstaff, possibly Will Kemp, a notable dancer. For a full account of the Epilogue, see pp. 142–6.

45 **FRANCIS** A drawer – that is, one who draws liquor to serve customers – at the Hostess's tavern, Francis was the object of mean-spirited mockery by the Prince and Poins in *1H4*. In *2H4*, they continue to mock him by mimicking his phrase *Anon, anon, sir* when they disguise themselves as drawers (2.4.285).

47 **BEADLES** sheriff's officers or under-bailiffs whose job it was to punish petty offenders. The SD in Q names the pale, skeletally thin John Sincklo as the actor intended for the speaking role, suggesting its comic dimension: see 5.4.0.1–2n.

48 **STREWERS** So listed in Q, but as 'Groomes' in F, these attendants were charged with strewing rushes on streets as a sign of deference before the passing of a royal procession.

KING HENRY IV

PART TWO

INDUCTION   *Enter* RUMOUR *painted full*
of tongues.

RUMOUR
  Open your ears; for which of you will stop
  The vent of hearing when loud Rumour speaks?

INDUCTION Act and scene divisions in this edition for the most part follow those in F. All variants are recorded in the textual notes. The first such variant occurs with the Induction, which F labels Scene 1 (*Scena Prima*), requiring subsequent scenes in Act 1 to be numbered 2, 3 and 4 (*Secunda*, *Tertia* and *Quarta*). The current edition adheres to scene divisions for Act 1 established by 18th-century editors; the numbers of these scenes appear in brackets to signal them as variants from F. Two other variants occur in Act 4, when this edition numbers as a separate scene (4.2) one which in F is indivisible from 4.1, requiring that the following scene also be renumbered (4.3). No act and scene divisions are provided by Q.

The Induction serves as a prologue to the play. Capell, taking his cue from 35–7, locates the scene specifically before Warkworth Castle, the Percys' principal seat, to which, according to Holinshed (3.524), Northumberland had retreated upon hearing news that Westmorland was advancing against him.

0.1–2 Rumour is akin to the allegorical figures of medieval Morality plays and Tudor interludes. The original source of the figure

here was probably Fama in Virgil's *Aeneid*, 4.181–90, an indiscriminate reporter of fact, fiction and gossip who was depicted as having many eyes and tongues: 'she is a vast, fearful monster, with a watchful eye miraculously set under every feather which grows on her, and for every one of them a tongue in a mouth which is loud of speech, and an ear ever alert'. As Shaaber demonstrates (*Variorum*, 10–11), Shakespeare's audiences would have been familiar with the appearance of such a figure. Thomas More, in a pageant devised *c.* 1492 and printed in 1557, portrayed Fame 'with tonges . . . compassed all rounde' (*Works*, 1.5); in 1509, Fame became 'A goodly lady, envyroned about / With tongues of fire' in Stephen Hawes's *Pastime of Pleasure* (156–7); and in a court pageant presented before Henry VIII in 1519, the figure of Report entered 'apparelled in crimson sattin full of toongs' (Holinshed, 3.849). By 1553, when the Revels Office paid 'for paintinge of a cote and a Capp w*ith* Ies [eyes] tonges and eares for fame' (Feuillerat, 142), the costume had hardened into a convention.

1–2 **stop . . . hearing** plug up your ear. Cf. 1.1.79.

TITLE] THE / Second part of Henrie / the fourth, continuing to his death, / *and coronation of Henrie* / the fift. / With the humours of sir Iohn Fal- / *staffe, and swaggering* / Pistoll. / *As it hath been sundrie times publikely* / acted by the right honourable, the Lord / Chamberlaine his seruants. *Q;* The Second Part of Henry the Fourth, / Containing his Death: and the Coronation / of King Henry the Fift. *F*
INDUCTION] *F (Actus Primus. Scoena Prima. /* INDVCTION*.); not in Q*   0.1–2 *painted . . . tongues*] *Q; not in F*   1 SP] *Capell; not in QF*

I from the orient to the drooping west,
Making the wind my post-horse, still unfold
The acts commenced on this ball of earth.   5
Upon my tongues continual slanders ride,
The which in every language I pronounce,
Stuffing the ears of men with false reports.
I speak of peace while covert enmity,
Under the smile of safety, wounds the world;   10
And who but Rumour, who but only I,
Make fearful musters and prepared defence
Whiles the big year, swoll'n with some other grief,
Is thought with child by the stern tyrant War?
And no such matter. Rumour is a pipe   15

---

3   Rumour follows the course of the sun,
    which rises in the east (*orient*) and drops,
    or 'droops', in the west; *drooping* is a trans-
    ferred epithet. By circling the earth, Rumour
    gains the status of a natural phenomenon.

4   **post-horse** horse kept at an inn for use by
    post-riders or for hire by travellers. The
    duty of post-riders, who were stationed at
    regular intervals along post-roads, was to
    ride as quickly as possible to the next post
    bearing packets, messages and letters
    (*OED sb.*² 1). Equestrian imagery is
    continued in *ride* (6).
    still always, continually

4–5 **unfold / The acts** *unfold* means to
    disclose, reveal or expose (*OED v.* 2).
    Metaphorically, Rumour regards itself as
    a theatrical producer, with *acts* referring
    to the performance of a play as well as to
    the actions of its characters.

5   **commenced** commencèd

6   **tongues** a probable reference to the
    tongues painted on, or affixed to,
    Rumour's costume. F's singular 'Tongue'
    may indicate a non-theatrical provenance
    for the F text.

12 **fearful ... defence** the conscription of
    soldiers and the preparation of defence
    predicated on fear. Such preparations
    were regularly made during 1595–7 in
    anticipation of a Spanish invasion that
    never occurred. *Make* and *prepared*,
    though different tenses, may be read as
    parallel verbs.

13 **big** pregnant, as the next line makes clear

15 **And ... matter.** Q's punctuation puts a
    full stop or period to the speculation
    advanced by the preceding question; F's
    punctuation makes the resolution more
    tentative.

15–16 **pipe / Blown** begins a musical
    metaphor in which a *pipe*, an archaic
    wind instrument akin to a recorder and
    consisting of a single tube made of reed,
    straw or wood, is said to be so simple in
    its fingering that anyone can play it (20).
    Cf. Hamlet's use of a similar metaphor
    in *Ham* 3.2.342–63: 'Do you think I am
    easier to be played on than a pipe? Call
    me what instrument you will, though
    you fret me you cannot play upon me'
    (361–3).

---

6 tongues] *Q;* Tongue *F*   8 men] *Q;* them *F*   13 Whiles] *Q;* Whil'st *F*   grief] *Q;* griefes *F*   14–15 tyrant
War? . . . matter.] *Q;* Tyrant, Warre, . . . matter? *F*

Blown by surmises, Jealousy's conjectures,
And of so easy and so plain a stop
That the blunt monster with uncounted heads,
The still discordant wav'ring multitude,
Can play upon it. But what need I thus　　　　　20
My well-known body to anatomize
Among my household? Why is Rumour here?
I run before King Harry's victory,
Who in a bloody field by Shrewsbury
Hath beaten down young Hotspur and his troops,　　　25
Quenching the flame of bold rebellion
Even with the rebels' blood. But what mean I
To speak so true at first? My office is
To noise abroad that Harry Monmouth fell
Under the wrath of noble Hotspur's sword,　　　　30

16 **Jealousy's conjectures** The capitalization of 'Iealousies' followed by the lower
case 'coniectures' in Q, and the fact that
the two words are not separated by a
comma as they are in F, suggest that
Jealousy is to be understood as an
allegorical possessive. The conjectures
prompted by Jealousy thus stand in
apposition to surmises. Jealousy here may
be more akin to suspicion (*OED sb.* 5)
than to Envy, its traditional double. See
1.3.23n.

17 **stop** the closing of an aperture or finger-
hole in a wind instrument to change the
pitch. The aural image is anticipated in
'stop / The vent of hearing' (1–2).

18 **blunt** stupid, insensitive, obtuse (*OED
adj.* 1)

18–19 **monster ... multitude** This unflattering image of the mob had proverbial
force: 'A multitude of people is a beast
of many heads' (Dent, M1308). Cf. the

allusion to 'this Hydra, son of war' at
4.1.266. Shakespeare used the image
twice in *Cor*: at 2.3.16–17: 'the many-
headed multitude', and 4.1.1–2: 'the
beast / With many heads'.

19 **still discordant** constantly bickering

20 **what ... I** what need is there for me to

22 **my household** here, the theatre audience,
with an implication that everyone present
would be familiar with, and perhaps
guilty of abusing, the 'well-known body'
(21) of Rumour.

23–7 **I ... blood** Rumour summarizes
events at the conclusion of *1H4* 5.3–4 to
set in relief the misinformation that
follows.

29 **noise** commonly used as a verb, meaning
to report, rumour, or spread (*OED v.* 1)
Harry Monmouth In 1387, Prince
Henry was born in, and therefore named
after, Monmouth in Wales.

16 Jealousy's conjectures] *Oxf (Shaaber);* Iealousies coniectures *Q;* Ielousies, Coniectures *F*
19 wav'ring] *Q;* wauering *F*　21 anatomize] *Q (*anothomize*), F (*Anathomize*), F4*　27 rebels'] *Theobald²*;
rebels *QF*

And that the King before the Douglas' rage
Stooped his anointed head as low as death.
This have I rumoured through the peasant towns
Between that royal field of Shrewsbury
And this worm-eaten hole of ragged stone   35
^FWhere^F Hotspur's father, old Northumberland,
Lies crafty-sick. The posts come tiring on,
And not a man of them brings other news
Than they have learnt of me. From Rumour's tongues
They bring smooth comforts false, worse than true   40
    wrongs.   *Exit.*

31 **the Douglas'** The article before Douglas's name distinguished him as the clan leader. The King's Scottish antagonist in *1H4* was the same Earl of Douglas.

33 **peasant** condescending term identifying the inhabitants as rude and ignorant, and presumably more susceptible to rumour

34 **royal** i.e. because the King did battle there

35 **hole** Theobald's emendation, 'Hold', meaning a castle or fortification, is plausible in view of the frequent misreading of *e* as *d* in Elizabethan secretary hand; but the agreement of Q and F on *hole*, if one assumes that Q was not F's source (see pp. 468–70), would seem to have more authority here, given the imaginative association of *hole* with *worm-eaten*. A rhetorical contrast is drawn between '*that* royal field' (34) and '*this* worm-eaten hole' before which Rumour apparently stands.
ragged stone denotes the rough projecting stonework typical of a fortress (Davison), but may also allude to the severe erosion of castles and city walls in Shakespeare's day (Cam¹).

37 **Lies crafty-sick** feigns illness. While Holinshed (3.522), Daniel (*CW*, 3.97)

and Shakespeare (in *1H4* 4.1.16) all give 'the sickness of Northumberland' as the reason for his absence from Shrewsbury, none of them accuses him of deception. Nevertheless, Northumberland's abandonment of his son at a critical moment seems strategic in *1H4*, and he is rebuked for it in this play by Hotspur's widow (2.3.10–16). Furthermore, Worcester's claim in *1H4* that some may suspect that the Earl's absence was prompted by 'wisdom, loyalty, and mere dislike / Of our proceedings' (4.1.61–4) rather than sickness introduces the possibility of craftiness – a possibility reinforced here by *Lies*.

posts express couriers (see 4n.)

tiring on riding hard, to the point of exhaustion; possibly, borrowing a term from hawking, *tiring* = tearing (Ard¹)

39 **of ... tongues** Q's punctuation, with a comma between 'me' and 'from' and another following 'tongues', creates a syntactic ambiguity; for the phrase 'from Rumour's tongues' could function in apposition to 'of me' instead of introducing the clause in 40. F's punctuation links the phrase to the final clause unambiguously.

34 that] *Q; the F* 35 hole] *QF*; Hold *Theobald* 36 Where] *F*; When *Q* 39 of me. From] *F*; of me, from *Q* 40 SD] *F*; *exit Rumours. Q*

1[.1]   *Enter the* LORD BARDOLPH *at one door.*

LORD BARDOLPH
  Who keeps the gate here, ho?

        [*Enter the* Porter *at another door.*]

                        Where is the Earl?
PORTER
  What shall I say you are?
LORD BARDOLPH   Tell thou the Earl
  That the Lord Bardolph doth attend him here.
PORTER
  His lordship is walked forth into the orchard.

1.1 The Induction locates this scene at a castle (35–7); historically, the Earl of Northumberland's principal residence was Warkworth Castle in Northumberland. Shakespeare almost never specifies locations in stage directions, instead using dialogue to identify a place to the degree it might be necessary, and otherwise allowing the unlocalized empty stage to ensure fluidity of action. The most notable exception to this rule occurs in 4.1, where an opening SD identifies a precise location.

0.1, 1 SD The nearly simultaneous entrances of Lord Bardolph and the Porter are resolved by F's yoking them together as one entrance, but Q's signalling the entrance of Lord Bardolph '*at one doore*' would suggest that the Porter enters from another door in response to Lord Bardolph's calling, not with him. The fact that Northumberland soon enters through a *gate* (5) at which Lord Bardolph is told to knock indicates that there may have

been three points of entry. In modern productions, Northumberland is often revealed standing or sitting centre stage as the scene begins, with Lord Bardolph entering to him from upstage; and as a result, lines 2–6 are cut.

0.1 LORD BARDOLPH here, as in Holinshed, Northumberland's closest ally, who conspired with him against the King in 1405 (presumably the date of this scene; cf. 189–209n.) and who, as is reported at 4.3.97–9, joined him in defeat at the Battle of Bramham Moor in 1408. When, in revising *1H4*, Shakespeare altered the name of Oldcastle's lowlife companion from Sir John Russell to Bardolph, he may not have envisaged using this section of Holinshed and risking confusion by having two characters with the name Bardolph in *2H4*. See 2.2.0.1n.

2 **What** who
3 **attend** wait for, await
4 **orchard** a garden for both herbs and fruit trees (*OED sb.* 1a *obs.*)

1.1] *Pope (Act I. Scene I.); Scena Secunda. F; not in Q*   **0.1**] *Q; Enter Lord Bardolfe, and the Porter. F; Porter before the Gate; Enter Lord* Bardolph. *Capell; The Porter above the Gate. Enter Lord Bardolph. / Singer² (Collier); Enter the* Lord Bardolph *at one door* [*, and the* Porter *at another*] *Cam²*   BARDOLPH] *QF (Bardolfe), Rowe*   **1 SD**] *this edn*

Please it your honour knock but at the gate,   5
And he himself will answer.

      Enter the Earl [of] NORTHUMBERLAND
      [*carrying a crutch and wearing a coif*].

LORD BARDOLPH   Here comes the Earl.
                        [*Exit Porter.*]

NORTHUMBERLAND
What news, Lord Bardolph? Every minute now
Should be the father of some stratagem.
The times are wild; contention, like a horse
Full of high feeding, madly hath broke loose   10
And bears down all before him.
LORD BARDOLPH   Noble Earl,
I bring you certain news from Shrewsbury.
NORTHUMBERLAND
Good, an God will.
LORD BARDOLPH   As good as heart can wish.
The King is almost wounded to the death,
And, in the fortune of my lord your son,   15

5   **Please it** if it would please; a stock
    deferential phrase
6.1–2 Northumberland enters before Lord
    Bardolph has a chance to knock for him.
    According to 145–7, he carries a *crutch*
    and is wearing a *coif* – a close-fitting cap
    tied under the chin, often worn by men as
    a nightcap (*OED sb.* 1) – both of which
    suggest illness.
8   **Should . . . of** is likely to beget. The
    image of paternity, used here for the
    first time, has relevance not only to
    Northumberland's having failed his son
    at Shrewsbury, but to Harry's fraught
    relationship with his father and his two

    father surrogates, Falstaff and the Lord
    Chief Justice.
    stratagem a violent or bloody deed;
    alternatively, an artifice or trick designed
    to outwit or surprise an enemy (*OED sb.*
    1–3). Both senses are appropriate here.
10 **of high feeding** with the eating of rich
    food (*OED* high *adj.* 8). The implication
    is that the political strife (*contention*)
    which led to war in *1H4* has been so well
    nourished that it is out of control.
11 **bears down** tramples
12 **certain** definite
13 **an God will** if God is willing
15 **fortune** case, situation

6 SD1.1] *Q; Enter Northumberland. F*   SD1.2] *Oxf subst.*   SD2] *Dyce; not in QF*   7 Every] *Q;* Eu'ry *F*
13 an God] and God *Q;* and heauen *F*

Prince Harry slain outright, and both the Blunts
Killed by the hand of Douglas. Young Prince John
And Westmorland and Stafford fled the field,
And Harry Monmouth's brawn, the hulk Sir John,
Is prisoner to your son. O, such a day!   20
So fought, so followed, and so fairly won,
Came not till now to dignify the times
Since Caesar's fortunes.

NORTHUMBERLAND   How is this derived?
Saw you the field? Came you from Shrewsbury?

LORD BARDOLPH
I spake with one, my lord, that came from thence,   25

---

16 **both the Blunts** evidence of garbled report or false rumour. In *1H4* Sir Walter Blunt is slain by Douglas at the Battle of Shrewsbury, where he was marching in the King's coat (5.3.13); and although Holinshed provides discrepant accounts of Sir Walter's death as though he were in fact two people, on the list of the slain only one Sir Walter Blunt is named (3.523). Daniel, on the other hand, reports that both Sir Walter and another Blunt, 'the kings Standard bearer', were killed at Shrewsbury (*CW*, 3.111, 112). Holinshed credits 'an English knight, one sir Iohn Blunt' with defending an English fortress in France in 1412 (3.540), and a John Blunt enters as a ghost character in the Qb issue of this play at 3.1.31. A Blunt is told to lead Collevile to execution in F (4.2.73) and is listed in a SD in Q (5.2.41).

17–18 **Young . . . field** another instance of false rumour. Sources agree that Stafford did not flee but was killed at Shrewsbury, fighting (like Walter Blunt) in the King's armour and apparel: see *1H4* 5.3.7–9; Holinshed, 3.523; and Daniel, *CW*, 3.113. They make no mention of Prince John or Westmorland at Shrewsbury.

19 **brawn** a swine or boar fattened for the table (*OED sb.* 4); cf. *1H4* 2.4.106–7: 'that damned brawn'. Appropriately, these and other epithets for Falstaff 'recall the chief stock-in-trade of the victuallers and butchers of Eastcheap, namely, meat of all kinds' (Wilson, *Fortunes*, 27).
   hulk a large merchant ship; figuratively, a big, unwieldy person (*OED sb.* 1, 4). For a comic expansion of the analogy, see 2.4.63–6.

20 **day!** Q's punctuation emphasizes the exclamatory nature of the phrase, though the syntax nevertheless requires *day* to be the subject of the sentence, as in F.

21 The triple alliteration echoes Caesar's '*veni, vidi, vici*' ('I came, I saw, I conquered'), anticipating not only the mention of *Caesar's fortunes* at 23, but Falstaff's parody and quotation of Caesar's line at 2.2.123–4 and 4.2.41–2.
   followed supported by loyal troops

23 **fortunes** victories
   How . . . derived? 'What is the source of your information?' See *OED* derive *ppl.a.*

A gentleman well bred and of good name,
That freely rendered me these news for true.

Enter TRAVERS.

NORTHUMBERLAND
Here comes my servant Travers, who I sent
On Tuesday last to listen after news.
LORD BARDOLPH
My lord, I overrode him on the way,   30
And he is furnished with no certainties
More than he haply may retail from me.

---

27 **freely** unreservedly, of his own accord
30 **overrode** Either overtook (*OED* over-
    ride *v.* 4) or out-rode (Cam¹). How one
    understands the context will determine
    which gloss is appropriate. There are two
    scenarios. In the first, 'overtook' suggests
    that Lord Bardolph and Travers were
    riding in the same direction, towards
    Warkworth – the former to impart to
    Northumberland the news he had heard
    from a *gentleman well bred* (26) who
    had come from Shrewsbury, the latter
    to bring a less sanguine report. Travers
    claims to have been *turned . . . back* (34)
    in his quest for news about the rebels'
    fate by Sir John Umfreville, possibly
    the same gentleman Lord Bardolph
    had encountered, who imparted *joyful
    tidings* (35) to him and then sped away
    (*Out-rode me*, 36). But on his ride back
    to Warkworth, during which he was
    overtaken by Lord Bardolph, Travers
    encountered another *gentleman* (37) who
    bore contrary news. The problem with
    this scenario is that Lord Bardolph
    claims that Travers 'is furnished with
    no certainties / More than he haply may
    retail from me' (31–2), which would
    contradict Travers's claim that he heard

the good news from Umfreville. If,
however, Bardolph and Umfreville are
one and the same (see 34n.), the scenario
changes, and 'out-rode' becomes the
more sensible gloss for *overrode*. Travers,
travelling towards Shrewsbury in search
of news, met Lord Bardolph on the way
and was *turned . . . back* by his reports of
the rebels' success. Lord Bardolph, *being
better horsed* (35), then out-rode Travers
(who in the meantime met the second
gentleman) and got to Northumberland
before him. In this case, Lord Bardolph's
claim that he *overrode* Travers would
simply anticipate, and make redundant,
Travers's report that Bardolph had
outridden him. Why would Shakespeare
have included this information twice,
and altered the verb in the process? The
second scenario is perhaps more attractive
because simpler, but it relies on speculation that Shakespeare meant to change
the name Umfreville to Bardolph, something which, however likely, neither Q
nor F confirms. Either scenario, however,
dramatizes the process by which historical fact is altered in the telling.
32 **retail** retell, recount

27.1] *Capell; opp. 25 Q; after 29 F; after 33 Pope*   28 who] *Q; whom F*   32 retail] *Q (*retale*), F (*retaile*)*

NORTHUMBERLAND

Now, Travers, what good tidings comes with you?

TRAVERS

My lord, Sir John Umfreville turned me back
With joyful tidings, and, being better horsed,   35
Out-rode me. After him came spurring hard
A gentleman almost forspent with speed,
That stopped by me to breathe his bloodied horse.
He asked the way to Chester, and of him
I did demand what news from Shrewsbury.   40
He told me that rebellion had bad luck,
And that young Harry Percy's spur was cold.
With that he gave his able horse the head,
And bending forward struck his armed heels
Against the panting sides of his poor jade   45

---

33 **tidings comes** Using singular verb forms with plural subjects was a not uncommon practice from the mid-16th to the mid-17th century, especially with nouns that could be thought of as collective (Abbott, 333). Cf. 5.5.47.

34 **Sir John Umfreville** a name most editors think Shakespeare replaced with Lord Bardolph, the change occurring in the course of revision. Evidence that Umfreville once figured in this scene is provided by Q, in which the SP for 161 (a line not in F) is *Vmfr*. At 1.3.81, the fact that Lord Bardolph is ignorant of news imparted to him in this scene (131–5) lends further support to the hypothesis that his role in 1.1 was originally written for someone else. Chambers speculates that Lord Bardolph had 'replaced Sir John Umfreville through a belated historical correction, not fully carried out' (*Shakespeare*, 1.379). The Oxford editors carry out that substitution here, thus

creating an octosyllabic line with an awkward repetition of 'Lord'.

37 **forspent** worn out

38 **breathe** allow to rest
bloodied i.e. its flesh torn by the rider's spurs

41 **bad** F's 'ill' is often preferred by editors because Northumberland uses the phrase *ill luck* at 51 in an apparent echo of Travers, and Shakespeare uses it elsewhere as well (cf. *MV* 3.1.89–91); but there is no compelling reason to reject Q.

42 **spur was cold** a play on Harry Percy's nickname, Hotspur: *cold* = dead. Cf. 50.

43 **able** strong, vigorous, powerful (*OED adj.* 5); perhaps, here, sufficiently recovered to proceed
the head freedom of rein, not restrained by a bridle

44 **armed** spurred; armèd

45 **jade** worn-out horse, hack; usually used contemptuously, but here, compassionately

---

33 with] *Q;* fro *F*   34 Sir John Umfreville] *Q (Vmfreuile),* F *(Vmfreuill);* Lord Bardolph *Oxf (Capell)*
36 hard] *Q;* head *F*   41 bad] *Q;* ill *F*   44 forward] *Q;* forwards *F*   armed] *Q;* able *F;* agile *Pope*

Up to the rowel head; and starting so
He seemed in running to devour the way,
Staying no longer question.

NORTHUMBERLAND   Ha? Again:
Said he young Harry Percy's spur was cold?
Of Hotspur, Coldspur? That rebellion   50
Had met ill luck?

LORD BARDOLPH   My lord, I'll tell you what:
If my young lord your son have not the day,
Upon mine honour, for a silken point
I'll give my barony. Never talk of it.

NORTHUMBERLAND

Why should that gentleman that rode by Travers   55
Give then such instances of loss?

LORD BARDOLPH   Who, he?
He was some hilding fellow that had stol'n
The horse he rode on, and, upon my life,
Spoke at a venture.

Enter MORTON.

Look, here comes more news.

---

46 **rowel head** spiked wheel at the end of a spur
47 **devour the way** eat up the road. Compare
    similar imagery in Job, 39.24: 'He [the
    war horse] swalloweth the grounde for
    fearcenes and rage' (Geneva Bible); also
    in Catullus' *Ode* 35.7 and in Jonson's
    Sejanus, 5.10.763–4 (Ard¹).
48 **Staying ... question** allowing no further
    conversation (*OED* stay *v.* 19). Cf. *MV*
    4.1.342: 'I'll stay no longer question.'
49–50 **Said ... Coldspur?** Daniel may have
    inspired the quibbles on hot and cold:
    'Such wracke of others bloud thou didst
    behold / O furious *Hotspur*, ere thou lost

thine owne! / Which now once lost that
heate in thine waxt cold' (*CW*, 3.114).
52 **have ... day** has not won the battle
53 **point** piece of lace for tying a garment;
    hence, a trifle
54 **Never ... it** 'Mark my words.'
55 ¹**that** possibly a case of compositorial
    anticipation, in which case F's 'the'
    would be correct
56 **instances** examples, evidence
57 **hilding** contemptible, worthless (*OED*
    sb. 2)
59 **at a venture** at random, recklessly, with-
    out due consideration (*OED* venture *sb.* 1c)

---

48 Ha? Again:] *F*; Ha? Again, *Q*; Ha! Again? *Capell*   55 ¹that] *Q*; the *F*   57 stol'n] *QF* (stolne)
59 Spoke] *Q*; Speake *F*; Spake *F2–4*   a venture] *Q* (a venter); aduenture *F*   SD] *this edn; opp.* 59 *Q;
after* 59 *F*

NORTHUMBERLAND

    Yea, this man's brow, like to a title-leaf,   60

    Foretells the nature of a tragic volume:

    So looks the strand whereon the imperious flood

    Hath left a witnessed usurpation.

    Say, Morton, didst thou come from Shrewsbury?

MORTON

    I ran from Shrewsbury, my noble lord,   65

    Where hateful death put on his ugliest mask

    To fright our party.

NORTHUMBERLAND   How doth my son and brother?

    Thou tremblest, and the whiteness in thy cheek

    Is apter than thy tongue to tell thy errand.

    Even such a man, so faint, so spiritless,   70

    So dull, so dead in look, so woebegone,

    Drew Priam's curtain in the dead of night

    And would have told him half his Troy was burnt;

---

60 **title-leaf** title-page. See TITLE t.n. for evidence of the descriptive nature of Elizabethan title-pages. Title-pages for tragedies frequently mentioned the fates of major characters.

62 **strand** shoreline, beach
imperious flood high tide. Cf. *imperious surge* at 3.1.20.

63 **witnessed usurpation** visible trace. The line of seaweed left along the shore is said to resemble the line of a furrowed brow. The word *usurpation*, apt for this play about a usurping king, is used to describe the encroachment of an abnormally high tide.

67 **brother** i.e. Thomas Percy, Earl of Worcester, who has been sentenced to death by the King in *1H4* 5.5.14, yet who, Morton falsely assures Northumberland, is still living (82)

70–4 Neither Homer nor Virgil includes this episode in recounting the sack of Troy. In Virgil, *Aen.*, 2.268–97, the ghost of Hector appears to Aeneas in his sleep to warn him of danger, and Aeneas awakes to find Troy on fire, but Priam is not mentioned. However, a revival of Kyd's *The Spanish Tragedy*, re-titled *Jeronimo* and acted on 7 January 1597, may have included, among other interpolated passages, the lines 'Draw me like old Priam of Troy, crying, "The house is a-fire, the house is a-fire, as the torch over my head"' (Fourth Addition, 156–8) – a possible source for the reference here (Ard²).

70 *Even* was certainly pronounced 'e'en' to ensure a pentameter line.

72 **curtain** i.e. the curtain around his bed

62 strand] *QF* (strond)   whereon] *Q;* when *F*   64 Morton] *F, Q* (Mourton)   68 tremblest] *Q;* trembl'st *F*
73 was burnt] *Q;* was burn'd *F;* had burnt *Cam²*

But Priam found the fire ere he his tongue,
And I my Percy's death ere thou report'st it.   75
This thou wouldst say: 'Your son did thus and thus;
Your brother thus; so fought the noble Douglas',
Stopping my greedy ear with their bold deeds.
But in the end, to stop my ear indeed,
Thou hast a sigh to blow away this praise,   80
Ending with 'Brother, son, and all are dead.'

MORTON

Douglas is living, and your brother yet;
But for my lord your son –

NORTHUMBERLAND   Why, he is dead?
See what a ready tongue suspicion hath!
He that but fears the thing he would not know   85
Hath by instinct knowledge from others' eyes
That what he feared is chanced. Yet speak, Morton;
Tell thou an earl his divination lies,
And I will take it as a sweet disgrace
And make thee rich for doing me such wrong.   90

MORTON

You are too great to be by me gainsaid;
Your spirit is too true, your fears too certain.

---

74 **ere ... tongue** before the man had time
to speak
78 **Stopping** filling
79 **stop** prevent from hearing anything
further, punning on the sense of 'stop' in
78. Cf. Ind.1–2.
83 **dead?** F's punctuation would change Q's
agonized question to a more resigned
statement.
84 spoken with reference to himself:
suspicion has led him to anticipate the
truth in the speech above (67–81).

85–7 **He ... chanced** The man who fears
a truth, and therefore would prefer not
to know it, instinctively reads (*Hath ...
knowledge*) in others' eyes what that
truth is.
87 **is chanced** has happened
88–9 Ordinarily it is an offence (*disgrace*) to
contradict an earl, but Northumberland
will consider it *sweet* for Morton to give
the lie to his intuition (*divination*) of what
happened at Shrewsbury.
92 **spirit** intuition, perception (*OED sb.* 12)

79 my] *Q*; mine *F*   83 son –] *Rowe³*; sonne: *Q*; Sonne. *F*   dead?] *Q*; dead. *F*   86 others'] *Capell*; others
QF   88 an] *Q*; thy *F*

NORTHUMBERLAND

Yet, for all this, say not that Percy's dead.
I see a strange confession in thine eye;
Thou shak'st thy head and hold'st it fear or sin   95
To speak a truth. If he be slain,
The tongue offends not that reports his death;
And he doth sin that doth belie the dead,
Not he which says the dead is not alive.
Yet the first bringer of unwelcome news   100
Hath but a losing office, and his tongue
Sounds ever after as a sullen bell,
Remembered tolling a departing friend.

LORD BARDOLPH

I cannot think, my lord, your son is dead.

MORTON

I am sorry I should force you to believe   105
That which I would to God I had not seen;
But these mine eyes saw him in bloody state,

---

94 **strange** reluctant (*OED adj.* 11b)
95 **shak'st thy head** Morton tacitly confesses the truth by nodding his head.
hold'st it believe it to be
fear a fearful act
96 F's 'say so' completes the pentameter line but is not necessary to the meaning (cf. 4.3.52n.), while Q's abbreviated line allows a brief pause for Northumberland to take in the painful prospect of his son's death.
98 **he ... dead** a proverbial sentiment ('To belie the dead is a sin') (Dent, D124.1), common in drama of this period
belie slander, calumniate (*OED v.* 2)
101 **Hath ... office** performs an unrewarding service or task
102 **sullen** deep, dull and mournful in tone (*OED adj.* 3b). Cf. *Son* 71.1–2: 'No longer mourn for me when I am dead /

Than you shall hear the surly sullen bell'.
103 **tolling** F's substitution of 'knolling' for *tolling* is not easy to explain, since the words are virtually synonymous. *OED* cites this line as the earliest instance of both words' use to mean ringing out for a dead or dying person.
105–6 In the contest for credibility, Morton upstages Lord Bardolph by arguing that second-hand reports must give way before his own eye-witness account of Hotspur's death. In *1H4*, however, only Falstaff is onstage to witness Harry's combat with Hotspur, and Harry infamously permits him to take credit for killing Hotspur at 5.4.156–8. Shakespeare's inconsistency allows Morton to render his more accurate account of Hotspur's death in the following lines (107–11).

---

96 slain,] *Q;* slaine, say so: *F*   102–3 bell, / Remembered tolling] *Q;* Bell / Remembred, knolling *F*
106 God] *Q;* heauen *F*

Rend'ring faint quittance, wearied and out-breathed,
To Harry Monmouth, whose swift wrath beat down
The never-daunted Percy to the earth,   110
From whence with life he never more sprung up.
In few, his death, whose spirit lent a fire
Even to the dullest peasant in his camp,
Being bruited once, took fire and heat away
From the best-tempered courage in his troops;   115
For from his metal was his party steeled,
Which once in him abated, all the rest
Turned on themselves, like dull and heavy lead.
And as the thing that's heavy in itself
Upon enforcement flies with greatest speed,   120

---

108 **Rend'ring faint quittance** making
meagre resistance; *quittance*, meaning a
return of blows, works as a financial
metaphor as well: the repayment of a
debt – here, what is owed to Harry.
out-breathed out of breath, possibly
implying that his opponent had more
stamina
109–11 Holinshed and Stow (*Annales*)
simply record that Hotspur was killed by
soldiers of the royal army. Shakespeare is
therefore unhistorical: in crediting Harry
with the prize – '*The Prince killeth
Hotspur.*' (*1H4* 5.4.75 SD) – he may have
been inspired by a passage in Daniel
wherein the King is told that at
Shrewsbury 'shall young *Hotespur* with
a fury led / Meete with thy forward sonne
as fierce as he' (*CW*, 3.97).
112 **In few** in a few words, in short
whose Hotspur, not death, is the implied
antecedent.
114 **Being bruited once** from the moment it
was reported
115 **best-tempered** having the hardness and
elasticity of steel, metaphorically forged
in the fire mentioned at 112

116 **metal** with a pun on mettle, meaning
courage, spirit or strength of character.
Anticipated by *tempered* in the previous
line, *metal* introduces a series of images,
continuing in this line with *steeled*, which
compares the rebel soldiers' conduct on
the field with heavy *lead* (118) and their
flight from the field with *arrows* (123).
F's 'Mettle', indistinguishable from Q's
'mettal' in the theatre, lacks its metaphoric richness in print.
party soldiers
117–18 The meaning is not clear. Possibly
the abatement – the blunting of the edge
(*OED* abate *v.* 8) – of Hotspur's *metal*
(sword or mettle) by his death caused
those soldiers who had once been steeled
by him to lose their edge: that is, to bend,
turn back on themselves, and become as
dull and heavy as they used to be. To be
as dull or heavy as lead was proverbial
(Dent, L133.1, 134).
120 **Upon enforcement** under compulsion;
when force is applied to it

---

109 Harry] *Q; Henrie F*   110 never-daunted] *F; neuer daunted Q*   116 metal] *Q (*mettal*), F4; Mettle*
F1–3

So did our men, heavy in Hotspur's loss,
Lend to this weight such lightness with their fear
That arrows fled not swifter toward their aim
Than did our soldiers, aiming at their safety,
Fly from the field. Then was that noble Worcester   125
So soon ta'en prisoner; and that furious Scot,
The bloody Douglas, whose well-labouring sword
Had three times slain th'appearance of the King,
'Gan vail his stomach and did grace the shame
Of those that turned their backs, and in his flight,   130
Stumbling in fear, was took. The sum of all
Is that the King hath won, and hath sent out
A speedy power to encounter you, my lord,
Under the conduct of young Lancaster
And Westmorland. This is the news at full.   135

121 **heavy in** dejected by, playing on *heavy*
as 'weighted down' at 119 and anticipating the quibble on *weight* at 122. The
phrase contrasts with the *lightness* of
their *fear* that propels them at 122–5.

123 **fled** ambiguously used here as the past
tense of both flee and fly (flew); likewise
the fleeing of soldiers is suggested at
125 by the verb *Fly*. By using these
verbs interchangeably, Shakespeare fuses
arrows and soldiers together, turning the
simile into a half-metaphor.

123 **aim** target or thing aimed at

125 **Then** two meanings, both apply: at that
time; for that reason. The latter better
explains *So soon* at 126.
   Worcester Thomas Percy, Earl of
Worcester and Northumberland's brother

128 Holinshed's report that Douglas 'slew Sir
Walter Blount, and three other apparelled
in the King's suit and clothing' (3.523)
is the source of this passage and two

passages in *1H4* (5.3.1–29, 5.4.24–37).
For references to the King's decoys in
this play, see 16n., 17–18n.

129 **'Gan ... stomach** began to lose his
courage (*OED* vail *v.*[2] 4a: abase, humble,
lower)
   grace sanction by fleeing with them,
used ironically in reference to Douglas's
noble title

131 **Stumbling ... took** an abbreviation of
Holinshed, who records Douglas's 'falling from the crag of an high mountain',
his capture and his subsequent release
by the King (3.523). The account in
1H4 5.5.17–31 spoken by Hal, who is
so impressed by Douglas's 'valours' that
he delivers him 'ransomless and free', is
closer to Holinshed than is Morton, who
attributes fear to Douglas.

133 **power** army (*OED sb.* 9)
   encounter confront, do battle with (*OED
v.* 1)

126 So] *Q;* Too *F*

NORTHUMBERLAND

For this I shall have time enough to mourn.
In poison there is physic; and these news,
Having been well, that would have made me sick,
Being sick, have in some measure made me well.
And as the wretch whose fever-weakened joints   140
Like strengthless hinges buckle under life,
Impatient of his fit, breaks like a fire
Out of his keeper's arms, even so my limbs,
Weakened with grief, being now enraged with grief,
Are thrice themselves. Hence, therefore, thou nice
    crutch!   145
    [*Tosses crutch aside.*]
A scaly gauntlet now with joints of steel
Must glove this hand. And hence, thou sickly coif!
    [*Snatches off coif.*]

137 **physic** medicine. Cf. a similar paradox in *RJ* 2.3.19–20: 'Within the infant rind of this weak flower / Poison hath residence and medicine power'; and in *Luc* 530–2: 'The poisonous simple sometimes is compacted / In a pure compound; being so applied, / His venom in effect is purified.'

137–9 **and . . . well** The syntax is ambiguous. *Having* and *Being* may arguably modify *me*, or an implied 'I', rather than *these news*. Northumberland affirms that Morton's report, poisonous enough to make him sick had he been well, has paradoxically given him the impetus (*physic*) to get out of his sickbed and take action. The structure of 138–9 produces, in Weis's phrase, 'a taut chiasmus'.

137 **these news** Though Morton has made *news* singular at 135, Northumberland's plural form was commonly used when the word referred to an account of recent

events rather than its dissemination (*OED sb.* 2a).

140 **wretch** miserable or unfortunate person (*OED sb.* 2)

141 **life** the weight of living

142 **Impatient . . . fit** modifies *wretch* at 140. *Impatient* means unable to endure the *fit*, a severe illness or a paroxysm brought on by fever (*OED* fit *sb.* 3a), an image enhanced by *fire* (142).

143 **keeper's** nurse's (*OED sb.* 1e)

144 **enraged** made hot or feverish (*OED* enrage *v.* 6b)

145 **nice** unmanly

146 **scaly gauntlet** A *gauntlet* is a glove worn as armour, usually made of leather and covered with steel plate, in this case *scaly* with overlapping pieces of metal (*OED* scaly *adj.* 5).

147 **sickly coif** For *coif*, see 6.1–2n.; *sickly* is transferred from Northumberland to the *coif*, a hypallage similar to that at 1.3.99.

137 these] *Q*; this *F*   143 keeper's] *Rowe*; keepers *QF*   145, 147 SD] *Oxf subst.*

Thou art a guard too wanton for the head
Which princes, fleshed with conquest, aim to hit.
Now bind my brows with iron, and approach   50
The ragged'st hour that time and spite dare bring
To frown upon th'enraged Northumberland!
Let heaven kiss earth! Now let not nature's hand
Keep the wild flood confined! Let order die!
And let this world no longer be a stage   155
To feed contention in a ling'ring act;

148 **guard** protection or defence, with a possible play on its obsolete meaning, ornamental trimming on a garment (*OED sb.* 11a)

   wanton of clothing: luxurious, self-indulgent, effeminate (*OED adj.* 4)

149 **fleshed with conquest** their taste of victory making them hunger for more bloodshed (*OED* flesh *v.* 1, 2a, 2c). Dogs were fed with raw meat (*fleshed*) to whet their appetites for the chase.

150 **bind . . . iron** fit my head with a helmet. More conventionally laurels, not iron, would bind one's brows: Northumberland imagines a perversely ceremonial scene of arming.

150–1 **approach . . . hour** the subjunctive form, meaning 'let the roughest hour approach'. Weis reads the line as 'let them approach', but there is no logical antecedent for 'them'. See a similar use of the subjunctive at 4.3.250–2.

153–60 Northumberland's hyperbolic call for the world to return to chaos anticipates the vaunting of later tragic heroes: Lear, who commands all nature's germens to spill at once because his daughters have proven ungrateful (*KL* 3.2.6–9); Timon, who bids the social fabric unravel because his friends have abandoned him (*Tim* 4.1.1–41); and Macbeth, who would risk chaos to learn

what his future holds (*Mac* 4.1.50–61). Macbeth's invocation of a moral as well as a natural disorder most closely echoes Northumberland's speech which, by willing a fratricidal *spirit* to *Reign in all bosoms*, hints at the moral degeneration of the rebels' cause. Northumberland himself has, through his treachery, contributed to the very unrest which has cost his son's life and led to his present despair.

153 **kiss** touch; an ironically delicate verb for the apocalyptic collapse of earth and sky

153–4 **Now . . . confined!** Nature, the principle of order, is bid to allow the ocean (*flood*) to encroach on the land and thus become *wild* because unconfined. Allusions to the flood in Genesis and to the great Stratford flood of 1588 are both possible.

155–6 The metaphor of the world as a stage was proverbial ('This world is a stage and every man plays his part', Dent, W882; cf. *AYL* 2.7.140–67), and *ling'ring act*, meaning both a prolonged performance and an extended struggle, extends the metaphor: cf. Henry's account of his own kingship as a performance at 4.3.326–7. But *To feed contention* – that is, to nourish or exacerbate a quarrel – makes it a mixed metaphor.

149 fleshed] *QF;* flush'd *Capell*   155 this] *Q;* the *F*

177

But let one spirit of the first-born Cain
Reign in all bosoms, that, each heart being set
On bloody courses, the rude scene may end
And darkness be the burier of the dead.   160

LORD BARDOLPH

This strained passion doth you wrong, my lord.

MORTON

Sweet earl, divorce not wisdom from your honour;
The lives of all your loving complices
ᶠLean on yourᶠ health, the which, if you give o'er

---

157 **one ... Cain** a universal impulse to
murder one's brother: see Genesis, 4.1–
8. Bolingbroke alludes to the Cain and
Abel story twice in *R2* (1.1.104–6, 5.6.43–
4), seemingly without being aware that
the reference alludes to himself as the
guilty murderer of his cousin (= brother).
159 **rude scene** barbarous and violent action;
or, in a continuation of the stage
metaphor, a bad performance
161–5 These warnings to Northumberland
not to succumb to passion are reminiscent of those spoken to Hotspur after he
has drowned his wisdom in a sea of rant
(*1H4* 1.3.208–36). Shakespeare draws
an implicit comparison between father
and son.
161 SP *Q assigns this line to Sir John
Umfreville, whose role was probably
conflated with Lord Bardolph's during
revision (see 34n.). This edition follows
Pope and many subsequent editors in
changing the SP to Lord Bardolph: cf.
162 SPn. Capell is clearly wrong to
assign the line to Travers, who, a mere
messenger, would not speak to a lord in
this way.
161 **strained passion** excessive or unnatural
outburst – whether of feeling or rhetoric,

either of which would apply (*OED*
strained *ppl.a.* 4; passion *sb.* 6c); strainèd
162 SP *Q assigns this line to Lord Bardolph,
and F follows suit; but in Q the line ends
with a comma, evidence that it belongs
both syntactically and logically with the
three lines that follow (which Q and F
assign to Morton) and should be spoken
by the same character. There may have
been confusion if '*Bard.*' was written
in the margin of the MS against 161–2
but was not understood as a substitution
for '*Vmfr.*', causing Q compositors to
assign one line to each of them and to
postpone Morton's SP to 163. Editors of
F, or of the copy on which it was based,
apparently realized that the SP '*Vmfr.*'
was anomalous and so omitted 161
entirely but kept 162 and 163 as they are
in Q. Most modern editors dismiss F and
divide the SPs as I do here; but Melchiori
assigns 161 to Morton and 162–5 to Lord
Bardolph, and the Oxford editors (Oxf,
TxC), reasoning that 162 was a marginal
addition intended to replace 161, omit
161, and assign 162 to Lord Bardolph
and 163ff. to Morton.
163 **complices** confederates, comrades (*OED*
sb. 1)

---

161 SP] *Pope (L. Bard.); Vmfr. Q; Tra. / Capell;* MORTON *Cam²; not in F*   161 This ... lord.] *Q; not in F*   162 SP] *Cam¹ (Daniel); Bard. Q; L. Bar. F*   163 The] *Cam¹ (Daniel); Mour. The Q; Mor. The F*   164 Lean on your] *F;* Leaue on you *Q*   which,] *Theobald;* which *QF*   164–5 o'er ... passion,] *F subst.;* ore, ... passion *Q*

To stormy passion, must perforce decay. 165
ᶠYou cast th'event of war, my noble lord,
And summed the account of chance before you said
'Let us make head.' It was your presurmise
That in the dole of blows your son might drop.
You knew he walked o'er perils, on an edge, 170
More likely to fall in than to get o'er.
You were advised his flesh was capable
Of wounds and scars, and that his forward spirit
Would lift him where most trade of danger ranged.
Yet did you say 'Go forth'; and none of this, 175
Though strongly apprehended, could restrain
The stiff-borne action. What hath then befall'n,
Or what hath this bold enterprise brought forth,

166–79 *lines omitted from Q, possibly in an attempt to lighten Morton's role, which suffers a more substantial and problematic cut at 189–209

166 **cast th'event** calculated the risk, or forecast the outcome; *cast* introduces a gambling metaphor appropriate to the discussion of rebellion and developed in the following lines.

167 **summed ... chance** added up figures to obtain a balance, thereby to reckon the odds of winning

168 **make head** raise an army. Cf. *1H4* 3.1.62.

presurmise presupposition

169 **dole** distribution (*OED sb.* 5b) or dealing out; a continuation of the gambling metaphor, with a possible pun on dole as 'sorrow' as in *MND* 5.1.267: 'What dreadful dole is here?'

170 **edge** likely a metonymy for sword, as in *Cor* 5.6.112: 'Stain all your edges on me'. Humphreys finds in this passage an allusion to the perilous sword-bridges of medieval romance which also, apparently, inform a passage in *1H4*, wherein Worcester comments to Hotspur that rebellion is 'As full of peril and adventurous spirit / As to o'erwalk a current roaring loud / On the unsteadfast footing of a spear' (1.3.190–2). The association of Hotspur with risk and even foolhardiness in Morton's speech may deliberately recall imagery used by Worcester.

172 **advised** aware

172–3 **capable / Of** susceptible or open to (*OED adj.* 3b)

173 **forward** ardent, eager, zealous (*OED adj.* 6a)

174 **trade of** trafficking in – another commercial term

176 **apprehended** understood, anticipated with fear or dread (*OED* apprehend *v.* 3, 11)

177 **stiff-borne** resolutely or obstinately undertaken

178 ***hath ... brought** F's 'hath . . . bring' is clearly wrong. Keeping 'hath' requires that 'bring' be changed to 'brought', as in F2. Alternatively, the Oxford editors

166–79] *F; not in Q*   166 You] *F;* MORTON You *Cam²*   178 hath . . . brought] *F2;* hath . . . bring *F;* did . . . bring *Riv;* doth . . . bring *Oxf*

More than that being which was like to be?[F]

LORD BARDOLPH

We all that are engaged to this loss   180
Knew that we ventured on such dangerous seas
That if we wrought out life 'twas ten to one;
And yet we ventured for the gain proposed,
Choked the respect of likely peril feared,
And since we are o'erset, venture again.   185
Come, we will all put forth body and goods.

(*TxC*) speculate that F's original word was 'doth', but that 'doth' was contaminated during the printing by *hath* in 177: replacing *hath* with 'doth' allows F's 'bring' to remain unchanged. While F2 has no particular authority, the presence of parallel *hath* phrases in 177 and 178 seems more defensible than an awkward shift in verb tense from *hath* . . . *befall'n* to 'doth . . . bring'.

179 'more than the outcome (*that being*) that was anticipated anyway' (*like to be* = likely to have occurred)

180–6 Lord Bardolph extends Morton's gambling metaphor (166–74) by alluding to the voyages of Elizabethan merchant venturers, evidence that Morton's lines were probably cut from Q or its source MS rather than added later.

180 **engaged to** involved in, committed to (*OED* engage *v.* 13); engagèd
loss invokes the idea of financial indebtedness

182 **wrought out life** survived to the end (*OED* work *v.* 38f)
ten to one i.e. the long odds of coming back alive. Rebellion is figured as the perilous voyage of a merchant ship.

183–5 *Capell's punctuation, by making *gain* the subject of a subordinate clause beginning *for* and meaning 'because the proposed gain overcame our fear of likely peril' (note its neat pairing of

participles in *proposed* and *feared*), creates an effective rhetorical balance between the two verbs remaining in the main clause: 'we ventured . . . And . . . venture again'. Like most editors, I prefer Capell's alternative to the less artful punctuation on which Q and F agree; but as that original punctuation also makes sense, with *we* serving as the subject of three verbs – *ventured, Choked* and *venture* – there is no compelling reason to change it.

184 **Choked the respect** blocked or smothered the contemplation

185 **o'erset** turned bottom up (continuing the nautical imagery), defeated, overwhelmed

186 *Q's punctuation unambiguously turns *body and goods* into direct objects – 'All of us shall put forth our bodies and our goods' – and better preserves the mercantile metaphor than F does. By separating the last three words from the rest of the line with a comma, causing 'we will all put forth' to be read as a complete clause, F sets *body and goods* in ambiguous apposition either to the subject *we* (if *all* modifies the subject) or to the direct object *all*.
put forth hazard, invest (as venture capital); if F's punctuation is adopted, possibly set out, as to sea

---

182 'twas] *Q* (twas); was *F*   183 ventured . . . proposed,] *QF*; ventur'd, . . . propos'd *Capell*   186 forth body] *Q*; forth; Body, *F*

MORTON

'Tis more than time. (*to Northumberland*) And,
    my most noble lord,
I hear for certain, and dare speak the truth,
^FThe gentle Archbishop of York is up
With well-appointed powers: he is a man   190
Who with a double surety binds his followers.
My lord your son had only but the corpse,
But shadows and the shows of men, to fight;
For that same word 'rebellion' did divide
The action of their bodies from their souls,   195
And they did fight with queasiness, constrained
As men drink potions, that their weapons only
Seemed on our side; but for their spirits and souls,

189–209 *lines omitted from Q, possibly for their political content, though they may have been deemed unnecessary because they anticipate 1.3 (see pp. 448–57). Their omission leaves Morton with only two lines of an unfinished sentence and makes Northumberland's reply at 210 unfathomable. The omitted lines telescope historical time and conflate Holinshed's accounts: Morton's report of the Archbishop's being 'up / With well-appointed powers' alludes to the Prelate's Rebellion – the result of deliberations dramatized in 1.3 – which occurred in May 1405, nearly two years after the Battle of Shrewsbury was fought on 21 July 1403.

189 **gentle** well-born and genteel, of noble character
Archbishop of York Richard Scrope, who, according to Worcester in *1H4* 1.3.265–6, 'bears hard / His brother's death at Bristol, the Lord [William] Scrope' – presumably at the hands of Bolingbroke. Shakespeare follows Holinshed in making the two Scropes

brothers, although they were in fact distant cousins. See List of Roles, 9n.

190 **well-appointed powers** a well-equipped army

191 **double surety** both temporal and spiritual authority. Hotspur's authority, in contrast, was only temporal, as the following lines explain.

192 **corpse** bodies without souls. F's 'Corpes' is an obsolete spelling of the plural form of 'corps', meaning body.

196–7 **constrained . . . potions** like men forced to take medicine

197–8 **that . . . Seemed** *only* probably modifies *weapons*, and *that* implies consequence: 'so that only their weapons seemed on our side'. This reading would contrast the physical alliance of *bodies* (195) and *weapons*, constrained to fight for the rebel cause, with the *spirits and souls* at odds with rebellion. Alternatively, if *only* modifies *Seemed*, the implication would be that the men's weapons, despite appearances, were not really engaged *on our side* because their souls were not in the fight.

---

188 dare] *Q; do F*   189–209] *F; not in Q*   192 corpse] *F (Corpes); corpse's Dyce; corpses Collier³*

This word, 'rebellion', it had froze them up
As fish are in a pond. But now the Bishop   200
Turns insurrection to religion,
Supposed sincere and holy in his thoughts.
He's followed both with body and with mind,
And doth enlarge his rising with the blood
Of fair King Richard scraped from Pomfret stones;   205
Derives from heaven his quarrel and his cause;
Tells them he doth bestride a bleeding land
Gasping for life under great Bolingbroke;
And more and less do flock to follow him.^F

NORTHUMBERLAND

I knew of this before, but, to speak truth,   210
This present grief had wiped it from my mind.
Go in with me, and counsel every man
The aptest way for safety and revenge.

198–9 **but . . . up** two possible readings: (1) As for their spirits and souls, rebellion had frozen them, or (2) Had it not been for their spirits and souls, rebellion would have frozen the men; *word, rebellion* and *it* are all in apposition.

201–2 *F's punctuation requires *Supposed* to look back syntactically and modify either *insurrection* (i.e. the Archbishop considers the insurrection to be sincere and holy) or *Bishop* (200), where Rowe's punctuation requires it to look forward and modify *He* (203). While most editors follow Rowe, F makes perfectly good sense.

202 **Supposed** considered (with no suggestion of scepticism)

204 **enlarge his rising** extend the scope of his uprising (*OED* enlarge *v.* 3a); or increase his own power and status

204–5 **with . . . stones** by invoking the murder of Richard II at *Pomfret* (Pontefract) Castle; see *R2* 5.5. The

Archbishop may also use Richard's blood as a holy relic to attract more followers.

206 **Derives** traces, obtains (*OED v.* 6a). The Archbishop claims that his quarrel is sanctioned by God.

207 **bestride** stand over so as to protect or defend. Cf. *1H4*, where Falstaff asks Hal to bestride him if he falls down in battle (5.1.121–2).

208 **Bolingbroke** the surname given to Henry Plantagenet in *R2* before he becomes King Henry IV

209 **more and less** people of all ranks, referring to social standing rather than numbers

210 **I . . . before** On the conflation of time, see 189–209n.

212 **counsel every man** let each man consider

213 **safety and revenge** These would seem to be incompatible goals, as Northumberland's behaviour in 2.3 demonstrates.

201–2 religion, . . . thoughts.] *F subst.* (Religion, . . . Thoughts:); religion, . . . thoughts, *Rowe*   208 Bolingbroke] *Pope; Bullingbrooke F*

Get posts and letters, and make friends with speed;   214
Never so few, and never yet more need.   *Exeunt.*

1[.2]   *Enter* Sir John ᶠFALSTAFFᶠ *alone, with his* PAGE
                   bearing his sword and buckler.

FALSTAFF   Sirrah, you giant, what says the doctor to my
        water?

PAGE   He said, sir, the water itself was a good healthy
        water, but for the party that owed it, he might have
        more diseases than he knew for.   5

---

214 **posts** express couriers; see Ind.4n. and
37.
   make . . . speed either (1) make friends
   (i.e. gather support) quickly, or (2) a
   personification: make speed your friend
215 **Never . . . few** hyperbolic for the small
   number of rebels. This lends weight to
   the first reading of *make friends* (214) as
   gathering more support.
1.2 The scene occurs on a London street,
   most probably in Eastcheap, where
   Mistress Quickly keeps her tavern.
0.1 **alone** Q's '*alone*' may be a vestige of an
   early draft of the scene in which Falstaff
   entered without his Page, though more
   probably '*alone*' signifies 'in advance of
   an attendant' (Shaaber, *Variorium*). Cf.
   the entry of the King at Qb 3.1.0, who
   also, while 'alone', is accompanied by
   his Page. The physical contrast of the
   diminutive Page and the fat knight is
   potentially humorous, and this humour is
   often magnified in performance when the
   Page struggles to drag onto the stage a
   sword and buckler as large as he is. The
   sword and buckler borne by the Page
   attest to both Falstaff's military exploits
   at Shrewsbury, where he is given credit
   for killing Hotspur (see *1H4* 5.5.156–8),
   and his status as a knight, which is at

issue in this scene. In some productions
Falstaff, hobbled by gout (see 229–30,
243–4), enters leaning on a walking stick
in a sly parody of Northumberland's
entrance with his *nice crutch* (see
1.1.145) at 1.1.6.
0.2 **buckler** small round shield, usually
   carried by a handle at the back; sometimes
   generalized to mean a larger shield
1   **Sirrah** a form of address to inferiors,
   sometimes contemptuous but usually less
   so when spoken to children (*OED sb.* 1).
   Compare its use at 2.1.5, 2.2.157 and
   2.4.15, 378.
   giant spoken ironically. Justice Shallow
   alludes to the Page's diminutive stature
   three times, once with similar irony: 'And
   welcome, my tall fellow!' (5.1.56; see
   also 5.3.30–1, 57). The fact that in *TN*,
   too, humorous reference is made to
   Maria's size – 'Some mollification for
   your giant' (1.5.199) – suggests that a
   small boy was acting in Shakespeare's
   company.
   to about
2   **water** urine. It was common practice for
   doctors to diagnose disease by inspecting
   the urine.
4   **party . . . it** person to whom it belonged
5   **knew for** was aware of (*OED* know *v.* 17)

215 and] *Q; nor F*   **1.2**] *Scene II. / Steevens; Scena Tertia. F; not in Q*   0.1–2] *Q (Enter sir Iohn*
alone, . . . buckler.); Enter Falstaffe, and Page. F   5 more] *F, Q (*moe*)*

FALSTAFF   Men of all sorts take a pride to gird at me. The brain of this foolish compounded clay-man is not able to invent anything that intends to laughter more than I invent or is invented on me; I am not only witty in myself, but the cause that wit is in other   10 men. I do here walk before thee like a sow that hath overwhelmed all her litter but one. If the Prince put thee into my service for any other reason than to set me off, why then I have no judgement. Thou whoreson mandrake, thou art fitter to be worn in my   15 cap than to wait at my heels. I was never manned with an agate till now, but I will inset you neither in

6   **to gird** jesting or gibing (*OED v.*[2] 4), but, considering Falstaff's girth, a possible play on confining with a belt or girdle (*OED v.*[1] 1)

6–11 **The brain ... men** As in *1H4* 2.4.466–7, Falstaff universalizes himself as the wellspring of humour and humanity.

7   **foolish ... clay-man** Man, whose flesh is clay, is made of folly. Pope's emendation to put *clay* and *man* in apposition has been widely adopted, but QF's agreement on the rarely used hyphen to form a compound noun is significant and should be preserved. The Bible regularly refers to flesh as clay: e.g. Isaiah, 64.8: 'we are the clay, and thou art our potter', and Job, 13.12: 'Your memories may be compared vnto ashes, and your bodies to bodies of clay'.

8   **intends to** tends to incite. The Oxford editors argue that *intends* tangles with the three uses of *invent* on 8–9 and was replaced by the more usual Shakespearean word 'tends' in F.

12 **overwhelmed** crushed under her body

14 **set ... off** set in relief, as if a foil, here

with reference to discrepant sizes; make conspicuous by contrast (*OED* set *v.*[1] 147e[*a*])

15 **whoreson** son of a whore, used as a coarsely abusive epithet (*OED sb.* b) but often with jocular familiarity. One of Falstaff's favourite words.
    mandrake poisonous plant whose forked roots were thought to resemble a man, especially his legs and lower torso; here, probably a glance at the Page's diminutive size – thus, midget. See 3.2.314n.

15–16 **worn ... cap** another reference to the Page's size. Falstaff alludes anachronistically to the Elizabethan fashion of wearing a jewel as decoration on the hat. Cf. *Tim* 3.7.110–11: 'He gave me a jewel th'other day, and now he has beat it out of my hat'.

16 **manned** attended, but here used ironically, for Falstaff regards his Page as less than a man

17 **agate** a semi-precious stone, at times carved with tiny figures, used for seals or set in brooches worn on the hat (see 15–16n.). For an analogous use of *agate* to signify size, see Mercutio's description

7 foolish ... clay-man] *QF;* foolish-compounded-clay, Man *Pope*   8 intends] *Q;* tends *F*   12 overwhelmed] *Q (*ouerwhelmd*);* o'rewhelm'd *F*   14 judgement. Thou] *F;* iudgement thou *Q*   17 inset] *Q (*in-set*);* sette *F*

gold nor silver, but in vile apparel, and send you back
again to your master for a jewel – the juvenal, the
Prince your master, whose chin is not yet fledge.   20
I will sooner have a beard grow in the palm of my
hand than he shall get one off his cheek, and yet he
will not stick to say his face is a face royal. God
may finish it when He will, 'tis not a hair amiss yet.
He may keep it still at a face royal, for a barber shall   25
never earn sixpence out of it; and yet he'll be crowing
as if he had writ man ever since his father was a
bachelor. He may keep his own grace, but he's almost

of Queen Mab, who comes 'In shape no
bigger than an agate-stone' (*RJ* 1.4.55).

inset wordplay: either to set a jewel
(*agate*) in a bezel, or rim, of precious
metal; or to dress the Page (*inset you* = set
you in)

18 **vile** suitable for a person of low rank

18–19 **send ... jewel** Falstaff will return
the Page, meanly attired, to the Prince
as a badly worked piece of jewellery:
for means 'as'. Cf. 2.2.68–9, where the
Prince observes that Falstaff has
transformed the Page into an ape.

19 **juvenal** juvenile, youth. If pronounced
'juv'nal', it might create a homophony
sufficient to pun on *jewel*, in which
case, as Weis notes, Falstaff uses a
chiasmus: 'master ... jewel ... juvenal
... master'.

20 **fledge** covered with feathers or down; so,
figuratively, a beard (*OED v.* 4). The
present here has adjectival force, standing
in for the past participle.

21–2 **a beard ... hand** Falstaff may be
alluding to the old wives' tale that males
who masturbate grow hair on their palms,
in which case he is bragging that he
doesn't need such an outlet to achieve
sexual satisfaction.

22 **off** from. Collier's 'of' would have meant
the same as 'on' when applied to parts of
the body.

23 **stick** hesitate, scruple (*OED v.* 15)

23, 25 **a face royal** an excellent face, but
with a double pun on (1) the face of a
king or prince, and (2) the image of the
monarch's face stamped on a coin, called
a *royal*, worth ten shillings

24 **finish it** complete the face by giving it a
beard

'tis ... yet because it has no hair on it:
Falstaff's quibble is humorous because
a hairless face cannot, of course, have
a hair out of place; *not a hair* also
conventionally meant 'not a whit'.

25 **He ... still** The Prince's face will retain
its full value – of a royal, or ten shillings
– because he will have no need to pay a
barber sixpence for a shave.

26–8 **and ... bachelor** Falstaff may be
insinuating, outrageously, that the Prince
is a bastard.

27 **writ man** attained manhood (*OED* write
v. 11b)

28 **grace** a pun on (1) his royal title, and
(2) favour, with a possible glance at
the Puritans' assumption of grace which
Falstaff implicitly mocks in his comments

18 vile] *Q;* vilde *F*   19 jewel – the juvenal] iewel, the iuuenall *Q;* Iewell. The *Iuuenall F*   20 fledge] *Q;*
fledg'd *F*   22 off] *Q;* on *F;* of *Sisson (Collier)*   and] *Q; not in F*   23 God] *Q;* Heauen *F*   24 'tis] *Q;* it
is *F*   26 he'll] *Q (*heele*);* he will *F*   28 he's] *Q (*hees*);* he is *F*

out of mine, I can assure him. – What said Master
Dommelton about the satin for my short cloak and   30
my slops?

PAGE   He said, sir, you should procure him better
assurance than Bardolph. He would not take his bond
and yours; he liked not the security.

FALSTAFF   Let him be damned like the glutton! Pray   35
God his tongue be hotter! A whoreson Achitophel, a

on London tradesmen, many of whom
were Puritans, at 35–42. Cf. 39n. on
smoothy-pates.

29–31 **What ... slops** Falstaff, in musing
about the Prince, seems to have been half
talking to himself; now, he fully addresses
the Page.

29–30 **Master Dommelton** The tailor's
name is derived from 'dommel' (or its
variant 'dumble', as in F's '*Dombledon*'),
a slang term for a blockhead.

30–1 **satin ... slops** evidence that Falstaff
wishes to cut a proud figure in the world
in the wake of winning honours at
Shrewsbury. The clothing he has ordered
is both fashionable and beyond his
means: a *short cloak* was probably the
waist-length, full-sleeved garment known
as a Dutch cloak; *slops* were baggy knee-
breeches; and the *satin* of which they are
to be made was extraordinarily expensive.
In *Annales*, Stow remarks that Henry IV's
reign took 'exceeding pride in garments,
gowns with deepe and broade sleeves'
(519); but as Humphreys notes, the
sartorial extravagance of which Falstaff is
guilty was common in Elizabeth's reign
as well. Her Privy Council periodically
inveighed against 'excesse in apparell'
because it led to 'the confusion of degrees
of all estates ... and finally to the
impoverishing of the Realme' (Dyson,
entries for 13 February 1597 and 6 July
1597).

32 **procure** acquire or obtain, here with the
force of offer (*OED v.* 1)

32–3 **better ... Bardolph** i.e. collateral; a
pledge of payment more reliable than
Bardolph's

33 **bond** promissory note; a legal agreement
to pay at some future date

34 **security** something deposited as a
guarantee of future payment, to be
forfeited in case of default. Master
Dommelton clearly is no dumb-bell.

35–6 **Let ... hotter!** Falstaff alludes to the
parable of Dives, the rich man who for
the sin of gluttony is damned to hell,
where he cries, 'sende Lazarus that he
may dippe the tippe of his fynger in
water, and coole my tongue; for I am
tormented in this flambe' (Luke, 16.24).
Falstaff invokes this parable to comment
on Bardolph's fiery nose in *1H4* (3.3.31–
5: see 48n. below) and again to condemn
his recruits as 'slaves as ragged as
Lazarus in the painted cloth where the
glutton's dogs licked his sores' (4.2.24–
6). His readiness to attribute gluttony to
others may be an unconscious projection
of his own propensity to excess: in
damning Bardolph, he ironically damns
himself.

36 **whoreson** See 15n.

Achitophel the Old Testament counsellor
who deserted King David for Absolom
(2 Samuel, 15–16). Falstaff implicitly
accuses the tailor of treachery.

30 Dommelton] *Q; Dombledon F*   31 my] *Q; not in F*   33 bond] *F (*Bond*); band Q*   35–6 Pray God] *Q;*
may *F*

rascal – yea forsooth knave – to bear a gentleman
in hand and then stand upon 'security'. The whoreson
smoothy-pates do now wear nothing but high shoes
and bunches of keys at their girdles; and if a man is   40
through with them in honest taking up, then they
must stand upon security. I had as lief they would put
ratsbane in my mouth as offer to stop it with security.
I looked 'a should have sent me two and twenty

---

37 ***rascal ... knave** – Q's punctuation is
ambiguous: the colon after 'rascall' may
suggest that the next phrase is a direct
address to the Page (the 'knaue'), in
which case Falstaff's use of the mild oath
yea forsooth may be a vestige of his
original incarnation as the proto-Puritan
Oldcastle (see pp. 64–70); yet the colon
also may be meant to set off *yea forsooth*
as mimicry of the tradesman's obsequious
manner of speaking, and to place 'knaue'
in apposition to 'rascall': that is the
option selected here. In F, 'Rascally-yea-
forsooth' becomes an adjectival phrase
modifying 'knaue', here unambiguously
referring to the tailor, whose use of
such oaths Falstaff mocks as a sign of
his fawning respectability. GWW's
conjecture that the article 'a' should
precede *knave* would allow *knave* to
stand in apposition to both *rascal* and
Achitophel.
   forsooth in truth
37––8 **bear ... hand** keep a man in
expectation; assure him or lead him on
(*OED* bear *v.* 3e). Falstaff insists on his
status as a gentleman – a man of gentle
birth, entitled to bear arms and so to
be extended credit without putting up
collateral – in contrast to a bourgeois
shopkeeper.
38 **stand upon** insist upon, demand (*OED*
stand *v.* 78m)

39 **smoothy-pates** Puritan tradesmen who,
in contempt of fashion, cropped their hair
short and later came to be known as
Roundheads. Falstaff's attack on Puritan
hypocrisy allows Shakespeare to satirize
the smug, increasingly vocal London
merchants who were opposed to the
theatre. See also 28n.
   high shoes High cork-soled shoes were
a sign of pride and would reveal the
tradesmen's social aspirations – especially ironic if the tradesmen are identified
as Puritans (see Linthicum, 252–3).
40 **bunches of keys** i.e. as tokens of weighty
business affairs; another wry glance at
the self-importance of the emergent
tradesmen class
   girdles belts worn around the waist to
secure garments, and to which articles
could be fastened
40–1 **is ... up** has come to an agreement
(*OED* through *adv.* 3b) with them to
make an honest puchase on credit (*OED*
take *v.* 93d)
42 **had as lief** would be just as glad if. Q's
'liue' is a variant spelling of F's 'lieve' or
'liefe' (*lief*).
43 **ratsbane** rat poison
   offer to stop presume to fill
44 **looked** expected
   'a the colloquial form of 'he', regularly
used by Falstaff
44–5 **two ... yards** an extravagant amount
of satin; see 30–1n.

---

37 rascal . . . knave –] *Q (*rascall: yea forsooth knaue,*);* Rascally-yea-forsooth-knaue, *F*   knave] a knave
(conj. GWW)   39 smoothy-pates] *Q;* smooth-pates *F*   42 lief] *F (*liefe*), Q (*liue*)*   44 'a] *Q;* hee *F*

yards of satin, as I am a true knight, and he sends   45
me 'security'! Well he may sleep in security, for he
hath the horn of abundance, and the lightness of his
wife shines through it – where's Bardolph? – and yet

45 **a true knight** Falstaff's staking his word
on his knighthood is defensive, for he is
often demeaned by the social inferiors
with whom he keeps company – and here,
by a lowly tailor. He represents a class
of knight, common in Elizabeth's reign,
who had a title but no land or money; yet
by claiming *true* knighthood, he protests
his credit-worthiness. His claim to gentility at 37–8 is similar. On the status of
knighthood in Elizabethan England, see
Stone, 71–81; on the failure of knights,
as gentlemen soldiers, to prosper under
Elizabeth, see A. Ferguson, 101–5; and
on the economic anxiety of war veterans
for whom pensions were not assured, see
Jorgensen, *World*, 210–13.

46 **Well he** Q's punctuation preserves the
irony of a husband's sleeping soundly
(*Well*) in ignorance of his wife's infidelity;
F's does not.
²**security** here used in a triple sense, each
one different from its meaning earlier in
the scene (cf. 34n., 42, 43): (1) freedom
from care, (2) financial well-being, and
(3) certainty of his wife's fidelity. Falstaff
may once again be using an ecclesiastical
idiom, for, as Humphreys notes, Archbishop Sandys in his eleventh sermon harps
on '[t]he sleep of error, or sin, and of
security' as tantamount to spiritual
lethargy (*Sermons*, 208, 210–12).

47 **horn of abundance** plays on various
meanings. As a cornucopia, it signifies
the tailor's financial prosperity. Horns
also provided the translucent material
used to make lanterns, or, in Shakespeare's
preferred spelling, 'lanthorns' (49). Most
suggestively, the horn was metonymic for
a cuckold, a derisive epithet for a husband

whose wife had committed adultery. The
man who has a *horn of abundance* is
therefore one who bears the shame of
having a promiscuous wife. Falstaff,
however, intimates that the tailor's
prosperity may be due to his willingness
to turn a blind eye to his wife's infidelities.
The cuckolding of fastidious tradesmen
by their sexually unsatisfied wives was a
common jest in city comedy.

47–50 **the lightness . . . him** The light which
shines through the lantern also betokens
the wantonness (*OED* lightness *sb*. 7b) of
a wife which metaphorically illuminates
her husband's *horn*; yet despite having
such a light on his own head, he remains
blind to his situation. QF's spelling of
lantern as *lanthorn* preserves the play on
horn and continues the passage's ridicule
of the tailor as a cuckold: pronouncing
the word as written would have made the
point clear.

48 **where's Bardolph?** F moves this question to the end of Falstaff's speech, but,
as Melchiori argues, Q's placement of it
is more subtle: it suggests an interruption
spurred by Falstaff's unconscious association of Bardolph with the imagery of
lighted lanterns, hell-fire and the parable
of Dives he has been using to characterize
the tailor. Cf. his speech to Bardolph
in *1H4*: '[T]hou art the Knight of the
Burning Lamp. . . . I never see thy face
but I think upon hell-fire and Dives that
lived in purple: for there he is in his robes,
burning, burning. . . . Thou hast saved me
a thousand marks in links and torches
walking with thee in the night betwixt
tavern and tavern' (3.3.25–43).

45 a] *Q; not in F*   46 Well he] *Q;* Well, he *F*   48 it . . . and] *Q (*it: wheres Bardolf, &*);* it, and *F*

cannot he see, though he have his own lanthorn to
light him.   50

PAGE   He's gone in Smithfield to buy your worship a
horse.

FALSTAFF   I bought him in Paul's, and he'll buy me a
horse in Smithfield. An I could get me but a wife in
the stews, I were manned, horsed and wived.   55

Enter Lord Chief JUSTICE ᶠ*and* Servantᶠ.

PAGE   Sir, here comes the nobleman that committed the
Prince for striking him about Bardolph.

FALSTAFF   Wait close, I will not see him.

JUSTICE   What's he that goes there?

SERVANT   Falstaff, an't please your lordship.   60

---

51 **in** to
  Smithfield from early times to 1855,
  the market for horses, cattle and sheep
  occupying a level or smooth (*smethe*)
  field of five to six acres north of Newgate
  and west of Aldgate. Smithfield horses
  were frequently the butt of jokes: cf.
  53–5n.

53–5 Falstaff echoes a proverb first recorded
  in Simon Robson's *Choise of Change*
  (1585): 'A man must not make choice of
  three things in three places: of a wife in
  Westminster, of a servant in Paul's, of
  a horse in Smithfield, least he choose
  a quean, a knave or a jade.' See Dent,
  W276.

53 **Paul's** The nave of St Paul's Cathedral
  had become a kind of employment office
  where servants without masters would
  advertise their services.

54 **An** if

55 **stews** brothels. For an explanation of the
  term, see 2.4.146–7n.

55.1 **and* Servant** Q's omission is clearly
  an oversight, since the Servant has a

speaking role. The Lord Chief Justice
is traditionally followed by a tipstaff
(a court officer or bailiff) whenever he
appears in public.

56–7 Elyot's *Gouernour* (2.6) and Stow's
  Annales (547–8) record that Prince
  Henry threatened but did not in fact strike
  the Lord Chief Justice. The legendary
  incident, a later accretion, was dramatized
  in *Famous Victories*, 4.69 – '*He giveth
  him a box on the ear*' – and Shakespeare's
  audience undoubtedly was familiar with
  it. Only here, however, is Bardolph named
  as the cause of the altercation; sources
  identify him merely as a servant to the
  Prince. See 5.2.67–82, and pp. 129–30.

56 **committed** imprisoned

58 **Wait close** 'Let's wait nearby.' That
  Falstaff is referring to himself rather than
  commanding his Page is evident from 'I
  will not [do not wish to] see him'.

59 **What's** who's

60 **an't** if it, conventionally followed by
  'please you' as a deferential phrase
  spoken to those of higher rank

---

49 lanthorn] *QF* (lanthorne)   50 him.] *Q*; him. Where's *Bardolfe? F*   51 in] *Q*; into *F*   54 An] *Q* (and);
If *F*   but] *Q*; *not in F*   55.1 Lord] *Q*; *not in F   and* Servant] *F*; *not in Q*

JUSTICE   He that was in question for the robbery?

SERVANT   He, my lord; but he hath since done good service at Shrewsbury and, as I hear, is now going with some charge to the Lord John of Lancaster.

JUSTICE   What, to York? Call him back again.   65

SERVANT   Sir John Falstaff!

FALSTAFF   Boy, tell him I am deaf.

PAGE   You must speak louder; my master is deaf.

JUSTICE   I am sure he is, to the hearing of anything good. [*to Servant*] Go pluck him by the elbow; I must speak   70 with him.

SERVANT   Sir John?

FALSTAFF   What, a young knave and begging? Is there not wars? Is there not employment? Doth not the King lack subjects? Do not the rebels need soldiers?   75 Though it be a shame to be on any side but one, it is worse shame to beg than to be on the worst side, were it worse than the name of rebellion can tell how to make it.

SERVANT   You mistake me, sir.   80

---

61 **in . . . robbery** under judicial inquiry for the robbery at Gad's Hill. Cf. *1H4* 2.4.492–510.

62–3 **good . . . Shrewsbury** a reference to his (unearned) reputation for having killed Hotspur; see 0.1n.

64 **charge** troops under his command. Cf. *1H4* 3.3.185: 'a charge of foot'.

65 **to York** information fleshed out at 200–2 and consistent with *1H4*, where the King dispatches Prince John and Westmorland 'Towards York . . . /To meet Northumberland and the prelate Scrope' (5.5.36–7).

70 **pluck** grab; not a decorous way of getting one's attention

73–4 **What . . . wars?** As a ruse to ignore the Lord Chief Justice, Falstaff pretends to mistake the servant for a young beggar who, because the country is at war, could easily find gainful employment as a soldier. Beholding such sloth, he feigns moral indignation. On the use of the singular verb *Is* with the plural noun *wars*, see 1.1.33n.

75 **lack subjects** i.e. owing to the number of rebels

76 **any . . . one** that is, the King's

78–9 **were . . . it** 'even if that side were worse than rebellion itself could devise'

80 **mistake me** are wrong about what I am: i.e. I am not a beggar.

---

61 robbery] *F, Q (*rob'ry*)   69 anything] *QF (*any thing*)   70 SD] *Oxf¹ subst.*   72 John?] *Q; Iohn. F*
73 begging] *Q; beg F*   75 need] *Q; want F*   soldiers?] *F; souldiers, Q*

FALSTAFF   Why, sir, did I say you were an honest man?
Setting my knighthood and my soldiership aside,
I had lied in my throat if I had said so.

SERVANT   I pray you, sir, then set your knighthood and
your soldiership aside and give me leave to tell you,   85
you lie in your throat if you say I am any other than
an honest man.

FALSTAFF   I give thee leave to tell me so? I lay aside that
which grows to me? If thou get'st any leave of me,
hang me; if thou tak'st leave, thou wert better be   90
hanged. You hunt counter. Hence! Avaunt!

SERVANT   Sir, my lord would speak with you.

JUSTICE   Sir John Falstaff, a word with you.

FALSTAFF   My good lord, God give your lordship good
time of day. I am glad to see your lordship abroad.   95

81   Falstaff deliberately misinterprets *mistake me* by claiming that he has not misjudged the servant's character.
82   **Setting … aside** i.e. because it is inconceivable that knights and soldiers would ever lie – a typically Falstaffian hyperbole. Cf. *1H4* 3.3.119–20: 'setting thy knighthood aside, thou art a knave to call me so'.
83   **had … throat** would have lied egregiously. To lie in one's throat was a familiar tag of which Tilley (T268) records numerous instances dating from 1590, and Wilson, *Dictionary*, from 1576 (460a).
85   **give me leave** allow me (*leave* = permission, liberty)
88–9 *I give … me?** Q's punctuation is problematic. It makes sense only if the two clauses can be seen to imply a subjunctive followed by a condition: 'If I were to give . . . , so I would lay aside . . . .'; and GWW speculates that an initial 'If' may indeed have been omitted in the copy-text for Q. F attempts to clarify the

relationship between the two clauses by turning them both into questions in which Falstaff responds with mock outrage to each of the things the Servant asks him to do: set aside his knighthood, and give him *leave* to call Falstaff a liar.
89   **grows to** belongs to, is an integral part of (that is, his dignity as a knight and soldier)
90   ²**thou … be** it would be better for you to be
91   **You hunt counter** in effect, 'You're barking up the wrong tree'. Dogs were said to hunt counter if they followed the scent in a direction opposite that in which the game had gone: in *CE*, for example, Antipholus of Ephesus is jailed by 'A hound that runs counter' (4.2.39). F's hyphenation, however, makes 'Hunt-counter' unambiguously an epithet meaning a catchpole, a petty officer in charge of arresting debtors. Equally derogatory, both alternatives – the verb phrase and the epithet – work in this context.
Avaunt! 'Begone! Away!'
95   **abroad** out of doors

81 sir, did] *Q;* sir? Did *F*   man?] *F;* man, *Q*   88 me so?] *F;* me, so *Q*   89 me? If] *F;* me, if *Q*   91 hunt counter] *Q;* Hunt-counter *F*   94 God] *Q; not in F*   95 of] *Q;* of the *F*

I heard say your lordship was sick: I hope your
lordship goes abroad by advice. Your lordship, though
not clean past your youth, have yet some smack of
an ague in you, some relish of the saltness of time
in you, and I most humbly beseech your lordship to   100
have a reverend care of your health.

JUSTICE   Sir John, I sent for you before your expedition
to Shrewsbury.

FALSTAFF   An't please your lordship, I hear his majesty
is returned with some discomfort from Wales.   105

JUSTICE   I talk not of his majesty. You would not come
when I sent for you.

FALSTAFF   And I hear moreover his highness is fallen
into this same whoreson apoplexy.

---

97 **by advice** with the permission of a doctor

98 **clean** entirely

98–9 **smack . . . ague** lingering signs of
sickness; that is, he does not look well.
Falstaff's impudent strategy in these lines
is to deflect the Justice's interrogation by
projecting his own infirmities onto him.
F's 'smack of age', however, stands in
more precise apposition to *the saltness of
time* (99) in contrast to *youth* (98).

99 **relish** trace. Both *smack* and *relish*
invoke taste.
saltness of unknown origin, but probably
referring to the tang of meat preserved in
brine; *saltness of time* would thus be an
unflattering metaphor for old age.

102–3 The Lord Chief Justice had summoned
Falstaff to appear before the King's Bench
on charges of robbery *before* Falstaff was
given a military command: see 61n.

104–5 **his majesty . . . Wales** probably a
conflation of (1) a march into Wales
against the forces of Glendower and the
Earl of March announced by the King
after the Battle of Shrewsbury in 1403
(see *1H4* 5.5.39–40) – a march which

never took place owing to lack of funds
(Holinshed, 3.524), and (2) the luckless
Welsh expedition made two years later,
as a follow-up to Gaultree, during which
the King lost fifty of his cannon in bad
weather (Holinshed, 3.530). Falstaff
once again attempts to divert the Justice's
interrogation, this time by discussing yet
another sick old man, the King; and he
succeeds in doing so until 132.

109 **whoreson apoplexy** King Henry's illness,
a paralysis whose symptoms and causes
Falstaff aptly catalogues at 112–18, was
chronicled by Otterbourne in 1408. Some
writers identified the disease as leprosy,
inflicted on Henry as divine punishment
for his murder of Richard II or execution
of Archbishop Scrope, but Hall dismisses
this as falsehood, as does Holinshed,
who argues that the King suffered 'a
sore sickness, which was not a leprosy
stricken by the hand of God . . . as
foolish friars imagined, but a very
apoplexy, of the which he languished
till his appointed hour' (3.541). For
whoreson, see 15n.

---

98 have] *Q;* hath *F*   99 an ague] *Q;* age *F*   100 in you] *Q; not in F*   102 for] *Q; not in F*   102–3 expedi-
tion] *Q;* Expedition, *F*   104 An't] *Q (Andt);* If it *F*   107 you.] *Q;* you? *F*

JUSTICE Well, God mend him. I pray you let me speak   110
with you.

FALSTAFF This apoplexy, as I take it, is a kind of lethargy,
an't please your lordship, a kind of sleeping in the
blood, a whoreson tingling.

JUSTICE What tell you me of it? Be it as it is.   115

FALSTAFF It hath it original from much grief, from study,
and perturbation of the brain. I have read the cause of
his effects in Galen: it is a kind of deafness.

JUSTICE I think you are fallen into the disease, for you
hear not what I say to you.   120

ᶠFALSTAFFᶠ Very well, my lord, very well; rather, an't
please you, it is the disease of not listening, the
malady of not marking, that I am troubled withal.

JUSTICE To punish you by the heels would amend the
attention of your ears, and I care not if I do become   125
your physician.

FALSTAFF I am as poor as Job, my lord, but not so

113–14 **sleeping ... blood** deprivation of
sense or motion
115 **What** why
116 **it original** its origin. Shakespeare never
used the possessive pronoun 'its'; 'it' as a
possessive was common. But 'his' was
the usual possessive, as at 118.
study worry, stress (*OED sb.* 3a)
117 **perturbation** disturbance. In Elizabethan
treatises on physiology, 'perturbation'
usually applies to the soul rather than the
body. Cf. 4.3.154, and *R3* 5.3.160–2, *MA*
2.1.238–9 and *Mac* 5.1.9–10.
118 **his** its
Galen Claudius Galen, Greek physician
(AD 129–99), regarded as the foremost
authority on medicine as late as the 16th
century

121 SP The survival of '*Old.*' in Q suggests
that Shakespeare may have begun writing *2H4* before Oldcastle's name was
changed to Falstaff or, alternatively, that
he simply forgot. See p. 40.
123 **marking** paying attention
124 **punish ... heels** put you in irons or in
the stocks (*OED* heel *sb.*[1] 18)
126 **physician** with an implication that a
judge, like a doctor, administers corrective medicine. Falstaff plays on the
analogy at 128–32.
127–8 **as poor ... patient** a conflation of
two proverbs drawn from Job, 1–2: 'As
poor as Job' and 'As patient as Job'
(Dent, J60, 59). Falstaff puns on *patient*
as someone under a physician's care.

110 God] *Q;* heauen *F* you] *Q; not in F* 112 as ... is] *Q (*as I take it? is*);* is (as I take it) *F* 113 an't
... lordship] *Q; not in F* in] *Q;* of *F* 115 it? Be] *F;* it, be *Q* 116 it] *QF1–2;* its *F3–4* 121 SP] *F
(Fal.); Old. Q* 125 do become] *Q;* be *F*

patient. Your lordship may minister the potion of
imprisonment to me in respect of poverty; but how
I should be your patient to follow your prescriptions,   130
the wise may make some dram of a scruple or indeed
a scruple itself.

JUSTICE   I sent for you, when there were matters against
you for your life, to come speak with me.

FALSTAFF   As I was then advised by my learned counsel   135
in the laws of this land-service, I did not come.

JUSTICE   Well, the truth is, Sir John, you live in great
infamy.

FALSTAFF   He that buckles himself in my belt cannot
live in less.   140

JUSTICE   Your means are very slender, and your waste
is great.

---

128 **minister the potion** administer the
medicine
129 **in . . . poverty** i.e. because I have no
money to pay any fine. Falstaff may be
implying that the practice of imprisoning
debtors is unfair.
   how in what way or manner, why (*OED
adv.* 1a, 1c)
131 **make . . . scruple** The *OED* cites this as
the first instance of 'scruple' being used
to mean 'hesitate to believe' (*sb.*² 2b), but
the sense of hesitation with regard to
right and wrong – 'scruple' indicating
moral compunction (*sb.*² 1) – also obtains.
In the first reading, Falstaff would imply
that the Justice's *prescriptions* have no
power to reform him, because Falstaff's
nature is unregenerate. In the second, he
would aver that *the wise* doubt whether
the Justice should administer corrective
measures to him, because such punishment is undeserved. In these two readings,
the force of *how* (129) would change
accordingly, from the degree to which

Falstaff *could* be reformed to why or
whether he *should* be so. With *dram* and
scruple he continues the play on medical
terminology: a dram in apothecaries'
weight was 60 grains, or one-eighth of
an ounce, and a scruple was one-third
of a dram. Cf. Malvolio in *TN*: 'no dram
of a scruple, no scruple of a scruple'
(3.4.76).
133–4 **matters . . . life** charges brought
against you (for the robbery at Gad's
Hill) which might, if proved, lead to the
death penalty
135–6 **learned . . . land-service** Falstaff may
point to his sword and buckler as the
learned counsel who advised him on
the laws of war, according to which a
military command, or *land-service* to the
King, took precedence over the Justice's
summons.
139–40 Falstaff quibbles on the Justice's
phrase *live in . . . infamy* as if it referred
to wearing garments, in which case *great*
at 137 would refer to clothing size.

---

136 land-service] *F*; land seruice *Q*   139 himself] *Q*; him *F*   141 are] *Q*; is *F*   waste] *Q*; wast *F*   142 is]
Q; not in F

FALSTAFF   I would it were otherwise; I would my means
were greater and my waist slender.

JUSTICE   You have misled the youthful Prince.   145

FALSTAFF   The young Prince hath misled me. I am the
fellow with the great belly, and he my dog.

JUSTICE   Well, I am loath to gall a new-healed wound.
Your day's service at Shrewsbury hath a little gilded
over your night's exploit on Gad's Hill. You may   150
thank th'unquiet time for your quiet o'erposting that
action.

FALSTAFF   My lord –

JUSTICE   But since all is well, keep it so: wake not a
sleeping wolf.   155

---

144 **greater** Following Betterton, Berger
and Williams (*Notes*, 3.240 ff.) argue
that 'great' provides a better rhetorical
balance with *slender* – and a closer echo
of the Justice's wording – than *greater*
does, that QF are therefore in error, and
that the error originated when the Q
compositor changed the term 'great' in
MS copy to accord with what he assumed
to be the comparative form *slender* (=
slenderer) in the same line.
*waist slender As the pun on *waist* is
homophonic, the QF spelling offers no
contradiction. Falstaff attempts to reverse
the Justice's appraisal of his character
with clever wordplay. Although F's use
of the comparative form 'slenderer'
balances *greater* more exactly than Q's
slender does, it is also consistent with the
scribe's attempt throughout the copy-text
for F to regularize grammar and to clear
up minor inconsistencies. Q's *slender*
makes perfectly good sense.

146–7 **I am ... dog** an obscure joke, now
lost, possibly referring to the man in the
moon (*the great belly* = the full moon)
who was said to be led (here, *misled*) by
a dog. Cf. *MND* 5.1.134–5. The joke is
extended at 2.2.104–5.

148 **gall** make sore by rubbing or chafing

149–50 **gilded over** to cover with liquid
gold or gold paint ('gilt'), and so,
figuratively, to conceal defects (*OED*
gild *v.*[1] 7); perhaps an intentional recollection of Hal's concession to Falstaff
in *1H4*: 'if a lie may do thee grace / I'll
gild it with the happiest terms I have'
(5.4.157–8).

151–2 **your ... action** the tacit overlooking
of your offence, with *quiet* balancing
unquiet. To 'overpost', a term drawn
from riding post (see Ind.4n.), meant to
move over the ground quickly (*OED v.*
1), or here, metaphorically, to dismiss
a matter without fuss. Cf. *2H6*: 'His
guilt should be but idly posted over /
Because his purpose is not executed'
(3.1.255–6).

154–5 **wake ... wolf** a variation on the
adage 'It is evil waking of a sleeping dog'
(Dent, W7); or, in modern parlance, 'Let
sleeping dogs lie.'

144 greater] *QF*; great *Betterton   waist*] *Hanmer²*; waste *QF   slender*] *Q*; slenderer *F*   150 Gad's Hill]
Gadshill *Q*; Gads-hill *F   151* th'unquiet] *Q*; the unquiet *F   153* lord –] *Q*; Lord? *F*

FALSTAFF   To wake a wolf is as bad as smell a fox.

JUSTICE   What? You are as a candle, the better part
burnt out.

FALSTAFF   A wassail candle, my lord, all tallow: if I did
say of wax, my growth would approve the truth.   160

JUSTICE   There is not a white hair in your face but should
have his effect of gravity.

FALSTAFF   His effect of gravy, gravy, gravy.

JUSTICE   You follow the young Prince up and down like
his ill angel.   165

FALSTAFF   Not so, my lord. Your ill angel is light, but
I hope he that looks upon me will take me without
weighing; and yet in some respects I grant I cannot

---

156 **smell a fox** proverbial for being suspici-
ous (Dent, F652.1), with an allusion to
the fox's legendary cunning

157–8 **You ... out** The burning candle which
consumes itself was a stock metaphor
for mortality. See Tilley, C39: 'A candle
lights others and consumes itself.'

159 **wassail candle** a candle big enough to
last through a night of revelry (*wassail*
= carousal, drinking healths). Falstaff
implies that his girth lends him a kind of
immortality.

   tallow animal fat used in making candles

160 **wax** Falstaff puns on (1) beeswax, an
alternative to tallow for making candles,
and (2) increase in size, joking about
his own corpulence. Contradicting the
Justice (157–8), Falstaff in effect claims
that his life is a candle that forever
sustains itself.

   approve the truth prove this assertion

162, 163 **his effect** the appearance: *his* = its.
Cf. 118n.

162 **gravity** possibly pronounced with a long
a, like its root word grave, thus allowing
a jingle with *gravy* (163)

163 **gravy** fatty juices from hot meat, an appropriate gastronomic image for Falstaff
following his recognition of a buried pun
on *hair* as 'hare' at 161: Falstaff humorously twists the Justice's admonition to
mean that his beard should always be
spattered with the fatty juices of a roasted
hare. 'To stew in one's own gravy' also
meant to be bathed in sweat (*OED sb.*
2b).

165 **ill angel** refers to an evil tempter like the
Vice of medieval Morality plays. Hal
uses a similar epithet for Falstaff in *1H4*:
'that reverend Vice, that grey Iniquity'
(2.4.441).

166 **Your ... light** a pun on Lucifer as 'an
angel of lyght' (2 Corinthians, 11.14),
and a coin that has been clipped and is
therefore not its full weight or value
(*light*). Tradesmen weighed coins to
make sure they were not counterfeit or
pared down. An *angel* was a gold coin so
called for the impression on it of the
archangel Michael slaying the dragon
(*OED* angel *sb.* 6).

---

156 smell] *Q;* to smell *F*   157 What? You] *F;* What you *Q*   161 in] *Q;* on *F*   165 ill] *Q;* euill *F*
167 without] *Q;* without, *F*

go. I cannot tell. Virtue is of so little regard in
these coster-mongers' times that true valour is turned   170
ᶠbearherdᶠ, pregnancy is made a tapster, and his
quick wit wasted in giving reckonings. All the other
gifts appertinent to man, as the malice of his age
shapes ᶠthem, areᶠ not worth a gooseberry. You that
are old consider not the capacities of us that are   175
young. You do measure the heat of our livers with the
bitterness of your galls; and we that are in the vaward
of our youth, I must confess, are wags too.

169 **go** pass as genuine currency (*OED v.*
12a); walk or move easily (a possible
allusion to the gout mentioned at 243–4)
cannot tell do not know what to think
or say
regard account, importance
170 **coster-mongers'** i.e. crassly commercial.
A *coster-monger* was an apple-seller
(costard = apple) or fruiterer who, as
opposed to a shopkeeper, sold produce in
the open street; thus, a petty tradesman.
171 **bearherd** keeper of performing bears.
This debasement of *true valour* (170)
would have had satirical point if it
alluded to Edward Alleyn, the actor of
heroic parts in Marlowe's tragedies, who
in 1594 acquired an interest in the bear-
baiting house at Paris Garden and,
according to Stow, on various occasions
took part in the baiting himself (Shaaber,
Variorum). Q's 'Berod' is possibly a
compositorial misreading but more likely
an aberrant spelling of 'bearherd'.
pregnancy ... tapster Fertility of intellect (*pregnancy*) has as little value as one
who taps beer for customers at a tavern.
his its
172 **wit** understanding, intellect
giving reckonings adding up how much
is owed; dispensing bills

173 **gifts appertinent to** qualities belonging
to
173–4 **as ... them** as the wickedness of the
present time fashions or corrupts them;
his age = the times in which a man lives
174 ***them, are** The Q compositor probably
misread MS 'are' as 'one', an easy
mistake occasioned by his failure to see
the tilde over the *e* of *them* (GWW).
not ... gooseberry Cf. *TC* 5.4.11: 'not
proved worth a blackberry'.
176–7 **You ... galls** From ancient times, the
liver was thought to be the source of love
and passion (cf. 4.2.102–3 and 5.5.31),
and gall (bile) the seat of anger. Falstaff
thus claims a physiological basis for old
age's misunderstanding of youth, and
in doing so he facetiously echoes Lyly's
Euphues: The Anatomy of Wit (1579),
wherein the dissolute young Euphues
remonstrates with the older Eubulus: 'Do
you measure the hot assaults of youth by
the cold skirmishes of age, whose years
are subject to more infirmities than our
youth? We merry, you melancholy; you
careful, we careless; we bold, you fearful;
we in all points contrary unto you, and ye
in all points unlike unto us' (40).
177 **vaward** vanguard, forefront
178 **wags** mischievous fellows

170 coster-mongers'] *Q (*costar-mongers*)*, *F (*Costor-mongers*)* times] *Q;* dayes *F3–4; not in F1–2*
171 bearherd] *F (*Beare-heard*)*; Berod *Q* and] *Q;* and hath *F*   172 reckonings] *Q;* Recknings *F*   173 his]
Q; this *F*   174 them, are] *F;* the one *Q*   176 do] *Q; not in F*   177 vaward] *QF;* van-guard *Pope*

JUSTICE   Do you set down your name in the scroll of
youth, that are written down old with all the characters   180
of age? Have you not a moist eye, a dry hand, a
yellow cheek, a white beard, a decreasing leg, an
increasing belly? Is not your voice broken, your wind
short, your chin double, your wit single, and every
part about you blasted with antiquity? And will you   185
yet call yourself young? Fie, fie, fie, Sir John!

FALSTAFF   My lord, I was born about three of the clock
in the afternoon, with a white head and something
a round belly. For my voice, I have lost it with
hallowing and singing of anthems. To approve my   190

180–1 **that . . . age** who are inscribed with
all the physical signs of old age. The
metaphor of writing involves a play on
characters, meaning both letters of the
alphabet and characteristics. The following description of Falstaff as an old man
may be indebted to the writings of
Theophrastus, a Greek philosopher who
mercilessly sketched various types of
human failings in his popular *Characters*.
The Justice would thus reprove Falstaff
with the force of classical authority.

180 **written down old** It is possible to hear
in this line an implicit reference to the
enforced name change of Oldcastle to
Falstaff. See pp. 139–40.

181–4 **moist . . . single** Cf. Hamlet's satirical
characterization of old men to Polonius:
'their eyes purging thick amber and
plumtree gum . . . they have a plentiful
lack of wit together with most weak
hams' (*Ham* 2.2.195–7).

181 **moist** watery, rheumy
   dry hand antithetical to the moist hand,
which was a sign of youth and health. Cf.
Oth 3.4.36–7.

182 **decreasing** shrivelling, perhaps in relation to his *increasing* belly

183–4 **wind short** breathing laboured (i.e.
he is short of breath)

184 **wit single** understanding slow; perhaps
owing to senility (*single* = slight, poor:
OED adj. 12b)

185 **blasted** withered, shrivelled, blighted
(*OED* blast *v.* 7)

187–8 **about . . . afternoon** i.e. when the
day was well advanced. As plays were
performed in the afternoon, Falstaff may
be humorously acknowledging that he
was *born* as a fully fleshed character
(R.G. White).

190 **hallowing** onomatopoeia for the shouting
Falstaff has done either while hunting,
as he urged on dogs to the chase, or in
battle. If one pairs it with *singing of
anthems*, *hallowing* may take on more
spiritual overtones, since 'hallow' literally
means 'to honour as holy' (*OED v.*[1] 3).
   singing of anthems An anthem was a
musical setting of a prose passage usually
taken from Scripture or the Liturgy.
Falstaff's anthem-singing may simply be
an irreverent joke; but it also may be a
survival of the original Falstaff, Sir John
Oldcastle, whose death as a Lollard in
1417 accorded him, nearly two centuries

184 your chin double] *Q; not in F*   186 yet] *Q; not in F*   187–8 about . . . afternoon] *Q; not in F*
190 hallowing] *QF1–2;* hollowing *F3–4;* hallooing *Dyce*[2]

youth further, I will not. The truth is, I am only old in judgement and understanding; and he that will caper with me for a thousand marks, let him lend me the money, and have at him! For the box of the ᶠearᶠ that the Prince gave you, he gave it like a rude prince, and 195 you took it like a sensible lord: I have checked him for it, and the young lion repents – marry, not in ashes and sackcloth, but in new silk and old sack.

later, the status of a Puritan martyr. It may contain, too, an implicit reference to Ephesians, 5.18–19, in which St Paul urges his followers to make 'melodie to the Lord in your hearts' by '[s]peaking vnto your selues in psalms, and hymnes, and spiritual songs'. Cf. the reference to Puritans' singing of psalms in *1H4*: 'I would I were a weaver; I could sing psalms or anything' (2.4.126–7). Many English weavers were Calvinist refugees from the Netherlands.

approve See 160n.

191–2 **old . . . understanding** a biblical aphorism. Cf. Job, 12.12: 'Among olde persons there is wysedome, and in age is vnderstanding', and 1 Corinthians, 14.20: 'but in vnderstanding bee of a ripe age'.

192–3 **caper with me** compete with me in cutting capers (leaping with a scissor-kick motion) or, more generally, in frolicsome dancing. Falstaff offers this as absurd proof of his youthful vigour.

193 **for . . . marks** As a mark was valued at thirteen shillings and four pence, this represented a vast sum; but with characteristic bravado, Falstaff wants the person who challenges him to caper also to lend him money for the bet. This anticipates his asking the Justice for an ever bigger loan of a thousand pounds at 222–3.

194 **have at him** an expression of defiance, announcing the speaker's intention to

attack an adversary (*OED* have *v.* 20); here, 'I'll take him on.'

box of the ear See 56–7n. Q's 'yeere' for *ear* suggests compositorial error.

195 **rude** discourteous, uncivil (*OED adj.* 4)

196 **sensible** a quibble on (1) reasonable, and (2) capable of feeling physical sensation (alluding to the pain inflicted by the Prince)

checked reprimanded

197 **lion** The iconic image of the King (or, in Harry's case, future king) as a lion was traditional. Cf. *1H4* 3.3.145–8.

marry Originally 'by the Virgin Mary', this had become a mild oath meaning 'to be sure'.

198 **ashes and sackcloth** Having ashes sprinkled on one's head and dressing in sackcloth, the coarsest of fabrics, were traditional signs of abject penitence (*OED* sackcloth *sb.* 1b; ash *sb.*² 7). Falstaff echoes Luke, 10.13, and Matthew, 11.21: 'They had repented long agone in sackcloth and ashes'.

new . . . sack echoes the proverb 'To mourn in sack and claret' (Dent, S13), meaning to lament outwardly but rejoice inwardly. Sack was a canary wine – Spanish white, named for the Canary Islands – which improved with age; and silk was material of which extravagant garments were fashioned (cf. 30–1n.). Playing on the *sack* in *sackcloth*, Falstaff makes the ironic point that Harry's self-indulgence betokens no penitence at all.

191 further] *Q;* farther *F*   194 him! For] *F (*him. For*);* him for *Q*   the ear] *F (*th'eare*);* the yeere *Q*
197 – marry] *Q (, mary), F (*: Marry*), Cam¹*

JUSTICE   Well, God send the Prince a better companion.

FALSTAFF   God send the companion a better prince;   200
I cannot rid my hands of him.

JUSTICE   Well, the King hath severed you: I hear you
are going with Lord John of Lancaster against the
Archbishop and the Earl of Northumberland.

FALSTAFF   Yea, I thank your pretty sweet wit for it. But   205
look you pray, all you that kiss my lady Peace at
home, that our armies join not in a hot day; for, by
the Lord, I take but two shirts out with me, and I
mean not to sweat extraordinarily. If it be a hot day,
and I brandish anything but a bottle, I would I might   210
never spit white again. There is not a dangerous
action can peep out his head but I am thrust upon
it. Well, I cannot last ever; but it was alway yet the

---

202 **severed** separated. F's 'and Prince
Harry' clarifies what is implicit in Q.

202–4 **I . . . Northumberland** See 65n.

205 **I . . . it** The *it* is ambiguous. Falstaff
probably means that he holds the Justice
responsible for separating him and the
Prince; but he may instead be offering the
Justice sarcastic thanks for an unwelcome
military assignment.

206 **look** make sure

kiss . . . Peace Falstaff disparages those
men remaining safely at home (like the
Justice), rather than going to battle, as
effete courtiers who make love to an
allegorized Lady Peace. Cf. Othello's
reference to 'the soft phrase of peace'
(*Oth* 1.3.83).

207 **join** encounter one another, meet in
conflict (*OED v.*[1] 12)

208–9 **¹I . . . extraordinarily** Falstaff warns
the Lord Chief Justice that if the day is
too hot, he will not exert himself in
battle, the implication being that without

Falstaff's exertion, the King's forces will
lose.

210 **¹I . . . bottle** Falstaff's bravado recalls
that at Shrewsbury, he kept a bottle
instead of a pistol in his holster, to
the Prince's dismay (*1H4* 5.3.52–6);
brandish is customarily used of swords.

211 **spit white** a phrase of uncertain meaning:
white may signify clear and therefore
healthy spit, as opposed to spit tainted
with blood from wounds or phlegm from
disease. Possibly, too, Falstaff is making
a bawdy reference to ejaculation, with
spit meaning 'emit semen' (Williams,
Dictionary, 3.1288, *spit 2*), incidentally
assuring the Justice of his sexual potency.

212 **action** military operation

213 **ever** forever

213–19 ***but . . . motion** On F's omission of
these lines, see p. 474.

213 **alway** archaism for 'always', the genitive
form which superseded it

---

199 God] *Q;* heauen *F*   200 God] *Q;* Heauen *F*   202 severed you] *Q;* seuer'd you and Prince *Harry F*
205 Yea] *Q;* Yes *F*   207–8 for . . . Lord, I] *Q;* for if I *F*   210 and] *Q;* if *F*   a] *Q;* my *F*   bottle,] *F;* bottle. *Q*
I would] *Q;* would *F*   213 ever;] euer, *Q;* euer. *F*   213–19 but . . . motion.] *Q; not in F*

trick of our English nation, if they have a good thing,
to make it too common. If ye will needs say I am   215
an old man, you should give me rest. I would to God
my name were not so terrible to the enemy as it is.
I were better to be eaten to death with a rust than to
be scoured to nothing with perpetual motion.

JUSTICE   Well, be honest, be honest, and God bless your   220
     expedition.

FALSTAFF   Will your lordship lend me a thousand pound
     to furnish me forth?

JUSTICE   Not a penny, not a penny. You are too impatient
     to bear crosses. Fare you well; commend me to my   225
     cousin Westmorland.

          [*Exeunt Lord Chief Justice and Servant.*]

214 **trick** habit, practice or custom, with a
   pejorative connotation (*OED sb.* 7)
215 **common** undervalued because too
   familiar, with the implication here of
   using up a good thing so that nothing is
   left of it. Falstaff complains that his value
   as a soldier has been cheapened through
   exploitation and overuse. Related to two
   proverbs, 'The more common a good
   thing is the better' (Dent, T142) and 'Too
   much of one thing is good for nothing'
   (Dent, T158).
   will needs are determined to (*OED* needs
   adv. e)
218–19 The image is of armour. In an ironic
   inversion of the proverb 'It is better to
   wear out than rust out' (Dent, W209),
   Falstaff claims that as an old soldier, he
   should be allowed to retire (*be eaten . . .
   with a rust*), not expected to wear himself
   out in battle (*be scoured to nothing*), the
   idea being that perpetual motion will act
   as an abrasive on the armour. As Cowl
   notes (Ard[1]), a number of treatises on
   perpetual motion were published in the
   late 16th century; and in a letter to Lord
   Burghley in 1594, Edmund Jentill claimed

to have invented a 'perpetuall motion'
able to 'dryve a myll'. Thus Falstaff's
words would have had topical resonance.
222 **a thousand pound** the exact sum Falstaff
   eventually borrows from Shallow but
   cannot repay (cf. 5.5.72–5), establishing
   an ironic link between the two Justices.
   For an anticipation of his determination
   to borrow a large amount, see 192–4.
223 **furnish me forth** equip me for the
   expedition. Falstaff's impudent request
   may convey an implicit challenge to the
   Justice: 'If you want me to be honest,
   you'll need to provide me with the means
   to remain so.'
225 **crosses** a play on (1) the term for silver
   coins stamped with a cross (Cf. *LLL*
   1.2.32–4 and *AYL* 2.4.11–12), and (2)
   afflictions, as in Luke, 14.27: 'whosoeuer
   doth not beare his crosse'. The Justice's
   willingness to answer Falstaff pun for
   pun indicates that he is in all ways a
   worthy adversary, and he continues his
   numismatic punning at 2.1.117–20.
226 **cousin** a term of respectful intimacy
   among people, especially of noble rank,
   not related by blood

220 God] *Q;* heauen *F*   226 SD] *Capell subst.; Exit. F2–4; not in QF*

FALSTAFF   If I do, fillip me with a three-man beetle. A
man can no more separate age and covetousness than
'a can part young limbs and lechery; but the gout
galls the one and the pox pinches the other, and so   230
both the degrees prevent my curses. – Boy?

PAGE   Sir?

FALSTAFF   What money is in my purse?

PAGE   Seven groats and two pence.

FALSTAFF   I can get no remedy against this consumption   235
of the purse. Borrowing only lingers and lingers it
out, but the disease is incurable. [*Hands letters to
Page.*] Go bear this letter to my Lord of Lancaster,
this to the Prince, this to the Earl of Westmorland,

---

227 **fillip … beetle** strike me (*OED* fillip *v.*
3) with a sledgehammer. A *beetle* was an
outsized hammer used to drive stakes or
ram paving stones; a beetle heavy enough
to require three men would be comically
appropriate to wield against a man of
Falstaff's size.

227–9 **A man … lechery** a mixture of
proverbial insights. Dent records 'Old
men are covetous by nature' (M568);
Dekker, in *2 Honest Whore*, observes
that 'Letchery loues to dwell in the
fairest lodging, and Couetousness in the
oldest buildings' (2.1.79–80). Falstaff,
who persists in calling himself both
old and young, attempts to justify the
avarice of which the Justice has just
accused him.

229 **'a** he

gout Falstaff here identifies the malady
which is causing him such physical pain
– and which he in typical fashion
universalizes as the bane of old age – as
gout, an inflammation of the small joints
that lodges in the big toe. Cf. 243–4.

230 **galls** See 148n.

the **pox** a sexually transmitted disease,
particularly syphilis

pinches hurts, causes physical pain to
(*OED v.* 5)

231 **degrees prevent** The meaning is unclear,
and various editors have emended *degrees*
to 'diseases'. But it probably refers to the
two stages of life, youth and age, both
of which anticipate (*prevent*) Falstaff's
curses because each is plagued with its
own ailment.

233 **What** how much

234 **groats** coins worth fourpence each

235 **consumption** a pun on the spending of
money and the wasting of the body by
disease

236–7 **Borrowing … incurable** Cf. an
analogous proverb, 'He is purse-sick and
lacks a physician' (Dent, P263).

238–9 **Go … Westmorland** Since winning
honours at Shrewsbury, Falstaff presumes a certain familiarity with the
nobility, as his letters to the two Princes
and the Earl attest. His impudent letter
to Harry lends itself to a comic reading
at 2.2.116–31.

---

227 fillip] *Q, F* (fillop)   229 'a] *Q;* he *F*   231 curses. – Boy?] *F;* curses, boy. *Q*   237–8 SD] *this edn;
(Giving letters) Oxf*

and this to old mistress Ursula, whom I have weekly 240
sworn to marry since I perceived the first white hair
of my chin. About it; you know where to find me.

[*Exit Page.*]

A pox of this gout, or a gout of this pox, for the one
or the other plays the rogue with my great toe. 'Tis no
matter if I do halt: I have the wars for my colour, and 245
my pension shall seem the more reasonable. A good
wit will make use of anything. I will turn diseases
to commodity. [*Exit.*]

1[.3] *Enter the* ARCHBISHOP [of York], Thomas MOWBRAY
(Earl Marshal), the Lord HASTINGS *and*
^FLORD^F BARDOLPH.

ARCHBISHOP

Thus have you heard our cause and known our means;
And, my most noble friends, I pray you all

240 **mistress Ursula** perhaps the Christian
name of Mistress Quickly, to whom
Falstaff has sworn marriage on 'Wednesday in Wheeson week' (2.1.87–8),
though in *H5* she is called Nell (2.1.19)
and is married to Pistol. Melchiori
speculates that Shakespeare confused
her name with that of Ursula, Hero's
attendant, in *MA*, which was printed at
the same time as the *2H4* Quarto; but it is
equally plausible that Falstaff is referring
to some other woman.

243 **A pox ... pox** 'A pox of [or on]
something' was a common curse, here
made more comic by a quibble on its
literal meaning. Cf. 230.

243–4 **for ... toe** a sure symptom of gout,
though Falstaff acknowledges that he

has syphilis (*pox*) as well. He ends the
scene as he began it, concerned about his
diseases.

245 **halt** limp
colour excuse, pretext. Falstaff will
claim that a war wound has made him
lame. Cf. more ominous punning on
colour at 5.5.84–7.

246 **my pension ... reasonable** i.e. the
evidence of injury will serve to justify
Falstaff's military pension, or, possibly,
to increase it – make it *more* considerable
(*OED reasonable adj.* 6b).

248 **commodity** profit, material advantage

1.3 Largely Shakespeare's invention, this
scene fleshes out Morton's report of
the Prelate's Rebellion at 1.1.189–209
– a report omitted from Q, perhaps

242 of] *Q;* on *F* SD] *Capell; not in QF* 244 the other] *Q;* th'other *F* 'Tis] *Q (*Tis*);* It is *F* 245 matter
if] *Q;* matter, if *F* halt] *Q (*hault*), F* 248 SD] *Capell; Exeunt F; not in Q* **1.3**] *Scene III. / Steevens;
Scena Quarta. F; not in Q* 0.1–3] *Capell subst.; Enter th'Archbishop, Thomas Mowbray (Earle Marshall)
the Lord Hastings, Fauconbridge, and Bardolfe. Q; Enter Archbishop, Hastings, Mowbray, and Lord
Bardolfe. F* 1 cause] *Q;* causes *F* known] *Q (*knowne*);* kno *F;* know *F2–4*

Speak plainly your opinions of our hopes.
And first, Lord Marshal, what say you to it?

MOWBRAY

I well allow the occasion of our arms   5
But gladly would be better satisfied
How in our means we should advance ourselves
To look with forehead bold and big enough
Upon the power and puissance of the King.

HASTINGS

Our present musters grow upon the file   10
To five and twenty thousand men of choice,
And our supplies live largely in the hope
Of great Northumberland, whose bosom burns
With an incensed fire of injuries.

because its substance is dramatized here – and may have been suggested by two paragraphs in Holinshed (3.529) which identified a location for the meeting (the Archbishop's palace in York) and the names of the conspirators: 'Richard Scroope archbishop of Yorke Thomas Mowbraie earle marshall . . . the lords Hastings, Fauconbridge, [and] Berdolfe'.

0.1–3 *Q reproduces verbatim the names in Holinshed, including Fauconbridge, a ghost character who is duly excised from F.

1 The scene begins in the middle of a debate, the Archbishop's *cause* (reason for rebellion) and *means* (military strength) having already been discussed.

4 **Lord Marshal** an officer charged with arranging ceremonies, especially with regulating combats in the lists. The son of the first Duke of Norfolk who had been banished by Richard II as a result of his quarrel with Henry Bolingbroke (see *R2* 1.3.148–53), Thomas Mowbray did not inherit his father's dukedom and was allowed to keep the title Earl Marshal

only in name, the office having been granted to Westmorland. See 4.1.111n.

5 **well . . . arms** grant that we have good reason to take up arms

7 **in our means** with the forces at our disposal

8 **forehead** figuratively, a commanding countenance; assurance (*OED sb.* 2). Dent cites 'To have an impudent forehead' as proverbial (F590.1). Cf. the 'moody frontier' of defiance put up by the Percys in *1H4* 1.3.19.

9 **puissance** strength

10 **musters** soldiers assembled for service
upon the file according to the enlistment roll (*OED sb.* 3c)

12 **supplies** reinforcement of troops (*OED sb.* 5)
live largely depend to a great extent. With reference to troop reinforcement, however, *largely* could also refer to large numbers of soldiers (which the rebels hope Northumberland will provide).

14 **incensed** figuratively, angered or enraged; incensèd. The line also plays on the literal meaning 'kindled', applied to the *fire of injuries*.

5 SP] *Mow. F; Marsh. Q*

LORD BARDOLPH

> The question then, Lord Hastings, standeth thus: 15
> Whether our present five and twenty thousand
> May hold up head without Northumberland.

HASTINGS

> With him we may.

LORD BARDOLPH   Yea, marry, there's the point.

> But if without him we be thought too feeble,
> My judgement is we should not step too far 20
> ᶠTill we had his assistance by the hand;
> For in a theme so bloody-faced as this,
> Conjecture, expectation and surmise
> Of aids incertain should not be admitted.ᶠ

ARCHBISHOP

> 'Tis very true, Lord Bardolph, for indeed 25
> It was young Hotspur's cause at Shrewsbury.

LORD BARDOLPH

> It was, my lord, who lined himself with hope,

15–17 Shaheen draws a parallel between these lines and Luke, 14.31–2, which becomes even more explicit at 41–62.

17 **hold up head** maintain self-respect (*OED* hold *v.* 30b); so, encounter the King's forces with confidence. Cf. 'look with forehead bold' (8) for earlier anthropomorphizing of the rebel force.

18 **marry** See 1.2.197n.

21–4, 36–55 *The reason for Q's failure to include these passages is unclear. Neither is of a particularly political nature, making censorship unlikely. Perhaps they were cut in an attempt to reduce the role of Lord Bardolph. See pp. 448–57.

22 **theme so bloody-faced** action so likely to cause bloodshed

23 An echo of Rumour's self-anatomy in Ind.16.

26 **young Hotspur's cause** the reason for Hotspur's death. Q's *cause*, meaning 'the case as it concerns anyone' (*OED sb.* 10), is probably correct, though F's 'case', adopted by many editors, averts a repetition of *cause* at 37. The Archbishop attributes Hotspur's death to his waging war before he had assurance of support: he relied too much on the expectation of aid. With Q's omission of 21–4, his attribution grows more pointed: Hotspur's death is blamed directly on Northumberland's failure to come to his assistance.

27 **who lined himself** who (referring to Hotspur) fortified himself: the metaphor is drawn from clothing, with lining as the reinforcement of a garment. Cf. Lady Percy's asking Hotspur whether her brother Mortimer 'hath sent for you / To

---

18 Yea] *Q;* I *F*   19 too] *Q;* to *F*   21–4] *F; not in Q*   24 incertain] *F1–2;* uncertain *F3–4*   26 cause] *Q;* case *F*   27 was, my lord,] was (my Lord) *F;* was my Lord, *Q*

Eating the air and promise of supply,
Flatt'ring himself in project of a power
Much smaller than the smallest of his thoughts;   30
And so with great imagination,
Proper to madmen, led his powers to death
And, winking, leapt into destruction.

HASTINGS

But by your leave, it never yet did hurt
To lay down likelihoods and forms of hope.   35

LORD BARDOLPH

ᶠYes, if this present quality of war –

line his enterprise' (*1H4* 2.3.79–80), and the French King's instructing the Dauphin 'To line and new-repair our towns of war' (*H5* 2.4.7).

28 **Eating ... promise** 'A man cannot live upon air' is proverbial for feeding on false hopes (Dent, M226). Hotspur's hope lay in the promise of supplies from his father (see 12n.) which never arrived. Q's *and* yokes *air* and *promise* in a hendiadys as if they were the same thing, the promise no more substantial than air, where F's 'on' more conventionally makes *promise* the cause of Hotspur's false hope. Cf. *Ham* 3.2.89–90: 'I eat the air, promise-crammed'.

29 **project** anticipation

29, 32, 71 **power, powers** army, troops

30 **Much smaller** i.e. which turned out to be much smaller

32 **Proper to madmen** befitting madmen. Cf. *MND* 5.1.7–8: 'The lunatic, the lover, and the poet / Are of imagination all compact'. Hotspur's crazed imagination of heroic exploits elicits comment from his confederates in *1H4*: 'Imagination of some great exploit / Drives him beyond the bounds of patience' (1.3.198–9); 'He

apprehends a world of figures here, / But not the form of what he should attend' (208–9).

33 **winking** closing his eyes to the truth; perhaps suggested by the proverbial 'Look ere you leap' (Dent, L429)

35 **lay down** consider
   forms of hope estimates of what we may hope for

36–41 ***Yes ... them** These lines have caused consternation among readers and editors alike, in part because the first two may be corrupt, possibly damaged when 36–55 was marked for deletion in the Q copy. The more important editorial interventions are recorded in the textual notes. I have adhered to F, changing the punctuation slightly to clarify what I take to be Lord Bardolph's rejoinder to Hastings's assertion that it does not hurt to nurse hopes: 'Yes, it does hurt, if the war we are contemplating – indeed, the impending campaign of foot – is grounded in hopes no surer than those we entertain of an early spring when we see the first buds, fully aware that they are likely to be blighted by frost before they have a chance to blossom.' It is possible

28 and] *Q;* on *F*   29 in] *Q;* with *F*   36–55 Yes ... else] *F; not in Q*   36–7] *F (*Yes, if ... warre, / Indeed ... action: a ... foot); Yes, if ... war / Impede ... act; a ... foot Pope; Yes, if the ... war / Impede the present action. A ... foot Capell; Yes, in ... war; – / Indeed ... action, (a ... foot) Malone*

Indeed, the instant action, a cause on foot –
Lives so in hope as in an early spring
We see th'appearing buds, which to prove fruit
Hope gives not so much warrant as despair   40
That frosts will bite them. When we mean to build,
We first survey the plot, then draw the model;
And when we see the figure of the house,
Then must we rate the cost of the erection
Which, if we find outweighs ability,   45
What do we then but draw anew the model
In fewer offices, or at least desist
To build at all? Much more in this great work,
Which is almost to pluck a kingdom down
And set another up, should we survey   50
The plot of situation and the model,
Consent upon a sure foundation,

to read Lord Bardolph's admonition as somewhat more conciliatory, with *Yes, if* understood differently: 'I agree, provided the war we are contemplating . . . is not grounded on hopes as unreasonable as those . . .'.

36 **quality** occasion, cause (*OED sb.* 8b)

37 **instant** imminent, impending (*OED adj.* 3)

cause on foot business (*OED* cause *sb.* 10) involving foot-soldiers (*OED* foot *sb.* 4); therefore, a campaign of foot. Oxf¹ reads the phrase more idiomatically: 'the matter that is now afoot'.

38 **so . . . as** F's punctuation suggests that *as* begins a new sentence, where I take it to introduce a simile which explains *so in hope.*

39–41 **to prove . . . them** Structured as an antithesis, these lines argue that hope for the buds' ripening (*to prove fruit*) is less warranted than despair that frost will kill

them. Both *Hope* and *despair* are subjects of the verb *gives.*

41–62 **When . . . tyranny** This elaborate analogy between preparing for war and constructing a building draws on the parable of the builder in Luke, 14.28–32.

42 **model** architectural plans or elevations (*OED sb.* 1)

43 **figure** design

44 **rate** calculate (*OED v.*¹ 2)

45 **ability** i.e. to meet expenses

47 **In fewer offices** with fewer rooms; specifically, perhaps, those rooms devoted to household work or service (*OED* office *sb.* 9)

at least at worst

48 **this great work** i.e. the war we are undertaking

49 **pluck** pull by force

51 **plot of situation** a play on (1) land site for building, and (2) plan of action

52 **Consent** agree

38 hope as] *Globe;* hope: As *F;* hope, as *Rowe*   39–40 fruit . . . as] *F* (fruit, . . . warrant, as)   47 offices, or] *Collier²;* offices? Or *F*   least] *F;* last *Capell*

Question surveyors, know our own estate,
How able such a work to undergo,
To weigh against his opposite; or else[F]   55
We fortify in paper and in figures,
Using the names of men instead of men,
Like one that draws the model of an house
Beyond his power to build it, who, half through,
Gives o'er and leaves his part-created cost   60
A naked subject to the weeping clouds
And waste for churlish winter's tyranny.

HASTINGS

Grant that our hopes, yet likely of fair birth,
Should be stillborn, and that we now possessed
The utmost man of expectation,   65
I think we are [F]a[F] body strong enough,
Even as we are, to equal with the King.

---

53 **surveyors** those who superintend the construction; contractors (*OED sb.* 2)
estate money, property, possessions; in this case, resources for war
54 'whether we are able to undertake, our resources to support, such a work'
55 **weigh against** counterbalance, countervail (*OED* weigh *v.*[1] 16d)
his opposite adverse conditions, or the resources of our enemy; *his* = its, and *estate* (53) its antecedent
56–62 *Although these lines provide an apt summary and conclusion of the analogy developed above, they stand on their own quite effectively. Q's omission of 36–55, therefore, a case of skilful splicing, does not disrupt the logic of the scene.
56 **fortify** strengthen structurally (a building), or augment (our forces)
in paper . . . figures a hendiadys: by means of figures on paper; *figures* are

numerical estimates backed by no actual support of troops, but may also refer to designs, as at 43.
59 **power** means
60 **part-created cost** metonymic for the half-finished house, *cost* referring to the money already spent on it
61–2 The rebels' concern about their own political disenfranchisement by an ungrateful king may lie behind the metaphor of the house as a *naked subject* abused by *winter's tyranny.*
62 **waste for** something wasted or destroyed by (*OED sb.* 6c)
63 **yet . . . birth** still likely to yield the desired results
65 'all the men we can expect'
66 **a body** understood as corporate: an organized force (*OED sb.* 16). Q's 'so' is probably a compositorial error.

---

55 To] *F;* How *Capell;* And *Hudson (Staunton)* opposite;] *Theobald;* Opposite? *F*   57 instead] *F, Q (*in steed*)*   58 one] *F;* on *Q*   an] *Q;* a *F*   59 through] *F;* thorough *Q*   66 we are a] *F;* we are so, *Q;* we're so a *(Collier)*

LORD BARDOLPH

What, is the King but five and twenty thousand?

HASTINGS

To us no more; nay, not so much, Lord Bardolph;
For his divisions, as the times do brawl,   70
^FAre^F in three heads: one power against the French,
And one against Glendower, perforce a third
Must take up us. So is the unfirm King
In three divided, and his coffers sound
With hollow poverty and emptiness.   75

ARCHBISHOP

That he should draw his several strengths together
And come against us in full puissance
Need not to be dreaded.

HASTINGS   If he should do so,
^FHe leaves his back unarmed, the French and Welsh^F

---

69 **To us** so far as concerns us
   nay ... much a phrase echoed in *Ham*
   1.2.138
70 **as ... brawl** responding to the present
   disturbances: *brawl* = wrangle, squabble
   (*OED v.* 1)
71 **Are** F's alternative to Q's 'And' is
   reasonable in view of the frequent *r/n* and
   e/d misreadings in Elizabethan secretary
   hand.
   heads gatherings of forces (*OED sb.* 30)
   against the French probably referring to
   the expedition led by the Earl of Kent and
   the Duke of Clarence in the summer of
   1405 (Holinshed, 3.528–9)
72 **Glendower** I adopt the QF spelling
   Glendower, which until recently has been
   sanctioned by editors, because it probably
   indicates the anglicized pronunciation of
   the Welsh *Glyndŵr* (pronounced *Glin-
   dwr '*), the authentic form embraced by

recent editors. The spelling *Glendour*
used at QbF 3.1.103 is a variant of
Glendower and no doubt pronounced the
same.
73 **take up** encounter, oppose (*OED* take *v.*
   93p)
74 **sound** possibly from the proverb 'Empty
   vessels sound most' (Dent,   V36).
   Holinshed refers numerous times to
   Henry's impecuniousness and to his
   desperate requests for funds from the
   clergy and laity alike (e.g. 3.525, 530).
   For similar use of the proverb, see *H5*
   4.4.69 and *KL* 1.1.154–5.
76 **strengths** forces, armies
79–80 ***the French ... heels** F corrects an
   obvious error in Q, in which the printer
   apparently misunderstood an intended
   substitution in the copy-text. 'French and
   Welch' had probably been written in the
   margin or interlined between 78 and 79 to

---

68 What,] *Q;* What *F*   71 Are] *F;* And *Q*   72 Glendower] *QF;* Glyndŵr *Oxf*   78 to] *Q; not in F*
78–80 If . . . that.] *F; prose Q*   79] *F;* French and Welch he leaues his back vnarmde, they *Q;* To *French,
and Welsh, he leaves his back unarm'd, / They Capell*

Baying him at the heels: never fear that.   80
LORD BARDOLPH
    Who is it like should lead his forces hither?
HASTINGS
    The Duke of Lancaster and Westmorland;
    Against the Welsh, himself and Harry Monmouth.
    But who is substituted against the French
    I have no certain notice.
^FARCHBISHOP   Let us on,   85
    And publish the occasion of our arms.

---

replace 'they', but instead was inserted
by the printer in the line above, resulting
in nonsense.

80 **Baying . . . heels** Hastings metaphorically views war as a hunt, with the King as
the fox and the French and Welsh as
hounds in close pursuit.

81 an anomalous line: Lord Bardolph asks
for information already provided him by
Morton at 1.1.132–5. For Shakespeare's
probable conflation of two roles –
Bardolph's and Umfreville's – during the
process of revision, and the resulting
confusion of which this line is evidence,
see 1.1.34n.

82 **Duke of Lancaster** a mistaken
designation for Prince John, who, though
born at Lancaster and so designated by
Holinshed – 'the lord Iohn of Lancaster'
(3.529) – was actually created Duke of
Bedford in 1411 (Holinshed, 3.546), after
the events dramatized in this play, and is
so named in *H5*. Shakespeare's confusion
may have originated in Stow, who in
describing Henry's coronation reports
that 'his second sonne was there made
duke of Lancast[er]' (*Annales*, 513).
Shakespeare apparently thinks of John as
next in line to Harry, but Henry's second
son was Thomas, also called the Duke

of Clarence (Ard²). John is referred to
as 'Lancaster' in *1H4* as well (5.4.0.2,
2, 16).

84 **substituted** deputed, delegated (*OED v.*
1c). GWW defends Ridley's reading by
conjecturing that 'substitute' was a noun
meant to parallel the proper names in
the preceding lines: i.e. Lancaster and
Westmorland against the northern rebels,
the King and Prince Henry against the
Welsh, and some substitute against the
French. F's ''gainst' may have been
intended to regularize the metrics of the
line.

85 **notice** information

85–108 *ARCHBISHOP . . . worst The Archbishop's speech appears only in F, but the
fact that the first three words (*Let us on*)
complete 85 as a line of iambic pentameter, which in Q remains an irregular
line, suggests that the speech, rather than
being a later addition, was cut from Q. It
may have been cut for political reasons,
or possibly to shorten the play for performance when it was not deemed
essential to draw historical connections
between *2H4* and *R2*. See pp. 448–57.

85 **on** proceed

86 **publish . . . arms** make known the
reasons for our insurrection

---

84 substituted against] *Q;* substituted 'gainst *F;* substitute against *Ridley*   85–108 ARCHBISHOP Let
. . . worst.] *F; not in Q*

The commonwealth is sick of their own choice;
Their over-greedy love hath surfeited.
An habitation giddy and unsure
Hath he that buildeth on the vulgar heart.   90
O thou fond many, with what loud applause
Didst thou beat heaven with blessing Bolingbroke
Before he was what thou wouldst have him be?
And being now trimmed in thine own desires,
Thou, beastly feeder, art so full of him   95
That thou provok'st thyself to cast him up.
So, so, thou common dog, didst thou disgorge

88 i.e. the people's allegiance (*love*) to Henry, excessive in its self-interest (*over-greedy*), has made them sick. The idea of surfeiting was commonly used to figure political disaffection; here, the Archbishop claims that the people have only themselves to blame.

89–90 a proverb from Luke, 6.49: 'But he that heareth and doeth not, is lyke a man, that without foundation, built an house vpon the earth, agaynst which the fludde dyd beate, and it fel immediatly: And the fall of that house was great'.

89 **giddy** foolish, mad

90 **vulgar** common, as opposed to aristocratic

91–3 possibly an echo of Daniel's account of the fickleness of the populace in changing their allegiance from Richard to Bolingbroke: 'the malecontented sort / That loue kings best before they haue them still' (*CW*, 1.71). Cf. the Duke of York's account of Bolingbroke's entry into London (*R2* 5.2.7–21).

91 **fond many** foolish multitude

93 **what ... be** i.e. king

94 **trimmed ... desires** dressed in the garments you yourselves wanted (*OED* trim *v.* 7); or possibly, in view of the imagery of feeding in 95–6, a reference to dressing food for the table (Cam[2]). In brief: 'Now that you have got what you wanted'.

95–6 The imagery of animal gluttony, incarnated in this play by Falstaff, returns to that of surfeit introduced at 87–8.

96 **cast him up** vomit him up, purge yourself of him; *provok'st thyself* implies that the vomiting is self-induced; cf. *H5* 3.2.60. These lines about surfeiting and sickness would have brought to mind Falstaff, whose fatness was emblematic of the kingdom's ills.

97–100 **So ... it** a common proverb (see Dent, D455) deriving from Proverbs, 26.11: 'Like as the dogge turneth agayne to his owne vomite: euen so a foole beginneth his foolishness agayne afresh'. It is repeated in 2 Peter, 2.22, which in turn is quoted in French by the Dauphin in *H5* 3.7.65–6. The portrayal of the multitude as a *common* or mongrel dog eager to devour the dead king it has just disgorged registers a disgust at the fickleness of the mob equalled in Shakespeare only by Coriolanus.

94 trimmed] *F* (trimm'd); trimm'd up *F2–4*

Thy glutton bosom of the royal Richard,
And now thou wouldst eat thy dead vomit up
And howl'st to find it. What trust is in these times?　　100
They that when Richard lived would have him die
Are now become enamoured on his grave.
Thou, that threw'st dust upon his goodly head
When through proud London he came sighing on
After th'admired heels of Bolingbroke,　　　　　　105
Cry'st now, 'O earth, yield us that king again
And take thou this!' O thoughts of men accursed!
Past and to come seems best; things present, worst.F

ᶠMOWBRAYᶠ

Shall we go draw our numbers, and set on?　　　　109

HASTINGS

We are time's subjects, and time bids be gone.　　*Exeunt.*

98　**bosom** stomach; but also a figurative play
　　on the breast as the seat of desire, where
　　first Richard, then Bolingbroke, has been
　　lodged in popular affection (*OED* bosom
　　sb. 6)
99　**dead vomit** The adjective, rightfully
　　belonging to Richard (98) and therefore
　　a hypallage, or transferred epithet, yields
　　a grotesque personification of vomit. Cf.
　　1.1.147n.
102　**on** of
103–5　a further recollection of the Duke of
　　York's report in *R2* 5.2 (cf. 91–3n.),
　　where 'rude misgoverned hands from
　　windows' tops / Threw dust and rubbish
　　on King Richard's head' (5–6), and 'dust
　　was thrown upon his sacred head' (30) as
　　he followed the triumphant Bolingbroke
　　through London. An echo of 2 Samuel,
　　16.13, is also possible (Ard²).
105　**th'admired** th'admirèd
107　**accursed** modifies either *thoughts* or *men*
108　F's italicization of and opening quotation
　　marks for this line lend it the force of

an aphorism; furthermore, the line completes a couplet, signalling the end of
the speech. As such, it might make an
appropriate exit line for the Archbishop:
he has begun his speech with *Let us on*
(85) and would logically exit at its conclusion, expecting the others to follow
immediately. But they do not: Mowbray's
Shall we . . . set on? (109) seems to
question whether they should follow the
Archbishop, just as he has earlier doubted
the wisdom of proceeding against the
King (5–9), while Hastings's reply (110)
affirms his obedience to a force greater
than himself. The absence of a final exit
SD in F leaves open the possibility of
staggered exits. Q precludes this possibility: see 109n.
　　seems For a singular verb used with a
　　plural subject, see 1.1.33n.
109　**draw our numbers** assemble our army.
　　Q, having omitted the Archbishop's long
　　speech at 85–108, assigns this final line to
　　him as the senior ranking person present.

---

106 Cry'st] *Ard²*; Cri'st *F*; Criest *Dyce*　　108] *italicized and with opening quotation marks F*　　109 SP]
Mow. F; Bish. Q　　110 SD] *Q (ex.); Theobald; not in F*

2.1 *Enter* HOSTESS *of the tavern, and an* Officer[, FANG].

HOSTESS   Master Fang, have you entered the action?
FANG   It is entered.
HOSTESS   Where's your yeoman? Is't a lusty yeoman?
    Will 'a stand to't?
FANG   Sirrah – Where's Snare?   5
HOSTESS   O Lord, ay, good Master Snare.

[*Enter* SNARE.]

2.1 Like 1.2, this scene takes place on a
street, presumably near the Hostess's
tavern in Eastcheap
0.1 *Q's permissive '*an Officer or two*'
makes it likely that the compositor was
working from a holograph: Shakespeare
intended the appearance of a second
officer, Snare, but had not yet decided
when to have him enter. F solves the
problem with its massed entry, but the
Hostess's questioning Snare's whereabouts at 3 and Fang's asking for him at 5
suggest than he has not yet entered.
Alternatively, he may merely be lagging
behind and make his presence known at
7.
1 **Master Fang** The Hostess confers on
Fang a title of respect not warranted by
the rank of constable (Ard²). She similarly
confers the title *Master* on Snare (6, 9), a
royal or ecclesiastical title (*your grace*)
upon the Lord Chief Justice (68–9) and a
captaincy on Pistol (2.4.138). Fang and
Snare are descriptive names for officers
of the law, who in this case are to arrest
Falstaff: fang = seize, apprehend (*OED v.*
1); snare = capture, catch by entangling
(*OED v.* 1).
    entered the action recorded the lawsuit;

brought the case before the court in
written form (*OED* enter *v.* 22a)
3 **yeoman** traditional second to a constable;
attendant or assistant to an officer (*OED
sb.* 1b)
    lusty (1) strong, vigorous and valiant;
(2) full of lust or sexual desire (*OED adj.*
5a, 4)
4 **stand to't** fight stoutly, apply himself
manfully (*OED* stand *v.* 76c); but a
bawdy play on 'get an erection' extends
the sexual connotation of *lusty* above.
5 Fang apparently turns around to address
Snare and discovers that he is not there.
That *Sirrah* may be addressed to a third
officer is unlikely, since no lines are given
to an officer other than Fang and Snare;
nor is Capell's silent '*Boy*' necessary
(0.1 t.n.). For *Sirrah* as a form of address,
see 1.2.1n.
6.1 Anticipated by the Hostess to be *a lusty
yeoman* (3), Snare would have cut a comic
figure at his delayed entrance if the role
was played by John Sincklo, the cadaverously thin actor who may have doubled
as the Beadle – ridiculed as a *starved
bloodhound* by Doll and the Hostess
(5.4.26) – and also as Feeble (Cam¹).

2.1] *Actus Secundus. Scoena Prima.* F; *not in* Q   0.1] *Q (Enter Hostesse of the Tauerne, and an Officer
or two.); Enter Hostesse, with two Officers, Fang, and Snare.* F; *Enter the* Hostess; Phang, *and his Boy,
with her; and* Snare *following. Capell*   1 Fang] *F*; Phang *Q (throughout)*   3 Is't] *Q*; Is it *F*   4 'a] *Q*;
he *F*   to't] *Q (*too't*);* to it *F*   5 Sirrah – Where's] *Ard² (Shaaber);* Sirra, where's *QF*; [*to the Boy.* Sirrah,
where's *Capell*   6 O Lord, ay] *Q (*O Lord I*);* I, I *F*   6.1] *this edn (Cam¹)*

213

SNARE   Here, here.

FANG   Snare, we must arrest Sir John Falstaff.

HOSTESS   Yea, good Master Snare, I have entered him
and all.   10

SNARE   It may chance cost some of us our lives, for he
will stab.

HOSTESS   Alas the day, take heed of him. He stabbed me
in mine own house, most beastly in good faith. 'A
cares not what mischief he does; if his weapon be   15
out, he will foin like any devil. He will spare neither
man, woman nor child.

FANG   If I can close with him, I care not for his thrust.

HOSTESS   No, nor I neither. I'll be at your elbow.

FANG   An I but fist him once, an 'a come but within my   20
    ᶠviceᶠ –

---

11 **chance** perhaps, perchance: a noun used
adverbially (*OED sb.* c)

13 **stabbed** The implication is that this
was with either his sword or his penis,
though the Hostess probably means to
speak metaphorically of the financial
hurt Falstaff has inflicted on her. Cf. a
similar pun in *JC* 1.2.272–4: 'if Caesar
had stabbed their mothers, they would
have done no less'. Here begins a series
of sexual *double entendres* in which
the Hostess may unwittingly reveal the
nature of her relationship with Falstaff.

14 **beastly** uncivilly; possibly a bawdy
allusion to a beast's position during coitus
– that is, mounting from the rear

16 **out, he** Q's punctuation, which puts
weapon and *foin* in the same sentence,
makes a more pointed joke than F's.
foin a fencing term meaning lunge or
thrust with a pointed weapon – hence,
pierce or prick – here with phallic
overtones: cf. 2.4.233. In Falstaff's

willingness to spare no one when his
weapon is *out*, the Hostess grants him a
kind of indiscriminate sexual appetite.
Partridge cites the proverb 'A standing
prick has no conscience.'

18 **close** grapple, engage in hand-to-hand
combat (*OED v.* 13), with a possible connotation of sexual embrace
thrust Referring to either swordplay or
sexual penetration, *thrust* continues the
bawdy *double entendre*, though inadvertently on Fang's part.

19 **No … neither** If by this the Hostess
means that she will be ready to receive
Falstaff's thrust, she has, perhaps uncon-
sciously, grasped the sexual innuendo of
the conversation.

20 **An … fist** If I just grab or punch (*OED*
fist *v.*¹ 2). A possible play on *fist* as
masturbate would lend bawdy meaning to
an 'a come but, and F's substitution of
vice (firm grip) for Q's innocuous 'view',
which may be a compositorial misreading

9 Yea] *Q;* I *F*   11 for] *Q; not in F*   14 most . . . faith] *Q;* and that most beastly *F*   'A] *Q;* he *F*   15 does]
Q; doth *F*   16 out, he] *Q;* out. Hee *F*   20 An . . . an 'a] *Q (*And . . . and a*);* If. . . if he *F*   21 vice –] *F*
(*Vice.*), *Capell;* view. *Q*

HOSTESS   I am undone by his going, I warrant you:
he's an infinitive thing upon my score. Good Master
Fang, hold him sure! Good Master Snare, let him not
scape! 'A comes ᶠcontinuantlyᶠ to Pie Corner, saving   25
your manhoods, to buy a saddle, and he is indited to

of *vice* as 'vue' (Cam[1]), continues the joke. *OED* records the first instance of 'come' as slang for achieving orgasm in 1650, but the term was popular well before that: Partridge and Williams (*Dictionary*) list other instances of it in Shakespeare. Fang thus seems to share the Hostess's proclivity for inadvertent *double entendres*. Fang's repetition of two conditional clauses beginning with *An* suggests a mounting frustration which would typically climax in a statement of resolve such as 'I'll show him!'

22 **undone ... going** financially ruined by Falstaff's going off to war; primarily because he owes her so much money, but possibly referring as well to a reputation ruined because he has promised to marry her. See 85–93.

I warrant you colloquial pledge of assurance of a fact (*OED* warrant *v.* 5)

23 **he's ... score** In the first of the Hostess's malapropisms, *infinitive* is a mistake for infinite. She means that Falstaff has countless debits recorded by means of chalk markings on a board or door (*OED* score *sb.* 9a); but there may be a hint of sexual indebtedness as well, her *score* being the number of times he has 'had' her with his *thing* (penis), and *infinitive* referring to the length of that *thing*. Cf. 31n. on *long one*.

24 **sure** secure

25 ***continuantly** Editors since Delius have preferred F's word over Q's 'continually' as a likely malapropism for 'incontinently' – meaning both unchastely (*OED adv.*[1]) and immediately (*adv.*[2]) – typical of the

Hostess. Davison speculates that a Q compositor mistakenly corrected what he took to be an error in the Hostess's speech, for it is easier to imagine a compositor substituting a common word ('continually') for an uncommon word (*continuantly*) in Q copy than inventing such a word in F.

Pie Corner The corner of Giltspur Street and Cock Lane in Smithfield (see 1.2.51–5), and so named for the cooks' shops there. Adjacent to a centre of horse-trading with many saddlers' shops, Pie Corner was a familiar resort of prostitutes. Known for its brothels since 1393, it was still mentioned in court records two centuries later: in 1586 a parson committed 'carnal copulation ... twice in one Theals house a cook by Pye Corner', and in 1608 a woman was seen 'occupied in a stable at Pye Corner' (Gowing, 'Gender', 16). Unsurprisingly, the phrase had become slang for the female pudendum (Williams, *Revolution*, 259).

25–6 **saving your manhoods** no offence meant to your manhoods; an apologetic formula (usually 'saving your reverence') excusing the mention of an indelicate subject, which in this case would be that Falstaff was 'buying a saddle', a euphemism for whoring

26 **indited** comic catachresis for 'invited' – cf. *RJ* 2.4.127, 'She will endite him to some supper' – but also a verbal slip evoking the Hostess's indictment of Falstaff for crimes committed, the domain of hospitality contaminated by her desire for legal retribution.

22 by] *Q;* with *F*   22–3 going ... he's] *Q subst.;* going: I warrant he is *F;* going; I warrant you, he is *Theobald*   25 'A] *Q;* he *F*   continuantly] *F;* continually *Q*   26 indited] *QF1–2;* invited *F3–4*

215

dinner to the Lubber's Head in Lumbert Street to
Master Smooths the silkman. I pray you, since my
exion is entered and my case so openly known to the
world, let him be brought in to his answer. A hundred   30
mark is a long one for a poor lone woman to bear; and
I have borne, and borne, and borne, and have been
fubbed off, and fubbed off, and fubbed off, from this
day to that day, that it is a shame to be thought on.
There is no honesty in such dealing, unless a woman   35

27 **Lubber's ... Lumbert Street** comic play on two names which the Hostess confuses. The Libbard's or Leopard's Head, which she calls Lubber's (a 'lubber' being an idle, clumsy lout), was located on Lombard Street, named for the merchants from Lombardy who settled there in the 13th century. The Leopard's Head may refer to the sign at Master Smooths the silkman's shop (28), since silken garments often had the head of a lion or leopard embroidered on them (cf. *LLL* 5.2.544), and Falstaff is having a new wardrobe made (1.2.29–31); but it may also refer to the sign of a tavern, since Falstaff plans to dine there.

28 **Smooths** Neither Q nor F offers justification for the possessive form favoured by recent editors.

29 **exion is entered** The word *exion* may be the Hostess's humorous attempt at a proper pronunciation, probably in three syllables, of 'action'. In addition to the legal meaning, the phrase plays on sexual penetration.
case legal case, but a vulgar term for the vagina as well, continuing the Hostess's inadvertent revelation of her own promiscuity. The slang probably derived from the meaning of 'case' as receptacle or seed-vessel (*OED sb.*² 1a, 2a).

30 **brought ... answer** put on trial; brought to court to answer the charges

30–1 **A hundred mark** about 66 pounds. For the value of Falstaff's debt, see 1.2.192–4.

31 **long one** substantial reckoning. For the tallying of an account, see 23n. The length of Falstaff's bill (with a glance at his penis length as well: cf. 'an infinitive thing', 23) may allow *mark* to be understood as the markings made to keep track of it.
lone The Hostess's marital status is problematic. In this scene, she reminds Falstaff of his repeated promise to marry her (cf. 1.2.240–1) and calls herself *a poor widow* (68); but in *1H4*, she identifies herself as 'an honest man's wife' (3.3.119). Shakespeare apparently was not concerned about the potential contradiction.

32–3 **borne ... fubbed off** The Hostess says that she has put up with (*borne*) Falstaff's debt and been put off by his excuses (*OED* fub *v*.¹ 3a) for an unconscionably long time, but the verbs also convey sexual innuendo: she has *borne* him – the full weight of his body – and he has *fubbed* her relentlessly. Cf. 'O happy horse, to bear the weight of Antony!' (*AC* 1.5.22).

27 Lubber's ... Lumbert] *Q;* Lubbars ... Lombard *F*   28 Master Smooths] *Q;* M. *Smoothes F*   pray you] *Q;* pray'ye *F*   29 exion] *QF1–2;* Action *F3–4*   31 one] *QF;* Lone *Theobald;* loan *Hanmer;* score *Collier*²; ow'n' *White*   33 and fubbed off, from] *Q;* from *F*

should be made an ass and a beast to bear every
knave's wrong.

Enter Sir John ᶠFALSTAFFᶠ, BARDOLPH
and the Boy [PAGE].

Yonder he comes, and that arrant malmsey-nose
knave Bardolph with him. Do your offices, do your
offices, Master Fang and Master Snare! Do me, do   40
me, do me your offices!

FALSTAFF   How now, whose mare's dead? What's the
matter?

FANG   I arrest you at the suit of Mistress Quickly.

FALSTAFF   Away, varlets! – Draw, Bardolph! Cut me off   45

---

36 **an ass ... beast** The analogy between a
woman and a beast of burden, bearing
every knave's wrong, recalls the Hostess's
image of bestial copulation at 14.

37 **wrong** In keeping with the bawdy
innuendo of the sentence, *wrong* may
mean penis or even illegitimate child
(Bate & Rasmussen).

37.1–2 *F's placement of the SD makes
more sense than Q's, for although Falstaff
does not speak until 42, the Hostess
acknowledges his entrance here, and the
intervening lines may have allowed him,
no doubt with comic flair, to cross the
stage to her.

38 **arrant** downright or notorious, usually
used with *knave* (*OED adj.* 3); cf. 5.1.30,
39; 5.4.1.
   malmsey-nose Malmsey was a strong,
sweet red wine; so, a reference to the
redness of Bardolph's nose, presumably
caused by drink.

39–40 **Do ... offices** i.e. arrest Falstaff.

40–1 **Do ... ²me** The Hostess's thrice-
repeated *do* carries a bawdy quibble on

'fuck' much loved by Shakespeare. With
me, she employs the ethical dative, an
archaic construction in which a pronoun
would seem to require a preposition –
e.g. 'Do ... *for* me'. The ethical dative
was often used colloquially when 'the
action implied in the verb ... [was]
perceived as having some effect on the
person referred to' (Hope, 100). See also
Abbott, 220.

42 **whose mare's dead?** proverbial for
'What's all the fuss?' (Dent, M657).

44 **Mistress Quickly** the first time she is so
identified in this play. In *1H4* she is only
once called by this name, at 3.3.92.

45 **varlets** knaves, rascals; but the word also
means sergeant (*OED sb.* 1d), in which
case it would be a particularly appropriate
epithet for Fang.
   Draw, Bardolph! If Fang and Snare are
trying to subdue Falstaff, he would call
on Bardolph, whose hands are still free,
to draw his sword.
   Cut me On use of the ethical dative, see
40–1n.

37.1–2] *Q (after 41) (Enter sir Iohn, and Bardolfe, and the boy.); Enter Falstaffe and Bardolfe. F; Enter
Sir John Falstaff, Page, and Bardolfe. Capell*   39 knave] *Q; not in F*   44 I] *Q; Sir Iohn, I F*   Mistress
Quickly] *Q(corr)F; mistris, quickly Q(uncorr)*

the villain's head! Throw the quean in the channel!
[*Fang and Snare attempt to apprehend Falstaff.
A brawl ensues.*]

HOSTESS   Throw me in the channel? I'll throw thee
in the channel! Wilt thou, wilt thou, thou bastardly
rogue? – Murder! Murder! – Ah, thou honeysuckle
villain, wilt thou kill God's officers and the King's?   50
Ah, thou honeyseed rogue! Thou art a honeyseed,
a man queller, and a woman queller!

FALSTAFF   Keep them off, Bardolph.

OFFICERS   A rescue, a rescue!

HOSTESS   Good people, bring a rescue or two! – Thou   55

46 **quean** impudent woman, often a harlot or strumpet; Falstaff's first insult to the Hostess's virtue
channel gutter or open sewer running along the street

48 **Wilt ... ²thou** The Hostess's repeated phrase either anticipates the sentence she cannnot spit out until 50 – 'wilt thou kill God's officers . . . ?' – or, more likely, is a sputtered response to Falstaff's threat to throw her in the channel.
bastardly humorous conflation of 'bastard' and 'dastardly'

49, 51 **honeysuckle, honeyseed** malapropisms for 'homicidal' and 'homicide'. The Hostess makes two stabs at it.

50 **wilt ... King's** Tudor homilies, echoing Romans, 13.3–6, often referred to rulers as 'God's ministers' and therefore to government officials as 'God's officers' (Shaheen, *History*, 160).

52 **queller** killer (*OED* quell *v.* 1), with a bawdy pun in *woman queller* as a man who quells, or subdues, a woman's lust

54 *Q's SP indicates that this line probably was spoken, though not in unison, by both officers rather than only by Fang, as in F. While elsewhere in Q Fang is named in SPs, here the more general SP '*Offic.*' suggests that both Fang and Snare are

calling for assistance in making the arrest. Alternatively, they may be expressing alarm that Bardolph is rescuing Falstaff from their grip. Such forcible 'rescues' of people or goods from legal custody were common in the London streets (*OED* rescue *sb.* 2). Ard² cites Dekker, *1 Honest Whore*, 4.3.141: 'A rescue Prentises, my master's catch-pold' (*Dramatic*, 2.84); and Cowl (Ard¹), Lodowick Barry, *Ram Alley*, 3.1, in which Captain Puff attacks the whore Taffeta – much as Pistol accosts Doll in 2.4 – and asks, 'do you bring / A rescue, goodman knight?' (Dodsley, 10.326).

55 **bring ... two** get someone to help. The Hostess has understood the Officers to be calling for reinforcements to rescue *them* from their own incompetence.

55–6 **Thou wot ... wot ta?** The Hostess lapses into dialect when entering the fray, here probably addressing Falstaff (see 57n.), whom Fang and Snare are having a hard time holding, or possibly Bardolph, whom she tries to prevent from rescuing Falstaff. In either case, the physical struggle involving the Hostess is comic. Her lines, in a modern idiom, mean 'You will, will you? Go ahead and try it, you rogue!' – suggesting perhaps that Falstaff

46 SD] *this edn; A brawl. Oxf*   48 in the channel] *Q; there F*   49, 51 Ah] *a Q; O F*   54 SP] *Q; Fang. F*
55 or two] *Q; not in F*   55–6 Thou . . . ta?] *Q; Thou wilt not? thou wilt not? F*

wot, wot thou? Thou wot, wot ta? – Do, do, thou
rogue! Do, thou hempseed!

PAGE [*to Hostess*]   Away, you scullion, you rampallian,
you fustilarian! I'll tickle your catastrophe.

Enter Lord Chief JUSTICE *and his Men.*

JUSTICE   What is the matter? Keep the peace here, ho!   60
HOSTESS   Good my lord, be good to me. I beseech you
stand to me.

JUSTICE

How now, Sir John? What are you brawling here?
Doth this become your place, your time and business?
You should have been well on your way to York.   65
[*to Fang*] Stand from him, fellow! Wherefore
hang'st thou upon him?

will not have an easy time escaping her
clutches or that she, though a woman,
will be a worthy match for any assailant.
Alternatively, she may be addressing the
Page, who verbally assaults her at 58–9.

57 **hempseed** an epithet that draws on both
honeyseed (the Hostess's blunder for
'homicide', 51) and hemp, used to make
the hangman's rope; thus, a gallows-bird
(*OED sb.*). The term thus logically fits
Falstaff, lending support to the hypothesis
that he is the addressee. Alternatively,
hempseed, as grain, could be a joke about
diminutive size (cf. Mustardseed in
MND), in which case the Hostess would
be addressing the Page.

58 **scullion** the most menial of kitchen servants; thus, a person of the lowest order
rampallian ruffian, villain, scoundrel,
usually applied to a woman

59 **fustilarian** Onions posits a comic
coinage drawn from 'fustilugs', a term
for a fat, frowzy woman.

tickle your catastrophe a jocular threat
meaning to beat or whip someone (Dent,
C187.1); i.e. 'make your backside tingle'
or, more vulgarly, 'whip your arse'; *tickle*,
used ironically, meant beat or chastise
(*OED v.* 6b), and *catastrophe* was a
euphemism for a person's posterior (*OED
sb.* 2b). This line hints at the farcical
nature of the scuffle the Page and the
Hostess are engaged in while Fang and
Snare try to subdue Falstaff and Bardolph.

61 **be good to** protect: an appeal made to
someone in authority (Ard¹)

62 **stand to** support, stand up for; also, given
the Hostess's proclivity for unintended
wordplay, a plea for him to get an
erection. Cf. her asking whether the lusty
Snare will 'stand to't' (4).

63 **What** why. Cf. 1.2.115.

64 **place** social rank, status as a knight

66 **Stand from** let go of: presumably
addressed to Fang, who has been trying to
apprehend Falstaff

58 SP] *F1–2; Boy. Q; Fal. F3–4*   SD] *this edn*   scullion] *Q (*scullian*), F*   59 fustilarian] *Q; Fustillirian F*
tickle] *Q; tucke F*   59.1] *Q; Enter Ch. Iustice. F*   60 What is] *Q; What's F*   63 What] *QF; what, Pope;*
what! *Keightley*   66 thou upon] *Q; vpon F; thou on Pope; on Collier*

HOSTESS   O my most worshipful lord, an't please your
grace, I am a poor widow of Eastcheap, and he is
arrested at my suit.

JUSTICE   For what sum?   70

HOSTESS   It is more than for some, my lord; it is for all
I have! He hath eaten me out of house and home.
He hath put all my substance into that fat belly of his;
[*to Falstaff*] but I will have some of it out again, or
I will ride thee a'nights like the mare.   75

FALSTAFF   I think I am as like to ride the mare if I have
any vantage of ground to get up.

67–8 **an't ... grace** The Hostess misapplies
a deferential phrase, *your grace* usually
reserved for royalty, dukes and archbishops. Cf. 1n. on *Master Fang.*

68 **Eastcheap** the street running eastward
from Cheapside, with fleshly associations
appropriate to Falstaff. According to
Stow's *Survey* (1598), 'This Eastcheape
is now a flesh Market of Butchers there
dwelling . . . it had sometime also Cookes
mixed amongst the Butchers, and such
other as solde victuals readie dressed of
all sorts' (216). It was here, too, that in
1410 the King's sons Thomas and John
reportedly raised a ruckus in a tavern late
one night which had to be quelled by the
mayor and sheriffs (217). In *Famous
Victories*, however, this 'bloody fray'
(2.88) is blamed on Prince Henry and
becomes the occasion of his first arrest.

71 **more ... some** Deaf to her own puns, the
Hostess quite innocently misinterprets
the word *sum* (70).

73 **substance** the food and drink she sells,
but more generally, everything she owns
(*OED sb.* 16)

74 **out** back, returned; i.e. in the form of
payment

75 **I will ... mare** The Hostess here
addresses Falstaff directly. Her simile is

jumbled. By *mare* she probably means
the nightmare or incubus which she will
resemble in her pursuit of him (*OED sb.*[2]
1); but also, through a pun she is ignorant
of, she may identify herself as a horse
(*mare*). Alternatively, by riding Falstaff
like the mare, she implies that he is a
horse she will sit astride until she has
satisfaction. The only certain thing is that
the Hostess inadvertently opens herself to
a bawdy interpretation in *ride thee a'
nights*.

76 **I am ... mare** Falstaff plays on the
sexual meaning of *ride the mare*, saying
that he is as likely (*like*) to do the riding
as she; and if she is the mare, he also
may play on its meaning 'hag' (*OED sb.*[2]
2). Enriching the comic riposte, riding
the wild mare (*OED sb.*[1] 2b) was a game
akin to leap-frog to which Falstaff alludes
at 2.4.249. He adds to these meanings
a possible allusion to hanging: the two-
or three-legged mare was a slang term
for the gallows (*OED sb.*[1] 2a). Falstaff
was concerned about hanging for thievery
in *1H4* (1.2.56–9) and appears to be so
still.

77 **vantage ... up** opportunity to mount –
the horse, the Hostess or the gallows

71 all] *Q (*al*); all:* all *F*   74 SD] *Oxf*[1]   75 a'nights] *Q (*a nights*);* o' Nights *F*

JUSTICE   How comes this, Sir John? What man of good
temper would endure this tempest of exclamation?
Are you not ashamed to enforce a poor widow to so   80
rough a course to come by her own?

FALSTAFF [*to Hostess*]   What is the gross sum that I owe
thee?

HOSTESS   Marry, if thou wert an honest man, thyself
and the money too. Thou didst swear to me upon a   85
parcel-gilt goblet, sitting in my Dolphin chamber at
the round table by a seacoal fire upon Wednesday in
Wheeson week, when the Prince broke thy head for
liking his father to a singing man of Windsor – thou

---

79   **temper** disposition
  exclamation outcry or protest
80   **enforce** compel, oblige (*OED v.* 10)
80–1   **to so ... course** to resort to such crude
  means. The Justice adopts Falstaff's
  imagery of horseback riding.
81   **come ... own** get what is owed her
86   **parcel-gilt** partly gilded, especially common in silverware such as bowls and cups
  whose inner surfaces would be gilt (*OED
  adj.*): cf. 1.2.149–50n. Weis suggests
  that a vow to marry made on such a
  goblet travesties the holy sacraments,
  the goblet possibly substituting for a
  chalice. Melchiori observes that the
  wealth of detail mustered by the Hostess
  may be prompted by her notion of what a
  legal deposition demands. Certainly this
  rambling speech captures her bourgeois
  social aspirations and her fascination with
  material possessions.
  Dolphin chamber Rooms at taverns and
  inns were frequently distinguished by
  names. Cf. the Half-moon and Pomegran-
  ate in *1H4* 2.4.26, 36.
87   **seacoal** generic term for mineral coal, as
  opposed to charcoal, possibly so named
  because it was transported to London by
  sea, usually from Newcastle (*OED sb.*

2a). There was social prejudice against
coal fires at this time because they were
thought to be more unpleasant and
unhealthy than wood fires, though economic pressures were extending their use.
According to Andrew Hope, a document
dated 1615 observed that 'the poorer sort
of the inhabitants of Bristol do use to burn
stone coal alias sea coal in their houses
... not being able to buy wood which is
very dear and scarce to be had'. The
Hostess's using coal for heat may thus
provide a telling detail about the social
standing of her establishment.
88   **Wheeson** northern or midland dialect
  for Whitsun, or Pentecost, the seventh
  Sunday after Easter commemorating the
  descent of the Holy Spirit upon the
  Apostles (Acts, 2). Cf. the Hostess's
  similar pronunciation of *Peesel* for Pistol
  at 2.4.162.
  broke cracked or wounded (*OED* break
  v. 5b). The fact that the Hostess washes
  Falstaff's wound (90) indicates that this
  was no small box in the ear.
89   **liking** likening, comparing (*OED* like
  *v.*² 1b). Though the word may reflect
  the Hostess's dialect, the Q compositor
  may have misread 'lik'ning', the form

---

78 What] *Q;* Fy, what a *F;* Fie, what *Rowe*   82 SD] *this edn*   87 upon] *Q;* on *F*   88 Wheeson] *Q;*
Whitson *F*   89 liking his father] *Q;* lik'ning him *F*

didst swear to me then, as I was washing thy wound,   90
to marry me and make me 'my lady', thy wife. Canst
thou deny it? Did not goodwife Keech the butcher's
wife come in then and call me gossip Quickly, coming
in to borrow a mess of vinegar, telling us she had
a good dish of prawns, whereby thou didst desire to   95
eat some, whereby I told thee they were ill for a
green wound? And didst thou not, when she was gone
downstairs, desire me to be no more so familiarity
with such poor people, saying that ere long they
should call me madam? And didst thou not kiss me,   100

printed in F, owing to confusion over
minims.
singing . . . Windsor This alludes to a
plot to dethrone Henry IV as a pretender.
In the first year of his reign, a priest impersonating Richard II took part in the Abbot
of Westminster's conspiracy to seize Henry
at Windsor, where he was celebrating
Christmas (Holinshed, 3.514–15; Stow,
Annales, 515). The priest has been identified as John Magdalen, who, although
not a professional musician (*singing man*),
was a chaplain of King Richard. The
identification of him as a musician may
have come from Sir Philip Sidney, whose
Discourse to the Queen's Majesty (1580)
warns Elizabeth against pretenders to the
throne: 'Lett the singing man in Henry
the IVths time . . . be sufficient to prove
that occasions geve mindes scope to
stranger thinges then ever would haue
ben imagined' (Feuillerat, 3.53). Singing
men of royal and university chapels
were often satirized as debauchees, as
in Earle's *Microcosmographie* (1628;
no. 69): 'Their pastime or recreation
is prayers, their exercise drinking, yet
herein so religiously addicted that they
serve God oftest when they are drunke'.
Cowl (Ard¹) and Humphreys (Ard², App.
3) review the evidence cogently.

91 **'my lady'** As the wife of a knight, the
Hostess would gain the title of Lady, such
social distinctions apparently of as great
value to her as to Sir John. In his *Description of England* (1577; 2.2) William
Harrison asserts, 'How soeuer one be
dubbed or made Knight, his wife is by
and by called *Madame*, or Ladye' (115).
The absurd prospect of the Hostess's
becoming a Lady glances obliquely at the
threats to gentility made by the merchant
class at this time.
92 **goodwife Keech** A civil form of address,
goodwife simply means mistress of the
house. A keech was a lump of suet which
a butcher would roll up for tallow. In *H8*,
Wolsey is called 'a keech' for being a
butcher's son (1.1.55).
93 **gossip** friend or neighbour, but also a
woman who delights in idle talk (*OED sb.*
2a, 3). Both would apply to the Hostess.
94 **mess** small quantity (*OED sb.* 1c)
95, 96 **whereby** whereupon (*OED adv.* 3b)
97 **green** fresh, unhealed (*OED adj.* 10a)
98 **familiarity** familiar; a stock malapropism
also occurring in Munday's *John a Kent
and John a Cumber* (*c.* 1590), 347–8
(Shaaber, *Variorum*)
100 **madam** a title given to a knight's wife.
Cf. 91n.

97 thou not] *Q;* not thou *F*   98 so familiarity] *Q;* familiar *F*

and bid me fetch thee thirty shillings? I put thee now
to thy book-oath; deny it if thou canst.

FALSTAFF   My lord, this is a poor mad soul, and she says
up and down the town that her eldest son is like you.
She hath been in good case; and the truth is, poverty   105
hath distracted her. But for these foolish officers, I
beseech you I may have redress against them.

JUSTICE   Sir John, Sir John, I am well acquainted with
your manner of wrenching the true cause the false
way. It is not a confident brow, nor the throng of   110
words that come with such more-than-impudent
sauciness from you, can thrust me from a level
consideration. You have, as it appears to me, practised
upon the easy-yielding spirit of this woman, and
made her serve your uses both in purse and in person.   115

HOSTESS   Yea, in truth, my lord.

JUSTICE   Pray thee, peace. [*to Falstaff*] Pay her the debt
you owe her, and unpay the villainy you have done
with her: the one you may do with sterling money,
and the other with current repentance.   120

FALSTAFF   My lord, I will not undergo this sneap

102 **book-oath** oath made on the Bible
104 **her ... you** Falstaff implies that the
     Hostess has accused the Justice of
     fathering her child, a baldly provocative
     attempt to discredit her testimony.
105 **in good case** well off financially, or in
     good physical and mental health (*OED*
     case *sb.* 5a, b). Falstaff implies that a
     sudden change in station has caused the
     Hostess to lose her wits (*distracted her*,
     106).
109 **true cause** truth of the matter
110 **brow** facial expression, countenance
     (*OED sb.* 5b, c)
112 **level** judicious, balanced, impartial
115 **in purse ... person** financially and sexu-

ally. By cutting the speech at *and made
her*, F sanitizes it.
118–19 **done with her** F's omission of *with*
     lessens the likelihood of a sexual reading.
     For *do* as a bawdy pun, see 40–1n.
119–20 **sterling ... current** When used to
     describe coins, both adjectives mean
     genuine or authentic as opposed to
     counterfeit. In them the Justice continues
     his 'numismatic punning' (Lee) begun
     at 1.2.224–5. Paired with *repentance*,
     current means both present and having
     the quality of current coin – that is, of
     money in circulation (*OED adj.* 5).
121 **sneap** rebuke; possibly dialectical for
     'snub'

103 mad] *Q* (*made*), *F*   113 You ... me,] *Q*; I know you ha' *F*   114–15 and ... person.] *Q*; *not in F*
116 Yea, in truth] *Q*; Yes in troth *F*   117 Pray thee] *Q*; Prethee *F*   SD] *Oxf¹*   119 with] *Q*; *not in F*

without reply. You call honorable boldness 'impudent
sauciness'. If a man will make curtsy and say nothing,
he is virtuous. No, my lord, my humble duty
remembered, I will not be your suitor. I say to you   125
I do desire deliverance from these officers, being
upon hasty employment in the King's affairs.

JUSTICE   You speak as having power to do wrong; but
answer in th'effect of your reputation, and satisfy the
poor woman.   130

FALSTAFF   Come hither, hostess. [*Takes her aside.*]

Enter a Messenger[, GOWER].

JUSTICE   Now, Master Gower, what news?

GOWER

The King, my lord, and Harry, Prince of Wales,
Are near at hand; the rest the paper tells.

[*Hands a paper to the Lord Chief Justice, who reads it.*]

FALSTAFF   As I am a gentleman!   135

122–3 **You ... sauciness** Falstaff exculpates
himself by employing a paradiastole, a
rhetorical figure by which, in George
Puttenham's words, 'we do excuse our
own vices, or other men's whom we
defend, by calling them virtues' (154).
Shakespeare apparently drew from Thomas
Hoby's translation of Castiglione's *The
Courtier*, which observes that everyone
praises or blames 'according to his fancie,
always covering a vice with the next
virtue to it ... as in calling him that is
saucie bolde' (see Skinner, 161–72).

123 **make curtsy** pay obeisance or bow to
one's superior (*OED* courtesy *sb.* 8,
curtsy *sb.* 2, 3)

124–5 [2]**my ... remembered** though I am
mindful of the respect due to you. F's

substitution of 'your' for *my* is clearly an
error.

125 **your suitor** one who asks you (sues)
for favours. The imagery of courtship
continues from *make curtsy*.

126 **deliverance** release

128 **as having power** as if you were entitled

129 **answer ... of** behave in a way that befits

131.1 **GOWER** Melchiori suggests that the name
may have been taken from a paragraph
about the poet John Gower in Holinshed's
life of Henry IV (3.541). Shakespeare
used the name again for his English
captain in *H5* and for the Chorus in *Per.*

135, 137 **As ... gentleman** The conversation
between Falstaff and the Hostess has
already begun. His twice-repeated oath –
presumably that he will repay the Hostess

---

123 make] *Q; not in F*   124 my] *Q;* your *F*   126 do] *Q; not in F*   deliverance] *Q;* deliu'rance *F*
129 th'effect] *Q;* the effect *F*   131 SD] *Capell ([taking her aside.); Aside. Pope*   131.1] *Q (after 134)
(enter a messenger); Enter M. Gower F*   133 Harry] *Q; Henrie F*   134 SD] *this edn; [delivering a packet.
Capell*

HOSTESS   Faith, you said so before.

FALSTAFF   As I am a gentleman; come, no more words
of it.

HOSTESS   By this heavenly ground I tread on, I must be
fain to pawn both my plate and the tapestry of my   140
dining chambers.

FALSTAFF   Glasses, glasses is the only drinking. And for
thy walls, a pretty slight drollery, or the story of the
prodigal, or the German hunting in waterwork is
worth a thousand of these bed-hangers and these fly-   145

---

what he owes her – has little credit. The
Justice has instructed Falstaff to *satisfy*
(129) the Hostess by repaying his debts
and perhaps by marrying her; Falstaff,
however, simply begs her for more
money.

136 The Hostess is probably expressing
scepticism, for Falstaff has not kept such
oaths in the past; but she may simply be
acknowledging that she has already
heard his promise.

139 **By . . . on** comic confusion of two oaths:
by the ground I tread on, and by this
heavenly light

140 **fain** content (*OED adj.* 2)
plate tableware: utensils and drinking or
serving vessels made most often of silver
or gold (*OED sb.* 16)

142 **Glasses . . . drinking** Falstaff, eager for
a loan, attempts to rationalize the
Hostess's having to pawn her plate and
tapestries by reassuring her that such
things are out of fashion. In the late 16th
century, glass was replacing metal (*plate*)
as the best quality or most proper (*only*)
drinking ware. In his *Description of
England* (1577; 2.6), William Harrison
reports that 'our gentilitie as lothing
those mettals [gold and silver] . . . do
now generallie choose rather the Venice
glasses both for our wine and beere. . . .

And as this is seene in the gentilitie, so in
the wealthie communaltie the like desire
of glasse is not neglected. . . . The poorest
also will haue glasse if they may' (147).
With her aspirations to bourgeois respectability, the Hostess certainly would not
want to be without.

143 **drollery** comic painting often depicting
coarse goings-on at taverns, country fairs
or soldiers' quarters

143–4 **the story . . . prodigal** Recorded in
Luke, 15.11–32, the parable of the
Prodigal Son was a popular subject
for Elizabethan wall decorations, here
sandwiched irreverently between two
more vulgar subjects.

144 **German . . . waterwork** scenes of boar-
or stag-hunting painted on cloth to
imitate tapestry (*OED waterwork sb.* 4).
The importation of such mass-produced
art from the Continent drew fire from
those who would protect English jobs.
Hall (586–7) records complaints made
during the reign of Henry VIII that 'the
Dutchemen bryng ouer . . . lether and
Weynskot ready wrought, with . . . painted
clothes so that if it were wrought here,
Englishmen mighte haue some worke &
lyuynge by it'.

145 **bed-hangers** cheap curtains around a
bed

---

136 Faith] *Q*; Nay *F*   143 slight] *Q* (sleight), *F*   144 German] *Q* (Iarman), *F* (Germane)   145 bed-
hangers] *Q*; Bed-hangings *F*

bitten tapestries. Let it be ten pounds, if thou canst.
Come, an 'twere not for thy humours, there's not a
better wench in England. Go wash thy face and draw
the action. Come, thou must not be in this humour
with me. Dost not know me? Come, come; I know 150
thou wast set on to this.

HOSTESS   Pray thee, Sir John, let it be but twenty nobles;
i'faith, I am loath to pawn my plate, so God save
me, la!

FALSTAFF   Let it alone; I'll make other shift. You'll be 155
a fool still.

HOSTESS   Well, you shall have it, though I pawn my
gown. I hope you'll come to supper. You'll pay me
all together?

FALSTAFF   Will I live? [*to Bardolph*] Go with her. With 160
her! Hook on, hook on.

---

146 **tapestries** DSK notes that 'tapestrie' was
occasionally used as a plural form, as
in Q: see, for example, John Baret's
Alvearie (1574), which refers to
'tapestrie, or hangings'.

ten pounds The amount Falstaff begs
from the Hostess here is far greater than
the 30 shillings he had bid her fetch when
proposing marriage to her (see 101).

147 **an ... humours** if it were not for your
moods (*OED* humour *sb.* 6c)

148 **wash thy face** evidence that the Hostess
has been crying

148–9 **draw the action** withdraw the lawsuit
(*OED* draw *v.* 37)

151 **set on** put up, incited (*OED* set *v.* 148c).
Whom Falstaff suspects of inciting her to
have him arrested, he does not say.

152 **twenty nobles** The noble being a gold
coin valued at one-third of a pound, the

Hostess tells Falstaff that she is prepared
to give him only six pounds 13 shillings.
Weis is inaccurate in calculating that her
offer is, ironically, exactly equivalent to
the ten pounds he has requested.

155 **Let it alone** 'Forget it.'

make other shift manage some other
way (Onions; *OED* shift *sb.* 6b). Falstaff
is attempting to make the Hostess feel
guilty, and his strategy works. In the next
line, she capitulates.

156 **still** always

159 **all together** everything you owe. The
Hostess wistfully asks for this reassurance from Falstaff before going to fetch
him more money.

160 **Will I live?** 'As sure as I live.'

161 **Hook on** 'Stick with her.' Falstaff
instructs Bardolph to make sure the
Hostess will return with the money.

---

146 tapestries] *F;* tapestrie *Q*   ten pounds] x.£ *Q;* tenne pound *F*   147 an 'twere] *Q (*and twere*);* if it
were *F*   there's] *Q;* there is *F*   149 the] *Q;* thy *F*   150 Dost . . . Come,] *Q; not in F*   152 Pray thee] *Q;*
Prethee *F*   153 i'faith . . . loath] *Q;* I loath *F*   153–4 so . . . me] *Q;* in good earnest *F*   157 though] *Q;*
although *F*   159 all together?] *Rowe;* al together. *Q;* al-together? *F*   160 SD] *Capell ([to Bard.)*

HOSTESS   Will you have Doll Tearsheet meet you at
    supper?
FALSTAFF   No more words; let's have her.
                    Exeunt Hostess and Sergeant [Fang with Snare,
                                           Bardolph and Page].
JUSTICE *[to Gower]*   I have heard better news.   165
FALSTAFF   What's the news, my lord?
JUSTICE *[to Gower]*   Where lay the King tonight?
GOWER   At ^FBasingstoke^F, my lord.
FALSTAFF   I hope, my lord, all's well. What is the news,
    my lord?   170
JUSTICE *[to Gower]*   Come all his forces back?

---

162 **Doll Tearsheet** Doll was a familiar name
for whores in plays of this period: cf.
Dol Common in Jonson's *The Alchemist*
and Doll Target in Dekker's *2 Honest
Whore*. Her surname reveals both her
profession and her temperament. Like the
names of other ahistorical characters who
appear in this play – Fang, Snare, Pistol,
Silence, Shallow and the Gloucestershire
recruits – hers suggests that Shakespeare
was drawing as never before from a
tradition of comically descriptive naming
which would soon be tapped by Jonson
in his comedies of humours. On the
dehumanizing use to which Shakespeare
puts this tradition in *2H4*, see A. Barton,
108–10.

164 SD *Q's placement of the SD after 161
seems to be an error. Perhaps the compositor misplaced a SD written in the
margin opposite 161–4, or conceivably,
if the error originated in a holograph,
Shakespeare added 162–4 as an afterthought but neglected to move the SD.
Sergeant While in Q Fang alone is
designated by '*Sergeant*', the list of
'Actors Names' in F identifies 'Phang,
and Snare' as '2 Serieants'.

165 **better** Q's word suggests that the Justice
is understating the case: the news con-
veyed in the letter is not good. F's 'bitter'
makes his sentiment more explicit.

167 **tonight** i.e. last night (*OED adv.* 3)

168 ***Basingstoke*** F's substitution for Q's
'Billingsgate', which is the London fish
market (and would make no sense as a
place for Henry to spend the night),
Basingstoke is a market town 46 miles
from London on the Great West Road.
The King's sojourn there is mentioned by
none of the sources, but Shakespeare
may have wished to convey that the
King was returning from his Welsh
campaign.

169–79 The Justice ignores Falstaff's attempts
to butt into his conversation with Gower.
When, in exasperation, he finally acknowledges Falstaff's interruption, Falstaff
pays him back by speaking only to
Gower – the dinner invitation is a ruse
– and by ignoring the Justice's attempt
at censure. He plays a comic game of
tit-for-tat.

171–4 Shakespeare deviates from Holinshed,
who reports that the King 'left his iournie
into Wales, and marched with all speed

---

164 SD] *Q (exit hostesse and sergeant.) (after 163);* [*Exeunt* Host. Bar. *Officers, and Boy. Capell*   165 SD]
this edn   better] *Q;* bitter *F*   166 my lord] *Q;* my good lord *F*   167 SD] *this edn*   tonight] *Q;* last night *F*
168, 172 SPs] *Rowe; Mess. Q; Mes. F*   168 Basingstoke] *F;* Billingsgate *Q*   171 SD] *this edn*

GOWER

No; fifteen hundred foot, five hundred horse
Are marched up to my lord of Lancaster
Against Northumberland and the Archbishop.

FALSTAFF

Comes the King back from Wales, my noble lord? 175

JUSTICE [*to Gower*]

You shall have letters of me presently.
Come, go along with me, good Master Gower.

FALSTAFF My lord!

JUSTICE What's the matter?

FALSTAFF Master Gower, shall I entreat you with me to 180
dinner?

GOWER I must wait upon my good lord here. I thank
you, good Sir John.

JUSTICE Sir John, you loiter here too long, being you
are to take soldiers up in counties as you go. 185

FALSTAFF Will you sup with me, Master Gower?

JUSTICE What foolish master taught you these manners,
Sir John?

towards the north parts' (3.529) where
the more dangerous adversaries were
mustering their forces. There is no
evidence of his returning to London
beforehand, nor of the division of troops
mentioned here.

173 **my ... Lancaster** Prince John. See
1.3.82n.

180 **entreat ... me** Modern usage would
require an infinitive such as 'to go' after
you.

182 **wait upon** accompany, attend (*OED* wait
v. 14k)

184–5 *Q's error in printing as irregular
verse lines what is patently prose (and
reads as prose in F) may have arisen
when a compositor assumed that the

Justice would continue to speak in verse,
as he has with Gower at 172–7.

being ... go Falstaff has been commanded to recruit soldiers on his way
north to York. The fact that he takes a
detour west to Gloucestershire to do so
(3.2) strongly suggests that the recruiting
scene may originally have been written
for an earlier draft of a *H4* play describing
Falstaff marching to Shrewsbury via
Coventry with a 'charge of foot' (*1H4*
4.2.1–47), and during which march a
stop in Gloucestershire would have made
more sense geographically.

185 **take soldiers up** enlist, recruit (*OED*
take *v.* 93j)

176 SD] *this edn* 177 Gower] *Q; Gowre F (also at 180, 186)* 184–5] *prose F; Q lines* long, / vp / go. /
185 counties] *Q; Countries F*

FALSTAFF   Master Gower, if they become me not, he
    was a fool that taught them me. – This is the right   190
    fencing grace, my lord: tap for tap, and so part fair.
JUSTICE   Now the Lord lighten thee, thou art a great fool.
                                         ᶠ*Exeunt*ᶠ [*at separate doors*].

2.2   *Enter* PRINCE [Henry *and*] POINS.

PRINCE   Before God, I am exceeding weary.
POINS   Is't come to that? I had thought weariness durst
    not have attached one of so high blood.

189–90 **Master . . . me** a humorous irony: by answering Gower, who did not ask him the question, rather than the Justice, who did, Falstaff gets away with calling the latter a fool for having taught him, by example, to ignore the person speaking to him (*these manners*, 187).

189 **become me not** are impolite or unsuitable (*OED* become *v.* 8b)

190–1 **right fencing grace** proper art of fencing

191 **tap for tap** A *tap* is a light but audible blow (*OED* tap *sb.²* 1); here, metaphoric – 'Tip for tap' (Dent, T352a) or 'Tit for tat' (Tilley, T356).
    fair on good terms, the implication being, 'Now we're even.'

192 **lighten** a pun: (1) enlighten spiritually (*OED v.²* 3), or (2) reduce in weight, followed by a play on *great* meaning fat. Cf. the play on *great* and *slender* at 1.2.141–4.

192 SD Presumably the three exit through two doors: Falstaff through one, the Justice and Gower through the other. On the question of whether the stage required two or three doors, see 1.1.0.1, 1 SDn.

2.2 Though editors tend to locate this scene in a room at the Prince's residence in London, a location is never specified in

the text: it must be private enough for Harry and Poins to have an intimate conversation, but public enough for them to observe the approach of Bardolph and the Page (66–7). The empty stage would have served both purposes and made the need to identify a specific location moot.

0.1 *The inclusion of the phantom '*sir Iohn Russel, with other*' in Q indicates that the compositor was working from unrevised copy in which Shakespeare, as he often did, listed characters who would not enter until later or for whom he then decided not to write a part. In an earlier draft of a *H4* play, Russell was probably the name given to Bardolph, who enters later in this scene and is listed in F's anticipatory entry in place of Russell. If, as Melchiori argues, this short section of Q was set from a sheet of that earlier draft, it would explain why Sir John Russell is silently supplanted by Bardolph at Q 66. Morgann notes that in *Famous Victories*, Harry's boon companions – Ned, Tom and Oldcastle – are three times called *Knights* in SDs (at 5.82, 9.6 and 9.51), and that this may have led Shakespeare to envision three such titled companions for Harry when working on an early draft of *H4*. Russell was the family name of the Earls

192 SD *Exeunt*] *F; not in Q   at separate doors*] *this edn*   **2.2**] *Scena Secunda. F; not in Q*   0.1] *Rowe; Enter the Prince, Poynes, sir Iohn Russel, with other. Q; Enter Prince Henry, Pointz, Bardolfe, and Page. F*   1 Before God] *Q; Trust me F*   2 Is't] *Q; Is it F*

PRINCE Faith, it does me, though it discolours the
complexion of my greatness to acknowledge it. Doth   5
it not show vilely in me to desire small beer?

POINS Why, a prince should not be so loosely studied as
to remember so weak a composition.

PRINCE Belike, then, my appetite was not princely got,
for, by my troth, I do now remember the poor creature   10
small beer. But indeed, these humble considerations
make me out of love with my greatness. What a
disgrace is it to me to remember thy name, or to

of Bedford, as Harvey (*1H4* 1.2.154) was
that of the third husband of the Earl of
Southampton's mother: these names
might have been altered to Bardolph and
Peto at the same time Oldcastle was
changed to Falstaff, and for the same
reason. See pp. 140, 157n, 26.

1 **I . . . weary** The Prince's weariness may
be a sign of despondency, or it may result
from his having just ridden back from
Wales. In *MV*, written perhaps in the
same year, both Antonio and Portia open
scenes (1.1, 1.2) with similar expressions
of weariness.

3 **attached** seized, laid hold of (*OED v.* 3b).
The word is used in its legal sense of
'take into custody' at 4.1.337.

3 **high blood** exalted rank. Poins is making
a facetious remark about the exemption
of royals from common complaints.

4–5 **discolours . . . greatness** makes my
royalty blush in shame

6 **vilely** unseemly, meanly (as of rank or
social condition)
small beer weak or watered-down beer,
typically only 3% or 4% proof and a
staple in the diet of women and children;
figuratively, trifling matters, small things
(*OED* beer *sb.* 1b) – the implication being
that a prince should by nature prefer
strong drink and manly pursuits

7 **loosely studied** badly educated, or
dissolute in his habits

8, 10 **remember** think of, or recall, with
longing (*OED v.* 2a)

8 **so . . . composition** a brew so low in
alcohol content, or a companion so low-
born. With more sarcasm than sympathy
for Harry's dilemma, Poins would perhaps
include himself among such companions.
The play on *composition* as a literary
exercise continues from *studied* (7).

9 **Belike** probably, perhaps
not princely got that is, adulterated by
behaviour (or by low-born companions)
unbefitting a prince

10 **creature** a substance which ministers
to the physical comfort of humankind,
and thus, humorously, liquor (*OED sb.*
1c, 1d). For a similar usage, see *Oth.*
2.3.304–5: 'good wine is a good familiar
creature, if it be well used'.

12 **out . . . greatness** unhappy with my exalted
position and responsibilities; or, unable to
fulfil the expectations of my rank

12–14 **What . . . tomorrow** an allusion to
the belief that a member of the royal
family should not mix with, or deign to
recognize, commoners; but such snobbery
was most typical among parvenus, as
Shakespeare implies in *KJ* 1.1.186–7: 'if
his name be George, I'll call him Peter; /
For new-made honour doth forget men's
names'. Cf. Middleton, *Your Five Gallants*,
2.3.87–9, and Jonson, *The Devil Is an
Ass*, 2.8.6–10.

4 Faith, it does] *Q;* It doth *F*   6 vilely] *F4;* vildly *Q;* vildely *F1–3*   10 by my troth] *Q;* (in troth) *F*

know thy face tomorrow! Or to take note how many
pair of silk stockings thou hast, with these and those   15
that were thy peach-coloured once; or to bear the
inventory of thy shirts, as: one for superfluity and
another for use. But that the tennis-court keeper
knows better than I; for it is a low ebb of linen with
thee when thou keepest not racket there, as thou hast   20
not done a great while, because the rest of the low

15 **with these** apart from these which you
have on
15–16 **these ... once** The implication is that
Poins has only two pairs of stockings, just
as he has only two shirts (17–18): the pair
he has on (*these*) and another pair (*those*)
that used to be *peach-coloured* – a shade
of pink favoured by courtiers – but have
faded from wear, the past tense *were*
justifying Q's *once*. Though F's substitution of 'ones' for *once* is elected by
most editors, perhaps because *thy* seems
to invite it, Q makes the Prince's critique
of Poins's wardrobe more pointed.
16 **bear** i.e. bear in mind
17–18 **one ... use** one for a spare, another to
wear. Harry may be mocking Poins for
owning only two; but like stockings, shirts
were costly markers of social status.
Stubbes, in *Anatomy of Abuses* (1583),
scathingly censures the extravagance of
those who wear them for fashion: 'Their
Shirtes ... are eyther of Camericke,
Holland, Lawne, or els of the finest cloth
that may be got. And of these kinds of
Shirts euery one now doth weare alike
... I haue heard of shirtes that haue cost,
some ten shillings, some twentie, some
fourty, some fiue pound, some twenty
Nobles & (which is horrible to heare)
some ten pound a peece' (94). Falstaff has
earlier bragged, 'I take but two shirts out
with me' to the wars (1.2.208), a sign that
he intends not to exert himself, unlike
Poins at tennis.

18 **that** direct object of *knows*
tennis-court Tennis had become a
popular sport in London, and courts
abounded, though Puritans tended to
frown on them as little different from
ale-houses, dicing-houses, brothels and
other dens of iniquity. Cf. the anonymous
Elizabethan play *Lingua: Or, The Combat
of the Tongue*, 3.4: 'In truth, sir, I was here
before, and missing you, went back into
the city, sought you in every alehouse, inn,
tavern, dicing-house, tennis-court,
stews, and such like places, likely to find
your worship in' (Dodsley, 9.391).
19–20 **it ... there** only running out of shirts
could prevent you from playing there.
Tennis players apparently changed shirts
frequently during a match: Cowl (Ard[1])
cites Fletcher, *Honest Man's Fortune*,
3.1: 'How long doth that [a lord's]
affection] last? perhaps the changing of
some three shirts in the Tennis-Court',
and Jonson, *Cynthia's Revels*, 2.1.66–8:
'he dares tell 'hem, how many shirts he
has sweat at *tennis* that weeke'.
20 **keepest not racket** a play on (1) holding
a tennis racket in hand (i.e. playing a
match), and (2) causing a disturbance
(*racket*), further linking tennis to other
forms of riotous behaviour (*OED* keep *v*.
36)
21–2 **the rest ... holland** The Prince's
wordplay is as intricate as it is scabrous.
The term *holland* refers both to the
Netherlands, where fine linen was made,

15 hast, with] *Q;* hast? (Viz. *F;* hast – videlicet *Oxf[1]*   16 once] *Q;* ones *F*   18 another] *Q;* one other *F*
20 keepest] *Q;* kept'st *F*   21 the low] *Q;* thy Low *F*

countries have ᶠmade a shift toᶠ eat up thy holland.
And God knows whether those that bawl out the
ruins of thy linen shall inherit His kingdom, but
the midwives say the children are not in the fault   25
whereupon the world increases and kindreds are
mightily strengthened.

POINS   How ill it follows, after you have laboured so
hard, you should talk so idly! Tell me, how many

and to the linen itself. The *rest of the low countries* which *eat up* holland may refer to the vexed political relations between Holland and the other Low Countries; but it also may mean that by pawning his shirts (*holland*), Poins has financed his sexual indulgences in brothels, so that *low countries* would play bawdily on 'cunt' (cf. *Ham* 3.2.110: 'Do you think I meant country matters?', and Jonson, *Every Man Out*, 3.6.54–5: 'This rapier, sir, has trauail'd by my side, sir, [to] the best part of *France* and the *low Countrey*'). A third alternative suggests that *the low countries* are Poins's own genitals which, either dirty from poor hygiene or suppurating from venereal disease, have ruined his undergarments which, like shirts, were sometimes made of linen. In any case, the conclusion is that Poins has not played tennis in a long time.

22 **made ... to** a punning phrase clearly authorial and perhaps inadvertently omitted by the Q compositor: without it, *eat* functions as a past participle; *made a shift* can be taken to mean both (1) contrived or managed (*OED* shift *sb.* 10a, 6b), and (2) changed shirts, or underwear. Cf. Falstaff: 'I'll make other shift' (2.1.155).

23–7 F omits these lines perhaps not so much on account of their bawdy innuendo as of their profanity. Bringing God into Poins's dirty linen was beyond the pale.

23–4 **those ... linen** The children Poins has fathered *bawl out* of – cry while wrapped in – his ruined linen, suggesting either that their swaddling clothes are made from his discarded shirts or that his pawning of those shirts led directly to the sexual congress by which the bastards were conceived.

24 **inherit His kingdom** go to heaven (Matthew, 25.34)

25–7 ***the children ... strengthened** Most editors adopt Theobald's punctuation, which oddly disjoins *whereupon* from *fault* and gives the final two clauses the force of aphorism: 'this is the way the world multiplies and families (*kindreds*) are fortified'. But Q's lack of punctuation implies a syntactically dependent relationship among the clauses which makes perfectly good sense: that the bastards 'are not in the fault whereupon' means that they 'are not to blame for being the cause that' the world multiplies.

28–9 **How ... idly!** Poins upbraids Harry for having so little substance to show for all the effort he has just exerted on witticisms at his expense. In essence, he is retaliating by telling Harry that his humour has failed to hit the mark.

28 **ill** unfortunately or unworthily, connoting deficiency of performance (*OED adv.* 5, 6)
   follows implies consequence or result: such hard labour has yielded such poor results (*OED v.* 16).

29 **idly** vacuously, ineffectively

22 made . . . to] *F; not in Q*   23–7] *Q; not in F*   23 bawl] *Q (*bal*); Pope*   out] *Q; out of Pope;* out from *Capell*   25 fault whereupon] *Q;* fault; whereupon *Theobald*   26 kindreds] *Q (*kinreds*); Pope*

good young princes would do so, their fathers being   30
so sick as yours at this time is?

PRINCE   Shall I tell thee one thing, Poins?

POINS   Yes, faith, and let it be an excellent good thing.

PRINCE   It shall serve among wits of no higher breeding
than thine.   35

POINS   Go to, I stand the push of your one thing that you
will tell.

PRINCE   Marry, I tell thee it is not meet that I should be
sad now my father is sick, albeit I could tell to thee,
as to one it pleases me for fault of a better to call my   40
friend, I could be sad, and sad indeed, too.

POINS   Very hardly, upon such a subject.

PRINCE   By this hand, thou thinkest me as far in the
devil's book as thou and Falstaff for obduracy and
persistency. Let the end try the man. But I tell thee,   45

30–1 **their . . . is** By bringing up the touchy
subject of the Prince's relationship with
his father, Poins continues to retaliate.
Though King Henry admits to being
'shaken' and 'wan with care' at the
opening of *1H4* (1.1.1), this the first
mention of the King's illness in either
play, and it helps prepare for his eventual
death in 4.3. Surprisingly, however,
when the King appears at 3.1 – a scene
omitted from the first issue of Q – there is
no acknowledgement of his illness. See
3.1n.

33 **an . . . thing** i.e. something worthier than
your recent quips

36 **Go to** an expression of disapproval,
remonstrance, protest or incredulity, akin
to 'Come, come!' (*OED* go *v*. 93b)
stand the push can withstand the
mockery. Cf. *1H4* 3.2.66.

38 **meet** fitting (*OED adj*. 3). Harry acknowledges that his rebellious behaviour in
1H4, which has so displeased his father,

might make his sympathy for him now
look hypocritical: cf. 50–1.

40 **fault** lack (*OED sb*. 1c; Dent, F106)

42 **Very hardly** with much difficulty (*OED*
hardly *adv*. 6). Poins is sceptical that Harry
feels genuine concern for his father.

43 **By this hand** a mild oath

43–4 **in . . . book** possibly a reference to the
superstition that the devil kept a register
with the names of all those subject to him;
but more likely derived from 'in a
person's books', meaning to be in favour
with (here) the devil (*OED* book *sb*. 15;
Tilley, B534)

44–5 **obduracy and persistency** i.e. persistence in evil. The *OED* defines both
words similarly and quotes this line as the
earliest example of each.

45 **Let . . . man** Judge things by their final
outcome; proverbial: 'The end tries all'
(Dent, E116.1). Cf. Ecclesiasticus,
111.27, 'In a mans ende, his workes are
discouered'.

30 being] *Q*; lying *F*   31 at this time] *Q*; *not in F*   33 faith,] *Q*; *not in F*   36–7 you will] *Q*; you'l *F*
38 Marry,] *Q (*Mary*);* Why, *F*   43 By this hand,] *Q*; *not in F*   thinkest] *Q*; think'st *F*

my heart bleeds inwardly that my father is so sick;
and keeping such vile company as thou art hath in
reason taken from me all ostentation of sorrow.

POINS   The reason?

PRINCE   What wouldst thou think of me if I should   50
weep?

POINS   I would think thee a most princely hypocrite.

PRINCE   It would be every man's thought, and thou art a
blessed fellow to think as every man thinks. Never a
man's thought in the world keeps the roadway better   55
than thine. Every man would think me an hypocrite
indeed. And what accites your most worshipful
thought to think so?

POINS   Why, because you have been so lewd and so
much engraffed to Falstaff.   60

PRINCE   And to thee.

POINS   By this light, I am well spoke on: I can hear it
with mine own ears. The worst that they can say of

---

47 **vile** unsuitably mean, of low rank. Cf.
1.2.18.

47–8 **in reason** accordingly, justifiably
(*OED* reason *sb.* 13b)

48 **ostentation** show, outward appearance
(*OED sb.* 2)

50–1 from the aphorism 'The weeping of
an heir is laughter under a visor' (Dent,
W248.1), which can be traced to the Latin
author Aulus Gellius (Ard¹)

52 **princely** an allusion both to Harry's title
and, as an intensifier, to the magnitude of
his hypocrisy

53–4 **thou ... thinks** Harry's phrase *blessed
fellow* is contemptuous, for he knows that
every man's thought is wrong and he
perhaps feels disappointment that Poins,
whom he calls friend (40–1), should so
misconstrue him.

55 **man's ... world**   The   prepositional
phrase *in the world* belongs with *man's*
rather than with *thought*.
keeps the roadway is more predictable

57 **accites** induces, incites; also a legal term
meaning to cite or to summon (cf.
5.2.140) which leads to further punning
below

57–8 **your ... thought**   Continuing   the
sarcasm begun at *blessed* (54), the Prince
invents a title of mock respect for Poins's
thought, representing it as 'a magistrate
... sitting in judgment on Hal's conduct'
(Cam¹).

59 **lewd** vulgar, base

60 **engraffed** closely attached; an image
from gardening (cf. 5.3.3)

62 **By this light** sometimes 'by this heavenly
light'; a mild oath
on of

me is that I am a second brother and that I am a proper
fellow of my hands, and those two things I confess   65
I cannot help. By the mass, here comes Bardolph.

Enter BARDOLPH *and* Boy [PAGE].

PRINCE   And the boy that I gave Falstaff. 'A had him
from me Christian, and look if the fat villain have not
transformed him ape.

BARDOLPH   God save your grace.   70

PRINCE   And yours, most noble Bardolph.

POINS   [*to Bardolph*]   Come, you virtuous ass, you
bashful fool, must you be blushing? Wherefore blush
you now? What a maidenly man at arms are you

64 **a second brother** Younger sons of the
gentry, according to the laws of primo-
geniture, inherited nothing of substance
and therefore had to eke out a living for
themselves.

64–5 **a proper . . . hands** good with my
fists (or with a sword). Dent (M163) cites
as proverbial: 'He's a tall man of his
hands.' In context, this phrase could
metaphorically define a man of valour,
skill or practical ability (*OED* hand *sb.*
30a).

66 **By the mass** a mild oath, referring to the
celebration of the Eucharist

67–8 **'A . . . Christian** i.e. the Page looked
like a normal boy (*Christian*) when Harry
gave him to Falstaff. *'A* = he.

69 **transformed him ape** dressed him up
fantastically as one would a performing
ape, with a hint that the Page is now an
imitator (*ape*) of Falstaff's own wit and
manners

71 **And yours** The Prince plays on *your
grace* as a mock form of address for
Bardolph, and in so doing may express

comic concern that Bardolph is a soul
whom God has not chosen to receive
grace.

72 SP *Although some editors, following
Theobald and Johnson, attribute this
speech to Bardolph as an attack on the
Page for being a 'maidenly man at arms',
a phrase which paradoxically grants him
soldiership and yet genders him female (a
demeaning emasculation commonly used
to characterize pre-pubescent boys), the
QF attribution of the speech to Poins need
not be changed, for it mercilessly mocks
Bardolph's *blushing* – the red face which
is his most noteworthy feature (cf.
1.2.48n.) – as a sign not of his excessive
drinking, but of his *bashful* modesty in
deflowering a pot of ale (see 75–6n.). The
Page confirms the import of Poins's joke
in the following speech.

72 **virtuous** preferable to F's 'pernitious' in
its proverbial association with blushing:
'Blushing (Bashfulness) . . . is virtue's
color' (Tilley, B480)

66 By the mass,] *Q;* Looke, looke, *F*   66.1] *Q; Enter Bardolfe. F (after 69); Enter Bardolph, and Page. /
Rowe (after 69)*   67 'A] *Q;* he *F*   68 look] *Q;* see *F*   70 God] *Q; not in F*   72 SP] *QF; Bard. /
Theobald*   SD] *Ard²; to the Boy / Johnson*   virtuous] *Q;* pernitious *F*

become! Is't such a matter to get a pottle-pot's   75
maidenhead?

PAGE   'A calls me e'en now, my lord, through a red
lattice, and I could discern no part of his face from
the window. At last I spied his eyes, and methought
he had made two holes in the ale-wife's petticoat and   80
so peeped through.

PRINCE [*to Poins*]   Has not the boy profited?

BARDOLPH [*to Page*]   Away, you whoreson upright
    ᶠrabbitᶠ! Away!

PAGE [*to Bardolph*]   Away, you rascally Althaea's dream!   85
    Away!

---

75 **matter** momentous act, big thing
75–6 **get . . . maidenhead** open and consume
    a pot of ale. Cf. *Mucedorus*, 3.5: 'I call'd
    for three pots of ale, as 'tis the manner of
    us courtiers. Now, sirrah, I had taken the
    maidenhead of two of them' (Dodsley,
    7.234). Poins continues to belittle Bardolph,
    implying that the only deflowering he is
    capable of is breaking the seal of an ale-pot.
75 **pottle-pot** two-quart pot or tankard
77 **'A . . . now** 'He called me just a little
    while ago.' The Page's use of the historic
    present (Sisson, 2.45) embellishes Poins's
    mockery of Bardolph by providing a scato-
    logical context for it. Q's 'enow', the plural
    form of 'enough', for 'e'en now' may
    have been a compositorial misreading.
    my lord The Page addresses the Prince
    specifically, not Poins, probably out of
    deference.
77–8 **red lattice** i.e. from inside an ale-house.
    Red lattice windows were traditional at
    taverns: the Page implies that he could
    not distinguish (*discern*) the colour of
    Bardolph's face from that of the window.
    Cowl (Ard¹) cites George Wilkins, *The
    Miseries of Enforced Marriage*, 3.1: 'Be
    mild in a tavern? 'tis treason to the red

lattice, enemy to their sign-post, and
slave to humour' (Dodsley, 9.510); and
Humphreys (Ard²) cites Marston, *Antonio
and Mellida*, 5.2.124–5: 'I am not as well
knowne by my wit, as an alehouse by a
red lattice' (Marston, 1.58).
80 **ale-wife's petticoat** The Page intimates
    that Bardolph was underneath the petti-
    coat of the barmaid, and thus perhaps
    engaged in a sexual act. Characterized
    as a prostitute by such activity, she
    may possibly be identified as Mistress
    Quickly, whose tavern was the favourite
    haunt of Falstaff and his companions.
82 **profited** i.e. from Falstaff's teaching, for
    the Page has just demonstrated a budding
    Falstaffian wit. The Prince is probably
    more sarcastic than admiring: see 69n.
83 **whoreson** See 1.2.15n.
84 ***rabbit** F's substitution of *rabbit* for
    'rabble' may correct a misreading by the
    Q compositor: a rabbit walking upright
    offers a humorous image of the Page,
    where Q's 'rabble', a contemptuous term
    usually used collectively for a mob,
    would make little sense.
85 **Althaea's dream** Shakespeare's confla-
    tion of two classical myths demonstrates

---

75 Is't] *Q;* Is it *F*   77 'A calls] *Q;* He call'd *F*   e'en now] *Cam;* euen now *F;* enow *Q*   80 ale-wife's]
Capell; ale wiues *Q;* Ale-wiues *F*   petticoat] *Q;* new Petticoat *F;* new red petticoat *(Collier);* red peticote
Oxf   81 so] *Q; not in F*   82, 83, 85 SDs] *this edn*   82 Has] *Q;* Hath *F*   84 rabbit] *F (*Rabbet*);* rabble *Q*

PRINCE   Instruct us, boy: what dream, boy?

PAGE   Marry, my lord, Althaea dreamt she was delivered
of a firebrand, and therefore I call him her dream.

PRINCE   A crown's worth of good interpretation; there   90
'tis, boy. [*Gives him a coin.*]

POINS   O, that this blossom could be kept from cankers!
Well, there is sixpence to preserve thee. [*Gives him
a coin.*]

BARDOLPH   An you do not make him hanged among
you, the gallows shall have wrong.   95

PRINCE   And how doth thy master, Bardolph?

BARDOLPH   Well, my lord. He heard of your grace's
coming to town. There's a letter for you. [*Hands
letter to Prince.*]

POINS   Delivered with good respect. And how doth the
Martlemas your master?   100

the Page's ignorance: (1) Hecuba, when
pregnant with Paris, prophetically dreamt
that she gave birth to a firebrand that set
fire to Troy (Ovid, *Heroides*, 16; cf. *TC*
2.2.110); and (2) Althaea, at the birth of
her son Meleager, was told by the Fates
that he would live so long as the brand
they had placed on the fire was not
burned. Althaea quenched the flame; but
when Meleager, as an adult, killed her
brothers, she in revenge threw the brand
into the fire and Meleager expired (Ovid,
Met., 8.425–525; cf. *2H6* 1.1.231–2). In
either case, the Page intends the firebrand to be a disparaging reference to
Bardolph's red face.

90–1 Harry's praise for the Page's scholarship is gently ironic. A *crown*, a coin
worth five shillings, was a not insignificant reward.

92 **cankers** pests or diseases which destroy
plants; figurative here for Falstaff,

Bardolph and the other roisterers who are
corrupting the Page. From the proverbial
'The canker soonest eats the fairest rose'
(Dent, C56).

93 **sixpence ... thee** an anachronistic allusion to the cross stamped on Elizabethan
sixpenny coins

94–5 **An ... you** 'if your collective influence doesn't manage to get him hanged'.
Bardolph is counter-attacking.

95 **have wrong** suffer an injustice. F's 'be
wrong'd' means the same thing.

99 **good respect** due deference. Poins uses
irony to criticize the unceremonious way
Bardolph delivers the letter to the Prince.
The letter is one of those Falstaff gave to
the Page at 1.2.238–42.

100 **Martlemas** a reference to Falstaff. The
feast of St Martin, or Martinmas (11 November), was associated with the slaughter
of hogs and cattle to ensure sufficient
meat for the winter. References to

88 Althaea] *Q* (Althear), *F*   dreamt] *Q* (dreampt); dream'd *F*   91 'tis] *Q*; it is *F*   91, 93 SDs] *this edn*
92 this] *Q*; this good *F*   94 An] *Q*; If *F*   him] *Q*; him be *F*   95 have wrong] *Q*; be wrong'd *F*   97 my]
Q; my good *F*   98 SD] *this edn*

BARDOLPH   In bodily health, sir.

POINS   Marry, the immortal part needs a physician, but
that moves not him: though that be sick, it dies not.

PRINCE   I do allow this wen to be as familiar with me as
my dog; and he holds his place, for look you how he   105
writes. [*Shows Poins the letter.*]

POINS [*Reads.*]   *John Falstaff, Knight.* – Every man
must know that, as oft as he has occasion to name
himself, even like those that are kin to the King; for
they never prick their finger but they say, 'There's   110
some of the King's blood spilt!' 'How comes that?'
says he that takes upon him not to conceive. The

Martlemas beef abound in writings of
this period, and Harry's labelling Falstaff
'my sweet beef' in *1H4* (3.3.176)
suggests that *Martlemas* may similarly,
if contemptuously, invoke Falstaff's
corpulence and gluttony. The term
possibly alludes as well to Falstaff's
being in the autumn of his life.

102–3 **the immortal ... not** a humorous
allusion to Matthew, 9.12: 'They that
be whole, nede not a phisition, but they
that are sicke'. The implication is that
Falstaff's soul is in peril.

103 **moves** troubles, disquiets, motivates to
change (*OED v.* 9a, 10a), with a possible
pun on bodily motion. Physical rather
than spiritual health would be responsible
for 'moving' Falstaff.

104 **wen** lump, wart or fatty tumour; thus, as
Johnson glosses, 'a swoln excrescence of
a man' (Ard[1])

105 **dog** a reversal of 1.2.147, where Falstaff
calls the Prince his dog

holds his place insists upon his rank

107 SP *Some editors assign this speech
to the Prince as a continuation of his

previous lines, but there is no reason
to think that Poins should not read the
salutation himself. Conceivably, he
takes the letter from the Prince when
invited to 'look ... how he writes'
(105–6), only to have the Prince snatch it
back at 116 when he tires of Poins's
lengthy commentary. Alternatively, Poins
may simply be reading over Harry's
shoulder.

107–9 **Every ... himself** As F's punctuation makes clear, *that* is the object of
know and refers to Falstaff's knighthood, which title he uses whenever
he names himself. In Q, the lack of a
comma between *that* and what follows
makes the syntax ambiguous, allowing
one to read *that* as the beginning of a
relative clause which is never completed.
As in 1.2.180, this line may contain
an implicit reference to the name by
which Falstaff was known originally,
Oldcastle.

112 **takes ... conceive** pretends not to
understand

105 how] *Q; not in F*   106 SD] *this edn*   107 SP] *QF; not in Sisson*   SD] *Rowe; Letter. F; not in Q*
Every] *QF; Poins.* Every *Sisson*   108 that, as] *F;* that as *Q*   has] *Q;* hath *F*   110 There's] *Q;* there is *F*
111–12 that?' ... that] *F4 subst., Rowe;* that (saies he) that *Q, F1–3 subst.*   112 conceive. The] *F4 subst.,
Rowe;* conceiue? the *F1–3;* conceiue the *Q*

answer is as ready as a borrower's cap: 'I am the
King's poor cousin, sir!'

PRINCE   Nay, they will be kin to us, or they will fetch   115
it from Japheth. But the letter: [*Reads.*] *Sir John*
Falstaff, Knight, to the son of the King nearest his
father, Harry, Prince of Wales, greeting.

POINS   Why, this is a certificate.

PRINCE   Peace! [*Reads.*] *I will imitate the honourable*   120
Romans in brevity.

POINS   He sure means brevity in breath: short-winded.

[PRINCE] [*Reads.*]   *I commend me to thee, I commend*

---

113 ***borrower's cap** Warburton's conjecture
has been widely accepted, because it
is customary to think of a borrower
as always having cap in hand: cf. *Tim*
2.1.16–19. Poins argues that those
who claim kinship with the King pre-
dictably find excuses to broadcast the
relationship. QF's 'borrowed cap' makes
little sense.

115–16 **fetch . . . Japheth** If they cannot
claim royal kinship, they will *fetch*
their lineage from Japheth, third son
of Noah, from whom all Europeans (or
Gentiles) were thought to have descended
(Genesis, 10.2–5).

119 **a certificate** In a letter, the name of the
addressee should come before that of the
writer. By putting his own name before
that of the Prince, Falstaff not only shows
presumption, but adopts the form of a
licence or patent (*certificate*) issued by a
sovereign to a subject.

121 **Romans** The allusion is disputed. It
may refer to Pliny the Younger, whose
style was epigrammatic; or to Brutus,
who, according to Plutarch, affected the
'brief compendious manner of speech of

the Lacedaemonians'; or to Julius Caesar,
whose terse summary of his victory at
Zela, used in his address to the senate in
47 BC, Falstaff parodies at 123–4 and
translates at 4.2.41–2. Given the plural,
Romans, Falstaff is probably alluding
not to an individual but to a general
trait, though Warburton's emendation to
a singular 'Roman' better introduces
Falstaff's parody of Caesar.

123 SP ***As Q and F omit this SP, it appears
that Poins continues to speak here, but
certainly this is an error. Not only
would the Prince probably read his
own letter, but Q prints '*Poynes*' in the
SP at 132, evidence that someone else
has been speaking the previous lines.
Without an intervening SP, printing
'*Poynes*' at 132 would be unnecessary.
Cf. 107 SPn.

123–4 ¹*I commend . . .* ²*thee* In his version
of Roman brevity, Falstaff parodies the
Latin tricolon known by every schoolboy,
veni, vidi, vici ('I came, I saw, I
conquered'), which Julius Caesar used in
addressing the senate. See 121n., and cf.
1.1.21n. and 4.2.41–2.

---

113 borrower's] *Theobald (Warburton);* borowed *Q;* borrowed *F*   115 or] *Q;* but *F*   116 Japheth] *QF*
*(*Iaphet*)   But] *Q;* But to *F*   letter: [*Reads.*] *Sir*] *Oxf¹ subst.;* letter, Sir *Q;* Letter: – *Sir F;* letter. / Poin.
Reads. Sir / Betterton;* letter. / *Poins.* Sir *Hanmer*   119 SP] *QF; not in Betterton*   120 SD] *McEachern*
121 Romans] *Q (*Romanes*), F (*Romaines*);* Roman *Warburton*   122 He sure] *Q;* Sure he *F*   123 SP]
Theobald; not in QF   SD] *McEachern*

thee, and I leave thee. Be not too familiar with Poins,
for he misuses thy favours so much that he swears   125
thou art to marry his sister Nell. Repent at idle times
as thou mayst, and so farewell.

> *Thine by yea and no – which is as much as to*
> *say, as thou usest him – Jack Falstaff with my*
> *family, John with my brothers and sisters, and*   130
> *Sir John with all Europe.*

POINS   My lord, I'll steep this letter in sack and make
him eat it!

PRINCE   That's to make him eat twenty of his words. But
do you use me thus, Ned? Must I marry your sister?   135

POINS   God send the wench no worse fortune, but I
never said so.

---

126 ***at idle times*** at your leisure; or possibly, for your idleness (Cam²). Falstaff parodies the pious wishes common in letters of the time.

128 ***by ... no*** a mild citizens' oath derived from Matthew, 5.34–7 – 'But I say vnto you, Sweare not at all, nether by heauen, for it is ye throne of God . . . But let your communication be Yea, yea: Nay, nay. For whatsoeuer is more then these, commeth of euil' – and consistent with Falstaff's other uses of Puritan pieties: cf. 1.2.37. It may be a vestige of the satire on Oldcastle's Lollardism (see pp. 67–70), though Shallow uses the same phrase at 3.2.9. For similarly parodic use of the phrase, see J. Cooke, *How a Man May Choose a Good Wife from a Bad* (Dodsley, 9.61–2).

129 ***as ... him*** i.e. depending on how you treat him. Dent cites 'To use as one is used' as proverbial (U25.1). Cf. *TN* 3.4.163–4.

130 *family* Though most editors prefer F's 'familiars', Q's *family* draws a distinction

between his blood relations and those Puritans who call one another brothers and sisters.

brothers and sisters another possible survival of satire on Puritanism manifest in Oldcastle. That Falstaff's Puritan *brothers and sisters* should call him *John* indicates a formality lacking in the more familiar *Jack* used by his blood relations.

131 ***Sir John*** Falstaff's letter ends as it began, by trumpeting his title. Cf. 107–9n.

132 **sack** See 1.2.198n. on *new . . . sack*, and cf. *canaries*, 2.4.27.

133 **eat it** Cowl cites other plays in which a character is forced to eat a letter or document onstage, though Falstaff is never made to do so (Ard¹). Most pertinent, the Summoner in *1 Oldcastle* is forced to swallow the summons he has come to serve on Sir John (6.42–76).

134 **twenty** a large number (*OED adj.* 1d)

135 **use** abuse

126 *Nell*] *Q (*Nel), *F*   130 *family*] *Q; Familiars F   sisters*] *Q; Sister F*   132 SP] *Q; not in F*   I'll] *Q (*Ile); I will *F*   136 God . . . wench] *Q; May the Wench haue *F*

240

PRINCE   Well, thus we play the fools with time, and the
spirits of the wise sit in the clouds and mock us. – Is
your master here in London?   140
BARDOLPH   Yea, my lord.
PRINCE   Where sups he? Doth the old boar feed in the
old frank?
BARDOLPH   At the old place, my lord, in Eastcheap.
PRINCE   What company?   145
PAGE   Ephesians, my lord, of the old church.
PRINCE   Sup any women with him?

138 **thus . . . time** Cf. *Son* 124.13–14: 'To
this I witness call the fools of time, /
Which die for goodness, who have lived
for crime'; and Ephesians, 5.15–16:
'Walke circumspectly, not as fooles, but
as wise, redeeming the time'.
138–9 **the . . . us** Cf. Psalms, 2.4: 'He that
dwelleth in heauen shal laugh them to
scorne: the Lorde shall haue them in
derision'.
142–3 **Doth . . . frank?** possibly proverbial,
though Tilley cites this as the earliest
instance: 'He feeds like a boar in a frank'
(B483), a *frank* being a sty or pig-pen.
Falstaff is elsewhere called a *brawn*
(1.1.19; *1H4* 2.4.107) and a *boar-pig*
(2.4.232). This line provides the only hint
in either part of *H4* that the location of
Falstaff's revelry may have been the
Boar's Head – what is called in *Famous
Victories* 'the old tavern in Eastcheap'
(1.74). Although there is no evidence that
a Boar's Head existed during the reign of
Henry IV, several taverns in Tudor
London bore the name, the first reference
to one dating from a lease in 1537 (Ard[2]).
Sugden writes that '[t]his famous hos-
telry' was located on the north side of
Great Eastcheap and abutted at the back
St Michael's Church in Crooked Lane
(66).
144 **Eastcheap** See 2.1.68n.

146 i.e. roistering companions or heavy
drinkers; with reference to Paul's warning
to the Ephesians against wickedness and
drunkenness (Shaheen cites Ephesians,
5.3–4, 5.7 and 5.18). Cf. *MW* 4.5.17,
where the Host of the Garter Inn calls
himself Falstaff's 'Ephesian'. The *old
church* most obviously refers to paganism
– that is, to the Ephesians' degeneracy
before their conversion; but there may
also be a sly glance at 'the prime church
of Ephesus' which was taken to provide
a model of church government for
the reform movement (Ard[1]). Such
irreverence informs a comic passage in
1 Oldcastle, 13.129–31: 'I am neither
heretic nor puritan, but of the old church.
I'll swear, drink ale, kiss a wench, go to
mass, eat fish all Lent, and fast Fridays
with cakes and wine' – such behaviours
as Falstaff and his companions practise
religiously. Still another possible reference is to the cult of Diana, called the
'olde religion' in marginal notes to the
Geneva Bible (Acts, 19.22–4), which
was identified with the period's officially
displaced old religion, Roman Catholicism, whose idolatrous practices and
grounding in worldly authority could be
understood as code for the transgres-
sive behaviours of Falstaff (R. Martin,
225–6).

141 Yea] *Q;* Yes *F*

PAGE   None, my lord, but old Mistress Quickly and
    Mistress Doll Tearsheet.

PRINCE   What pagan may that be?   150

PAGE   A proper gentlewoman, sir, and a kinswoman of
    my master's.

PRINCE   Even such kin as the parish heifers are to the
    town bull. – Shall we steal upon them, Ned, at
    supper?   155

POINS   I am your shadow, my lord; I'll follow you.

PRINCE   Sirrah – you boy, and Bardolph – no word to
    your master that I am yet come to town. There's for
    your silence. [*Gives them coins.*]

BARDOLPH   I have no tongue, sir.   160

PAGE   And for mine, sir, I will govern it.

PRINCE   Fare you well. Go.   [*Exeunt Bardolph and Page.*]
    This Doll Tearsheet should be some road.

POINS   I warrant you, as common as the way between
    Saint Albans and London.   165

---

150 **pagan** heathen, a continued reference
to the Ephesians. It could also mean
'whore' (*OED sb.* 2b), though it would
then anticipate the exchange between the
Prince and Poins at 163–5.

151 **proper gentlewoman** woman of good
breeding and respectable character

154 **town bull** a bull kept at parish or town
expense to service the local heifers; used
figuratively for promiscuous men or
whoremasters. Tilley cites later instances,
such as 'The town bull is as much a
bachelor as he' (B716); Dent dates the
phrase from Harington's 1591 translation
of Ariosto's *Orlando Furioso*: 'the towne
Bull of the Parish' (B716).
steal upon surprise through stealth

160 'I won't say a word.'

163 **should be** is likely to be
road whore: a woman whose body bears
the traffic of men indiscriminately. Cf.
Tilley, 'As common as the highway'
(H457), or Dent, 'As common as the
cartway' (C109), an expression that dates
back at least as far as *Piers Plowman*,
3.127. Cowl (Ard[1]) cites Wilkins's *The
Miseries of Enforced Marriage*, 3.3, in
which the Sister complains, 'Shall I be
left then like a common road, / That
every beast that can but pay his toll / May
travel over?' (Dodsley, 9.522).

164–5 **the way ... London** the Great North
Road, particularly heavily travelled

---

149 Tearsheet] *Q (*Tere-sheet*),* F *(Teare-sheet)*   153–5] *prose Q; F lines* Towne-Bull? / Supper? /
153 heifers] *Q (*Heicfors*),* F *(*Heyfors*)*   157–9] *prose Q; F lines* your / Towne. / silence. /   158 come to] *Q;*
in *F*   159 SD] *Capell subst.; not in QF*   162 you] *Q;* ye *F*   SD] *Capell subst.; not in QF*   162–3] *prose
Q; F lines* go. / Rode. /

PRINCE   How might we see Falstaff bestow himself
tonight in his true colours and not ourselves be seen?
POINS   Put on two leathern jerkins and aprons, and wait
upon him at his table as drawers.
PRINCE   From a god to a bull? A heavy descension: it   170
was Jove's case. From a prince to a prentice? A low
transformation: that shall be mine, for in everything
the purpose must weigh with the folly. Follow me, Ned.

Exeunt.

2.3   *Enter* [*the* Earl of] NORTHUMBERLAND,
his wife[, LADY NORTHUMBERLAND], *and the*
wife to Harry Percy[, LADY PERCY].

NORTHUMBERLAND
I pray thee, loving wife and gentle daughter,
Give even way unto my rough affairs.

---

166 **bestow** employ, comport (*OED v.* 5)
167 **in . . . colours** proverbial for 'according
to his real nature' (Dent, C520.1),
'colours' probably originally referring to
the distinguishing insignia of a knight
(*OED* colour *sb.* 6a, b)
168 **jerkins** close-fitting jackets or jerseys
169 **drawers** tapsters; young men who draw
(tap) ale at a tavern, usually apprenticed
to a publican. Cf. *prentice*, 171.
170–1 **From . . . case** an allusion to Ovid,
Met., 2.846–76, where Jove transforms
himself into a bull to rape Europa. The
Prince's recollection of Ovid may have
been prompted by his mention of the
town bull at 154.
170 **heavy descension** weighty descent,
serious falling off
171 **prentice** apprentice. See 169n.
   low ignoble or trivial, in contrast to
heavy at 170. The Prince envisages his

own metamorphosis as a comic reduction
of Jove's.
173 **weigh with** be weighed against,
counterbalance
2.3 Like 1.1, this scene presumably takes
place in Warkworth Castle, the Earl of
Northumberland's principal residence.
According to Holinshed (3.530), 'too
much haste of the Archbishop' was the
primary reason that Northumberland
failed to join his confederates at Gaultree
Forest, and only after the routing of the
rebels there did he resolve to flee north
to Berwick in Scotland. By having
Northumberland bow to the will of his
wife and daughter-in-law and decide for
reasons of personal safety not to join
forces with the Archbishop (65–7),
Shakespeare in this scene fashions his
own history, turning the *result* of defeat at
Gaultree into a *cause* of that defeat and

---

168 leathern] *Q;* Leather *F*   169 as] *Q;* like *F*   170 descension] *Q;* declension *F*   171 prince] *F;* pince *Q*
172 everything] *F* (euery thing*); enery thing *Q*   **2.3**] *Scena Tertia. F; not in Q*   0.1–3] *Q (Enter*
Northumberland his wife, and the wife to Harry Percie.); Enter Northumberland, his Ladie, and Harrie
Percies Ladie. F   1 pray thee] *Q;* prethee *F*   2 even] *Q;* an euen *F*

Put not you on the visage of the times
And be like them, to Percy, troublesome.

LADY NORTHUMBERLAND

I have given over. I will speak no more.   5
Do what you will; your wisdom be your guide.

NORTHUMBERLAND

Alas, sweet wife, my honour is at pawn,
And but my going, nothing can redeem it.

LADY PERCY

O yet, for God's sake, go not to these wars.
The time was, father, that you broke your word,   10
When you were more ^Fendeared^F to it than now –
When your own Percy, when my heart's dear Harry,
Threw many a northward look to see his father
Bring up his powers; but he did long in vain.
Who then persuaded you to stay at home?   15

attributing a motive and culpability to Northumberland absent in Holinshed.
The scene's most notable feature, however, is the strength of its women. It is the only scene in Shakespeare's second history tetralogy in which women prevail. Lady Northumberland has clearly tried already to convince her husband to flee; here, Lady Percy chastises her father-in-law for dishonouring his son and shames him into compliance with her will. Shakespeare draws a sharp contrast between these aristocratic women, whose chief concern is honour and family loyalty, and the Hostess of the tavern, who in the scenes that flank this one is obsessed with material goods and bourgeois respectability.

1   **daughter** daughter-in-law, the widow of Harry Percy (Hotspur); also at 46

2   **Give even way** Generally, 'give way' means to indulge or allow scope to; but *even*, signifying smooth, plays against

rough to activate a reading of *way* as a passage or access. Northumberland is begging the women to let him join the Archbishop without protest.

3   **not** goes with both *Put* and *be* (4): 'Do not put on a mask of cheerfulness and so be troublesome to me.'

4   **Percy** The Earl refers to himself by his family name.

5   **given over** given up, ceased trying to persuade him (*OED* give v. 63a)

7   **at pawn** held as a pledge (*OED* pawn *sb.*² 2a)

8   **but my going** i.e. apart from my joining the other rebel forces

10   On Northumberland's broken promise to assist the rebel cause at Shrewsbury, see Ind.37n. and *1H4* 4.1.13–84.

11   **endeared** bound by obligation – in this case, familial (*OED* v. 6b)

13   **to see** in hopes of seeing. The infinitive implies expectation.

14   **powers** Cf. 1.1.133n.

9 God's] *Q;* heauens *F*   10 that] *Q;* when *F*   11 endeared] *F (*endeer'd*);* endeere *Q*   12 heart's dear Harry] *Q;* heart-deere-*Harry F*   14 powers] *Q;* Powres *F*

There were two honours lost: yours and your son's.
For yours, the God of heaven brighten it!
For his, it stuck upon him as the sun
In the grey vault of heaven, and by his light
Did all the chivalry of England move   20
To do brave acts. He was indeed the glass
Wherein the noble youth did dress themselves.
ᶠHe had no legs that practised not his gait;
And speaking thick, which nature made his blemish,

16 **There** on that occasion. The honour lost by Northumberland was ethical, for he betrayed his son; that lost by Hotspur was mortal, for with his death, all his 'proud titles' were won by Hal (*1H4* 5.4.78).

17 **the God ... it** i.e. may God redeem, or allow you to burnish to its former brightness, your tarnished honour.

18 **stuck** a verb which indicates the fixity of a heavenly body in its sphere. Cf. *AC* 5.2.78–9: 'His face was as the heavens, and therein stuck / A sun and moon'.

19 **grey** not dull, but the colour of the light morning sky. Cf. *Tit* 2.1.1: 'the morn is bright and grey'; *RJ* 2.3.1: 'The grey-eyed morn'; and *Son* 132.5–6: 'And truly, not the morning sun of heaven / Better becomes the grey cheeks of the East'.

light both literal and metaphoric: shining example

20 **Did ... move** were motivated; but with a continuing play on celestial motion. The *chivalry* (horsemen, knights) are likened to heavenly bodies proceeding in their course under the influence of Hotspur (*OED* move *v.* 16b).

21 **glass** mirror. Cf. *Ham* 3.1.152, 'The glass of fashion and the mould of form' (*OED sb.* 8a).

23–45 **He ... grave** This poignant extension of Lady Percy's eulogy for her dead husband and chastisement of her father-in-law was undoubtedly in the original

text: the fact that the opening words of Northumberland's reply at 45 complete Lady Percy's partial line makes that clear. Why, then, was her speech cut so drastically for Q? Practically, the cut may have been intended to shorten Lady Percy's role in performance so that the boy who played her, and who in the next scene was to double as Doll Tearsheet, would have fewer lines to learn. Alternatively, political sensitivity may have been the cause. If Hotspur was identified with the Earl of Essex, whose failed expedition to Ireland in 1599 would have been fresh in the public's mind when Q was published in 1600, a glorification of Hotspur could have been deemed inappropriate.

23 i.e. the legs belonging to the *noble youth* for whom Hotspur provided a role-model

24 What Shakespeare meant by *speaking thick* has generated great debate. Probably *thick* means fast (*OED adv.* 3) and without pause – appropriate for the impetuous Hotspur – in contrast to those who speak *low and tardily*, which style is termed *perfection* (26–7). Nevertheless, the fact that Lady Percy calls speaking thick a *blemish* of *nature* has prompted critics to argue that Hotspur must have had a speech defect: Schlegel translated thick as *stottern*, or stutter, and thus inspired a stage tradition of stuttering German Hotspurs which was imported

17 the . . . heaven] *Q; may heauenly glory F*   23–45 He . . . grave.] *F; not in Q*

Became the accents of the valiant, 25
For those that could speak low and tardily
Would turn their own perfection to abuse
To seem like him – so that in speech, in gait,
In diet, in affections of delight,
In military rules, humours of blood, 30
He was the mark and glass, copy and book,
That fashioned others. And him – O wondrous him!
O miracle of men! – him did you leave,
Second to none, unseconded by you,
To look upon the hideous god of war 35
In disadvantage, to abide a field
Where nothing but the sound of Hotspur's name
Did seem defensible: so you left him.
Never, O never do his ghost the wrong
To hold your honour more precise and nice 40
With others than with him. Let them alone!
The Marshal and the Archbishop are strong.

to England most famously by Laurence
Olivier in 1945. Conceivably, too, *thick*
could refer to Hotspur's northern accent,
which would make his speech difficult for
London audiences to understand, as has
been the case in some recent productions.
25 **Became the accents** 'was adopted as
the preferred speaking style'. Ironically,
those who aspired to be valiant emulated
Hotspur's defects as well as virtues: cf.
26–8.
26 **low and tardily** quietly, deliberately, and
presumably with clear diction
27 **turn ... abuse** renounce their decorous
manner of speaking
29 **affections of delight** disposition or inclination (*OED* affection *n.*[1] 3 – online version)
towards pleasure or entertainment
30 **humours of blood** disposition or
temperament: *blood* was identified as the
seat of emotion or passion (*OED sb.* 5).
For *humours*, see 2.1.147n.

31 **mark** standard; object by which to take
one's bearing, as in 'sea-mark' (*OED*
mark *sb.* 9)
copy pattern, example (*OED sb.* 8c)
book guide, source of instruction (*OED
sb.* 4a). Cf. *AYL* 2.1.16: 'books in the
running brooks'.
34 **unseconded** not reinforced or supported,
with a play on *Second*
36 **abide a field** encounter an enemy in
battle (*OED* abide *v.* 14; field *sb.* 8)
38 **defensible** able to provide defence; or
possibly, as an ethical judgment, worth
defending
40 **precise and nice** scrupulously or fastidi-
ously (*OED* precise *adj.* 2) and strictly or
carefully (*OED* nice *adj.* 7b): both
adjectives have adverbial force. The
nearly synonymous terms lend emphasis
to Lady Percy's warning.
42 **Marshal** i.e. Thomas Mowbray. See
1.3.4n.

32 O wondrous him!] *Rowe;* O wondrous! him, *F*

Had my sweet Harry had but half their numbers,
Today might I, hanging on Hotspur's neck,
Have talked of Monmouth's grave.^F

NORTHUMBERLAND   Beshrew your heart,   45
Fair daughter; you do draw my spirits from me
With new lamenting ancient oversights.
But I must go and meet with danger there,
Or it will seek me in another place
And find me worse provided.

LADY NORTHUMBERLAND   O, fly to Scotland   50
Till that the nobles and the armed commons
Have of their puissance made a little taste!

LADY PERCY

If they get ground and vantage of the King,
Then join you with them like a rib of steel
To make strength stronger. But, for all our loves,   55
First let them try themselves. So did your son:
He was so suffered. So came I a widow;

---

45 **Monmouth's** Prince Harry's: see Ind.29n.
This implicit reference to Hotspur's combat
with Prince Harry suggests that Lady
Percy, like Morton (1.1.109), may know
that the Prince, not Falstaff, killed her
husband; but to honour the disparate
requirements of comedy and history,
Shakespeare allows us to have it both
ways.
Beshrew a mild, sometimes affectionate curse meaning 'the devil take' or
'a plague on', often spoken before an
admission or confession (*OED v.* 3b)
46 **draw my spirits** 'sap my vital energy';
i.e. depress
47 **With** by
new again, freshly
ancient past, bygone
50 **provided** prepared
51 **armed commons** i.e. soldiers; armèd.
Lady Northumberland, attentive to rank,

distinguishes between those with titles
and those without.
52 **of ... taste** tested their strength
53 **get ... of** gain a position of superiority or
advantage over (*OED* get *v.* 5b; vantage
sb. 3a); *ground and vantage* may be a
hendiadys for 'vantage-ground'.
54 **rib of steel** The image is of reinforcing a
barrel with a steel band: cf. 4.3.43, *MA*
4.1.151, *Ham* 1.3.62 and *AC* 2.2.122. The
expression 'to be hooped with (have ribs
of) steel' had acquired proverbial force
(Dent, S844.1).
55 **all our loves** both our sakes. For *all*
meaning two, cf. 3.1.35 (Ard¹).
56 **try** test – that is, without the help of
Northumberland. Cf. 50–2.
56–7 **So ... so ... So** thus
57 **suffered** forced (i.e. to test his strength
unassisted)
came became

47 oversights] *Q, F (*Ouer-sights*)   49 another] *F, Q (*an other*)

247

And never shall have length of life enough
To rain upon remembrance with mine eyes,
That it may grow and sprout as high as heaven   60
For recordation to my noble husband.

NORTHUMBERLAND

Come, come, go in with me. 'Tis with my mind
As with the tide swelled up unto his height
That makes a still stand, running neither way.
Fain would I go to meet the Archbishop,   65
But many thousand reasons hold me back.
I will resolve for Scotland: there am I
Till time and vantage crave my company.   *Exeunt.*

2.4   ^F*Enter two* Drawers^F[, FRANCIS *and* Drawer,
                    who carries a dish of apple-johns].

FRANCIS   What the devil hast thou brought there? Apple-
johns? Thou knowest Sir John cannot endure an
apple-john.

---

59 **rain ... eyes** water with my tears the
plant of *remembrance* (rosemary). Cf.
Ham 4.5.169: 'There's rosemary: that's
for remembrance'.

61 **For recordation to** in memory of

62 **go in** Northumberland's instruction serves
as a pretext for the characters to exit. It
does not suggest that the scene is meant
to take place outdoors, as some editors
indicate by locating it 'Before the castle'
(Ard¹) or 'Outside Northumberland's
castle at Warkworth' (Norton).

63 **his** its

64 **a still stand** a standstill, the precise point
from which the tide, having reached its
height (63), will begin to ebb; possibly, in
this context, an impasse

65 **Fain** gladly

67–8 Here, as at Shrewsbury, Northumberland's abandonment of his allies helps to
seal the rebellion's fate. Cf. 2.3n.

67 **for** to flee to
am I I shall I stay: an implied future tense

68 **vantage** advantage, opportunity (*OED
sb.* 4b)

2.4 The scene is located in a room at the
Hostess's tavern in Eastcheap, and in
many ways it parallels both the structure
and content of the great tavern scene –
also 2.4 – in *1H4*.

0.1–2 *Q's permissive '*or two*' suggests that
in the copy-text, Shakespeare had not yet
resolved how many drawers would be
involved in the scene, just as there seems
to have been similar indecision over how
many officers enter at the top of 2.1, and
how many strewers of rushes at the top of
5.5. Two drawers might seem warranted,
because the Prince and Poins will replace
them later in the scene, and clearly two
are required at the outset: Francis, the
drawer who was humiliated by Harry and

2.4] *Scaena Quarta. F; not in Q*   0.1 *Enter two* Drawers] *F; Enter a Drawer or two. Q*   0.1–2 FRANCIS
... apple-johns] *Oxf¹ subst.*   1, 10 SPs] *Q; 1. Drawer. F*   the devil] *Q; not in F*

DRAWER   Mass, thou sayst true. The Prince once set
a dish of apple-johns before him and told him there   5
were five more Sir Johns and, putting off his hat, said,
'I will now take my leave of these six dry, round, old,
withered knights!' It angered him to the heart, but he
hath forgot that.

FRANCIS   Why then, cover and set them down, and see   10
if thou canst find out Sneak's noise. Mistress Tearsheet
would fain hear some music.

Poins in *1H4* 2.4, and another drawer
whose SP at 4 is '*Draw.*'. Editing is
complicated, however, by Q's SD '*Enter
Will.*' at 18. Most editors take '*Will*' to be
either the name of a third drawer or the
name of the actor designated to play him;
but as there are no lines assigned to a
third drawer, the substance and placement
of the SD are open to question. Mahood
suggests that a third drawer may have
been introduced 'to give work experience
to a new young actor' (*Bit Parts*, 19–20).
Greg (*First Folio*, 273), on the contrary,
speculates that '*Will*' might refer to the
actor Will Kemp who, playing Falstaff,
may be crossing the stage on his way to
relieve himself, thus preparing for his
entry line, 'Empty the Jordan!' (34). Alternatively, the SD might have been mistakenly copied from a marginal note made
in the playhouse to anticipate the arrival
of Falstaff 14 lines later. F eliminates the
confusion in Q by omitting the enigmatic
SD and redistributing lines between the
two drawers. F designates Francis simply
as '1. *Drawer*', cuts 13–14, assigns
Francis's lines at 15–18 and 21 to '2.
Draw.', and assigns those of the second
drawer at 19–20 to '1. *Draw*'. F thus stream-
lines the exchange and clears up the
problem of Francis's asking the drawer to
fetch the musicians (10–11) and then
doing so himself (21). But this problem is

more apparent than real (see 21n.). There
is no compelling reason to alter Q or to
reassign speeches when the simple deletion of '*Enter Will.*' allows Francis and
the Drawer to proceed with their preparations without editorial intervention.

1–2 **Apple-johns** apples, possibly so named
because ripe around St John's Day (27
December), that are not eaten until they
are shrivelled. They are said to keep for
up to two years.

4–9 *OED* cites Phillips's *Cider* (1708) on the
metaphoric significance of an apple-john,
'whose wither'd rind, entrench'd by
many a furrow, aptly represents Decrepid
age'. Cf. *1H4* 3.3.3–4: 'I am withered
like an old apple-john'. Wilson (Cam[1])
suggests that the apple-john may also
signify impotence, thus exacerbating
Harry's insult and Falstaff's anger.

4   **Mass** See 2.2.66n.

6   **putting . . . hat** removing his hat, a
gesture here of mock deference

10   **cover** spread a cloth on the table. Diners
at a tavern would often conclude their
meal with an 'after-supper', a course of
fruit and wine taken in a different room.
This would appear to be the case with
Falstaff and Doll.

11   **find out** fetch, discover the whereabouts
of (*OED* find *v.* 20b)
     Sneak's noise Sneak's band: *noise* was a
term for a group of musicians (*OED sb.*

4 SP] *Draw. Q;* 2. *Draw. F*   Mass,] *Q (*Mas*); not in F*   7–8 old, withered] *Q;* old-wither'd *F*   12 hear]
Q; haue *F*

DRAWER   Dispatch! The room where they supped is too
    hot; they'll come in straight.
FRANCIS   Sirrah, here will be the Prince and Master Poins   15
    anon, and they will put on two of our jerkins and
    aprons, and Sir John must not know of it. Bardolph
    hath brought word.
DRAWER   By the mass, here will be old utas! It will be
    an excellent stratagem.   20

5b). In *Famous Victories*, the Prince three
times sends for 'a noise of musicians'
(2.83, 4.72, 5.82). Lindley observes that
noise was most often associated in the
theatre with the viol or fiddle and cites
John Cooke, *Green's Tu Quoque* – 'there
will be good company, a noise of choice
Fidlers' (Dodsley, 11.190) – though a
mixed consort may have been employed,
always likely to contain players on the
treble and tenor viol as well as wood-
winds. It is uncertain whether the *noise*
here was made up of actors working in
the Lord Chamberlain's company or was
instead a pick-up band hired for performances (Lindley, 'Sneak?'). If the latter,
then *Sneak* may have been the actual
name of a person who had such a band;
otherwise, it may have been a generic
name. Either way, its endurance is proven
by Heywood's allusion to 'Sneakes noise'
in *1 Iron Age*, 3.1 (*c.* 1613). The musicians
do not arrive until 226.

13 **Dispatch!** 'Hurry up!' This command
would make more sense if spoken by a
third drawer who bursts in with news of
Falstaff and Doll's imminent arrival – cf.
the Third Strewer's similar injunction at
5.5.4 – and it provides further evidence
that Shakespeare left this portion of the
scene to be tidied in performance. See
also 0.1–2n.

16 **anon** at once, straight away (*OED adv.*

4), a term the Prince and Poins mercilessly
mock Francis for using in *1H4* (2.4.28–66)
and which they themselves adopt when disguised as drawers later in this scene (285).
jerkins See 2.2.168.

18 Q's SD '*Enter Will.*' may have signalled
that Will Kemp, as Falstaff, was to cross
the stage at this point, or it may have been
mistakenly copied from a marginal note
scribbled in the playhouse to anticipate
the entrance of Kemp at 32: see 0.1–2n.
Q2 and Q3 of *RJ* similarly list an entrance
for Will Kemp instead of Peter, the character he played (4.5.99); and the Q of *2H4* lists
actor John Sincklo instead of the Beadle,
the character he played, in the SD at 5.4.0.

19 **By the mass** a mild oath invoking the
'old religion', Catholicism, whose rituals
and practices were often identified with
the festive calendar: cf. *old utas*, below.
old utas rare sport (Ard[1]); a high old time
(Ard[2]); a time of festivity or merriment.
OED gives 'utis' as a variant of 'utas' (*sb.*
1c), a reduced form of the plural 'utaves',
or octaves, referring to the eight days of a
(Catholic) festival. The aberrant spelling
'utis' is found only in *2H4*; and without a
good reason for preserving it, I revert to
the normal spelling. The adjective *old*
serves as an intensifier but also gestures
nostalgically to days gone by – here, to
the merry tavern scenes of *1H4*.

20 **stratagem** scheme, trick

13–14] *Q; not in F, Oxf*   14 straight.] *Q; straight. Enter* WILL. *Cam[2]*   15 SP] *Q;* 2. *Draw. F;* WILL *Cam[2]*
18 word.] *F; word. Enter Will. Q; word. Enter Third Drawer. / Alexander (Ridley)*   19 SP] *Q;* 1. *Draw. F;*
3 *Draw. / Alexander (Ridley);* FRANCIS *Davison*   By the mass,] *Q; Then F*   old] *Q(corr)F;* oll *Q(uncorr)*
utas] *this edn;* utis *QF*

FRANCIS   I'll see if I can find out Sneak.   *Exit.*

Enter [the HOSTESS] Mistress Quickly
and DOLL Tearsheet.

HOSTESS   I'faith, sweetheart, methinks now you are in
an excellent good temporality. Your pulsidge beats
as extraordinarily as heart would desire, and your
colour, I warrant you, is as red as any rose, in good   25
truth, la! But, i'faith, you have drunk too much
canaries, and that's a marvellous searching wine, and
it perfumes the blood ere one can say, 'What's this?'
How do you now?
DOLL   Better than I was. Hem!   30
HOSTESS   Why, that's well said. A good heart's worth
gold. Lo, here comes Sir John.

---

21 Perhaps Francis's decision to find Sneak's
noise himself after he has already told the
Second Drawer to do so (10–12) is
motivated by the Drawer's news that
Falstaff and Doll are to enter imminently.
23 **temporality, pulsidge** Quicklyisms for
'temper' and 'pulse', each word made to
sound richer and more Latinate by the
addition of syllables
24 **extraordinarily** ordinarily, regularly.
The Hostess cannot seem to control the
contradictory work done by her extra
prefixes and suffixes.
27 **canaries** a sweet wine from the Canary
Islands – hence, the plural. Cowl (Ard¹)
speculates that the Hostess may be
confusing wine with a lively dance called
'canaries'.
searching potent; capable of finding out
one's weak points – i.e. making one
drunk (*OED ppl.a.* 1b)

28 **perfumes** The Hostess either conflates
'suffuses' and 'permeates' or else means
'perfuses' (permeates): the fragrance
of her malapropism adds an olfactory
agency to the inebriating power of
wine.
'What's this?' 'What's happened to me?'
30 **Hem!** conventional notation for a vulgar
noise such as a belch or hiccup which
Doll, having eaten and drunk her fill,
would be prone to make. Elsewhere in the
play, the word is used as a call to drink
a draught, akin to 'Drink up!' (cf.
3.2.217–18 and *1H4* 2.4.16). In some
performances, however, *Hem* has been
taken as a cue for Doll to vomit into a
chamber pot, allowing Falstaff to make
comic business of the line he speaks on
entering, *Empty the jordan!* (34).
31–2 **A . . . gold** confusion of two aphorisms:
'A good heart conquers ill fortunes' and

---

21 SP] *Q; 2. Draw. F;* DRAWER *Cam²*   SD] *QF; Exit with third drawer. / Alexander; Exit [with Francis]*
Cam²; Exeunt / Rowe   21.1–2] *Q (Enter mistris Quickly, and Doll Tere-sheet.); Enter Hostesse, and*
Dol. F   22 I'faith] *Q (*Yfaith*); not in F*   25–6 in . . . la!] *Q (*in . . . law:*); not in F*   26 i'faith] *Q (*yfaith*);*
not in F   28 one] *Q; wee F*   31 that's] *Q; that was F*   32 Lo] *Q (*loe*);* Looke *F*

Enter Sir John [FALSTAFF].

FALSTAFF [*Sings.*] 'When Arthur first in court' –
Empty the jordan!   [*Exit Drawer.*]
– 'and was a worthy king' – How now, Mistress   35
Doll?

HOSTESS   Sick of a calm, yea, good faith.

FALSTAFF   So is all her sect. An they be once in a calm,
they are sick.

DOLL   A pox damn you, you muddy rascal! Is that all the   40
comfort you give me?

'A good name is better than gold' (Tilley, H305, N22). Cf. Proverbs, 22.1.

33–5 **'When . . . king'** The lines from the popular ballad *Sir Lancelot du Lake*, according to the first extant version printed in Thomas Deloney's *Garland of Good Will* (1586), are not quite as Falstaff remembers: 'When Arthur first in court began / And was approved king, / By force of arms great victories won / And conquest home did bring'. For those who knew the song, Falstaff's singing even a garbled version might have seemed evidence of his revived bravado. See Duffin, 435–7, and Lindley, *Music*, 147.

34 **jordan** chamber pot. Tavern rooms were furnished with such necessities, according to Earle's *Microcosmographie* (1628), and Falstaff has probably filled one. He shouts the command either to someone offstage or, as I take it, to the Drawer onstage, who exits to do Falstaff's bidding. For an alternative staging possibility, see 30n.

35 **How now** elliptical for 'How are you now?'

37, 38 **calm** The Hostess means its homophone 'qualm' (a sudden fit of faintness or illness), but Falstaff pretends to understand her to mean 'calm waters'.

38 **her sect** Another of the Hostess's malapropisms, *sect* seems to mean both 'sex' (*OED* sect *sb.* 1d) and 'profession' – that is, prostitution – with a wry glance at its reference to a group of adherents to a particular religious faith (*OED* sect *sb.* 4). Calvinist banter about the state of Doll's soul resumes at 323–44.

38–9 **An . . . sick** a paradoxical metaphor: 'if they are ever in calm waters, they get seasick'. Falstaff seems to mean one of the following: (1) women who are quiet must be sick, because otherwise they would be talking, or (2) prostitutes fail to ply their trade only when sick, or (3) prostitutes who aren't doing any business feel out of sorts (Ard²).

40 **A pox** an imprecation akin to 'the plague': *pox* = syphilis
muddy rascal abusive epithet meaning 'dirty rogue' but originally referring to a young male deer (*rascal*), lean and sluggish (*muddy*) because out of season

---

32.1] *Q; Enter Falstaffe. F; Enter* Falstaff, *singing. Capell*   33 SD] *Capell (singing); not in QF*   34 jordan] *Q (*iourdan*), F (*Iordan*)*   SD] *Capell; Exit Francis / Alexander; Exit Will / Davison; not in QF*   37 good faith] *Q; good-sooth F*   38 An] *Q (*and*); if F*   40 A . . . you,] *Q; not in F*

FALSTAFF You make fat rascals, Mistress Doll.

DOLL I make them? Gluttony and diseases make; I make them not.

FALSTAFF If the cook help to make the gluttony, you   45
help to make the diseases, Doll. We catch of you, Doll, we catch of you. Grant that, my poor virtue, grant that.

DOLL Yea, Jesu, our chains and our jewels.

FALSTAFF [*Sings.*] 'Your brooches, pearls and ouches!'   50

(Puttenham, 3.17). There may be a further implication that the rascal is sexually inferior to the full-grown antlered buck, the term derived from the Italian *rascaglione*, a man without testicles (Williams, *Dictionary*, 3.1143–4): cf. Hamlet's self-chastisement as '[a] dull and muddy-mettled rascal' (2.2.502). Doll uses *muddy* in a different sense at 55.

42 **make fat rascals** continues the play on *rascal* as a lean deer, which Falstaff says Doll fattens (*fat rascals* has the force of an oxymoron). Figuratively, he is alluding to the bloating which may result from the sexually transmitted diseases (43) she bequeaths to her customers.

43 **diseases make** F's provision of 'them' as a direct object here may suggest an inadvertent omission by the Q compositor.

46 **catch of** catch (the diseases) from

47 **poor virtue** *poor* was a term of endearment; *virtue* meant 'virtuous person' (cf. *Tim* 3.6.7).

49 ***Yea, Jesu** F's substitution of 'I [Ay] marry' for Q's innocuous 'Yea ioy' suggests to Ridley that 'ioy' may have been a compositor's misreading of the profane 'Iesu' which appeared in the

copy-texts of Q and F but was altered following the Act of 1606. The Oxford editors accept *Jesu* as the probable reading. See similar uses of *Jesu* by the Hostess at 296 and by Shallow at 3.2.33 and 43: pronounced *Jē-zū*.

our chains ... jewels understood to be the object of 'We catch of you' (46): Doll turns Falstaff's wit back on him by accusing him of stealing ('catching') her valuables.

50 Falstaff makes light of Doll's accusation by turning it into a line from a song, perhaps a snatch of a loosely remembered ballad such as 'The Boy and the Mantle' which contains the phrase, 'With brauches and ringes'. Falstaff's *brooches, pearls* and *ouches* are all types of jewellery, an 'ouch' being a clasp or brooch often set with precious stones; but they also are euphemisms for the carbuncles, skin sores and pimples or pustules caused by sexually transmitted diseases. Falstaff thus continues to slander Doll as a carrier of disease. For comparison, Oxf[1] cites Nicholas Udall's translation of *The Apophthegmes of Erasmus* (1564): 'little pimples . . . in the noses and faces . . . are called the Saphires and Rubies of the Tauern'.

43 make;] *Q*; make them. *F*   45 cook . . . make] *Q*; Cooke make *F*   49 Yea, Jesu] *Oxf (conj. Ridley)*; Yea joy *Q*; I marry *F*   50 SD] *this edn*   ouches] *Q, F (Owches)*

– For to serve bravely is to come halting off, you
know; to come off the breach with his pike bent
bravely, and to surgery bravely, to venture upon the
charged chambers bravely –

DOLL   Hang yourself, you muddy conger, hang yourself!   55
HOSTESS   By my troth, this is the old fashion. You two
never meet but you fall to some discord! You are both,
i'good truth, as rheumatic as two dry toasts; you
cannot one bear with another's confirmities. What

51 **to serve ... off** Falstaff introduces an elaborate network of military *double entendres* to defend his potency which reaches a climax in the conversation he has with Doll and Pistol at 110–39. 'Brave service' can be taken in both a military and a sexual sense, as either distinction in battle or skilful copulation. In asserting that the proof of such bravery is to *come halting off*, Falstaff refers both to a wound that makes one limp off the field and to ejaculation ('coming off') which leaves a penis limp and unable to stand. On *come* as slang for achieving orgasm, see 2.1.20n.

52 **to come ... bent** makes the point of the previous *double entendre* even more explicit. In a military sense, a *breach* is a gap in a fortification made during an assault from which the soldier returns with his *pike* – a weapon with a wooden shaft and a pointed head of steel or iron – *bent* after engaging the enemy. In a sexual sense, the *breach* is the vagina, from which the penis (*pike*) emerges *bent* from vigorous copulation.

53 **surgery** medical treatment, necessary for both the war wound and the pox

53–4 **to venture ... chambers** either (1) to dare to face the loaded guns of the enemy (*OED* venture *v.* 9), or (2) to penetrate a woman's vagina (*chambers*) which is *charged* because filled with discharged

semen (Partridge). Weis notes that while *charged chambers* – as a loaded piece of ordnance – might seem more obviously to be a phallic reference, a cannon has a bore-hole in front of its breech, and a loaded cannon would therefore be seen as a dangerous hole, signifying 'infected female genitalia'. Cf. similar punning on women as the vector of sexually transmitted disease in Sonnet 144: 'Till my bad angel fire my good one out' (14).

55 **muddy conger** An abusive epithet Doll likes to apply to Falstaff (see 40n.), *muddy* here refers to the muddy shallows that large sea-eels (*congers*) inhabit. But the phrase is bawdy: since *conger* was a slang term for penis, she in effect calls him a 'dirty prick': cf. Dekker, *Shoemakers' Holiday*, 1.4.111: 'you sowsed cunger'. The line is omitted in F.

58 **rheumatic ... toasts** another Quickly-ism. A *rheumatic* humour is cold and wet: the Hostess means 'choleric', and makes the same error in *H5* 2.3.36. Because the choleric humour is hot and dry, Doll and Falstaff are bound to 'grate one another' (Johnson). 'As hot as toast' was proverbial (Dent, T363).

59 **confirmities** a malapropism for 'infirmities'. The Hostess abuses the language of the Geneva Bible: 'We that are strong, ought to beare the infirmities of the weake' (Romans, 15.1).

51–2 off ... come] *Rowe subst.;* off, you know to come *Q;* off: you know, to come *F*   55] *Q; not in F*
56 By my troth] *Q;* Why *F*   58 i'good truth] *Q;* in good troth *F*

the goodyear! One must bear, [*to Doll*] and that must   60
be you: you are the weaker vessel, as they say, the
emptier vessel.

DOLL   Can a weak empty vessel bear such a huge full
hogshead? There's a whole merchant's venture of
Bordeaux stuff in him! You have not seen a hulk   65
better stuffed in the hold. Come, I'll be friends with
thee, Jack: thou art going to the wars, and whether I
shall ever see thee again or no there is nobody cares.

Enter Drawer.

DRAWER   Sir, Ancient Pistol's below and would speak
with you.   70

59–60 **What the goodyear!** a mild imprecation, probably akin to 'What the devil!'
According to the *OED*, 'goodyear'
denotes 'some undefined malefic power
or agency' (*sb. b*).

60–1 **One . . . vessel** 'A woman is the
weaker vessel' was proverbial and
derived from 1 Peter, 3.7 (Dent, W655).
The Hostess yokes it to the cliché that
'Women are made to bear' (*TS* 2.1.200),
in which the implied objects of bearing
are children, household burdens and men.
Here, she admonishes Doll to suffer
indignities in silence – that is, to put up
with Falstaff. In addition to denoting a
woman's body, *vessel* is a pun meaning
(1) a receptacle or container, or (2) a
merchant ship – on both of which
meanings Doll plays at 63–6.

63 **empty vessel** a ship with no cargo, or a
woman's body unoccupied sexually

64 **hogshead** literally, a wine barrel; figuratively, a swinish lout. Doll implies that so
weak a vessel as she may not be able to
bear the weight of Falstaff.

64–5 **merchant's . . . stuff** shipload of
Bordeaux wine; *merchant's venture*

alludes to the risk of losing both ship and
cargo at sea.

65–6 **hulk . . . hold** transport ship with more
cargo crammed below decks; so, figuratively, a hulking man with so fat a gut.
The image of Doll as a vessel is here
silently transferred to Falstaff: cf. 1.1.19.

68.1 *F does not clarify which, if either, of
the drawers who speak at the opening
of the scene returns; in Q, however, it
may be inferred that because Francis is
regularly named in SPs, the unnamed
drawer enters here.

69 **Ancient Pistol** Ensign Pistol: a military
rank, but perhaps, as with Corporal
Bardolph, an honorific title either self-
conferred or conferred by Captain
Falstaff. All three titles are inappropriate
and unearned (Jorgensen, *World*, 65).
Pistol, however, is appropriately named.
The early pistol was a noisy weapon
likely to go off at half-cock; and if
pronounced *Peesel* or 'Pizzle' (as the
Hostess insists at 162), it is a pun on a
slang term for penis as well: hence,
Ancient Pistol can mean 'old prick'.
Davison suggests a possible derivation

60 goodyear] *Q* (goodyere), *F* (good-yere)   60 SD] *Rowe (after 62), Hudson; not in QF*   65 Bordeaux]
QF (Burdeux)   69 Pistol's] *Q; Pistoll is F*

DOLL　Hang him, swaggering rascal! Let him not come hither. It is the foul-mouth'dst rogue in England!

HOSTESS　If he swagger, let him not come here! No, by my faith, I must live among my neighbours; I'll no swaggerers. I am in good name and fame with　75 the very best. – Shut the door! – There comes no swaggerers here. I have not lived all this while to have swaggering now. – Shut the door, I pray you!

FALSTAFF　Dost thou hear, hostess?

HOSTESS　Pray ye pacify yourself, Sir John; there comes　80 no swaggerers here.

FALSTAFF　Dost thou hear? It is mine ancient.

HOSTESS　Tilly-fally, Sir John, ne'er tell me. An your ancient swagger, 'a comes not in my doors! I was

---

from the Italian *pistolfo*, which John Florio defined in 1611 as 'a roguing beggar, a cantler, an upright man that liveth by cozenage'.

71　**swaggering** bullying, boastful. Pistol is stereotyped as a 'roaring boy', a traditional braggart soldier or *miles gloriosus* who, according to Dekker's *Diuels Last Will and Testament* (*Non-Dramatic*, 3.354), is noted for 'swaggering, or swearing three pil'd oathes in a Tauerne'. Humphreys cites Nashe's *Terrors of the Night*, which admonishes such quarrellers, who 'beare the name of souldiers, and liue baselie swaggering in euerie alehouse, hauing no other exhibition but from harlots and strumpets', to 'seeke some newe trade, and leaue whoring and quarrelling, least besides the nightly guilt of youre owne banqurout consciences, Bridewell or Newgate prooue the ende of your caueleering' (*Works*, 1.384). Chapman, in *Achilles Shield* (1598, sig. B²), identifies swaggering as a 'new word' privileged 'with much imitation'.

72　**It** he
74–5　**I'll no** A verb such as 'allow' is understood.
76　**the very best** people of repute. The Hostess is defensive about her reputation: cf. 84–96.
80　**pacify yourself** be satisfied; keep quiet
83　**Tilly-fally** a silly exclamation akin to 'nonsense' or 'fiddlesticks'. Cf. *TN* 2.3.77: 'Tilly-vally, lady!'
　　ne'er tell me an expression of incredulity or impatience
83–4　***An . . . 'a** Q's syntax does not make sense. Humphreys was the first editor to accept Maxwell's emendation of Q's 'swaggrer' to *swagger a* (*a* = he), words which might easily have been misread by a compositor. Q's ampersand ('&') for *An* (= if), furthermore, would seem to require a conditional clause to follow: Maxwell's emendation provides that. F omits 'and', thus allowing the Hostess simply to repeat her warning from 76–7.

73–4 No . . . faith,] *Q; not in F*　74 among] *Q; amongst F*　80 Pray ye] *Q;* 'Pray you *F*　83 ne'er] *Q;* neuer *F*　An] *Q (&); not in F*　84 swagger, 'a] *Ard² (Maxwell);* swaggrer *Q;* Swaggerer *F*

before Master Tisick the debuty t'other day, and as 85
he said to me – 'twas no longer ago than Wed'sday
last, i'good faith – 'Neighbour Quickly,' says he –
Master Dumbe our minister was by then – 'Neighbour
Quickly,' says he, 'receive those that are civil, for',
said he, 'you are in an ill name.' Now 'a said so; I 90
can tell whereupon. 'For', says he, 'you are an honest
woman, and well thought on; therefore take heed
what guests you receive. Receive', says he, 'no
swaggering companions.' There comes none here!
You would bless you to hear what he said. No, I'll no 95
swaggerers.

FALSTAFF He's no swaggerer, hostess. A tame cheater,
i'faith: you may stroke him as gently as a puppy
greyhound. He'll not swagger with a barbary hen if

85 **Master ... debuty** The spelling of 'deputy' in Q probably reveals the Hostess's pronunciation. *Tisick* (or 'phthisic'), meaning consumptive or racked by a cough, makes a satirical name for a deputy, a petty magistrate who served a City ward in the same capacity as an alderman. Apparently Tisick has summoned the Hostess for keeping a disorderly house; the warning she received would explain why she is so defensive about her reputation. The discursive style of her speech, with its interruptions and piling up of homely detail, recalls that of her speech at 2.1.84–102 and is much like that of Juliet's Nurse in *RJ* 1.3.16–48.

88 **Master Dumbe** probably an allusion the Puritan term 'dumb dogs' for those unzealous clergymen who did not preach their own sermons, or failed to preach at all: 'Their watchemen are all blinde: they haue no knowledge: they are all domme dogs: thei can not barke' (Isaiah, 56.10, Geneva Bible).

89 **receive ... civil** admit (to your tavern) only those who behave decently

90 **are ... name** have earned a bad reputation. The Hostess has protested her own *good name* at 75.

91 **whereupon** the reason why
honest spoken of a woman, *honest* usually means chaste. Here, it means respectable.

94 **companions** fellows; probably said contemptuously

95 **bless you** say 'Bless me!', or make the sign of the cross; i.e. be shocked

97 **tame cheater** cant phrase for a con artist who appears innocuous so as not to dissuade others from gaming with him, as opposed to a *swaggerer* who might drive them off with quarrelling

99 **swagger** quarrel
barbary hen guinea fowl, whose feathers are easily ruffled; also slang for a prostitute

85 debuty t'other] *Q;* Deputie, the other *F* 86 'twas] *Q;* it was *F* Wed'sday] *Q (*wedsday*);* Wednesday *F*
87 i'good faith] *Q (*I good faith*);* ay, good faith *Cam²; not in F* 88 Dumbe] *Q, F (*Dombe*)* 90 said] *Q;*
sayth *F* 'a] *Q;* hee *F* 98 i'faith] *Q;* hee *F* 99 He'll] *Q (*heele*);* hee will *F*

her feathers turn back in any show of resistance. –   100
Call him up, drawer!   [*Exit Drawer.*]

HOSTESS   Cheater, call you him? I will bar no honest
man my house, nor no cheater; but I do not love
swaggering, by my troth. I am the worse when one
says 'swagger'! Feel, masters, how I shake. Look   105
you, I warrant you!

DOLL   So you do, hostess.

HOSTESS   Do I? Yea, in very truth do I, an 'twere an
aspen leaf. I cannot abide swaggerers.

Enter Ancient PISTOL, ᶠBARDOLPH *and*ᶠ Boy [PAGE].

PISTOL   God save you, Sir John.   110
FALSTAFF   Welcome, Ancient Pistol. Here, Pistol, I

102–3 **I . . . cheater** By distinguishing an
honest man from a *cheater*, the Hostess
seems to understand the latter to be
dishonest: see 97n. But immorality does
not seem to bother her; swaggering
does. Warburton (after Theobald) spied
another Quicklyism here, arguing that
she confuses *cheater* with *escheater*, the
collector of escheats due to the Crown.

104 **by my troth** Though most editors
punctuate so that this phrase belongs to
the clause that follows, Q punctuates so
that it reaffirms the previous declaration.
I . . . worse 'I feel ill.'

106 **I warrant you** See 2.1.22n.

108–9 ¹**an . . . leaf** as if I were an aspen leaf:
a proverbial simile (Dent, L140)

109.1 *Q's '*Bardolfes boy*' may be a compositor's misreading of '*Bardolfe & boy*',
for otherwise Bardolph's entrance would
not be noted. The boy could be Bardolph's
own attendant, but more likely he is
Falstaff's page, who accompanied

Bardolph at 2.2.66 and would probably
do so again here.

111–13 **I . . . hostess** The puns yoking military and sexual behaviour begun at 51
resume here, this time focusing on the
multiple potentials of Pistol's name (see
69n.): *charge* means both to offer a toast
and to load a pistol; *discharge* means to
empty the cup, to fire the pistol and to
ejaculate – with the Hostess in each
instance receiving the shots. Other plays
of the period had similar puns. Cf. John
Cooke, *Green's Tu Quoque*: '*Purse*:
Here, Mistress Tickleman, shall I charge
you? *Tickle*: Do your worst, serjeant'
(Dodsley, 11.197); Chapman, *Gentleman
Usher*: 'Come pledge me wench, for I
am drie againe, / And strait will charge
your widdowhod fresh ifaith' (2.1.18–
19); and Webster, *Duchess of Malfi*: 'a
Switzer . . . with a pistol in his great cod-
piece' (2.2.36–8).

---

101 SD] *Capell; not in QF*   104 by my troth] *Q; not in F*   108 an 'twere] *Q (*and twere*); if it were F*
109.1] *Rowe subst.; Enter antient Pistol, and Bardolfes boy. Q; Enter Pistol, and Bardolph and his Boy. F*
110 God save] *Q;* 'Saue *F*

258

charge you with a cup of sack; do you discharge
upon mine hostess.

PISTOL   I will discharge upon her, Sir John, with two
bullets.   115

FALSTAFF   She is pistol-proof; sir, you shall not hardly
offend her.

HOSTESS   Come, I'll drink no proofs, nor no bullets; I'll
drink no more than will do me good. For no man's
pleasure, I.   120

PISTOL   Then to you, Mistress Dorothy! I will charge
you.

DOLL   Charge me? I scorn you, scurvy companion.
What, you poor, base, rascally, cheating, lack-linen
mate? Away, you mouldy rogue, away! I am meat for   125
your master.

PISTOL   I know you, Mistress Dorothy.

114–15 **with two bullets** literally, from his
pistol; metaphorically, from his testicles
or, by extension, with two shots of semen
116 **pistol-proof** 'immune to pricks, pox,
pregnancy, and Pistol himself' (Williams,
Glossary, 58)
116–17 **not . . . her** (1) not injure her in any
way (*not hardly* = scarcely); but also (2)
not harm her with your hardness, with
hardly as a bawdy pun on erection
118 **I'll . . . bullets** The Hostess seems to
mistake *bullets* for a term like *proofs*,
meaning, in context, small measures of
distilled spirits; but the sexual innuendo
suggests that she is unwilling to swallow
Pistol's semen. That she realizes the banter
is bawdy becomes clear when she protests,
'For no man's pleasure, I' (119–20).
121–3 **Then . . . me?** Rebuffed by the
Hostess, Pistol decides to toast (*charge*)
Doll instead (*to you*). Doll, however,
takes *charge* to mean sexually accost.
123 **scurvy companion** *scurvy*, meaning

covered with scabs, was a term of abuse:
worthless, contemptible. For *companion*,
see 94n.
124–5 **lack-linen mate** fellow who cannot
afford a shirt or, possibly, underwear.
Cf. the inventory of Poins's linen at
2.2.14–24.
125, 130 **mouldy** literally, covered with mould,
as at 146; figuratively, decaying or rotten
– clearly one of Doll's favourite insults
125–6 **meat . . . master** Containing a pun on
'mete' and possibly on *mate*, for the
words would have been nearly homophonic, this was proverbial for 'too good
for you' (Dent, M837); but *meat* understood as 'flesh' keeps up the bawdy
innuendo. Doll privileges Falstaff over
Bardolph (*your master*) but in the process
defines herself as a possession, and her
value as a factor of her owner's rank in
the male hierarchy.
127 **I know you** perhaps implying that he
could reveal things to Doll's discredit

116 pistol-proof; sir,] pistoll proofe: sir, *Q;* Pistoll-proofe (Sir) *F;* pistol-proof, sir; *Capell*   not] *Q; not
in F*   118 ²I'll] *Q;* I will *F*

DOLL   Away, you cutpurse rascal! You filthy bung, away! By this wine, I'll thrust my knife in your mouldy chaps an you play the saucy cuttle with me.   130
Away, you bottle-ale rascal, you basket-hilt stale juggler, you! Since when, I pray you, sir? God's light, with two points on your shoulder? Much!

PISTOL   God let me not live, but I will murder your ruff for this!   135

FALSTAFF   No more, Pistol; I would not have you go off here. Discharge yourself of our company, Pistol.

HOSTESS   No, good Captain Pistol; not here, sweet captain!

---

128 **cutpurse** pickpocket, thief
  filthy bung thieves' cant for a pickpocket: *bung* means purse. Melchiori speculates that *filthy* may originally have been 'filch'; so, 'filch-bung'. Since a bung also was a plug for a barrel (cf. *Ham* 5.1.194), the term may have had scatalogical force, as in the crude epithet bung-hole (for arsehole).
130 **chaps** cheeks
  an . . . cuttle if you try your dirty tricks; 'cuttle' or 'cuttle-bung' was a cant term for a knife used to slit the straps holding purses, which usually hung from the girdle.
  saucy impertinent, rude
131 **bottle-ale** possibly meaning cheap ale. Cf. small beer (2.2.6).
131–2 **basket-hilt stale juggler** unfashionable buffoon (*stale juggler*) of the sort found at country fairs, who entertained the crowd by fencing with swords fitted with hilts in the shape of a basket to protect the hand: thus, an impostor
132 **Since when** probably (1) 'Since when have you known me, as you claim?' (127), but possibly (2) 'Since when have you been a soldier?'
133 **two . . . shoulder** *points* were tags or laces used to fasten armour to the chest (cf. 1.1.53), so Doll is probably ridiculing Pistol's makeshift military uniform.

Melchiori speculates that she may be deriding her *lack-linen mate* (124–5), much as Falstaff does his recruits in *1H4* 4.2.41–4, for wearing two napkins instead of a shirt (which he cannot afford) and securing them by *points* across the *shoulder* to make a half-shirt.
  Much! an expression of scornful incredulity: 'What a lot you have to show (for your soldiership)!'
134 **murder your ruff** Prostitutes during Elizabeth's reign were known for wearing large ruffs around their necks, and the tearing off (*murder*) of such ruffs signified sexual assault in drama of the period. As an item of costume, the ruff is anachronistic in this play.
136–7 The reason that these lines are omitted in F is unclear: they are bawdy, but no bawdier than many others. Davison suggests that the compositor's eye-skip may have been responsible.
136 **go off** more sexual play on Pistol's name: (1) fire, and (2) ejaculate
137 **Discharge . . . company** leave us; with a pun on *discharge* (see 111–13n.)
138 **Captain** The Hostess, perhaps to pacify him, inflates Pistol's rank, but her echo of Falstaff's warning at 136–7 continues the *double entendre*.

130 an] *Q (and); if F*   132–3 God's light] *Q; what F*   134 God . . . but] *Q; not in F*   136–7] *Q; not in F*

DOLL　Captain! Thou abominable damned cheater, art　140
　　　thou not ashamed to be called captain? An captains
　　　were of my mind, they would truncheon you out for
　　　taking their names upon you before you have earned
　　　them! You a captain? You slave, for what? For tearing
　　　a poor whore's ruff in a bawdy house? – He a captain?　145
　　　Hang him, rogue! He lives upon mouldy stewed
　　　prunes and dried cakes. A captain? God's light, these
　　　villains will make the word as odious as the word

142 **truncheon you out** 'truncheon' (a club
or cudgel) used as a verb: i.e. 'beat you
out of their ranks'

142–4 **for . . . them** Pistol is not guilty as
charged: the Hostess, not he himself, has
commissioned him *captain*. Doll's accusations, however, were warranted by bogus
captains satirized in numerous other
plays, in whose company an audience
might justifiably have placed Pistol.

144 **slave** term of contempt akin to rogue

146–7 **stewed . . . cakes** scraps from brothels
and pastry shops; *stewed prunes* were
associated with brothels because they
were thought to be 'part of the cure for
venereal disease' and possibly a preventa-
tive against it, according to W. Clowes,
The Cure of . . . Lues Venerea (1596), 161.
Ard² cites Dekker, *Seven Deadly Sinnes*
(*Non-Dramatic*, 2.44), 'a house where
they set stewed Prunes before you', and
extended discussion of Mistress Elbow's
craving for stewed prunes in *MM*
2.1.88–112. The term came to signify
bawds – Falstaff insults Mistress Quickly
by comparing her to 'a stewed prune' in
1H4 3.3.112–13 – and brothels were
commonly called 'the stews' (cf. 1.2.55).
Williams (*Glossary*, 61) identifies *cake*
as a term used for 'woman in her sexual
capacity': thus *dried cakes* may mean
whores past their prime – a term Doll
employs to continue belittling Pistol's
sexual prowess.

147–8 **these villains** base-minded scoundrels
such as Pistol who, according to Doll,
denigrate language by giving reputable
words disreputable meanings. Shakespeare
indulges in wry irony, since no scene in
the entire canon plays with bawdy *double
entendres* more than this one.

148–50 **¹as . . . ill-sorted** The word *occupy*
fell into bad company (*ill-sorted*) when
it became a popular euphemism for
fornicate, as it is, Cowl observes (Ard¹),
in Heywood's *2 If You Know Not Me,
You Know No Body*: 'a prentise must
not occupy for himself but for his
master. . . . And he cannot occupy for his
master, without the consent of his mistris'
(Heywood, 1.311); and in *RJ* 2.4.98–9:
'for I was come to the whole depth of
my tale and meant indeed to occupy
the argument no longer'. In *Discoveries*,
Jonson, a strange bedfellow for Doll,
echoes her complaint that 'Many, out
of their owne obscene Apprehensions,
refuse proper and fit words; as *occupie*,
nature, and the like' (8.610). The *OED*
verifies this observation by illustrating
how quickly *occupy* fell into disuse:
194 quotations exemplify its use in the
16th century, and only eight in the 17th
(Cam²). Doll's censure of the term is
especially ironic, given her occupation.
Cf. similar wordplay with *accommodated*,
3.2.66–72.

141 An] *Q (*and*); If *F*　147 God's light] *Q; not in *F*　148–50 word¹ . . . ill-sorted]*Q;* word Captaine
odious *F*

'occupy', which was an excellent good word before
it was ill-sorted; therefore captains had need look   150
to't.

BARDOLPH   Pray thee go down, good ancient.

FALSTAFF   Hark thee hither, Mistress Doll.

PISTOL   Not I! I tell thee what, Corporal Bardolph, I
could tear her! I'll be revenged of her!   155

PAGE   Pray thee go down.

PISTOL   I'll see her damned first! To Pluto's damned

150–1 **need look to't** better beware

153 **Hark thee hither** As 'hark' means 'give
ear', Falstaff may be urging Doll to listen
to him; more likely, he is beckoning to
her to prevent a fray with Pistol.

154 **Corporal** Pistol bestows a rank upon
Bardolph beyond his deserts, much as
the Hostess has done for him (cf. 138).
Bardolph holds no military rank in *1H4*
or *MW*, though in *H5* Nym addresses him
as Lieutenant (2.1.2).

155 **tear** tear apart; do violent injury to.
Pistol's threat to Doll's ruff is now
transferred to her person: cf. 134–5.

157–200 *In a sudden metamorphosis, Pistol's
language hereafter parodies the exaggerated heroic diction of plays written
in the 1580s and early 1590s by Greene,
Peele, Kyd, Marlowe and others – a
fustian that was mercilessly mocked in
John Eliot's *Ortho-epia Gallica* (1593),
whose Braggart provided a prototype for
Pistol (see Lever, 'French'). Though a
few specific sources for Pistol's lines are
recorded here, the humour of his rant lies
in its absurdly eclectic hodgepodge of
classical tags, songs and bombast – in
its burlesque of an outmoded style rather
than particular passages. Through it,
Shakespeare exposes Pistol's soldiership
as no more than theatrical imposture, the
misremembered scraps of unfashionable
plays. Editors since Pope and Capell

have chosen to change all Pistol's fustian
– printed as prose in QF – into parodic
verse lines: the textual notes record some
of their decisions about what constitutes
(often irregular) lines of iambic verse.
But as George Wright has demonstrated,
prose can often scan as iambic pentameter, and Pistol's speech, though
relentlessly iambic, does not have the
hallmarks of verse: 'The point seems to
be that Pistol has heard such iambic rant
in the theater and has adopted it as his
personal style without realizing that for
words to be verse they must come not
only in iambs but in lines. Pistol's iambic
word-strings are often not pentameter or
hexameter or anything' (110–11). Thus
there is no good reason to deviate from
QF by printing Pistol's speeches as
anything other than prose.

157–9 **To ... also** an echo of the infernal
imagery found in plays such as Peele's
Battle of Alcazar, in which Muly
Mahamet personifies Erebus, son of
Chaos and Night, as a hell full of
torments, tortures, plagues and pains
(2.2.73–97); *Locrine*, in which cursed
ghosts are dragged through the foul
rivers of Erebus (3.6.65–6); Marlowe's *1
Tamburlaine*, with a similar allusion to
'the blasted banks of Erebus' (5.1.244);
Greene's *Alphonsus, King of Arragon*, in
which '*Plutoes* loathsome lake' probably

---

151 to't] *Q;* to it *F*   155 of] *Q;* on *F*   157–61] *prose QF; Capell lines* first! / deep, / also. / Down! / here?
/ ; *Oxf lines* first / hand, / deep, / also. / I. / faitours! / here? /   157 damned] *Q (*damnd*), F (*damn'd*), Rowe*

lake – by this hand – to th'infernal deep, with Erebus
and tortures vile also! Hold hook and line, say I!
Down! Down, dogs! Down, faitours! Have we not   160
Hiren here? [*Draws his sword.*]

HOSTESS   Good Captain Peesel, be quiet; 'tis very late,
i'faith. I beseek you now, aggravate your choler.

PISTOL   These be good humours indeed! Shall pack-

figures as the River Styx (3.955: Greene,
13.368); and Kyd's *Spanish Tragedy*,
where Hieronimo vows to 'Knock at the
dismal gates of Pluto's court' (3.13.110).

159 **Hold ... line** a proverbial tag from
angling (Dent, H589) which wishes the
fisherman good luck; perhaps taken from
a ballad couplet, 'Hold hook and line, /
Then all is mine'. A similar reference in
KL 3.6.6–7, 'Nero is an angler in the lake
of darkness', suggests that Pistol's line
may follow from his allusion to Pluto's
lake (157–8).

160 **Down! Down, dogs!** Possibly an allusion
to Cerberus (cf. 168), this is more likely
a comic echo of vaunt such as 'Down,
dog, and crouch before the feet / Of great
Morocco', from *The Famous History of
the Life and Death of Captain Thomas
Stukeley* (Edelman, 22.61–2), or 'Now
crouch, ye kings of greatest Asia', from
2 Tamburlaine (4.3.98), with Pistol appropriating the role of conqueror.

faitours obsolete term for traitors or
rogues. F's 'fates' is probably a compositor's misreading.

160–1 **Have ... here** Probably borrowed
from a lost play by Peele, *The Turkish
Mohamet and Hiren the Fair Greek* (c.
1594), this line was repeated as a comic
tag in later plays such as Middleton's
Old Law, 4.1.52–5 ('CLOWN: No dancing
with me; we have Siren here. COOK:

Siren? 'Twas Hiren the fair Greek, man');
Jonson, Chapman and Marston's
Eastward Ho, 2.1.107–8 ('*hast thou not
Hyren here?*'; Jonson, 4.539); and
Dekker's *Satiromastix*, 4.3.243–4 ('we
have Hiren here') – evidence of Pistol's
lingering popularity as a fantastic. Hiren
(or Irene) came to mean whore and thus,
here, may refer to Doll. Pistol, however,
is more likely naming the sword he
brandishes *Hiren*, playing on the homophony with 'iron'; he does so again at
175. In doing so, he follows the chivalric
practice of Amadis du Gaul, who, according to Theobald, named *his* sword Hiren.

162 **Peesel** colloquial pronunciation of Pistol
which emphasizes an already latent pun
on 'pizzle' (from piss), meaning penis.
Cf. 111–13n., and the tavern scene in
1H4 when Falstaff calls the Prince 'You
bull's pizzle' (2.4.239). The Hostess's
pronunciation both here and at 2.1.88
(*Wheeson* for Whitsun) possibly indicates
a northern or midland dialect.

163 **beseek, aggravate** The Hostess is in
rare malapropian form: she confuses
beseek with beseech and *aggravate* with
its opposite, assuage or placate.

164 **good humours** fine sentiments

164–6 **Shall ... day** Pistol butchers one of
Tamburlaine's most famous lines, in
which he bullies the captive kings who
drag his chariot: 'Holla, ye pampered

158 by this hand] *Q; not in F*   th'infernal] *Q;* the Infernall *F*   with] *Q;* where *F*   159 vile] *Q;* vilde *F*
160 faitors] *Q (*faters*), Capell;* Fates *F*   161 SD] *Oxf¹; [clapping his Hand to his Sword. Capell; not
in QF*   162 'tis] *Q;* it is *F*   163 i'faith] *Q; not in F*   164–9 Shall ... toys?] *prose QF; Pope lines*
packhorses, / Asia, / day, / Cannibals, / with / roar! / toys? / ; *Oxf lines* pack-horses, / Asia, / day, / cannibals,
/ Greeks? / Cerberus, / toys? /

263

horses, and hollow pampered jades of Asia, which   165
cannot go but thirty mile a day, compare with Caesars
and with Cannibals and Troyant Greeks? Nay, rather
damn them with King Cerberus, and let the welkin
roar! Shall we fall foul for toys?

HOSTESS   By my troth, captain, these are very bitter   170
words.

BARDOLPH   Be gone, good ancient! This will grow to
a brawl anon.

PISTOL   ^FDie^F men like dogs, give crowns like pins!
Have we not Hiren here?   175

HOSTESS   A'my word, Captain, there's none such here.

---

jades of Asia! / What, can ye draw but
twenty miles a day . . . ?' (*2 Tamburlaine*,
4.3.1–2).

165 **hollow** an apparent echo of Tamburlaine's
'Holla'

   jades contemptuous term for worn-out
   horses

166 **compare with** rival. The implication is
that the kings who draw Pistol's imaginary chariot should, by their breeding, be
able to cover far more territory than
ordinary horses.

166–7 **Caesars . . . Greeks** Attempting to
outdo Tamburlaine in heroic rant, Pistol
borrows the ludicrously bungled classical
names dropped by the Braggart in Eliot's
Ortho-epia Gallica. Particularly amusing is the substitution of *Cannibals* for
Hannibals (the appropriate pairing with
Caesars) and his conflation of Trojans
with Greeks.

168 **King Cerberus** Cerberus was not a king,
but the three-headed dog who guarded
the gates of the underworld.

168–9 **let . . . roar** a popular refrain in drinking songs, meaning 'Let the heavens

resound' or, more secularly, 'Let the clouds
thunder'. Cf. *1 Tamburlaine*, 4.2.45, 'the
welkin crack'.

169 **fall . . . toys** quarrel over trifles (*OED*
fall *v.* 87b)

174 **Die . . . dogs** proverbial fustian: 'To die
like a dog (a dog's death)' (Dent, D509).
Either the Q compositor or his copy-text
apparently omitted a word; for without
Die, Pistol's two imperative clauses form
one declarative sentence – 'Men like
dogges give crowns like pins' – which
makes no sense.

   give . . . pins Pistol attempts to outdo the
   largesse of Tamburlaine, who gives conquered kingdoms to his loyal followers
   as though they were trifles: cf. *1
   Tamburlaine*, 4.4.114–21.

176–7 **there's . . . her?** The Hostess takes
Hiren to be the name of a whore and, by
assuring Pistol that she would never deny
such a woman to him, inadvertently
confesses what she has tried so hard
to deny: that she runs a brothel. Her
humorous confusion may have given rise
to Hiren's reputation in later plays: see
160–1n.

---

166 mile] *Q*; miles *F*   Caesars] *Q*; *Caesar F*   167 Cannibals] *QF1–2*; Canniball *F3–4*   167–9 and
Troyant . . . toys?] *prose QF*; *Capell lines* Greeks? / Cerberus; / *toys*? /   167 Troyant] *Q (*troiant*)*; Troian *F*
170 captain] captaine *Q(corr)*; captane *Q(uncorr)*; Captaine *F*   174–5] *prose QF*; *Oxf lines* pins! / here? /
174 Die] *F*; *not in Q*   dogs, give] *F*; dogges giue *Q*   176 A'my] *Q (*A my*)*; On my *F*

What the goodyear, do you think I would deny her?
For God's sake, be quiet.

PISTOL   Then feed and be fat, my fair Calipolis! Come,
give's some sack. *Si fortune me tormente sperato*   180
me contento. Fear we broadsides? No, let the fiend
give fire! Give me some sack; – and sweetheart [*to
his sword*], lie thou there. – Come we to full points
here? And are etceteras no things?

177 **What the goodyear** See 59–60n.

179 **feed . . . Calipolis** Pistol echoes a speech
in Peele's *Battle of Alcazar* in which
Muly Mahamet enters with raw meat
on the tip of his sword, 'forcèd from a
lioness', to offer to his starving wife:
'Feed then and faint not fair Calypolis,
/ . . . Feed and be fat that we may meet
the foe / With strength and terror to
revenge our wrong' (2.3.71–102 *passim*).
As Cowl observes (Ard¹), the scene was
sensational enough to inspire parody in
other plays such as Dekker's *Satiromastix*, 4.1.150: 'Feede and be fat my
faire Calipolis', Marston's *What You Will*
(exactly the same line, 5.1.1) and Thomas
Heywood's *The Royall King, and the
Loyall Subiect*, 2.2: 'Here I do meane to
cranch, to munch, to eate. / To feed, and
be fat my fine *Cullapolis*'. Wilson (Cam¹)
speculates that Pistol is offering the
Hostess an apple-john on the tip of his
sword.

180–1 *Si . . . contento* an ungrammatical
mix of Italian, Spanish and French for 'If
fortune torments me, hope contents me',
a popular motto which Pistol repeats
as his exit line at 5.5.95, though with
enough deviation to suggest that he has
no idea what he is saying. Melchiori, who
rewrites the line in grammatically correct
Italian, suggests that Pistol is singing a
snatch of an Italian madrigal, but there is

scant justification for such emendation.
See Dent, F614, and, for earlier instances,
Wilson, *Dictionary*, 282b.

181 **broadsides** the full array, or simultaneous
discharge, of artillery on one side of a
warship (*OED sb.* 2)
fiend figurative for the artillery in
broadsides

182 **give fire** shoot
sack See 1.2.198n. on *new . . . sack.*

182–3 **sweetheart . . . there** Weapons were
commonly personified by their bearers.
Cf. Jonson, *Every Man Out*, where
Cavalier Shift protests, 'Sell my rapier?
no, my deare, I will not bee diuorc't from
thee, yet' (3.6.80–1), and *Mucedorus*,
2.3, in which the wild man Bremo says to
his club, 'lie thou there, / And rest thyself,
till I haue further neede' (Dodsley,
7.220).

183–4 **Come . . . no things?** 'Are we to stop
here? Is there no further entertainment?'
Pistol may be responding to the others'
attempts to quiet him. The phrase *full
points* puns on the tips of swords and
on full stops (periods) as marks of punctuation, while *etceteras* and *things* are
both bawdy references to the female
pudendum. Cf. Q1 of *RJ*, 'O that she
were / An open etcetera' (2.1.37–8) and
'to sink in it, should you burden love – /
Too much oppression for a tender thing'
(1.4.23–4). F's 'nothing' may diminish

177 goodyear] *Q;* good-yere *F*   178 For God's sake] *Q;* I pray *F*   179–84] *prose QF; Capell lines*
Calipolis! / sack. / *contento.* / there. / nothing? /   180 give's] *Q (*giues*);* giue me *F*   180–1 *Si . . . contento.*] *Q,*
*F (*contente*); [Sings] Se fortuna mi tormenta, ben sperato mi contenta – Cam²* (*Keightley*)   182–3 sweetheart,
lie] *Q(corr)F;* sweet hartlie *Q(uncorr)*   SD] *Capell subst.; not in QF*   184 no things] *Q;* nothing *F*

FALSTAFF   Pistol, I would be quiet.   185

PISTOL   Sweet knight, I kiss thy neaf. What! We have
seen the seven stars.

DOLL   For God's sake, thrust him downstairs! I cannot
endure such a fustian rascal.

PISTOL   Thrust him downstairs? Know we not Galloway   190
nags?

FALSTAFF   Quoit him down, Bardolph, like a shove-groat
shilling. Nay, an 'a do nothing but speak nothing, 'a
shall be nothing here.

BARDOLPH   Come, get you downstairs.   195

PISTOL   [*Snatches up his sword.*]   What, shall we have
incision? Shall we imbrue? Then death rock me

the sexual innuendo, but if 'thing'
denotes a penis, as it does elsewhere in
Shakespeare, then Q's *no things*, with its
buried pun on 'O things', vaginal orifices,
would signify the lack of a penis, and so,
a vagina. This is the sense in which
Hamlet plays on 'nothing' in his banter
with Ophelia (*Ham* 3.2.111, 114).

186 **neaf** northern dialect for hand or fist: cf.
MND 4.1.19: 'Give me your neaf'. Pistol
vulgarizes the chivalric Spanish custom
of kissing the hand of a fellow knight.

186–7 **We ... stars** a nostalgic claim of good
fellowship: 'We have caroused together
till all hours': cf. Falstaff's 'We have
heard the chimes at midnight' (3.2.214)
and, more pertinent, his admission, 'we
that take purses go by the moon and the
seven stars' (*1H4* 1.2.12–13). By *the
seven stars*, Pistol means the Pleiades, or
Great Bear, a point of reference in the
night sky. But 'The Seven Stars' was
also the name of an Elizabethan tavern
near the Inns of Court that figured in
the anonymous *Timon* comedy (Bulman,
'Timon', 115–16), an appropriate – if

anachronistic – venue for Pistol and
Falstaff to drink in.

189 **fustian** bombastic, ranting. The term
derived from a coarse cloth of cotton and
flax, worn by those who could not afford
better.

190–1 **Galloway nags** small horses bred in
Scotland, used in London to draw light
carriages and often for hire. But *nag* was
also slang for prostitute, a woman who
could be easily ridden (cf. *AC* 3.10.10:
'Yon ribaudred nag of Egypt'): so in
effect, Pistol asks, 'Don't we know a
whore when we see one?'

192 **Quoit** toss like a quoit, a discus of metal
or stone thrown into a ring. Cf. 247.

192–3 **shove-groat shilling** a coin (usually
an Edward VI shilling) propelled by hand
along a polished board into pockets at the
end during a game (*shove-groat*) akin to
shuffleboard

193–4 **an ... here** if he does nothing but
speak nonsense, he'll have to leave. By
thrice repeating *nothing*, Falstaff satiric-
ally echoes Pistol's *no things* at 184.

197 **incision** blood-letting (a term from
medicine)

188 For God's sake] *Q; not in F*   189 endure] *Q (*indure*), F*   192 Quoit] *Q (*Quaite*), F*   193 an 'a ... 'a]
*Q (*and*); if hee ... hee F*   196 SD] *Rowe subst. (after 200), Capell subst.; not in QF*   196–200] *prose
QF; Capell lines* imbrue? / days! / wounds / say! /   197 imbrue] *Q (*imbrew*), F (*embrew*)

asleep, abridge my doleful days! Why then, let
grievous, ghastly, gaping wounds untwine the sisters
three! Come, Atropos, I say!   200

HOSTESS   Here's goodly stuff toward.

FALSTAFF   Give me my rapier, boy!

DOLL   I pray thee, Jack, I pray thee, do not draw!

FALSTAFF   Get you downstairs!

> [*Falstaff draws his sword and exchanges thrusts
> with Pistol.*]

HOSTESS   Here's a goodly tumult! I'll forswear keeping   205
house afore I'll be in these tirrits and frights. So!
Murder, I warrant now! Alas, alas, put up your naked
weapons! Put up your naked weapons!

> [*Exit Pistol, pursued by Bardolph.*]

---

imbrue shed blood, wound one another.
In a similarly silly situation, Thisbe cries,
'Come, blade, my breast imbrue!' (*MND*
5.1.331).

197–8 death . . . asleep the opening line of a
song attributed to both Anne Boleyn and
her brother as they awaited execution in
1536 ('O Death! rocke me on slepe') but
also included in a volume written by
Arnold Cosbie as he lay in the Marshalsea
prison in 1591 (Ard¹). See Duffin, 281–3.

198 abridge . . . days burlesques the laments
in heroic plays such as *Locrine*, 'I my
selfe . . . Meane to abridge my former
destenies' (5.4.238–9, in Brooke) and
1 Tamburlaine, 'Now Bajazeth, abridge
thy baneful days' (5.1.286).

198–9 let . . . wounds parody of alliterative
verse found in old-fashioned heroic
tragedies, already lampooned by Bottom
in *Pyramus and Thisbe*

199–200 untwine . . . I say The *sisters three*
refers to the three Fates of classical
mythology, whose functions Pistol has

confusedly intertwined: Clotho held the
spindle on which life's thread was spun,
Lachesis drew the thread and Atropos cut
it. Invocations to Atropos were frequent:
cf. *Locrine*, 'Sweet *Atropos*, cut off my
fatall thred' (5.4.222, in Brooke) and
Sackville's 'Complaint of Henry, Duke
of Buckingham', which abounds in
allusions to doleful days, the sisters three
and Atropos cutting the thread.

201 goodly . . . toward said with irony: a fine
'to do' in the making

205–6 keeping house carrying on a business; i.e. the tavern, but with a possible
play on *house* as brothel

206 tirrits perhaps a Quicklyism conflating
terrors and *fits* (Ard²), though similar
words were current in dialect: e.g. 'ter'
for anger, 'tirrivee' for commotion
(Wright, *Dictionary*)

208 put . . . weapons more inadvertent *double
entendre* from the Hostess. *Put up* means
to sheathe or erect; *naked weapons* refers
to unsheathed swords or exposed penises.

---

199 untwine] *F3;* vntwinde *Q;* vntwin'd *F*   201 goodly] *Q;* good *F*   203 pray thee . . . pray thee] *Q;*
prethee . . . prethee *F*   204 SD] *this edn; Drawing, and driving Pistol out. / Rowe; Falstaff thrusts at
Pistol. Cam¹; not in QF*   206 afore] *Q;* before *F*   208 SD] *Oxf;* [*Exeunt* Pistol *and* Bardolph. *Capell; Exit
Bardolph, driving Pistol out. / Collier³; not in QF*

DOLL   I pray thee, Jack, be quiet. The rascal's gone. Ah,
    you whoreson little valiant villain, you!   210
HOSTESS   Are you not hurt i'th' groin? Methought 'a
    made a shrewd thrust at your belly.

[Enter BARDOLPH.*]*

FALSTAFF   Have you turned him out a'doors?
BARDOLPH   Yea, sir; the rascal's drunk. You have hurt
    him, sir, i'th' shoulder.   215
FALSTAFF   A rascal, to brave me!
DOLL   Ah, you sweet little rogue, you! Alas, poor ape,
    how thou sweat'st! Come, let me wipe thy face. Come
    on, you whoreson chops! Ah, rogue, i'faith, I love
    thee. Thou art as valorous as Hector of Troy, worth   220
    five of Agamemnon, and ten times better than the
    Nine Worthies! Ah, villain!

209 **be quiet** The Hostess urges Falstaff to
    calm down rather than to be silent:
    apparently he is still going through the
    motions of fighting Pistol.
210 **whoreson** an abusive epithet, similar
    to the modern 'sonofabitch', which, in
    context, becomes a term of endearment.
    Cf. 219, 232.
211 **groin** probably a euphemism for the
    genitals. The Hostess's solicitude is under-
    standable, given her hopes of marrying
    Falstaff.
212 **shrewd** vicious, nasty
216 **brave** challenge, threaten or defy
217, 219 **rogue** a term of reproach, here used
    affectionately to indicate a mischief-
    maker (*OED sb.* 3).
    ape fool. Cf. similarly playful usage in
    1H4, 2.3.74: 'you mad-headed ape!'.

219 **chops** a person with fat cheeks, also
    applied to Falstaff at *1H4* 1.2.129
220–1 **Hector ... Agamemnon** two heroes
    of the Trojan War. Hector, eldest son of
    King Priam, was the most valiant of the
    Trojans; Agamemnon was a king and
    general of the Greek armies.
222 **Nine Worthies** a mixture of historical,
    legendary and biblical heroes celebrated
    as the noblest of their type in chivalric
    romances: three pagans (Hector,
    Alexander, Julius Caesar); three Jews
    (Joshua, David, Judas Maccabeus); and
    three Christians (Arthur, Charlemagne,
    Godfrey of Bouillon). Shakespeare
    celebrates them in a comic masque of the
    Worthies in *LLL* 5.2.531–711.

209 pray thee] *Q;* prethee *F*   rascal's] *Q;* Rascall is *F*   210 valiant] *Q (*vliaunt*), F*   211 'a] *Q;* hee *F*
212.1] *Capell; not in QF*   213 a'doors] *Q (*a doores*);* of doores *F*   214 Yea] *Q;* Yes *F*   215 i'th'] *Q;* in
the *F*   217 Ah, you] *F, Q (*A you*)*   219 Ah, rogue] *F, Q (*a rogue*)*   i'faith] *Q (*yfaith*); not in F*   222 Ah,
villain] *F, Q (*a villaine*)*

FALSTAFF   ^FA^F rascally slave! I will toss the rogue in a
  blanket.

DOLL   Do, an thou dar'st for thy heart. An thou dost, I'll   225
  canvas thee between a pair of sheets.

Enter [FRANCIS *with*] *Music*[, *Sneak's band*].
  [*Bardolph and Hostess talk aside.*]

PAGE   The music is come, sir.

FALSTAFF   Let them play. – Play, sirs! [*Music*] Sit on my
  knee, Doll. A rascal, bragging slave! The rogue fled
  from me like quicksilver.   230

DOLL   I'faith, and thou follow'dst him like a church.

---

223 *A Q's interjection 'Ah' is wrong here,
  because Falstaff is not directly addressing
  Pistol: F's article is correct. Somewhat
  confusingly, though, Q's 'A' at 217 and
  'a' at 219 and 222, obviously meant to be
  interjections, apparently are a variant
  spelling of 'Ah'.

223–4 I . . . blanket Falstaff is still reliving
  his victory over Pistol: tossing in a
  blanket was a punishment for cowards.
  Dent cites as proverbial 'To toss like a
  dog in a blanket' (D513.1).

225 an . . . heart 'as if your life depended
  on it' (*OED* for *conj.* 9c); or perhaps
  more literally, 'if you don't fear having a
  heart attack'. Doll is indulging Falstaff's
  fantasy.

225–6 I'll . . . sheets Ironically, Doll will
  turn Pistol's punishment into Falstaff's
  reward by tossing the latter between a
  pair of sheets as a sexual favour. There is
  a pun on *canvas* meaning (1) to entangle
  or catch within a net, a term from
  hawking, and (2) the material of which
  sheets are made. To make the irony clear,
  Doll's emphasis should be on *thee*.

226.1–2 *Whether the musicians play onstage
  or in the music gallery above is unclear
  (cf. *1H4* 3.1.226n.). Also unclear is how
  long they continue to play, though it is
  certainly long enough to provide back-
  ground music for the dialogue between
  Falstaff and Doll (228–83). The use of
  musical underscoring to establish mood
  was rare in Elizabethan drama; here, the
  mood is likely to have been gently
  melancholic, the musical selections
  associated with old age and declining
  performance – themes picked up again in
  the snatches of song sung by Silence in
  5.3 (Lindley, *Music*, 147). The musicians
  may have played beyond 283, for Falstaff
  doesn't instruct the Page to pay them
  until 378.

229–30 fled . . . quicksilver   proverbial
  (Dent, Q14.1, 'To run like quicksilver',
  i.e. like mercury). Cf. *Ham* 1.5.66.

231 like a church an odd simile, possibly,
  according to Cowl (Ard¹), inspired
  by Nashe's *Summer's Last Will and
  Testament* (1030–1; *Works*, 3.266), in
  which Bacchus is said to have a

---

223 A] *F*; Ah *Q*   225 an . . . An] *Q* (and . . . and*)*; if . . . if *F*   dar'st] *F*; darst *Q*   226.1] *this edn*; enter
musicke. Q (after 227); Enter Musique. *F*   226.2] *this edn*; *Bardolph talks to Hostess.* / *Collier*³ *(after
267)*; *not in QF*   228 SD] *Singer*²; *not in QF*   231 I'faith] *Q (*Yfaith*)*; *not in F*

Thou whoreson little tidy Bartholomew boar-pig,
when wilt thou leave fighting a'days and foining
a'nights and begin to patch up thine old body for
heaven?   235

> *Enter* PRINCE [Henry] *and* POINS
> [*dressed as drawers, and standing apart*].

FALSTAFF   Peace, good Doll. Do not speak like a
death's-head: do not bid me remember mine end.
DOLL   Sirrah, what humour's the Prince of?
FALSTAFF   A good shallow young fellow. 'A would have
made a good pantler; 'a would ha' chipped bread well.   240
DOLL   They say Poins has a good wit.

'paunch . . . built like a round church'
and filled with 'tunnes of wine'. In
contrasting Pistol's *quicksilver* exit with
Falstaff's laborious pursuit, Doll may be
gently ridiculing Falstaff's hulking size;
but quite possibly the joke is now lost.

232 **tidy** plump, fat
  Bartholomew boar-pig a humorous gloss
  on Falstaff's visits to the Pie Corner
  district of Smithfield (cf. 1.2.51n., 2.1.25n.),
  site of Bartholomew Fair, a carnival held
  annually on St Bartholomew's Day (24
  August), at which roast pig was sold by
  vendors. A boar pig is a young boar; Doll
  is thus flattering Falstaff, who elsewhere
  is called an 'old boar' (2.2.142).
233 **leave** stop, give up
233–4 **foining a'nights** nocturnal thrusting
  (sexual) in contrast to diurnal thrusting
  (*fighting*); see 2.1.16n. on *foin.*
234–5 **patch . . . heaven** remedy your physical ailments in preparation for death, with
  a possible hint of doing penance as well
235.2 **dressed as drawers** The Prince's and
  Poins's disguise presumably consisted of

no more than drawers' aprons and leather
jerkins (see 2.2.168), sufficient to convey
in dramatic shorthand that they would
pass unrecognized, as do Shakespeare's
comic heroines when disguised as young
men. But Francis knows about the
planned trick on Falstaff (see 15–18),
and presumably all the tavern personnel
are in on it. Doll's plying Falstaff with
questions about the Prince and Poins
immediately after their entrance suggests
that she either is already aware of the
ruse or has recognized them and is
playing along. Her questions otherwise
are too coincidental.

237 **death's-head** skull used as a *memento
  mori*, a reminder of one's mortality
238 **humour** here, character or temperament
240 **pantler** servant of the pantry, a menial
  position
  ha' have
  chipped bread removed the hard crusts
  from a loaf of bread before serving it
241 **wit** understanding, intellect

233–4] a'days . . . a'nights] *Q;* on dayes . . . on nights *F*   235.1–2] *this edn; Enter Prince and Poynes.
Q; Enter the Prince and Poines disguis'd. F*   238 humour's] *Q;* humor is *F*   239–40 'A . . . 'a] *Q;*
hee . . . hee *F*   240 a'] *Q (*a*);* haue *F;* ha' *Cam²*   241 has] *Q;* hath *F*

FALSTAFF   He a good wit? Hang him, baboon! His wit's
as thick as Tewkesbury mustard! There's no more
conceit in him than is in a mallet.

DOLL   Why does the Prince love him so, then?   245

FALSTAFF   Because their legs are both of a bigness, and
'a plays at quoits well, and eats conger and fennel,
and drinks off candles' ends for flap-dragons, and
rides the wild mare with the boys, and jumps upon

243 **thick ... mustard** *thick* means dense
and is thus pejorative when applied to
Poins's wit. Tewkesbury mustard, however, was as famous for its sharp taste as
for its texture: Tilley cites a proverbial
simile at odds with Falstaff's usage:
'He's as sharp, as if he liv'd upon
Tewksbury-Mustard' (M1333).

244 **conceit** imagination, wit (*OED sb.* 8d)
mallet heavy wooden hammer, figuratively associated with mental dullness.
Compare 'As dull as a beetle' (Tilley,
B220); a *beetle*, a large mallet, is
mentioned at 1.2.227, and also in *TS*
4.1.144: 'beetle-headed ... knave'.

246 **both ... bigness** the same size. Before
the advent of trousers, the size of one's
calf was important to men of fashion
and was emphasized by the choice of
stocking. Cf. 2.2.14–16.

247 **plays at quoits** a game in which *quoits*
(see 192n.) were thrown into a ring, the
object being to come as close as possible
to hitting a stake in the ground, much as
in a game of horseshoes (*OED sb.* 2). Here
begins Falstaff's comic itemization of all
those self-indulgent behaviours for which
the Prince enjoys Poins. The expressions
are a catalogue of tavern and brothel cant.
conger and fennel sea-eel (cf. 55n.)
seasoned with fennel to make it
digestible. Unless well cooked, *conger*
was thought to blunt the wits – another
crack at Poins's lack of intelligence.

Cf. *1 Oldcastle*, 4.24: 'I could eat this
conger'.

248 **drinks ... flap-dragons** Poins participates in foolishly risky tavern games; *flap-
dragons* were flaming objects – here,
lighted candle wicks – afloat on liquor
which the drinker, to prove his dexterity,
had either to dodge or, in Poins's case, to
dowse in his mouth (*drink off*). As Cowl
(Ard¹) observes, the dangers of such
behaviour are recorded by W.R. in *A
Match at Midnight* 2.1: 'our Flemish
corporal was lately choked at Delft with a
flap-dragon' (Dodsley, 13.44).

249 **rides ... mare** an allusion to one of two
different games: either see-saw or, more
likely, a variant on leap-frog, 'wherein
the person who acts the mare, slides over
the shoulders of several others, who are
linked together; and is strapped with
leathern aprons, and the like, while he is
getting over' (Wright, *Dictionary*, mare
*sb.*² 1). Falstaff has earlier used the
phrase as a bawdy metaphor for fornica-
tion: see 2.1.75–7.

249–50 **jumps upon joint-stools** indulges in
rowdy behaviour at taverns. A *joint-stool*
was made of parts joined together; to
jump over one was taken as a sign of high
spirits, as in Middleton's *Chaste Maid in
Cheapside*: 'when you come to your inn,
if you leaped over a joint-stool or two,
'twere not amiss; (*Aside*) – although you
break your neck, sir' (3.3.122–4).

242 wit's] *Q; Wit is F*   243 There's] *Q; there is F*   245 does] *Q; doth F*   247 'a] *Q; hee F*

joint-stools, and swears with a good grace, and wears   250
his boots very smooth like unto the sign of the Leg,
and breeds no bate with telling of discreet stories;
and such other gambol faculties 'a has that show a
weak mind and an able body, for the which the Prince
admits him. For the Prince himself is such another.   255
The weight of a hair will turn ᶠtheᶠ scales between
their *haber de poiz*.

PRINCE   Would not this nave of a wheel have his ears cut
off?

POINS   Let's beat him before his whore.   260

PRINCE   Look whe'er the withered elder hath not his
poll clawed like a parrot.

POINS   Is it not strange that desire should so many years
outlive performance?

FALSTAFF   Kiss me, Doll. [*She kisses him.*]   265

---

250 **swears ... grace** is adept at profanity; *good grace* meaning both (1) proficiency and (2) God's grace

251 **smooth ... Leg** tight-fitting like the boot on the sign over a boot-maker's shop called the Leg. Poins, apparently vain about his calves, wears boots to show them off: cf. 246n.

252 **breeds ... stories** causes no offence (*OED* bate *sb.* = strife, discord) by telling pointless tales about people. Although Falstaff may mean precisely what he says, he probably means the opposite, that Poins delights his companions with slanderous gossip, *discreet stories* being those that ought to be kept private.

253 **gambol faculties** frivolous inclinations

255 **admits** i.e. to his company

257 *haber de poiz* Falstaff's anglicized

pronunciation of the French *avoirdupois*, meaning weight or degree of heaviness (*OED sb.* 3)

258 **nave ... wheel** hub of a wheel: a pun on Falstaff's knavery (*nave*) and an allusion to his girth (*wheel*)

258–9 **ears cut off** 'A Star Chamber penalty for defaming royalty' (Winstanley, cited in Ard²)

260 **before** in front of

261 **whe'er** archaic contraction of 'whether'
withered elder shrivelled old man, or sapless elder tree. The suggestion of sexual impotence becomes explicit at 263–4. Cf. similar references to Falstaff as an *apple-john* (3–8) and a *dead elm* (335).

262 **poll clawed** hair tousled (by Doll), with a play on *poll*/'Poll' as the name of a parrot

---

250 joint-stools] *QF (*ioynd-stooles)*   251 boots] *Q;* Boot *F*   253 'a has] *Q;* hee hath *F*   256 a hair] *Q;* an hayre *F*   the] *F; not in Q*   257 haber de poiz] *Q, F (Haber-de-pois);* avoirdupois *Var '03*   260 Let's] *Q;* Let vs *F*   261 whe'er] *Neilson;* where *Q;* if *F*   265 SD] *Capell; not in QF*

PRINCE   Saturn and Venus this year in conjunction?
What says th'almanac to that?

POINS   And look whether the fiery trigon his man be not
lisping to his master's old tables, his notebook, his
counsel-keeper.   270

FALSTAFF   Thou dost give me flattering busses.

DOLL   By my troth, I kiss thee with a most constant
heart.

FALSTAFF   I am old, I am old.

DOLL   I love thee better than I love e'er a scurvy young   275
boy of them all.

FALSTAFF   What stuff wilt have a kirtle of? I shall receive

---

266 **Saturn ... conjunction** The Prince mocks
Doll and Falstaff's relationship with a
play on *conjunction* as (1) an astrological
term for the apparent proximity of two
planets which, when viewed from the
earth, appear to overlap, and (2) a term
for sexual intercourse. The reference to
Saturn and Venus is satiric because the
two planets are almost never in conjunction, and in mythology they are opposite
in temper: Saturn, patriarch of the gods,
is cold and morose in his old age; Venus,
goddess of love, hot and libidinous.

267 **th'almanac** then, as now, a cheaply
printed book widely read for making
astrological predictions

268 **fiery trigon** an astrological name sneer-
ingly given to Bardolph to mock his
burning complexion and red nose. The
twelve signs of the Zodiac were divided
into four groups of three (*trigon* = a
triangle), of which the *fiery trigon*, hot
and dry, included Aries, Leo and
Sagittarius. For similar references to
Bardolph's complexion, see 333, 336–8,
and 2.2.72–89 *passim*.

269 **lisping** whispering sweet nothings. During the conversation between Doll and
Falstaff, Bardolph has apparently taken
the Hostess aside for an intimate conversation. Sexual liaisons at the tavern seem
to be more casual than committed:
Falstaff has promised to marry the
Hostess yet carries on with Doll through
the Hostess's good offices; Bardolph here
appears to be courting the Hostess, yet by
H5 she will have married Pistol.

269–70 **old ... counsel-keeper** phrases which
define Falstaff's deep and long-standing
friendship with the Hostess. She has
served as his *tables* (tablets, possibly
used for recording assignations) and
notebook (akin to a private diary), and in
both instances has been his *counsel-
keeper* (confidante). That she is *old*
distinguishes her from Doll.

271 **flattering busses** insincere kisses

275–6 **a ... all** any boy. For *scurvy*, see 123n.

277 **What ... of?** 'What material would you
like your gown to be made of?' A *kirtle*
was a bodice and skirt worn over the
petticoats and farthingale.

---

267 th'almanac] *Q;* the Almanack *F*   269 master's] *F (*Masters*);* master, *Q*   272 By my troth] *Q;* Nay
truely *F*   277 wilt] *Q;* wilt thou *F*

money a'Thursday: shalt have a cap tomorrow. –
A merry song! – Come, it grows late; we'll to bed.
Thou't forget me when I am gone.   280

DOLL   By my troth, thou't set me a-weeping an thou
sayst so. Prove that ever I dress myself handsome till
thy return! Well, hearken a'th' end.

FALSTAFF   Some sack, Francis!

PRINCE, POINS [*coming forward*]   Anon, anon, sir!   285

FALSTAFF   Ha? A bastard son of the King's? – And art
not thou Poins his brother?

PRINCE   Why, thou globe of sinful continents, what a
life dost thou lead?

FALSTAFF   A better than thou: I am a gentleman, thou art   290
a drawer.

277, 278 **wilt, shalt** In Q, 'thou' is the implied
subject for each verb; F provides it.

279 **A merry song!** probably a comment on
the song being played (228 SD) rather
than a request for a new one

281 **an** if

282–3 **Prove … return** Doll urges a trial of
her constancy: 'Witness (*Prove*) whether
I'll wear attractive clothes, and thus
entice other men, in your absence.'

283 **hearken a'th' end** proverbial for 'judge
by the outcome', and a variant of the
Latin *respice finem* (Dent, 'Mark the
end', E125; cf. Ecclesiastes, 7.36); cf. *CE*
4.4.41. Doll enjoins Falstaff to wait until
his return to judge her fidelity, though the
line may carry a secondary injunction to
listen to the end of the piece of music,
following Falstaff's comment on the
music at 279.

285 **Anon, anon, sir!** The Prince and Poins
mimic the answer Francis invariably
gives when called: see 16n. In answering

Falstaff's call, they presumably do not
need to doff their aprons and jerkins for
him to identify them – the only time in
Shakespeare when persons who have
disguised themselves are instantly
recognized.

287 **Poins his brother** archaic form of the
possessive: Poins's brother and lookalike,
a companion to the bastard son of the
King who resembles the Prince (286).

288 **globe … continents** an allusion to
Falstaff's girth, but also to his universality: cf. *1H4* 2.4.466–7: 'Banish plump
Jack and banish all the world'. Falstaff's
universality, however, is of the fallen
variety: his *sinful continents* not only
refer to the geography of his body,
but play on three other meanings as
well: receptacles for sin ('continent' =
container); sinful contents ('continent' =
what is contained); and, oxymoronically,
'continence', its homophone and a virtue
at odds with sin.

---

278 a'Thursday] *Q* (a Thursday); on Thursday *F*   shalt] *Q*; thou shalt *F*   279 we'll] *Q* (weele); wee
will *F*   280 Thou't] *Q*; Thou wilt *F*   281 By my troth] *Q*; *not in F*   thou't] *Q*; Thou wilt *F*   an] *Q* (and);
if *F*   283 a'th'] *Q*; the *F*   285 SD] *Capell*; *not in QF*   287 Poins his] Poynes his *Q*; *Poines*, his *F*

PRINCE   Very true, sir, and I come to draw you out by
the ears.

HOSTESS   O, the Lord preserve thy grace! By my troth,
welcome to London. Now the Lord bless that sweet   295
face of thine! O Jesu, are you come from Wales?

FALSTAFF   Thou whoreson mad compound of majesty,
by this light flesh and corrupt blood [*Indicates Doll.*],
thou art welcome!

DOLL   How? You fat fool, I scorn you!   300

POINS [*to Prince*]   My lord, he will drive you out of
your revenge and turn all to a merriment if you take
not the heat.

PRINCE [*to Falstaff*]   You whoreson candle-mine, you!
How vilely did you speak of me now before this   305
honest, virtuous, civil gentlewoman!

HOSTESS   God's blessing of your good heart, and so she
is, by my troth.

292–3 **to . . . ears** with a pun on what
drawers do: to stretch out by the ears as a
form of torture, or to drag to the gallows
– a punishment for traitors (*OED* draw v.
87c, 4). Cf. 258–9n.
296 **come from Wales** Cf. references to the
King's Welsh campaign at 1.2.104–5,
1.3.79–83 and 2.1.133–4.
297 **compound** mass, lump
298 **by . . . blood** Attempting to divert attention from himself to Doll, who perhaps
sits on his knee, Falstaff 'jokingly extends
the common oath *by this light* by adding
flesh and blood' (Delius). As a result,
light becomes an adjective meaning
promiscuous and modifies *this* – that is,
her – flesh; and *corrupt blood* may refer
to the diseases Doll is said to carry: cf.
42–7. Doll's retort at 300 is understandably contemptuous.

302 **merriment** comic jest
302–3 **if . . . heat** 'if you don't strike while
the iron is hot' – a metaphor from
the blacksmith's forge (Craig). Cf. *KL*
1.1.309: 'We must do something, and i'
the heat'.
304 **candle-mine** a heap of tallow for making
candles: an allusion to Falstaff's fat. Cf.
1.2.159–60 and *1H4* 2.4.220–1: 'thou
whoreson obscene greasy tallow-catch'.
306 **honest . . . gentlewoman** chaste, moral,
polite and well-bred woman. The Prince
contradicts Falstaff and speaks courteously of Doll, though perhaps with
tongue in cheek, both here and at 330.
For comparable uses of these terms, see
89 (*civil*), 91 (*honest*) and 2.2.151
(*gentlewoman*).

---

294 grace] *Q;* good Grace *F*   By my troth,] *Q; not in F*   295 the Lord] *Q;* Heauen *F*   296 O Jesu] *Q;*
what *F*   298 light flesh] *F;* light, flesh, *Q*   SD] *this edn; Leaning his hand upon Dol. / Rowe*   301 SD]
Oxf¹ subst.   304 SD] *Oxf¹*   305 vilely] *F3–4;* vildly *QF1–2*   me] *Q;* me euen *F*   307 God's blessing of]
Q; 'Blessing on *F*

FALSTAFF [*to Prince*]   Didst thou hear me?

PRINCE   Yea, and you knew me as you did when you ran   310
away by Gad's Hill. You knew I was at your back
and spoke it on purpose to try my patience.

FALSTAFF   No, no, no, not so; I did not think thou wast
within hearing.

PRINCE   I shall drive you then to confess the wilful   315
abuse, and then I know how to handle you.

FALSTAFF   No abuse, Hal, a'mine honour; no abuse.

PRINCE   Not to dispraise me, and call me pantler and
bread-chipper and I know not what?

FALSTAFF   No abuse, Hal.   320

POINS   No abuse?

FALSTAFF   No abuse, Ned, i'th' world! Honest Ned,
none. I dispraised him before the wicked, [*to Prince*]
that the wicked might not fall in love with thee – in

310–11 ¹**you . . . Hill** an allusion to Falstaff's
comic exposure in *1H4* when, to excuse
his cowardly behaviour during the Gad's
Hill robbery, he claims to have recognized that the Prince was his assailant: 'By
the Lord, I knew ye as well as he that
made ye' (2.4.259–60). Falstaff makes
no such claim here.

318 **Not . . . ¹me** *Not* carries over the negative
from Falstaff's previous line, so the
meaning is, 'You intended no abuse in
disparaging me?'

322, 327 **Ned** a nickname for Poins by which
Falstaff, cornered, attempts to ingratiate
himself; used also by the Prince at
2.2.135, 154 and 173

323 **the wicked** parody of the Puritan idiom
– *the wicked* being the reprobate or
infidels – by which Falstaff attempts to
flatter the Prince as one of the elect and
distance himself from his tavern companions. His method is akin to claiming

that he was a coward 'on instinct' at
Gad's Hill because, as a lion, he would
never harm the 'true prince' (*1H4*
2.4.260–6). Falstaff's excuse is a pale
echo of his bravura self-justification in
1H4, however. He uses the same strategy
of turning lies to advantage by flattery,
but here the strategy is telescoped, the
joke quickly passes and Falstaff does not
expect to be believed. His use of Puritan
terms may be a residue of his earlier
incarnation as Oldcastle. Cf. 1.2.36,
2.2.128n., and his confession to being
'little better than one of the wicked' in
1H4 1.2.91. See also p. 68.

324 **with thee** Falstaff turns from speaking to
Poins *about* Harry – *I dispraised him*
(323) – to address Harry directly. Since
the sentence continues in the second
person (*thy father*, 326), F's 'with him' is
a less sensible option. See a similar shift
of address at 2.1.72–5.

309 SD] *Oxf¹ subst.*   310 Yea] *Q*; Yes *F*   317 a'mine] *Q (*a mine*);* on mine *F*   319 bread-chipper] *Q;*
Bread-chopper *F*   322 i'th'] *Q;* in the *F*   323 SD] *Sisson subst.; not in QF*   324 thee] *Q;* him *F*

which doing I have done the part of a careful friend   325
and a true subject, and thy father is to give me thanks
for it. No abuse, Hal; none, Ned, none. No, faith,
boys, none.

PRINCE   See now whether pure fear and entire cowardice
doth not make thee wrong this virtuous gentlewoman   330
to close with us. Is she of the wicked? Is thine hostess
here of the wicked? Or is thy boy of the wicked? Or
honest Bardolph, whose zeal burns in his nose, of the
wicked?

POINS   Answer, thou dead elm, answer!   335

FALSTAFF   The fiend hath pricked down Bardolph
irrecoverable, and his face is Lucifer's privy kitchen,
where he doth nothing but roast malt-worms. For the

326 **is to** should
329 **entire** unalloyed, pure (*OED adj.* 6b)
331 **to close with** in order to pacify (*OED close v.* 14)
  Is . . . wicked? The Prince may speak only partly in earnest, for by Puritan standards, the denizens of the tavern would all be among (*of*) the wicked, their souls unregenerate. His use of words such as *virtuous* (330) and *honest* (333) is ironic; cf. 306n.
333 **zeal** Burning *zeal* was a Puritan virtue, but here it is reduced to the red glow of Bardolph's nose. Cf. 268n. and Dekker, *If This Be Not a Good Play*, 5.4.262: '''Tis a burning zeal must consume the wicked' (*Dramatic*, 3.210).
335 **dead elm** an image of old age and decay: cf. *withered elder* at 261. Shakespeare twice uses 'elm' for a man to whom a woman clings – *CE* 2.2.174: 'thou art an elm, my husband, I a vine', and *MND* 4.1.42–3: 'the female ivy so / Enrings the barky fingers of the elm' – though the implication here is that Falstaff is no longer of service to women. The topos

of the elm and vine is traditional: see Demetz.
336–7 **pricked . . . irrecoverable** listed Bardolph in his book as unredeemable. 'To prick' meant to make a mark next to a name on a list (*OED v.* 14, 15); Falstaff uses it in this sense during the recruitment scene at Justice Shallow's farm (3.2.111–79 *passim*). For the legend of the devil's book, see 2.2.43–4n. Falstaff continues to play on the Puritan notion that the souls of his companions are reprobate.
337 **Lucifer's privy kitchen** the devil's private kitchen, i.e. hell, extending the Prince's joke about the inflammation in Bardolph's face (333). Occurring only once in Scripture, *Lucifer* is the name used to compare Nebuchadnezzar with the morning star (Isaiah, 14.12); but by Shakespeare's time 'the title "Lucifer" was mistakenly applied to Satan' (Shaheen, 165).
338 **he . . . malt-worms** he (*Lucifer*) spends all his time punishing (roasting) lovers of malt liquor – drunkards such as Bardolph.

327 faith] *Q; not in F*   329 entire] *Q (*intire*), F*   332 thy] *Q; the F*

277

boy, there is a good angel about him, but the devil
blinds him too.   340

PRINCE   For the women?

FALSTAFF   For one of them, she's in hell already and
burns poor souls. For th'other, I owe her money,
and whether she be damned for that I know not.

HOSTESS   No, I warrant you.   345

FALSTAFF   No, I think thou art not. I think thou art quit
for that. Marry, there is another indictment upon
thee, for suffering flesh to be eaten in thy house

The antecedent for *he* is ambiguous, but
in context it would make no sense if
Bardolph were doing the roasting.

339–40 **there...too**   an   image   from
Morality plays, in which the figure of
mankind is caught in a tug-of-war
between allegorical good and evil; *about*
= hovering near

340 ***blinds** Most editors are dissatisfied with
both the Q and F verbs, and some offer
substitutions of their own, recorded in the
t.n.; but Q's reading is defensible – the
devil blinds the boy (*too* = like everyone
else) to the good angel's presence.
Shaheen cites as a source 2 Corinthians,
4.4 – 'The God of this worlde hath
blinded the minds . . . of the infidels' –
arguing that 'the cluster of biblical
references that follow one another in
rapid succession' within these lines
suggests that the Q reading is correct
(*History*, 165). Sisson would alter Q to
read 'but the devil blinds him to't',
reasoning that Q's *too* is a 'graphically
plausible error' for a MS 'to't' (*Readings*,
48) – an alteration which would more
pointedly identify Falstaff as the *good
angel* (339) to whose presence the devil
blinds the boy. Falstaff may indeed imply
that he himself is the boy's good angel, in
contrast to the Lord Chief Justice's

accusing him of being the Prince's *ill
angel* at 1.2.165.

343 **burns poor souls** a reference to Doll,
implying that she both damns (*burns*)
the souls of her clients by practising
her profession and infects (*burns*) those
clients with sexually transmitted diseases
(*OED v.* 14e)

344 **damned for that** Lending money at
interest, or usury, was condemned as a
sin, especially and most hypocritically
by Puritans; but Falstaff is once again
muddling the notion of culpability, for
the Hostess has not charged him interest
on his loans, and he has no intention of
paying them back.

346–7 **quit for that** either (1) acquitted of
the sin of usury, or (2) cleared of the debt
I owe you (because it will never be
repaid)

347 **indictment upon** charge brought against

348–9 **suffering...law** i.e. allowing meat
to be consumed at your tavern when
doing so was prohibited during Lent;
or metaphorically, running a brothel.
'Eating flesh' was a euphemism for
fornicating with prostitutes: cf. *MM*, in
which the Duke is called 'a fleshmonger'
(5.1.331). The sale of meat during Lent
was forbidden by law, though the law
was honoured more in the breach than in

339–40 devil blinds] *Q;* Deuill outbids *F;* devil's behind *(Cam¹);* devil bloats *(W. Walker);* devil attends
Ard²; devil binds *Davison;* devil bids *Oxf¹;* devil brands *(GWW conj.)*   342 she's] *Q (*shees*);* shee is *F*
343 th'other] *Q;* the other *F*

contrary to the law, for the which I think thou wilt
howl.   350

HOSTESS   All vict'lers do so. What's a joint of mutton or
two in a whole Lent?

PRINCE   You, gentlewoman.

DOLL   What says your grace?

FALSTAFF   His grace says that which his flesh rebels   355
against.

    Peto knocks at door.

HOSTESS   Who knocks so loud at door? Look to th'
door there, Francis.   [*Exit Francis.*]

                                      ^F*Enter* PETO.^F

PRINCE   Peto, how now, what news?

the observance. In frustration, the Privy
Council issued a proclamation in 1588,
and nearly every year thereafter, that 'her
Maiesties pleasure is, vpon the vnderstanding of the great disorders heretofore
and especially the last Lent committed in
killing and eating flesh in the time of
Lent', that innkeepers be fined a hundred
pounds – a huge sum – for serving meat
to any customers except those especially
licensed to eat it (Dyson).

350 **howl** suffer at the hands of the law; or
biblically, suffer the tortures of the
damned

351–2 These lines are a wonderful expression of the Hostess's moral laxity. As
usual, she understands only the literal
meaning of Falstaff's words; and while
she intends to admit to a minor infringement of the Lenten law, she in fact confirms the more serious charge of running
a brothel with unintentional *double
entendres*: *vict'lers* (owners of eating
establishments) also means bawds; *a
joint of mutton*, a whore; and fasting

during Lent, sexual abstinence. For
further use of *mutton* as slang for a
prostitute, see *TGV* 1.1.94–6 and *MM*
3.2.174–6.

355–6 Falstaff's allegation has two possible
meanings: (1) the Prince feels revulsion
at calling a whore a gentlewoman; or, (2)
especially given the sexual significance
of *flesh* at 348, the Prince pays her a
courtesy at odds with his desire for her.
The contrast between his spiritual grace
and fleshly lust may spring from
Galatians, 5.17: 'For the flesh lusteth
against the Spirit, and the Spirit against
the flesh'. For earlier puns on *grace*, see
1.2.28–9 and *1H4* 1.2.15–17; and for a
similar play on fleshly rebellion, see *MV*
3.1.31–2: 'JEW My own flesh and blood
to rebel! SALANIO Out upon it, old carrion,
rebels it at these years?'

356 SD **Peto** This is the sole appearance
of Peto in this play, and he serves only
as a court messenger. For a discussion
of his identity, see 2.2.0.1n. and *1H4*
1.2.154n.

351 vict'lers] *Q (*vitlars*), F (*Victuallers*), Kittredge* What's] *Q;* What is *F*   356 SD] *Q (Peyto); not
in F*   357 to th'] *Q (*too th'*); to the F*   358 SD] *this edn; not in QF*   358.1] *F; not in Q*   359 Peto] *Q
(*Peyto*), F*

PETO

> The King your father is at Westminster,   360
> And there are twenty weak and wearied posts
> Come from the north; and as I came along
> I met and overtook a dozen captains,
> Bare-headed, sweating, knocking at the taverns,
> And asking every one for Sir John Falstaff.   365

PRINCE

> By heaven, Poins, I feel me much to blame
> So idly to profane the precious time
> When tempest of commotion, like the south,
> Borne with black vapour, doth begin to melt
> And drop upon our bare unarmed heads.   370
> Give me my sword and cloak. – Falstaff, good night.
>   *Exeunt Prince and Poins [with Peto].*

361 **twenty** i.e. many: used to signify an indefinite number (Ard¹)

posts express couriers

363 **a dozen** like *twenty* (361), probably signifies an indefinite number

364 **Bare-headed** a detail demonstrative of urgency and haste (Cam¹). Hats were *de rigueur* for gentlemen (certainly those with the status of captain), who would wear them even at church and mealtimes and remove them only at court or in the presence of royalty.

365 **asking . . . Falstaff** possibly an allusion to Falstaff's neglect of duty, but just as possibly a wry glance at the reputation for valour Falstaff falsely won at Shrewsbury – a reputation which would make his services sought for the wars in the north, as he himself notes with pride at 379–82.

368 **tempest of commotion** a storm of insurrection (*OED* commotion *sb.* 4). Cf. 4.1.36.

south south wind, bringer of storms. Cf. *1H4* 5.1.3–6: 'The southern wind / . . . Foretells a tempest and a blustering day',

and *AYL* 3.5.51: 'Like foggy south, puffing with wind and rain'.

369 **Borne . . . vapour** laden with dense fog or black clouds

melt dissolve into rain (*OED v.* 2c)

370 **unarmed** unprotected, unprepared for battle; unarmèd

371 **Falstaff, goodnight** The Prince's pointed words of farewell are the last he speaks to Falstaff before repudiating him in 5.5. Revealing his regret for having so profaned the time (367), they signal his determination to redeem the time from idleness (a promise he has made in *1H4* 1.2.206–7 and will honour when he next appears, at court, in 4.3), and they recall his exit from the comparable scene in *1H4*, when, leaving Falstaff in a drunken sleep and affirming his duty to the King, he vows, 'I'll to the court in the morning' (2.4.530).

371 SD *As the t.n. attests, editors disagree about who should exit at this point. F specifies only the Prince; Q, the Prince and Poins. More recent editors, following

360 SP] *Q (Peyto), F* Westminster] *QaF;* Weminster *Qb* 371] *Q; F lines* Cloake: / night. / 371 SD *Exeunt . . . Poins] Q; Exit. F; [Exeunt* Prince, Poi. Pet. *and* Bar. *Capell*

FALSTAFF   Now comes in the sweetest morsel of the
night, and we must hence and leave it unpicked.

                 [*Knocking within. Exit Bardolph.*]
More knocking at the door?

              [*Enter* BARDOLPH.]

How now, what's the matter?   375
BARDOLPH
You must away to court, sir, presently.
A dozen captains stay at door for you.
FALSTAFF [*to Page*]   Pay the musicians, sirrah.

               [*Exit Page, with Sneak's band.*]
Farewell, hostess; farewell, Doll. You see, my good
wenches, how men of merit are sought after. The   380
undeserver may sleep when the man of action is
called on. Farewell, good wenches! If I be not sent
away post, I will see you again ere I go.
DOLL   I cannot speak! If my heart be not ready to
burst . . . Well, sweet Jack, have a care of thyself.   385

Capell, add Peto and Bardolph to the list,
though there is little reason for Bardolph
to exit with the Prince, whose parting line
suggests that he turns his back on Falstaff
and his companions.

372–3 **the sweetest . . . night** in this context,
if spoken to Doll, suggests a time most
conducive to intimacy or pleasure. Cf.
5.3.49–50: 'the sweet a'th' night'.

373 **must hence** The verb 'go' is understood.
unpicked applied to *morsel*, with the
sense of its going untasted or unenjoyed

376 **presently** at once

377 **A dozen captains** The fact that all the
captains would converge on the door
together is perhaps inadvertently comic.
For the number, see 363n.
stay wait

378 addressed to the Page, who would have
carried his master's purse. Cf. 1.2.233–4.

378 SD2 *The exit of the Page with the
musicians at this point allows the stage to
be cleared of superfluous players before
the scene's final focus on Falstaff's farewell. If the musicians were in a gallery
above (see 226.1–2n.), presumably they
would exit from there.

380–2 **The undeserver . . . on** humorous
anticipation of a sentiment in the King's
soliloquy which follows shortly, wherein
he meditates on why *the great* remain
sleepless while the *poorest subjects* sleep
soundly (3.1.12, 4). It is characteristic of
Shakespeare to precede the main event
with an ironic precursor.

383 **post** post-haste, right away

373 SD *Knocking within.*] *Capell subst; not in QF*   *Exit Bardolph.*] *Ard.²; not in QF*   374.1] *Capell; not
in QF*   378 SD1] *Capell (after* sirrah*.); not in QF*   SD2] *this edn; not in QF*

FALSTAFF   Farewell, farewell.   *Exit [with Bardolph].*
HOSTESS   Well, fare thee well. I have known thee
these twenty-nine years, come peascod time; but
an honester and truer-hearted man . . . Well, fare thee
well.   390

[*Enter* BARDOLPH.]

BARDOLPH   Mistress Tearsheet!
HOSTESS   What's the matter?
BARDOLPH   Bid Mistress Tearsheet come to my master.
HOSTESS   O, run, Doll! Run, run, good Doll! Come. –
She comes blubbered! – Yea, will you come, Doll?   395
Exeunt.

386 SD *Neither Q nor F signals an exit for Bardolph, but his departure with Falstaff allows Doll and the Hostess to be onstage alone for a few poignant moments before he returns at 390.

387–90 The Hostess's valedictory to a man she has known for nearly 30 years speaks volumes about the depth of her loyalty and attachment to him. The play may offer little evidence of the honesty and true-heartedness she claims to find in him, but her lines are no doubt sincere, as the thought she leaves unfinished at 389 – her syntax choked with emotion – attests. Doll's and the Hostess's sorrow at Falstaff's departure stands in marked contrast to the bitter tone of Lady Northumberland's and Lady Percy's farewell to Northumberland in 2.3.

388 **peascod time** early summer, when peas form in their pods. Thomas Tusser, in *A Hundred Good Pointes of Husbandrie* (1557), identifies the month precisely:

'Good peason and leakes, to make poredge in Lent / And pescods in July, save fish to be spent'. Duffin (218–20) prints lyrics to a song called 'In Peascod Time', or 'The Shepherd's Slumber', a pastoral fantasy first published in *England's Helicon* (1600). The precision with which the Hostess dates her first meeting with Falstaff is touching.

395 **blubbered** covered with tears. The fact that Doll is weeping probably explains her reluctance to go to Falstaff. The Hostess's exhortation for her to *run* yields to the more sympathetic *come* as she encourages Doll to accompany her as she moves to the door – a credible motivation for clearing the stage. The fact that the Hostess's lines address two different auditors has prompted some editors (see t.n.) to assign *Come* and *Yea . . . Doll?* to Bardolph and to leave only the explanatory *She comes blubbered* for her; but the import of the Hostess's dialogue in Q is clear.

386 SD *Exit] QbF; not in Qa   with Bardolph] Capell subst; not in QF   390.1] this edn; not in QF   391 SP] QF (Bard.); Bard. [within. Capell; Bard. [At the door] Cam¹   394–5 Come . . . Doll?] Q; not in F; Bardolph. Come! / Hostess. She . . . blubbered. / Bardolph. Yea . . . Doll? (Vaughan), Cam¹   395 SD] QbF; not in Qa*

3.1   *Enter the* KING *in his nightgown* [F]*with a Page*[F].

KING

Go, call the Earls of Surrey and of Warwick;
But ere they come, bid them o'er-read these letters
And well consider of them.   [*Gives letters to Page.*]

3.1 *On the omission of this scene from the first issue of Q, see pp. 440–7. Though it contributes virtually no new material to the plot other than false report of Glendower's death at 103, the scene introduces a much-needed royal presence to weigh against the Prelate's Rebellion. It depicts the King – now at the palace in Westminster (2.4.360) – and his nobles as political strategists, and fleshes out the official history with Richard's prophecy that civil war will be the wages of Henry's usurpation. Perhaps more important, the scene reinforces the themes of sickness, betrayal, guilt and political necessity which, as embodied in Henry, lend the play a tragic resonance to balance the comedy of the Falstaff plot. Without it, Henry would not appear until his deathbed scene in 4.3, leaving the rebels to bustle without a visible dramatic antagonist and causing a juxtaposition of two major comic scenes with Falstaff – 2.4 in Eastcheap and 3.2 in Gloucestershire – which would allow no time, theatrically, for him to travel from one place to the other.

0.1 *Qb's *'alone'* is probably meant to suggest that the King is the only person of consequence to enter; it does not preclude attendance by the Page, who is needed to do his bidding at 3. Cf. the SD at Q 1.2.0, where Falstaff enters 'alone, with his page bearing his sword and buckler'.

nightgown not in the modern sense of sleepwear, but, according to Linthicum, a rich 'ankle-length gown with long sleeves and collar varying in size from the shawl-collar of the men's modern dressing-gown to the fur collar on ladies' coats. It was worn for warmth both indoors and out. Previous to the reign of Henry VIII, it was frequently of worsted or woolen materials, sometimes made with a hood' (184).

1 **Earls . . . Warwick** The two Earls, Surrey and Warwick, play no role in *1H4* and are not mentioned as the King's counsellors in any known source. Shakespeare may have confused Warwick with 'the king-maker' of that title in *3H6*, whose family name was Richard Neville – the name Henry mistakenly gives to the present Earl (see 66n.). Surrey, however, who is mute in this scene and does not appear elsewhere, is unlikely to have been confused with the Duke of Surrey in *R2* 4.1: Shakespeare may simply have pulled the name out of a hat (Cam[2]). Holinshed records the death of 'Thomas Beauford earle of Surrie' in 1410 (3.536).

2 **these letters** Though not identified, the letters Henry holds may have been brought by the *posts* mentioned late in the previous scene (2.4.361–2); alternatively, they may be letters Henry himself has written to Surrey and Warwick. To judge from remarks made in 36–44, they contain news of the Prelate's Rebellion and Northumberland's role in it. Because 2.3 has dramatized Northumberland's decision to abandon the rebel cause, however, he no longer poses a threat to the King – an irony which robs this scene of much of its tension.

3.1] *Actus Tertius. Scena Prima. F; not in Q*   0.1] *Qb* (*Enter the King in his night-gowne alone.*), *F* (*Enter the King, with a Page.*); *not in Qa*   1–108] *QbF; not in Qa*   1 Warwick] *Qb* (*War.*), *F*   3 SD1] *this edn*

> Make good speed.
>
> ^F*Exit*^F [*Page*].
>
> How many thousand of my poorest subjects
> Are at this hour asleep? O sleep! O gentle sleep!   5
> Nature's soft nurse, how have I frighted thee,
> That thou no more wilt weigh my eyelids down
> And steep my senses in forgetfulness?
> Why rather, sleep, liest thou in smoky cribs,
> Upon uneasy pallets stretching thee   10
> And hushed with buzzing night-flies to thy slumber,
> Than in the perfumed chambers of the great,
> Under the canopies of costly state
> And lulled with sound of sweetest melody?
> O thou dull god, why li'st thou with the vile   15
> In loathsome beds and ^Fleav'st^F the kingly couch

4–31 Henry's apostrophe to sleep echoes Sidney's sonnet 'Come Sleepe, o Sleepe, the certaine knot of peace' (*Astrophel*, 39) in expressing a sentiment – that the great sleep uneasily – also found in Daniel (*CW*, 3.115): 'But now the king retires him to his peace, / A peace much like a feeble sicke mans sleepe' (Ard², Cam¹). Furthermore, it anticipates Henry V's address to ceremony wherein he envies the life of the unencumbered peasant (*H5* 4.1.263–81) and Macbeth's famous lines about sleep which emphasize, more than here, the guilt of the speaker (*Mac* 2.2.34–42).

5 **O sleep!** These words, in both Q and F, make the line oddly hypermetric, leading Dyce to speculate that they must have been interpolated. Without them, the line would be a regular iambic pentameter.

7 **That** so that, or with the result that. Cf. 1.1.197.

9 **cribs** hovels (*OED sb.* 3a)

10 **uneasy** uncomfortable, with an ironic anticipation of the moral or spiritual discomfort implicit in the same word at 31

     pallets simple beds or mattresses, usually made of straw (*OED sb.*² 1)

11 **hushed ... night-flies** Qb's punctuation, adopted here, allows personified sleep to be hushed to its slumber by buzzing flies. F's alters the sense by having sleep, hushed by 'bussing' Night (a maternal image of kissing), fly to its slumber. But as sleep is addressed in the second person, F's third-person verb 'flyes' is not in agreement; this suggests that Qb's use of 'flies' as a noun is correct.

13 **state** splendour or magnificence, befitting a person of rank (*OED sb.* 17a)

15 **dull** heavy, drowsy, insensible (*OED adj.* 3). Cf. 4.1.250 and 4.2.96.

     vile people of mean estate, peasants. See also its adjectival use at 1.2.18 and 2.2.47.

3 SD2] *Rowe; Exit. F; not in Qb*   10 pallets] *Qb;* Pallads *F*   11 hushed ... night-flies] *Qb (*husht*);* huisht with bussing Night, flyes *F*   12 Than] Then *QbF*   great,] *Qb;* Great? *F*   14 sound] *Qb;* sounds *F* 15 li'st] *Qb (*li'ste*); F (*lyest*)   vile] *Qb;* vilde *F*   16 leav'st] *F;* leauest *Qb*

A watch-case or a common 'larum bell?
Wilt thou upon the high and giddy ᶠmastᶠ
Seal up the ship-boy's eyes and rock his brains
In cradle of the rude, imperious surge   20
And in the visitation of the winds,
Who take the ruffian ᶠbillowsᶠ by the top,
Curling their monstrous heads and hanging them
With deafing clamour in the slippery clouds,
That, with the hurly, death itself awakes?   25

17 The term *watch-case* compares the canopied bed of state in which the King lies awake with an ornamental case for a pocket watch wherein the wound-up mechanism, like the King, prepares to strike the alarm bell. Such watches were becoming common in Shakespeare's time – witness Middleton, *A Mad World, My Masters*, 5.2.251–2: 'the watch rings alarum in his pocket' (Ard¹) – though the reference would be anachronistic for a medieval king to make. The *or* indicates either that *watch-case* and *'larum bell* are alternate terms for the same thing, or that they are distinctly different, in which case the reference to a pocket watch may lead Henry to imagine a more public (*common*) type of alarm, the bell rung by a sentinel to signal a disturbance or warn of approaching danger. Cf. *Mac* 2.3.75.

18–20 Shakespeare draws the image of the young sailor asleep on the topmast from a passage in Proverbs (23.34) warning against the evils of drinking too much wine – 'Yea, thou shalt be as though thou layest in the middest of the sea, or sleepest vpon the top of the mast of a shyp' – possibly filtered, as Humphreys observes, through the 'Homily Against Gluttony and Drunkenness' which appeared in a volume of sermons in 1574 (*Certain Sermons*, 208) and which is more closely echoed in *R3*: 'Who builds

his hope in air of your good looks / Lives like a drunken sailor on a mast, / Ready with every nod to tumble down / Into the fatal bowels of the deep' (3.4.98–101).

19 **Seal up** make blind; aurally indistinguishable from 'seel up', which in falconry meant to stitch a hawk's eyelids together as part of its training (*OED v.²* 1). Cf. *Oth* 3.3.213: 'To seel her father's eyes up, close as oak'.

20 **In cradle** Abbott discusses the omission of the article in a prepositional phrase with a dependent genitive (89).

21 **visitation** violent or destructive force visited upon a people or country (*OED sb.* 8)

24 **deafing** archaic form, meaning to drown out one sound with a louder one (*OED deaf v.* 3). Cf. *KJ* 2.1.147: 'What cracker is this same that deafs our ears?'
   slippery a suggestive epithet over which editors have argued for centuries: it may refer to the clouds' gliding swiftly through the sky, or to their capacity to change shape, or to their moisture. The image of gargantuan waves mingling with the clouds, a commonplace in Shakespeare's day, has been variously attributed to Virgil (*Aen.*, 1.102–3, 3.564–7), Ovid (*Met.*, 11.497–8) and Lucan (*Pharsalia*, 5.642).

25 **That** See 7n.
   hurly uproar or tumult

18 mast] *F;* masse *Qb*   22 billows] *F;* pillowes *Qb*   24 deafing clamour] *Qb;* deaff'ning Clamors *F* slippery] *Qb;* slipp'ry *F*

Canst thou, O partial sleep, give then repose
To the wet sea-son in an hour so rude,
And in the calmest and most stillest night,
With all appliances and means to boot,
Deny it to a king? Then happy low, lie down!   30
Uneasy lies the head that wears a crown.

Enter WARWICK, *Surrey and Sir John Blunt.*

WARWICK

Many good morrows to your majesty.

KING

Is it good morrow, lords?

26 **partial** unfair in favouring one person over another (*OED adj.* 1a)
   *then As there is no clear plural antecedent for Qb's 'them', F's 'thy' is possibly correct; but the simplest explanation is that the compositor made an error in reading minims, substituting an *m* for an *n*. Alternatively, if Qb's 'season' in the next line is an error for *sea-son* (see 27n.), the compositor might have conceivably misread 'him' as 'them'.

27 **sea-son** The suggested readings *sea-son* and 'sea's son' are plausible alternatives for Qb's 'season' and preferable to F's 'Sea-Boy', a term suspiciously close to the *ship-boy* (19) for which it substitutes (Davison).

29 **appliances** things applied as means to an end; aids (*OED sb.* 3). Presumably such aids to sleep would include music to dull the senses, a blindfold to keep out light, and drugs.
   to boot to advantage; or, as in modern parlance, in addition (*OED* boot *sb.* 1)

30 This line contains 12 syllables. Shaaber (*Variorum*) speculates that the parentheses surrounding 'happy' in Qb may have been deletion marks misunderstood by the

compositor; without that word, the line would be a regular iambic pentameter.
   low people of mean estate. Cf. 15n. on *vile.*

31 proverbial: 'Crowns have cares' (Dent, C863)

31.1 *F omits Sir John Blunt from its SD, presumably because he is a ghost character who has no lines in the scene. Neither, however, does the Earl of Surrey; the reason modern editors include him but jettison Blunt is that the King calls for Surrey at line 1. At 35, however, the King's 'good morrow to you all' suggests that Warwick may be accompanied by two other nobles: although *you all* may arguably refer to only two addressees, as in *2H6* 2.2.26, it typically requires at least three. Dramatically, therefore, there is justification for both Surrey and Blunt to accompany Warwick. Q has Blunt enter again, as a mute attendant on the new King, at 5.2.41; and as Cam[1] and subsequent editions indicate, he must attend Prince John at Gaultree as well (though Blunt is not listed in the entry at 4.2.23 in either Q or F), for the Prince instructs him to lead Collevile to York at 4.2.73.

26 then] *Riv;* them *Qb;* thy *F*   27 sea-son] *Chester;* season *Qb;* Sea-Boy *F;* sea's son *Ridley*   30 happy] *F;* (happy) *Qb*   31.1] *Qb;* Enter Warwicke and Surrey. *F*

WARWICK

'Tis one a'clock, and past.

KING

Why then, good morrow to you all, my lords. 35

Have you read o'er the letter that I sent you?

WARWICK

We have, my liege.

KING

Then you perceive the body of our kingdom,

How foul it is, what rank diseases grow,

And with what danger, near the heart of it. 40

WARWICK

It is but as a body yet distempered

Which to his former strength may be restored

With good advice and little medicine.

My Lord Northumberland will soon be cooled.

KING

O God, that one might read the book of fate 45

And see the revolution of the times

Make mountains level, and the continent,

---

36 **letter** Most editors accept F's plural form, assuming a compositorial error in Qb; but Qb's singular would make sense if the King sent copies of the *same* letter – presumably one he has written – to Surrey and Warwick (see 2n.). Thus he would logically refer to the letter as plural when giving copies to his page, but as singular when asking whether the nobles had read it.

38–43 Elaborate metaphors of the state as a body politic, subject to diseases analogous to those that weaken a physical body such as the King's, were commonplace in Elizabethan writings.

39 **rank** foul, festering (*OED adj.* 14b)

41 **yet distempered** still sickened: by a disproportion of the four bodily humours

(blood, phlegm, black and yellow bile) which, according to medieval physiology, were thought to regulate a person's health and temperament; *distempered* also suggests having a fever.

43 **little** The article 'a' is understood. Cf. *TN* 5.1.167: 'Hold little faith, though thou hast too much fear'.

44 **cooled** with a play on reducing the fever implicit in *distempered* (41)

46 **revolution ... times** passage of time, or perhaps changes wrought by time. Cf. *alteration*, 52.

47–9 **Make ... sea** The imagery of natural features losing their distinct properties, melting or metamorphosing into something else, anticipates the apocalyptic

---

34 a'clock] *Qb (*a clocke*), F (*a Clocke*);* o' clock *Theobald*   36 letter] *Qb;* Letters *F*   40 it.] *Qb;* it? *F*
45 God] *Qb;* Heauen *F*

287

Weary of solid firmness, melt itself
Into the sea; and other times to see
The beachy girdle of the ocean   50
Too wide for Neptune's hips. How chances, mocks
And changes fill the cup of alteration
With divers liquors! O, if this were seen,
The happiest youth, viewing his progress through –
What perils past, what crosses to ensue –   55
Would shut the book and sit him down and die!
'Tis not ten years gone

imagery of later tragic heroes such as
Hamlet and Antony, much as it echoes
that of Sonnet 64: 'When I have seen the
hungry ocean gain / Advantage on the
kingdom of the shore, / And the firm soil
win of the wat'ry main, / Increasing store
with loss, and loss with store' (5–8).
Behind such imagery may lie Ovid, *Met.*,
15.261–3, either in the original Latin or
in Golding's 1567 translation (Ard²).

47 **continent** dry land (*OED sb.* 3b), or that
which contains or holds (1a) as the shore
does the sea.

50–1 **The ... hips** The shore is personified
as a belt wrapped around Neptune's
waist, which, as the sea recedes, grows
too wide for him: cf. 1.2.40n. on *girdles.*
OED glosses *beachy* as 'pebbly'.

51–2 ***chances ... changes** In the absence
of any punctuation in Qb and F separating
chances from *mocks*, editors have been
inclined (1) to alter *mocks* to 'mock' as a
plural verb for the subject *chances*, creating a parallel construction, 'chances mock
/ And changes fill' – but causing a
problem with the direct object *cup*, which
can be filled but not mocked; or (2) to
assume that *mocks* is a contraction of
mock us, thus creating parallel direct objects
as well; or (3) taking a hint from F's

capitalization of 'Chances', to personify
it as a possessive so that 'chance's mocks'
refers to the ironic tricks played by
accident. Each of these solutions is more
complicated than the one chosen here,
which is to treat the three nouns in Qb as
parallel subjects of the verb *fill.*

53–6 ***O ... die!** Found only in Qb, these
lines were probably interpolated, perhaps
as a marginal addition, in MS copy (Ard²,
lxxxii). The fact that without them, as
in F, the half-line at 53 ('With divers
liquors!') joins the half-line at 57 (''Tis
not ten years gone') to yield an iambic
pentameter – and further, a line which
marks a logical transition in thought –
supports this conjecture. Their inclusion,
however, allows Henry to voice an almost
suicidal despair ('sit him down and die')
akin to Richard's meditation on the deaths
of kings and thus marks an effective
transition into Henry's recollection of
Richard's fortunes beginning at 57
(Oxf¹). Alternatively, though less likely,
these lines may have been edited out of
the copy-text used for F, as happened
with the reference to Blunt at 31.1.

55 **crosses** trials or misfortunes (*OED* cross
sb. 10), derived from Jesus's bearing the
Cross (e.g. in Matthew, 16.24)

51 chances, mocks,] chances mockes, *Qb;* Chances mocks *F;* chances mock *Rowe;* chances mock us
(Vaughan); chance's mocks *Cam¹*   53–6 O ... die!] *Qb; not in F*   54–5 through – ... ensue –] *this edn;*
through, ... ensue? *Qb; not in F*

Since Richard and Northumberland, great friends,
Did feast together, and in two year after
Were they at wars. It is but eight years since   60
This Percy was the man nearest my soul,
Who like a brother toiled in my affairs
And laid his love and life under my foot;
Yea, for my sake, even to the eyes of Richard
Gave him defiance. But which of you was by –   65
[*to Warwick*] You, cousin Neville, as I may
     remember –
When Richard, with his eye brimful of tears,

60 **eight years** Henry's placement of Richard II's deposition (1399) eight years earlier would put the present scene at 1407. But as the Battle of Shrewsbury, news of which opens this play, was fought in 1403, and as the Gaultree episode (1405) dramatized in 4.1 had not yet occurred, Shakespeare clearly is not attending carefully to historical time. See 103n. on *that . . . dead* and pp. 119–22.

64 **even . . . eyes** i.e. in person and without fear, in spite of Richard's claim to divine right

66 **cousin Neville** Henry misremembers, or Shakespeare does. No Earl of Warwick appears in *R2*, and the family name of Warwick in this play was Beauchamp, not Neville. On the other hand the Earl of Westmorland, who plays a key role at Gaultree, was named Rafe Neuill in both Holinshed (3.529) and Stow (*Annales*, 529); and, as Wilson reports (Cam¹), an Earl of Warwick named Richard Neville plays a king-making role in *3H6* (see 1n.). Thus there was ample reason for confusion, and it is likely that Shakespeare meant to include Westmorland in this scene, not Warwick. The term *cousin* was used both for blood relatives (as at 71) and as a mark of intimacy among people who were not related.

67–79 A conflation of scenes in *R2*. Richard is *checked and rated* in the deposition scene (*R2* 4.1.222–52) when Northumberland attempts to get him to confess his crimes against the state. The lines Henry quotes, however, are from *R2* 5.1.55–65, a confrontation scene from which he was absent. Furthermore, the lines themselves are misquoted: 'The mounting Bolingbroke', with its overtones of predatory ambition, here becomes the familiar 'My cousin Bolingbroke'; and Richard's poetic 'The time shall not be many hours of age / More than it is' becomes a more prosaic 'The time shall come'. Various explanations for the misquotation are possible, from the exculpatory (Henry was not present and therefore is simply reporting hearsay) to the machiavellian (Henry calculatedly revises Richard's words to play down his own role as usurper). In any case, the effect of these snatches of misremembered quotation is of thought-in-process, so that Henry's speech, with its self-interruptions akin to those in Hamlet's first soliloquy, has a veneer of authenticity. This recollection of events in *R2* also contributes to the network of reports by which this play interrogates the nature of historical truth and invention.

59 year] *Qb*; yeeres *F*   66 SD] *Rowe; not in QbF*   67 eye brimful] eye-brimme full *Qb*; Eye, brim-full *F*

Then checked and rated by Northumberland,
Did speak these words, now proved a prophecy?
'Northumberland, thou ladder by the which   70
My cousin Bolingbroke ascends my throne' –
Though then, God knows, I had no such intent,
But that necessity so bowed the state
That I and greatness were compelled to kiss –
'The time shall come', thus did he follow it,   75
'The time will come that foul sin, gathering head,
Shall break into corruption' – so went on,
Foretelling this same time's condition
And the division of our amity.

WARWICK

There is a history in all men's lives   80
Figuring the natures of the times deceased,
The which observed, a man may prophesy
With a near aim of the main chance of things

---

68 **checked and rated** reprimanded (cf. 1.2.196) and berated (cf. 5.2.69)

73 **necessity** Henry invokes the principle of necessity, of inevitable cause and effect, to justify his usurpation – a principle which had gained popularity in post-Machiavellian Europe. Whether he is sincere is debatable, despite his appeal to God as witness (72). In *R2* he swears that he has returned from banishment only to claim his father's dukedom (2.3.113–14), yet simply by returning, he has challenged royal authority; furthermore, he proceeds to raise an army and sentence Richard's favourites to death before proffering Richard 'allegiance and true faith of heart' (3.3.37) at Flint castle. Davison cites a speech made by Oliver Cromwell to Parliament in 1654 as a gloss on such principle: 'Necessity hath no law. Feigned necessities, imaginary necessities . . . are the greatest cozenage that men can put upon the Providence of God, and make pretences to break known rules by'. Such cozenages are sanctioned by Warwick's speech at 80 and embraced by Henry as *necessities* at 92–3.

74 **were compelled** Henry's use of the passive voice – he declines to say by whom he was compelled – illustrates how cunningly he avoids responsibility and evades the charge of usurpation (GWW).

78 **time's condition** Cf. 4.1.101 and 5.2.11.

80–5 Warwick invokes the classical concept of *Historia magistra vitae*: history as the teacher of life (Cam²). By giving form (*Figuring*) to the events of ages past (*times deceased*), history allows the observant person to predict (*prophesy*) what is in store (*intreasured*) for the future.

83 **a near aim** reasonable accuracy
main chance likelihood of occurrence

---

69 prophecy?] *Capell;* prophecie: *QbF*   71 Bolingbroke] *Pope;* Bolingbrooke *Qb; Bullingbrooke F*   72 God] *Qb;* Heauen *F*   79 division] *Qb (*deuision*), F*   81 natures] *Qb;* nature *F*

As yet not come to life, who in their seeds
And weak beginning lie intreasured.   85
Such things become the hatch and brood of time;
And by the necessary form of this
King Richard might create a perfect guess
That great Northumberland, then false to him,
Would of that seed grow to greater falseness,   90
Which should not find a ground to root upon
Unless on you.

KING   Are these things then necessities?
Then let us meet them like necessities,
And that same word even now cries out on us.
They say the Bishop and Northumberland   95
Are fifty thousand strong.

WARWICK   It cannot be, my lord.
Rumour doth double, like the voice and echo,
The numbers of the feared. Please it your grace
To go to bed. Upon my soul, my lord,
The powers that you already have sent forth   100
Shall bring this prize in very easily.
To comfort you the more, I have received
A certain instance that Glendower is dead.

---

84 **who** a frequent substitution for 'which' in personification. Cf. 22.
in their seeds Cf. *Mac* 1.3.58: 'If you can look into the seeds of time'.
85 **intreasured** stored safely, as in a treasury (*OED* entreasure *v.* 1); intreasurèd
86 **hatch ... time** a metaphor for offspring, drawn from egg-laying animals; also used to characterize the unknown outcome of Hamlet's melancholy (*Ham* 3.1.163–6). The terms *hatch* and *brood* are synonymous.
87 **necessary ... this** inevitable pattern of cause and effect

90 **of that seed** from that beginning
97 **double ... echo** Despite confusing variations in punctuation between Qb and F, *voice* and *echo* are most easily explained as parallel objects of *like*, leaving *double* as the sole verb: Rumour doubles the number of the enemy, like the voice and its echo.
100 **powers** army. Cf. 1.1.133.
103 **instance** proof
that ... dead another example of historical inaccuracy. Owen Glendower did not die until 1415–16 (R. Davies, 326–7); and even Holinshed's error in putting

---

84 who] *Qb;* which *F*   85 beginning] *Qb;* beginnings *F*   intreasured] *Qb, F (*entreasured*)*   97 double, ... echo,] *Ard²;* double like the voice, and eccho *Qb;* double, like the Voice, and Eccho, *F*   99 soul] *Qb;* Life *F*   100 powers] *Qb;* Pow'rs *F*   103 Glendower] *F3;* Glendour *QbF;* Glyndŵr *Oxf*

> Your majesty hath been this fortnight ill,
> And these unseasoned hours perforce must add   105
> Unto your sickness.
> KING   I will take your counsel;
> And were these inward wars once out of hand,
> We would, dear lords, unto the Holy Land.   *Exeunt.*

3.2   *Enter* Justice SHALLOW *and* Justice SILENCE.

> SHALLOW   Come on, come on, come on; give me your
> hand, sir, give me your hand, sir. An early stirrer, by
> the rood! And how doth my good cousin Silence?

his death at 1409 (3.536) does not explain its report here, for this scene is imagined to have occurred before the defeat of the rebels at Gaultree in 1405: see 60n. Holinshed's account of a Welsh massacre at Usk in 1405 in which Glendower's son was captured (3.527) could possibly have been the source of confusion (Ard²). I use the spelling of Glendower's name as it was printed in QF 1.3.72, rather than the variant spelling used by QbF in this scene: see 1.3.72n.

104 For earlier references to the King's illness, see 1.2.104–10 and 2.2.38–48.

105 **unseasoned hours** troublesome times

107 **inward** domestic, civil

out of hand resolved, finished

108 **would** An additional verb such as 'go' or 'march' is understood.

the Holy Land Henry returns to the crusade he proposed at the conclusion of *R2* (5.6.49–50) and again at the opening of *1H4* (1.1.19–27) but which rebellion made impossible. Holinshed (3.540–1) reports that Henry assembled ships, men, treasure, munitions 'and all things necessarie for such a roiall iournie as he pretended to take into the holie land' 'to

recouer the citie of Jerusalem from the Infidels' in 1412, significantly later than events depicted here; and Henry alludes to such preparations at 4.3.1–10. This would have been the last crusade. By leading it, Henry presumably would secure absolution from his sin of usurpation. Providence, however, thwarts his plan. For the prophecy that he would die in Jerusalem, see 4.3.360–8n.

3.2 The comic premise of this scene, Falstaff's corrupt conscription of soldiers, was probably inspired by a scene in *Famous Victories* and reflects a growing concern with such abuses at the end of the 16th century. The scene occurs on Justice Shallow's farm, located – according to evidence at 4.2.79–80 which is reinforced throughout by references to names and places associated with the Cotswolds and their environs – in Gloucestershire. For a discussion of the illogic of Falstaff's recruiting soldiers in Gloucestershire for wars in the north, and evidence that the scene may have originally been written for *1H4* or for an early draft of a single *H4* play which was later divided into two parts, see pp. 12–13.

3.2] *Scena Secunda. F; not in Q*   0.1] *Qa (*Silens*), Qb; Enter Shallow and Silence: with Mouldie, Shadow, Wart, Feeble, Bull-calfe. F*   1 ³come on] *Qa F;* come on sir *Qb*   3, 5 doth] *Q (*dooth*), F*   3 Silence] *QaF;* Silens *Qb*

SILENCE   Good morrow, good cousin Shallow.

SHALLOW   And how doth my cousin your bedfellow?   5
And your fairest daughter and mine, my god-
daughter Ellen?

SILENCE   Alas, a black woosel, cousin Shallow.

SHALLOW   By yea and no, sir. I dare say my cousin
William is become a good scholar. He is at Oxford   10
still, is he not?

0.1 *F's massed entry may reveal its provenance in a theatrical copy, though it may
not necessarily reflect theatrical practice,
as the Oxford editors assert (*TxC*, 352,
361). The grouping of characters at the
head of a scene in which they will appear
may have served as a convenient annotation for the playhouse, but not as an
indication of their actual entry. Alternatively, the massed entry, a tradition in
classical drama, may reflect the intervention of a literary scribe who prepared
the text for F. Were the five recruits to
enter here, they would stand mute onstage
for nearly 100 lines. Q, on the other hand,
lists only the entry of the two justices: it is
understood from Falstaff's request to see
the recruits (96), and from Shallow's
subsequent directive (99–100), that they
will enter individually as they are called.
Some editors, adapting F, announce a
massed entry when Mouldy is called
(101), so that the recruits gather onstage
and merely step forward as they are
named. But this would substitute one
comic surprise – the collective appearance
of a humorously rag-tag group – for five
individual such surprises and thus would
make little theatrical sense.

1   **Come ...³on** Shallow's thrice repeated
come echoes the Hostess's bidding Doll
to come at the end of 2.4, hinting that
these scenes may once have been consecutive, and 3.1 inserted as an afterthought.
See pp. 440–7 and 3.1n. The 'sir'

following the third *come on* in Qb
may have been attracted from the twice
repeated *sir* in the following line.

2–3 **by the rood** by the Cross; a mild and
already archaic (because Roman Catholic)
oath

3   **cousin** See 3.1.66n. The exact relationship between the two justices is not
established.

5   **bedfellow** familiar term for one's spouse

8   **black woosel** black ousel, or blackbird.
OED records 'woosel' as a 16th-century
spelling for ousel. Through it, Q may be
indicating Silence's rustic pronunciation:
cf. the spelling 'Woosell' in the F version
of Bottom's song about 'The ousel cock,
so black of hue' (*MND* 3.1.120). The
import of Silence's remark is his regret,
perhaps feigned, that his daughter is dark
rather than fair, because blondes traditionally were thought more beautiful,
more desirable, and thus more eligible for
marriage.

9   **By ... no** Shallow repeats a mild
citizen's oath which Falstaff has used
earlier: see 2.2.128n.

10   **William** though not identified as such,
presumably Silence's son. Unless he
had his children at an advanced age,
Silence must be considerably younger
than Shallow, who was a student at
Clement's Inn when Falstaff was just a
boy (24–5). On the matter of the age of
these characters, see 210n.

---

8 woosel] *Q;* Ouzell *F*   9 no] *Q;* nay *F*

SILENCE   Indeed, sir, to my cost.

SHALLOW   'A must then to the Inns a'Court shortly. I was once of Clement's Inn, where I think they will talk of mad Shallow yet.   15

SILENCE   You were called lusty Shallow then, cousin.

SHALLOW   By the mass, I was called anything; and I would have done anything indeed, too – and roundly, too. There was I, and little John Doyt of Staffordshire, and black George Barnes, and Francis Pickbone, and   20 Will Squele, a Cotsole man: you had not four such swinge-bucklers in all the Inns a'Court again! And I may say to you, we knew where the bona robas were and had the best of them at commandment. Then was

13–14 **Inns . . . Inn** Oxford and Cambridge often sent their best students to study law at the Inns of Court, the intellectual centres of London life where lawyers were trained, tested and called to the bar. Clement's Inn, at the time Shallow attended it, was one of eight Inns of Chancery, lesser institutions which provided legal training to those students who had not gained admission to the Inns of Court. In Shakespeare's time, the Inns of Chancery were being taken over by lawyers excluded from the Inns of Court. Shallow thus inadvertently identifies himself, in contrast to the Lord Chief Justice, as a legal mind of no great acuity.

16 **lusty** full of life, or lascivious: both meanings reflect ironically on Shallow's present condition. Underlying the following recollection of his days at Clement's Inn is the classical trope *Ubi sunt?*, or 'Where is the life that late I led?' See especially 33–4, 211–19 and Pistol's ironic recapitulation of the theme at 5.3.140–1.

18 **roundly** thoroughly, to the full (*OED adv.* 2)

19–21 **little . . . man** The names of Shallow's companions are comic. A 'doit' is a coin worth half a farthing and so, metaphorically, a trifle; a 'pickbone' is a starving or avaricious person; and squealing (*Squele*) is associated with pigs. Shallow's mentioning the midland homes of two companions, Staffordshire and the Cotswolds, like his later inclusion of Wart among the recruits (see 137n.), reinforces the placement of the scene in Gloucestershire. *Cotsole* is a phonetic variant of Cotswold, indicative perhaps of Shallow's rustic speech.

22 **swinge-bucklers** daring adventurers, rowdy mischief-makers

23 **bona robas** from the Italian for good dresses, or, as defined by Florio in *A World of Wordes* (1598), 'good stuffe, a good wholesome plum-cheeked wench'. Shallow's assertion that he *had the best* of the bona robas *at commandment* implies that they were high-class whores. See also 204n. and cf. Dekker, *2 Honest Whore*, 1.1.55–6: 'our Country Bona Robaes, oh! are the sugrest delicious Rogue'.

24 **at commandment** at our beck and call

13 'A] *Q;* Hee *F*   a'Court] *Q (*a court*);* of Court *F*   17 By the mass] *Q; not in F*   19 Doyt] *Q; Doit F*
20 Barnes] *Q; Bare F*   21 Cotsole man] *Q;* Cot-sal-man *F;* Cot'swold man *Pope*   22 a'Court] *Q (*a court*);*
of Court *F*   23 bona robas] *Q (*bona robes*), F (Bona-Roba's)*

Jack Falstaff – now Sir John – a boy, and page to   25
Thomas Mowbray, Duke of Norfolk.

SILENCE   This Sir John, cousin, that comes hither anon
about soldiers?

SHALLOW   The same Sir John, the very same. I see him
break Scoggin's head at the court gate when 'a was a   30
crack not thus high; and the very same day did I fight
with one Samson Stockfish, a fruiterer, behind Gray's
Inn. Jesu, Jesu, the mad days that I have spent! And
to see how many of my old acquaintance are dead.

SILENCE   We shall all follow, cousin.   35

SHALLOW   Certain, 'tis certain; very sure, very sure.
Death, as the psalmist saith, is certain to all; all shall
die. How a good yoke of bullocks at ᶠStamfordᶠ fair?

25–6 **page . . . Norfolk** Shakespeare creates
a fictional history for Falstaff that eventually attached itself to both the historical
John Fastolfe and John Oldcastle. Mowbray,
banished in *R2* (1.3), was the enemy of
Bolingbroke, now Henry IV, so that Falstaff
by association stands once again in opposition to Bolingbroke. There is no evidence
that Falstaff's original, Sir John Oldcastle,
was in any way connected to Mowbray.

29 **see** saw. On the use of the 'complete
present' tense for the past, see Abbott,
346, and Hope, 149–50.

30 **Scoggin's** Henry Scogan, friend to Chaucer
and court poet to Henry IV, reportedly sent
a ballad to Prince Harry when he and his
brothers were dining in London (Stow,
Survey, 1.214). Shakespeare's audience,
however, would have been more familiar
with John Scoggin, jester to Edward IV,
whose name, owing to the publication of
an apocryphal jestbook called *Scoggin,
his iestes* in 1565–6, came to be synonymous with 'buffoon'. Falstaff apparently
has always brawled with fools.

31 **crack** lively lad, rogue or wag (*OED sb.*[3]
11)

32 **Samson Stockfish** a humorously paradoxical name. The biblical hero Samson
is yoked to a stockfish, a dried, salted cod
which needed to be beaten before cooking
and which had come to signify cowardice:
'To beat one like a stockfish' was
proverbial (Dent, S867). Falstaff used the
term to insult the Prince in *1H4* – 'you
bull's pizzle, you stock-fish!' (2.4.239);
and see similar uses in *MM* 3.2.105 and
Tem 3.2.69. Shallow's courage is thus no
greater than Falstaff's, and his adversary's
being a fruit-seller adds to the comedy.

32–3 **behind Gray's Inn** i.e. in Gray's Inn
Fields, which stretched north of Gray's
Inn, one of the Inns of Court

37 **Death . . . all** The closest reference is to
Psalms, 89.47: 'What man is he that
lyueth, and shall not see death', but the
sentiment was a commonplace: cf. Dent,
D142: 'Death is common to all.'

38 **How** how much for; what is the price of
yoke of bullocks A yoke is a contrivance

27 This . . . cousin] *QaF;* Coosin, this Sir Iohn *Qb*   29 see] *Q;* saw *F*   30 Scoggin's] *Q (*Skoggins*), F
(*Scoggan's*)   'a] *Q;* hee *F*   32 Samson] *Q, F (*Sampson*)*   33 Jesu, Jesu] *Q;* Oh *F*   34 my] *Q;* mine *F*
37 as . . . saith] *Q; not in F*   38 Stamford] *F;* Samforth *Q*

SILENCE   By my troth, I was not there.

SHALLOW   Death is certain. Is old Dooble of your town   40
living yet?

SILENCE   Dead, sir.

SHALLOW   Jesu, Jesu, dead! 'A drew a good bow, and
dead? 'A shot a fine shoot. John a'Gaunt loved him
well and betted much money on his head. Dead!   45
'A would have clapped i'th' clout at twelve score
and carried you a forehand shaft ᶠatᶠ fourteen and
fourteen and a half, that it would have done a man's
heart good to see. How a score of ewes now?

by which animals are coupled together to draw a plough; here, it is metonymic for a pair. Shallow's incongruous leap from considering mortality to expressing a lively interest in bullocks may have been inspired by Ecclesiasticus, 38.24–5: 'How can he get wisdome that holdeth the plough . . . and his talke is but of the breeding of bullocks?' (Geneva Bible).

Stamford fair Stamford, a market town in Lincolnshire 90 miles from London on the Great North Road, was noted for its horse and cattle fairs held each February, Lent and August.

39 **By my troth** by my faith: a mild oath, omitted in F

40, 52 **Dooble** Q's spelling is a variant of, and may indicate Shallow's rustic pronunciation of, 'double'.

43 **'A . . . bow** He was a good archer; *bow* possibly means a longbow, the weapon of choice used against the French during the time of John of Gaunt, who here is said to have bet money on Dooble's ability (44–5). Shallow prefers *'a* to *he* throughout.

44 **John a'Gaunt** Duke of Lancaster, who figures prominently in *R2*; fourth son of Edward III and father of Henry IV. For

a disparaging gloss on Shallow's presumed familiarity with him, see Falstaff at 318–24.

46–8 **clapped . . . half** According to Shallow, Dooble was an skilled archer. He hit (*clapped*) the bullseye (a *clout* was a piece of cloth marking the centre of the target) from a distance of 240 yards (*twelve score*) and, by shooting the arrow straight ahead rather than in a high arc – keeping the target in sight above his bow hand (*a forehand shaft*) – could hit the target even from 280 or 290 yards away, a remarkable feat. Shallow is no doubt exaggerating Dooble's skills, his memory of a youthful companion coloured by the same hyperbole with which he describes his own conquest of women.

47 **carried you** ethical dative, used for emphasis and here meaning *shot*. Cf. 2.1.40–1n.
   *at Q's erroneous 'a' may have resulted from the printer's eye-skip from the *a* preceding *forehand*.

48 **that** so that

49 **How . . . now?** Shallow's continued interest in market prices even as he laments the death of old friends emphasizes his will to live in the face of his own mortality.

39 By my troth] *Q;* Truly Cousin *F*   40, 52 Dooble] *Q; Double F*   43 Jesu , Jesu, dead!] *Q;* Dead? See, see: *F*   43–4 'A . . . 'A] *Q;* hee . . . hee *F*   44 fine] *QbF;* fiue *Qa*   a'Gaunt] *Q (*a Gaunt*);* of Gaunt *F*   46 'A] *Q;* hee *F*   i'th'] *Q (*ith*);* in the *F*   47 at] *F;* a *Q*

SILENCE   Thereafter as they be; a score of good ewes   50
     may be worth ten pounds.
SHALLOW   And is old Dooble dead?
SILENCE   Here come two of Sir John Falstaff's men, as
     I think.

Enter BARDOLPH *and one with him.*

Good morrow, honest gentlemen.   55
BARDOLPH   I beseech you, which is Justice Shallow?
SHALLOW   I am Robert Shallow, sir, a poor esquire of
     this county and one of the King's justices of the
     peace. What is your good pleasure with me?
BARDOLPH   My captain, sir, commends him to you: 60
     my captain Sir John Falstaff – a tall gentleman, by
     heaven, and a most gallant leader.

50   **Thereafter ... be** 'It depends on their
     quality.'
54.1 *The man who accompanies Bardolph
     is mute and, like other ghost characters
     who populate the Q SDs of this play
     (1.3.0.1–3, 2.2.0.1, 3.1.31.1, 4.3.0.1–3),
     provides evidence that the copy-text for
     Q may have been an uncorrected
     holograph. F's attempt to correct the SD
     by identifying the '*one with him*' (Q) as
     '*his Boy*' may spring from Bardolph's
     appearance with '*his Boy*' in F at 2.4.109,
     but Silence's reference to *two ... men* at
     53 suggests that the person accompanying
     Bardolph is not a page.
55   *Sisson (*Readings*) defends F's attribu-
     tion of this line to Shallow rather than
     Silence, arguing that it is 'surely Shallow's
     place' to greet newcomers as master of the
     estate. Humphreys adds that the greeting
     is in the idiom of Shallow, who uses the
     phrase *Honest gentleman* while speaking
     to Pistol at 5.3.107. Yet as Silence employs
     the same form of greeting earlier in the

scene – 'Good morrow, good cousin
Shallow' (4) – there is no compelling
reason to alter the attribution of the line to
him in Qb and corrected Qa. Uncorrected
Qa, on the other hand, assigns the line to
'*Bardolfe*'; but as the SP in the following
line also reads '*Bard.*', this is clearly an
error. Berger and Williams ('Variants', 115)
speculate that the SP at 55 in uncorrected
Qa may have been attracted from the SP
at 56; but Berger (*Second Part*, viii) later
argues that the attraction was more likely
from the SD at 54, and this would account
too for uncorrected Qa's printing of
Bardolph's full name in 55 SP rather than
its abbreviation, as in 56 SP.
57   **esquire** ordinarily a member of the
     gentry ranked just below a knight; here, a
     country squire (*OED sb.* 2b). Shallow's
     poor betrays false modesty.
60   **him** himself. See 2.2.123 for compar-
     able use of the objective to replace the
     reflexive pronoun.
61   **tall** valiant

54.1] *Q; Enter Bardolph and his Boy. F (after 52)*   55 Good] *Qa (corr), Qb; Bardolfe. Good Qa (uncorr);*
Shal. Good F   59 your good] *QaF; your Qb*   61–2 by heaven] *Q; not in F*

SHALLOW   He greets me well, sir. I knew him a good
   backsword man. How doth the good knight? May
   I ask how my lady his wife doth?   65
BARDOLPH   Sir,   pardon;   a   soldier   is   better
   ᶠaccommodatedᶠ than with a wife.
SHALLOW   It is well said, in faith, sir, and it is well said
   indeed, too: 'better accommodated' – it is good; yea,
   indeed is it. Good phrases are surely, and ever were,   70
   very commendable. 'Accommodated': it comes of
   accommodo. Very good, a good phrase.
BARDOLPH   Pardon, sir, I have heard the word. Phrase,
   you call it? By this day, I know not the phrase; but I
   will maintain the word with my sword to be a soldier-   75
   like word and a word of exceeding good command,
   by heaven! 'Accommodated': that is, when a man is,
   as they say, accommodated, or when a man is being

---

64 backsword man a fencer who used a
sword with only one cutting edge, or,
alternatively, who for practice used a
stick with a basketwork hilt rather than a
sword. Cf. 2.4.131.

64–5 May . . . doth In his effort to be
genteel, Shallow begins the same kind of
polite interrogation he used with Silence.

67 accommodated outfitted, supplied: a
word coming into fashion at the end of
the 16th century, as Ben Jonson notes
in *Discoveries*, when he condemns the
improper use of such 'perfumed termes of
the time, as *Accommodation*' (Jonson,
8.632). Like the Hostess in Jonson's
Every Man In His Humour (see 75–6n.),
however, Bardolph does not know its
meaning, as he reveals at 73–80 when
he admits only to having *heard the word*
and defines it tautologically. Cf. similar
consideration of the word *occupy* at
2.4.148–50.

70, 72 phrases, phrase The term could
denote a single word, as in *Ham*:
'"beautified" is a vile phrase' (2.2.110).
Bardolph does not understand what
Shallow means by *phrase* and thus
defends 'accommodate' as a *word* (73–6).

72 accommodo In pouncing on the word's
etymology – offering the first person
present tense of the Latin *accommodare*,
meaning to fit or make comfortable –
Shallow flaunts his schoolboy erudition.

75–6 soldier-like word Corroborative evidence that 'accommodate' was used as
military jargon, at least in stage comedy,
appears in Jonson's *Every Man In*, where
Bobadill commands, 'Hostesse, accommodate vs with another bed-staffe here,
quickly: Lend vs another bed-staffe. The
woman do's not vnderstand the wordes of
Action' (1.5.125–8). See also 67n.

76 word . . . command either (1) proper military term, or (2) term that comes in handy

---

63 well, sir. I] wel, sir, I *Q*; well: (Sir) I *F*   67 accommodated] *F*; accommodate *Q*   68 in faith] *Q*; *not
in F*   70 ever were] *Q*; euery where *F*   73 Pardon] *QaF*; Pardon me *Qb*   74 this] *QaF*; This good *Qb*
77 by heaven] *Q*; *not in F*   78 is being] *Qa*; is, beeing *QbF*

whereby 'a may be thought to be accommodated,
which is an excellent thing.   80

Enter FALSTAFF.

SHALLOW   It is very just. Look, here comes good Sir
John! – Give me your good hand, give me your
worship's good hand! By my troth, you like well and
bear your years very well. Welcome, good Sir John!
FALSTAFF   I am glad to see you well, good Master   85
Robert Shallow. [*to Silence*] Master Soccard, as
I think?
SHALLOW   No, Sir John, it is my cousin Silence, in
commission with me.
FALSTAFF   Good Master Silence, it well befits you   90
should be of the peace.

---

79 **'a ... thought** F's reduction of Q's
phrasing to 'he thought' lessens the
humour of Bardolph's stumbling through
an attempt to define a word he does not
know. His confusion is evident in
whereby ... to be, which apparently
qualifies *is being* but makes little sense.

81 **just** true

83 **like** are thriving (*OED v.* 4). F's substitution of 'look' is an unnecessary
simplification.

86 **Soccard** Though most editors regard the
name as meaningless, it may derive from
the term 'socage' or 'soccage', which the
OED defines as a form of tenancy – the
holding of land in payment for certain
services other than knight-service. Thus
'soccard' may have been a colloquial
term for 'tenant'. In substituting the name
'Sure-card', the scribe for F was probably
trying to make sense of an unfamiliar
word, though there is scant agreement on

what 'Sure-card' means. Malone asserted
that it meant 'boon companion' in the
early 17th century (*Suppl.*), though there
has been no corroboration. Onions
glosses it as a 'person certain to bring
success'; but again, no corroboration.

88 **Silence** Here and eight other times in Q,
Silence's name appears as 'Scilens' or
'Silens', aberrerant spellings also found
in 146 lines of the *Sir Thomas More*
MS often thought to be written in
Shakespeare's hand, but otherwise
unknown. This has been taken by some
editors as evidence that the copy-text
for Q may have been Shakespeare's
holograph. See 4.3.163n. and pp. 432–40.

88–9 **in commission** i.e. holding the office
of Justice of the Peace (*OED sb.*[1] 2c)

90–1 **it ... peace** Falstaff puns on Silence's
name: as a Justice of the Peace, it is
appropriate that he keep peace – that is,
remain silent.

---

79 whereby] *F;* whereby, *Q*   'a may be] *Q;* he *F*   80.1] *QaF; Enter sir Iohn Falstaffe. Qb*   82 your good] *Q;*
your *F*   83 By ... like] *Q;* Trust me, you looke *F*   86 SD] *Oxf¹*   Soccard] *Q;* Sure-card *F*   88, 90 Silence]
F; Scilens *Qa;* Silens *Qb*

SILENCE   Your good worship is welcome.

FALSTAFF   Fie, this is hot weather, gentlemen! Have you
provided me here half a dozen sufficient men?

SHALLOW   Marry, we have, sir. Will you sit?   95

FALSTAFF *[Sits.]*   Let me see them, I beseech you.

SHALLOW   Where's the roll? Where's the roll? Where's
the roll? Let me see, let me see, let me see: so, so, so,
so, so, so, so. Yea, marry, sir. Rafe Mouldy! Let them
appear as I call; let them do so, let them do so. Let   100
me see. Where is Mouldy?

[Enter MOULDY.]

MOULDY   Here, an't please you.

SHALLOW   What think you, Sir John? A good-limbed
fellow, young, strong and of good friends.

FALSTAFF   Is thy name Mouldy?   105

MOULDY   Yea, an't please you.

FALSTAFF   'Tis the more time thou wert used.

SHALLOW   Ha, ha, ha! Most excellent, i'faith: things
that are mouldy lack use! Very singular good; in
faith, well said, Sir John, very well said.   110

93 **Fie . . . gentlemen** possibly a broad hint
that Falstaff is thirsty (Cam[1])
94 ***half a dozen** Inconsistencies in the
number of recruits being discussed were
never ironed out. Five, not six, men are
called in this scene, from whom Falstaff
is presumably to select four recruits.
Shallow mentions four at 189, 243 and
247, but also claims at 188 that he has
called two more than this number. In the
event, by allowing the two ablest men to
buy out their services, Falstaff winds up
with only three.
sufficient fit, able

98–9 **see: so . . . so.** Shallow is presumably
reading through the roll as he speaks. His
most salient habit of speech is repetition;
his most ardent wish, to ingratiate himself
with Falstaff.
104 **friends** kin, family. Coming from a
respectable family was regarded by Sir
John Smythe, in a letter to Lord Burghley
dated 28 January 1589/90, as crucial for
military discipline, so that 'footmen [i.e.
foot soldiers] do enrol none but such as
are gentlemen, yeomen, yeomen's sons,
and artificers of some haviour' (*Hist.
Mss, Salisbury Papers*, 4.4–5).

92 SP] *Sil. F; Scil. Qa; Silens Qb*   94 dozen] *Q;* dozen of *F*   96 SD] *Oxf[1] (after 96)*   97–8 [1, 2, 3]roll] *F;*
roule *Qa;* rowle *Qb*   98 let me see: so] *QaF;* so *Qb*   99 so, so, so. Yea] so (so, so) yea *Q;* yea *F*   Rafe]
Q; Raphe F   101.1] *Davison; not in QF*   102 an't] *Qa (and't); and it Qb; if it F*   106 an't] *Q (and't); if
it F*   108 i'faith] *Q (yfaith); not in F*   109–10 in faith] *Q; not in F*

^FFALSTAFF   Prick him.^F

MOULDY   I was pricked well enough before, and you
could have let me alone. My old dame will be undone
now for one to do her husbandry and her drudgery.
You need not to have pricked me. There are other   115
men fitter to go out than I.

FALSTAFF   Go to! Peace, Mouldy. You shall go, Mouldy.
It is time you were spent.

MOULDY   Spent?

SHALLOW   Peace, fellow, peace! Stand aside. Know you   120
where you are? – For th'other, Sir John, let me see
Simon Shadow.

111 *i.e. choose him by putting a mark next
to his name. The Q compositor apparently
mistook this line as a SD.

112 **pricked** Mouldy puns on the various
meanings of 'prick', as (1) provoked or
henpecked; (2) turned sour or mouldy
(usually said of wine or beer: *OED*
pricked *ppl.a* 2); but most important for
this context, (3) endowed with a penis,
for the sexual wordplay continues in the
following lines. Cf. Sonnet 20, where
Nature is said to have 'pricked thee out
for women's pleasure' (13), and Dekker,
1 Honest Whore, 5.2.267–8: 'you prickt
her out nothing but bawdy lessons, but
Ile prick you all'.

113 **My . . . undone** Mouldy seems to be intent
on deceiving the recruiters. While the *old
dame* he mentions at 229–32, incapable
of helping herself, may be his mother, the
old dame he mentions here would seem,
in this bawdy context, to be a slang term
for his wife (akin to 'my old lady' in
modern parlance), whose being *undone*
puns on the sexual meaning of 'do': she
will be left both devastated and unfucked
if he is recruited. Cf. 2.1.22 and 40–1n.

114 **husbandry . . . drudgery** common *double
entendres*; *husbandry* means both man-

aging a farm and fulfilling a husband's
role sexually, while *drudgery* has even
more comic overtones, as Dent (L57)
reports, quoting an early modern source:
'To dig anothers [*sic*] garden' means
'to Cuckold one, to do his work and
drudgery, as they say for him.' Cf. *AW*
1.3.42–4: 'He that ears my land spares
my team, and gives me leave to in the
crop; if I be his cuckold, he's my drudge'.

116, 117 **go** For a comparably latent pun on
go meaning 'fuck', reinforced here by the
pun on *spent* (118), see 166.

117 **Go to!** an expression of remonstrance or
derisive incredulity, akin to 'Come,
come!' (*OED* 93b). Cf. 228, 234.

118 **spent** used up, consumed; also a term for
achieving orgasm (Williams, *Dictionary*,
3.1281–2: spend = shed seed), and thus
a fitting consummation of the bawdy
innuendo above

121 **th'other** the others: collective plural

121–2 ***let . . . Shadow** Editors are virtually
unanimous in adopting F's punctuation,
so that *let me see* suggests Shallow is
looking over the roll before choosing a
name to call. Q's punctuation, however,
is just as defensible: *let me see* becomes a
command for Simon Shadow to appear,

111 FALSTAFF Prick him.] *F; Iohn prickes him. Q (SD after 110)*   112 and] *Q; if F*   121 th'other] *Q; the
other F*   121–2 see Simon] *Q; see: Simon F*

FALSTAFF   Yea, marry, let me have him to sit under. He's
    like to be a cold soldier.

SHALLOW   Where's Shadow?   125

[*Enter* SHADOW.]

SHADOW   Here, sir.

FALSTAFF   Shadow, whose son art thou?

SHADOW   My mother's son, sir.

FALSTAFF   Thy mother's son! Like enough, and thy
    father's shadow; so the son of the female is the   130
    shadow of the male. It is often so indeed, but much
    of the father's substance.

SHALLOW   Do you like him, Sir John?

FALSTAFF   Shadow will serve for summer. Prick him,
    for we have a number of shadows fill up the muster   135
    book.

and Falstaff's *let me have him* (123)
echoes that command.

122 **Shadow** The name implies thinness or
emaciation. The role would have been appropriate for John Sincklo, an actor who
used his thinness to comic effect (see
5.4n.). The name may also allude to the
practice of recruiting *shadows* in order to
swindle the public coffers: see 135–6n.

123–4 **let . . . soldier** Falstaff plays on
'shadow' as shade to sit under to escape
the heat (cf. 93), therefore making
Shadow a cool or *cold soldier*; but 'cold'
can also mean indifferent, cowardly or,
more ominously, dead.

124 **like** likely

127–30 **son** punning on the opposition of
sun and shadow

129–32 an esoteric joke about Shadow's
paternity, punning on his name. He is
doubtless his mother's son and the image
(*shadow*) of his father; but sons are only
reflections of their fathers, and often poor

ones. In Shadow's case the father, as a
mere *shadow* by name, may have no
substance: that is, the father may not
exist, thus making Shadow, in effect, a
shadow of a shadow, or a bastard. For a
similar use of *much* to mean 'You have
little to show', see 2.4.133n.

129 **son!** As the punctuation mark in Q is
crowded between 'sonne' and 'like', it
could conceivably be a colon, as in F; but
most editors treat it as an exclamation
point.

134 **serve** a triple pun: (1) suffice (to provide
shade for a summer's day), (2) do military service, or (3) have sexual intercourse

135–6 **shadows . . . book** The term *shadows*
referred to fictitious or dead men whose
names were entered in the muster rolls so
that corrupt captains could collect their
pay, a form of graft. Falstaff's ready admission to such a fraudulent practice suggests
how common it was. See pp. 84–5.

135 **fill** to fill

123 Yea, marry] Q *(*Yea mary*);* I marry F   125.1] *Davison; not in QF*   129 son!] Q *(*sonne!*);* sonne: F
131 but much] Q; but not F; but not much *Capell*   135 fill] Q; to fill F

SHALLOW Thomas Wart!
FALSTAFF Where's he?

[*Enter* WART.]

WART Here, sir.
FALSTAFF Is thy name Wart?   140
WART Yea, sir.
FALSTAFF Thou art a very ragged wart.
SHALLOW Shall I prick him, Sir John?
FALSTAFF It were superfluous, for ^Fhis^F apparel is built
    upon his back, and the whole frame stands upon pins. 145
    Prick him no more.
SHALLOW Ha, ha, ha! You can do it, sir, you can do it!
    I commend you well. – Francis Feeble!

[*Enter* FEEBLE.]

FEEBLE Here, sir.
SHALLOW What trade art thou, Feeble?   150

137 **Thomas Wart** A Thomas Warter from
    Chipping Camden, a village near
    Stratford-upon-Avon, is included on a list
    of men from Gloucestershire deemed
    '*Able and Sufficient*' for military service
    in 1608 (MS quoted in Ard²). Aged
    50–60, Warter was a carpenter by trade
    and 'of lower stature fitt to serve with
    a Calyver', details consistent with the
    description of Wart at 144–5, 261–5 and
    271–7. It is conceivable that Shakespeare,
    in his quest for authentic detail in the
    recruiting scene, modelled Wart on a man
    he knew.
142 **ragged** tattered in his dress, or full of
    rough lumps, like a wart (*OED adj.* 2).
    Conceivably, Falstaff also puns on
    ragwort, the popular name of several

species of the plant Senecio, or ragweed
(*OED* ragwort *sb.* 1), which was believed
to be an aphrodisiac.
144–6 The punning on *pins* and 'pricks'
    leads Falstaff into a carpentry metaphor,
    wherein Wart's rags (*apparel*) are said to
    be built upon his back and precariously
    held together by *pins*, pegs used to join
    timbers; *pins* may also refer to Wart's
    skinny legs, on which his whole *frame*
    stands. Any more pricking might cause it
    to collapse.
147 **You . . . it!** 'You have a way with words.'
    Shallow is flattering Falstaff's verbal
    dexterity.
150 SP *Following Theobald, many editors
    assign this line to Falstaff, thinking the
    question rightly to be his: as Humphreys

138.1] *Davison; not in QF* 143 him, Sir John?] *Q*; him downe, / Sir *Iohn? F* 144 his] *F; not in Q*
148 well. – Francis] well: Francis *Q*; well. / *Francis F* 148.1] *Davison; not in QF* 150 SP] *Shal. QF;*
Fal. *Theobald*

FEEBLE A woman's tailor, sir.

SHALLOW Shall I prick him, sir?

FALSTAFF You may; but if he had been a man's tailor,
he'd a' pricked you. [*to Feeble*] Wilt thou make as
many holes in an enemy's battle as thou hast done in   155
a woman's petticoat?

FEEBLE I will do my good will, sir; you can have no
more.

FALSTAFF Well said, good woman's tailor! Well said,
courageous Feeble! Thou wilt be as valiant as the   160
wrathful dove or most magnanimous mouse. –
Prick the woman's tailor well, Master Shallow, deep
Master Shallow.

FEEBLE I would Wart might have gone, sir.

FALSTAFF I would thou wert a man's tailor, that thou   165

asserts, 'Shallow's office is to produce the recruits, Falstaff's to question them'. But Q and F agree that it is Shallow's line, and there is no compelling reason to alter the SP.

151–6 As the name Feeble suggests, women's tailors were ridiculed for being effeminate cowards, as in the proverb 'It takes nine tailors to make a man.' They were also mocked as sexual deviants, witness Jonson's *The New Inn* wherein Nick Stuffe, the ladies' tailor, makes love to his wife while dressed in finery commissioned by his rich clients. Tailors were also said to seize the opportunities of their trade for purposes of sexual conquest: the term thus signified a fornicator, a man who used his 'tail' or penis to penetrate a client, and, by extension, the penis itself. Therefore, just as a man's tailor could make a suit of clothes (*OED* prick v. 20) for Shallow, so could that same tailor thrust him through with sword or prick (*OED v.* 1). Falstaff's

asking Feeble how many holes he has made in a woman's petticoat alludes to both his sewing skills and his sexual prowess.

155 **battle** army. Cf. 4.1.154, 179.

157 **my good will** my best. Inadvertently invoking the bawdy meaning of *will* as sexual desire, Feeble extends Falstaff's run of *double entendres*.

160–3 **courageous ... Shallow**   Falstaff indulges in demeaning oxymorons at the expense of the recruits.

161 **magnanimous** valiant

162 ***tailor well** F's punctuation is preferable to Q's, for *well* used adverbially to advise Shallow how to prick Feeble makes better sense than for *well* to serve as an interjection addressed to Shallow for no apparent reason.

164 **would** wish. Feeble's line, indicating that he knows Wart was not pricked, may be evidence that he was already onstage. See discussion of F's massed entry at 0.1n.

153 may; but] may, but *Q;* may: / But *F*   154 he'd a'] *Q (*hee'd a*);* he would haue *F*   SD] *Oxf¹*   162 tailor well] *F;* tailer: wel *Q*

mightst mend him and make him fit to go. I cannot
put him to a private soldier, that is the leader of
so many thousands. Let that suffice, most forcible
Feeble.

FEEBLE   It shall suffice, sir.   170

FALSTAFF   I am bound to thee, reverend Feeble. – Who
is next?

SHALLOW   Peter Bullcalf o'th' green.

FALSTAFF   Yea, marry, let's see Bullcalf.

[*Enter* BULLCALF.]

BULLCALF   Here, sir.   175

FALSTAFF   'Fore God, a likely fellow! Come, prick
Bullcalf till he roar again.

BULLCALF   O Lord, good my lord captain –

FALSTAFF   What, dost thou roar before thou art pricked?

BULLCALF   O Lord, sir, I am a diseased man!   180

FALSTAFF   What disease hast thou?

BULLCALF   A whoreson cold, sir; a cough, sir, which
I caught with ringing in the King's affairs upon his
coronation day, sir.

---

166 **mend . . . go** mend his clothes to make
him presentable as a soldier, with a pun
on *mend* meaning to reform him or free
him from defect, and a bawdy play on *fit
to go* meaning able to fuck. Cf. 116, 117.
167 **put him to** enlist him as
167–8 **leader . . . thousands** probably referring to the lice which infest Wart's clothes.
Falstaff jokes that a man who has so
many at his command should not be
enlisted as a mere soldier.
168 **suffice** be reason enough (for not recruiting Wart)
171 **reverend** worthy of great respect.

Falstaff is continuing his ironic praise of
the recruits begun at 159.
173 **green** the village green
176 **likely** able, suitable: cf. 256.
176–7 **prick . . . roar** another play on *prick*
as (1) choose, or (2) stab. 'To roar like a
bull' was proverbial (Dent, B715), and in
1H4 Falstaff 'roared, as every I hear bullcalf' (2.4.260).
177 **again** in response
182 **whoreson** See 1.2.15n.
183–4 **ringing . . . day** literally, the ringing
of church bells on the annual observance
of the monarch's coronation, a holiday

170 sir] *Q; not in F*   172 next] *Q;* the next *F*   173 o'th' green] *Q;* of the Greene *F*   174 let's] *Q;* let vs *F*
174.1] *Davison (after 173); not in QF*   176 'Fore God] *Q;* Trust me *F*   prick] *Q;* pricke me *F*   178, 180 O
Lord] *Q;* Oh *F*   179 thou art] *Q;* th'art *F*

305

FALSTAFF   Come, thou shalt go to the wars in a gown.   185
We will have away thy cold, and I will take such
order that thy friends shall ring for thee. – Is here all?

SHALLOW   Here is two more called than your number.
You must have but four here, sir; and so I pray you
go in with me to dinner.   190

FALSTAFF   Come, I will go drink with you, but I cannot
tarry dinner. I am glad to see you, by my troth, Master
Shallow.

SHALLOW   O Sir John, do you remember since we lay
all night in the Windmill in Saint George's Field?   195

FALSTAFF   No more of that, Master Shallow.

SHALLOW   Ha, 'twas a merry night! And is Jane
Nightwork alive?

FALSTAFF   She lives, Master Shallow.

---

which signalled the beginning of a new
administrative year (*affairs* = business)
and often was celebrated with riotous
partying. The reference is anachronistic,
since the custom was instituted only
during the reign of Queen Elizabeth
(GWW).

185 **gown** dressing gown worn by the sick:
cf. 3.1.0.1n. on *nightgown*.

186 **have away** get rid of (possibly, as the
following line implies, through death)

186–7 **take such order** make such
arrangements

187 **ring for thee** Falstaff continues his
cynical wordplay: (1) ring in your place
while you do military service, or, more
slyly, (2) ring bells at your funeral

188 On the number of recruits, see 94n.

192 **tarry** stay for; evidence perhaps that
despite his delay in leaving London,
Falstaff is not loitering on his way to
York. Cf. 290.

195 **Windmill . . . Field** John Norden's map
of London dated 1600 shows a windmill
in St George's Field (Cam[1]), which lay
south of the Thames between Southwark
and Lambeth: Shallow may be referring
to a tavern or an inn named for it.
More probably, though, the Windmill
was a brothel. Southwark was noted for
its brothels, and Shallow's phrase *lay all
night* and his mention of Jane Nightwork
(197–8), whose name no doubt signalled
her profession, increase the probability.

198 **Nightwork** As Cowl and Humphreys
observe (Ard[1], Ard[2]), the term was
common: cf. Jonson, *Every Man Out*,
5.8.30–2: 'I mar'le what peece of
nightwork you haue in hand . . . what, is
this your Pandar?'; Middleton, *A Mad
World*, 1.2.1: 'She may make night-work
on't'; and Massinger, *The Guardian*,
3.5.39: 'I had ever a lucky hand in such
smock night-work'.

188 Here] *Q;* There *F*   192 by my] *Q;* in good *F*   196 Master Shallow.] *Q;* good Master *Shallow*: No
more of that. *F*   197 'twas] *Q;* it was *F*

SHALLOW   She never could away with me.   200

FALSTAFF   Never, never. She would always say she
could not abide Master Shallow.

SHALLOW   By the mass, I could anger her to th' heart.
She was then a bona roba. Doth she hold her own
well?   205

FALSTAFF   Old, old, Master Shallow.

SHALLOW   Nay, she must be old. She cannot choose but
be old. Certain she's old, and had Robin Nightwork
by old Nightwork before I came to Clement's Inn.

SILENCE   That's fifty-five year ago.   210

SHALLOW   Ha, cousin Silence, that thou hadst seen that
that this knight and I have seen! – Ha, Sir John? Said
I well?

FALSTAFF   We have heard the chimes at midnight,
Master Shallow.   215

---

200 **away with** endure, put up with (*OED*
away *adv.* 16), or bear, with a possible
sexual innuendo

204 **bona roba** Cf. 23n. Its use here
strengthens the likelihood that Shallow
means high-class whore.

204–5 **Doth ... well?** 'Is she still in good
health?' Falstaff's reply indicates either
that he is still in touch with her or that he
is simply humouring Shallow with an
answer.

208–9 **had ... by** *had* means 'gave birth to';
by indicates paternity.

210 As Melchiori notes, Silence's observation is telling. If Shallow was a student at
Clement's Inn 55 years earlier, he must
now be over 70, Jane Nightwork even
older, and Falstaff, then a page, at least in
his late 60s. In *1H4* Falstaff gives his age
as 'some fifty, or, by'r Lady, inclining to
threescore' (2.4.412–13), but it would be

characteristic of him to shave a few years
off his age, and Falstaff in *2H4* clearly is
meant to appear older and more disease-
ridden than in *1H4*. Silence's perspective
is that of a younger man: 211–12 implies
that he has not lived as long, nor seen as
much, as Shallow and Falstaff. See also
10n.

214 **heard ... midnight** stayed up till all
hours: a nostalgia for night-time revelry
reminiscent of Pistol's 'We have seen the
seven stars' (2.4.186–7). In the context
of *Ubi sunt?*, however, the lateness of the
hour also signifies old age. Orson Welles
took the American title of his film *Chimes
at Midnight* from this line: see pp. 482–5.
chimes In clocks of Shakespeare's time,
a two-note descending third sounded
incrementally at each quarter hour, so
that eight notes would have chimed at
midnight (GWW).

---

203 By the mass] *Q; not in F*   to th'] *Q* (too'th*); to the *F*   209 Clement's] *Q(corr), F;* Clemham
Q(uncorr)   210 SP] *Scilens Q; Sil. F*   year] *Q;* yeeres *F*   211 Silence] *F; Scilens Q*

SHALLOW   That we have, that we have, that we have; in
faith, Sir John, we have. Our watchword was 'Hem,
boys!' Come, let's to dinner; come, let's to dinner.
Jesus, the days that we have seen! Come, come.
Exeunt [Falstaff, Shallow and Silence].
BULLCALF   Good Master Corporate Bardolph, stand my   220
friend and here's four Harry ten shillings in French
crowns for you. [*Offers coins.*] In very truth, sir, I
had as ᶠliefᶠ be hanged, sir, as go; and yet for mine
own part, sir, I do not care, but rather because I am

217 **watchword** password
217–18 **Hem, boys** Tyrwhitt writes that
'hem' was a 'vulgarism' which meant
'to cry courage' as one lifted one's cup
(30–1), equivalent to 'Drink up!' or
'Down the hatch!' Cf. *1H4* 2.4.16; Eliot,
Ortho-epia Gallica (2.41); and an old
drinking song used in Brome's *Jovial
Crew* which concludes, 'He cheered up
his heart when his goods went to wrack, /
With a "hem boy, hem" and a cup of old
sack' (2.2.100–1). Duffin (192–3) argues
that Shallow's line makes explicit reference to this song. D.S. Bland speculates
that 'hem' may also have served as the
password by which students at the Inns of
Court and Chancery were let through the
City gates late at night (132). For 'hem'
as notation of a vulgar noise such as a
belch or hiccup, see 2.4.30n.
220 **Corporate** Corporal: a malapropism akin
to Mistress Quickly's, and evidence that
Bullcalf is ignorant of military terminology. Mouldy confuses Bardolph's rank
further by promoting him to *Corporal
Captain* at 229. See also 2.4.138n.
220, 230 **stand** act as (*OED v.* 15c)
221–2 **four . . . crowns** perhaps a sleight of
hand on Bullcalf's part. Harry 10 shilling
coins were Tudor in origin (Harry =

Henry VII: the denomination is thus
anachronistic). By the 1590s, however,
they had been devalued and were worth
only five shillings (Ard²). By offering
Bardolph their worth in French crowns
(which also had been devalued), Bullcalf
could claim to pay him 40 shillings, or
two pounds, while Shakespeare's audience would recognize that the coins were
worth only half that, or one pound.
Mouldy doubles Bullcalf's offer at 232–
3. Thus Bardolph would receive three
pounds in bribes, the amount he reports
to Falstaff at 245. Earlier editors,
believing Bullcalf to have paid a full
two pounds, assumed that Bardolph was
pocketing a pound for himself by under-
reporting the amount to Falstaff; but this
would be true only if the Harry 10
shillings and French crowns had kept
their original value.
223–7 **and yet . . . much** comically circular
reasoning which hinges on the thrice
repeated 'for mine own part'. Bullcalf
uses the phrase twice parenthetically, as
if to qualify his reasons for not wanting
to serve, and then as a climactic admission that 'care for mine own part' –
concern for his own person – prompts
him to be a coward.

216 that we have; in] *Q;* in *F*   217–18 Hem, boys] *Theobald;* Hemboies *Q;* Hem-Boyes *F*   219 Jesus] *Q;*
Oh *F*   SD *Exeunt*] *Q;* [*Exeunt* Falstaff, *and* Justices. *Capell; not in F*   221 here's] *Q;* heere is *F*   222 SD]
this edn   223 lief] *F;* liue *Q*

unwilling, and for mine own part have a desire to   225
stay with my friends; else, sir, I did not care for mine
own part so much.

BARDOLPH [*Takes coins.*]   Go to, stand aside.

MOULDY   And good Master Corporal Captain, for my
old dame's sake, stand my friend. She has nobody   230
to do anything about her when I am gone, and she
is old and cannot help herself. [*Offers coins.*] You
shall have forty, sir.

BARDOLPH [*Takes coins.*]   Go to, stand aside.

FEEBLE   By my troth, I care not. A man can die but once.   235
We owe God a death. I'll ne'er bear a base mind.
An't be my destiny, so; an't be not, so. No man's too
good to serve 's prince; and let it go which way it
will, he that dies this year is quit for the next.

BARDOLPH   Well said. Th'art a good fellow.   240

FEEBLE   Faith, I'll bear no base mind.

228, 234 **Go to** come on (*OED* go *v.* 93a); a
milder remonstrance here than at 117

230 **old dame's sake** The *old dame* Mouldy
refers to here may be his mother rather
than his wife (cf. 113). In either case,
it intensifies his appeal for a family
hardship deferment.

231 **do . . . her** wait upon her. If, however,
one takes his *old dame* to be his wife,
then a gloss implying sexual service is
likely: cf. 2.1.40–1n.

233 **forty** 40 shillings, or two pounds.

235–9 **A man . . . next** With typically
Shakespearean irony, Feeble refutes the
stereotype of cowardice by stoically
citing two common proverbs – 'A man
can die but once' (Dent, M219) and 'I
owe God a death' (G237) – and, in his
final clause, echoing two more: 'Death pays
all debts' (D148) and 'He that dies this

year is excused for the next' (D326.1).
Feeble's pun on death as a debt owed to
God, for 'death' was pronounced 'debt'
by Elizabethans, yokes a commercial
image to a spiritual accounting. Versions
of this sentiment appeared earlier in *1H4*:
'thou owest God a death' (5.1.126) and
'the end of life cancels all bonds'
(3.2.157). Henry Smith, in his *Sermons*
(1609), explains the theological concept
of debt: 'I owe God a death, as his Son
died for me' (598, cited in Kittredge).
Between these proverbs Feeble stuffs
two popular tags also found in *Famous
Victories*: 'Dost think that we are so base-
minded to die among Frenchmen?'
(10.47–8) and 'I am sure he is not too
good to serve the king' (10.4).

239 **quit** exempted, excused

---

228 SD] *this edn*   230 old] *Q(corr), F; not in Q(uncorr)*   has] *Q;* hath *F*   232 SD] *this edn*   234 SD]
this edn   235 By my troth] *Q; not in F*   236 God] *Q; not in F*   I'll ne'er] *Q (*ile nere*);* I will neuer *F*
237 An't . . . an't] *Q (*and't . . . and't*);* if it . . . if it *F*   237 man's] *Q;* man is *F*   238 serve 's] *Q;* serue his *F*
240 Th'art] *Q;* thou art *F*   241 Faith, I'll] *Q (*Faith ile*);* Nay, I will *F*

Enter FALSTAFF *and the* Justices.

FALSTAFF　Come, sir, which men shall I have?

SHALLOW　Four of which you please.

BARDOLPH *[apart to Falstaff]*　Sir, a word with you.
　I have three pound to free Mouldy and Bullcalf.　　　245

FALSTAFF *[apart]*　Go to, well.

SHALLOW　Come, Sir John, which four will you have?

FALSTAFF　Do you choose for me.

SHALLOW　Marry, then: Mouldy, Bullcalf, Feeble and
　Shadow.　　　250

FALSTAFF　Mouldy and Bullcalf! For you, Mouldy, stay
　at home till you are past service; and for your part,
　Bullcalf, grow till you come unto it. I will none of
　you.　　　　　　　*[Exeunt Mouldy and Bullcalf.]*

SHALLOW　Sir John, Sir John, do not yourself wrong!　255
　They are your likeliest men, and I would have you
　served with the best.

FALSTAFF　Will you tell me, Master Shallow, how to
　choose a man? Care I for the limb, the thews, the

---

248 a ruse, apparently to disguise the fact that Bardolph has already taken bribes from the two ablest recruits

252 **past service** too old to do either military service or domestic service, the latter with a pun on the sexual service Mouldy renders his wife. Cf. similar plays on *husbandry* and *drudgery* in 114.
　for your part Falstaff wryly echoes Bullcalf's reiterated phrase from 223–7.

253 **till ... it** until you reach maturity, from a bullcalf to a bull; or – continuing the pun on *service* – until you are ready to perform the duties of the town bull (cf. 2.2.153–4), with *come* meaning ejaculate (cf. 2.1.20n.). With characteristic audacity, Falstaff excuses Mouldy as too old, and Bullcalf too young, to be recruited.

256 **likeliest men** ablest or most suitable recruits. Cf. 176.

259–61 **Care ... spirit** In rationalizing his illogical choice of recruits, Falstaff brazenly echoes 1 Samuel, 16.7, in which God prefers David over his bigger brothers: 'But the Lorde sayde vnto Samuel: Loke not on his fashion, or on the height of his stature, because I haue refused him: for God seeth not as man seeth. For man loketh on the outward appearaunce, but the Lorde beholdeth the heart'. Humphreys argues that the passage parodies contemporary recruitment manuals such as Thomas Proctor's *Of the Knowledge and Conducte of Warres* (1578), which holds it 'most vayne' to choose a soldier by 'his shoulders, brest, armes, thyghes,' or other physical attributes, for 'the courage & mynde is as much to bee respected, as the bodye'.

259 **thews** 'bodily proportions, lineaments,

241.1] *Q; not in F*　244 SD] *Davison subst.*　246 SD] *this edn*　250 Shadow] *Q (*Sadow*), F*　254 SD] *Oxf subst.; not in QF*

310

stature, bulk and big assemblance of a man? Give   260
me the spirit, Master Shallow! Here's Wart: you see
what a ragged appearance it is. 'A shall charge you
and discharge you with the motion of a pewterer's
hammer, come off and on swifter than he that gibbets
on the brewer's bucket. And this same half-faced   265
fellow Shadow? Give me this man! He presents no
mark to the enemy: the foeman may with as great
aim level at the edge of a penknife. And for a retreat,
how swiftly will this Feeble, the woman's tailor, run
off! O, give me the spare men, and spare me the great 270

or parts, as indicating physical strength'
  (*OED* thew *sb*[1]. 3b)
260 **assemblance** build, appearance
262 **ragged** See 142n.
262–3 **charge . . . discharge you** load and
  fire, with a play on sexual assault and
  ejaculation: cf. the puns in 2.4.111–13.
  On the use of *you* as an ethical dative, see
  2.1.40–1n.
263–4 **the motion . . . hammer** i.e. very
  rapid strokes
264 **come . . . on** possibly a military phrase
  meaning to retreat and advance, or
  perhaps, in light of the image at 262–3,
  to lower and raise his gun. In any case,
  coming off and on, like charging and
  discharging, is bawdily suggestive of
  copulation.
264–5 **gibbets . . . bucket** This enigmatic
  phrase probably refers to hoisting onto
  one's shoulders (*gibbets* = hangs) a yoke
  or beam which carries counterbalanced
  buckets of beer for transport from the vat
  to the barrel (Shaaber, *Variorum*, 264), an
  act which had to be performed with speed
  and precision to avoid spillage.
265 **half-faced** i.e. with a face so thin it can
  only be seen in profile, as on a coin

266–70 **Give . . . off** Falstaff again parodies
  military manuals such as Matthew
  Sutcliffe's *The Practice, Proceedings,
  and Lawes of Armes* (1593): 'Men of
  meane stature are for the most parte more
  vigorous and couragious . . . and commonly excell great bodied men in swift-
  nesse and running, which is a matter
  in a souldier verie requisite and commendable' (65); and Sir John Smythe's
  Instructions . . . and Orders Mylitarie
  (1596), which observes that small-arms
  men are 'of the smallest sorte and size of
  men, because they should be the lesser
  markes in the sightes of their enemies
  in skirmish near at hand' (188). See
  Jorgensen, 'Rank', 34–5.
267 **mark** target
267–8 **as great aim** either (1) as much
  chance of success, or (2) as large a target
  level aim or shoot (*OED v.* 7a, b)
269–70 **how . . . off** an ironically inaccurate
  appraisal. Falstaff and Shallow were not
  present to hear Feeble contradict the
  stereotype of the cowardly women's
  tailor at 235–9.
270 **spare** puns on *spare* first as an adjective
  (lean, thin) and then as a verb: 'relieve
  me from having to endure'

261 Here's Wart:] *Q; Where's Wart? F*   262 'A] *Q(a); hee F*   268 retreat] *Q (retraite), F (Retrait)*

311

ones! – Put me a caliver into Wart's hand, Bardolph.
[*Bardolph hands Wart a caliver.*]

BARDOLPH   Hold, Wart! Traverse! Thas, thas, thas!

FALSTAFF   Come, manage me your caliver. So. Very
well. Go to, very good, exceeding good. – O, give
me always a little, lean, old, chopped, bald shot. –   275
Well said, i'faith, Wart! Th'art a good scab. Hold,
there's a tester for thee. [*Gives Wart a coin.*]

SHALLOW   He is not his craft's master; he doth not do it
right. I remember at Mile End Green, when I lay at
Clement's Inn – I was then Sir Dagonet in Arthur's   280

---

271 **me** On use of the ethical dative, see
   2.1.40–1n.
   caliver a light musket – other than the
   pistol, the lightest portable firearm. See
   also 137n.
272 Bardolph shouts commands as if Wart
   were in his platoon. To traverse was to
   march to and fro (*OED v.* 5). *Thas* may be
   an aberrant spelling of 'thus', but just as
   likely, it imitates the nearly unintelligible
   orders barked by drill sergeants to their
   troops.
273 **manage me** show me how you can
   handle (ethical dative, see 2.1.40–1n.)
274–5 **give . . . shot** Falstaff's argument
   continues to burlesque advice given in
   recruitment manuals of the day (see
   259–61n., 266–70n.). Though small stature
   and agility may have been regarded as
   virtues in a musketeer (*shot*), it was never
   recommended that he be old, dried up
   (QF 'chopt' was a variant of 'chapt' =
   chapped), or bald. Furthermore, *shot* was
   a term, common in dialect, for 'a refuse
   animal left after the best of the flock
   or herd have been selected' (*OED sb.*[3]),
   and thus a derogatory epithet for an
   older man.
276 **Well said** 'Well done.' Cf. 5.3.9.

scab a mild epithet meaning rascal or
   scoundrel, with a pun on Wart's name
277 **tester** sixpence. Falstaff gives money
   to Wart probably as a reward for his
   performance, not as press-money.
278 **not . . . master** i.e. not skilled in his
   handling of a caliver
279 **Mile End Green** an open field in London
   now known as Stepney Green, formerly
   used for fairs and shows and as a drill
   ground for training the citizen militia.
   Contemporary references to the military
   exercises performed there are often
   contemptuous: see, for example, Barnabe
   Riche, *Souldiers Wishe to Britons Welfare*
   (1604): 'God blesse me, my countrey,
   and frendes, from his direction that hath
   no better experience than what hee
   hath atteyned unto . . . from a traynyng at
   Mile-end-greene' (cited in Steevens[4]).
   Shallow's using such exercises as the
   standard by which to judge Wart's
   expertise is thus ludicrous.
   lay lodged, lived
280–1 **Sir . . . Show** Sir Dagonet was King
   Arthur's fool in Malory's *Morte d'Arthur*
   (9.18), a figure whose name elicited
   derisive laughter in Jonson's *Every
   Man Out* (4.4.118–19), *Cynthia's Revels*

---

271 SD] *this edn*   272 Thas, thas, thas] *Q;* thus, thus, thus *F*   275 chopped, bald] *F (*chopt, bald*), Q (*chopt
Ballde*)   276 i'faith] *Q (*yfaith*); not in F*   Th'art] *Q;* thou art *F*   277 there's] *Q;* there is *F*   SD] *Oxf¹
subst.*

Show – there was a little quiver fellow, and 'a would
manage you his piece thus; and 'a would about and
about, and come you in, and come you in. 'Rah, tah,
tah!' would 'a say; 'Bounce!' would 'a say; and away
again would 'a go, and again would 'a come. I shall   285
ne'er see such a fellow.

FALSTAFF   These fellows ^Fwill^F do well, Master Shallow.
God keep you, Master Silence; I will not use many
words with you. Fare you well, gentlemen both; I
thank you. I must a dozen mile tonight. – Bardolph,   290
give the soldiers coats.

SHALLOW   Sir John, the Lord bless you; God prosper
your affairs; God send us peace. At your return, visit

(5.4.549) and Beaumont and Fletcher's
Knight of the Burning Pestle (4.46).
Arthur's Show was a popular archery
exhibition held at Mile End Green by
the Society of Arthur's Knights, each
member of which adopted the name of
a knight of the Round Table. Shallow
unselfconsciously remembers playing
the fool.

281 **quiver** nimble

281–5 **'a . . . come** Shallow here attempts to
re-enact – *thus* (282) – and no doubt
to comic effect, how the *quiver fellow*
would execute single-handedly the drill
of an entire company of musketeers. In
order to maintain a constant barrage
on the enemy, and because Elizabethan
muskets took a long time to reload, the
front rank of men would fire and then run
to the rear to reload (*about and about*)
while the next rank fired, each subsequent
rank doing the same until the first rank
had its turn again (*come you in*). *Rah, tah,
tah!* imitates the noise either of gunfire or

of reloading the caliver. *Bounce*, a newly
fashionable onomatopoeia, was equivalent
to 'bang'. Cf. Thomas Heywood, *1 Fair
Maid of the West*, 4.1: 'Bounce quoth the
guns' (Heywood, 2.315).

282 **manage . . . piece** handle his firearm. On
you as the ethical dative, see 2.1.40–1n.

285–6 **I . . . fellow** 'again' is understood.
Shallow continues to be nostalgic for
the golden days of his youth: cf. his
conversation with Falstaff at 194–219.

287 **These fellows** i.e. his three recruits

288–9 **I . . . you** another play on Silence's
name

290 **I . . . tonight** The verb 'ride' is implied.
Cf. 191–2.

291 **coats** linen or leather jackets which could
be reinforced with chainmail or steel
plates. Because it is unlikely that an army
in Elizabeth's day would have carried
stores of clothing, *coats* may be short
for 'coat and conduct money' given to
recruits to outfit themselves.

281–5 'a . . . 'a . . . 'a . . . 'a . . . 'a . . . 'a] *Q*; hee . . . hee . . . hee . . . hee . . . hee . . . he *F*   286 ne'er] *Q*
*(*nere*)*; neuer *F*   287 will] *F*; wooll *Q*   288 God . . . Silence] *Q (*Scilens*)*; Farewell Master *Silence F*
292–3 the Lord . . . God . . . God] *Q*; Heauen . . . and . . . and *F*   293 peace. At your] *Collier*; peace at
your *Q*; Peace. As you *F*

our house; let our old acquaintance be renewed.
Peradventure I will with ye to the court.   295
FALSTAFF   'Fore God, would you would.
SHALLOW   Go to, I have spoke at a word. God keep you.
FALSTAFF   Fare you well, gentle gentlemen.
                                                                Exit [Shallow with Silence].
On, Bardolph, lead the men away.
                        [Exit Bardolph with Shadow, Wart and Feeble.]
As I return I will fetch off these justices. I do see   300
the bottom of Justice Shallow. Lord, Lord, how
subject we old men are to this vice of lying! This
same starved justice hath done nothing but prate to
me of the wildness of his youth and the feats he hath
done about Turnbull Street, and every third word a   305
lie, duer paid to the hearer than the Turk's tribute. I
do remember him at Clement's Inn like a man made
after supper of a cheese paring. When 'a was naked

---

295 **Peradventure** perhaps. 'Go' is implied after *will*.
296 **would you would** I wish you would
297 **I . . . word** I mean what I say
298–9 *Q reads '*exit*' at the end of 298 and begins 299 with the SP '*Shal.*' Shaaber (*Variorum*) speculates that the copy-text read '*exit Shal.*' but that the words were so positioned that the compositor mistook '*Shal.*' for a SP. Falstaff is clearly the speaker at 299.
300 **As** when. On the illogic of Falstaff's returning from Lincolnshire to London through Gloucestershire, see pp. 12–13.
fetch off fleece, con
301 **bottom . . . Shallow** punning on his name and playing on the shallowness of his character
301–2 ¹**Lord . . . lying** lines ironically spoken by a master. Cf. his similar

sentiment in *1H4* 5.4.145–6: 'Lord, Lord, how this world is given to lying!'.
303 **starved justice** a comment on Shallow's scrawny physique, but metaphorically on his impoverished sense of ethics
prate prattle, talk idly
305 **Turnbull Street (now Turnmill Street)** notorious haunt of thieves and whores near Smithfield market in London
duer more duly
306 **Turk's tribute** conventionally xenophobic reference to the barbaric practice by which the Sultan supposedly put to death those subjects who were delinquent in paying dues to him. Cf. 5.2.47–8.
307–10 **a man . . . knife** Falstaff disparages Shallow's slight build – and the insignificant figure he cut – by likening him to man moulded from a scrap of cheese rind left after dinner. Radishes

---

294 our] *Q*; my *F*   295 ye] *Q*; you *F*   296 'Fore God] *Q*; I *F*   you would.] *Q*; you would, Master
Shallow. F   297 God keep you.] *Q*; Fare you well. *F*   298 SD *Exit] Q*; *after 297 F; Exeunt Shallow and
Silence. / Dyce*   299 On] *F; Shal.* On *Q*   SD] *Capell subst.; not in QF*   301 Lord, Lord] *Q; not in F*
305 Turnbull] *Q (*Turne-bull*); Turnball F*   308 'a] *Q;* hee *F*

he was for all the world like a forked radish with
a head fantastically carved upon it with a knife. 'A   310
was so forlorn that his dimensions to any thick sight
were invincible. 'A was the very genius of famine,
yet lecherous as a monkey, and the whores called
him mandrake. 'A came ^Fever^F in the rearward of the
fashion, and sung those tunes to the overscutched   315

had split (*forked*) roots: by imagining
legs carved from the roots and a head
grotesquely (*fantastically*) fashioned
from the radish itself, Falstaff implies
that Shallow, when naked, looked like a
figure without a body, all head and legs.
Root carving was a common diversion in
Shakespeare's day.

311 **forlorn** wretchedly thin, meagre (*OED
adj.* 5b)
    thick sight faulty vision. Cf. *JC* 5.3.21:
'My sight was ever thick'.

312 *****invincible** QF's word is defensible if
understood to mean incapable of being
perceived and to imply the defeat a short-
sighted person would suffer in struggling
to see Shallow. But Rowe's emendation
'invisible' is often adopted by editors
because it is the more obvious choice:
invincible may have been a catachresis
(*OED* invincible *adj.* 3) or possibly a
compositor's misreading of 'invisible' in
the copy-text. Elsewhere in Shakespeare,
invincible always carries its ordinary
meaning.
    genius embodiment

313 **lecherous ... monkey** This commonly
held belief also underlies Iago's taunt
about Desdemona's sexuality: 'as prime
as goats, as hot as monkeys' (*Oth*
3.3.406).

314 **mandrake** The application to Shallow is
twofold. First, *mandrake* is glossed in the
Geneva Bible (Genesis, 30.14) as 'a
kinde of herbe whose rote hath a certeine

likenes of ye figure of a man', analogous
to the radish to which Falstaff has already
compared Shallow's form (309–10).
Gerard's *Herball* (1597; 2.280) explains
why the mandrake was so regarded:
'The roote is long, thick, whitish, diuided
many times into two or three parts,
resembling the legs of a man, with other
parts of his body adioining thereto as the
priuie parts, as it hath been reported.'
Perhaps owing to this last association,
the mandrake from ancient times was
thought to be an aphrodisiac: cf. 1.2.15.
Falstaff thus implies that the whores
ridiculed Shallow's insatiable lust.

314–15 **'A came ... fashion** either (1) he
wore styles only after they had gone out
of fashion, or (2) he was always socially
inept. Partridge suggests that 'came . . . in
the rearward' may also hint that Shallow
was 'perverted in his sexual practices'
(145) – that is, he practised buggery.

315–17 **tunes ... goodnights** melodies whistled
in the street by *car-men* (drivers of carts,
wagons or carriages) that Shallow passed
off as his own impromptus (*fancies*) and
serenades (*goodnights*) to the whores he
wished to impress. Henry Chettle in *Kind-
Heartes Dreame* lists 'The Carman's
Whistle' as a popular bawdy song of this
era; and Duffin (90–4) prints lyrics for
two different ballads about the car-man,
the tune for which is found in several
settings of this period. In a manner
similar to Shallow, young Bartholomew

309 radish] *Q (*reddish*), F*   310 'A] *Q;* Hee *F*   312 invincible] *QF;* invisible *Rowe*   'A] *Q;* Hee *F*
genius] *Q(corr), F;* gemies *Q(uncorr)*   313–14 yet ... mandrake] *Q; not in F*   314 'A] *Q;* hee *F*   ever]
F; ouer *Q*   315–17 and sung ... goodnights.] *Q; not in F*

housewives that he heard the car-men whistle, and
sware they were his fancies or his goodnights. And
now is this Vice's dagger become a squire and talks
as familiarly of John a'Gaunt as if he had been sworn
brother to him; and I'll be sworn 'a ne'er saw him   320
but once in the tilt-yard, and then he burst his head for
crowding among the marshal's men. I saw it and told
John a'Gaunt he beat his own name, for you might
have thrust him and all his apparel into an eel-skin.
The case of a treble hautboy was a mansion for him,   325

Cokes in Jonson's *Bartholomew Fair* (1.4.77–81) picks up 'vile tunes' from carters 'which hee will sing at supper, and in the sermon-times': 'if hee meete but a Carman i' the streete, . . . hee will whistle him, and all his tunes ouer, at night in his sleepe!'

315–16 **overscutched housewives** washed-up whores. Pronounced 'hussies' or 'hussifs', *housewives* was a common term for prostitutes; and *overscutched* meant either thoroughly whipped, as is to be Doll's punishment at 5.4.5, or simply used up, with a possible play on the word 'scut', the tail of a hare, which became a slang term equivalent to cunt. Falstaff reveals that Shallow consorted not with the bona robas he brags about at 23–4, but with the lowest, and perhaps oldest, of the profession.

318 **Vice's dagger** an allusion to the dagger of lath (thin, flat wood) comically brandished by the Vice figure in Moralities and Tudor Interludes. Cf. *1H4*, where Falstaff threatens to 'beat [Hal] out of [his] kingdom with a dagger of lath' (2.4.130–1), and Feste's song in *TN*: 'like to the old Vice / . . . Who with dagger of lath, in his rage and his wrath, / Cries 'Aha!' to the devil' (4.2.123–6). Falstaff mocks Shallow for his wraith-like appearance.

319 **John a'Gaunt** Ironically, Falstaff himself claims such familiarity at 322–3. As page to Mowbray, he might at times have been in the company of John of Gaunt: see 25–6n.

319–20 **sworn brother** companion-in-arms; one who has taken a vow of friendship

321 **tilt-yard** a ground for tournaments and jousts close to Whitehall in Westminster

321–2 **he . . . men** Shallow appears to have been beaten about the head for trying to enter an area of the tilt-yard reserved for tournament officials – clear proof that he held no sway with John of Gaunt. The antecedent of *he*, however, is unclear and might possibly refer to Gaunt, who thus would have beaten Shallow himself. For discussion of the marshal's function, see 1.3.4n.

323 **he . . . name** strained Falstaffian word-play. Shallow surpassed (*beat*) Gaunt by being even more gaunt (emaciated) than the name suggests.

324 **thrust** stuffed
eel-skin used as a tight-fitting sheath, thus suggestive of comically exaggerated thinness. In *1H4* Falstaff calls Harry 'you starveling, you eel-skin' (2.4.238), and in *KJ* Faulconbridge's skinny arms are mocked as 'eel-skins stuff'd' (1.1.141).

325 **case . . . hautboy** The treble was the slenderest of the three Elizabethan

319, 323 a'Gaunt] *Q (a Gaunt)*; of Gaunt *F*   320 'a ne'er] *Q (a nere)*; hee neuer *F*   324 thrust] *Q*; truss'd *F*   eel-skin] *Q(corr), F*; eele-shin *Q(uncorr)*   325 hautboy] *Q (hoboy)*, *F (Hoeboy)*

a court; and now has he land and beefs. Well, I'll be
acquainted with him if I return, and 't shall go hard,
but I'll make him a philosopher's two stones to me.
If the young dace be a bait for the old pike, I see no
reason in the law of nature but I may snap at him. Let   330
time shape, and there an end.   [*Exit.*]

4.1   *Enter the* ARCHBISHOP [of York],
            MOWBRAY, HASTINGS [*and a Captain*]
            within the Forest of Gaultree.

ARCHBISHOP
What is this forest called?

---

hautboys (ancestor of the oboe), its case, like the eel-skin, long and narrow.

326 beefs cattle, oxen

326–7 be acquainted with find occasion to swindle; an ominous recasting of Shallow's invitation to 'let our old acquaintance be renewed' (294) which implies that Falstaff will make himself acquainted with Shallow's wealth. Cf. 'I will fetch off these justices' (300).

327–8 't shall . . . I'll 'it will be to my discredit if I don't' (*OED* hard *adv.* 2c); more colloquially, 'I'll be damned if I don't'

328 philosopher's two stones Alchemists believed that one of these stones would confer eternal youth; the other – presumably the one Falstaff is more interested in – would transmute base metals into gold. Falstaff thus intends to grow rich by Shallow, and in Act 5 he manages to secure his first instalment. The mention of *two* stones (when he is really interested in only one) increases

the likelihood that Falstaff is also playing on *stones* as slang for testicles, a *double entendre* in line with his other dismissive characterizations of Shallow.

329–30 If . . . him The law of nature to which Falstaff alludes is epitomized in a proverb, 'The great fish eat the small' (Dent, F111). The *dace* is a small freshwater fish used for bait.

330 but I may that says I shouldn't
   ***Let** While corrected Q's 'till' may make colloquial sense if regarded as an extension of the previous clause – Falstaff will snap at Shallow until time shapes his destiny – uncorrected Q's and F's introduction of an independent clause with 'let' rounds out Falstaff's speech more aphoristically, an option preferred by most editors.

4.1.0.1–3 *Q indicates Lord Bardolph's entrance here, though he plays no part in the scene and, according to Holinshed (3.530), had fled to Scotland with Northumberland. F deletes Bardolph's

325–6 for . . . court;] for him: a Court. *F*; for him a Court. *Q*   326 has] *Q*; hath *F*   beefs] *Q*; Beeues *F*
I'll] *Q* (ile); I will *F*   327 't] *Q*; it *F*   328 I'll] *Q* (ile); I will *F*   330 him. Let] *F, Q(uncorr)*(him: let);
him, till *Q(corr)*   331 SD] *Capell; Exeunt. F; not in Q*   **4.1**] *Actus Quartus. Scena Prima. F; not in Q*
0.1–3] *Q (Enter the Archbishop, Mowbray, Bardolfe, Hastings, within the forrest of Gaultree.); Enter the
Arch-bishop, Mowbray, Hastings, Westmerland, Coleuile. F*   0.1 *and a Captain*] *this edn*

HASTINGS

'Tis Gaultree Forest, an't shall please your grace.

ARCHBISHOP

Here stand, my lords, and send discoverers forth
To know the numbers of our enemies.

HASTINGS

We have sent forth already.

ARCHBISHOP   'Tis well done.   5

My friends and brethren in these great affairs,
I must acquaint you that I have received
New-dated letters from Northumberland,
Their cold intent, tenor and substance thus:
Here doth he wish his person with such powers   10
As might hold sortance with his quality,
The which he could not levy; whereupon
He is retired, to ripe his growing fortunes,
To Scotland, and concludes in hearty prayers

name from the SD but adds those of
Westmorland, who does not enter until
24, and Collevile, who does not speak
until his encounter with Falstaff in 4.2.
Though one could argue that Collevile's
inclusion is justified because he is a
famous rebel (4.2.61) worthy of partici-
pating in the councils of war (see *TxC*,
363, and Oxf¹), F's listing of Westmorland
and Collevile in the SD is more likely
anticipatory: cf. the massed entry at F
3.2.0. For evidence of scribal error in F,
see 4.2n.

0.3 Holinshed places this episode on 'a plaine
within the forrest of Galtree' (3.529).
Originally spelled 'Galtres', the forest,
established by Norman kings, lay just to
the north of York and by the time of
Henry IV's reign covered 100,000 acres.
Identification of a locale in an introductory SD is rare in Shakespeare; here,

the opening lines of the scene make it
superfluous.

2   **an't shall please** if it suits; an expression
of deference

3   **discoverers** scouts

8   **New-dated** recent. The letters are
Shakespeare's invention.

9   **cold** chilling, dispiriting (*OED adj.* 9,
10a)

10 **powers** forces, troops. Cf. 1.1.133.

11 **hold sortance with** be appropriate for
quality rank

12 **whereupon**   for   which   reason.
Northumberland's excuse is patently
false: cf. 2.3.65–8.

13–14 **to ripe ... Scotland** The meaning of
growing fortunes is ambiguous. It may
imply optimism that Scotland will yield
Northumberland such powers as he could
not levy in England, but the Archbishop's
account may be tinged with sarcasm.

2 Gaultree] *Q*; Gaultre *F*   an't] *QF* (and't)   9 tenor] tenure *QF*; tenour *Theobald*   12 could] *Q(corr)F*;
would *Q(uncorr)*

That your attempts may overlive the hazard   15
And fearful meeting of their opposite.

MOWBRAY

Thus do the hopes we have in him touch ground
And dash themselves to pieces.

Enter Messenger.

HASTINGS   Now, what news?

MESSENGER

West of this forest, scarcely off a mile,
In goodly form comes on the enemy,   20
And, by the ground they hide, I judge their number
Upon or near the rate of thirty thousand.

MOWBRAY

The just proportion that we gave them out.
Let us sway on and face them in the field.

Enter WESTMORLAND.

ARCHBISHOP

What well-appointed leader fronts us here?   25

MOWBRAY

I think it is my Lord of Westmorland.

WESTMORLAND

Health and fair greeting from our general,

---

15 **attempts** enterprise
overlive survive, outlive
15–16 **hazard . . . meeting** probably a
hendiadys: 'the peril (*hazard*) and fear-
inducing (*fearful*) risk of encountering'
16 **opposite** adversary
17 **touch ground** run aground; a metaphor
from shipwrecks (*OED* ground *sb*. 2b)
20 **goodly form** proper formation, used of
the military (*OED* form *sb*. 8)

21 **ground they hide** amount of space they
take up
22 **Upon** close to
rate total
23 'The exact number we estimated.'
24 **sway on** advance, move ahead (*OED*
sway *v*. 4b)
25 **well-appointed** 'in full military regalia'
(Cam²). Cf. 1.1.190 and *H5* 3.Chorus.4.
fronts confronts, meets (us) face to face
(*OED v*. 3a)

15 overlive] *QF (*ouer-liue*)   18 SD *Enter*] *Q; Enter a F*   24.1] *F, Q (after 25)*

The prince Lord John and Duke of Lancaster.

ARCHBISHOP

Say on, my Lord of Westmorland, in peace,

What doth concern your coming.

WESTMORLAND   Then, my lord,   30

Unto your grace do I in chief address

The substance of my speech. If that rebellion

Came like itself, in base and abject routs

Led on by bloody youth, guarded with rage

And countenanced by boys and beggary –   35

I say, if damned commotion so appear

In his true, native and most proper shape,

You, reverend father, and these noble lords

Had not been here to dress the ugly form

Of base and bloody insurrection   40

With your fair honours. You, Lord Archbishop,

---

30 **What . . . coming** 'why you have come'

32 **If that** if

33 **like itself** in its true colours
    routs disorderly mobs, rabble

34 **bloody** passionate, excitable, possibly
    bloodthirsty
    guarded with rage extends the person-
    ification of rebellion as a figure progres-
    sing through a mob, led by youth, protected
    (*OED* guard *v.* 7) by rage, and attended
    by beggary. In similar fashion, *rage and
    hot blood* are said to be the Prince's
    counsellors at 4.3.63. Although Q and F
    agree on *rage*, some editors, arguing that
    the word is an error springing from a
    common source, prefer Singer's emenda-
    tion 'guarded with rags', because 'rags'
    would sort well with beggary and *guarded*
    would assume its sartorial meaning of
    trimmed or ornamented with lace and
    embroidery (*OED ppl.a.* 3a), thus yield-
    ing a metaphor picked up in 'dress the
    ugly form / Of . . . insurrection' at 39–40.

35 **countenanced** approved
    by boys by no one *but* boys. Westmorland
    implies that only the young would be
    taken in by the Archbishop's hypocrisy.

36 **commotion** rebellion, insurrection. Cf.
    2.4.368.
    appear were to appear: the subjunctive
    mood

37 **his** its
    true . . . proper a redundancy typical
    of Westmorland, as in the *If* clauses
    beginning at 32 and 36, the four *Whose*
    clauses at 42–5, and the four parallel
    phrases at 50–2. Westmorland's habit of
    syntactical repetition is reminiscent of
    John of Gaunt's in *R2*.

39 **Had not been** would not be

40 **bloody** Unlike its use at 34, *bloody* here
    signifies the bloodshed for which these
    rebels will be responsible.

41 **fair honours** refers to the rebels' exalted
    ranks, but glances ironically at their
    dishonourable motives as well. As the

30–1 Then . . . address] *F; one line Q(corr)*   30 Then, my lord] *Q(corr)F; not in Q(uncorr)*   34 rage]
QF; rags Singer² (W.Walker)   36 appear] *QF; appear'd Pope*

Whose see is by a civil peace maintained,
Whose beard the silver hand of peace hath touched,
Whose learning and good letters peace hath tutored,
Whose white investments figure innocence, 45
The dove and very blessed spirit of peace:
Wherefore do you so ill translate yourself
Out of the speech of peace that bears such grace
Into the harsh and boist'rous tongue of war,
Turning your books to graves, your ink to blood, 50
Your pens to lances, and your tongue divine
To a loud trumpet and a point of war?

ARCHBISHOP

Wherefore do I this? So the question stands.
Briefly, to this end: we are all diseased,
^FAnd with our surfeiting and wanton hours 55
Have brought ourselves into a burning fever,

culmination of the sartorial metaphor begun at 39, *fair honours* would mean handsome garments.

44 **good letters** erudition

45 **white investments figure** 'ecclesiastical robes symbolize'. On the sacrilege of the Bishop's support of rebellion against the King, see 1.1.200–9.

46 **dove** See Matthew, 3.16: 'the spirite of God descendying lyke a doue'.

47 **translate** a triple pun: (1) translate one language (*peace*) into another (*war*), (2) transform (from a cleric to a soldier), and (3) transfer your See (from church to battlefield), a technical meaning of *translate* used for the movement of bishops (Ard²).

52 **point of war** short phrase sounded on a trumpet or bugle as a signal in the field (*OED* point *sb.* A 9a)

55–79 *The omission of these lines from Q is probably the result of censorship (self- or enforced) owing to political

sensitivities surrounding either the deposition of Richard II or the treachery of an Archbishop (see pp. 448–53). Without them, the imagery of disease introduced at 54 – and with it, the Archbishop's promised justification for rebellion – go undeveloped, and the movement from 54 to 80 is abrupt.

55–8 The Archbishop's comparison of the rebels' situation to that of Richard works two ways: (1) he admonishes them for having wasted their time, like Richard, in 'surfeiting and wanton hours' – here meaning not excess and debauchery, but inattention to their political purpose – which may, as a result, bring about their deaths; (2) he ironically identifies them as targets of an ambitious Bolingbroke who, as he did with Richard, will fabricate charges of corruption (*disease*) in order to eliminate them. The withering sarcasm with which Richard's fate is phrased – he *being infected, died* – occludes the fact that he was killed.

45 figure] *Q(corr)F;* figures *Q(uncorr)* 54 end: we] *F;* end we *Q* 55–79] *F; not in Q*

And we must bleed for it; of which disease
Our late King Richard, being infected, died.
But, my most noble Lord of Westmorland,
I take not on me here as a physician,   60
Nor do I as an enemy to peace
Troop in the throngs of military men,
But rather show a while like fearful war
To diet rank minds sick of happiness
And purge th'obstructions which begin to stop   65
Our very veins of life. Hear me more plainly.
I have in equal balance justly weighed
What wrongs our arms may do, what wrongs
     we suffer,
And find our griefs heavier than our offences.
We see which way the stream of time doth run   70

57 **bleed** play on blood-letting as a medical cure, and shedding blood in battle. Throughout this passage (54–66) the Archbishop uses imagery of curing the sick body as a metaphor for purging the state of its ills through civil war.

60 **take ... physician** do not assume the role (*OED* take *v.* 16a) of physician – i.e. military commander (cf. 57n.). The Archbishop is being disingenuous here, for lines 64–5 confirm that he is indeed acting as a physician (Ard²). This passage was influenced by the Archbishop's claim in Holinshed 'that he tooke nothing in hand against the kings peace, but that whatsoeuer he did, tended rather to aduance the peace and quiet of the commonwealth ... and therefore he maintained that his purpose to be good & profitable, as well for the king himself, as for the realme' (3.529).

62 **Troop** march

63 **show ... war** temporarily put on the frightening mask of war

64 Continuing the imagery of 'surfeiting and wanton hours' in 55–8, this line probably

means 'to discipline minds bloated, and thus sickened, with excess': *diet* = regulate, return to health; *rank* = swollen, puffed up (*OED adj.* 6); *sick of* = sick with; *happiness* = excess.

65 **purge**   **th'obstructions**   medically, cleanse the blood of impurities; politically, rid the state of corrupting influences. For a similar metaphor of purging, with the same use of *rank*, see Sonnet 118: 'to prevent our maladies unseen / We sicken to shun sickness when we purge', bringing 'to medicine a healthful state / Which, rank of goodness, would by ill be cured' (3–4, 11–12). **stop** block, close up

66 **Hear ... plainly** Aware that his heavily metaphoric speech may not have been fully understood, the Archbishop here offers to translate it.

67 **justly** precisely (*OED adv.* 5)

70 **which ... run** probably a reference to speed rather than direction: 'how things are going'. The line echoes a proverb, 'How runs the stream?' (Dent, S925). Cf. *TN* 4.1.59.

And are enforced from our most quiet there
By the rough torrent of occasion,
And have the summary of all our griefs,
When time shall serve, to show in articles,
Which long ere this we offered to the King   75
And might by no suit gain our audience.
When we are wronged and would unfold our griefs,
We are denied access unto his person
Even by those men that most have done us wrong.[F]
The dangers of the days but newly gone,   80
Whose memory is written on the earth
With yet-appearing blood, and the examples
Of every minute's instance, present now,

---

71 **enforced** driven by force (*OED v.* 7a)
most quiet there With *most* functioning
as an adjective and *there* referring to *the
stream of time* (70), F's phrase suggests
that the pressure of political circumstance
(*torrent of occasion*) has driven the
rebels from a state of calm (*most quiet*)
into action. Some editors have adopted
Hanmer's emendation of *there* to
'sphere', and Wilson's (Cam¹) 'shore' has
also won adherents, assuming a compositor's (unlikely) misreading of *s* for *t*
and *o* for *e*.

72 **rough torrent** a violent onrush of water
which sweeps the rebels out of their calm.
The image of a river flooding its banks is
answered at 175–6.
occasion events, circumstance

74 **When . . . serve** when the time is appropriate; when the occasion arises
articles written complaints

76 **suit** supplication, entreaty
audience i.e. with the King. Shakespeare
strengthens the rebels' case beyond what
sources warrant. Holinshed (3.529) writes
that the rebels took their grievances to
the nobility and even published them 'in

the publike streets of the citie of Yorke';
but no evidence of their taking articles to
the King and being turned away is
recorded.

77–9 The Archbishop's sudden shift to the
present tense emphasizes the urgency of
his case.

77 **unfold** make clear, explain

79 Cf. the Archbishop's complaint in
Holinshed that 'he could have no free
accesse' to the King 'by reason of such a
multitude of flatterers as were about him'
(3.529).
Even . . . men by those very men

80 **dangers** conflicts, probably referring to
the battle at Shrewsbury
newly recently

82 **yet-appearing blood** either (1) blood
shed during past conflicts has indelibly
stained the earth as a portent, or (2) those
conflicts have continued to result in the
spilling of more blood

82–3 **examples . . . now** a crux for which
Steevens's gloss is as good as any:
'examples (of injustice) which every
minute press on our notice, even this very
moment' (Steevens⁴)

---

71 there] *F*; sphere *Hanmer*; chair *Collier² (Theobald)*; shore *Cam¹ (Vaughan)*; flow *Sisson*   80 days] *F*;
daie's *Q*

Hath put us in these ill-beseeming arms
Not to break peace, or any branch of it,   85
But to establish here a peace indeed,
Concurring both in name and quality.

WESTMORLAND

Whenever yet was your appeal denied?
Wherein have you been galled by the King?
What peer hath been suborned to grate on you,   90
That you should seal this lawless, bloody book
Of forged rebellion with a seal divine
And consecrate commotion's bitter edge?

84 **Hath** Use of a singular verb with a plural subject (*dangers*, 80) was common conversational practice from the mid-16th century to the mid-17th.
ill-beseeming unseemly, inappropriate

87 i.e. so that *peace* will exist both in name and in reality

89 **galled** annoyed, perhaps with overtones of abuse or injury; gallèd

90 **suborned** bribed, treacherously induced
grate on harass, oppress

91–2 **seal . . . divine** a possible allusion to the function of bishops as licensers, or censors, of published books; *seal* = authorize

92 **forged** organized, with an implication of fraudulence

93, 95 *These two lines, which appear only in uncorrected Q, are problematic. Their omission from corrected Q may indicate that they were marked for deletion; their omission from F, if F used an independent copy-text, would corroborate corrected Q. Why 93 should have been marked for deletion is puzzling, because it makes sense as a culmination of Westmorland's reproof to the Archbishop. Line 95, however, appears to be corrupt. It is unlikely that a compositor would have been asked to delete these two lines during the printing of Q, because it is much more difficult to remove two lines of type from either side of an intervening line than to remove two adjacent lines. This has led to speculation (Walker, 'Cancelled', 115–16, and *Textual*, 104–5) that a proofreader who had been instructed to cut 101–2, which directly precede the long deletion of Westmorland's speech (103–39), mistakenly cut 93 and 95 instead, perhaps because they begin with the same words as 101–2 (*And* and *To*). Alternatively, Weis speculates that Shakespeare himself marked 93 and 95 for deletion before the book of the play was copied from his holograph, but that the compositor of uncorrected Q carelessly reintroduced them. The deletion of 95, however, does not make 94 and 96, which now become consecutive, any more sensible a reply to Westmorland's questions; and the lack of an adequate referent for *any such redress* (97) adds to the enigmatic nature of the passage, suggesting that at some stage more lines must have been cut.

93 **commotion's bitter edge** the injurious (*OED* bitter *adj.* 5a) sword of rebellion. For a similar use of *edge* as a metonymy for sword, see 1.1.170; for *commotion* as rebellion, see 36 and 2.4.368.

93] *Qa; not in QbF*   bitter edge] *Qa;* Civil Page *Theobald;* Civil Edge *Warburton;* title-page *Herford;* evil page *(Vaughan)*

ARCHBISHOP

My brother general, the commonwealth.
To brother born, an household cruelty, 95
I make my quarrel in particular.

WESTMORLAND

There is no need of any such redress;
Or if there were, it not belongs to you.

MOWBRAY

Why not to him in part, and to us all

94–6 This passage seems to be built on a double antithesis: general vs. particular and brother general vs. brother born (Cam²). The Archbishop quarrels over wrongs done both to the commonwealth (personified as his *brother general*, his fellow subjects) and to William Scroop (le Scrope), Earl of Wiltshire, whom Shakespeare, following Holinshed (3.522), erroneously believed to be brother to the Archbishop (*1H4* 1.3.265–6; he was in fact the Archbishop's cousin) and who was beheaded by Bolingbroke (*R2* 3.2.141). On the other hand, *brother general* may be a calculatedly unctuous form of address to Westmorland; and if so, 95 may stand in apposition to *commonwealth*, which is not separated from it by any punctuation in uncorrected Q. The passage thus might mean that the Archbishop makes the subject of his particular quarrel the commonwealth itself, which has degenerated into civil unrest that cruelly pits brothers from the same household against one another. DSK suggests that for clarity, a simple 'is' added after *born* might allow 94–5 to be read together as a sentence meaning 'the commonwealth is become a cruelty to my brother' and 96 to stand as a separate assertion that the Archbishop is therefore making his quarrel *particular* – that is, personal.

95 **an household** Bulloch suggests 'unhouseled', meaning not allowed to receive the last sacrament, which would have added insult to injury in the case of the Archbishop's brother. Cf. *Ham* 1.5.76–7: 'Cut off even in the blossoms of my sin, / Unhouseled, disappointed, unaneled'. Bulloch's emendation wins support in West, 'Scroop's quarrel'.

96 **quarrel** ground for complaint

97 **such redress** The referent is unclear, because the Archbishop has not detailed what particular grievances he wants to be redressed.

98 **it ... you** Westmorland counters not only that the Archbishop's grievances are unfounded (97), but that the King himself may have suffered wrongs at the hands of the Archbishop which need to be redressed. Holinshed faults the Archbishop for 'the reforming whereof did not yet apperteine vnto him' (3.529) and in so doing echoes Tudor policy, which censured rebellious clerics: 'it is evident that men of the Cleargie . . . ought both themselues specially, and before other, to be obedient vnto their princes, and also to exhort al others vnto the same' (*Certain Sermons*, 598).

99 **Why ... him** 'Why shouldn't the Archbishop be entitled to redress?'

94] *QF;* My brother general, [*shewing* Mowbray.] the common-wealth; *Capell;* My quarrel general, the commonwealth, *(conj. Johnson)* 95] *Qa; not in QbF* an household] *Qa;* unhouseled *(Bulloch)*

That feel the bruises of the days before   100
And suffer the condition of these times
To lay a heavy and unequal hand
Upon our honours?
^FWESTMORLAND   O my good Lord Mowbray,
Construe the times to their necessities
And you shall say indeed it is the time,   105
And not the King, that doth you injuries.
Yet for your part, it not appears to me
Either from the King or in the present time
That you should have an inch of any ground
To build a grief on. Were you not restored   110
To all the Duke of Norfolk's signories,
Your noble and right well-remembered father's?
MOWBRAY
What thing, in honour, had my father lost

---

100 **days before** Cf. 'days but newly gone'
(80).

101 **condition . . . times** Cf. 3.1.78 and
5.2.11.

102 **unequal** unjust

103–39 ***O . . . King** These lines were cut
from Q probably owing to political
censorship, or fear of it. Not only do they
recall events leading to the deposition of
Richard II, about which Elizabeth was
acutely sensitive; they also anticipate,
in Mowbray's situation (107–14), the
plight of the son of the most recent Duke
of Norfolk, to whom Elizabeth restored
the lands but not the title of his father,
whom she had executed in 1572 for plotting treason against her. Without these
lines, which digress from the immediate
purpose, Westmorland's reply to Mowbray
at 140 makes no sense.

104 i.e. understand the current situation in
terms of what present circumstances
demand. Cf. 3.1.92–4.

107 **for your part** a direct reply to Mowbray's
allegation beginning at 99

111 **signories** estates. In *R2* Bolingbroke
repeals the banishment of his rival
Thomas Mowbray, Duke of Norfolk, and
restores to him 'all his lands and
signories' (4.1.90) just prior to hearing of
his death (92–101). Carlisle reports that
before his death, the banished Mowbray
fought 'Many a time . . . / For Jesu Christ
in glorious Christian field' (93–4) on a
pilgrimage to the Holy Land that, ironically, his opponent King Henry is
prevented from making in this play.
Though inheriting his father's estates,
Mowbray is not given the dukedom nor
made Lord Marshal other than in name:
see 1.3.4n.

113 **in honour** a defence of his family's
reputation injured when Richard II
banished Thomas Mowbray, the Duke of
Norfolk: cf. *R2* 1.3.148–77.

102–3 To . . . honours?] *Q; one line F*   103–39 WESTMORLAND O . . . King.] *F; not in Q*

That need to be revived and breathed in me?
The king that loved him, as the state stood then,   115
Was force perforce compelled to banish him;
And then that Henry Bolingbroke and he,
Being mounted and both roused in their seats,
Their neighing coursers daring of the spur,
Their armed staves in charge, their beavers down,   120
Their eyes of fire sparkling through sights of steel,
And the loud trumpet blowing them together –
Then, then, when there was nothing could have
        stayed
My father from the breast of Bolingbroke –
O, when the King did throw his warder down,   125

---

114 **breathed** reinvigorated. Mowbray's point
  is that his father, though banished, had
  never lost his titles and signories; thus
  they were not Bolingbroke's to restore.

115–29 Mowbray vividly recalls the scene at
  Coventry in *R2* (1.3) – imagining details
  beyond the scope of the Elizabethan
  playhouse – and thus provides both a
  continuity of historical narrative, doubtless for the sake of audiences who had
  seen the earlier play, and a justification
  for the present rebellion.

115 **state** political situation

116 ***force perforce** willy-nilly. Theobald's
  emendation of F, an adverbial phrase
  which appears at 4.3.46, makes sense,
  since F's 'forc'd' and 'compell'd' form
  an awkward tautology.

117–26 Mowbray begins a string of participial phrases (*Being mounted*) and
  absolute constructions (*coursers daring*)
  which ultimately does not result in a
  sentence: the clause beginning 'Henry
  Bolingbroke and he' is never completed.
  The *then* at 117 is repeated twice at 123,
  followed by a *when* clause that breaks off
  after two lines to be replaced by a new,
  more coherent attempt at a sentence, this
  time about King Richard, at 125. The
  rushed syntax is probably intended
  to convey the intensity of Mowbray's
  feeling in describing a scene that resulted
  in his father's banishment and eventual
  death in exile. In 117, *that* serves either
  as a demonstrative intensifier for Henry
  or, less likely, as the false start of a
  relative clause.

118 **roused** raised, with overtones of excitement; rousèd

119 **daring . . . spur** eager for the charge: the
  horses are awaiting the spur (metonymic
  for rider) to prick them into action.

120 **armed . . . charge** lances poised in
  readiness; armèd
  beavers visors or faceguards of their
  helmets

121 **sights** visors (*OED sb.* 13b *obs.*); here,
  slits in the beavers

123 **stayed** kept

125 **warder** mace, staff of command. Cf. *R2*
  1.3.118, which this line echoes. Richard's
  calling a halt to the confrontation,
  from Mowbray's point of view, kept
  Bolingbroke alive, who otherwise would
  have died in the tilt.

116 force . . . compelled] *Theobald;* forc'd, . . . compell'd *F*

327

His own life hung upon the staff he threw;
Then threw he down himself and all their lives
That by indictment and by dint of sword
Have since miscarried under Bolingbroke.

WESTMORLAND

You speak, Lord Mowbray, now you know not what.   130
The Earl of Hereford was reputed then
In England the most valiant gentleman.
Who knows on whom Fortune would then have
    smiled?
But if your father had been victor there,
He ne'er had borne it out of Coventry;   135
For all the country in a general voice
Cried hate upon him, and all their prayers and love
Were set on Hereford, whom they doted on,
And blessed and graced indeed more than the King.[F]
But this is mere digression from my purpose.   140
Here come I from our princely general
To know your griefs, to tell you from his grace

---

127 threw . . . down metaphorically, sacrificed
   all their lives the lives of all those. See
   Abbott, 218.
128 by indictment . . . sword through legal
   (in Mowbray's view, illegal) prosecution,
   or by force of arms. For an illustration of
   Bolingbroke's abuse of power, see his
   indictment of Bushy and Green in *R2*
   3.1.2–30.
129 miscarried perished
131 Earl of Hereford In *R2*, Bolingbroke's
   title was Duke (not Earl) of Hereford
   before he assumed the title of his father
   John of Gaunt, Duke of Lancaster. For
   the sake of metrics, Hereford is a
   dissyllable, and is so spelled in F at 138
   ('Herford').
135 ne'er . . . it would never have been able
   to maintain that victory (owing to public

censure: cf. 136–7). Coventry was the
place where Bolingbroke and Mowbray's
father met for the trial by combat which
Richard aborted: see 115–29n.
136 country . . . voice a personification of
   public sentiment; *country* is understood
   as a collective noun, signifying the people.
138 Hereford disyllabic: see 131n.
138–9 doted . . . King For evidence of
   Bolingbroke's popularity and his courtship of the common people, see *R2*
   1.4.23–36.
140 *digression . . . purpose See 103–39n.
   This line makes no sense without the
   previous speeches' recapitulation of
   events that led to the present rebellion.
141 princely general i.e. Prince John
142 know your griefs listen to your
   grievances

139 indeed] *Theobald (Thirlby);* and did *F*   140 But] *F; West.* But *Q*

328

That he will give you audience; and wherein
It shall appear that your demands are just,
You shall enjoy them, everything set off   145
That might so much as think you enemies.

MOWBRAY

But he hath forced us to compel this offer,
And it proceeds from policy, not love.

WESTMORLAND

Mowbray, you overween to take it so.
This offer comes from mercy, not from fear;   150
For lo, within a ken our army lies,
Upon mine honour, all too confident
To give admittance to a thought of fear.
Our battle is more full of names than yours,
Our men more perfect in the use of arms,   155
Our armour all as strong, our cause the best;
Then reason will our hearts should be as good.
Say you not, then, our offer is compelled.

MOWBRAY

Well, by my will, we shall admit no parley.

WESTMORLAND

That argues but the shame of your offence: 160
A rotten case abides no handling.

---

143 **wherein** in so far as

145 **You ... them** i.e. they will be granted
(*enjoy* = be satisfied)
everything set off an ambiguous phrase
which probably means that anything
proving an obstacle to amity will be
excepted or removed (*OED* set *v.*[1] 147a)

146 **think you** hint that you are

147 **forced ... compel** an apparent tautology,
though *compel* probably here means
'accept under duress'

148 **policy** expedience, but with connotations
of cunning or dissimulation. Here, as at
183–4, Mowbray is prescient.

149 **overween** are presumptuous or arrogant
(*OED v.* 1)

151 **ken** normal range of vision (*OED sb.* 2)

154 **battle** army. Cf. 179 and 3.2.155.
more ... names probably (1) replete
with more men of rank (cf. *H5* 4.8.106),
but possibly (2) of greater size

156 **all** every bit

157 **reason will** it stands to reason
hearts courage, spirit (*OED sb.* 11a)

159 **by my will** i.e. if it's up to me
admit no parley refuse any conference

161 Westmorland puns on *case* to mean the
rebels' cause or claim: he suggests that

159 parley] *Q (*parlee*), F*

329

HASTINGS

Hath the Prince John a full commission,
In very ample virtue of his father,
To hear and absolutely to determine
Of what conditions we shall stand upon?   165

WESTMORLAND

That is intended in the general's name.
I muse you make so slight a question.

ARCHBISHOP [*Offers a paper.*]

Then take, my Lord of Westmorland, this schedule,
For this contains our general grievances.
Each several article herein redressed,   170
All members of our cause both here and hence
That are ensinewed to this action,
Acquitted by a true substantial form
And present execution of our wills,
To us and our purposes confined   175

their refusal to discuss it attests to its weakness. Cf. the proverb 'It is a bad sack (case) that will abide no clouting' (Dent, S6), where 'case' refers to a box or container and 'clouting' means mending or patching.
  rotten weak or unsound (*OED adj.* 8a)
162 **commission** probably pronounced as four syllables
163 **In . . . virtue** with the full authority
164 **absolutely** with binding force
164–5 **determine / Of** make a decision about
165 **stand** insist
166 **intended . . . name** signified (*OED v.* 20) by the title of general
167 'I am surprised [*OED* muse *v.* 3a] you entertain so frivolous a doubt [*OED* question *sb.* 1a]'; *question* is pronounced as three syllables.
168 **schedule** document, list. The term may

come from Stow's account in *Annales*, 529; Holinshed uses 'scroll'.
169 **general** common, shared
170 an absolute construction: 'Once every article has been redressed': *several* = individual
171–3 another absolute construction: 'Once all members . . . have been acquitted . . . .' The Archbishop's syntax is formal in its parallelism.
171 **here and hence** now and in the future
172 **ensinewed to** joined as by strong sinews to; alternatively, bound to one another in
172, 192 **action** pronounced as three syllables
173–4 i.e. pardoned (*Acquitted*) by both a legally binding agreement (*OED* form *sb.* 13) and the immediate implementation (*execution*) of our demands (*wills*)
175 *The placement of this line has caused the whole passage to be misread or declared unintelligible. It belongs not

168 SD] *this edn*   172 ensinewed] *Q, F (*insinewed*)*   175 our] *Q*; to our *F*   purposes confined] *QF*; purposes, confin'd *Theobald²*; properties confirm'd *Hanmer*; properties, confin'd *Warburton*; purposes, confirm'd *Capell*; purposes, consign'd *Malone*; purposes consigned *Oxf*

We come within our awful banks again
And knit our powers to the arm of peace.

WESTMORLAND [*Takes the paper.*]

This will I show the general. Please you, lords,
In sight of both our battles we may meet
And either end in peace – which God so frame! –   180
Or to the place of diff'rence call the swords
Which must decide it.

ARCHBISHOP   My lord, we will do so.

Exit Westmorland.

MOWBRAY

There is a thing within my bosom tells me
That no conditions of our peace can stand.

with the lines above – for the 'execution of [their] wills' to be 'confined' would make little sense – but with those that follow. If read in conjunction with 176, it signals the rebels' willingness to return to orderly conduct, within prescribed bounds and restricted (*confined*) again to their own affairs (*purposes*), once the conditions outlined in the two absolute phrases above have been met (see 170n., 171–3n). Had this line followed rather than preceded 176, it would have caused less confusion (Ard²).

and our F's additional 'to' helps to ensure a pentameter line, but there is no compelling reason to alter Q's metrical variation.

176 **come ... banks** The image of a river that has flooded its banks becoming once again *confined* within them harks back to imagery at 70–2. See a similar metaphor in the section of *Sir Thomas More* thought to be in Shakespeare's hand: 'Whiles they [the rebels] are o'er the bank of their obedience / Thus will they bear down all things' (6.47–8).

*awful Recent editors have tended to adopt Q's spelling 'awefull' in order to capture the word's original sense of reverence or due respect, which in this case would be owed to the King. The word is used similarly at 5.2.85. In performance, however, it would prove nearly impossible to aurally distinguish the old form from the new.

177 **knit ... arm** The metaphor is inchoate. The idea of knitting (fastening) something to an arm suggests clothing, but in the context of *powers*, *arm* carries a military connotation.

178 **Please you** a deferential phrase: 'If it pleases you'

179 **battles** See 154n.

180 ***And** Theobald's emendation makes *end in peace* a verb phrase parallel to *call the swords* (181). QF's 'At', on the other hand, requires *end* to be a noun and is difficult to explain: meeting 'at either end' makes little sense here.

frame bring to pass (*OED v.* 8d)

181 **place of diff'rence** i.e. battlefield; *diff'rence* = contention

swords metonymy for soldiers

176 awful] *Q (*awefull*), F (*awfull*)   178 SD] *Oxf subst.*   general. Please!] *F*; Generall, please *Q*   180 And] *Theobald (Thirlby);* At *QF*   God] *Q*; Heauen *F*   182 SD] *Q (after* decide it.*), Rowe; not in F*

331

HASTINGS

    Fear you not that: if we can make our peace   185
    Upon such large terms and so absolute
    As our conditions shall consist upon,
    Our peace shall stand as firm as rocky mountains.

MOWBRAY

    Yea, but our valuation shall be such
    That every slight and false-derived cause –   190
    Yea, every idle, nice and wanton reason –
    Shall to the King taste of this action,
    That, were our royal faiths martyrs in love,
    We shall be winnowed with so rough a wind
    That even our corn shall seem as light as chaff   195
    And good from bad find no partition.

ARCHBISHOP

    No, no, my lord, note this: the King is weary
    Of dainty and such picking grievances,
    For he hath found to end one doubt by death
    Revives two greater in the heirs of life;   200

186 **large** generous, broad
187 **consist** stand or insist (*OED v.* 4c)
189 **our valuation** 'the way we are regarded'
190 **false-derived** wrongly attributed (to us); derivèd
191 **nice** petty, insignificant
    wanton frivolous
192 **to . . . taste** remind the King
193 'so that even if we martyred ourselves to prove our loyalty (*faiths*) to the King'
194–5 Winnowing, a process for separating wheat from chaff, required a gentle wind to blow off the lighter husks and leave the grain (*corn*) for milling. Mowbray, however, anticipates a wind so severe (*rough*) that corn and chaff will be blown away together. His point is that the King, in his suspicions, will not be able to distinguish the rebels' loyal service from their past actions.

196 **partition** distinction; pronounced as four syllables
198 'of such finicky and pernickety fault-finding'. The adjectives are redundant, and *such* might logically precede both of them. Some editors have regarded *such picking* as a scribal or compositorial misreading, though *picking* was in use at the time and is appropriate in context, akin to the modern phrase 'nit-picking'. The *grievances* of which the King is said to be weary are probably not those catalogued by the rebels (which are far from *dainty*), but his own niggling suspicions.
199 **doubt** source of fear or suspicion
    death putting someone to death
200 **greater** i.e. doubts
    heirs of life supporters who survive the person executed

185 not that:] *Pope*; not, that *QF*; not that, *F2*   189 Yea] *Q*; I *F*   198 dainty . . . picking] *QF*; picking out such dainty *(conj. Johnson)*

And therefore will he wipe his tables clean
And keep no tell-tale to his memory
That may repeat and history his loss
To new remembrance. For full well he knows
He cannot so precisely weed this land   205
As his misdoubts present occasion.
His foes are so enrooted with his friends
That, plucking to unfix an enemy,
He doth unfasten so and shake a friend,
So that this land, like an offensive wife   210
That hath enraged him on to offer strokes,
As he is striking, holds his infant up
And hangs resolved correction in the arm
That was upreared to execution.

201 **tables** records or writing tablets. Cf.
2.4.269 and *Ham* 1.5.98, 107.

202 **tell-tale . . . memory** tattle-tale (reminding the King of deeds he has tried to
blot from memory). This line may mean
that the King will not resume the kind
of behaviour that will lead to more
bloodshed and regret.

203 **history** preserve or record: the only use
of *history* as a verb in Shakespeare (*OED
v.* 1 *trans.*)
his loss This may refer to the concessions
which the King is willing to make to the
rebels (Shaaber, *Variorum*); it may mean
the sacrifice – of men, of trust, of honour
– incurred by the King during the civil
insurrection; or it may signify more
generally those things that the King will
try to erase from his memory.

204 **new remembrance** presumably the King's,
but possibly the collective memory of his
country

205–6 **precisely . . . occasion** completely
(*precisely*) eradicate from England everything that his fears or suspicions (*misdoubts*) give rise to (*present occasion*)

205 **weed this land** The metaphor of the state
as an unweeded garden was common,

most fully developed in *R2* 3.4.24–101,
and most famously in *Ham* 1.2.132–7.

207–9 probably inspired by the parable of
the wheat and the tares in Matthew, 13.29:
'Nay: lest whyle ye geather vp the tares,
ye roote vp also the wheate with them';
enrooted suggests an entangling of roots.

209 **so** by this action
shake lose, alienate

210 **offensive** i.e. who has offended her
husband

211 **offer strokes** threaten a beating. A simile
comparing England to the offending wife
of an abusive monarch would, in an
Elizabethan context, have been politically daring.

213–14 **hangs . . . execution** By her action,
the wife stops in mid-air (*hangs*) the
blow (*correction*) that her husband has
resolved to administer even as his arm
was raised (*upreared*) to do it (*execution*);
execution is pronounced as five syllables.
Cf. a similar suspension of an intended
blow in the Player's account of Pyrrhus's
slaughter of Priam: '*For lo, his sword /
Which was declining on the milky head /
Of reverend Priam seemed i'th'air to
stick*' (*Ham* 2.2.415–17).

HASTINGS

> Besides, the King hath wasted all his rods   215
> On late offenders, that he now doth lack
> The very instruments of chastisement,
> So that his power, like to a fangless lion,
> May offer but not hold.

ARCHBISHOP   'Tis very true;

> And therefore be assured, my good Lord Marshal,   220
> If we do now make our atonement well,
> Our peace will, like a broken limb united,
> Grow stronger for the breaking.

Enter WESTMORLAND.

MOWBRAY   Be it so.

> Here is returned my Lord of Westmorland.

WESTMORLAND

> The Prince is here at hand. Pleaseth your lordship   225
> To meet his grace just distance 'tween our armies?

215 **wasted ... rods** used up all his punish-
ments. Cf. Psalms, 89.32: 'I will visite
their offences with the rod'.
216 **late** recent, or, more ominously, deceased.
Cf. 199.
   that so that
219 **offer ... hold** threaten violence (as at
211) but not carry out the threat
221 **atonement** reconciliation
222–3 **a broken ... breaking** proverbial:
'A broken bone (leg) is the stronger when
it is well set' (Dent, B515)
223 **for** as a result of
225 **Pleaseth** 'would it please'; a variant of
please it (*OED* please v. 3). Cf. 178.
   your lordship This line is addressed to
the Archbishop, whom Westmorland cannot call 'your grace' because *grace* in his
speech is reserved for Prince John. The

line would certainly not be addressed
to Mowbray, *pace* Capell, because
Westmorland's earlier conversation with
Mowbray (97–161) would discourage
him from regarding Mowbray as a
spokesman for the rebel cause.
226 **just distance** half way (*just* = exact:
cf. 23n.). The source is Holinshed, 3.530:
'iust in the midwaie betwixt both the
armies'.
226.1 *I preserve Q's placement of Prince
John's entrance to ensure the fluidity of
action. As Q and F agree that the scene
is continuous and stipulate no break in
the action, the rebels presumably walk
forward to meet Prince John at centre
stage, their lines (227–8) indicating movement simultaneous with his entrance.
Many editors, however, have adopted F's

223 SD] *QF (after 224)*   223–4 Be ... Westmorland.] *F; one line Q*   225 Pleaseth] *QF;* [*to* Mow.
Pleaseth *Capell*   226 .1] *Q; Enter Prince Iohn. F (after 228)*

Enter Prince JOHN *and his Army.*

MOWBRAY

Your Grace of York, in God's name, then, set forward.

ARCHBISHOP [*to Mowbray*]

Before, and greet his grace.

[*to Westmorland*]   My lord, we come.

[*Led by Mowbray, they cross to meet Prince John.*]

JOHN

You are well encountered here, my cousin Mowbray.

Good day to you, gentle Lord Archbishop,   230

And so to you, Lord Hastings, and to all.

My Lord of York, it better showed with you

When that your flock, assembled by the bell,

Encircled you to hear with reverence

Your exposition on the holy text   235

^FThan^F now to see you here, an iron man,

Cheering a rout of rebels with your drum,

---

later placement of the SD and, following Capell, begun a new scene after 228, with a general exit followed by the return of the rebels on one side of the stage and the entrance of Prince John on the other.

228 **Before** go before. Berger and Williams ('Variants') conjecture that the Archbishop directs this to Mowbray, who then would move across the stage to greet the Prince in advance of the others.

229–30 Prince John addresses Mowbray first presumably because he arrives first; he then greets the others by order of rank.

229 **cousin** a form of address common among the nobility, not necessarily indicative of blood relationship. Cf. 306, 311, and see 3.1.66n.

230 **gentle** See 1.1.189.

232–8 Prince John's attack on the Archbishop echoes that of Westmorland at 41–52.

232 **better . . . you** suited you better

233 **When that** when; *that* serves as an intensifier.

assembled . . . bell a reference to church bells calling a congregation to mass

236 **iron** i.e. clad in armour, as in Holinshed, 3.529; or, possibly, merciless, as in *1H4*: 'tales of iron wars' (2.3.47). The Archbishop is dressed for battle, with armour over his clerical garb, as in Holinshed.

*man Q's 'talking', a flat word which makes the line hypermetric, was probably meant to be cancelled in favour of *Cheering* (237), which stands in apposition to it.

237 **rout** See 33n.

227 God's] *Q*; heauen's *F*   set] *Q; not in F*   228 SD1] *(Berger&Williams); not in QF*   grace. My lord,] grace (my lord) *QF*; Grace; my lord, *Theobald*; Grace. – My lord, *(Johnson)*   SD2] *this edn; not in QF* SD3] *this edn; not in QF; They go forward. Cam¹; They march over the stage. Oxf*; [*Exeunt. Capell* 229 encountered] *Q (* incountred*), F*   236 Than] Then *F*; That *Q*   man] *F*; man talking *Q*

Turning the word to sword and life to death.
That man that sits within a monarch's heart
And ripens in the sunshine of his favour,   240
Would he abuse the countenance of the king,
Alack, what mischiefs might he set abroach
In shadow of such greatness? With you, Lord Bishop,
Is it even so. Who hath not heard it spoken
How deep you were within the books of God –   245
To us, the speaker in His parliament;
To us, th'imagined voice of God Himself,
The very opener and intelligencer
Between the grace, the sanctities of heaven,
And our dull workings? O, who shall believe   250
But you misuse the reverence of your place,

238 **Turning . . . sword** turning Scripture
(the word of God) into a call to war. The
homophonic play on *word* and *sword* is
now lost to us but may have informed
Ephesians, 6.17: 'The sword of the Spirit,
which is the worde of God' (Geneva
Bible). Cf. *MW* 3.1.41–2: 'What, the
sword and the word? Do you study them
both, Master Parson?'
240 **ripens . . . favour** possibly influenced by
Nashe, *Pierce Penilesse his Supplication
to the Diuell*, 1.186: 'which of them all
[famous men] sate in the sun-shine of his
souereignes grace' (Ard¹)
241 **Would he** has subjunctive force: if he
were to
241, 252 **countenance** protection, support,
favour (*OED sb.* 8)
242 **set abroach** set afoot, stir up (*OED*
abroach *adv.* 2)
243 **In . . . greatness** when out of the King's
favour
245 **within . . . God** both (1) in the study of
theology (Holinshed, 3.529, mentions the
Archbishop's 'incomparable learning'),
and (2) in God's good graces. Cf. the

proverb 'To be in (out of) one's books'
(Dent, B534).
246 **speaker . . . parliament** the person who
represents the nation before God. To a
greater degree in Tudor times than today,
the Speaker served as intermediary
between the monarch and the House of
Commons (Ard²).
247 **th'imagined** QF's 'th'imagine' may have
resulted from a scribal or compositorial
misreading of a *d* as an *e*.
248 **opener** interpreter, exegete
intelligencer messenger, mediator (*OED
sb.* b)
249 **sanctities** holiness; but possibly, too, the
hierarchy of saints sitting in God's
parliament. Cf. *Paradise Lost*, 3.60–1:
'Above him all the Sanctities of Heaven /
Stood thick as Stars.'
250 **our dull workings** the limits of our
earthly understanding: *dull* = slow (*OED
adj.* 1; cf. 3.1.15); and *workings* =
functions or operations, as of the brain
(*OED vbl. sb.* 5)
251 **But you** that you do not

245 God] *Q*; Heauen *F*   246 His] his *QF*   247 th'imagined] *Rowe*; th'imagine *QF*   God Himself] *Q*;
Heauen it selfe *F*

Imply the countenance and grace of heaven,
As a false favourite doth his prince's name,
In deeds dishonourable? You have ta'en up,
Under the counterfeited zeal of God,   255
The subjects of His substitute, my father,
And both against the peace of heaven and him
Have here upswarmed them.

ARCHBISHOP   Good my Lord of Lancaster,
I am not here against your father's peace;
But, as I told my Lord of Westmorland,   260
The time misordered doth, in common sense,
Crowd us and crush us to this monstrous form
To hold our safety up. I sent your grace
The parcels and particulars of our grief,

252 **Imply** involve, implicate (*OED v.* 1), with a moral imputation stronger than F's 'Employ'
countenance See 241n.
253 **false** duplicitous
254 **ta'en up** levied, enlisted; *subjects* (256) is the direct object. Cf. 2.1.185.
255 **counterfeited zeal** Herford suspects a pun on 'seal' which would imply that the Archbishop is only pretending to act with God's approval. The phrase may echo Romans, 10.2: 'They haue the zeale of God' (Geneva Bible).
256 **His substitute** Tudor doctrine insisted that the monarch was God's anointed deputy in the state; but as the Archbishop claims to be acting on God's behalf, Prince John chastises him by invoking the long-standing conflict between royal absolutism and ecclesiastical authority. Cf. *R2* 1.2.37–41: 'God's is the quarrel, for God's substitute, / His deputy anointed in His sight, / Hath caused his death, the which if wrongfully, / Let heaven revenge, for I may never lift / An

angry arm against His minister.' In Romans, 13.3–6, earthly rules are called 'God's ministers'.
257 **against . . . him** possibly a formulaic phrase. Cf. Sir Thomas Smith, *De Republica Anglorum* (1583), 3.3: 'The Prince . . . must see iustice executed against all . . . offenders against the peace, which is called Gods and his.'
258 **upswarmed** caused to swarm, like bees
261 **in common sense** an ambiguous phrase: (1) as anyone can see; or (2) in our shared feeling of grievance
262 **Crowd . . . crush** a redundant phrase. *OED* cites this line as the earliest use of 'crowd' to mean 'crush' (*v.* 6d).
monstrous form distorted or unnatural course of action. The phrase anticipates the image of monstrosity at 266–7.
263 **hold . . . up** ensure our safety
264 **parcels** details. Perhaps because it inflates his case, the Archbishop is fond of redundancy: *parcels* and *particulars* mean the same thing. Cf. 262n.
grief grievances

252 Imply] *Q;* Employ *F*   253–4 name, . . . dishonourable? You] *F;* name: . . . dishonorable you *Q*
254 ta'en] *Q (*tane*);* taken *F*   255 God] *Q;* Heauen *F*   256 His] *Q (*his*);* Heauens *F*

The which hath been with scorn shoved from
    the court,   265
Whereon this Hydra, son of war, is born,
Whose dangerous eyes may well be charmed asleep
With grant of our most just and right desires,
And true obedience, of this madness cured,
Stoop tamely to the foot of majesty.   270

MOWBRAY

If not, we ready are to try our fortunes
To the last man.

HASTINGS   And though we here fall down,
We have supplies to second our attempt;
If they miscarry, theirs shall second them,
And so success of mischief shall be born,   275

---

265 **hath** On the use of singular verbs with plural subjects, see 84n. on *Hath*.

266 **Hydra . . . war** 'many-headed monster born of war'. The Hydra was proverbially identified with the *wav'ring multitude* (see Dent, H278; also Ind.18–19), but here seems to signify the unchecked growth of – and difficulty of quelling – civil war (see *OED* hydra *sb*. 2). Ovid (*Met.*, 9.70–4) recounts that the Hydra was a snake of the Lernaean marshes whose heads grew back faster than they could be cut off, and which was finally killed by Hercules. The image may have been inspired by Daniel, *CW*, 3.86: 'And yet new *Hydraes*, lo, new heades appeare / T'afflict that peace reputed then so sure' (Ard²).

267 In a conflation of classical myths, the Archbishop metamorphoses the many-headed Hydra into the hundred-eyed monster Argus, Juno's watchman who was guarding Io when he was charmed asleep by the music of Mercury (Ovid, *Met.*, 1.622–721).

269–70 Here, *True obedience* is personified as a loyal subject 'stooping' (bowing) before the King, its *madness* (rebellion) *cured* by the granting of the rebels' desires (268). The syntax is obscure: 'eyes may . . . be charmed asleep' (267) and 'obedience . . . Stoop tamely' seem to be paralleled as consequences of the rebels' conditions being met.

272–7 **And . . . generation** These lines extend the analogy begun at 266 of war to a many-headed Hydra, and also prophesy the Wars of the Roses, which Shakespeare had dramatized in his first tetralogy.

272 **though . . . fall down** even if . . . fail

273 **supplies to second** reinforcements to renew. Cf. 1.3.12.

274 **miscarry** are turned back
theirs . . . them analogous to the Hydra's growing new heads; also perhaps a recollection of the Archbishop's claim that one rebel killed 'Revives two greater in the heirs of life' (200)

275 **success of mischief** a succession of troubles

266 Hydra, son] *Q; Hydra-Sonne F*

And heir from heir shall hold his quarrel up
Whiles England shall have generation.

JOHN

You are too shallow, Hastings, much too shallow,
To sound the bottom of the after-times.

WESTMORLAND

Pleaseth your grace to answer them directly   280
How far forth you do like their articles.

JOHN

I like them all and do allow them well,
And swear here, by the honour of my blood,
My father's purposes have been mistook,
And some about him have too lavishly   285
Wrested his meaning and authority.
[*to Archbishop*] My lord, these griefs shall be with
    speed redressed;
Upon my soul, they shall. If this may please you,
Discharge your powers unto their several counties,

---

276 **hold . . . up** perpetuate the quarrel
277 **Whiles** so long as
   generation offspring, or the power to produce offspring. Pronounced as five syllables.
279 **sound the bottom** plumb the depths (*OED* sound *v.*² 2a, 5); what a sailor does to find out how deep the water is. The nautical play on *shallow* and *bottom* as opposing terms invests *shallow* (278) with a double meaning: England's future is too deep for Hastings to fathom.
280–93 Westmorland may interrupt Prince John for fear that any further insults will turn the rebels away and thereby spoil the plot to trap them. In essence, Westmorland tells Prince John to get to the point, and the Prince picks up the cue at 282. This exchange indicates that Westmorland has masterminded the plot,

as Holinshed attests (3.530). In both Stow and Holinshed, Westmorland himself negotiates with the rebels at Gaultree, Prince John being only 16 at the time. By having Prince John – here clearly older than the historical prince – negotiate the peace, Shakespeare suggests a fellowship of deceit and attaches to the royal household a duplicity not attributed to it in the sources.
280 **Pleaseth** See 225n.
281 **How far forth** to what extent
281, 282 **like** approve of
282 **allow** accept as reasonable or valid (*OED v.* 4a)
285 **about** in attendance on
   lavishly loosely, freely
286 **Wrested** twisted, perverted (*OED v.* 5)
289 **powers** soldiers, troops. Cf. 1.1.133n.
   several respective

276 his] *Q;* this *F*   278] *Q; F lines* (*Hastings*) / shallow, /   287 SD] *Oxf¹ subst.*   288 soul] *Q;* Life *F*

As we will ours; and here, between the armies,   290
Let's drink together friendly and embrace,
That all their eyes may bear these tokens home
Of our restored love and amity.
   [Attendant passes cups.]

ARCHBISHOP

I take your princely word for these redresses.

^FJOHN^F

I give it you and will maintain my word,   295
And thereupon I drink unto your grace.   *[Drinks.]*

^FHASTINGS^F

Go, captain, and deliver to the army
This news of peace. Let them have pay, and part.
I know it will well please them. Hie thee, captain!
              ^F*Exit*^F *[Captain]*.

ARCHBISHOP

To you, my noble Lord of Westmorland.   *[Drinks.]*   300

WESTMORLAND

I pledge your grace;   *[Drinks.]*
           and if you knew what pains

---

292 **That** so that
293 SD As Prince John and Westmorland have known from the first that they would negotiate a peace, drinks may have been brought on by an attendant when Prince John entered at 226.
295–9 *Q's attribution of the first two lines to the Archbishop as a continuation of 294 is wrong, because they are clearly Prince John's response *to* the Archbishop: the compositor may inadvertently have transferred to 297 the SP intended for 295. Q's attribution of 297–9 to Prince John, therefore, is also wrong, because he issues a command to discharge the royal army at 320. F correctly attributes these

lines to a rebel leader: without Hastings's instructions here to dismiss the rebel army, the report of their behaviour at 330–3 would make no sense.
298 **part** depart
299 **Hie thee** make haste, go quickly (*OED* hie *v.* 2).
300–1 **To … grace** Formal pledges of faith or friendship were made while raising a cup. Cf. 306.
301–4 **if … hereafter** With an irony undetected by the rebels, Westmorland acknowledges his role in the trick about to be played on them. See 280–93n.
301–2 **pains … breed** The imagery suggests childbirth.

293 SD] *this edn* 294 redresses.] *F*; redresses, *Q* 295 SP] *F*; *not in Q* 296 SD] *Collier²*; *not in QF*; [*drinks and gives the cup to the* Archbishop. *Capell* 297 SP] *F (Hast.)*; *Prince Q* 299] *Q*; *F lines* them. / Captaine. / SD] *Exit. F*; *not in Q* Captain] *Steevens³*; *Colevile. / Rowe*; Officer. *Capell* 300 SD] *Oxf subst.*; *not in QF* 301 SD] *this edn*; *not in QF* 301–2] *Q*; *F lines* Grace: / bestow'd / Peace, /

I have bestowed to breed this present peace,
You would drink freely. But my love to ye
Shall show itself more openly hereafter.

ARCHBISHOP

I do not doubt you.

WESTMORLAND   I am glad of it.   305
Health to my lord and gentle cousin Mowbray!
[*Drinks.*]

MOWBRAY

You wish me health in very happy season,
For I am on the sudden something ill.

ARCHBISHOP

Against ill chances men are ever merry,
But heaviness foreruns the good event.   310

WESTMORLAND

Therefore be merry, coz, since sudden sorrow
Serves to say thus: some good thing comes tomorrow.

ARCHBISHOP

Believe me, I am passing light in spirit.

---

303 **freely** liberally
307 **happy season** appropriate or fitting time (*OED* happy *adj.* 5b)
308 **something** somewhat
309–10 These lines are one version of a proverbial sentiment common in literature of the period, as illustrated in 'A lightening before death' (Dent, L277), or 'When men are merriest death says "checkmate"' (Dent, M599), or an amalgamation of the two in *RJ* 5.3.88–90: 'How oft when men are at the point of death / Have they been merry! Which their keepers call / A lightning before death.'
309 **Against** in the face of
    chances events

310 **heaviness** sadness, sorrow, with an implicit glance at *merry* (309), meaning light, as its antithesis. Cf. *passing light* at 313.
311–12 The rhyming couplet reinforces the sentiment as an aphorism but also hints at Westmorland's artifice.
311 **coz** a fond abbreviation of cousin. Westmorland's feigned familiarity has nothing to do with kinship; rather, it disguises his darker purpose.
312 **some good thing** a deliberate ambiguity. The meaning of *good* depends on whether one is of the King's or the rebels' party.
313 **passing light** surpassingly cheerful. Cf. 309–10.

306 SD] *Collier²; not in QF;* [*drinks, and gives to* Mow. *Capell*   311 coz] *Q (*coze*), F (*Cooze*), Rowe*

341

MOWBRAY

    So much the worse, if your own rule be true.

      Shout [within]

JOHN

    The word of peace is rendered. Hark how they shout!   315

MOWBRAY

    This had been cheerful after victory.

ARCHBISHOP

    A peace is of the nature of a conquest,

    For then both parties nobly are subdued

    And neither party loser.

JOHN *[to Westmorland]*   Go, my lord,

    And let our army be discharged too.   320

                    ^F*Exit*^F *[Westmorland]*.

    [to Archbishop] And, good my lord, so please you,
      let our trains

    March by us, that we may peruse the men

    We should have coped withal.

ARCHBISHOP   Go, good Lord Hastings,

    And ere they be dismissed, let them march by.

                     ^F*Exit*^F *[Hastings]*.

JOHN

    I trust, lords, we shall lie tonight together.   325

---

314 **your own rule** Mowbray refers to the Archbishop's aphorism at 309–10. Mowbray's suspicion of Westmorland's motives and his unease with a negotiated peace are consistent throughout. See especially his premonition at 183–4.

315 **rendered** proclaimed

316 **had been** conditional: would have been

318 **For then** in so far as

    nobly i.e. because peace is a noble end

320 **discharged** dischargèd

321 **so please you** See 178n.

    trains ranks of soldiers (*OED sb.* 11)

322 **peruse** inspect

323 **coped withal** encountered, fought with (*OED* cope *v*.² 2 *obs.*)

325 **lie tonight together** spend the night in the same place, as a sign of accord. The veiled pun in *lie*, however, hints at duplicity.

314 SD] *Capell ([Shouts within]; Shout. Q; not in F*   319 loser] *QF (looser)* SD] *Oxf¹*   320 SD] *Rowe³; Exit. F (opp. 322); not in Q*   321 SD] *Oxf¹ subst.*   324 SD] *Rowe subst.; Exit. F; not in Q*

Enter WESTMORLAND.

Now, cousin, wherefore stands our army still?

WESTMORLAND

The leaders, having charge from you to stand,
Will not go off until they hear you speak.

JOHN

They know their duties.

Enter HASTINGS.

HASTINGS [*to Archbishop*]

My lord, our army is dispersed already.   330
Like youthful steers unyoked they take their courses
East, west, north, south; or like a school broke up,
Each hurries toward his home and sporting place.

WESTMORLAND

Good tidings, my Lord Hastings, for the which
I do arrest thee, traitor, of high treason.   335

---

326 **wherefore** why

329–33 This incident plays out as an object lesson in good and bad governance. The royal army, disciplined in war, knows the hierarchy of command and so awaits the order from Prince John, while the rebel army, lacking both loyalty and discipline, behaves in a manner emblematic of insurrection itself (see 330–3). Yet this lesson is qualified by deviousness on the part of Westmorland, who has instructed the troops not to disperse until they have had the royal order.

331–2 **take ... south** i.e. fly in all directions

332 **broke up** that has just been let out

334 **tidings** news. Westmorland, not Prince John, swoops in for the kill: see 280–93n.

335, 340 **thee** the objective case of *thou*, still used in the 16th century as a form of

address to one's intimates or inferiors. When addressing Lord Hastings and the Archbishop, Westmorland and Prince John twice substitute *thee* for *you*, which heretofore they have used exclusively. These exceptions may connote a disdain of the rebels which now, in victory, they are free to express.

335 **high treason** defined in 1350–1 as an act 'compassing or imagining' the death of a king, a member of his immediate family or one of his judges, and the levying of war against the king or aiding of his enemies (Davison). As all treason was punishable by death, the *capital treason* mentioned at 337 presumably signifies high treason as well.

325.1] *F, Q (after 324)*   330 SD] *this edn*   My lord,] *Q; not in F*   already] *Q; not in F*   331 take ... courses] *Q;* tooke ... course *F*   333 toward] *Q;* towards *F*

And you, Lord Archbishop, and you, Lord Mowbray,
Of capital treason I attach you both.

MOWBRAY

Is this proceeding just and honourable?

WESTMORLAND

Is your assembly so?

ARCHBISHOP

Will you thus break your faith?

JOHN   I pawned thee none.   340
I promised you redress of these same grievances
Whereof you did complain, which, by mine honour,
I will perform with a most Christian care.
But for you rebels, look to taste the due
Meet for rebellion.   345

337 **capital** punishable by death
   attach arrest
339 **assembly** As Humphreys notes, this
   refers to legislation against unlawful
   assembly, which 'is where people
   assemble themselves together to do some
   vnlawfull thing against the peace' (*An
   exposition of certaine . . . Termes of the
   Lawes*, 1598; fol. 120ʳ).
340 **pawned thee none** pledged no faith to
   you. Prince John draws a distinction
   between the deed and the doer: he has
   promised only to redress the rebels'
   grievances (287), not to pardon the rebels
   themselves. Treachery, he implies, is a
   separate and unpardonable offence.
   Whether this constitutes acting in good
   faith is debatable. Technically he is
   fulfilling the *letter* of his pledge to the
   rebels. Davison cites a decree by the
   Council of Constance (1410–15) issued
   while Henry IV was on the throne, that
   faith need not be kept with heretics, in
   whose company the rebels, by disobeying
   the divinely anointed King, may be
   counted. On the other hand, because

Prince John has spoken reassuringly of
the 'restored love and amity' (293)
between himself and the rebels which
will result from redressing their grievances, he seems to violate the *spirit* of his
pledge to them. Shakespeare's audience
may have regarded John's distinction
between deed and doer as false, a perfidious expedient for trapping the enemy
and an illustration of the machiavellian
policy that the Prince would have learned
from his father.
343 **with . . . care** Whether or not the Prince
   intends it, his use of *Christian* sounds
   ironic in light of his implicit betrayal of
   the rebels in the following lines.
344 **look . . . due** i.e. expect to suffer the
   punishment
345 ***Meet** appropriate. Most editors flesh out
   Q's hemistich as F does, but the words
   may be a scribal afterthought. As Weis
   argues, the arresting of the line at
   rebellion creates an emphatic caesura
   appropriate in this context. It also marks
   a major shift from blank verse to rhymed
   couplets: cf. 346–51n.

345 rebellion.] *Q; Rebellion, and such Acts as yours. F*

Most shallowly did you these arms commence,
Fondly brought here and foolishly sent hence.
Strike up our drums! Pursue the scattered stray!
God, and not we, hath safely fought today.
Some guard ᶠthese traitorsᶠ to the block of death –   350
    [*Soldiers arrest the Archbishop, Hastings and
        Mowbray.*]
Treason's true bed and yielder-up of breath.   ᶠ*Exeunt.*ᶠ

[4.2]   *Alarum. Excursions. Enter* FALSTAFF
                    ᶠ*and* COLLEVILEᶠ.

FALSTAFF   What's your name, sir? Of what condition
    are you, and of what place?

346–51 *The fact that this speech ends in
    three rhymed couplets suggests that it
    concludes a scene, despite the fact that
    neither Q nor F indicates a break in the
    action. See 4.2n.
346 **shallowly** frivolously, ill-advisedly, with-
    out consideration. As at 278, Shakespeare
    may keep echoes of the name Shallow in
    circulation as a reminder that injudicious
    behaviour is not exclusive to the rebels.
    these arms commence possibly means
    'begin these hostilities', but the next line
    requires a meaning such as 'raise these
    armies'.
347 **Fondly . . . foolishly** parallel verb phrases
    introduced by adverbs which mean the
    same thing
348 **scattered stray** fleeing stragglers. Prince
    John's command anticipates the alarum
    and excursions that follow at 4.2.0.1.
    Since the rebel leaders have been
    arrested, one might expect the Prince
    to excuse the common soldiers; but
    John permits no leniency. See Falstaff's
    assessment of him at 4.2.84–94.

349 A traditional attribution of victory to
    divine intervention, as in *H5* 4.8.107–13.
    In the circumstances, since no battle has
    been fought and the rebels have been
    defeated through guile, the sentiment
    rings hollow. As so often in this scene,
    language serves to mask hidden pur-
    poses: it is used strategically to obscure
    rather than clarify intention.
350 **Some guard** some (of you) escort
    *these traitors Q's 'this traitour' seems
    to suggest that the Archbishop alone is
    intended for the block; but as Stow and
    Holinshed agree, and as the play makes
    clear (cf. 334–7, 4.3.84–5), several
    rebels are executed.
    block of death block of wood on which
    the condemned are beheaded (*OED*
    block *sb.* 3b)
351 SD *Although F indicates that the stage
    is cleared, Q does not. On the division of
    scenes, see 4.2n.
4.2 *Although neither Q nor F marks this as
    a new scene, a general exit is clearly
    intended at the end of 4.1 (and is so

349 God] *Q;* Heauen *F*   hath] *Q;* haue *F*   350 these traitors] *F;* this traitour *Q*   SD] *this edn; The
captains guard Hastings, the Archbishop, and Mowbray. Oxf (after 337); not in QF*   351 SD] *F; not in Q*
4.2] *Oxf; SCENE III. Capell; not in QF*   0.1–2] *Alarum Enter Falstaffe excursions Q; Enter Falstaffe and
Colleuile. F*   0.2] *F; not in Q*   2 place?] *Q;* place, I pray? *F*

COLLEVILE I am a knight, sir, and my name is Collevile
of the Dale.

FALSTAFF Well, then: Collevile is your name, a knight   5
is your degree, and your place the dale. Collevile
shall be still your name, a traitor your degree, and the
dungeon your place – a place deep enough so shall
you be still Collevile of the Dale.

COLLEVILE Are not you Sir John Falstaff?   10

FALSTAFF As good a man as he, sir, whoe'er I am. Do
ye yield, sir, or shall I sweat for you? If I do sweat,

designated in F), and the completion of the previous action is signalled by three rhyming couplets (4.1.346–51). Yet Shakespeare may have envisaged an unbroken sequence of episodes at Gaultree, much as he does at Shrewsbury in *1H4*. Between the exit of the leaders and the entry of Falstaff and Collevile come an alarum and excursions during which the royal army, as commanded at 4.1.348, rounds up the rebels' *scattered stray*. Good battle scenes were crowd pleasers, as Shakespeare knew; and although there is little to motivate the skirmishes here – far less hangs on them than hung on the battles at Shrewsbury or Bosworth Field – they add colour and excitement, and they also serve to bring Falstaff and Collevile onstage for their encounter.

0.1 ***Alarum. Excursions.*** A SD common in Shakespeare's history plays denoting the trumpet call to arms (*OED* alarm *sb.* 4a) and the confusion of sallies, sorties and skirmishes (*OED* excursion *sb.* 3) by which a few actors represented the clashes of entire armies.

0.2 F's placement of Collevile's entry here offers strong evidence that the inclusion of his name in the massed entry at F 4.1.0 was a scribal error. Editors since Capell have often expanded the SD to read '*Enter Falstaff and Colevile, meeting*';

but as Davison suggests, it is equally plausible that they enter together with swords drawn, one of them backing the other onto the stage.

1 **condition** social rank (*OED sb.* 10a)

3–4 **Collevile of the Dale** Holinshed (3.530) includes a 'sir Iohn Colleuill of the Dale' among those rebels beheaded for conspiracy at Durham, after the King had marched there from York on his way to attack the Earl of Northumberland. The historical Collevile played no part at Gaultree. Though editors typically standardize the spelling of his name to 'Coleville', the spelling most frequently used in QF and the demands of scansion (cf. 60, 61, 71) suggest that the name was pronounced as three syllables (kŏl-ĕ-vīl).

8–9 **dungeon . . . Dale** The joke is predicated on dales' being known as deep places and possibly, like dungeons, as pits associated with hell (Cam[1]). I delete punctuation between *enough* and *so* in order to clarify the comparison being made: the dungeon will be sufficiently deep for Collevile still to be called 'of the Dale'.

12 **sweat for you** 'have to exert energy (fight) to overcome you'. This anticipates the use of *sweat* in the second Epilogue, which promises a sequel in which 'Falstaff shall die of a sweat' (30), perhaps incurred by syphilis.

3–4] *prose Q; F lines* Sir: / Dale. /   7 shall be still] *Q (*shalbe*); shall be still *F*   8 enough so] enough, so *Q;* enough: so *F*

they are the drops of thy lovers and they weep for thy
death. Therefore rouse up fear and trembling, and do
observance to my mercy.   15

COLLEVILE   I think you are Sir John Falstaff, and in that
thought yield me.

FALSTAFF   I have a whole school of tongues in this belly
of mine, and not a tongue of them all speaks any
other word but my name. An I had but a belly of any   20
indifferency, I were simply the most active fellow
in Europe. My womb, my womb, my womb undoes
me. Here comes our general.

Enter ᶠPrinceᶠ JOHN, WESTMORLAND,
[*Sir John Blunt*] *and the rest.*

JOHN

The heat is past; follow no further now.

---

13 **they . . . lovers** 'The drops of sweat I
shed in overcoming you will provoke
tears in your friends' (*OED* lover *sb.* 1a).
14 **rouse up** stir up, awaken within yourself
(*OED v.* 4)
   fear and trembling a biblical phrase –
see Ephesians, 6.5: 'Seruantes obey them
that are [your] bodily maisters with feare
& trembling' – and possibly a vestige of
Falstaff's parody of Puritan cant
14–15 **do observance** pay homage (as by
kneeling)
18–20 **I . . . name** 'The size of my belly
proclaims my name to the world in every
language'; *school* is figurative for a large
number (*OED sb.*[2] 2a), as of fish, but also
plays on the idea of a place where those
who teach languages gather. Recalling
the image of 'ʀᴜᴍᴏᴜʀ *painted full of
tongues*' (Ind.0.1–2), Falstaff shamelessly trades on the false report of his
valour at Shrewsbury.

20 **An . . . but** if only I had
21 **indifferency** ordinary size
   were conditional: would be
   active in the military sense. Falstaff
claims that if he were thinner, he would
perform heroic deeds exceeding those for
which he is famous.
22 **womb** belly (*OED sb.* 1a). Falstaff humorously compares his own paunch with the
rounded belly of a pregnant woman.
   undoes me prevents me being the most
active (*OED* undo *v.* 8)
23.2 *Sir John Blunt* No doubt intended to
be among '*the rest*' in Q's SD, Blunt is
addressed at 73, though he remains mute.
He is similarly included in SDs at 3.1.31
and 5.2.41, though he is mute in both scenes.
Shakespeare apparently found Blunt a
convenient character to swell a scene.
24 **heat** most intense period (as of fighting:
see *OED sb.* 12a)
   follow pursue the enemy

17 thought] *Q(corr), F;* thoght *Q(uncorr)*   18 tongues] *Q(corr), F;* tongs *Q(uncorr)*   23.1] *Enter Iohn
Westmerland, and the rest. Q; Enter Prince Iohn, and Westmerland. F; Enter Prince John of Lancaster,
Westmoreland, Blunt, and others. Cam*   24 further] *Q;* farther *F*

Call in the powers, good cousin Westmorland.   25
                                            [*Exit Westmorland.*]
                                            [*Sound*] *retreat.*
Now, Falstaff, where have you been all this while?
When everything is ended, then you come.
These tardy tricks of yours will, on my life,
One time or other break some gallows' back.

FALSTAFF   I would be sorry, my lord, but it should be   30
thus. I never knew yet but rebuke and check was the
reward of valour. Do you think me a swallow, an
arrow or a bullet? Have I, in my poor and old motion,
the expedition of thought? I have speeded hither
with the very extremest inch of possibility; I have   35
foundered nine score and odd posts; and here, travel-

---

25 **powers** soldiers, troops. Cf. 1.1.133n.

25 SD2 *retreat* trumpet signal to call back an army in pursuit. Sounding a retreat would make sense after Prince John has ordered that the pursuit be stopped ('Call in the powers'). Q's '*Retraite*' is separated from the SD for Westmorland's entry at 23, close to the right margin, suggesting that it may have been written in the margin of the copy-text and subject to compositorial error in its placement.

28 **tardy tricks** delaying tactics

29 **break . . . back** i.e. get you hanged. The common nickname for the gallows, the wooden horse, summons a humorous image of Falstaff as a rider whose weight will prove too much for the horse to bear.

30–1 **but . . . thus** if this were not the case. Falstaff is being ironic: he means that he would be sorry if either (1) the gallows did *not* break under his weight (thus making hanging impossible), or (2) he weren't subject to the Prince's rebuke, since, in these thankless times, rebuke is itself proof of one's valour (31–2).

31 **I . . . but** double negative: 'I always knew that'

check reproof

33 **motion** movement of the body

34 **expedition** speed. Falstaff asks rhetorically whether the Prince thinks he has the ability to move as swiftly as the mind can think. Cf. *Ham* 1.5.29–31: 'that I with wings as swift / As meditation or the thoughts of love / May sweep to my revenge'.

35 **very . . . possibility** conflation of time and distance: *extremest inch* is transferred from the ground Falstaff covered to the nearly impossible speed with which he covered it. His use of *very* to intensify a superlative form insists that he could move no faster.

36 **foundered . . . posts** lamed more than 180 post-horses, presumably with hard riding. As post-horses were established (or 'posted') at every 10 miles, Falstaff claims to have ridden nearly 2,000 miles – an absurd boast, but one in keeping with his exuberantly false claims elsewhere. See also *1H4* 2.4.236, where Prince

---

25 SD1] *Rowe; not in QF*   SD2 *Sound*] *this edn   retreat*] *Q (Retraite) (after 23)*   36 foundered] *Q (foundred), F (fowndred)*

tainted as I am, have in my pure and immaculate
valour taken Sir John Collevile of the Dale, a most
furious knight and valorous enemy. But what of that?
He saw me and yielded, that I may justly say with the   40
hook-nosed fellow of Rome, 'There, cousin: I came,
saw and overcame.'

JOHN   It was more of his courtesy than your deserving.
FALSTAFF   I know not. Here he is, and here I yield him.

Harry calls Falstaff a 'horse-back-breaker', and 29 above. For *posts*, see Ind.4n. and *OED sb.*[2] 1.

36–7 **travel-tainted** weakened or wearied from riding (*OED* taint *v.* 2a, 3a)

37 **immaculate** unstained (in reputation)

40 **He . . . yielded** Falstaff's truthful admission, so different from his lie about killing Hotspur in combat, may spring from his pride that Collevile surrendered owing to fear of Falstaff's fierce reputation.
that so that

41 **hook-nosed . . . Rome** an irreverent characterization of Julius Caesar. The nose is the most prominent feature of Caesar's profile in his medallion portrait, printed in North's translation of Plutarch's *Lives* (1579), one of Shakespeare's favourite sources.
*There, cousin Falstaff, impersonating Caesar and, as ever, delighting in effrontery, uses these words to address Prince John as a familiar: cf. 25. Editors, however, have not been happy with them, conjecturing that the writing in Q's copytext wasn't clear, that the compositor misread (finding further evidence in the catchword's variant spelling 'their') and that F, or its copy-text, omitted the words owing to their unintelligibility. Humphreys's 'three words' has been widely accepted, in part because he plausibly argues that Shakespeare bor-

rowed the phrase from North's translation of Plutarch's 'Life of Julius Caesar', where, against a marginal note that 'Caesar wryteth three wordes to certifie his victory [over King Pharnaces]', the text reports that Caesar 'onely wrote three words vnto *Antius* of Rome, *Veni, Vidi, Vici*; to wit, I came, I saw, I ouercame' (*Lives*, 787). Falstaff's translation of the Latin, of course, has five words, not three. GWW speculates that Falstaff may present Collevile to – or make him kneel before – the Prince on *There, cousin*, an intriguing staging possibility. It is presumptuous for a commoner, even one as irreverent as Falstaff, to address royalty as *cousin*.

41–2 **I . . . overcame** The original Latin is from Caesar's *War Commentaries*, though Shakespeare may have derived his translation from North: see 41n. above. Falstaff anticipates the tripartite pattern at 2.2.123–4.

43 The line has proverbial force. Cf. 'It is more of your goodness than my desert' (Dent, G337).

44 **Here . . . him** Falstaff's ready surrender to the Prince of a prisoner he is entitled to keep is a magnanimous gesture. It stands in marked contrast to Hotspur's refusal to hand his prisoners over to the King in *1H4* (1.1.90–4).

41 There, cousin:] *Q* (there cosin*,*) *(catchword* their*); there, Caesar, – Theobald;* your cousin, – *Capell;* my cousin *Collier;* their true consul *(Vaughan);* the cozener *Ard[1];* their Caesar, *Sisson;* three words, *Ard[2];* not in F

And I beseech your grace let it be booked with the   45
rest of this day's deeds, or, by the Lord, I will have it
in a particular ballad else with mine own picture on
the top on't, Collevile kissing my foot. To the which
course if I be enforced, if you do not all show like
gilt twopences to me and I, in the clear sky of fame,   50
o'ershine you as much as the full moon doth the
cinders of the element which show like pins' heads to
her, believe not the word of the noble. Therefore let
me have right, and let desert mount.

45 **booked** recorded
47 **particular ballad** ballad written especially about me. Ballads on all sorts
of subjects, printed as broadsides and
illustrated with woodcuts, were hawked
in the streets by ballad-mongers (cf. *WT*
4.4.262ff.), and it was not uncommon
for a person to commission a ballad
glorifying his own adventures. Bottom
imagines singing just such a ballad before
the Duke in *MND* 4.1.212–17. In *1H4*
Falstaff threatens to have ballads written
to expose his accomplices in the Gad's
Hill robbery and 'sung to filthy tunes'
(2.2.43–4); and in Jonson's *Bartholomew
Fair*, Joan Trash threatens Leatherhead,
'and thou wrong'st mee, . . . I'll finde a
friend shall right me, and make a ballad
of thee' (2.2.15–17).
48–53 **To . . . noble** The tortuous syntax
requires explanation. The first *if* clause
sets a condition (i.e. if I am forced to have
this ballad written) which, once met, will
result in the next two *if* clauses: (1) you
will 'all show like gilt twopences to me',
and (2) I shall outshine you as a *full moon*
does the stars. But Falstaff expresses
these results as hypothetical negatives: if
these things don't happen, 'believe not
the word of the noble'. The main clause

thus, in typically Falstaffian fashion,
challenges the listener to take his word as
that of a man nobly born. Following Cowl
(Ard[1]), Humphreys suggests that Falstaff
is parodying the grandiloquent style of
earlier stage heroes and especially, in the
final lines, Basilisco's boast in *Soliman
and Perseda*, 1.3.81–2: 'I repute myself
no coward; / For humilitie shall mount'.
49–50 **like . . . me** like counterfeits compared
to me. Silver twopences were sometimes
gilded and passed off as half-crowns,
which were the same size but worth 30
pence.
51 **o'ershine** outshine
52 **cinders . . . element** stars of heaven, *element* harking back to the *clear sky* at 50
52–3 **show . . . her** 'look no bigger than the
heads of pins compared with the full
moon (*her*)'
53 **the noble** Falstaff caps his bravado with a
coinage pun: he has out-performed other
nobles in battle just as a *noble*, a gold coin
valued at six shillings eight pence,
outshines the *gilt twopences* whose value
he has just disparaged (cf. 49–50n.).
54 **let desert mount** let my deserving rise to
its rightful place in 'the clear sky of fame'
(50). Falstaff requests nothing less than
an apotheosis.

46 by the Lord] *Q;* I sweare *F*   47 else] *Q; not in F*   48 on 't] *Q;* of it *F*   52 pins' heads] *Q (*pinnes
heads), *F (*Pinnes-heads)

JOHN   Thine's too heavy to mount.   55

FALSTAFF   Let it shine, then.

JOHN   Thine's too thick to shine.

FALSTAFF   Let it do something, my good lord, that may
do me good, and call it what you will.

JOHN

Is thy name Collevile?

COLLEVILE   It is, my lord.   60

JOHN

A famous rebel art thou, Collevile.

FALSTAFF   And a famous true subject took him.

COLLEVILE

I am, my lord, but as my betters are
That led me hither. Had they been ruled by me,
You should have won them dearer than you have.   65

---

55   **heavy** either substantial in merit (spoken
ironically) or heinous (as in *Ham* 4.1.12:
'O heavy deed!'). In either case the
Prince is punning about Falstaff's weight.
The subject of this and the next four lines
is *desert* (54).

57   **thick** another pun: opaque, or of great
bulk (like Falstaff's body)

59   **do me good** promote my fortunes
(Shaaber, *Variorum*). For similar use of
the phrase, cf. *R3* 4.3.33, *MA* 1.1.271 and
MV 3.5.6. Humphreys cites a letter
written to Sir Robert Cecil on 28 April
1595, recommending for preferment a
Mr Buck, 'whom Her Majesty . . . herself
named, showing a gracious disposition
to do him good, and think him fit . . . for
one of two offices' (*Hist. Mss, Hatfield
Papers*, 5.189).

    what you will whatever you want

60, 61, 71 **Collevile** Here, trisyllabic pronunciation ensures a pentameter line. See
3–4n.

61   **famous rebel** There is nothing in the
sources to confirm this assessment of

Collevile; indeed, his alacrity in sur-
rendering may seem cowardly. Nevertheless, the compliment inflates Falstaff's
achievement and invites the next line.

62   **true** loyal. Falstaff may be reminding the
Prince of his gesture at 44: 'here I yield
him.'

63   **betters** those of higher rank

64   **led me hither** both physically, to
Gaultree, and politically, to the point of
capture. The line implies reproach.

64–5   **Had . . . have** Collevile intimates that
he, like Mowbray (see 4.1.147–59,
183–96), argued against a negotiated
peace settlement, leading some editors to
believe that Shakespeare may once have
intended a role for him in 4.1, where F
includes his name in the initial SD.
Alternatively, he may speak simply as a
disgruntled soldier who thinks he knew
better than his commanders.

64   **been . . . me** taken my advice

65   **should** would
    dearer at greater cost; i.e. not without a
fight

FALSTAFF   I know not how they sold themselves, but
thou, like a kind fellow, gavest thyself away gratis,
and I thank thee for thee.

Enter WESTMORLAND.

JOHN
Now, have you left pursuit?

WESTMORLAND
Retreat is made and execution stayed.   70

JOHN
Send Collevile with his confederates
To York, to present execution.
Blunt, lead him hence and see you guard him sure.
                    ᶠ*Exit [Blunt] with Collevile.*ᶠ
And now dispatch we toward the court, my lords;
I hear the King my father is sore sick.   75
Our news shall go before us to his majesty,

66–78 Falstaff deflates Collevile's bravado
with a withering comparison: where the
rebel leaders *sold* themselves, Collevile
'gave' himself away. Falstaff's thanks to
Collevile for making a gift of himself is
satirical.

69 **left pursuit** stopped your pursuit (of the
rebel soldiers)

70 **Retreat is made** The signal for retreat
has been sounded: cf. 25 SD2.
execution stayed i.e. the massacre of
the *scattered stray* (4.1.348) halted or
prevented

72 **To York** elision of events that occurred in
1405. Holinshed reports that both the
Archbishop and Mowbray were 'beheaded
the morrow after Whitsundaie in a place
without the citie' of York (3.530), while
Collevile and others were beheaded in
Durham some time later. See 3–4n.

present immediate

73 **Blunt** the only time in the play he is
mentioned by name in a speech. See
23.2n.
sure securely

74 **dispatch we** let us hasten (*OED v.* 8)

75 **the King ... sick** This is unhistorical.
Holinshed reports that after Gaultree, the
King himself supervised the executions
of the rebels at York, 'punished by
greeuous fines the citizens of Yorke
(which had borne armour on their
archbishops side against him)', and then
led 'an armie of thirtie and seuen
thousand fighting men' north to encounter
Northumberland (5.530). Cf. Stow,
Annales, 530.
sore dangerously (*OED adv.* 1b)

76 **go before** precede

---

67 gratis] *Q; not in F*   69 Now,] *Q; not in F*   73 SD] *Exit with Colleuile. F; Exeunt Blunt and others with
Colevile. Cam; Exit Colevile guarded. / Collier; not in Q*

[*to Westmorland*] Which, cousin, you shall bear to
   comfort him,
And we with sober speed will follow you.

FALSTAFF   My lord, I beseech you give me leave to
   go through Gloucestershire and, when you come to   80
   court, stand my good lord in your good report.

JOHN

Fare you well, Falstaff. I, in my condition,
Shall better speak of you than you deserve.

                  [*Exeunt all but Falstaff.*]

FALSTAFF   I would you had the wit; 'twere better than
   your dukedom. Good faith, this same young sober-   85
   blooded boy doth not love me, nor a man cannot
   make him laugh. But that's no marvel: he drinks no

---

78 **sober** unhurried; showing no trace of
urgency (*OED adj.* 5b)

79–81 *Though Q and F print these lines
as metrical prose, like Pistol's (cf.
2.4.157–200n.), F's arrangement of them
on the page and its addition of 'pray' to
make a decasyllabic line at 81 have
encouraged some editors to print them
as three regular verse lines ending at *go*,
court and *report*, the final two forming a
rhymed couplet. But the effect is forced:
Falstaff does not speak verse elsewhere
and has no reason to do so here.

79 **leave** permission

80 **Gloucestershire** the first identification in
the play of Gloucestershire as the home
of Justice Shallow. At 3.2.38, Shallow's
mention of Stamford Fair suggests a
Lincolnshire location more appropriate
for the play. Conceivably, Falstaff's line
is a vestige of an early draft of the play in
which he visited Shallow on his way from
London to Coventry, making a stop in
Gloucestershire feasible. See 3.2n.

81 **stand … lord** 'act the part of a friend'
(*OED* stand *v.* 15c); cf. 3.2.220–1, 230.

82–3 **I … deserve** a pledge not unlike the
one Hal makes to Falstaff at Shrewsbury.
Cf. *1H4* 5.4.157–8.

82 **condition** (1) capacity as commander-in-
chief, (2) role as duke (cf. 84–5), or (3)
disposition to be charitable

84 **would … wit** wish you had the intelligence (to do so)
'twere better it would be worth more

85 **dukedom** Falstaff may be alluding to
Prince John's *condition* mentioned at 82
(Ard¹).

85–8 **Good … wine** plays on the proverbial
expression that 'Good wine makes good
blood' (Dent, W461). In this epilogue
to his military career, Falstaff wryly
acknowledges his 'Dutch courage' or 'pot
valour': if wine makes men brave, he
jokes, then those who do without it are
fools and cowards (93).

85–6 **sober-blooded** temperate, or humourless

---

77 SD] *Craig subst.; not in QF*   80 Gloucestershire] *Q (Glostershire), F*   81 lord in] *Q;* Lord, 'pray, in *F*
82–3] *F; prose Q*   83 SD] *Capell subst.; Exit. F; not in Q*   84 had the] *Q;* had but the *F*

wine. There's never none of these demure boys come
to any proof, for thin drink doth so over-cool their
blood, and making many fish meals, that they fall   90
into a kind of male green-sickness; and then, when
they marry, they get wenches. They are generally
fools and cowards – which some of us should be, too,
but for inflammation. A good sherris sack hath a
twofold operation in it. It ascends me into the brain,   95

88 **never none** F standardizes this colloquial-
ism to 'never any'.
demure serious, reserved (*OED adj.* 2)
88–9 **come ... proof** (1) 'who amount to
much or fulfil their potential' (*OED proof
sb.* 7); but also, with a pun on *proof* as the
strength of alcoholic content (*OED sb.*
10a), (2) 'who ever take a drink'. Cf.
2.4.118.
89–91 **for ... green-sickness** The syntax is
awkward: *making many fish meals* parallels *thin drink* as a subject of the verb
doth ... over-cool. Humphreys suggests
that these lines may be indebted to a
speech by Bacchus in Nashe's *Summer's
Last Will and Testament* (1094–8): 'I
beseech the gods of good fellowship,
thou maist fall into a consumption with
drinking smal beere. Euery day maist
thou eate fish and let it sticke in the midst
of thy maw, for want of a cup of wine to
swim away in. Venison be *Venenum* to
thee' (*Works*, 3.268).
89 **thin drink** beer, and perhaps small beer, a
weak or watered-down drink disparaged
by the Prince at 2.2.5–11. The effect on
the blood of wine versus ale (barley-broth),
a drink stronger than beer, is debated in
H5 when the French Constable, amazed
by the courage of the English forces,
asks, 'Can sodden water, / A drench for
sur-reined jades, their barley-broth, /
Decoct their cold blood to such valiant
heat? / And shall our quick blood, spirited
with wine, / Seem frosty?' (3.5.18–22).

90 **making ... meals** eating a lot of fish.
Falstaff subscribes to the belief that red
meat makes a man virile and courageous;
fish, the opposite.
91 **green-sickness** chlorosis, a form of
anaemia mostly affecting girls at the
onset of puberty, so named because it
turns the skin a greenish tint
92 **get wenches** beget daughters. Falstaff's
claim that weak drink and a fish diet
cause a man to father children of the
'weaker sex' is contradicted by the
proverbial wisdom of the day, which held
that 'Who goes drunk to bed begets but a
girl' (Dent, B195).
93 **should** would
94 **but for inflammation** 'if it weren't for
the spirit that drink inflames in us'
sherris sack a Spanish white wine (*OED
sack sb.³* 1a, b) imported from Xeres
(hence, *sherris*, modern Jerez). See
1.2.198n. on *new ... sack*.
95 **twofold operation** The powers over the
brain and blood which Falstaff attributes
to sack are not entirely his own invention.
He freely draws from medical lore of
the day (which was in turn indebted to
Hippocrates), and particularly from Timothy
Bright's *Treatise of Melancholy* (1586; 93–
9), which details how 'wine, and strong
drinke ... haue a power to comfort the
braine, and hart, and affect all our bodie
throughout with celeritie and quicknesse'.
95, 96 **ascends me, dries me** On use of the
ethical dative, see 2.1.40–1n.

88 none] *Q;* any *F*

dries me there all the foolish and dull and crudy
vapours which environ it, makes it apprehensive,
quick, forgetive, full of nimble, fiery and delectable
shapes, which, delivered o'er to the voice, the tongue,
which is the birth, becomes excellent wit. The second   100
property of your excellent sherris is the warming of
the blood, which before, cold and settled, left the liver
white and pale, which is the badge of pusillanimity
and cowardice. But the sherris warms it and makes
it course from the inwards to the parts' extremes. It   105

96 **dull** sluggish

96–7 **crudy vapours** thick or dense – *crudy*
is an obsolete form of 'curdy' (*OED
adj.* 2) – spirits or exhalations which
were said to develop within bodily
organs, especially the stomach, and then
rise to the brain, obstructing it and
causing ill health (*OED* vapour *sb.pl.* 3a).
Humphreys cites Timothy Bright's
analogous description of melancholy:
'grosse, dull, and of fewe comfortable
spirits; and plentifully replenished with
such as darken all the clernesse of those
sanguineous, and . . . defile their pure-
nesse with the fogge of that slime'
(*Treatise*, 100). Cf. 95n.

97 **environ** envelop
apprehensive alert, discerning, responsive (*OED adj.* 3)

98 **quick** lively
forgetive imaginative, inventive;
apparently a Shakespearean coinage from
'forge'. Cf. *H5* Chorus.5.23: 'the quick
forge and working-house of thought', and
Ham 4.7.88: 'in forgery of shapes and
tricks'. Pronounced with a soft *g* and with
emphasis on the first syllable.
fiery ardent, spirited

99 **shapes** imaginary or spectral forms
(*OED sb.* 6c)

99–100 **which . . . wit** The syntax is confusing. If *which* refers to *shapes*, then it is
probably the subject of the verb *becomes*
– a common use of a singular verb with
a plural subject (cf. 1.1.33n.). If *which*
refers to *sherris sack*, however, the subject and verb are in agreement, though the
antecedent is more distant. The *tongue*
would seem to be in apposition to the
voice to which these fanciful shapes are
delivered o'er; the collective voice and
tongue then give utterance, or *birth*,
to wit, with *delivered* reinforcing the
birthing metaphor. Conceivably, though
less grammatically, *tongue* stands not in
apposition to *voice* but as itself the
subject of *becomes*: once the shapes have
been delivered to the voice, the tongue –
as agent of the voice – gives birth to them
as speech and thus becomes wit.

102 **settled** not flowing, coagulated (*OED
ppl.a.* 6)
liver by classical tradition, the seat of the
passions. See 1.2.176–7n.

103 **white** On whiteness as a badge of
cowardice, see *R3* 4.4.464: 'White-
livered runagate', and *H5* 3.2.32: 'For
Bardolph, he is white-livered and red-
faced'.

105 **parts' extremes** the extremities of
different parts of the body

96 crudy] *Q, F (*cruddie*)*

illumineth the face, which as a beacon gives warning
to all the rest of this little kingdom, man, to arm; and
then the vital commoners and inland petty spirits
muster me all to their captain, the heart, who, great
and puffed up with this retinue, doth any deed of   110
courage. And this valour comes of sherris, so that
skill in the weapon is nothing without sack, for that
sets it a-work; and learning, a mere hoard of gold
kept by a devil till sack commences it and sets it in

106 **illumineth the face** a reference to the
flush which frequently accompanies too
much drink and is characteristic of
alcoholics, as in descriptions of Bardolph
(cf. 2.2.73, 2.4.333 and 337). Falstaff
ennobles the red face as a *beacon* that
inspires courage in the rest of the body.

107 **little kingdom, man** The notion of the
human body as a microcosm of the body
politic was a popular trope in Renaissance
literature, and this passage develops it
with comic and physiological flair. For
more serious applications, see *R2* 5.5.1–
11, *KJ* 4.2.245–6, *JC* 2.1.68–9, and
especially Menenius' fable of the belly in
Cor 1.1.95–159.

108–9 **vital ... heart** The heart is, by analogy, the commander of lively troops
(*vital commoners*) who, coming from the
interior of the country (*inland*), gather
together (*muster*) to serve him: *commoners* here is another term for *spirits*,
highly refined fluids which were said to
come in three forms – natural, animal and
vital – and were 'supposed to permeate
the blood and chief organs of the body'
(*OED* spirit *sb.* 16a), thereby determining
both physical and spiritual characteristics.

108 **petty** of lesser importance, subordinate
(*OED adj.* 3a)

109 **muster me** 'assemble for the purpose of
enlistment' (*OED v.* 2c), here with the
ethical dative

109–10 **great ... up** tautology: swollen and
inflated (as with courage or pride)

112–15 **skill ... use** Falstaff attributes to
sack the power to teach the soldier how
to wield his weapon bravely and to enable
the scholar to use his hoard of learning.
Syntactically, *so that* appears to introduce
two dependent clauses which detail the
consequences of not drinking sack: (1)
'skill is nothing', and (2) 'learning, a
mere hoard', with the comma replacing
the verb. Wilson (Cam[1]) points out a
parallel passage in Nashe's *Summer's
Last Will and Testament* (984–90): 'So,
I tell thee, giue a soldier wine before he
goes to battaile ... it makes him forget
all scarres and wounds, and fight in the
thickest of his enemies, as though hee
were but at foyles amongst his fellows.
Giue a scholler wine, going to his booke,
or being about to inuent, it sets a new
poynt on his wit, it glazeth it, it scowres
it, it giues him *acumen*' (*Works*, 3.265).

113–14 **hoard ... devil** alludes to the superstition that buried treasure was guarded
by evil spirits

114–15 **commences ... act** possibly puns
on graduation exercises at Cambridge
and Oxford. William Harrison, in his
Description of England, 2.3, comments
that 'In Oxford this solemnitee is called
an Act, but in Cambridge they vse the
French word Commensement' (75). See

106 illumineth] *Q*; illuminateth *F*   110 with this] *Q*; with his *F*   111 sherris, so that] *Q*; Sherris. So, that *F*
113 hoard] *Q (whoord), F (Hoord)*

act and use. Hereof comes it that Prince Harry is   115
valiant; for the cold blood he did naturally inherit
of his father he hath like lean, sterile and bare
land manured, husbanded and tilled with excellent
endeavour of drinking good and good store of fertile
sherris, that he is become very hot and valiant. If   120
I had a thousand sons, the first human principle I
would teach them should be to forswear thin potations
and to addict themselves to sack.

Enter BARDOLPH.

How now, Bardolph?
BARDOLPH   The army is discharged all and gone.   125
FALSTAFF   Let them go. I'll through Gloucestershire,
and there will I visit Master Robert Shallow, Esquire.
I have him already temp'ring between my finger and

also Tyrwhitt, 97–8). Falstaff thus
humorously implies that sack confers the
same distinction as a university degree.
See Cowl *(*Ard[1]*)* and Humphreys (Ard[2]);
also *OED* commence *v.* 4c; act *sb.* 8.
in act into action
115 **Hereof comes it** 'thus it happens'
117–18 **he hath ... manured** an echo of the
Bishop of Carlisle in *R2*, who prophesies
that 'The blood of English shall manure
the ground' (4.1.138). Falstaff avouches
that the manuring (with sherry) has
happened already.
118 **husbanded** cultivated. Cf. 3.2.114.
119 **endeavour** exertion, effort: humorous
application of a word for physical labour
to the labour of drinking
good store a large quantity (*OED* store
sb. 4). In *Famous Victories*, the Vintner's
Boy reports that 'the young Prince and
three or four more of his companions . . .
called for wine good store' (2.81–3).

fertile extends the agrarian simile and
means, figuratively, promoting thought
and action
120 **that** so that
hot ardent, passionate, hot-blooded (*OED
adj.* 6a) and possibly sexually active (6c),
in contrast to the cold-bloodedness of his
father and his brother John
121 **human** secular, as opposed to divine. Q's
'humane' was the common spelling of
'human' until the 18th century.
122 **thin potations** weak or watered-down
liquor (*OED sb.* 2). Cf. *thin drink* at 89.
126 **Gloucestershire** See 80n.
127 **Master, Esquire** The compounding of
titles is sarcastic: Falstaff is mocking the
man he is about to fleece. *Esquire* was a
term for a member of the landed gentry.
See 3.2.57n.
128 **temp'ring** warming, softening. Wax was
softened between the fingers to prepare it
for use as a seal (*OED* temper *v.* 13).

117 sterile] *Q, F (*stirrill*)*   121 human] *Q (*humane*); not in F*   123.1] *Q (after 124), F*   128 temp'ring] *Q
(*tempring*); tempering F*

my thumb, and shortly will I seal with him. Come   129
away.   ᶠ_Exeunt._ᶠ

4[.3]   _Enter the_ KING, WARWICK, Thomas,
                   Duke of CLARENCE, Humphrey[, Duke] of
                      GLOUCESTER [, _and Attendants_].

KING

Now, lords, if God doth give successful end
To this debate that bleedeth at our doors,

---

129 **seal with him** play on words: (1) reach
   an agreement with him, or, continuing
   the metaphor of tempering, (2) mould
   him, like wax, to my purposes
4.3 This scene between father and son is an
   imaginative fusion of several sources.
   Holinshed briefly recounts that the Prince
   'tooke awaie' his father's crown after
   attendants had told him the King was
   dead (3.541). The dramatization of this
   episode in _Famous Victories_ is closer to
   Shakespeare's version and may have
   provided the source for the Prince's reply
   to the King's denunciation of him. In
   Daniel, the King himself addresses the
   crown before going to sleep; but portions
   of his advice to the Prince, after he has
   awoken, are echoed closely by Shakespeare (_CW_, 3.119–30). Shakespeare
   makes little direct use of an episode
   narrated by Holinshed, dated 1412, in
   which the Prince, seeking to allay his
   father's suspicion that he wants to usurp
   the throne, kneels before him, hands him
   a dagger and vows 'that his life was not
   so deare to him, that he wished to liue one
   daie with his [father's] displeasure'
   (3.539); but the dramatization of this
   episode in _Famous Victories_ may have
   inspired the overall shape and tone of
   Shakespeare's scene. See pp. 122–9.

The location of the scene is identified as
the Jerusalem Chamber (360–2), mentioned by Holinshed (3.541) as the room
in which the King died. The chamber
itself, however, is not in the royal palace
at Westminster, where this scene takes
place, but in Westminster Abbey. The
reference to Jerusalem brings full circle
Henry's wish to make a journey to the
Holy Land on a crusade he first proposed
at the conclusion of _R2_, here ironically
fulfilled. See pp. 127–8.

0.1–3 *Q's inclusion of the ghost character
Kent in the entry is further evidence that
the copy-text for Q was Shakespeare's
holograph: cf. the entries in Q of
Fauconbridge at 1.3.0 and Blunt at 3.1.31.
The name Kent, like that of Harcourt at
93, was apparently chosen at random out
of Holinshed. An Edmund, Earl of Kent,
rescued Thomas, Duke of Clarence, in an
action against the French in 1405, and his
son led a raid against the French with
Warwick in 1412. See 3.1.1n.

The King's illness has seemed to many
editors to require that he be carried in on
a chair or even a bed, and usually his
entry is staged in this way. In the corresponding scene in _Famous Victories_, the
King is apparently too weak to walk and
refers to his chair (8.26); and here his

---

130 SD] _F; not in Q_   **4.3**] _Oxf; Scena Secunda F; SCENE IV. Capell; not in Q_   0.1–3 _Enter . . ._ GLOUCESTER]
_Q (Enter the King, Warwike, Kent, Thomas duke of Clarence, Humphrey of Gloucester.); F (Enter King,
Warwicke, Clarence, Gloucester.)_   0.3 _and Attendants_] _Cam² subst.; and others. / Capell; not in QF_   1 God]
Q; Heauen F

358

We will our youth lead on to higher fields
And draw no swords but what are sanctified.
Our navy is addressed, our power collected, 5
Our substitutes in absence well invested,
And everything lies level to our wish;
Only we want a little personal strength,
And pause us till these rebels now afoot
Come underneath the yoke of government. 10

WARWICK

Both which we doubt not but your majesty
Shall soon enjoy.

KING   Humphrey, my son of Gloucester,
Where is the Prince your brother?

GLOUCESTER

I think he's gone to hunt, my lord, at Windsor.

---

unawareness that Clarence is present may suggest that the he is indeed sitting or reclining by 16–17, and thus unable to look around. There is no compelling reason, however, that the King should not enter under his own power. It makes theatrical sense for him to sit at the point he mentions feeling unwell and calls those in attendance to come near him (102–11).

2 **debate** struggle

3 **higher fields** battlefields in which they will fight in a holy (*higher*) rather than a civil cause. Henry had intended to undertake a crusade early in his kingship (*R2* 5.6.49–50) but had had to break off his plans in order to cope with civil rebellion (*1H4* 1.147–8). He has renewed his wish to go to the Holy Land at 3.1.108, but once again rebellion, compounded by his own ill health (cf. 3.1.104–6), prevents him from acting on it. His motives for undertaking a crusade are debatable. In *R2* they seem penitential, sprung from his need to atone for King

Richard's murder, and there is no reason to think that his desire to war against the infidel in *1H4* is any less genuine. Similarly, his motives in this scene would be less seriously in doubt if he did not advise Prince Harry at 338–44 to undertake foreign wars as a shrewd means to deflect political opposition. The machiavellianism of such deathbed advice, probably inspired by Daniel's account in *CW*, 3.127, encourages a more cynical reassessment of Henry's motives and potentially colours his earlier references to a crusade with political opportunism.

4 **sanctified** i.e. because used in a holy cause

5 **addressed** prepared
 power army. Cf. 1.1.133.

6 **substitutes in absence** deputies
 invested furnished with royal authority

7 **level** readily accessible (*OED adj.* 3a)

8 **we want** I lack

9 **pause us** The verb is used reflexively.

10 **Come underneath** can be restrained by

12–13 Humphrey . . . brother?] *Pope; prose QF*   12 Gloucester] *Q (*Gloster*), F*

KING

    And how accompanied?

GLOUCESTER   I do not know, my lord.   15

KING

    Is not his brother Thomas of Clarence with him?

GLOUCESTER

    No, my good lord; he is in presence here.

CLARENCE [*Steps forward.*]

    What would my lord and father?

KING

    Nothing but well to thee, Thomas of Clarence.

    How chance thou art not with the Prince thy brother?   20

    He loves thee, and thou dost neglect him, Thomas.

    Thou hast a better place in his affection

    Than all thy brothers. Cherish it, my boy,

    And noble offices thou mayst effect

    Of mediation, after I am dead,   25

    Between his greatness and thy other brethren.

    Therefore omit him not, blunt not his love,

    Nor lose the good advantage of his grace

    By seeming cold or careless of his will;

---

17 **presence** attendance
18 **would** wishes
19–48 Political subtext enriches the signi-
    ficance of this speech. Stow reports that
    the King on his deathbed expressed a fear
    to Prince Harry that 'after my departure
    from this life, some discord shall grow
    and arise between thee and thy brother
    Thomas duke of Clarence, whereby the
    realme may be brought to destruction and
    misery'; for both princes have 'great
    stomacke and courage' and Clarence,
    'through his high mind,' may 'make some
    enterprise against thee, intending to vsurp
    vpon thee' (*Annales*, 545). Shakespeare
    makes little of the potential for fraternal
    betrayal, but the King's conversation with

Harry in Stow is the probable source of
his admonition to Clarence here, and the
Prince's sober pledge in Stow to 'honor &
loue my brethren aboue al men, as long as
they be to me true, faithfull and obedient'
(545) may prompt the King's charitable
assessment of him at 30–41.
20 **chance** does it happen (*OED v.* 1a)
24 **offices** functions
    effect perform
26 **greatness** kingship
27 **omit** neglect
    blunt make less of (*OED v.* 2); put at risk
28 **grace** sovereign favour
29 **careless ... will** indifferent to his
    interests

18 SD] *this edn*   28 lose] *QF(*loose*)*

For he is gracious, if he be observed: 30
He hath a tear for pity and a hand
Open as day for meting charity.
Yet notwithstanding, being incensed, he is flint,
As humourous as winter, and as sudden
As flaws congealed in the spring of day.   35
His temper therefore must be well observed.
Chide him for faults, and do it reverently,
When you perceive his blood inclined to mirth;
But being moody, give him time and scope
Till that his passions, like a whale on ground,   40
Confound themselves with working. Learn this,
          Thomas,

30 **gracious** merciful, compassionate: a term conventionally applied to royalty

30, 36 **observed** shown due respect

32 **meting** doling out (*OED* mete *v.*¹ 6). Q's 'meet' was an alternate spelling for 'mete', though it is possible, as Furnivall (1909) does, to keep the original spelling to signify 'meeting the need of charity' or giving alms. Other editors, suspecting a scribal or compositorial misreading of *e* for *l*, prefer F's 'melting' as an attribute of charity: yielding to tender emotion.

33 **flint** hard, implacable

34 **humourous** capricious, playing on the belief in four bodily humours whose changes were thought to govern our dispositions, and one of which, moisture, is appropriate for winter

35 **flaws ... day** icy squalls at daybreak. *OED* glosses 'flaw' as both a snowflake (*sb.*¹ 1) and a sudden gust of wind (*sb.*² 1): *sudden* at 34 makes the latter gloss preferable. Metaphorically, flaws can be sharp bursts of passion (*sb.*² 2), but a literal reading seems to be required for the simile to work.

congealed cold or icy; congealèd

36 **temper** disposition, mood

38 **blood** passion, mood

39 **time** F's 'line', preferred by some editors, suggests that Clarence may play his brother like a fish, but the image seems inappropriate and at odds with the whale simile at 40.

40 **Till that** until

whale on ground Holinshed (3.1259) reports that a whale was stranded near Ramsgate in 1574.

41 **Confound** exhaust

working exertion

41–8 **Learn ... gunpowder** Henry's exhortation to Clarence is akin to Polonius's aphoristic advice to Laertes in its rapid metamorphosis of images and puns: 'Those friends thou hast ... / Grapple them unto thy soul with hoops of steel' (*Ham* 1.3.61–2). As Wilson notes (Cam¹), the hoop of steel used to make barrels (cf. *rib of steel*, 2.3.54) here melts into a ring of gold, emblematic of Clarence's power to ensure fraternal union, and then into a chalice (*vessel*) filled with the communal blood of the princes. As at Gaultree, however, the

32 meting] *Q (*meeting*)*; melting *F*   33 notwithstanding, being] *F*; notwithstanding being *Q*   he is] *Q*; hee's *F*   38 inclined] *Q (*inclind*)*, *F (*enclin'd*)*   39 time] *Q*; Line *F*

And thou shalt prove a shelter to thy friends,
A hoop of gold to bind thy brothers in,
That the united vessel of their blood,
Mingled with venom of suggestion –   45
As force perforce the age will pour it in –
Shall never leak, though it do work as strong
As aconitum or rash gunpowder.

CLARENCE

I shall observe him with all care and love.

KING

Why art thou not at Windsor with him, Thomas?   50

CLARENCE

He is not there today. He dines in London.

KING

And how accompanied?

CLARENCE

With Poins and other his continual followers.

KING

Most subject is the fattest soil to weeds,

chalice used for pledging amity may in fact be tainted with *venom*; but just as the chalice of family loyalty *Shall never leak*, so the united blood vessel of the princes should be able to withstand all attempts to make it burst.

45 **suggestion** suspicion, promptings to disloyalty (*OED sb.* 1a); probably pronounced as four syllables

46 **force perforce** willy-nilly. Cf. 4.1.116. The King thinks it inevitable that political circumstances will work to turn the princes against one another: see 19–48n.

47–8 **though . . . gunpowder** Cf. *RJ* 5.1.60–5: 'A dram of poison, such soon-speeding gear / . . . that the trunk may be discharged of breath / As violently as hasty powder fired / Doth hurry from the fatal cannon's womb'.

47 **though it** even though the venom

48 **aconitum** aconite, commonly called wolfsbane, a potently poisonous plant which Elizabethans thought invented by Hecate
   rash violent; operating quickly and strongly (*OED adj.* 2b)

49 **observe** See 30, 36n.

52 While F's addition of 'Canst thou tell that?' to complete the line metrically is consistent with its regularizing of lines elsewhere in the scene (cf. 120, 132, 180), the additional words do not enhance the meaning of the *Q* line.

54–66 As Humphreys notes, the despair of the King's speech here and at 222–67 echoes that of the King in *Famous Victories*, who fears that the Prince's riotous behaviour 'with grief will end his father's days' (3.38, also 6.4–5) and bring 'ruin and decay' to 'this noble realm of England' (5.65–7).

52 accompanied?] *Q*; accompanied? Canst thou tell that? *F*   53 Poins] *Q (Poines)*, *F (Pointz)*

362

And he, the noble image of my youth, 55
Is overspread with them; therefore, my grief
Stretches itself beyond the hour of death.
The blood weeps from my heart when I do shape
In forms imaginary th'unguided days
And rotten times that you shall look upon 60
When I am sleeping with my ancestors;
For when his headstrong riot hath no curb,
When rage and hot blood are his counsellors,
When means and lavish manners meet together,
O, with what wings shall his affections fly 65
Towards fronting peril and opposed decay!

WARWICK

My gracious lord, you look beyond him quite.
The Prince but studies his companions
Like a strange tongue, wherein, to gain the language,
'Tis needful that the most immodest word 70
Be looked upon and learnt, which, once attained,
Your highness knows, comes to no further use

54 proverbial: 'Weeds come forth on the fattest soil if it is untilled' (Dent, W241). Cf. Lyly, *Euphues*: 'The fattest ground bringeth forth nothing but weeds if it be not well tilled' (92).
fattest most fertile
58 **The blood ... heart** It was commonly believed that every sigh drew a drop of blood from the heart: *weeps* here means issues in drops, like tears (*OED v.* 4b).
58–9 **shape ... imaginary** imagine
59 **th'unguided** without proper rule, riotous
63 **rage, hot blood** roughly synonymous with unbridled passions
64 'When licentious habits have the power to satisfy themselves'; *means* denotes both royal authority and wealth; *lavish manners*, unrestrained and lewd behaviour.
65 **affections** inclinations

66 **fronting ... decay** the danger facing (*fronting*) him and ruinous (*opposed*) degradation
67 **look beyond** misconstrue (*OED* beyond *prep.* 3)
quite completely, entirely (*OED adv.* 1)
68–78 Warwick springs to the Prince's defence by echoing Harry's own self-exculpation in *1H4* 1.2.185–207, wherein he professes his intention to cast his followers off. Warwick also excuses the Prince's proficiency in learning the base language of drawers, a proficiency Harry acknowledges with regret in *1H4* 2.4.6–19. For an amusing analogue in which another royal learns *immodest* words (70), see Katherine's English lesson in *H5* 3.5.
68 **companions** pronounced as four syllables to ensure a pentameter line

69 wherein, . . . language,] *F;* wherein . . . language: *Q*   71 learnt] *Q;* learn'd *F*   72 further] *Q;* farther *F*

But to be known and hated. So, like gross terms,
The Prince will in the perfectness of time
Cast off his followers, and their memory   75
Shall as a pattern or a measure live
By which his grace must mete the lives of other,
Turning past evils to advantages.

KING

'Tis seldom when the bee doth leave her comb
In the dead carrion.

Enter WESTMORLAND.

Who's here? Westmorland?   80

WESTMORLAND

Health to my sovereign, and new happiness
Added to that that I am to deliver.
Prince John your son doth kiss your grace's hand:
Mowbray, the Bishop Scroop, Hastings and all
Are brought to the correction of your law.   85
There is not now a rebel's sword unsheathed,

---

73 **gross terms** i.e. the *immodest* words Hal
has learned
74 **in . . . time** at the appropriate moment,
when he is ready; *perfectness* suggests
ripeness or maturity, as applicable to
Harry as to time.
76–7 **measure . . . other** Cf. Mark, 4.24:
'with what measure ye meate, with the
same shall it be measured to you agayne'.
77 **mete** appraise, judge
other a collective plural: others
79–80 **'Tis . . . carrion** i.e. one shouldn't
expect to find sweetness in a rotten place,
because the agency producing sweetness
will not have put it there. The King means
that the Prince will be unlikely to
renounce his corrupt pleasures: probably
a reference to Judges, 14.8, in which

Samson 'turned out of the way to see the
carkasse of the Lion: And beholde, there
was a swarme of bees and hony in the
carkasse of the Lion'. Elizabethans, however, might also have been mindful that
the honey in the lion led to Samson's
riddle, 'Out of the eater came meate, and
out of the strong came sweetnesse' (Judges,
14.14), a titillating promise that good things
may come from corruption, readily applicable to the myth of Hal's regeneration.
79 **leave** deposit
84 **Scroop** While some editors prefer the
spelling 'Scrope', the QF spelling
'Scroope' probably reflects how the name
was pronounced. Theobald's regularizing
the spelling to *Scroop* preserves that
pronunciation.

77 other] *Q;* others *F*   80 SD] *F, Q (after 80)*   84 Bishop Scroop] *Theobald;* Bishop, Scroope *QF*

But Peace puts forth her olive everywhere.
The manner how this action hath been borne
Here at more leisure may your highness read,
With every course in his particular.   [*Offers a paper.*]   90

KING

O Westmorland, thou art a summer bird
Which ever in the haunch of winter sings
The lifting up of day!

Enter HARCOURT.

Look, here's more news.

HARCOURT

From enemies heavens keep your majesty,
And when they stand against you, may they fall   95
As those that I am come to tell you of.
The Earl Northumberland and the Lord Bardolph,
With a great power of English and of Scots,

---

87 **olive** olive branch, symbol of peace
90 'with each incident described in detail'. The word *course* has been variously glossed as phase, proceeding, or line of action; but as Melchiori notes, it was also a technical term used in bear-baiting to mean an attack, which would be appropriate in describing the rebels' actions. Shakespeare uses it in this sense in *KL* 3.7.53: 'I am tied to the stake and I must stand the course', and in *Mac* 5.7.1–2: 'They have tied me to the stake: I cannot fly, / But, bear-like, I must fight the course'. **his** its Cf. 1.2.117.
92 **haunch** buttock; hind part; latter end. Shakespeare's use of similar phrases is typically comic: '[t]he posteriors of this

day' (*LLL* 5.1.84) and 'the buttock of the night' (*Cor* 2.1.51).
92–3 **sings … day** celebrates daybreak. Though no particular bird is identified, the lark was thought to be the bird that sang first in the morning and ushered in the spring.
93 SD **HARCOURT** a name apparently picked at random from Holinshed; cf. GOWER at 2.1.131.1. The arrival of messengers in quick succession parallels 1.1, in which a string of messengers bring Northumberland reports from Shrewsbury.
97–9 This brief reference to the Battle of Bramham Moor in 1408 is the last mention of Northumberland. Holinshed reports that the Earl fought 'with great manhood' (3.534).

---

90 SD] *this edn;* [*Kneels, and gives a Packet. Capell (after 89); not in QF*   93 SD] *F; enter Harcor. Q* (*after 93*)   94 heavens] *Q;* Heauen *F*

Are by the Shrieve of Yorkshire overthrown.
The manner and true order of the fight   100
This packet, please it you, contains at large.   [*Offers
    packet.*]

KING

And wherefore should these good news make me sick?
Will Fortune never come with both hands full,
But wet her fair words still in foulest terms?
She either gives a stomach and no food –   105
Such are the poor, in health; or else a feast
And takes away the stomach – such are the rich,
That have abundance and enjoy it not.
I should rejoice now at this happy news,
And now my sight fails and my brain is giddy.   110
O me, come near me, now I am much ill.   [*Swoons.*]

---

99 **Shrieve** sheriff

101 **at large** in full

102 **sick** On the King's illness, see 1.2.109n.

103 **Fortune** the goddess Fortuna, who
personified the workings of chance

104 *Q makes general sense if one assumes
that good news (*fair words*) may be
tainted – *wet* meaning daubed or soiled,
as with ink – by unfavourable conditions
(*foulest terms*). But F's substitution of
'write' for 'wet' and 'Letters' for 'termes',
the latter possibly a scribe's attempt to
correct the apparent redundancy of *words*
and *terms*, has won many adherents; and
even editors who prefer Q attempt to
find a better word than *wet*. Hilda Hulme
ingeniously suggests *wit* in its legal sense
of bequeath, understanding *words* to mean
that which is granted and *terms* as conditions (295); Cam² offers 'whet', meaning
sharpen, for which *wet* was an alternate
spelling; and Oxf¹ replaces *wet* with 'set'
in the sense of setting out or putting

down on paper. All these options are
reasonable, but they do not necessarily
improve on Q.
    still always. Cf. Ind.4.

105–8 proverbial: 'The rich man walks to
get a stomach to his meat, the poor man
to get meat for his stomach' (Dent,
M366)

105 **stomach** appetite

110 **And** but
    giddy confused, dizzy (*OED adj.* 2a)

111 SD *The King's giddiness suggests that
he feels faint and, if he is standing, about
to fall. His calling those assembled to
come near him would seem to be the
latest point at which he would sit on a
chair, unless he slumps to the floor
instead. The Oxford editors (Oxf) have
him swoon at this point, and the alarmed
responses of Gloucester, Clarence and
Westmorland, compounded by Warwick's
calling the King's sudden seizure a fit
(114), seem to justify a dramatic bout of

---

99 Shrieve] *Q (shrieve)*; Sherife *F*   101 SD] *this edn; Giving a packet. / Collier²; [kneels, and delivers it.
Capell; not in QF*   102] *Q; F lines* newes / sicke? /   104 wet . . . terms] *Q; write . . . letters F;* whet . . .
terms *Cam²*; set . . . terms *Oxf¹*   111 SD] *Oxf subst.; sinks, and falls into a Fit. / Capell; not in QF*

GLOUCESTER

    Comfort, your majesty.

CLARENCE   O, my royal father!

WESTMORLAND

    My sovereign lord, cheer up yourself. Look up!

WARWICK

    Be patient, princes. You do know these fits

    Are with his highness very ordinary.   115

    Stand from him; give him air. He'll straight be well.

CLARENCE

    No, no, he cannot long hold out these pangs.

    Th'incessant care and labour of his mind

    Hath wrought the mure that should confine it in

    So thin that life looks through.   120

GLOUCESTER

    The people fear me, for they do observe

    Unfathered heirs and loathly births of nature.

fainting. The King himself refers to it as swooning at 361. It is probable, too, that if the King has been wearing the crown, some noble would remove it here so that it would not fall on the floor. Thus the King's instruction at 137 would be directed to the person who holds the crown.

113 **Look up!** Davison glosses this as 'cheer up', but that would repeat what Westmorland has just said. The context suggests that the King's eyes are shut or vacantly staring.

114 **fits** seizures, fainting spells. Cf. 1.1.142n.

116 **straight** soon, immediately

117 **hold . . . pangs** endure these seizures

118–20 a metaphor for physical fragility in which the King's flesh is figured as a wall (*mure*). Mental anguish has beaten so thin the wall which should contain such anguish that it has become transparent and life can see through it (i.e. life might leave the body). Shakespeare borrows

from Daniel here: 'paine, and griefe . . . / Beseiged the hold that could not long defend, / . . . Wearing the wall so thin that now the mind / Might well looke thorow, and his frailty find' (*CW*, 3.116). F's completion of 120 as a fully metrical line roughly corresponds to the final line in Daniel.

120 On F's addition of words to complete the line metrically, see 52n.

121 **fear** frighten

    observe report seeing

122 These portents announced the death of kings. *Unfathered heirs* are children monstrously conceived, either through miraculous virgin births (as in Montaigne, *Apology for Raymond Sebonde*) or through the intercourse of a witch with an incubus; *loathly births* signifies hideously malformed infants, often the result of such parthenogenesis. Other prodigies portend the deaths of

112] *Steevens; prose QF* 116] *Q; F lines* ayre: / well. /   117 out these pangs.] *Q;* out: these pangs, *F*
120 through.] *Q;* through, and will breake out. *F*

The seasons change their manners, as the year
Had found some months asleep and leapt them over.

CLARENCE

The river hath thrice flowed, no ebb between,   125
And the old folk, Time's doting chronicles,
Say it did so a little time before
That our great-grandsire Edward sicked and died.

WARWICK

Speak lower, princes, for the King recovers.

GLOUCESTER

This apoplexy will certain be his end.   130

KING

I pray you, take me up and bear me hence
Into some other chamber.

[A bed is thrust forth; the King is moved to it.]

Julius Caesar (*JC* 1.3.5–32) and King Hamlet (*Ham* 1.1.112–24), and, in Daniel, the deposition of Richard II (*CW*, 1.114–16).

123–4 Shakespeare uses the image of seasonal chaos resulting from a disturbance in rule in *MND*, when Titania observes that 'the spring, the summer, / The childing autumn, angry winter, change / Their wonted liveries; and the mazed world, / By their increase, now knows not which is which' (2.1.111–14).

123 **as** as if

125–8 Holinshed records that on 12 October 1412 there 'were three flouds in the Thames . . . and no ebbing betweene: which thing no man liuing could remember the like to be seene' (3.540), but no chronicler associates this event with the death of Edward III in 1377. Editors note the association as Shakespeare's invention, but see 126n. for a correction.

126 **doting chronicles** senile witnesses to history. By calling into question the

reliability of the *old folk* who associate the floods with Edward's death, Clarence mocks, rather than confirms, Gloucester's belief in the people's report of unnatural portents.

128 **sicked** fell ill

130 **apoplexy** See 1.2.109n. The King's symptoms confirm the diagnosis of apoplexy as a sudden attack, caused by an effusion of blood or serum in the brain and preceded by giddiness, which arrests all powers of sense and motion (*OED sb.* 1).

132 On F's addition of words to complete the line metrically, see 52n.

132 SD *Editions since Cam have tended to begin a new scene here, but Q and F clearly signal that the action is continuous: no SDs indicate exits or entrances, and it makes little sense to interrupt the King's speech with a scene change. In most recent stagings, those in attendance carry the King in his chair to another part of the stage – or simply circle back to centre stage – and carefully move him

124 leapt] *Q*; leap'd *F*   132 chamber.] *Q*; Chamber: softly 'pray. *F*   SD] *this edn*; [*Attendants, and Lords, take the King up; convey him into an inner Room, and lay him upon a Bed. Capell; not in QF*

Let there be no noise made, my gentle friends,
Unless some dull and favourable hand
Will whisper music to my weary spirit.   135

WARWICK

Call for the music in the other room.

[*Exit Attendant. Music within.*]

KING

Set me the crown upon my pillow here.

CLARENCE

His eye is hollow, and he changes much.

WARWICK

Less noise, less noise.

Enter ᶠPRINCE Henry.ᶠ

PRINCE   Who saw the Duke of Clarence?

to a bed which has been brought on, his
head raised to face the audience as he
speaks at 133. The bed was probably thrust
through the curtains located between the
stage doors (GWW). See 178 SD1n.

134 **dull** slow, soothing
favourable kindly, well-disposed

135 'will play soft music to lull me to sleep'.
Music was thought to have the power to
soothe those whose spirits were over-
wrought: cf. *KL* 4.7.21–5. The King's
request for music is but the first of several
details which suggest that Shakespeare
closely followed a scene in *Famous
Victories* as his source: 'Good my lords,
draw the curtains, and depart my chamber
awhile; and cause some music to rock me
asleep' (8.8–10).

136 **the other room** perhaps a music gallery
or the upper stage

137 Despite recent stage practice and the
sanction of a SD in Oxf¹, it is unlikely

that the King, in his enfeebled state,
would remove his own crown. Rather, a
noble who has removed it earlier would
now place it on the pillow next to the
King's head. Cf. 111 SDn.

138 **changes much** i.e. grows pale

139–354 **Who ... father** In Holinshed (3.541),
those attending on the King believe him
to be dead and so inform the Prince, who
takes away the crown. Shakespeare's
dramatization of this incident is much
closer to the version in *Famous Victories*,
sc. 8, which was based on Hall. Speeches,
though longer, have much the same
pattern and tone, and the Prince's reply to
the King at 268–306 closely parallels
that in *Famous Victories*. In Daniel the
King, not the Prince, addresses the
crown, but their exchange after the King
has awoken includes political advice
which closely parallels that given by the
King at 331–44. See 3n.

136 SD] *Oxf subst. (Exit one or more. Still music within.);* [*to an Attendant who goes out. Capell; not in
QF*   139 SD] *F; Enter Harry Q*

CLARENCE

   I am here, brother, full of heaviness.   140

PRINCE

   How now, rain within doors and none abroad?

   How doth the King?

GLOUCESTER   Exceeding ill.

PRINCE

   Heard he the good news yet? Tell it him.

WARWICK

   He altered much upon the hearing it.

PRINCE   If he be sick with joy, he'll recover without   145

   physic.

WARWICK

   Not so much noise, my lords. Sweet prince, speak low;

   The King your father is disposed to sleep.

CLARENCE

   Let us withdraw into the other room.

WARWICK

   Will't please your grace to go along with us?   150

PRINCE

   No, I will sit and watch here by the King.

               [Exeunt all but the King and Prince.]

   Why doth the crown lie there upon his pillow,

---

140 **heaviness** sadness, sorrow. Cf. 4.1.310.

141–8 *Owing to metrical irregularities, line divisions in these speeches are at best tentative. Q and F disagree on which lines are prose and which, verse. I elect to keep the Prince's lines at 145–6 prose, as in Q, because rhythmically they break the regularity of Warwick's lines, just as the noise made by the Prince intrudes on the solemnity of those he bursts in on.

141 **rain** i.e. tears
    abroad out of doors

144 **altered** Warwick's reply sounds ironic, since one would expect the King to have rallied, not worsened, on hearing news that the rebels had been crushed. Cf. the King's questioning his own response to the *good news* at 102. The Prince picks up on the irony at 145–6.

146 **physic** medicine. Cf. 1.1.137.

141–2] *Q; prose F*   143] *Q; F lines* yet? / him. /   144 altered] *Q(corr), F;* vttred *Q(uncorr)*   145–6] *one line Q; F lines* Ioy, / physic. /   147–8] *Pope; F lines* (My Lords) / lowe, / sleepe. / ; *prose Q*   151 SD] *Oxf¹ subst.; Exeunt all but P. Henry. / Rowe (after 152); not in QF*

Being so troublesome a bedfellow?
O polished perturbation, golden care,
That keep'st the ports of slumber open wide 155
To many a watchful night, sleep with it now –
Yet not so sound and half so deeply sweet
As he whose brow with homely biggen bound
Snores out the watch of night. O majesty!
When thou dost pinch thy bearer, thou dost sit 160
Like a rich armour worn in heat of day
That scald'st with safety. By his gates of breath
There lies a downy feather which stirs not;
Did he suspire, that light and weightless down
Perforce must move. My gracious lord? My father? 165
This sleep is sound indeed. This is a sleep
That from this golden rigol hath divorced
So many English kings. Thy due from me

154–9 The Prince's apostrophe to the crown echoes his father's apostrophe to sleep at 3.1.4–31. As possible sources, see the King's address to the crown in Daniel, *CW*, 3.119–20, and the Prince's in *Famous Victories*, 8.11–21.

154 **perturbation** The crown is personified as a bringer of unrest.

155 **ports** gates, here meaning eyes

156 **watchful** wakeful, sleepless. Watching is crucial to this scene: it signifies attendance on the dying King (151) and the passage of the night (159).
   sleep . . . now Presumably the King is the unspoken subject of the Prince's injunction: may you sleep in spite of the presence of the crown.

158 **homely biggen** coarse nightcap. The word *homely* identifies the wearer as a poor subject, perhaps a peasant. The vulgarity of *Snores* (159) reinforces this class distinction.

159 **watch of night** The night was divided into several intervals, called watches, for sentry duty.

160 **pinch** torment; or more literally, if *majesty* (159) is taken to mean 'crown', the physical pain caused by the weight of the crown on one's head

162 **scald'st with safety** a paradox: the crown burns its wearer even as it provides the protection of sovereignty.
   gates of breath i.e. mouth and nose

163 **downy** For some editors, the peculiar spellings 'dowlny' in Q, 'dowlney' in F, and their common 'dowlne' at 164 provide evidence that the copy-text for this play may have been a Shakespearean holograph. For further evidence, see 3.2.88n. and p. 469.

164 **suspire** breathe

167 **rigol** circle. Cf. Macbeth's 'golden round' (*Mac* 1.5.28)

163 downy] *F4*; dowlny *Q*; dowlney *F1–3* 164 down] *F4*; dowlne *QF1–3* 165 move. My . . . father?] *Rowe subst.*; moue. My . . . Lord, . . . Father, *F*; moue my . . . lord . . . father: *Q* 168 due] *Q (deaw), F*

Is tears and heavy sorrows of the blood,
Which nature, love and filial tenderness   170
Shall, O dear father, pay thee plenteously.
My due from thee is this imperial crown,
Which, as immediate from thy place and blood,
Derives itself to me.   [*Puts crown on his head.*]
                    Lo where it sits,
Which God shall guard; and put the world's whole
    strength   175
Into one giant arm, it shall not force
This lineal honour from me. This from thee
Will I to mine leave, as 'tis left to me.   *Exit.*
    [*The King awakes.*]
KING   Warwick! Gloucester! Clarence!

Enter WARWICK, GLOUCESTER [*and*] CLARENCE.

CLARENCE
    Doth the King call?

169 **blood** perhaps, as elsewhere, emotion or passion; but there is also a play on kinship – blood relationship – confirmed by the following line. See the Prince's use of *blood* to refer to lineal succession at 173.

170 **nature** the natural affection of a son for his father

173 **immediate from** next in succession to

174 **Derives itself** descends

174 SD The Prince's crowning himself in the presence of his insensible, dying father has a certain symbolic import. Critics with a psychoanalytic bent argue that Harry is enacting an unconscious patricidal wish, as his father accuses him at 222. Weis interprets Harry's action as 'political autogenesis' (48) which ensures that, at least in this private coronation, he will

not receive the crown from the hands of a usurper. Yet this contrasts with Harry's explicit justification for inheriting the crown at 349–52. Ironically, in taking possession of the crown before it is rightly his, the Prince follows in his father's footsteps.

175–6 **and . . . arm** The clause has subjunctive force: 'were the world's whole strength put'. Cf. *Famous Victories*, 8.58–61.

178 SD1 The Prince exits through a different door from that taken by the others at 151. Warwick, by noting that '*This* door is open' (186), implies that it is not the same door through which he, Gloucester and Clarence have re-entered.

180 *F's addition of words to complete Warwick's line is explicable if one

174 SD] *Johnson subst. (after 174); not in QF*   where] *Q; heere F*   175–8] *Q; F lines* guard: / Arme, / from me. / leaue, / me. /   175 God] *Q; Heauen F*   178 SD2] *Oxf; not in QF*   179.1] *QF (after 178)*
180 majesty?] *Q; Maiestie? how fares your Grace? F*

WARWICK   What would your majesty?   180

KING

    Why did you leave me here alone, my lords?

CLARENCE

    We left the Prince my brother here, my liege,

    Who undertook to sit and watch by you.

KING

    The Prince of Wales? Where is he? Let me see him.

    He is not here.   185

WARWICK

    This door is open; he is gone this way.

GLOUCESTER

    He came not through the chamber where we stayed.

KING

    Where is the crown? Who took it from my pillow?

WARWICK

    When we withdrew, my liege, we left it here.

KING

    The Prince hath ta'en it hence. Go, seek him out.   190

    Is he so hasty that he doth suppose

    My sleep my death?

    Find him, my Lord of Warwick; chide him hither.

                                             [Exit Warwick.]

---

regards the King's and Clarence's speeches at 179–80 as comprising one regular line of verse. It makes more sense, however, to take Clarence's and Warwick's half-lines together as one verse line (180), separated from the King's part-line (179) by the amount of time it takes for them to enter and respond. On F's frequent completion of partial lines in Q, see 52n.

185 *F omits this line probably in the interest of preserving metrical regularity, just as it adds words for that purpose at 52, 120, 132 and 180. The King in his sickness speaks in part-lines here and at 192, 197 and 199.

190–5 *F's distribution of lines unsuccessfully attempts to regularize the metre of what, in Q, is an idiosyncratic alternation of regular and irregular lines.

182–4] *F; prose Q*   185] *Capell; prose Q; not in F*   190] *Q; F lines* hence: / out. /   191–2] *Capell; one line Q; F lines* suppose / (my Lord of Warwick) /   193–5] *Q; F lines* Chide . . . conioynes / me. / . . . are: /   193 SD] *Capell; not in QF*

This part of his conjoins with my disease
And helps to end me. See, sons, what things you are, 195
How quickly Nature falls into revolt
When gold becomes her object?
For this the foolish, over-careful fathers
Have broke their sleep with thoughts,
Their brains with care, their bones with industry. 200
For this they have engrossed and pill'd up
The cankered heaps of strange-achieved gold.
For this they have been thoughtful to invest
Their sons with arts and martial exercises,
When, like the bee tolling from every flower, 205

194 **part** conduct (*OED sb.* 11)
196 **Nature** personified as Mother Nature; here, the bonds of kinship and filial loyalty. Cf. 170.
199 **thoughts** worries
200 **industry** physical exertion, hard work
201 **engrossed** amassed, collected; engrossèd
pill'd pillaged or plundered, as in *R2* 2.1.246: 'The commons hath he pilled with grievous taxes' and *Tim* 4.1.11–12: 'Large-handed robbers your grave masters are / And pill by law'. The King's implicit admission that his wealth is tainted, perhaps because ill-gotten, is confirmed in 202. Q's 'pilld', although it would not typically be followed by *up*, is a more interesting, if less conventional, word than F's 'pyl'd' (piled), which only repeats the sense of *engrossed*.
202 **cankered** tarnished or morally corrupt, a common aspersion cast on gold; here, it may indict the means by which the gold was got. Cf. 2.2.92.
strange-achieved an ambiguous epithet meaning acquired (1) in foreign lands, (2) through extraordinary effort, or,

most likely, (3) by crooked means; achievèd
203 **thoughtful** careful, mindful
invest provide, endow
204 **arts ... exercises** The two branches of a gentleman's education during the Renaissance. Humphreys cites Middleton's masque *The World Tossed at Tennis*: 'I am Minerva, / Pallas to both, goddess of arts and arms, / Of arms and arts, for neither has precedence. / For he's the complete man partakes of both' (161–4).
205 *F's appending 'The vertuous Sweetes' to this line may have been the result of a scribe's or compositor's having misread *tolling* as 'culling' and deciding that a direct object needed to be supplied. Given the moral ambiguity with which the gold was said to have been got, however, the bee's 'culling virtuous sweets' would be naively inappropriate phrasing. F's consequent relineation of 205–9 results in a hemistich at 209.
tolling exacting a toll or tribute, collecting (i.e. pollen). The verb is here used intransitively.

199–200] *QF; Capell lines* care, / industry; / 199 sleep] *Q;* sleepes *F* 201 engrossed] *QF (*ingrossed*)* pill'd] *Q (*pilld*), F (*pyl'd*)* 205 tolling] *Q (*toling*);* culling *F* 205–6 flower, / Our] *Q;* flower / The vertuous Sweetes, our *F*

Our ᶠthighsᶠ packed with wax, our mouths with
    honey,
We bring it to the hive and, like the bees,
Are murdered for our pains. This bitter taste
Yields his engrossments to the ending father.

Enter WARWICK.

Now, where is he that will not stay so long   210
Till his friend Sickness have determined me?
WARWICK
My lord, I found the Prince in the next room
Washing with kindly tears his gentle cheeks,
With such a deep demeanour in great sorrow
That tyranny, which never quaffed but blood,   215
Would, by beholding him, have washed his knife
With gentle eye-drops. He is coming hither.

208 **murdered** The drones, not the workers,
are killed off by bees when swarming is
over, as Shakespeare accurately reports
in *H5* 1.2.202–4. The King is no doubt
more concerned with the dramatic force of
his patricidal simile than with its accuracy.
208–9 **This . . . father** confusing syntax: his
engrossments (amassed wealth; cf. 201),
the subject, *Yields* (a singular verb for a
plural subject) a *bitter taste* (the direct
object) in the mouth of the dying (*ending*)
father. The singular verb form may have
been erroneously induced by *taste*, which
takes the position usually accorded the
subject. By giving syntactical pride of
place to the *bitter taste*, Shakespeare
emphasizes the unnatural inversion of
what a father has a right to expect from
his sons, gratitude and filial obligation,
and reverses the proverb 'The bee sucks
honey out of the bitterest flowers' (Dent,
B205).

211 **friend . . . me* Sickness* is personified as
the Prince's friend who will put an end to
(determine = terminate) the King. I follow
Ridley in regarding Q 'hands' as a likely
misreading of 'haue' caused by confusions
of *n/u* and *d/e* common in secretary hand.
213 **kindly** natural, filial
214 **deep demeanour** look of profound
feeling; *deep* attaches to the following
phrase, i.e. 'deep in great sorrow'.
215–17 **tyranny . . . eye-drops** Humphreys
identifies a reference to Plutarch's 'Life
of Pelopides', a story also recounted in
Sidney's *Defence of Poesie*, in which the
blood-thirsty tyrant Alexander of Pherae
was moved to tears by a performance of
Euripides' *Troades*.
215 **tyranny** cruelty or, as personified, the
tyrant himself
    quaffed drank
    but anything but
217 **eye-drops** tears

206 thighs] *F;* thigh *Q;* thighs are *Pope;* thighs all *Hanmer*   206–9] *Q; F lines* Wax, / Hiue; / paines. /
engrossments, / Father. /   208 murdered] *Q (*murdred); *murthered *F*   209.1] *QF (after 211)*   211 have]
Ridley; hands *Q;* hath *F*

375

KING

   But wherefore did he take away the crown?

          Enter ᶠPRINCE Henryᶠ [*carrying the crown*].

   Lo where he comes. Come hither to me, Harry.
   – Depart the chamber; leave us here alone.   220
               Exeunt [*Gloucester, Clarence and Warwick*].

PRINCE

   I never thought to hear you speak again.

KING

   Thy wish was father, Harry, to that thought.
   I stay too long by thee; I weary thee.
   Dost thou so hunger for mine empty chair
   That thou wilt needs invest thee with my honours   225
   Before thy hour be ripe? O foolish youth,
   Thou seek'st the greatness that will overwhelm thee!
   Stay but a little, for my cloud of dignity
   Is held from falling with so weak a wind
   That it will quickly drop. My day is dim.   230
   Thou hast stol'n that which after some few hours
   Were thine without offence, and at my death

---

218 **wherefore** why

218.1 Since Warwick, on royal command, has told him that the King is alive and has asked for him (193), the Prince would of course have removed the crown from his head before entering. This logic is not always followed in performance.

222–67 On the debt of this speech to *Famous Victories*, see 54–66n.

222 To the proverbial sentiment 'We soon believe what we desire' (Dent, B 269), Shakespeare adds the pointed metaphor of paternity.

224 **chair** throne

225 **wilt needs** must

invest . . . with appropriate (*v.*); more literally, dress yourself in. Cf. 6, 203.

228–30 **for . . . drop** Clouds were thought to be held aloft by the wind. The King's *cloud of dignity* – a high estate which is both real and insubstantial – is supported by so *weak a wind* (i.e. his own faint breath) that it will soon plummet to earth.

230 **dim** growing dark. Metaphorically, his life is drawing to a close; perhaps, too, his eyesight is failing.

231 **stol'n** The King repeats a verb he has used to characterize his own strategy for advancement in *1H4* 3.2.50: 'And then I stole all courtesy from heaven'.

218.1] *this edn; Enter Prince Henry. F; Enter Harry. Q (after 217)*   220 SD] *exeunt Q; Exit. F; Ex. Lords. / Theobald; [Exeunt Warwick and the rest. Capell*   224 mine] *Q; my F*   225 my] *Q; mine F*   231 stol'n] stolne *QF*

Thou hast sealed up my expectation.
Thy life did manifest thou lov'dst me not,
And thou wilt have me die assured of it.   235
Thou hid'st a thousand daggers in thy thoughts,
Whom thou hast whetted on thy stony heart
To stab at half an hour of my life.
What, canst thou not forbear me half an hour?
Then get thee gone and dig my grave thyself,   240
And bid the merry bells ring to thine ear
That thou art crowned, not that I am dead.
Let all the tears that should bedew my hearse
Be drops of balm to sanctify thy head:
Only compound me with forgotten dust;   245

233 **sealed ... expectation** confirmed my worst fears; sealèd. For other instances of negative expectation, see 5.2.30–2, 124–8.

236 **a thousand daggers** Shakespeare may have had in mind Holinshed's account of an incident occurring in 1412 in which the Prince, seeking to alleviate the King's suspicion that he planned to usurp the throne, handed him a dagger and invited him to kill him, reassuring his father 'that his life was not so deare to him, that he wished to liue one daie with his displeasure' (Holinshed, 3.539). *Famous Victories* bases sc. 6 on this account: in it, when the Prince enters with a dagger, the King rebukes him for intending him harm. There is no evidence in either *H4* play that the Prince wished harm to his father, though the rumour surfaces in *1H4* when Harry, having rescued the King from Douglas, protests, 'they did me too much injury / That ever said I hearkened for your death' (5.4.50–1).

237 **Whom** In Q, the daggers are personified.
stony heart proverbial: 'A heart of (as hard as) stone' (Dent, H311)

238 The gist is that since the King has only a half hour of life left, the daggers' achievement of their purpose would be meaningless.

239 **forbear** spare; tolerate

241 **merry bells** The King witheringly suggests that the bells that should toll his death will be supplanted by those rung in celebration of his son's coronation.

242 **crowned** crownèd

244 **drops of balm** consecrated oil used to anoint a king at his coronation. Henry's irony is heightened by the uncertainty of his own claim to divine right. If he has violated the sanctity of kingship by usurping God's anointed monarch Richard (see *R2* 4.1.233–42), can lineal succession alone ensure that his son will have a legitimate claim to divine right? Cf. 349–52.

245–6 Cf. Job, 21.26: 'They shall sleepe both in the dust, and the wormes shall couer them' (Geneva Bible).

245 **compound** mix. Cf. *Ham* 4.2.3–5: 'ROSENCRANTZ What have you done, my lord, with the dead body? HAMLET Compound it with dust, whereto 'tis kin'.

237 Whom] *Q;* Which *F*   238 hour] *Q (*hower*), F (*howre*)   life] *QF1–2;* fraile life *F3–4, Rowe*   241 thine] *Q;* thy *F*

Give that which gave thee life unto the worms.
Pluck down my officers, break my decrees;
For now a time is come to mock at form.
Harry the Fifth is crowned! Up, vanity!
Down, royal state! All you sage counsellors, hence,   250
And to the English court assemble now
From every region apes of idleness!
Now, neighbour confines, purge you of your scum.
Have you a ruffian that will swear, drink, dance,
Revel the night, rob, murder, and commit   255
The oldest sins the newest kind of ways?
Be happy! He will trouble you no more.
England shall double gild his treble guilt;
England shall give him office, honour, might;
For the fifth Harry from curbed licence plucks   260
The muzzle of restraint, and the wild dog
Shall flesh his tooth on every innocent.
O my poor kingdom, sick with civil blows!

---

246 **that . . . life** i.e. Henry's own flesh

247 **Pluck down** dismiss; possibly an anticipation that the Prince will, in revenge, remove
the Lord Chief Justice from office

248 **form** law and order

252 **apes of idleness** fools who follow the
fashion of sloth, tainted by every vice
that idleness was said to foster. For a
similar use of *ape*, see 2.2.69.

253 **neighbour confines** neighbouring regions
– i.e. those close to London

254 **dance** Dancing was associated with such
lewd behaviours as drinking and swearing and thus was often included in
Puritan attacks on the stage. Cowl (Ard¹)
cites the 1601 Q of Jonson's *Every Man
In*: 'He, and his wilde associates, spend
their houres, / In repetition of lasciuious
iests, / Sweare, leape, and dance, and
reuell night by night' (1.4.56–8).

258 **double . . . guilt** To *gild* meant to cover
up or paint over, as with gold; the pun on
guilt was common. Cf. *H5* Chorus.2.0.26:
'the gilt of France, – O guilt indeed!', and
Mac 2.2.54–5: 'I'll gild the faces of the
grooms withal, / For it must seem their
guilt'.

260–1 **from . . . restraint** Excessive liberty
or the abuse of law (*OED* licence *sb*. 3b)
is figured as a dog whose rage has thus
far been checked by a muzzle: *plucks* =
removes. Cf. 247 and 1.2.70.

260 **curbed** restrained, checked; curbèd

262 **flesh . . . on** tear into the flesh of. Cf.
1.1.149.

263 **sick . . . blows** riven by internal conflicts.
The metaphor of sickness links the
state of the kingdom to that of the King
himself.

---

249 Harry the Fifth] *Q* (fift); Henry the fift *F*   252 every] *Q*; eu'ry *F*   254 ruffian] *Q* (ruffin), *F*   will] *Q*;
swill *F*   258 gild] *Q*, *F* (gill'd)   guilt] *Q* (gilt), *F*   261 muzzle] *F*, *Q* (mussel)   262 on] *Q*; in *F*

When that my care could not withhold thy riots,
What wilt thou do when riot is thy care? 265
O, thou wilt be a wilderness again,
Peopled with wolves, thy old inhabitants.
PRINCE [*Kneels.*]
O pardon me, my liege. But for my tears,
The moist impediments unto my speech,
I had forestalled this dear and deep rebuke 270
Ere you with grief had spoke and I had heard
The course of it so far. There is your crown,
And He that wears the crown immortally
Long guard it yours! If I affect it more
Than as your honour and as your renown, 275
Let me no more from this obedience rise,
Which my most inward, true and duteous spirit
Teacheth this prostrate and exterior bending.
God witness with me, when I here came in

264–5 **my care ... care** Structured as an epanalepsis, a rhetorical figure wherein words are repeated after intervening matter, these lines oppose the King's will to maintain order (*care*), which failed to curb his son's debauchery (*riots*), to the civil disobedience (*riot*) that is likely to be the legacy and affliction (*care*) of the Prince when he is king. Though these lines are ostensibly addressed to *my poor kingdom* (263), they are actually directed at the Prince, who serves to personify the kingdom's downfall. Cf. 5.5.59–61.

268–306 These lines are closely modelled on a speech in *Famous Victories* (8.39–47) in which the Prince returns the crown to his father, expressing reluctance to have it, sheds tears, appeals to God as witness and prays for his father. Yet Shakespeare alters his source in striking ways: see pp. 128–9.

268 SD That the Prince has knelt before his father is indicated in 276–8. When he rises is unclear, though he would certainly respond to his father's request that he come and sit by his bed at 310. Often, in performance, he rises before then, while delivering his long self-defence.

268 **But** had it not been

270 **had** would have
dear severe, grievous (*OED adj.*[2] 2)

272 **There ... crown** Whether the Prince returns the crown to his father on this line, or has placed it next to his father earlier in the speech when he has knelt (268) or even as early as his entrance (218), is open to interpretation.

273 **He ... immortally** i.e. God, or perhaps Christ

274 **affect** desire

276 **obedience** obeisance; i.e. kneeling in submission (*OED sb.* 3)

268 SD] *Rowe (after 268); [Kneeling and presenting it. Capell (after 272); not in QF* 268] *Q; F lines* (my Liege) / Teares, / 269 moist] *Q;* most *F* 277 inward, true and] *Q;* true, and inward *F* 278–9 bending. ... me,] *F;* bending, ... me. *Q* 279 God] *Q;* Heauen *F*

And found no course of breath within your majesty,   280
How cold it struck my heart. If I do feign,
O let me in my present wildness die
And never live to show th'incredulous world
The noble change that I have purposed.
Coming to look on you, thinking you dead,   285
And dead almost, my liege, to think you were,
I spake unto this crown as having sense
And thus upbraided it: 'The care on thee depending
Hath fed upon the body of my father;
Therefore thou best of gold art worse than gold: 290
Other, less fine in carat, more precious,

280 **course** current

281 **If . . . feign** The Prince may protest too much. This second of his *If* clauses, both of them intended to exculpate himself and impress the King with his sincerity, anticipates Iago's protestations of sincerity: 'If ever I did dream / Of such a matter, abhor me'; 'Despise me / If I do not' (*(Oth* 1.1.4–5; 6–7). It bids for belief in a version of events at odds with what the audience has just witnessed: cf. 285–306n.

282 **wildness** In addition to unruly behaviour, the word connotes an unregenerate spirit, so that were the Prince to die, he would presumably be damned.

284 See 68–78n. The Prince, of course, has already backslid on the reformation he has promised in *1H4* (3.2.129–59), and in this play has thus far been seen only with his tavern companions.
purposed purposèd

285–306 The Prince's account of what transpired at 152–78 differs significantly from what really occurred. In that speech, his surprise at discovering that his father was no longer breathing was balanced by a calculated decision to assume the crown as his *due* (172), an assurance that *God shall guard* it (175), and a pledge that nothing will 'force / This lineal honour' from him (176–7). And although he mentions tears and sorrow as debts owed to his father, he intends to pay them in the future, not at present (168–71). Now, speaking through tears (268–9), he confesses to have been struck *dead almost* (286) upon discovering his father (as he thought) dead; he claims to have accused the crown of murder (297) and tried it on reluctantly, to 'quarrel' (298) with it; and he disclaims any *joy, pride* or *entertainment to the might of it* (299–303), enlisting God to bear witness to his truth (304). Most of all, his verbatim recollection of what he spoke to the crown (288–94) invites a sceptical assessment of his whole speech, though in performance it often proves as convincing to an audience as it does to the King.

287 **as having sense** as if it could hear

288 **The . . . depending** the burdens of state that depend on you. The crown is personified as the weight of responsibility.

291 **carat** quality, value (*OED sb.*4)

281 struck] *QF (*strooke*)*   287 this] *Q; the *F   290 worse than] *Q (*then*); worst of *F   291 Other, . . . carat,] Other lesse fine, in karat *Q; *Other, lesse fine in Charract, is *F

Preserving life in med'cine potable;
But thou, most fine, most honoured, most renowned,
Hath eat thy bearer up.' Thus, my most royal liege,
Accusing it, I put it on my head   295
To try with it, as with an enemy
That had before my face murdered my father,
The quarrel of a true inheritor.
But if it did infect my blood with joy
Or swell my thoughts to any strain of pride,   300
If any rebel or vain spirit of mine
Did with the least affection of a welcome
Give entertainment to the might of it,
Let God forever keep it from my head
And make me as the poorest vassal is   305
That doth with awe and terror kneel to it.

KING

God put in thy mind to take it hence,
That thou mightst win the more thy father's love,

---

292 **med'cine potable** *aurum potabile*, a drug
thought to contain liquid gold and to have
great restorative powers. The Prince's
point is that the crown, though made of
pure gold, is in fact less precious than the
impure drug because it consumes rather
than heals the body.

294 **eat** eaten, pronounced *ĕt*, a normal past
tense of 'eat' used as a participle (Abbott,
343)

296–8 'to dispute with it the rights of a
legitimate heir'; *try* = ascertain the truth
of (*OED v.* 5c)

298 **quarrel** claim, argument: the direct
object of *try* (296)

300 **strain** degree, pitch; *swell* works with
strain to suggest a latent musical
metaphor.

302 **affection** inclination (*OED sb.* 5)

303 'show a willingness to assume its power'.
The images of welcome and entertainment turn the crown into a guest whom
the Prince professes to repudiate.

307 *F's additional half-lines here ('O my
Sonne!') and at 349 ('My gracious
Liege'), embraced by many editors, are
hypermetrical vocatives. Although they
may be authorial, Davison's speculation
that they were actors' interpolations is
more plausible, for they would help
actors to register the suddenness of the
King's change of heart at 307 and the
sincerity of the Prince's reply at 349. Cf.
the King's 'Oh, my son, my son!' in
Famous Victories, 6.2.

308 **win** Humphreys argues that F's 'ioyne'
was probably a misreading of MS
'winne'.

294] *Q; F lines* vp. / (my Royall Liege) / thy] *Q;* the *F*   most] *Q; not in F*   304 God] *Q;* heauen *F*
305 vassal] *QF (*vassaile*)*   307 God] *Q;* O my Sonne! / Heauen *F*   308 win] *Q;* ioyne *F*

Pleading so wisely in excuse of it.
Come hither, Harry; sit thou by my bed   310
And hear, I think, the very latest counsel
That ever I shall breathe. God knows, my son,
By what bypaths and indirect, crook'd ways
I met this crown; and I myself know well
How troublesome it sat upon my head.   315
To thee it shall descend with better quiet,
Better opinion, better confirmation,
For all the soil of the achievement goes
With me into the earth. It seemed in me
But as an honour snatched with boist'rous hand,   320
And I had many living to upbraid

310–48 The King's lengthy deathbed counsel to the Prince appears in both Stow (*Annales*, 545–6) and Daniel, but not in Holinshed. Stow (*Chronicles*, 578) cites as his authority early 16th-century MS additions to Tito Livio's *Vita Henrici Quinti*. Stow in turn influenced *Famous Victories*, Shakespeare's most immediate source: 310–15 strikingly echo *Famous Victories*, 8.48–51 and 56–7.

310 The Prince should rise here if, as seems likely, he is still kneeling at 306 when he compares himself to *the poorest vassal* who kneels *with awe and terror* before the crown. In performance, however, he often rises earlier, while delivering his impassioned self-defence, and on this line simply moves closer to sit by the King.

311 **latest** last

312–14 **God ... crown** Though these lines have parallels in Holinshed and *Famous Victories*, Shakespeare alone uses the phrase *crook'd ways*, an indication that the King may be thinking scripturally: cf. Psalms, 125.5: 'These that turne aside by their crooked wayes' (Geneva Bible).

313 **crook'd** tortuous; possibly devious or dishonest (*OED adj.* 1a, 3a). Pronounced as a monosyllable.

314 **met** With this verb, Henry implies that he did not usurp the crown; rather, it derived to him by chance or necessity: cf. 3.1.67–79. Yet his admission that he used *indirect, crook'd ways* (313), his acknowledgement of *the soil of the achievement* (318), and his calling it *an honour snatched* (320) all suggest that he knows better. Furthermore, audiences who had seen *R2* would have remembered the abdication scene – if indeed it was performed – in which Richard forced Bolingbroke to 'seize the crown' (4.1.182). On the omission of the deposition scene from Elizabethan Quarto editions of *R2*, see Forker, *R2* (Ard³), 165–6 and 506–8.

316 **better quiet** less dispute or discord

317 **Better opinion** more favourable reputation, more solid support (i.e. among the nobility)
    confirmation legitimacy or right to possession (*OED sb.* 2)

318 **soil ... achievement** i.e. taint of my acquisition of the crown; *soil* also puns on *earth* (319).

320 **boist'rous** violent (*OED adj.* 9a *obs.*)

321–2 **upbraid ... assistances** 'censure me for usurpation even though I gained the crown with their help'

312 God] *Q;* Heauen *F*   313 crook'd] *F, Q (*crookt*)*   315 sat] *QF (*sate*)*

My gain of it by their assistances,
Which daily grew to quarrel and to bloodshed,
Wounding supposed peace. All these bold fears
Thou see'st with peril I have answered,   325
For all my reign hath been but as a scene
Acting that argument. And now my death
Changes the mood, for what in me was purchased
Falls upon thee in a more fairer sort.
So thou the garland wear'st successively;   330
Yet, though thou stand'st more sure than I could do,
Thou art not firm enough, since griefs are green,
And all my friends, which thou must make thy
    friends,
Have but their stings and teeth newly ta'en out,

323 **Which** who
324 **supposed peace** the peace that Henry's
    succession was presumed to bring;
    supposèd
    fears threats
325 **answered** countered, put down; answerèd
326–7 **a scene . . . argument** a theatrical
    simile: *argument* means theme or subject
    but was also a term for the summary
    prefixed to the text of a play. Cf.
    1.1.155–60.
328 **mood** emotional pitch, or perhaps
    political climate. *OED* cites this line as
    using *mood* in the sense of a musical
    scale, or 'mode' (*sb.*[2] 3d); F3 and F4
    actually adopt that term.
    purchased a legal term meaning
    'acquired otherwise than by inheritance
    or descent' (*OED* purchase *v.* 5a). In *R2*
    Henry's father sent him forth 'to purchase
    honour' (1.3.282) where ordinarily one
    would regard honour as something to be
    earned, not bought. The word can also
    imply theft, as in *H5* 3.2.35–6: 'They
    will steal anything and call it purchase'.

329 **more fairer** Use of the double com-
    parative intensifies the King's point.
330 **garland** crown, with an implication of
    victorious deserving. Cf. 5.2.83.
    successively by right of succession
331 **stand'st more sure** have a greater claim
    to legitimacy in the public eye
332 **griefs are green** grievances are still
    fresh. For *grief*, cf. 4.1.264.
333 ***my** QF's 'thy' is probably an error ori-
    ginating as far back as Shakespeare's
    holograph and caused by anticipation of
    thy later in the line. That *my* was intended
    is confirmed by 335–7, where the King
    discusses how his friends advanced *him*;
    for him to refer to those friends only as
    the Prince's would make little sense. Weis
    makes a case for preserving 'thy' as the
    King's insistence that his son not take
    these alliances for granted, but constantly
    reinforce them. This reading would
    make sense only if *make* were heavily
    emphasized.

324] *Q; F lines* Peace. / Feares, /   325 answered] *F, Q* (answerd)   328 mood] *Q, F1–2 (*Moode*);* Mode
F3–4   333 my friends] *Rann (Tyrwhitt);* thy friends *QF;* the foes *Keightley;* my foes *Dyce*[2]; thy foes *(W.
Walker)*   334 ta'en] *Q (*tane*);* tak'n *F*

By whose fell working I was first advanced   335
And by whose power I well might lodge a fear
To be again displaced; which to avoid,
I cut them off, and had a purpose now
To lead out many to the Holy Land,
Lest rest and lying still might make them look   340
Too near unto my state. Therefore, my Harry,
Be it thy course to busy giddy minds
With foreign quarrels, that action hence borne out
May waste the memory of the former days.
More would I, but my lungs are wasted so   345
That strength of speech is utterly denied me.
How I came by the crown, O God forgive,
And grant it may with thee in true peace live.

PRINCE

You won it, wore it, kept it, gave it me;
Then plain and right must my possession be,   350
Which I with more than with a common pain
'Gainst all the world will rightfully maintain.

335 **fell working** ruthless scheming. The King attributes his political rise to the machinations of his friends, taking none of the blame himself. Cf. 322–3.

336 **lodge** harbour. Cf. *R3* 2.1.66: 'If ever any grudge were lodged between us'.

338–41 **a purpose ... state** Henry's machiavellian rationale for undertaking a crusade, admitted here for the first time, was suggested by Daniel, *CW*, 3.127. Cf. 3.1.108n. on *the Holy Land*.

340–1 **look ... state** 'scrutinize my kingship too closely', with an implicit threat of rebellion

342–3 **Be ... quarrels** That Harry takes his father's cynical advice is evident from Prince John's report at 5.5.104–7.

342 **course** course of action, strategy
giddy restless. Cf. 110n.

343 **action ... out** military action undertaken in foreign lands (*hence* = abroad)

344 **waste** expunge

345 **would I** 'speak' is understood.
wasted weakened; picks up on *waste* at 344

347–52 Though the scene continues briefly, these three rhyming couplets formally signal the end of the royal exchange. The Prince's lines are closely modelled on those spoken by his counterpart in *Famous Victories*, 8.58–61. For a similar use of three rhyming couplets to mark the end of an action, after which the scene continues, see 4.1.346–51 and 4.2n.

349 *On F's additional half-line, see 307n.
won it, wore it 'Win it and wear it' was proverbial (Dent, W 408).

351 **pain** effort

341] *Q; F lines* State. / (my *Harrie*) /   347 God] *Q;* heauen *F*   349 You] *Q;* My gracious Liege: / You *F*

Enter [Prince JOHN of] Lancaster.

KING

Look, look! Here comes my John of Lancaster.

JOHN

Health, peace and happiness to my royal father.

KING

Thou bringst me happiness and peace, son John;   355
But health, alack, with youthful wings is flown
From this bare, withered trunk. Upon thy sight
My worldly business makes a period.
Where is my Lord of Warwick?

PRINCE   My Lord of Warwick!

[*Enter* WARWICK.]

KING

Doth any name particular belong   360
Unto the lodging where I first did swoon?

357 **bare, withered trunk** For an analogous image of a tree trunk from whose bare branches birds have flown as a metaphor for the ageing human body, see Sonnet 73, in which the poet is figured as leafless winter 'boughs' likened to 'Bare ruined choirs where late the sweet birds sang' (3–4).

Upon thy sight on seeing you

358 **makes a period** comes to an end

360–8 Holinshed (3.541) is the source for these lines. The King comments on the irony of his having believed that the prophecy meant that he would die on a crusade rather than at home, in bed. Though there is no historical record of the prophecy he claims, it has parallels in the cases of other famous men. Edward I, for example, who expected to die in the 'burgh' of Jerusalem, met his end at Burgh-on-the-Sands near Carlisle in 1307 (Barbour, *The Bruce*, IV.207–10, EETS 1870, Extra ser. xi.84); in *2H6*, Suffolk reports that 'A cunning man did calculate my birth / And told me that by water I should die' (4.1.34–5), a prophecy punningly fulfilled as he dies by 'Walter' (31); and in *R3*, Richard 'started' at hearing Richmond's name, 'Because a bard of Ireland told me once / I should not live long after I saw Richmond' (4.2.103–5).

361 **swoon** See 111 SDn.

352.1] *Q (enter Lancaster); Enter Lord Iohn of Lancaster, and Warwicke. F; Enter Prince John, Warwick, Lords, and Others. Capell* 353–4] *Q; F lines* looke, / Lancaster: / Happinesse, / Father. / 359.1] Enter *Warwick, and others. Cam; come forward War. / (Collier); not in QF* 361 swoon] *Q (*swound*), F (*swoon'd*)*

385

WARWICK

'Tis called Jerusalem, my noble lord.

KING

Laud be to God, even there my life must end.
It hath been prophesied to me many years
I should not die but in Jerusalem,   365
Which vainly I supposed the Holy Land.
But bear me to that chamber: there I'll lie.
In that Jerusalem shall Harry die.   ᶠ*Exeunt.*ᶠ

5.1   *Enter* SHALLOW, FALSTAFF, BARDOLPH
                    [*and*] ᶠPAGEᶠ.

SHALLOW   By cock and pie, sir, you shall not away
    tonight. – What, Davy, I say!
FALSTAFF   You must excuse me, Master Robert Shallow.
SHALLOW   I will not excuse you. You shall not be excused.

362 **Jerusalem** Located in Westminster Abbey and not, as here, in the palace, the Jerusalem chamber was the Abbot's private drawing-room and so named for the mention of Jerusalem in inscriptions around the fireplace.

365 **not ... but** only

366 **vainly** foolishly

5.1 The location is Shallow's farm.

0.1–2 SD F's block entry, like that in the first Gloucestershire scene (3.2.0), differs from Q and, in bringing on Davy and Silence, is probably in error. Davy is twice called by Shallow (2, 6) and presumably should not enter until 'Here, sir' (7), while Silence does not figure in the scene at all.

1   **By ... pie** by God and the church ordinal: a silly oath which immediately signals a shift in the play from the *de casibus*

tragedy of the King's death to a scene of comedy. The term *cock*, a perversion of the word God (as in 'cock's body'; see *OED sb.* 8), was already slang for penis (Williams, *Dictionary*, 1.258–9), and was so used in *H5* (2.1.53–4); *pie* (*OED sb.* 3) was idiomatic for the book of rites used by the Roman Catholic Church for the ordination of priests and bishops, but also, appropriately, denotes a dish of food, Shallow's obsession in this scene.

2   **What** 'Come here!' or 'I need you now!' *What* was commonly used to introduce an exclamation. Cf. *Why* (6).

4–6 **I ... excused** Shallow's speech is characterized by repetitions such as these, common among old people and often comic in their accumulation. F typically reduces them.

363] *Q; F lines* heauen: / end. / God] *Q;* heauen *F*   368 SD] *F; not in Q*   **5.1**] *Actus Quintus. Scoena Prima. F; not in Q*   0.1–2] *Capell subst.; Enter Shallow, / Falstaffe, and Bardolfe Q (opp. 4.3.367–8); Enter Shallow, Silence, Falstaffe, Bardolfe, Page, and Dauie. F*   1 sir,] *Q; not in F*

386

Excuses shall not be admitted. There is no excuse   5
shall serve. You shall not be excused. – Why, Davy!

[*Enter* DAVY, *with papers in hand.*]

DAVY   Here, sir.

SHALLOW   Davy, Davy, Davy, Davy, let me see, Davy,
let me see, Davy, let me see. Yea, marry, William
Cook: bid him come hither. – Sir John, you shall not   10
be excused.

DAVY   Marry, sir, thus: those precepts cannot be served.
And again, sir, shall we sow the hade land with
wheat?

SHALLOW   With red wheat, Davy. But for William Cook   15
– are there no young pigeons?

DAVY   Yes, sir. Here is now the smith's note for shoeing
and plough-irons.

6.1 Davy's attempt to draw Shallow's attention to *those precepts* 12) and especially
to a bill for shoeing and plough-irons –
'Here is now the smith's note' (17) –
suggests that he has them in his hand
when he enters, or at least gestures to
them elsewhere, as on a table.

9–10 **William Cook** William the cook.
For other characters named after their
occupations, cf. Doll Tearsheet, Robin
Ostler (*1H4* 2.1.10) and Jeremy Butler
(Jonson, *Alchemist*, 5.1.27).

12 **precepts** writs, warrants (*OED sb.* 4)

13–14 Here begins a string of questions by
which Davy insists that the management
of the farm and matters of law take prior-
ity over preparation of the meal which
preoccupies Shallow. While not totally
ignoring Shallow's injunctions, Davy is
clearly used to keeping his master
focused in this way.

13 **hade land** Q's *hade land*, as Cowl points

out (Ard[1]), was the term used for 'high-
lying land' or 'land on a hill-side' to which
Drayton refers in *Poly-Olbion*, 13, when
he distinguishes 'higher Hades' from 'lower
Leas'. F's 'head-land' normalizes Q's
spelling to signify the strip of land at the
end of furrows on which the plough makes
its turns, and therefore tillable only after
the main crop has been planted. If F's
reading is correct, one may assume Q's
hade to be a countrified form of 'head':
see Wright, *Dictionary*, hade *sb.* (Ard[2]).

15 **red wheat** a variety deeper in colour than
ordinary wheat and called 'red Lammas'
in Gloucestershire, where it was sown in
late summer (Lammas Day falling on 1
August) or early autumn (Madden, 373,
citing Marshall's *Rural Economy of
Cotswold* [1796]).

17 **note** bill

18 **plough-irons** ploughshares; blades used
for cutting furrows in the soil

6 Why, Davy!] *Q; separate line F*   6.1 *Enter* DAVY] *Theobald; not in QF   with papers in hand*]
this edn   8 Davy, let me see, Davy,] *Q; not in F*   9 Yea, marry,] *Q (*yea mary*); not in F*   10 Cook] *QF
(*Cooke*)*   13 hade land] *Q; head-land F*   17–18] *prose Q; F lines* Sir. / Shooing, / Plough-Irons. /

387

SHALLOW   Let it be cast and paid. – Sir John, you shall
not be excused.   20

DAVY   Now, sir, a new link to the bucket must needs be
had. And, sir, do you mean to stop any of William's
wages about the sack he lost at ᶠHinckleyᶠ Fair?

SHALLOW   'A shall answer it. Some pigeons, Davy, a
couple of short-legged hens, a joint of mutton and   25
any pretty little tiny kickshaws, tell William Cook.

DAVY   Doth the man of war stay all night, sir?

SHALLOW   Yea, Davy, I will use him well. A friend i'th'
court is better than a penny in purse. Use his men
well, Davy, for they are arrant knaves and will   30
backbite.

DAVY   No worse than they are back-bitten, sir, for they
have marvellous foul linen.

---

19 **cast** calculated, added up

21 **link** rope or chain, possibly to attach the
bucket to a yoke. Cf. 3.2.265.

23 ***sack … Fair** Hinckley, a market town
30 miles northeast of Stratford-upon-
Avon, was noted for its cattle fairs held on
Whit Monday and in late August. Q's
spelling '*Hunkly*' may have resulted from
the compositor's misreading of minims.
The word *sack* may refer to a bag containing grain or some other product of the
farm, but possibly it refers to canary
wine, the implication being that the cook
has drunk the sack he claims to have lost
at the fair. See 1.2.198n. on *new . . . sack*.

24 **'A … it** 'He shall be charged for it.'

25 **short-legged hens** presumably meatier
than long-legged hens
joint leg or shoulder (*OED sb.* 8)

26 **kickshaws** fancy dishes, dainties; from
the French *quelques choses*

27 **man of war** (1) soldier, meaning Falstaff;
and perhaps, with a sly glance at his bulk,
(2) warship

28–9 **A … purse** proverbial: 'Better is a
friend in court than [A friend in court is
worth] a penny in purse' (Dent, F687).
Shallow reveals an ulterior motive for
entertaining Falstaff which in part
undercuts his country largesse.

29 **Use** treat

30 **arrant knaves** one of Shallow's favourite
phrases. Cf. 39 and 2.1.38n. on *arrant*.

31 **backbite** slander, traduce, speak ill of
others. Shallow is concerned lest any lack
of hospitality be reported to Falstaff.

32 **back-bitten** bitten on the back by lice.
Davy cleverly plays on Shallow's word
and makes light of his concern.

33 **marvellous** used adverbially to mean
'extremely'
foul linen dirty shirts or underwear. Cf.
2.2.19–27.

---

19 paid] *Q* (payed*)*, *F* (payde*)*   21 Now,] *Q; not in F*   23 lost] *Q;* lost the other day, *F*   Hinckley] *F;*
Hunkly *Q*   24 'A] *Q;* He *F*   it. Some] it: some *Q;* it: / Some *F*   26 tiny] *Q* (tinie*)*, *F* (tine*)*   28 Yea,
Davy,] *Q;* Yes *Dauy: F (separate line)*   32 back-bitten] *Q;* bitten *F*   33 marvellous] *Q* (maruailes*)*, *F*
*(*maruellous*)*

SHALLOW   Well conceited, Davy. About thy business,
Davy.   35
DAVY   I beseech you, sir, to countenance William Visor
of Woncote against Clement Perkes a'th' hill.
SHALLOW   There is many complaints, Davy, against
that Visor. That Visor is an arrant knave, on my
knowledge.   40
DAVY   I grant your worship that he is a knave, sir; but
yet God forbid, sir, but a knave should have some
countenance at his friend's request. An honest man,
sir, is able to speak for himself when a knave is not.
I have served your worship truly, sir, this eight years.   45
An I cannot once or twice in a quarter bear out a
knave against an honest man, I have little credit with
your worship. The knave is mine honest friend, sir;
therefore I beseech you let him be countenanced.

---

34 **Well conceited** wittily said. Cf. *conceit*,
2.4.244.
About The verb 'go' is understood.
36 **countenance** find in favour of (*OED v.*
5a). Cf. 43, 49.
36–7 **William ... a'th' hill** Shakespeare
takes pains to root his two litigants in
Gloucestershire. *Visor* (or Vizard) was
a common name in the region, and a
family by that name was recorded living
in Woodmancote (locally pronounced
'Woncot'), near Dursley, in 1612, while
a family named Perkis (or Purchase)
lived not far away, on Stinchcombe
Hill, known locally as simply 'The Hill'
(Huntley, 22, and Madden, 85–9, 372–4).
The hamlet of Wincot, four miles south
of Stratford-upon-Avon and mentioned in
TS Ind.2.20, has also been offered as the
original of Woncote. Rarely so specific in
his regional references, Shakespeare may

have used a Gloucestershire name for one
of Falstaff's recruits as well (Oxf[1]): see
3.2.137n.
38 **is** On singular verbs with plural subjects,
see 1.1.33n.
39 **arrant knave** See 30n.
42 **but ... should** that ... should not
42–3 **have some countenance** 'have the
court rule in his favour'. Cf. 36, 49.
43–4 **An ... not** Davy is either explaining
why Visor cannot get a fair hearing in
court, or referring to himself, who, as a
man of probity, can speak on behalf of his
knavish friend.
46 **quarter** division of the legal calendar
(*OED sb.* 8a). Cf. 78–80n.
bear out defend, support (*OED* bear *v.*[1] 3a)
48 **honest** In contrast to its use at 43 and 47,
in which Visor is seen to typify a dishonest man, *honest* seems here to refer to
personal loyalty rather than moral integrity.

36 I ... sir,] *Q; separate line F* 37 Woncote] *Q, F (*Woncot*)* a'th'] *Q; of the F* 38 is] *Q; are F*
42 God] *Q; heauen F* 45 this] *Q; these F* 46 An] *Q (and); and if F* 47 have little] *Q; haue but a very
litle F* 49 you] *Q; your Worship F*

SHALLOW   Go to, I say; he shall have no wrong. Look   50
    about, Davy.   [*Exit Davy.*]
    Where are you, Sir John? Come, come, come; off with
    your boots! – Give me your hand, Master Bardolph.
BARDOLPH   I am glad to see your worship.
SHALLOW   I thank thee with my heart, kind Master   55
    Bardolph. [*to Page*] And welcome, my tall fellow!
    Come, Sir John.
FALSTAFF   I'll follow you, good Master Robert Shallow.
                                                        [*Exit Shallow.*]
    Bardolph, look to our horses.
                                    [*Exeunt Bardolph and Page.*]
    If I were sawed into quantities I should make four   60
    dozen of such bearded hermits' staves as Master
    Shallow. It is a wonderful thing to see the semblable
    coherence of his men's spirits and his. They, by
    observing him, do bear themselves like foolish

50 **he ... wrong** If taken as assurance that he will decide the case in favour of Visor, Shallow's line provides proof of petty corruption in the magistracy, in contrast to the ethical integrity of the Lord Chief Justice. A more benign interpretation is that Shallow promises only to treat Visor fairly.
50–1 **Look about** look sharp; get moving
52–3 **off ... Bardolph** Shallow's urging Falstaff to remove his boots signals his determination to have him stay to dinner. Indeed, the line may invite comic stage business in which Shallow helps Falstaff off with his boots. Furthermore, 'Give me your hand' could be Shallow's request that Bardolph help him to remove Falstaff's boots, in which case Bardolph's

taking the line as a greeting (54) and shaking Shallow's hand would play as a humorous misunderstanding.
56 **tall** valiant, as at 3.2.61. If the greeting is addressed to the Page, as seems likely, it is also a joke about his small stature. Cf. *you giant* at 1.2.1.
60 **quantities** little pieces
    make equal
61 **hermits' staves** The suggestion that Shallow is as long and thin as a hermit's staff recalls Falstaff's earlier comparison of him to a *Vice's dagger*, an *eel-skin* and an hautboy case (3.2.318, 324, 325). Here, Falstaff contrasts Shallow's emaciation with his own amplitude.
62–3 **semblable coherence** strong similarity
63, 66 **spirits** dispositions, modes of behaviour

50–3] *prose Q; F lines* too, / *Dauy.* / Boots. / *Bardolfe.* /   50 Go . . . he] *Q* (Go to I say, he*)*; Go too, / I say he *F*   51 SD] *Capell; not in QF*   52 Come, come, come;] *Q;* Come, *F*   55 with my] *Q;* with all my *F*   56 SD] *Rowe (after* fellow*); not in QF*   58, 59 SDs] *Capell; not in QF*   64 observing] *Q;* obseruing of *F*

justices; he, by conversing with them, is turned into   65
a justice-like servingman. Their spirits are so married
in conjunction with the participation of society that
they flock together in consent like so many wild
geese. If I had a suit to Master Shallow, I would
humour his men with the imputation of being near   70
their master; if to his men, I would curry with
Master Shallow that no man could better command
his servants. It is certain that either wise bearing or
ignorant carriage is caught, as men take diseases one
of another; therefore, let men take heed of their   75
company. I will devise matter enough out of this
Shallow to keep Prince Harry in continual laughter
the wearing out of six fashions, which is four

65 **conversing** consorting (*OED* converse *v.* 2)
66–7 **are ... society** 'have become so similar through constant interaction with one another'
68–9 **flock ... geese** proverbial: 'Birds of a feather will flock (fly) together' (Dent, B393)
68 **in consent** in agreement, as one
69 **suit to** favour to ask of
70 **with ... near** (1) 'by emphasizing in how much confidence their master holds them'; or (2) 'by implying that I myself am a close friend of his'. Falstaff's goal of buttering up the servants makes the first meaning more likely.
71 **curry with** flatter. The metaphor comes from grooming (currying) a horse (Ard[1]).
74 **carriage** behaviour, demeanour (*OED* 14a), roughly synonymous with *bearing* (73). Falstaff is contrasting wisdom and ignorance.
   caught learned by example
   take catch
75–6 **therefore ... company** See Proverbs, 13.20: 'He that goeth in the companie of

wise men, shalbe wise: but who so is a companion of fooles, shalbe afflicted'; and cf. 'Draw to such company as you would be like' (Dent, C565.1). Falstaff does not seem aware of how fitly this proverb will apply to the Prince and his friendship; cf. 5.5.46–50.
76–7 **matter ... Shallow** play on words: *matter* denotes substance; 'shallow', of little substance.
78–80 **the wearing ... intervallums** i.e. for a whole year, without a break. Falstaff mocks both the rapid changes in fashions of clothing (six times per year) and the snail's pace at which lawsuits (*actions*) are settled. Two such actions may occupy an entire legal year, which was divided into four terms – Michaelmas, Hilary, Easter and Trinity. The long recesses between court sessions were called *intervallums*, Latin for intervals. As Wilson suggests (Cam[1]), Falstaff's satirical barbs may have appealed particularly to the fashionable students at the Inns of Court, London's law schools, for whom Shakespeare's company frequently performed.

74 diseases one] *Q*; diseases, one *F*

terms, or two actions; and 'a shall laugh without
intervallums. O, it is much that a lie with a slight   80
oath and a jest with a sad brow will do with a fellow
that never had the ache in his shoulders! O, you
shall see him laugh till his face be like a wet cloak ill
laid up!

SHALLOW [*within*]   Sir John!   85

FALSTAFF   I come, Master Shallow. I come, Master
Shallow.   [*Exit.*]

5.2   *Enter* WARWICK [*at one door, and the*]
              Lord Chief JUSTICE [*at another door*].

WARWICK
How now, my Lord Chief Justice, whither away?
JUSTICE
How doth the King?
WARWICK
Exceeding well. His cares are now all ended.

---

81   **sad brow** straight face
81–2   **a fellow ... shoulders** probably a
reference to the Prince, who is not old
enough to have suffered the pangs of age
and is still willing to indulge Falstaff's
foolishness. These lines reveal both
Falstaff's abiding affection for the Prince
and his assumption of privilege at a time
when Harry is poised to deny him
everything.
83–4   **like ... up** as wrinkled as a wet cloak
not properly hung to dry
5.2   The scene occurs in a place where members
of the royal family and the nobility meet,
perhaps the palace at Westminster.
0.1–2   *Q's massed entry may reveal
Shakespeare's early intention to have all

the mourners gather at once. It is contradicted by the entry of the King's three
sons at QF 13, possible evidence that only
as he wrote did Shakespeare decide to
begin the scene with the Lord Chief
Justice in private conversation with
Warwick. The inclusion of Westmorland
in Q's SD suggests that he was initially to
have been among the mourners; his
exclusion from Act 5 entirely is odd,
though he may have taken part in the
coronation procession (5.4) as one of the
King's train.
3   **Exceeding well** The sentiment was
commonplace. Cf. 'He is well since he is
in Heaven' (Dent, H347) and 'she is well
and nothing can be ill' (*RJ* 5.1.17).

---

79 'a] *Q; he F*   without] *Q; with F*   82 ache] *Q (*ach*), F*   85 SD] *Theobald; not in QF*   87 SD] *Exeunt
F; not in Q*   **5.2**] *Scena Secunda. F; not in Q*   0.1–2] *Oxf¹ subst.; Enter the Earle of Warwicke, and the
Lord Chiefe Iustice. F; Enter Warwike, duke Humphrey, L. chiefe Iustice, Thomas Clarence, Prince Iohn,
Westmerland. Q*   1 whither] *Q; whether F*   3] *Q; F lines* Cares / ended. /

JUSTICE

   I hope not dead.

WARWICK   He's walked the way of nature,

   And to our purposes he lives no more.   5

JUSTICE

   I would his majesty had called me with him.

   The service that I truly did his life

   Hath left me open to all injuries.

WARWICK

   Indeed, I think the young King loves you not.

JUSTICE

   I know he doth not, and do arm myself   10

   To welcome the condition of the time,

   Which cannot look more hideously upon me

   Than I have drawn it in my fantasy.

      Enter [Prince] JOHN, Thomas[, Duke of CLARENCE],

        and Humphrey[, Duke of GLOUCESTER].

WARWICK

   Here come the heavy issue of dead Harry.

   O, that the living Harry had the temper   15

   Of he, the worst of these three gentlemen!

---

5 **to our purposes** 'in terms of his influence on us'

6 **would** wish

7–8 The Justice refers to his arrest and imprisonment of Harry for boxing him on the ear, the consequences of which now give him pause. Though the legend is not dramatized in this play, Shakespeare's audience would have been familiar with it, and it was reported in *Famous Victories*, when the Chief Justice, 'for fear of my lord the young Prince' on his accession, releases the thief for whose imprisonment the Prince had boxed his ear (9.1–5). Here, the Justice shows no such fear, but great dignity. Cf. 67–71 and 1.2.56–7n. See also pp. 129–30.

7 **truly** loyally

11 **condition** temper, character. The Justice fortifies himself stoically against a hostile political climate. The condition of the time is one of the play's preoccupations: cf. 3.1.78 and 4.1.101.

13 **fantasy** imagination

14 **heavy issue** sorrowful children. For *heavy*, cf. 1.1.121n.

15 **temper** disposition

16 **worst** i.e. least worthy

13.1–2] *Q; Enter Iohn of Lancaster, Gloucester, and Clarence. F*   16 he] *Q; him F*

How many nobles then should hold their places
That must strike sail to spirits of vile sort?

JUSTICE

O God, I fear all will be overturned.

JOHN

Good morrow, cousin Warwick; [*to Justice*] good
    morrow.   20

CLARENCE, GLOUCESTER

Good morrow, cousin.

JOHN

We meet like men that had forgot to speak.

WARWICK

We do remember, but our argument
Is all too heavy to admit much talk.

JOHN

Well, peace be with him that hath made us heavy.   25

JUSTICE

Peace be with us, lest we be heavier.

GLOUCESTER [*to Justice*]

O good my lord, you have lost a friend indeed,
And I dare swear you borrow not that face
Of seeming sorrow. It is sure your own.

JOHN [*to Justice*]

Though no man be assured what grace to find,   30
You stand in coldest expectation.
I am the sorrier. Would 'twere otherwise.

CLARENCE [*to Justice*]

Well, you must now speak Sir John Falstaff fair,

---

17 **hold their places** maintain their rightful
    positions
18 'who must submit (lower their sails in
    surrender) to vulgar ruffians'
20, 21 **cousin** See 1.2.226n.
22 **forgot to** forgotten how to
23 **argument** theme, topic. Cf. 4.3.326–7.

24, 25 **heavy** Cf. 14.
28–9 **you . . . sorrow** your sorrowful visage
    is not feigned
30 **what . . . find** what royal favour to expect
31 'your hopes are bleakest'
33 **speak . . . fair** address courteously, with
    respect

18 vile] *Q*; vilde *F*   19 O God] *Q*; Alas *F*   20 SD] *this edn*

Which swims against your stream of quality.

JUSTICE

Sweet princes, what I did I did in honour,   35
Led by th'impartial conduct of my soul;
And never shall you see that I will beg
A ragged and forestalled remission.
If truth and upright innocency fail me,
I'll to the King my master that is dead   40
And tell him who hath sent me after him.

Enter Prince ^FHenry^F [*as* KING] *and Blunt.*

WARWICK

Here comes the Prince.

JUSTICE

Good morrow, and God save your majesty.

KING

This new and gorgeous garment, majesty,

34 **swims . . . quality** 'affronts your sense of
dignity'; adapted from the proverbial 'To
swim against the stream' (Dent, S930.1)

36 **th'impartial**   the   fair-minded,
unimpeachable

38 **ragged** base, beggarly. Cf. 3.2.142, 262.
forestalled remission either (1) pardon certain to be refused even before requested,
or (2) pardon secured in advance by some
cowardly gesture of submission (such as
the Chief Justice's release of the thief and
Prince's servant in *Famous Victories*; see
7–8n. above); *remission* should be spoken
as four syllables.

41.1 ***Prince** QF's reference to Henry as
'*Prince*' rather than '*King*' in SPs
throughout the scene, and Warwick's
calling him *the Prince* at 42, are puzzling.
They may indicate that Shakespeare thought
that Harry would assume the title of King

only at his coronation; yet Warwick refers
to him as *the young King* at 9, and Harry
himself admits to feeling uncomfortable
in his new role as *majesty* at 44–5.

***and Blunt** Q brings on Blunt as a mute
attendant: cf. similar ghost appearances
by Blunt at 3.1.31 and 4.2.73. I retain Q's
direction because it is unlikely that the
new King would enter, as in F, unattended.

44–5 **new . . . me** The metaphor of kingship
as attire, a robe to be put on and taken
off, counters the traditional belief that
the king's two bodies were indissolubly
united – a belief underlying Richard's
mock divestiture of his own authority
in *R2* 4.1.203–21. That kingship is now
something less than sacramental is suggested in Henry V's identification of it
as an 'idol ceremony' (*H5* 4.1.237); and
the metaphor of kingship as clothing

36 th'impartial] *Q;* th'Imperiall *F*   38–9 remission. . . . me,] *F;* remission, . . . me. *Q*   39 truth] *Q;*
Troth *F*   41.1] *Enter the Prince and Blunt Q (opp. 41–2); Enter Prince Henrie. F; Enter the new* King,
attended. Capell; Enter King Henry V. | Malone   43 God] *Q;* heauen *F*   44 SP] *K. Henry. | Theobald²;
Prince. | QF passim*

Sits not so easy on me as you think.   45
Brothers, you ^Fmix^F your sadness with some fear.
This is the English, not the Turkish, court:
Not Amurath an Amurath succeeds,
But Harry, Harry. Yet be sad, good brothers,
For, by my faith, it very well becomes you.   50
Sorrow so royally in you appears
That I will deeply put the fashion on
And wear it in my heart. Why then, be sad;
But entertain no more of it, good brothers,
Than a joint burden laid upon us all.   55
For me, by heaven, I bid you be assured,
I'll be your father and your brother too:
Let me but bear your love, I'll bear your cares.
Yet weep that Harry's dead, and so will I;
But Harry lives that will convert those tears   60
By number into hours of happiness.

---

reappears in the tragedy of the usurper Macbeth, whose title 'Hang[s] loose about him, like a giant's robe / Upon a dwarfish thief' (*Mac* 5.2.21–2).

48 a topical reference to the accession of Mohamet III to the Turkish Sultantate in January 1595. Just as his father Murad III (*Amurath*) had done at his own accession in 1574, Mohamet ordered all his brothers killed. The name *Amurath* had thus become a byword for barbaric tyranny, as in Jonson, *The Case is Altered*, 4.10.30–1: 'I tell thee if *Amurath* the greate Turke were here I would speake, and he should here me'. The King seeks to reassure his brothers that in England, a civilized country, the succession will be decorous and their lives safeguarded. Richard Hillman, however, argues that the allusion to Amurath serves 'as a powerful subversive emblem of the shadow-side of English monarchy' under the Lancastrians (167).

49 Harry, Harry The new King's reference to himself as *Harry* confirms his ownership of the public name by which he and his father have been called throughout the play and marks a contrast with *1H4*, in which he has more commonly been called *Hal*, the nickname by which his tavern companions presume familiarity with him. Notably, he is addressed as *Hal* only four times in *2H4*, and exclusively by Falstaff, who employs that name most inappropriately to interrupt the King's coronation procession (5.5.39); cf. also 2.4.317, 320, 327.

52 deeply solemnly, feelingly. In yet another sartorial metaphor (cf. 44–5) Harry praises his brothers' fashion of mourning and vows to 'wear it in [his] heart'.

54 entertain take upon yourselves

56 For as for

58 Let ... bear[^1] if you'll only let me have

61 By number one by one

46 mix] *F (*mixe); mixt *Q*   48 Amurath an Amurath] *Q; Amurah, an Amurah F*   50 by my faith] *Q; (*to speake truth) *F*   55 burden] *Q;* burthen *F*   59 Yet] *Q;* But *F*

BROTHERS

We hope no otherwise from your majesty.

KING

You all look strangely on me, [*to Justice*] and
    you most.

You are, I think, assured I love you not.

JUSTICE

I am assured, if I be measured rightly,   65

Your majesty hath no just cause to hate me.

KING

No? How might a prince of my great hopes forget

So great indignities you laid upon me?

What – rate, rebuke and roughly send to prison

Th'immediate heir of England? Was this easy?   70

May this be washed in Lethe and forgotten?

JUSTICE

I then did use the person of your father.

The image of his power lay then in me;

---

63 **strangely** in a cold or unfriendly manner,
as one might look upon a stranger (*OED*
adv. 2)
65 **measured** judged
67–71 For the incident of the Justice's arrest
of Prince Henry, see 1.2.56–7n.
67 **great hopes** i.e. expectation to succeed
my father as King
69 **rate** berate, chide
70 **easy** insignificant, of little importance
(*OED adj.* 15)
71 **washed in Lethe** In classical mythology,
drinking from – not washing in – the
water of Lethe, a river in Hades, induces
oblivion in souls entering the underworld
(Cam²). In Shakespeare, however, Lethe
drowns memory: cf. *R3* 4.4.251–3: 'So in
the Lethe of thy angry soul / Thou drown
the sad remembrance of those wrongs /
Which thou supposest I have done to

thee'; and *TN* 4.1.61: 'Let fancy still my
sense in Lethe steep'. Scansion demands
– and Q's spelling 'lethy' confirms – that
the final *e* in *Lethe* be pronounced. Cf. *R3*
4.4.251, *Ham* 1.5.33 and *TN* 4.1.61.
72 **did ... of** represented, acted in the name
of. Technically, judges were thought to
be personations of the king, himself the
fountain of all justice. Humphreys cites
a similar Latin phrase in John Case,
Sphaera Ciuitatis (1588; 179), defining
the locus of justice, '*iudexque[m] inuadis
personam tui patris gerit*'. The Lord
Chief Justice in *Famous Victories* utters
an approximate translation of this
sentiment to the Prince: 'your father,
whose lively person here in this place I do
represent' (4.79–80).
73, 78, 88 **image** symbol

And in th'administration of his law,
Whiles I was busy for the commonwealth,　　　　75
Your highness pleased to forget my place,
The majesty and power of law and justice,
The image of the king whom I presented,
And struck me in my very seat of judgement,
Whereon, as an offender to your father,　　　　80
I gave bold way to my authority
And did commit you. If the deed were ill,
Be you contented, wearing now the garland,
To have a son set your decrees at naught?
To pluck down justice from our awful bench?　　　　85
To trip the course of law and blunt the sword
That guards the peace and safety of your person?
Nay, more: to spurn at your most royal image

75 **busy ... commonwealth** working on behalf of the state. The Lord Chief Justice presided over the Court of King's Bench.

76 **pleased** thought it permissible (*OED* please *v.* 6a); pleasèd

78 **presented** represented

79 **struck** Shakespeare follows Holinshed here, where the Prince 'had with his fist striken the cheefe iustice for sending one of his minions (vpon desert) to prison, when the iustice stoutlie commanded him-selfe also streict to ward, & he (then prince) obeied' (3.543). In Elyot and Stow, the Prince does not act on his threat to strike the Lord Chief Justice. Holinshed's is the account reported in *Famous Victories*: see 1.2.56–7n.
　in ... judgement literally, 'even as I sat on the bench'; metaphorically, 'in my position as upholder of the law of the land'

80 **as an offender** This misplaced phrase modifies not the Justice himself (*I*, 81), but the Prince (*you*, 82).

82 **commit you** sentence you to prison
　ill blameworthy

83 **Be you** would you be
　garland crown. Cf. 4.3.330n.

84 **set ... at naught** violate

85 **awful** worthy of respect or reverence. Though F's spelling 'awefull' suggests this meaning, it would be aurally indistinguishable from Q's *awful* in performance. See also 4.1.176n.
　bench See 75n.

86 **trip ... law** pervert justice. The image is from running a race.

86, 102, 113 **sword** an emblem of justice: metaphorically, the power to enforce the law and punish offenders. Literally, as Davison observes, the Sword of Spiritual Justice is offered by the presiding Archbishop to the King at his coronation with the words, 'With this sword do justice'.

88 **spurn at** trample on, reject disdainfully (*OED* spurn *v.* 5, 3)

75 commonwealth] *Q* (common wealth*), F* (Commonwealth)　　79 struck] *QF1–2* (strooke*), F3*　　85 awful] *Q, F* (awefull)

And mock your workings in a second body?
Question your royal thoughts, make the case yours,   90
Be now the father and propose a son,
Hear your own dignity so much profaned,
See your most dreadful laws so loosely slighted,
Behold yourself so by a son disdained;
And then imagine me taking your part   95
And in your power soft silencing your son.
After this cold considerance, sentence me;
And as you are a king, speak in your state
What I have done that misbecame my place,
My person, or my liege's sovereignty.   100

KING

You are right, Justice, and you weigh this well;

---

89 **your . . . body** 'the performance of your royal will by a deputy'. On judges as the King's second body, see 72n.

91 **propose** imagine

92 **profaned** debased, blasphemed. Any offence against the King's holy personage was deemed a sacrilege (Cam²).

93 **dreadful** inspiring awe or reverence; formidable. Cf. *awful*, 85.

96 **in your power** with your authority
soft gently

97 **cold considerance** sober reflection, due consideration
sentence me The Justice thinks it likely that the new King will imprison and execute him. Cf. 35–41.

98 **in your state** impartially, according to your royal office

101–2 The King's decision to acquit the Justice as a consequence of his eloquent self-defence is Shakespeare's invention. One may reasonably suspect, however, that the King has already decided to retain the Justice and is simply toying with him, forcing him – with a sadism characteristic of his humour – to plead

for his life. By retaining the Justice as a surrogate 'father to his youth' (117), the King in effect displaces forever the anarchy of Falstaff, an assurance that lends even deeper irony to Falstaff's bravado in 5.3. Although Stow (*Annales*, 547–8), notes the Prince's willing submission to the Lord Chief Justice at the time of his arrest, he reports no further meeting between the two; and Holinshed, though observing that Henry V 'elected the best learned men in the lawes of the realme, to the offices of iustice' (3.543), makes no specific mention of the Lord Chief Justice. Shakespeare's closest source is *Famous Victories*, in which the King appoints the Lord Chief Justice 'Protector over my realm' (9.145) during his expedition to France.

101 *****right, Justice** Some editors, swayed by the lack of punctuation between these words in QF, argue that the phrase is an abstraction, 'right Justice' meaning an ideal personification of justice. In light of the previous dialogue's emphasis on symbolic identity, their case has merit;

95 your] *Q*; you *F*   101 right, Justice] *Hanmer*; right Iustice *QF*

Therefore still bear the balance and the sword.
And I do wish your honours may increase
Till you do live to see a son of mine
Offend you and obey you as I did;   105
So shall I live to speak my father's words:
'Happy am I that have a man so bold
That dares do justice on my proper son,
And not less happy having such a son
That would deliver up his greatness so.'   110
Into the hands of justice you did commit me,
For which I do commit into your hand
Th'unstained sword that you have used to bear,
With this remembrance: that you use the same
With the like bold, just and impartial spirit   115
As you have done 'gainst me. There is my hand.

but it would make more sense for the King, after listening to the Justice's logic, to assure him that he is right, as a result of which he may keep his job.
weigh consider

102 **balance** scales, emblem of judicial impartiality, picking up on *weigh* in 101. For the significance of the sword, see 86, 102, 113n.

107–10 As Humphreys observes, King Henry's speech, as recited by his son, resembles what is reported in Stow (*Annales*, 547–8), who drew nearly verbatim from Elyot's *Gouernour*, and it also resembles the account in Case's *Sphaera Ciuitatis* (see 72n.). How Harry remembers word for word a speech his father spoke when he was probably not present is unclear, but his quoting it is consistent with his ostensible reciting from memory his own speech to the crown, artfully altered, at 4.3.288–94, and with his father's politically adept misquotation of Richard II at 3.1.70–7. Self-serving (mis)quotation appears to be a family habit.

108 **do justice on** administer correction to, punish
proper own

110 **deliver . . . greatness** humble his eminence. Cf. 3.1.74.

110–11 ***so . . . justice** Modern editors often prefer F's punctuation, in which *so* (meaning 'thus') introduces the next line as a continuation of the sentence, ending with *justice*. Q's punctuation, however, is equally logical, allowing for a rhetorical parallelism in the four lines quoted by the King as a complete sentence (107–10) and creating an epanalepsis in the next two lines addressed to the Justice: 'Into the hands . . . you did commit me, / For which I do commit into your hand' (111–12). Cf. 4.3.264–5.

113 **th'unstained** the uncorrupted, never sullied by unjust use; unstained
have . . . bear are accustomed to carry

114 **remembrance** reminder

115 **like** same

109 not] *Q;* no *F*   110–11 so.' / Into . . . justice you] *Q subst.;* so, / Into . . . Iustice. You *F*

You shall be as a father to my youth;
My voice shall sound as you do prompt mine ear,
And I will stoop and humble my intents
To your well-practised, wise directions. 120
– And, princes all, believe me, I beseech you,
My father is gone wild into his grave,
For in his tomb lie my affections;
And with his spirits sadly I survive
To mock the expectation of the world, 125
To frustrate prophecies and to raze out
Rotten opinion, who hath writ me down
After my seeming. The tide of blood in me
Hath proudly flowed in vanity till now:

117 By adopting the Justice as a surrogate father, the King replaces his royal father, with whom he was reconciled only at his death, and also displaces Falstaff, who has provided a father figure less remote, more tolerant and more affectionate than his own. The way in which Harry wrestles with the authority of these three father figures has long been debated by psychoanalytic critics.

118 'My decisions will reflect your advice.'

119 **stoop and humble** bow and submit; a redundancy
my intents what I want to do

120 **well-practised** experienced

122–3 Harry asserts that he has buried his youthful misrule with his father; thus his father, as the receptacle of his son's riot, has 'gone wild into his grave'. Harry apparently believes in a consensual transfer of wildness from the prodigal son to the usurping father which permits the 'instantly reformed son to become the legitimate heir' (Crewe, 'Reforming', 236). The term *affections* signifies primarily the passions and riotous behaviour for which King Henry has upbraided his son (4.3.249–67), but it may also refer to

a natural disposition that now must be tutored by the civilizing influences of the court (*OED* affection *sb.* 3, 4). This speech bears a resemblance to Ephesians, 6.13–16, about shedding the old Adam and rising anew clad in 'the whole armour of God', and 'taking the shielde of faith, wherewith ye may quenche all the fierie dartes of the wicked'.

124 **spirits** character. The King suggests that he has replaced his own wild disposition with his father's more serious one (*his* spirits), an idea expanded at 128–32. In essence, he claims that he and his father have exchanged personae: the father has assumed the son's wildness in death; and in Harry, his father's sobriety survives.
sadly soberly, gravely

125 **mock** disprove

127–8 **who … seeming** 'which has reviled me because of the way I appeared'; *writ down* means condemned or disparaged (*OED* write *v.* 14b). The implication is that past behaviour has not painted a true picture of the new King.

128 **blood** passion

129 **proudly** vigorously: the image is of a swelling floodtide. Cf. *MND* 2.1.88–92:

118 ear] *QF* (eare)   126 raze] *Theobald;* race *QF;* rase *Pope;* 'rase *Capell*

Now doth it turn and ebb back to the sea,   130
Where it shall mingle with the state of floods
And flow henceforth in formal majesty.
Now call we our high court of parliament,
And let us choose such limbs of noble counsel
That the great body of our state may go   135
In equal rank with the best-governed nation,
That war or peace or both at once may be
As things acquainted and familiar to us,
In which you, father, shall have foremost hand.
Our coronation done, we will accite,   140
As I before remembered, all our state;
And, God consigning to my good intents,
No prince nor peer shall have just cause to say,
'God shorten Harry's happy life one day!'   ^F*Exeunt.*^F

'the winds . . . / . . . have suck'd up from the sea / Contagious fogs; which, falling in the land, / Hath every pelting river made so proud / That they have overborne their continents'.

131 **state of floods** majesty of oceans (Onions)

133 **we** From this point on, the King speaks of himself in the plural: following his assurances to his brothers and the Justice in the more familiar first person singular, he now shifts to a more public form of address to discuss matters of state.

134 **limbs . . . counsel** Cf. Holinshed: 'he chose men of grauitie, wit and high policie, by whose wise counsell he might at all times rule to his honour and dignitie' (3.543); *limbs* means members, anticipating the metaphor of the state as a body politic at 135.

135–6 **go . . . rank** march side by side. For a metaphor of the state as a body in less robust health, see 3.1.38–43.

137 **That** so that

139 **you, father** In performance, these words are almost always addressed to the Justice, assuring him yet again (cf. 117) that he has won the contest with Falstaff over who will be the young King's surrogate father and chief adviser. In some productions, however, the King looks away from the others to speak these words to the memory of the dead King, revealing an unresolved struggle with the father whose love he failed to win in life and whose will, for him, is still a dominant force. Harry's decision to act on his father's advice to make wars against France (5.5.104–7) lends some credibility to the idea that he addresses 137–9 to the memory of his father.

140 **accite** summon. Cf. 2.2.57.

141 **remembered** mentioned (*OED v.*¹ 3a)
state men of rank, noblemen (*OED sb.* 26a)

142 **consigning to** endorsing, setting His seal on (*OED v.* 5)

139 you] *Q(corr), F*; your *Q(uncorr)*   142 God] *Q*; heauen *F*   144 God] *Q*; Heauen *F*   SD] *F*; *exit. Q*

5.3   *Enter* Sir John ᶠFALSTAFFᶠ, SHALLOW, SILENCE,
DAVY, BARDOLPH [*and*] PAGE.

SHALLOW   Nay, you shall see my orchard, where, in an
arbour, we will eat a last year's pippin of mine own
graffing with a dish of caraways and so forth. Come,
cousin Silence, and then to bed.

FALSTAFF   'Fore God, you have here goodly dwelling,   5
and rich.

SHALLOW   Barren, barren, barren; beggars all, beggars
all, Sir John. Marry, good air. – Spread, Davy; spread,
Davy. [*Davy spreads a tablecloth.*] Well said, Davy.

FALSTAFF   This Davy serves you for good uses. He is   10
your serving-man and your husband.

5.3 The scene takes place in the garden of
Shallow's farm.

0.1–2 F's inclusion of Pistol, who does not
enter until 82, is the kind of anticipation
characteristic of F's block entrances at
2.2.0 and 4.1.0. Throughout the scene, as
in 3.2, Q uses the spellings 'Scilens' and
'Silens', thought to be idiosyncratically
Shakespearean, for Silence. Cf. 3.2.88n.
and pp. 439–40.

1   **orchard** See 1.1.4n.

2   **arbour** shady retreat; grassy plot of
ground
last year's pippin Humphreys cites
Thomas Cogan, *Haven of Health* (1584),
who considers 'pepins' among 'the best
Apples that we haue in England' and
advises that apples 'may be eaten with
least detriment, if they be gathered full
ripe, and well kept untill the next winter,
or the yeare following' (89).

3   **graffing** grafting. Cf. 2.2.60.

caraways sweets made with caraway
seeds, or just the seeds themselves. Cogan
(see 2n. on *last year's pippin*) cites flatu-
lence as the reason for eating them: 'We
are woont to eate Carawayes or Biskettes,
or some other kinde of Comfittes, or
seedes together with Apples, thereby to
breake winde engendred by them' (89).

5   **goodly** splendid or handsome, often with
reference to size

7–8   **Barren . . . air** With courteous modesty,
Shallow deflects Falstaff's compliment
by claiming that the land yields little and
its inhabitants live in poverty; all the
place has to recommend it, he claims, is
good air. Here and throughout, his most
notable speech habit is repetition: see
5.1.4–6n.

8   **Spread** set the table (*OED* v. 8b). Cf.
2.4.10n. (on *cover*).

9   **Well said** well done. Cf. 3.2.276.

11   **husband** steward or, in Davy's case,
manager of the farm

5.3] *Scene Tertia. F; not in Q*   0.1–2] *Q (Enter sir Iohn, Shallow, Scilens, Dauy, Bardolfe, page.);
Enter Falstaffe, Shallow, Silence, Bardolfe, Page, and Pistoll. F*   1 my] *Q; mine F*   2 mine] *Q; my F*
4 Silence] *F; Scilens Q (also at 37, 48, 52, 128)*   5 'Fore God] *Q; not in F*   5–6 goodly . . . rich] *Q;
a goodly . . . a rich F*   9 SD] *this edn; Davy begins to spread the table Oxf; not in QF*

SHALLOW   A good varlet, a good varlet, a very good
            varlet, Sir John. By the mass, I have drunk too much
            sack at supper! A good varlet. Now sit down, now sit
            down. [*to Silence*] Come, cousin.   15
SILENCE   Ah, sirrah, quoth 'a, we shall
            [*Sings.*] Do nothing but eat and make good cheer,
                        And praise God for the merry year,
                        When flesh is cheap and females dear,
                        And lusty lads roam here and there   20
                        So merrily,
                        And ever among so merrily.
FALSTAFF   There's a merry heart, good Master Silence!
            I'll give you a health for that anon.
SHALLOW   Give Master Bardolph some wine, Davy.   25
DAVY   Sweet sir, sit; I'll be with you anon. – Most sweet
            sir, sit. – Master Page, good Master Page, sit. – Proface!

12 **varlet** literally, servant; but Shallow may
    be playing affectionately on its derogatory
    meaning, knave. Cf. 2.1.45n.
16 **Ah, sirrah** an exclamation addressed to
    no one in particular and having the same
    force as 'Yes, sir!' F's spelling *Ah*
    regularizes Q's 'A'.
    quoth 'a said he – often the preface to a
    proverb; here, to a song
17–22 *All Silence's songs, or snatches of
    song, are printed as prose in QF, with the
    exception of 32–6 which appear as verse
    in F. Although only one of the songs (see
    73–5n.) can be identified, the others sound
    traditional and may have been familiar to
    an Elizabethan audience. John H. Long
    (86–9) speculates that the verses here and
    at 32–6 may be parts of the same Shrovetide
    wassail song, sung to the tune of 'Be
    merry, be merry'. See also Duffin, 63–4.
19 **flesh** meat

dear expensive, but also desirable. The
line contrasts the cheapness of meat with
the high price of women (presumably prostitutes), both marketable commodities.
22 **ever among** all the while
24 **give . . . health** drink to your health, lift a
    glass
26–7 **Sweet . . . ¹sit** Playing the role of host,
    Davy attempts to get the men to sit down,
    but who is specifically being addressed
    is unclear. The first addressee may be
    Bardolph, whom Shallow has asked him
    to serve (25); but other candidates are
    Falstaff and Shallow himself. Davy seems
    to address two different people before
    speaking to the Page and, beginning with
    Proface!, to address the guests in general.
27 **Proface** 'Welcome to it': a traditional
    salute spoken before a meal, from the
    obsolete French *bon prou vous fasse* (may
    it do you good)

13 By the mass] *Q; not in F*   15 SD] *Capell; not in QF*   16 Ah] *F, Q* (A)   17 SD] *Rowe subst. (also
at 32, 45, 73); not in QF*   17–22] *Rowe subst. (lines* chear / Year; / dear, / there: / merrily. /)*; prose QF*
18 God] *Q;* heauen *F*   21 merrily] *Q (*merely), *F*   23 Silence] *F;* Silens *Q*   25 Give Master Bardolph] *Q;*
Good M. *Bardolfe: F*

What you want in meat we'll have in drink, but you
must bear. The heart's all. [*Exit.*]

SHALLOW   Be merry, Master Bardolph; [*to Page*] and   30
my little soldier there, be merry.

SILENCE [*Sings.*]

> Be merry, be merry, my wife has all,
> For women are shrews, both short and tall.
> 'Tis merry in hall when beards wags all;
> And welcome merry Shrovetide!   35
> Be merry, be merry.

FALSTAFF   I did not think Master Silence had been a
man of this mettle.

SILENCE   Who, I? I have been merry twice and once ere
now.   40

Enter DAVY.

DAVY   There's a dish of leather-coats for you.

---

28 **What . . . drink** proverbial: 'What they
want in meat let them take in drink'
(Dent, M845)
want lack
meat food

29 **bear** put up with things as they are
The heart's all 'Good intentions are all
that count' (*OED* heart *sb.* 7).

32–6 On the origin of this song, see 17–22n.

34 The sentiment in this line (that talk and
laughter set men's beards wagging) was
proverbial – 'It is merry in hall when
beards wag all' (Dent, H55) – and found
as early as *Kyng Alisaunder* in 1312:
'Mery swithe it is in halle, / whan that
berdes waweth alle' (EETS, Orig. ser.
227, 67).
wags On the use of a singular verb with a
plural subject, see 1.1.33n.

35 **Shrovetide** the three days preceding Ash
Wednesday and the beginning of Lent, a
time for feasting and drinking

39 **merry** tipsy, pleasantly drunk. On the historical significance of *merry*, see pp. 88–90.
twice and once a stock inversion which
is a jocular way of saying 'now and then'.
If taken literally, however, the phrase
reveals how seldom Silence has been
inebriated or allowed himself to act
without inhibition. In performance, this
admission tends to arouse both humour
and pathos, especially if Silence is
played, as he so often is, as a decrepit old
man. But on Silence's age, see 3.2.210n.

41 **leather-coats** russet apples, so named for
their rough skin. It is unclear to whom, if
anyone in particular, Davy is offering
them.

29 must] *Q; not in F*   SD] *Theobald; not in QF*   30 SD] *this edn*   32–6] *Capell; F lines* all: / tall: / all;
/ merry. / ; *prose Q*   34 wags] *Q;* wagge *F*   38 mettle] *Q (*mettall*), F*   40.1] *Q; not in F*   41 There's] *Q;*
There is *F*

SHALLOW   Davy!

DAVY   Your worship, I'll be with you straight. – A cup
of wine, sir?

SILENCE [*Sings.*]

>   A cup of wine, that's brisk and fine,   45
>   And drink unto thee, leman mine;
>   And a merry heart lives long-a.

FALSTAFF   Well said, Master Silence.

SILENCE   And we shall be merry, now comes in the
sweet a'th' night.   50

FALSTAFF [*Drinks.*]   Health and long life to you, Master
Silence!

SILENCE [*Sings.*]

>   Fill the cup and let it come!
>   I'll pledge you a mile to th' bottom.

SHALLOW   Honest Bardolph, welcome! If thou want'st   55
anything and wilt not call, beshrew thy heart. [*to*

---

43 **straight** right away, immediately

43–4 **A cup . . . sir** Davy may offer the wine
to Bardolph, as Shallow has instructed
him to do at 25, but he probably fills
cups all round. Davy's attentive service
and assured control of the festivities
contrast with the ineptitude of the
drawers, especially Francis in *1H4* 2.4.
The same actor may have played Davy
and Francis.

45–7 No known setting for this drinking
song is extant, though Duffin (114–15)
offers two possible tunes that would fit
the metrical pattern of Silence's lines. See
also 53–4n.

46 **thee** QF's 'the' is a frequent Elizabethan
spelling of 'thee'.
   leman mistress, sweetheart

47 proverbial: 'A merry heart lives long'
(Dent, H320a). Cf. *LLL* 5.2.18: 'a light
heart lives long'.

49–50 **the . . . night** Cf. Falstaff's similar
sentiment at 2.4.372–3.

53–4 Though no original setting for these
lines exists, Duffin (145) suggests that
they may come from a second stanza of
'A cup of wine'. Alternatively, he offers a
melody from another 'Fill the cup' round
(which survives in the Lant Roll, 1580)
whose lyric matches the number of
syllables in Silence's lines.

53 **let it come** pass it round: a popular
drinking cry. Cf. *2H6* 2.3.66: 'Let it
come, i' faith, and I'll pledge you all'.

54 **pledge . . . bottom** drain the whole cup,
even if it is a mile deep: tavern cant also
used by Jonson in the 1601 Q of *Every
Man In* 5.3.153: 'I pledge M. Doctor and
't were a sea to the bottome'. Cf.
proverbial 'To set all a going if it were a
mile to the bottom' (Dent, A207).

55 **want'st** need. Cf. 28.

45–7] *Capell; Rowe lines* Wine, / fine, / mine; / long-a. / ; *prose QF*   46 thee,] *Cam¹*; the *QF*   49 And]
Q; If *F*   50 a'th'] *Q*; of the *F*   51 SD] *this edn; not in QF*   53–4] *Capell; prose QF*   54 to th'] *Q (too
th)*; to the *F*

Page] Welcome, my little tiny thief; and welcome
indeed, too. I'll drink to Master Bardolph and to all
the cabileros about London. [*Drinks.*]

DAVY   I hope to see London once ere I die.   60

BARDOLPH   An I might see you there, Davy!

SHALLOW   By the mass, you'll crack a quart together,
ha? Will you not, Master Bardolph?

BARDOLPH   Yea, sir, in a pottle-pot.

SHALLOW   By God's liggens, I thank thee. The knave   65
will stick by thee. I can assure thee that 'a will not
out, 'a; 'tis true bred!

BARDOLPH   And I'll stick by him, sir.

SHALLOW   Why, there spoke a king! Lack nothing; be
merry!   70

   One knocks at door.

Look who's at door there, ho! Who knocks?   [*Exit Davy.*]

FALSTAFF   Why, now you have done me right.

---

56   **call** ask for it
   beshrew See 2.3.45n.
57   **thief** scoundrel, said affectionately to the
   Page. See a similar use in *1H4*, when Lady
   Percy calls Hotspur a thief (3.1.231).
59   **cabileros** gallants, a humorous term for
   drinking companions; from the Spanish
   caballeros
60   **once** one day, or one time
61   **An** would that
62   **crack** drink, empty (*OED v.* 10)
64   **pottle-pot** two-quart tankard, double the
   size Shallow mentions at 62. Cf. 2.2.75.
65   **By God's liggens** As Cowl notes (Ard[1]),
   this oath is recorded nowhere else.
   Possibly *liggens* is a corruption of the
   diminutive for eye-lid, i.e. 'lidkins'. The
   expression 'By God's lid' occurs in *TC*
   1.2.203. A similar diminutive for 'God's
   body' was 'bodikins'.

66–7   **'a will . . . bred** He will not drop out
   (of a drinking bout) because he is a
   purebred. The implicit metaphor is of
   a hunting dog sticking with the pack or
   to the scent; but elsewhere Shakespeare
   applies the phrase to drinking, as when
   Lepidus vows, 'I am not so well as
   I should be, but I'll ne'er out' (*AC*
   2.7.30–1).
69   **there . . . king** i.e. well said. Possibly,
   too, Shallow's mention of a king's loyalty
   is an ironic anticipation that the new King
   will *not* 'stick by' his former companions.
72   **done me right** kept up with me in
   drinking. *Do me right* was a phrase commonly used to challenge a person to
   drink. Cf. Jonson, *Every Man Out*,
   5.4.79–81; Dekker, *1 Honest Whore*,
   1.5.167–8; and Marston, *Antonio and
   Mellida*, 5.2.26–7.

56–7 SD] *Capell (after* thief*); not in QF*   57 tiny] *Q, F (*tyne*), Rowe (*tyny*)*   59 cabileros] *Q;* Cauileroes *F*
SD] *Oxf subst.; not in QF*   61 An] *Q (*And*); If F*   62 By the mass] *Q; not in F*   64 Yea] *Q;* Yes *F*
65 By God's liggens,] *Q; not in F*   66 that 'a] *Q;* that. He *F*   67 out, 'a; 'tis] *Ard[2];* out, a tis *Q;* out, he
is *F*   70 SD] *Q (opp. 68); not in F*   71 Look who's] *Q;* Looke, who's *F*   SD] *Capell; not in QF*

SILENCE [*Sings.*]

> Do me right
> And dub me knight,
> Samingo.   75

Is't not so?

FALSTAFF   'Tis so.

SILENCE   Is't so? Why then, say an old man can do
somewhat.

[*Enter* DAVY.]

DAVY   An 't please your worship, there's one Pistol   80
come from the court with news.

FALSTAFF   From the court? Let him come in.

Enter PISTOL.

How now, Pistol?

PISTOL   Sir John, God save you.

FALSTAFF   What wind blew you hither, Pistol?   85

PISTOL   Not the ill wind which blows no man to good.

73–5 Silence sings the refrain of a popular
French drinking song, 'Monsieur Mingo',
set to music by Orlando di Lasso and
published in 1570. *Samingo* is Silence's
slurred pronunciation of Sir Mingo,
whose name derives from the Latin
mingo = 'I urinate' (Sisson, 2.54). The
song is thus about one Sir Pisser who is
knighted for his drinking capacity.
Snatches of it appear in plays by Jonson,
Chapman and Marston, and a fuller
text in Nashe's *Summer's Last Will and
Testament*, 968–71: '*Mounsieur Mingo
for quaffing doth surpasse, | In Cuppe,
in Canne, or glasse. | God Bacchus, doe*

*mee right, | And dubbe me Knight
Domingo*' (*Works*, 3.264). For the
complete musical setting, see Duffin,
263–5. The phrase *dub me knight* refers
to the Elizabethan tavern practice of
knighting, on his knees, whoever had
drunk the most sack.

79 **somewhat** something noteworthy (as a
drinker)

80 **An 't please** See 1.2.60n.

85 proverbial: 'What wind blows you
hither?' (Dent, W441)

86 Pistol answers Falstaff proverb for
proverb: 'It is an ill wind that blows no
man good' (Dent, W421).

73–5] Malone; prose QF   79.1] Capell subst.; not in QF   80 An't] Q (And't); If it F   82.1] F, Q (opp.
81)   84 God save you.] Q; 'saue you sir. F   86 no man] Q; none F   86–7 good. Sweet knight,] Q subst.;
good, sweet Knight: F

Sweet knight, thou art now one of the greatest men in
this realm.

SILENCE   By'r Lady, I think 'a be, but goodman Puff of
Bar'son.   90

PISTOL   Puff?

Puff i'thy teeth, most recreant coward base!
Sir John, I am thy Pistol and thy friend,
And helter skelter have I rode to thee;
And tidings do I bring, and lucky joys   95
And golden times and happy news of price.

FALSTAFF   I pray thee now, deliver them like a man of
this world.

PISTOL

A foutre for the world and worldlings base!
I speak of Africa and golden joys.   100

FALSTAFF

O base Assyrian knight, what is thy news?
Let King Cophetua know the truth thereof.

---

87 **greatest** Pistol means most powerful or
important, owing to Falstaff's relationship
with the new King, but Silence takes
him to mean biggest, as his comparison of
Falstaff with a fat man named Puff makes
clear (89).

89 **but** except for
goodman yeoman or farmer, below the
rank of gentleman

90 **Bar'son** Shakespeare may intend no particular place, but a Barston lies 15 miles
northeast of Stratford-upon-Avon, and a
Barcheston-on-the-Stour (locally pronounced
'Bar'son'), 10 miles to the southeast.

91, 92 **Puff** Pistol, altering the name to a verb
meaning to boast or swagger, turns it
against Silence as an insult.

92 **recreant** faint-hearted, dishonourable

94 **helter skelter** in disorderly haste

96 **of price** of great value (*OED* price *sb.* 7)

97–8 **like … world** 'as an ordinary mortal
would'; i.e. in plain English

99 **A foutre** a phrase of contempt stronger
than a 'fig' (cf. 118), from the French
foutre meaning to fuck: so, 'Fuck the
world and all the people in it!'

100 **Africa** a source of fabulous wealth in
the two parts of Marlowe's *Tamburlaine*,
which exerted a strong influence on
Pistol's rant in 2.4.157–200.

101 **Assyrian** a biblical term with which
Falstaff begins his mimicry of Pistol's
bombastic style. Assyrians were identified as brigands by Elizabethans, and in
drama were sometimes associated with
luxury and excess (Oxf[1]), as in Jonson's
Masque of Queenes, 766: 'Th' *Assyrian*
pompe, the *Persian* pride'.

102 **King Cophetua** The legend of this
African king, who 'cared not for

---

88 this] *Q;* the *F*   89 By'r Lady] *Q;* Indeed *F*   'a] *Q;* he *F*   92–6] *Pope; prose QF*   92 i'thy] *Neilson;*
ith thy *Q;* in thy *F*   94 And] *Q; not in F*   97 pray thee] *Q;* prethee *F*   99–102] *F; prose Q*
102 Cophetua] *Pope;* Couetua *Q;* Couitha *F*

SILENCE [*Sings.*]
> And Robin Hood, Scarlet and John.

PISTOL
> Shall dunghill curs confront the Helicons?
> And shall good news be baffled?   105
> Then, Pistol, lay thy head in Fury's lap!

SHALLOW   Honest gentleman, I know not your breeding.

PISTOL   Why then, lament therefor.

SHALLOW   Give me pardon, sir. If, sir, you come with
news from the court, I take it there's but two ways: 110
either to utter them or conceal them. I am, sir, under
the King in some authority.

PISTOL
> Under which king, besonian? Speak or die!

SHALLOW
> Under King Harry.

---

womenkind' yet fell in love with and married a beggar girl, was the subject of a popular ballad, 'A Song of a Beggar and a King', first printed in Richard Johnson's *Crowne Garland of Goulden Roses* (1612) but cited repeatedly before then by Shakespeare: cf. *LLL* 1.2.104–5 and 4.1.65–79; *RJ* 2.1.14; and *R2* 5.3.79. For the history and a complete setting of the ballad, see Duffin, 235–40.

103 A line from the second stanza of a ballad printed in 1632 as 'Robin Hood and the Jolly Pinder of Wakefield' (Child, 3.131): see J. Long, 92. For an earlier setting of fragments of a Robin Hood song contemporary with the play, see Duffin, 339–41.

104 Pistol, irritated by Silence's interruption, calls him a dog ('cur') who lives in a shitpile (*dunghill*) for daring to match wits against his own inspired muse. *Helicons* refers to the Muses who, in Greek mythology, lived on the sacred Mount Helicon.

105 **baffled** foiled, treated so disrespectfully. Cf. *TN* 5.1.363: 'Alas, poor fool. How have they baffled thee!'

106 **lay . . . lap** give yourself up to the forces of revenge. The Furies were mythological creatures who punished those who broke natural or moral laws. Pistol calls on one of them again at 5.5.35.

108 **therefor** for that (i.e. your ignorance)

113 **besonian** base fellow, beggar or, in military parlance, a recruit of the lowest rank: a term of contempt derived from the Italian *bisognoso* through the Spanish *bisoño*, meaning a soldier who lacked both skill and training – one of many Spanish military terms which, according to Cowl (Ard[1]), infiltrated English in the 16th century. Cf. Robert Barret, who, in *Theorike and Practike of Moderne Warres* (1598), repeatedly refers to Besonians as 'rawe men' (16) with no expertise in weaponry (Ard[2]).

---

103 SD] *Johnson; not in QF*   104–6] *F; prose Q*   107] *Q; F lines* Gentleman, / breeding. /   108 therefor] *Bullen;* therefore *QF*   109 Give . . . sir.] *Q; separate line F*   110 there's] *Q;* there is *F*   111 or] *Q;* or to *F*   113] king, besonian?] *Q;* King? / *Bezonian, F*   114–15] *Steevens; four prose lines QF*

PISTOL   Harry the Fourth or Fifth?

SHALLOW

   Harry the Fourth.

PISTOL   A foutre for thine office!   115

   Sir John, thy tender lambkin now is King.

   Harry the Fifth's the man! I speak the truth.

   When Pistol lies, do this [*Makes the fig.*]

      and fig me like

   The bragging Spaniard.

FALSTAFF   What, is the old King dead?

PISTOL

   As nail in door. The things I speak are just.   120

FALSTAFF   Away, Bardolph! Saddle my horse! Master

   Robert Shallow, choose what office thou wilt in the

   land; 'tis thine! Pistol, I will double charge thee with

   dignities.

BARDOLPH   O joyful day! I would not take a ᶠknighthoodᶠ   125

   for my fortune!

PISTOL   What? I do bring good news.

FALSTAFF [*to Davy*]   Carry Master Silence to bed.

                              [*Exeunt Davy and Silence.*]

---

115 **A ... office** Pistol tells Shallow that his
   position as Justice of the Peace is worthless. At the death of a king, all judicial
   offices were terminated (Cam¹), and Pistol
   implies that the new king will fill them
   with his cronies. For *foutre*, see 99n.

118–19 **do ... Spaniard** To *fig*, an insult
   akin to 'giving the finger' (or two) in contemporary Western cultures, meant to
   make an obscene gesture by thrusting the
   thumb between the index and middle
   fingers or, alternatively, into the mouth. A
   variant of the verb *foutre* (99, 115), 'fig'
   derived from the Spanish *higos dar* –
   hence the 'bragging Spaniard'.

120 **As ... door** proverbial: 'As dead as a
   doornail' (Dent, D567)
   just true

122–3 **choose ... thine** Falstaff's reassurance that Shallow may have the office of
   his choice counters Pistol's insult at 115.

123 **double charge** overload – a play on
   charging (loading) a pistol. Cf. similar
   puns on Pistol's name at 2.4.112–17.

127 **What** See 5.1.2n.

128–37 Falstaff's torrent of staccato commands and ejaculations indicates the
   excitement of the moment. Coming at the
   end of a leisurely scene, they imply a
   great deal of stage business – carrying

116–19] *F; prose Q*   118 SD] *Oxf subst.; not in QF*   120] *prose Q; F lines* doore. / iust. /   121–4] *prose*
Q; F lines Horse, / wilt / thee / Dignities. /   125–6] *prose Q; F lines* day: / Fortune. /   125 knighthood]
F; Knight *Q*   128 SD1] *Oxf¹*   128 SD2] *Oxf subst.; not in QF*

411

Master Shallow – my Lord Shallow – be what thou
wilt: I am Fortune's steward. Get on thy boots; we'll   130
ride all night. O sweet Pistol! Away, Bardolph!
                                                    [Exit Bardolph.]
Come, Pistol, utter more to me, and withal devise
something to do thyself good. Boot, boot, Master
Shallow!   *[Exit Shallow.]*
I know the young King is sick for me. Let us take   135
any man's horses: the laws of England are at my
commandment. Blessed are they that have been my
friends, and woe to my Lord Chief Justice!
                                                    [Exit with Page.]

Silence to bed, going off to saddle the
horses, putting on boots – which concludes the scene in ecstatic confusion.

128 *probably addressed to Davy, since
Shallow, Pistol and Bardolph are given
commands in subsequent lines. This
instruction serves not only as a SD but
also as a cue that Silence will not be a
part of the retinue accompanying Falstaff
to London. Although some productions
include him in 5.5, Silence appropriately
makes his final exit here.

128–38 SDs *Typically, in performance,
Falstaff, Shallow, Silence, Pistol and
Davy exit as a group at the end of the
scene; but the staggered exits indicated
here are appropriate to the moment and
add dramatic intensity, leaving Pistol
alone onstage to deliver his final lines.

130 **Fortune's steward** the chief admin-
istrator of Fortune's estate; i.e. the person
in control of others' futures

132 **withal** in addition

133–4 **Boot . . . Shallow** Falstaff's repeated
injunction for Shallow to hurry off and
put on his boots for travel (130–4)
should be sufficient motivation for him to
exit. In the urgency to depart for London,
he would be unlikely to linger onstage
after this (GWW).

135 **sick** longing

135–6 **Let . . . horses** According to Davison,
it is conceivable that Falstaff means only
to conscript horses in the King's name,
which would require the owners to forgo
a hiring fee but not ownership of the
horses themselves. Nevertheless, given
Falstaff's bravado, especially in the following line, audiences are justified in
thinking that he means to steal horses for
the trip to London. Falstaff is clearly
speaking this and the following lines to
Pistol, one of his accomplices, and not
to Shallow, who fawningly trusts in
Falstaff's integrity.

136–7 **the laws . . . commandment** This line,
more than any other, might have prepared
an Elizabethan audience for Falstaff's
rejection in 5.5. By arrogating all power
unto himself, Falstaff oversteps the bounds
beyond which even a king was not allowed
to go; for, according to Holinshed, among
the grievances urged against Richard II to
justify his deposition was his claim that
'all the lawes of England should come
foorth of his mouth' (3.432) and that
'neither law, iustice, nor equitie could
take place, where the kings wilfull will
was bent vpon any wrongfull purpose'
(3.496). To contemporary sensibilities,

131 SD] *Capell; not in QF*   134 SD] *this edn (GWW); not in QF*   137 Blessed . . . that] *Q;*
Happie . . . which *F*   138 to] *Q;* vnto *F*   SD] *this edn (GWW); not in QF*

PISTOL

  Let vultures vile seize on his lungs also!

  'Where is the life that late I led,' say they?   140

  Why, here it is! Welcome these pleasant days!   *Exit.*

5.4   *Enter* ^FBeadles^F [*dragging in*] ^FHOSTESS Quickly^F
               [*and*] ^FDOLL Tearsheet^F.

HOSTESS No, thou arrant knave, I would to God that
  I might die that I might have thee hanged! Thou
  hast drawn my shoulder out of joint.

therefore, Falstaff's presumption would have sounded shockingly anarchic.

137–8 **Blessed . . . friends** a phrase patterned on Scripture: e.g. Matthew, 5.5: 'Blessed are the meek'

138 **woe . . . Justice** Cf. *Famous Victories*, sc. 9, in which Oldcastle, upon hearing news of the King's death, exclaims 'we shall all be kings!', and Ned boasts, 'I shall be Lord Chief Justice of England' (7, 8). Since Harry has already embraced the Justice as his father and counsellor, Falstaff's line is heavily though unwittingly ironic, and so hubristic that even his staunchest defender condemns him for it: 'After this we ought not to complain if we see Poetic Justice duly executed upon him, and that he is finally given up to shame and dishonour' (Morgann, *Falstaff*, 179; cited in Ard²).

139 an allusion to either of two possible myths: that of Prometheus, who, as punishment for stealing the fire of the gods, was chained to a rock and every day suffered an eagle to gnaw out his liver, which grew back at night; or that of Tityus, a giant who, as punishment for trying to rape the mother of Apollo and Artemis, was consigned to Hades where two vultures tore out his liver. The myths are found in Virgil, *Aen.*, 6.595–600, and Ovid, *Met.*, 4.457–8; but numerous references to them occur in plays of the period, and even Pistol alludes to them again in *MW* 1.3.82: 'Let vultures gripe thy guts!'

140 **Where . . . led** a line from a lost poem or ballad, perhaps the one registered in March 1566 as 'A New ballad of one who misliking his liberty sought his own bondage through his own folly' (Duffin, 453). The line is also quoted in *TS* 4.1.127.

5.4 The scene occurs on a street outside the tavern in Eastcheap.

0.1–2 *The Hostess's opening lines indicate that she and Doll are being dragged onto the stage by the Beadles, not without a struggle. Q's SD looks authorial in its mistaken omission of the Hostess and Doll, in the indeterminacy of its numbers ('*three or foure officers*'), and in naming Sincklo both here and in all those SPs that F assigns to the Beadle. John Sincklo (or Sinclair) was the actor Shakespeare must have intended for the role. His skeletal thinness and pale complexion made him an easy comic butt, as the Hostess's and Doll's insults make clear; and he may have doubled in two other roles requiring an emaciated actor, Snare and Shadow.

139–41] *F; prose Q*   139 vile] *Q;* vil'de *F*   141 these] *Q;* those *F*   SD] *Q; Exeunt F*   **5.4**] *Scena Quarta. F; not in Q*   0.1–2] *Ard²; Enter Hostesse Quickly, Dol Teare-sheete, and Beadles. F; Enter Sincklo and three or foure officers. Q*   0.1 *dragging in*] *Capell*   1 to God that] *Q; not in F*

413

BEADLE   The constables have delivered her over to me,
and she shall have whipping-cheer, I warrant her.   5
There hath been a man or two killed about her.
DOLL   Nut-hook, nut-hook, you lie! Come on. I'll tell
thee what, thou damned tripe-visaged rascal: an the

Because Sincklo is not listed among the 'Principall Actors' in the 1623 Folio, he is likely to have played only minor character parts for the Lord Chamberlain's Men; but unusually, he is mentioned by name in the SDs of several other plays: in two earlier plays by Shakespeare, as a Keeper in *3H6* 3.1.0 and as a Player in *TS* Ind.98 (F); in the plot of Dekker's *2 Seven Deadly Sins*; and in the Induction (17 SD) to Marston's *The Malcontent*, acquired by the King's Men in 1604. Davison speculates that Shakespeare wrote other roles for him as well, such as Pinch in *CE*, Holofernes in *LLL* and the Apothecary in *RJ*.

0.1 **Beadles** sheriff's officers, under-bailiffs empowered to punish petty offences. Cf. *KL* 4.6.156–7: 'Thou, rascal beadle, hold thy bloody hand; / Why dost thou lash that whore?'

1 **arrant** See 2.1.38n.

2 **that ... hanged** so that you would be hanged as a result. The Hostess argues that the Beadle's rough manhandling of her ought to be punished. If it were to result in her accidental death, as she threatens here, he would be tried and executed.

3 **drawn ... joint** Constables and other officers of the law were noted for grabbing offenders by the shoulder. Cf. Chapman, *May Day*, in which sergeants are called 'peuter-button'd shoulder-clappers' (4.1.21).

5 **whipping-cheer** a '"banquet" of lashes with the whip' (Onions): *cheer* = a meal. Whipping was the standard punishment for whores.

I warrant her See 2.1.22n.

6 **about her** either (1) on account of her, or (2) in her company. In either case, Doll's alleged involvement in the death of one or two men comes as disturbing, if not surprising, news. Quarrels in brothels that resulted in killing were not uncommon (Ard[1]): cf. Dekker, *1 Honest Whore*, 3.3.77–80, 'O how many thus / ... haue let out / Their soules in Brothell houses, fell downe and dyed / Iust at their Harlots foot'. If Doll is seriously implicated in a capital offence (see 15–17 and n.), however, it is odd that she has been handed over to a beadle, who punishes non-felonious crimes, rather than brought before a justice.

7 **Nut-hook** hooked pole, similar to a shepherd's crook, used to pull down branches for gathering nuts; figuratively applied to constables and beadles (who were also called *catchpoles*), and particularly apt for this beadle who, as played by Sincklo, would have looked as thin as a pole

8 **tripe-visaged** with a face like *tripe* (the stomach of a cow, goat, or sheep which, when boiled and bleached for eating, took on a whitish colour), and therefore pale or pock-marked

8–9 **an ... with** 'if the child in my belly'. Doll's claiming pregnancy, while comic, nevertheless reminds us that pregnancy was the only condition that could spare a condemned woman, at least until the birth of her child, from corporal punishment and hanging.

4+ SP] *Rowe (Bead.), Malone; Sincklo. Q; Off. F*   5 whipping-cheer] *Q (whipping cheere);* Whipping cheere enough *F*   6 killed] *Q; (lately)* kill'd *F*   7 SP+] *F (Dol.); Whoore Q*   8 an] *Q (and);* if *F*

child I go with do miscarry, thou wert better thou
hadst struck thy mother, thou paper-faced villain!　　10

HOSTESS　O the Lord, that Sir John were come! I would
make this a bloody day to somebody. But I pray God
the fruit of her womb miscarry.

BEADLE　If it do, you shall have a dozen of cushions
again. You have but eleven now. Come, I charge you　　15
both go with me, for the man is dead that you and
Pistol beat amongst you.

DOLL　I'll tell you what, you thin man in a censer, I will

9–10 **thou ... mother** 'it would be better
for you to have hit your mother'; figuratively, 'you'll have hell to pay'. Doll's
warning, probably an idle threat, may be
meant to imply that the child is Falstaff's.
Cf. the Hostess's warning at 11–13.

10 **paper-faced** pale, sallow. Cf. 8n.

11 **I** Though F's 'hee' may be the preferable
reading because it explains why the
Hostess wishes that Falstaff were there,
Q's *I* is both playable and intelligible.

12 **make ... somebody** i.e. 'get even with
you' or 'make you pay for this'. The
phrase is akin to the proverbial 'To be
(make) a black (bloody) day to somebody'
(Dent, D88). Cf. *R3* 5.3.280: 'A black day
will it be to somebody.'

13 **fruit of her womb** a common biblical
phrase: e.g. Psalms, 127.3: 'The fruite of
the wombe' (Geneva Bible)
miscarry a typical blunder for Quickly,
if, as seems likely, she means *not* miscarry

14–15 **a dozen ... now** The beadle insinuates
that Doll's stuffing a cushion up her gown
to feign pregnancy has left the Hostess
with only 11. In performance, the Beadle
sometimes struggles to reach up inside
Doll's gown and pull the cushion out –
stage business which may be played for
laughs or gasps, depending on how violently it is executed.

15–17 **Come ... you** The beating and subsequent death of a man help to explain the
reference to 'a man or two killed' at 6.
Whether the Hostess was involved in the
beating is unclear. In 4–6, it appears that
only Doll is implicated and arrested; yet
amongst you (17) is an ambiguous phrase
which may implicate the Hostess as well,
who after all is charged to go with the
Beadle (15–16), presumably to prison.
Her ownership of the tavern where the
death occurred might provide sufficient
grounds for her arrest. Pistol's involvement in the beating is not mentioned
again, nor is he arrested for this reason in
5.5; yet the surprising evidence of his
continued patronage of the Hostess's
tavern after his eviction in 2.4 may lay
the groundwork for their being married
in *H5*.

18–21 Doll never completes her first sentence: *as soundly swinged* requires another
'as' phrase; but as she gets carried away
with epithets for the Beadle, she forgets
the logic of her syntax, returns to the
same verb now in a subjunctive clause,
and concludes a new sentence vowing to
forswear half-kirtles.

18 **thin ... censer** figure embossed on an
incense burner. Shakespeare frequently
compared low-relief figures on coins,

---

9 I] *Q;* I now *F*　wert] *Q;* had'st *F*　11 the Lord] *Q; not in F*　I] *Q;* hee *F*　12 pray God] *Q;* would *F*
13 womb] *Q;* Wombe might *F*　17 amongst] *Q;* among *F*　18 you ... you] *Q;* thee ... thou *F*

have you as soundly swinged for this – you bluebottle
rogue, you filthy famished correctioner! If you be   20
not swinged, I'll forswear half-kirtles.

BEADLE   Come, come, you she-knight-errant, come!

HOSTESS   O God, that right should thus overcome
might! Well, of sufferance comes ease.

DOLL   Come, you rogue, come; bring me to a justice.   25

HOSTESS   Ay, come, you starved bloodhound.

DOLL   Goodman death! Goodman bones!

HOSTESS   Thou atomy, thou!

DOLL   Come, you thin thing. Come, you rascal.   29

BEADLE   Very well.   *ᶠExeunt.*ᶠ

---

brooches and flasks to thin men. Cf.
3.2.265–6, *1H4* 1.3.207, *LLL* 5.2.606–11
and *KJ* 1.1.141–3. Here begins Doll's
series of attacks on the Beadle's thinness.

19, 21 **swinged** thrashed; pronounced with a
soft *g*

19 **bluebottle** anachronistic reference to the
blue coats worn by Elizabethan beadles

20 **correctioner** officer who inflicts punishment at the so-called House of Correction
at Bridewell. The Beadle's taking these
women to Bridewell would reinforce the
idea that their crime was a misdemeanour,
not a felony, and that they are being
rounded up as part of an effort to purge
London of its baser elements, those *misleaders* of the Prince whose banishment
is confirmed at 5.5.62–4.

21 **forswear half-kirtles** give up wearing
skirts. Since a *kirtle* consisted of a skirt
and bodice (see 2.4.277n.), a *half-kirtle*
was the skirt alone (Cam²). Although Doll
uses the expression to attest to the sincerity of her threat, the line is humorously
ironic, since Doll, in her line of work,
would be out of her kirtle as much as she
is in it.

22 **she-knight-errant** In medieval romance,
a knight errant wandered about in search
of adventure: *errant* is from the Latin
verb for travel or wander. The Beadle
punningly calls Doll both a heroine of
romance and a woman who *errs* (walks
the streets, sins) at night (*knight*); thus, a
night-wandering prostitute.

23–4 **right ... might** As at 13, the Hostess
says the opposite of what she means and
in so doing garbles the proverb 'Might
overcomes right' (Dent, M922).

24 **of ... ease** proverbial (Dent, S955),
meaning that suffering will merit a
heavenly reward

27 For *Goodman*, see 5.3.89n.; *death* and
bones imply that the Beadle looks cada-
verous. The images invoke the medieval
memento mori.

28 **atomy** a Quicklyism for 'anatomy', meaning skeleton; but *atomy* is ironically appropriate too, as the Elizabethan form for
'atom', meaning a mote or a diminutive
being. F misses the joke and prints
'anatomy'.

29 **rascal** lean deer. See Doll's use of the
term at 2.4.40.

---

19 bluebottle] *Q* (blewbottle*); blew-Bottel'd *F*   23 God] *Q; not in F*   overcome] *Q;* o'recome *F*   25] *Q;
F lines* come: / Iustice. /   26 Ay, come] *Capell;* I come *Q;* Yes, come *F*   28 atomy] *Q;* Anatomy *F*
29] *Q; F lines* Thing: / Rascall. /   30 SD] *F; not in Q*

5.5　　　　　*Enter [three]* Strewers *of rushes.*

1 STREWER　　More rushes, more rushes!
2 STREWER　　The trumpets have sounded twice.
3 STREWER　　'Twill be two a'clock ere they come from
　　the coronation. Dispatch, dispatch!　　　　　*ᶠExeunt.ᶠ*

Trumpets sound, and the KING *and his train pass over
the stage. After them enter* FALSTAFF, SHALLOW,
PISTOL, BARDOLPH *and the* Boy [PAGE].

FALSTAFF　　Stand here by me, Master Shallow! I will　　　　5

5.5 The location is a street near Westminster Abbey. Though there is no historical source for the scene, it is based loosely on *Famous Victories*, sc. 9, in which Harry's former companions rejoice at his succession (cf. 5.3.116–37) before being banished by the new King, and the bishops encourage the King to wage war against France after the episode of the tennis balls (cf. *H5* 1.2.259–98). Holinshed reports that the King 'banished' his 'misrulie mates of dissolute order and life from his presence (but not vnrewarded or else vnpreferred) inhibiting them vpon a great paine, not once to approch, lodge, or soiourne within ten miles of his court or presence' (3.543).

0.1 *Q indicates that three strewers of rushes were intended by listing them in SPs as 1, 2 and 3 (see t.n.). As with the drawers in 2.4, however, F reduces the number of strewers from three to two. This may reflect an economy of staging or may have been a scribe's attempt to tidy up the text. As Davison observes, rushes were strewn on streets as a sign of deference before the passing of a royal procession.

4.1–3 *Q has two royal processions: this one, apparently *en route* to the King's coronation at Westminster Abbey, and another returning from it at 38. F omits both the first procession and, since there is now no need for the Strewers to hurry, the command to 'dispatch' (4). Two possible reasons for the omission have been offered. First, as Jowett argues (285), it may reflect the exigencies of casting. Second, the Third Strewer's statement that the procession will come *from* the coronation (3–4) could anticipate its arrival at 38 and make its first appearance unnecessary. The trumpets sound twice, however; first (4) signalling that the King and his party are on their way to Westminster Abbey, and after some time (37) signalling that the coronation is over and that they are returning. Thus it is likely that Shakespeare intended two processions. Pageantry and rich costumes were popular with audiences, and he was not one to forgo such effects, as the coronation procession in *H8* makes clear.

5.5] *Scene Quinta. F; not in Q*　0.1] *Q; Enter two Groomes. F; Enter certain Grooms, strewing Rushes. / Capell; Enter three Grooms, strewing rushes. / Dyce²*　1 SP] *Q (1);* 1. *Groo. F*　2 SP] *Q (2);* 2. *Groo. F*　3 SP] *Q (3);* 1. *Groo. F*　'Twill] *Q;* It will *F*　a'clock] *Q (a clocke);* of the Clocke *F;* o' clock *Capell*　4 Dispatch, dispatch!] *Q; not in F*　SD] *F (Exit Groo.), F3 (Exeunt Groomes.); not in Q*　4.1–3] *Q; Enter Falstaffe, Shallow, Pistoll, Bardolfe, and Page. F*　5 Master Shallow] *Q (maister);* M. *Robert Shallow F*

make the King do you grace. I will leer upon him as
'a comes by, and do but mark the countenance that
he will give me.

PISTOL   God bless thy lungs, good knight!

FALSTAFF   Come here, Pistol; stand behind me. [*to*   10
Shallow] O, if I had had time to have made new
liveries, I would have bestowed the thousand pound
I borrowed of you! But 'tis no matter. This poor show
doth better; this doth infer the zeal I had to see him.

PISTOL   It doth so.   15

FALSTAFF   It shows my earnestness of affection –

PISTOL   It doth so.

6   **do you grace** honour you, presumably
with a high office
     leer upon him cast a knowing glance at
him, to catch his attention. As a subject
Falstaff *ought* to bow his head when the
King passes.

7   **countenance** approving look, favour
(*OED sb.* 4, 8)

11–12   **have . . . liveries** that is, to have them
made, so that Falstaff and his cronies
could have dressed for the occasion.
Liveries are uniforms of royal service.

12   **bestowed** spent

12–13   **thousand . . . you** We learn here that
Falstaff has succeeded in defrauding
Shallow (cf. 3.2.326–31, 4.2.126–9) of
the same amount he had earlier begged
from the Lord Chief Justice (1.2.222–3).
Although he has apparently not yet spent
the money (11–12), he later claims to be
unable to refund it to Shallow (72–6), a
contradiction which suggests either that
he has already spent it on something other
than new liveries for his friends, or that
he intends to.

13   **poor show** ordinary apparel

14   **infer** imply, demonstrate

15   SP *Although Falstaff has probably
addressed the previous lines to Shallow

(the *you* at 13), Q has Pistol respond to
them. It is conceivable that Falstaff
addresses 'But . . . him' (13–14) either
more generally to those assembled or
even to Pistol in particular, making Q's
assignment of 15 logical. Some editors,
however, assign not only 15 but also 17
and 19 to Shallow, arguing that these
lines reveal Shallow's habit of repeating
himself and must have been intended for
him (see 5.1.4–6n.). Others, following F,
assign 15 to Shallow and rationalize that
Pistol is mimicking him in 17 and 19.
Weis, who follows Q in assigning all
three lines to Pistol, suggests that his
rapid-fire exchange with Falstaff is a
way of prompting the reluctant Shallow
to agree with them, as he finally does
at 23, and thus to distract him from
asking where the money has gone. But
Pistol's rush to answer Falstaff also
reveals his impatience to tell him the
news of Doll's arrest – news that must
await the conclusion of Falstaff's conversation with Shallow, which Pistol
in effect is trying to interrupt. Pistol's
delivery of the lines, therefore, is
probably more urgent than calculated,
a form of butting in.

7 'a] *Q; he F*   9 God] *Q; not in F*   10–11 SD] *Collier; not in QF*   13 'tis] *Q; it is F*   15 SP] *Q; Shal. F*
16 of] *Q; in F*   17, 19 SPs] *QF; Shal. / Betterton*

FALSTAFF   My devotion –

PISTOL   It doth, it doth, it doth.

FALSTAFF   As it were to ride day and night and not to   20
deliberate, not to remember, not to have patience to
shift me –

SHALLOW   It is best, certain.

^FFALSTAFF^F   – but to stand stained with travel and sweat-
ing with desire to see him, thinking of nothing else,   25
putting all affairs else in oblivion, as if there were
nothing else to be done but to see him.

PISTOL   'Tis *semper idem*, for *absque hoc nihil est*; 'tis
in every part.

SHALLOW   'Tis so indeed.   30

PISTOL   My knight, I will inflame thy noble liver and
make thee rage! Thy Doll and Helen of thy noble
thoughts is in base durance and contagious prison,

---

21 **remember** i.e. how I am dressed
22 **shift me** change my clothes
24 SP *Q's omission of a new SP is
inadvertent, and perhaps a compositorial
error, for the lines clearly do not belong to
Shallow. Rather, they continue Falstaff's
rationalization, begun at 13, for appearing
so dishevelled and meanly attired before
the new King.
28 *semper idem* 'ever the same': a Latin
motto popular with Queen Elizabeth
absque . . . est 'apart from this, there is
nothing'. QF's '*obsque*' is a spelling
error, probably introduced by a compositor, for *absque*, a common Latin
preposition.
28–9 **'tis . . . part** a rough translation of the
second Latin phrase, possibly allied with
the proverb 'All in all and all in every
part' (Dent, A133), which expressed

absolute perfection. F adds 'all', perhaps
to bring Pistol's sentiment in line with the
proverb.
31–6 As Pistol's lines echo the fustian
spoken in old heroic plays, editors since
Pope have understandably tried to divide
them into something approximating verse
lines. But they have failed: metrically the
lines are so irregular that Q and F rightly
print them as prose.
31 **liver** the seat of passion. Cf. 1.2.176–7,
4.2.102–3.
32–3 **Helen . . . thoughts** your own Helen
of Troy. The name of Helen, a woman so
beautiful that the Greeks and Trojans
went to war over her, was often used
humorously for wives or mistresses.
33 **durance** confinement
contagious foul, noxious

20–2] *prose Q; F lines* night, / remember, / me. /   23 best,] *Q; most F*   24 SP] *F; not in Q   – but] this edn;
. But F; : but Q*   26 else] *Q; not in F*   28 absque] *F2; obsque QF*   'tis] *Q; 'Tis all F*   31–2] My . . . rage!]
prose QF; Johnson lines liver, / rage. /   31 inflame] *Q, F (*enflame*)*   32–6 Thy . . . truth.] *prose QF; Pope
lines* thoughts / prison; / hands. / snake, / truth. / ; *Capell lines* thoughts, / prison; / thither / hand: – / snake,
/ truth. /

haled thither by most mechanical and dirty hand.
Rouse up Revenge from ebon den with fell Alecto's   35
snake, for Doll is in. Pistol speaks nought but truth.

FALSTAFF   I will deliver her.

> *[Shouts within.]* ᶠ*Trumpets sound.*ᶠ

PISTOL

There roared the sea, and trumpet clangour sounds.

> *Enter the* KING *and his train*[, *his* ᶠBrothers,ᶠ
> *the* ᶠLord Chief JUSTICEᶠ *and others*].

FALSTAFF

God save thy grace, King Hal, my royal Hal!

PISTOL   The heavens thee guard and keep, most royal   40
imp of fame!

---

34   **haled** violently dragged (*OED* hale v.[1] 1b). Q's 'halde' might conceivably be a compositor's erroneous reading of 'haul'd', since 'haul' was spelled 'hall', as in F, until the 17th century (Ard[2]). It is curious that Pistol himself has not been arrested, since, according to the Beadle at 5.4.16–17, he is as guilty as Doll of beating a man to death. But his crime is never mentioned again; and here, his indignation is all on behalf of Doll.
mechanical base, vulgar; characteristic of a manual labourer. Cf. 'rude mechanicals' in *MND* 3.2.9.

35   **Rouse up Revenge** a probable echo of Kyd's *Spanish Tragedy*, in which the Ghost of Andrea repeatedly enjoins the character Revenge to take action with 'Awake, Revenge!' (3.15.8, 10, 29)
ebon den dark cave; i.e. hell
fell terrible, dreadful. Cf. 4.3.335.
Alecto's snake Alecto is one of the three Furies described by Virgil (*Aen.*, 7.346)

as having snakes writhing in their hair. Cf. 5.3.106n. and *AC*, 'Thou shouldst come like a Fury crowned with snakes' (2.5.40).
in in prison (*OED adv.* 6a)

38   a metaphor for the roar of approval heard when crowds lining the street catch a glimpse of the new King
trumpet clangour sounds 'A blast or clang of trumpets is heard', marking the return of the royal procession from Westminster Abbey.

39   **King Hal** Falstaff's calling the new King by his nickname is evidence of how profoundly he misunderstands both the nature of the occasion and how his world has changed. The familiarity of 'Prince Hal' was possible in the tavern; *King Hal* is an unforgivable breach of decorum. Cf. 5.2.49n. and A. Barton, 113–15.

41   **imp of fame** scion of a noble house (*OED sb.* 3). Cf. Peele, *Battle of Alcazar*, 2.1.374: 'the impe of roiall race'. The

---

34 haled] *Q (*halde*); Hall'd F1–3; Hal'd F4; Hauld Pope*   36 truth] *Q;* troth *F*   37 SD *Shouts within.*] *Steevens⁴; not in QF   Trumpets sound.*] *F (after 38); not in Q*   38.1–2 *Enter . . . train*] *Q; Enter King Henrie the Fift, Brothers, Lord Chiefe Iustice. F*   39 God] *Q; not in F*   40–1] *QF; Cam² lines* keep, / fame. /

FALSTAFF   God save thee, my sweet boy!

KING

My Lord Chief Justice, speak to that vain man.

JUSTICE (*to Falstaff*)

Have you your wits? Know you what 'tis you speak?

FALSTAFF

My King, my Jove, I speak to thee, my heart!   45

KING

I know thee not, old man. Fall to thy prayers.
How ill white hairs becomes a fool and jester!
I have long dreamt of such a kind of man,
So surfeit-swelled, so old and so profane;
But being awaked, I do despise my dream.   50

word *fame* here probably is meant to flatter the King's illustrious name, but it may also glance at the classical figure of Fama. Cf. Ind.0.1–2n.

43 **vain** foolish. By delegating the Justice to speak to Falstaff, the King manages to avoid doing so himself. When Falstaff ignores the Justice's warning at 44, however, the King has no choice but to address him personally.

46–71 The new King's speech is justly famous. In it, he adopts a formal public persona and speaks with a moral authority no doubt prompted by the Justice (cf. 5.2.117–20). Yet the first half of his speech – the rejection of Falstaff – is riddled with puns that remind one of Harry's playful relationship with Falstaff in *1H4* and threaten the calculated sobriety of the moment. In the second half, as if checking himself, the King implicitly addresses his wider audience in an attempt to convince them, as he has done his father in 4.3 and his brothers in 5.2, of the sincerity of his reformation. He invokes God as witness, and his rhetorical challenge to Falstaff to approach him only when he reverts to his former beha-

viour (59–60) could apply to others in the crowd as well. Although the final lines soften Falstaff's banishment with an offer of rehabilitation, the speech nonetheless succeeds in erasing the public perception of Harry as a madcap prince. If, in it, he struggles to overcome his desire to play with Falstaff still, that struggle makes his victory over his past riots all the more creditable, because hard won.

46 **I . . . not** a strong echo of the opening line of the Prince's soliloquy in *1H4* 1.3 – 'I know you all' (185) – in which he vows one day to abjure his riotous companions

47 **ill . . . becomes** poorly . . . suit. His point is that white hair should betoken the gravity that comes with age. On the use of a singular verb with a plural subject, see 1.1.33n.

48–50 inspired by Psalms, 73.19–20 (DSK): 'How suddenly are they destroyed, perished and horribly consumed, / As a dreame when one awaketh! O Lord, when thou raisest vs vp, thou shalt make their image despised' (Geneva Bible).

49 **surfeit-swelled** swollen by overeating; *surfeit* may also imply an excess of sensual indulgence.

42 God] *Q; not in F*   44] *Q; F lines* wits? / speake? /   47 hairs] *F, Q (*heires*)*   becomes] *Q;* become *F*
50 awaked] *Q (*awakt*);* awake *F*

Make less thy body hence, and more thy grace.
Leave gormandizing: know the grave doth gape
For thee thrice wider than for other men.
Reply not to me with a fool-born jest.
Presume not that I am the thing I was,   55
For God doth know, so shall the world perceive,
That I have turned away my former self;
So will I those that kept me company.
When thou dost hear I am as I have been,
Approach me, and thou shalt be as thou wast,   60
The tutor and the feeder of my riots.
Till then, I banish thee on pain of death,
As I have done the rest of my misleaders,

51 Typical of Harry's humour, this plays on the opposition between the flesh and the spirit. For Falstaff to make his body *less* means both to lose weight and to remove himself from the King's presence; to make his grace *more* means to behave more virtuously.
hence henceforth

52 **Leave gormandizing** 'Stop eating like a glutton'; the only sure way for Falstaff to make his body less (51).

52–3 **the grave … men** Harry jokes about Falstaff's corpulence in a manner reminiscent of his punning epitaph over Falstaff's corpse at Shrewsbury: 'I should have a heavy miss of thee / If I were much in love with vanity. / Death hath not struck so fat a deer today' (*1H4* 5.4.104–6). Metaphorically, the line implies that Falstaff's grave gapes *thrice wider* because he is far worse a sinner. The threat of damnation looms large. The phrasing here echoes Isaiah, 5.14: 'Therefore gapeth hell, and openeth her mouth maruelous wide that [they] may descende into it'.

54 a defensive line. As Warburton noted, the King, suddenly aware that he has lapsed

into a tone of jocular familiarity with his old friend, pulls himself up short by warning Falstaff not to reply in kind – an indication that Falstaff, seeing an opportunity at the end of 53, may have been about to interrupt him. In the following line, the King protests that he is *not* the same person he was, yet this speech has already revealed the struggle within.

55–8 Cf. a similar assurance at 5.2.124–8 and a similar enlisting of God as witness at 4.3.279 and 304. The Prince promised to turn away his former companions as early as his soliloquy in *1H4* 1.2.185–207; here, he honours that promise.

57 **turned away** dismissed, repudiated

61 **feeder** continues the digestive metaphor: cf. 49, 51–2.
riots Henry IV used this word to impugn his son's prodigal, licentious behaviour at 4.3.62 and 264–5. The new King's borrowing it here signals his appropriation of his father's perspective: Harry has succeeded Harry (5.2.48–9).

63 **the rest … misleaders** The identity of this group is never made clear; certainly the chief *misleaders* of Harry's youth are those present.

56 God] *Q;* heauen *F*

Not to come near our person by ten mile.
[also addressing Falstaff's companions]
For competence of life I will allow you,   65
That lack of means enforce you not to evils;
And as we hear you do reform yourselves,
We will, according to your strengths and qualities,
Give you advancement. *[to Justice]* Be it your
    charge, my lord,
To see performed the tenor of my word.   70
Set on.   F*Exit King*F *[with his train]*.

FALSTAFF   Master Shallow, I owe you a thousand pound.

SHALLOW   Yea, marry, Sir John, which I beseech you to
let me have home with me.

FALSTAFF   That can hardly be, Master Shallow. Do not   75

---

64 **ten mile** This number is specified in both Holinshed (3.543) and *Famous Victories* (9.47).

65 SD The addressee up to this point has been Falstaff alone. Here, however, the King's shift from the familiar *thee* (62) to the formal (and possibly plural) *you* (65) and the plural *yourselves* (67) indicates that he is also addressing, and presumably intends to banish, those who accompany Falstaff – Bardolph, Pistol and others. Cf. 90–1.

65 **For . . . life** 'sufficient means to enable you to live'
    allow you The implied object is an amount of money. The King's gesture is reported in Holinshed – 'but not vnrewarded or else vnpreferred' (3.543) – and Stow – 'to every one of whom he gaue rich and bounteous gifts' (*Annales*, 549) – but not in *Famous Victories*.

66 **That** so that
    enforce . . . evils will not compel you to resort to crime (*OED* enforce *v.* 10)

67–9 The King's promise to advance his old companions according to their reformation does much to allay the severity of their banishment, though his qualifying phrase (68) places a potent restriction on that promise. Dramatically, Falstaff's fate is sealed: he has no capacity to be other than what he is, nor would an audience wish him to be. For him, Harry's offer is moot.

67 **we** On the King's switching to the royal plural in public address, cf. 5.2.133n. He returns to the more familiar *my* when instructing the Justice (70).

70 **tenor** substance

72 Falstaff's response to the shock of rejection demonstrates his abiding capacity to recover, or to *act* as if he has recovered, his equilibrium.

74 **have home** i.e. have to take home

75 **That . . . be** If Falstaff has not had time to 'bestow' (12) the money yet, there is presumably no reason why Shallow shouldn't have it back; but see 12–13n.

---

65 SD] *this edn; not in QF*   66 evils] *Q;* euill *F*   68 strengths] *Q;* strength *F*   69 SD] *Capell subst.; not in QF*   70–1] *Pope; one line QF*   70 my] *Q;* our *F*   71 SD] *Capell subst.; Exit King. F; not in Q*   73 Yea] *Q;* 1 *F*

you grieve at this: I shall be sent for in private to him.
Look you, he must seem thus to the world. Fear not
your advancements. I will be the man yet that shall
make you great.

SHALLOW   I cannot perceive how, unless you give me   80
your doublet and stuff me out with straw. I beseech
you, good Sir John, let me have five hundred of my
thousand.

FALSTAFF   Sir, I will be as good as my word. This that
you heard was but a colour.   85

SHALLOW   A colour that I fear you will die in, Sir John.

FALSTAFF   Fear no colours. Go with me to dinner. Come,

Shakespeare's point seems to be that one
way or another, Falstaff has no intention
of returning the thousand pounds he
worked so cunningly to get.

75–7 **Do ... world** Falstaff's excuse for the
King's action is transparent, just as his
admonition to the others not to grieve
is an obvious attempt to disguise his
own grief. Even the most moralistic of
audiences finds it difficult not to respond
to the pathos of Falstaff's situation.

77–8 **Fear ... advancements** Do not doubt
the promotions I have promised you
(cf. 5.3.121–37). Falstaff's reassurance
sounds ironic in light of the King's
promise of conditional advancement at
67–9.

80–1 **I ... straw** Shallow deflates Falstaff's
claim by playing on the meaning of *great*
(79) as 'fat'. Such punning in a man not
noted for his wit robs Falstaff of a riposte:
in a reversal of roles both here and at
86–7, Falstaff plays straight man to
Shallow's comedian.

81 **doublet** close-fitting jacket

84 **as ... word** proverbial (Dent, W773.1)

85 **colour** pretext, pretence. Cf. 1.2.245.

86 **colour ... in** Shallow replies with a
double pun: (1) a *colour* (pretence) or
collar (hangman's noose) that Falstaff
will *die* in; and (2) a *colour* (hue) or collar
(article of clothing) which he will 'dye'
(change colour; so spelled in F) in.
Q's spelling 'collor' suggests that in
his holograph, Shakespeare may have
intended to make Shallow's pronunciation
of the word an obvious pun.

87 **Fear no colours** Falstaff retakes the
comic initiative by punning on *colours*
as military standards (cf. 2.2.167n.). His
expression was proverbial for 'fear no
enemy' or more generally, as here, 'have
no fear' (Dent, C520). In this passage
colours also refers to 'the brave shows
and excesses of rhetoric that wrap or
re-fashion the bare ribs of truth'
(Hattaway, 'Falstaff', 75–87).

78 advancements] *Q*; aduancement *F*   80 cannot] *Q*; cannot well *F*   you] *Q*; you should *F*   85 colour]
Q (collour), *F*   86 colour] *Q* (collor), *F*   that I fear] *Q*; I feare, that *F*   die] *Q, F* (dye)   87–9] *prose*
Pope; QF line dinner: / Bardolfe, / night. /   87 colours] *QF*

Lieutenant Pistol; come Bardolph. I shall be sent for
soon at night.

Enter [the Lord Chief*]* JUSTICE
and Prince JOHN *[with Officers].*

JUSTICE *[to Officers]*
  Go, carry Sir John Falstaff to the Fleet.   90
  Take all his company along with him.
FALSTAFF   My lord, my lord!

88 **Lieutenant** Falstaff's promotion of Pistol
from ancient to lieutenant is perhaps
intentional: it bestows a dignity which
he has promised him at 5.3.123–4 but
cannot now deliver except as a meaningless act of verbal ingratiation.

89 **soon at night** proverbial for 'tonight'
(Dent, S639.1). Falstaff, who in *1H4* calls
himself a 'squire of the night's body'
and a 'minion of the moon' (1.2.23–5),
remains a creature of the night even here,
not comprehending that the sun of
majesty has risen and shaken off 'the
base contagious clouds' (188) that had
smothered him.

89.1–2 *By indicating an exit only for the
King at 71, F allows Prince John and
the Justice to remain onstage during
Falstaff's conversation with Shallow. It
makes more theatrical sense, however,
for them to exit with the King at 71,
leaving the stage to Falstaff, and, as in Q,
to return here.

90 **the Fleet** a prison just north of the
intersection of Fleet Street and Ludgate
Hill where, in *Famous Victories*, 4.81, the
Prince is committed for striking the Lord
Chief Justice (Ard²). Here, it serves as a
place where Falstaff and his companions
will be held in temporary custody until
they appear at a formal hearing at which

the Lord Chief Justice will presumably
perform the *tenor* of the King's *word*
(70). Yet it nevertheless is a prison, and
what offences are charged to Falstaff
and the others that might warrant their
confinement remain unexplained. Falstaff
may be wanted for the Gad's Hill robbery
(1.2.133–4), and Pistol for beating a
man to death (5.4.16–17), but neither
of those crimes is mentioned here. Since
Queen Elizabeth used to imprison favourites simply for incurring her displeasure,
Falstaff's punishment may not have seemed
unduly severe to an Elizabethan audience;
yet following hard on his public humiliation by the King, his imprisonment is
unexpected and therefore tends to elicit
sympathy for him. In some productions
the arrest of Falstaff and his companions
has been made to seem consistent with
the brutal arrest of Doll Tearsheet and
Mistress Quickly (5.4) as evidence of a
new totalitarian repression.

91 **all his company** Why Shallow should be
among those taken to the Fleet is unclear.
His inclusion may have been an oversight
on Shakespeare's part, or a consequence
of the Lord Chief Justice's having not yet
had time to distinguish among Falstaff's
retinue.

89.1–2] *Enter Iustice / and prince Iohn Q (opp. 87–9); Re-enter Prince* John, *and the* Chief Justice;
Officers with them. Capell; not in F   90 SD] *Capell subst.; not in QF*

JUSTICE

I cannot now speak. I will hear you soon.

Take them away.

PISTOL _Si fortuna me tormenta, spero contenta._ 95

Exeunt [Officers with Falstaff, Pistol,

Shallow, Bardolph and Page].

JOHN

I like this fair proceeding of the King's.

He hath intent his wonted followers

Shall all be very well provided for,

But all are banished till their conversations

Appear more wise and modest to the world. 100

JUSTICE

And so they are.

JOHN

The King hath called his parliament, my lord.

JUSTICE

He hath.

JOHN

I will lay odds that, ere this year expire,

We bear our civil swords and native fire 105

---

95 See 2.4.180–1n. Pistol's reprise of a Latin tag about the torments of fortune and the solace of hope adds a poignant gloss to the arrest of Falstaff and his companions.

96 **fair proceeding** judicious conduct. Such praise in the mouth of Prince John makes the fairness of the proceeding suspect, for he has been aptly characterized by Falstaff as cold-blooded (4.2.85–7) and knows as well as anyone that Falstaff will find it virtually impossible to meet the conditions set for his release from banishment.

97 **wonted** accustomed

99 **conversations** behaviour (_OED sb._ 6)

105–6 **We . . . France** evidence that the King has accepted his father's advice to make foreign wars as a matter of policy (cf. 4.3.341–4) and that Shakespeare had already planned a play about Henry V's French wars.

105 **civil swords** citizens' swords, or swords used until now in civil strife. Cf. _civil blows_, 4.3.263 (Cam²).

native fire i.e. English guns

93–4] _F; prose Q_ 95] _Q; Si fortuna me tormento, spera me contento. F; Se fortuna mi tormenta, ben sperato mi contenta – Cam²_ SD _Exeunt] Q (after 94); Exit. Manet Lancaster and Chiefe Iustice. F Officers . . . Page] Capell subst._ 102] _Q; F lines_ Parliament, / Lord. /

426

As far as France. I heard a bird so sing,
Whose music, to my thinking, pleased the King.
Come, will you hence?   ᶠ*Exeunt.*ᶠ

EPILOGUE [1]   [*Enter the* Speaker of the EPILOGUE.]

First my fear, then my curtsy, last my speech.
My fear is your displeasure; my curtsy, my duty;
and my speech, to beg your pardons. If you look for
a good speech now, you undo me; for what I have to
say is of mine own making, and what indeed I should   5
say will, I doubt, prove mine own marring. But to the
purpose, and so to the venture. Be it known to you,
as it is very well, I was lately here in the end of a
displeasing play to pray your patience for it and to
promise you a better. I meant indeed to pay you with   10
this, which, if like an ill venture it come unluckily

---

106 **I . . . sing** proverbial (Dent, B374)

EPILOGUE **1, 2** *As printed in Q and F, this epilogue is unusual because it is written in prose and is uncommonly long. Its length may be explained, however, by its being a conflation of two discrete epilogues composed at different times and for different occasions – the first possibly for a court performance, to be spoken by Shakespeare himself; the second for a public performance, to be spoken by the actor playing Falstaff (Shapiro, 32–6). The two are uncomfortably conjoined in Q and F. For a discussion of the dramatic function and integrity of these independent epilogues, and the problem of their conflation in print editions, see pp. 142–6.

1, 2 **curtsy** bow: a sign of obeisance or respect. Cf. 2.1.123.

4 **undo me** cause me to despair

5–6 **making . . . marring** a frequent antithesis. Cf. the proverbial 'To make or (and) mar' (Dent, M48).

6 **doubt** fear

7 **purpose** matter at hand
venture risk, gamble. Here begins a series of images drawn from the commerce of merchant venturers. Cf. 1.1.180–6.

8 **in the end** at the end, presumably also to speak an epilogue

9 **displeasing play** The absence of records for the Lord Chamberlain's Men in 1596–7 makes it impossible to know what play might be referred to. For speculation that it may have been *1H4*, see p. 133–42.

10 **pay** i.e. repay, as for a debt

11–12 **ill . . . home** 'unsuccessful voyage, the ship returns to home port without the expected cargo'

106 heard] *Q;* heare *F*   108 SD] *Exeunt / FINIS. F; not in Q*   EPILOGUE 1] *this edn; Epilogue. QF; Epilogue / Spoken by a Dancer. / Pope*   Epil.0.1] *Oxf subst.*   1 curtsy] *Q (*cursie*), F (Curtsie)*   2 curtsy] *Q (*cursy*), F (Curtsie)*   10 meant] *Q; did meane F*

home, I break, and you, my gentle creditors, lose.
Here I promised you I would be, and here I commit
my body to your mercies. Bate me some, and I will
pay you some and, as most debtors do, promise you   15
infinitely. And so I kneel down before you [*Kneels.*]
– but, indeed, to pray for the Queen.

[EPILOGUE 2]

If my tongue cannot entreat you to acquit me, will
you command me to use my legs? And yet that were
but light payment, to dance out of your debt. But a   20

12 **break** go bankrupt. Cf. *MV* 3.1.103–5:
'Antonio's creditors . . . swear, he cannot
choose but break'. The breaking of a
promise (see 10) is also implicit.
   my . . . lose The audience is compared to
investors in the venture who stand to lose
if the play fails to please.
13–14 **commit . . . mercies** typically an actor's
appeal for applause
14 **Bate me some** forgive a part of my debt
(*OED* bate v.² 4)
15–16 **promise you infinitely** i.e. make any
promises to repay the remainder of what
I owe. The speaker is trying to strike a
bargain with the audience.
17 **to pray . . . Queen** Praying for the Queen
signals the end of the epilogue that may
have been spoken at a court performance.
F honours this convention by moving the
prayer to the end of the combined
epilogue. This transposition, however,
has little justification other than to tie the
two epilogues together as if they were
originally meant to be one, which they
were not: see p. 144.
18 **If . . . me** The opening of this epilogue
sounds a bit abrupt, as if the actor were
in mid-speech. GWW speculates that the
second epilogue may have begun with

the same lines as the first (from *First my
fear* to *pardons*, 1–3), continued with
further lines from that epilogue (from
here I commit to *infinitely*, 13–16), and
then moved to the lines printed here
as Epilogue 2 (GWW). If, however,
Epilogue 2 was written to be spoken by
the actor playing Falstaff, its opening
line, 'If my tongue cannot entreat you to
acquit me,' might been understood by an
audience to refer directly to Falstaff's
failure to win the acquittal of the King
and might therefore have sounded less
abrupt. On the occasion of the two epilogues, see pp. 143–5.
19 **use my legs** i.e. dance. The references
to dancing here, at 20, and again at 33
provoked Pope's speculation that the
speaker was a dancer. Of all the Lord
Chamberlain's Men, Will Kemp, who
was with the company until 1599, was
most renowned for his skill as a dancer
of jigs.
19–20 **were but** would be only
20 **light payment** either (1) insufficient
repayment, or (2) an entertainment too
nimble to be satisfying (cf. light of foot:
OED light *adj.*¹ 14). To *dance out of . . .
debt* is, in effect, to deceive one's creditors.

12 lose] *Q (*loose), *F*   16–17 And . . . Queen.] *Q, F (after 34)*   16 I] *Q; not in F*   SD] *this edn; not in
QF*   17. I] *this edn*   18 entreat] *Q (*intreate), *F*

good conscience will make any possible satisfaction,
and so would I. All the gentlewomen here have for-
given me. If the gentlemen will not, then the gentlemen
do not agree with the gentlewomen, which was never
seen in such an assembly.   25

One word more, I beseech you. If you be not too
much cloyed with fat meat, our humble author will
continue the story with Sir John in it and make
you merry with fair Katherine of France, where, for
anything I know, Falstaff shall die of a sweat unless   30
already 'a be killed with your hard opinions; for
Oldcastle died martyr, and this is not the man. My
tongue is weary. When my legs are too, I will bid you
good night.   [*Dances a jig, then exits.*]

22–5 **All ... assembly** The appeal to women
in the audience to prevail with the men
resembles the epilogue in *AYL*, in which
the actor playing Rosalind conjures the
men and women in the audience to please
one another by liking the play (10–16).
The final line wryly mocks the battle of
the sexes.

27 **cloyed ... meat** surfeited with fatty meat
or sweaty flesh: a humorous allusion to
the speaker

28–30 **continue ... sweat** The promise to
continue the saga of Falstaff in a play
about Henry V's French campaign indicates that this epilogue was written before
Shakespeare completed *H5*, for Falstaff
never appears in that play, his death being
reported by the Hostess at 2.3.9–25. Why
Shakespeare chose not to revive Falstaff's
fortunes in *H5* has been much debated.

30 **sweat** either (1) the sweating-sickness, a
disease characterized by fever; (2) syphilis,
for which sweating in a tub of hot water
was ostensibly a cure; or (3) exertion,
from the energy he has expended doing

military service or, with reference to
the actor himself, performing his role
on the stage. Falstaff has been associated
with sweat on other occasions: 1.2.209,
4.2.11–14, 5.5.24–5. On the applicability
of a sweating death to the historical
Oldcastle, see 31–2n.

31 **killed ... opinions** an appeal for applause:
cf. Epil.8–9. Presumably an audience's
disapproval could prove as fatal to
Falstaff as to the actor playing him.

31–2 **for ... man** On this disclaimer that
the historical Oldcastle was the model
for Falstaff, and the censorship that led
Shakespeare to change his name, see
pp. 133–42. Oldcastle was burned as a
heretic in St Giles' Field on Christmas
Day 1417. The oblique allusion to death
by fire at 30 thus provides one last, ironic
glimpse of the submerged identity of
Falstaff that the speaker is trying to
disavow: it affirms even as it denies.

33 **When ... too** A clear indication that the
speaker concludes the epilogue by
dancing a jig.

22 would] *Q; will F*   25 seen] *Q; seene before F*   31 'a] *Q; he F*   32 died] *Q; dyed a F*   34 SD] *this edn;*
[*He dances, then kneels for applause.*] *Exit / Oxf; FINIS Q; not in F*

APPENDIX 1

The text

Establishing a text for an edition of *Henry IV, Part Two* is notoriously difficult. There are two, arguably three, different versions of the play, but for various reasons none of them provides a fully authoritative basis for an edition. The first edition of the play, the Quarto of 1600 (Q), which has been widely, if doubtfully, thought to bear the marks of a holograph (a manuscript in the author's hand, often referred to by previous editors as foul papers)[1] or a copy made from it, seems in many ways the most reliable text, though it contains obvious errors. It appeared in two issues, termed Qa and Qb. For sheets A–D and F–L2, the printing is identical in both issues; but Qb provides a new scene (3.1) set in sheet E and introduces other, inadvertent changes occasioned by the resetting of type to include that scene. The Folio of 1623 (F) provides eight passages not included in the Quarto in addition to scene 3.1 from Qb; furthermore, it adds or clarifies stage directions, makes speech prefixes consistent and tidies the text in a manner once thought to be indicative of stage practice, suggesting to some editors its possible provenance in a playbook (anachronistically called a promptbook)[2] used by the Lord Chamberlain's company for theatrical performance, but which is actually more indicative of scribal preparation of a text for publication. The F text also bears the marks of unusual scribal interference: it sanitizes

---

1 Paul Werstine, in 'Post-theory', demonstrates that W.W. Greg's use of the term 'foul papers' to refer to completed plays rather than separate sheets is a violent departure from the term's use in the seventeenth-century documents he cites.

2 William Long challenges the use of the term 'promptbook' – a term first recorded in the nineteenth century – for the playbooks used by Elizabeth theatre companies in 'Stage', 124–5, and 'Precious', 415. See also Werstine's refutation of Greg's anachronistic use of 'prompt-book' in 'Plays', 484–5.

THE
Second part of Henrie

the fourth, continuing to his death,
and coronation of Henrie
the fift.

With the humours of *ſir* Iohn Fal-
ſtaffe, *and ſwaggering*
Piſtoll.

As it hath been ſundrie times publikely
acted by the right honourable, the Lord
Chamberlaine his ſeruants.

Written by William Shakeſpeare.

LONDON
Printed by V.S. for Andrew Wiſe, and
William Aſpley.
1600.

21   Title-page of the 1600 Quarto (sig. A1^r)

profanities found in Q, normalizes grammar and regularizes
forms with a propriety inconsistent with other Shakespearean
plays. Moreover, it shows evidence of compositorial contamination resulting from problems with typesetting. The editor
is thus confronted with a dilemma: how to establish a text
that might reasonably accord with what was performed by
Shakespeare's company in 1597, when finding a fully authoritative text is clearly not possible. The following pages weigh
the relative merits of Qa, Qb and F and the claims that each of
them can make to be the preferred copy-text for an edition.

THE QUARTO

Qa

A copy of the play was entered by Andrew Wise and William
Aspley in the Stationers' Register on 23 August 1600 and
printed that year by Valentine Simmes as a quarto bearing the
title 'THE / Second part of Henrie / the fourth, continuing to his
death, / *and coronation of Henrie* / the fift. / With the humours
of sir Iohn Fal- / *staffe, and swaggering* / Pistoll'. The text
shows signs that have been used in the past to claim that it was
copied from a draft of the play based on an authorial manuscript.
Its inconsistencies – missing or inadequate stage directions,
variant spellings and speech prefixes, ghost characters – are of
the sort one finds in the quarto of *Much Ado*, a copy of which
was entered by Wise and Aspley at the same time as *Part Two*;
and generations of editors have speculated that the source of
the Q text must have been a holograph kept by the Lord
Chamberlain's men as a safeguard against the theft of the play
by a rival company until they were ready to sell that holograph
to a stationer for publication.[1] The company would have been
reluctant to part with its annotated playbook, Greg reasoned,

---

1   The idea that acting companies secured holographs to guard against theft was first
    advanced by Pollard, *Shakespeare*, 53–7.

because that document alone would contain the licence from the Master of the Revels authorizing performance.[1] Although, as Fredson Bowers countered, 'There is no evidence whatever . . . that an author ever submitted for payment anything but a fair copy, or that the company required a dramatist to turn over his original foul sheets along with the fair copy' (Bowers, 15), this narrative of textual transmission has continued to enjoy wide currency, and virtually all editors of the play since Wilson (Cam¹), including the most recent Oxford and Cambridge editors, have subscribed to the theory that Q was based on Shakespeare's uncorrected holograph. Thus it must be dealt with.

The evidence that editors have found to support their argument that Q is based on a holograph rather than a playbook is predicated on the anachronistic belief that a copy used in the playhouse would, like a modern promptbook, record details of decisions made in rehearsal, especially stage directions. The stage directions in Q are infrequent and far less regular than one finds in a modern promptbook, but those that are included offer unusual descriptive detail, as if an author were writing notes to himself for staging or costuming: '*Enter Rumour painted full of tongues*' (Ind.0); '*Enter the Lord Bardolfe at one doore*' (1.1.0); '*Enter sir Iohn alone, with his page bearing his sword and buckler*' (1.2.0); '*Enter the King in his night-gowne alone*' (3.1.0). Authorial idiosyncrasy may account for unnecessary information provided in the opening stage direction of 4.1, which places the scene '*within the forrest of Gaultree*' – a location established by the first two lines of dialogue – and for an odd reminder of a character's function following his name at the entrance of '*Thomas Mowbray (Earle Marshall)*' (1.3.0). A few sound cues, too, may conceivably indicate the author's occasional attentiveness to stage practice, although they may just as well be annotations made by a theatrical bookkeeper.

1 Werstine, 'Editing', 33, cites Greg's argument in *First Folio.*

A '*Shout*' of soldiers is indicated when peace is made at Gaultree (4.1.314), an '*Alarum*' and '*Excursions*' follow the arrest of the rebels (4.2.0), a *Retraite* is sounded to signal the end of fighting (4.2.25), and '*Trumpets sound*' when the new King and his train pass over the stage on the way to his coronation (5.5.4), as they do again, according to Pistol (though without a stage direction), after the coronation (5.5.37).[1]

The variety of speech prefixes in Q also was thought to be typical of a holograph but atypical of a playbook used for performance. As McKerrow asserted, a theatrical promptbook 'would surely, of necessity, be accurate and unambiguous in the matter of character-names' – so the variable naming of characters in speech prefixes and stage directions in Q indicates that it must have been set from Shakespeare's 'original MS'.[2] Characters in Q are signalled by a profusion of designations. Falstaff has seven different speech prefixes: '*Iohn*', '*sir Iohn*', '*Falstaffe*', '*Falst.*', '*Fal.*', '*Fa.*' and, once, '*Old.*', a vestige of his earlier incarnation as Oldcastle. The Lord Chief Justice is designated by four ('*Iustice*' and '*Iust.*', '*Lord*' and '*Lo.*'); Prince Henry by three ('*Harry*', '*Prince*' and finally, '*King*'); and his brothers likewise by both their Christian names and their titles: Thomas of Clarence is '*Clar.*' (or '*Cla.*') and '*Tho.*'; Humphrey of Gloucester, '*Hum.*' (or '*Humph.*') and '*Glo.*'; John of Lancaster, '*Prince*' and '*Iohn*' and, to distinguish him from Prince Henry in 4.3, '*Lanc.*'. Shallow is designated by '*Shallow*', '*Shall.*', '*Shal.*' and '*Sha.*'; Silence, by three unabbreviated forms, '*Silence*', '*Silens*' or '*Scilens*'. Designations for the women move even more fluidly between individuation and occupation or type. Mistress Quickly is

---

1 For the presence of descriptive stage directions in playhouse manuscripts and in quartos annotated in the playhouse, see Werstine, *Manuscripts*, 132. He notes, moreover, that sound calls were added to all but two of the twenty-one extant playhouse texts (243).

2 McKerrow, 464, cited by Werstine in 'McKerrow's', 154, and also in Long, 'Perspective', 26–7.

called '*Quickly*' or '*Qui.*', but, far more often, '*Hostesse*' (or three abbreviations of it), while Doll Tearsheet has no fewer than eight speech prefixes including, most generically, '*Whoore*' in 5.4. Such variations may provide a glimpse into the mind of an author at work, conceiving each character in different ways as he writes; but, it is argued, they would not have survived the regularizing practices of those involved in preparing a playbook for performance. Recent scholarship, however, has shown this long-held assumption to be false. The eighteen playhouse manuscripts and three quartos with playhouse annotations surviving from this period are notably inconsistent in their use of speech prefixes and in the names used in stage directions,[1] and the variable forms found in Q are fully consistent with those found in these manuscript playbooks.

Ghost characters – intended for inclusion in a scene, but then apparently forgotten – are similarly thought to reveal a writer at work and, it is believed, would have been purged from a text used for theatrical performance. *Part Two* is haunted by such characters. Fauconbridge (1.3), Kent (4.3) and Sir John Russell (2.2), all named in stage directions, remain mute and presumably were abandoned, though not erased, in the course of composition. Sir John Umfrevile is given a line at 1.1.161 but otherwise is not heard from, his role apparently conflated with that of Lord Bardolph but his one speech prefix overlooked. Other characters are more problematic because, though mute, they may serve a function. Sir John Blunt enters twice (3.1.31, 5.2.41) when his presence seems only to swell a scene; yet, though unnamed, he apparently accompanies Prince John when the latter enters at 4.2.23, for the Prince instructs him to guard Collevile fifty lines later. The presence of the mute Surrey at

---

1   W. Long counts sixteen such manuscripts in 'Stage' (135), and increases the number to eighteen in 'Precious' (414). Werstine, in *Manuscripts*, adds the three annotated quartos to that number and collects all the examples of multiple designations of roles in these texts (359–64).

3.1.31 is required too, in response to the King's calling for him at 3.1.1. And both Lord Bardolph (4.1) and Lord Westmorland (5.2) are listed to enter scenes where they have no lines. One other anomalous name has been said to attest to the unfinished nature of the copy for Q: that of the actor John Sincklo, whose name substitutes for the character he plays – '*Beadle*' – in both the initial stage direction and the speech prefixes of 5.4. Repeated reference to the Beadle's emaciated appearance suggests that Shakespeare wrote the role with a comically thin member of his company in mind; and apparently, in his holograph, the name of the actor loomed larger for him than the character did. This does not provide proof, however, as has commonly been held, that Q was based on an uncorrected holograph rather than on a copy of playhouse provenance. As William Long has demonstrated ('Precious'), ghost characters repeatedly appear in the surviving manuscript playbooks of this period, and there is no evidence that scripts prepared for performance would have been systematically purged of them.

If ghost characters reveal Shakespeare having second thoughts or simply being inattentive, imprecise or inadequate stage directions for those characters who *do* speak may suggest that he finds their entrances and exits implicit in the dialogue and not worth noting for performance purposes. Indeed, actors could be counted on to work out their own comings and goings in rehearsal: such things would not need to be recorded in a playbook. Some unnoted entrances and exits in Q, however, are not so self-evident: among them, the entrance and exit of the Porter at 1.1.1 and 6; the entrance of an attendant for the Lord Chief Justice at 1.2.55; in 2.4, the Drawer's exit at 34, Pistol's at 208 and Bardolph's comings and goings in that same scene at 109, 208, 212 and 373; the various entrances and exits of the recruits in 3.2; Collevile's entrance at 4.2.0; Warwick's exit at 4.3.193; Davy's exits at 5.3.29 and 71 and Bardolph's at 131; the entrance of Mistress Quickly and Doll Tearsheet at 5.4.0; and the entrance of officers attending on Prince John and the Lord Chief Justice at 5.5.89. Other stage directions are misplaced. For example, at 2.1.163, the Hostess and Sergeant are signalled to exit before her last exchange with Falstaff; *Enter Will* makes no sense at 2.4.18 and should probably come six lines earlier; and in 5.2 the initial stage direction mistakenly lists '*Humphrey*', '*Clarence*' and '*Prince Iohn*', whose entrance is repeated at 13. Still other stage directions imperfectly correspond with speech prefixes: 2.1.132 instructs '*enter a messenger*', who is immediately named '*Gower*'; and '*the wife to Harry Percie*' listed at the top of 2.3 speaks as '*Kate*'.[1]

Even more symptomatic of a holograph, editors have argued, are so-called permissive stage directions, whose indeterminacy suggests an author making up a scene as he writes or leaving details to be worked out by the actors. The opening of 2.4, '*Enter a Drawer or two*', is the most problematic of these, for the ensuing division of speeches among the Drawers – one of whom is named Francis, and another, who enters later, Will – is far from clear. But other stage directions are equally permissive: 2.1 brings on the Hostess with '*an Officer or two*'; in 2.2 the Prince and Poins are accompanied by the phantom '*sir Iohn Russel, with other*'; in 3.1, the King enters '*alone*' but at once addresses his Page; at 3.2.54, '*Enter Bardolfe, and one with him*'; at 4.2.23, '*Enter Iohn Westmerland, and the rest*'; at 5.4, '*Enter Sincklo and three or foure officers*'; and 5.5 opens with the indeterminate '*Enter strewers of rushes*'.

For generations of editors, this accumulation of evidence pointed to the likelihood that Q was based on an uncorrected authorial draft insufficiently detailed or reliable to have been used for theatrical performance. McKerrow and Greg first advanced the theory that a playbook (or promptbook, as they

---

1 For many comparable instances of inconsistencies in other playhouse texts – missed or indefinite entrances and exits, omission of necessary characters from entrances, stage directions either permissive or misplaced or imperfectly corresponding to speech prefixes, etc. – see Werstine, *Manuscripts*, 359–88.

called it) would have included more complete and accurate stage directions, uniform speech prefixes and consistent entrances and exits; further, it would have tied up loose ends and would not have allowed permissive directions to stand. These assumptions have been embraced by the Oxford editors, who in their *Textual Companion* affirm that in playbooks, 'stage directions tend to be more systematically supplied . . . [and] more practically, and laconically worded' and 'characters tend to be more consistently identified in speech-prefixes' (12).[1] Following this logic, it is reasonable to conclude with Humphreys, as all subsequent editors of the play have done, 'that Shakespeare's manuscript was not used as the prompt-copy, and that the printer received it . . . in an interestingly original condition' (lxx).

Recent textual scholarship, however, has discovered that the assumptions underlying this hypothesis do not bear scrutiny, for those playbooks of this period that have survived in manuscript form all manifest the same inconsistences and irregularities that Greg and his followers attributed to 'foul papers'. Playbooks used by acting companies were not scrupulously shorn of their irregularities: stage directions often were minimal, speech prefixes typically inconsistent, ghost characters common, permissive stage directions the norm and entrances and exits often not accounted for. Nor were there consistent annotations for stage properties, music and other effects (Long, 'Stage', 123). The standards for regularity and accuracy in playbooks imposed by modern editors disregard Elizabethan practice, wherein a playwright could assume 'the abilities of the players to handle his play', trust them to translate the text into stage action, have confidence in their ability to figure out when to enter and exit, know that they would recognize their own speech prefixes (players having been given

1 Cited in Werstine, 'Post-theory', 104. In 'Plays', Werstine deems the Oxford editors 'uncritically enthralled by Greg's general theory' of textual transmission (492).

only part copies anyway) and accept that they would 'add or delete according to their needs' with no requirement for a playhouse bookkeeper to record such changes in the script (Long, 'Stage', 127). The persistence in playbooks of those characteristics long thought to be exclusive to holographs, therefore, erases a distinction that is fundamental to the claim that Q of *Part Two* was based on an untidy authorial manuscript. Indeed, the quest for consistency, accuracy and completeness, qualities one expects of a modern promptbook, would have benefited readers more than actors in the Elizabethan age, so that those very regularities that Greg argued were characteristic of a 'prompt-book' may have been provided by a scribe preparing the play for publication instead.[1]

This same logic works to dispel the final evidence that Q was based on an uncorrected holograph: that it preserves what are thought to be characteristically Shakespearean spellings of 'Scilens' for Silence, 'mas' for mass, 'on' for one and 'yeere' for ear. If these spellings are indeed peculiar to Shakespeare, it is nevertheless prudent to remember that apart from three pages in the manuscript of *Sir Thomas More* said to have been written in Shakespeare's hand (Hand D) – and evidence for this identification has been widely disputed – no Shakespearean holograph (apart from six signatures and the words 'By me' in his will) exists, so any identification of idiosyncratic spellings must remain highly conjectural. Furthermore, two peculiar features of the spelling of 'Silence' as 'Scilens', common to Hand D in *Sir Thomas More* and the quarto of *Part Two*, as Wilson and Pollard observed in 1919,[2] though highly unusual, were not unprecedented during this period. Most spellings of 'silence' recorded in the *OED* begin with *sci* or end with *lens*;

---

1   Long, 'Perspective', argues that McKerrow's 'requirements for the stage much better fit alterations made for readers' (27).

2   Cited by Werstine, 'Shakespeare', 133. Werstine observes that 'the slightly more common spelling of Justice Silence's name is "Silens", which is not a Hand-D spelling' (141–2, n. 4).

and moreover, the spelling 'Silens' occurs more often in Q than 'Scilens'. There is no compelling evidence, then, that an uncorrected holograph served as the copy-text for Q. Any editor examining the evidence must acknowledge the difficulty of trying to identify what kind of manuscript served as the copy-text for Q. As H.R. Woudhuysen has observed, 'Of the surviving theatrical manuscripts of the period, none exactly conforms to the generally established definition of "foul papers"'; furthermore, 'if compositors were capable of setting in type "foul-paper" features . . . scribes were equally capable of copying and reproducing them by hand. The only way by which scholars could be absolutely certain that a text was set from some kind of authorial draft or fair copy would be if the printer's copy and the resulting print were both to survive. Unfortunately, no scribal let alone authorial manuscript copy for a printed play survives from this period'.[1] Thus it is equally plausible, I would argue, that the playbook of *Part Two* for Shakespeare's company served as the copy-text for Q, and that it might, in addition to preserving authorial idiosyncrasies, bear the marks of theatrical annotation as well.

Qb

The insertion of 3.1 in the middle of sheet E was presumably the main reason for the new issue of Q. The survival today of nearly equal numbers of Qa and Qb texts, eleven of the former and ten of the latter,[2] may suggest that the addition was made about half-way through the printing of the Quarto (Humphreys, xii). A scene of 114 lines in Qb in which the King first soliloquizes about the burdens of office and then entertains reports of rebel activity, it was probably a part of the copy-text from which Qa was printed: without it, the King would not

---

1   Woudhuysen, 320, quoted in Werstine, 'Editing', 35.
2   See Berger (*Second Part*, v). A twenty-second copy is a fragment of Q which cannot be identified as a first or second issue.

appear until his deathbed scene at 4.3, and two long Falstaff scenes would be juxtaposed – 2.4 in the tavern and 3.2 on Shallow's farm – allowing Falstaff to dominate the entire middle section of the play, some 658 lines in Qa, uninterrupted by any intervening chronicle history. The idea of Falstaff's pre-eminence is theatrically attractive – the concluding lines in 2.4, 'Come. . . . Yea, will you come, Doll?' (394–5), are echoed by Shallow's opening line in 3.2, 'Come on, come on, come on; give me your hand, sir' (1–2) – and in fact became a feature of eighteenth- and nineteenth-century productions of the play, some of which moved the first appearance of the King to 4.3 and salvaged only his soliloquy from 3.1 with which to open that scene. Furthermore, Shakespeare may simply have been following his major source for the King's appearance: Daniel's *Civil Wars* moves from the Battle of Shrewsbury directly to the King's deathbed, so Shakespeare's delaying the King's entrance to 4.3 – his deathbed scene – would not have been unprecedented (see pp. 125–7).[1]

It can be objected that the juxtaposition of 2.4 and 3.2 gives Falstaff scant time to journey from London to Gloucestershire (a mere 46 lines in Qa), yet this would not be an insurmountable leap of imagination for an audience to make. A more plausible argument is that it would have been unusual for Shakespeare to write a history play that keeps the eponymous King on the margins until Act 4. Positioned as a royal centre for the play, and illustrating the debilitation of the state and the ill health of the King, both physical and metaphoric, 3.1 balances earlier scenes with the rebels – indeed, the reports brought to the ill King echo those brought to the ill Northumberland in 1.1 – with a dramatization of the centralized power against which they chafe. More important, it continues the alternation of high

1 Jowett & Taylor discuss the link between Daniel's poem and the play, arguing that without 3.1, 'Shakespeare would take up the King's role at exactly the point where it is taken up in the source which most influenced his presentation of the King' (35–6).

scenes with low which was a structural hallmark of *Part One* and has been, up to now, of *Part Two* as well. Falstaff has anticipated the King's meditation on sleep in 3.1 by wryly observing near the end of 2.4, 'You see, my good wenches, how men of merit are sought after. The undeserver may sleep when the man of action is called on' (379–82); so when the King laments that sleep lies 'with the vile / In loathsome beds' (15–16) but is denied 'to a king' (30), his sentiments have already been ironically glossed by Falstaff. It seems highly likely, then, that 3.1 was originally intended to be included in the play.

Why, then, was it omitted from the printing of Qa and inserted soon thereafter? The simplest explanation is that during the printing a manuscript page had been misplaced and, when found, prompted the issue of Qb.[1] The 114 lines of the scene in Qb are estimated to have been the normal length for a manuscript sheet, recto and verso;[2] thus, if the sheet had been misplaced,

---

1 GWW conjectures that during the printing of Q, when the compositor had set as far as into sheet F and possibly to the end of 3.2, he discovered the misfiled manuscript sheet bearing 3.1. By that time both formes of sheet E had gone to the printer and had perhaps been printed. Using persuasive evidence of damaged types, John Hazel Smith argues that upon discovering the misplaced scene, Valentine Simmes, determined to correct the error for which his shop was responsible, interrupted the printing of *Much Ado* to print the new sheet E, copies of which replaced copies of the original E in the yet unbound sheets of the Quarto. GWW suggests that half the print run remained unbound and could therefore incorporate the additional scene (Qb); the other half had already been bound and possibly sent to the booksellers (Qa). Smith's hypothesis is strengthened by the fact that the cancel is printed on paper stock with a watermark not known to Qa but standard for *Much Ado*. It appears, then, that the issue of Qb followed not long after the discovery of the missing scene. There is no evidence to support Humphreys's speculation that Qb was not issued until copies of the defective Qa 'had been sold off' (xii).

2 Pollard was the first to propose that Shakespeare wrote about 54 lines per page, so that the scene would have fitted neatly on the two sides of a single sheet ('Variant'). Numerous scholars have attempted to confirm Pollard's hypothesis by examining the pages in *Sir Thomas More* thought to be in Shakespeare's handwriting (Hand D), but such attempts have been successfully challenged: see Werstine's account in 'Shakespeare'.

The second part of

Dol I cannot fpeake, if my hart be not ready to burft: wel fweete Iacke, haue a care of thy felfe.

Fal. Farewell, farewell.

Hoft. Wel, fare thee wel, I haue knowne thee thefe twentie nine yeeres, come peafe-cod time, but an honefter, and truer hearted man: wel, fare thee wel.

Bard. Miftris Tere-fheete.

Hoft. Whats the matter?

Bard. Bid miftris Tere-fheete come to my maifter.

Hoft. O runne Doll, runne, runne good Doll, come, fhee comes blubberd, yea? wil you come Doll?   *exeunt*

Enter Iuftice Shallow, and Iuftice Silens.

Sha. Come on, come on, come on, giue me your hand fir, giue me your hand fir, an early ftirrer, by the Roode: and how doth my good coofin Silence?

Si. Good morrow good coofine Shallow.

Sha. And how doth my coofin your bedfellow? and your faireft daughter and mine, my god-daughter Ellen?

Si. Alas, a blacke woofel, coofin Shallow.

Sha. By yea, and no fir, I dare fay my coofin William is become a good fcholler, he is at Oxford ftil, is he not?

Si. Indeede fir to my coft.

Sha. A muft then to the Innes a court fhortly: I was once of Clements Inne, where I thinke they wil talke of mad Shallow yet.

Si. You were calld Lufty Shallow then, coofin.

Sha. By the maffe I was calld any thing, and I would haue done any thing indeede too, and roundly too: there was I, and little Iohn Doyt of Staffordfhire, and blacke George Barnes, and Francis Pickebone, and Will Squele a Cotfole man, you had not foure fuch fwinge-bucklers in all the Innes a court againe, and I may fay to you, wee knewe where the bona robes were, and had the beft of them all at commaundement : then was Iacke Falftaffe, now fir Iohn, a boy, and page to Thomas Mowbray duke of Norffolke.

Si. This fir Iohn, coofin, that comes hither anone about
fouldi-

The second part of

Bar. You muſt away to court ſir preſently,
A dozen captaines ſtay at doore for you.

Fal. Pay the muſitians ſirra,farewel hoſteſſe,farewel Dol,
you ſee (my good wenches)how men of merit are ſought after,the vndeſeruer may ſleepe, when the man of action is calld
on,farewell good wenches, if I bee not ſent away poſte, I will
ſee you againe ere I goe.

Dol. I cannot ſpeake:if my heart be not ready to burſt:wel
ſweete Iacke haue a care of thy ſelfe.

Fal. Farewell farewell. *exit.*

Hoſt. Well, fare thee well,I haue knowne thee theſe twenty
nine yeares, come peaſe-cod time, but an honeſter, and truer
hearted man:wel fare thee weL

Bard. Miſtris Tere-ſheete.

Hoſt. Whats the matter?

Bard. Bid miſtris Tere-ſheete come to my maſter.

Hoſt. O runne Doll; runne, runne good Doll, come, ſhe
comes blubberd,yea!will you come Doll?

exeunt.

*Enter the King in his night-gowne
alone.*

King Go call the Earles of Surrey and of War.
But ere they come, bid them o're-reade theſe letters,
And well conſider of them,make good ſpeed.
How many thouſand of my pooreſt ſubiects,
Are at this howre aſleepe? ô ſleepe ô gentle ſleep!
Natures ſoft nurſe,how haue I frighted thee,
That thou no more wilt weigh my eye-liddes downe,
And ſteep my ſences in forgetfulneſſe,
Why rather ſleepe lieſt thou in ſmoaky cribbes,
Vpon vneaſie pallets ſtretching thee,
And huſht with buzzing night-flies to thy ſlumber,
Then in the perfumde chambers of the great,

Vnder

23   Sig. E3ᵛ from Quarto B, 1600

444

there would have been no tell-tale signs in surrounding manuscript pages to alert the compositor to an omission. More speculatively, Melchiori argues that the sheet was retrieved from an early draft of a single play in which Shakespeare set out to dramatize the reign of Henry IV: when the material proved too unwieldy for one play and Shakespeare divided it after the Battle of Shrewsbury, he 'decided at the last moment, when the printing of the foul papers [for *Part Two*] was already at an advanced stage, to insert among them the recovered leaf containing the scene [3.1]', but too late for the first printing, since 'the insertion was made when the reviser who had been at work on the rest of the foul papers had already completed his job, so that they escaped his attention' (Melchiori, 201). Equally speculatively, Jowett and Taylor conjecture that Shakespeare wrote the scene as an 'afterthought' – part of an effort to expand the play's historical material – because a scene composed in sequence would have begun on the leaf where the previous scene ended and not on a new sheet, unless it had been written at a different time; and further, that the compositor, finding no indication of where the new leaf should be inserted, might simply have 'set it aside, without bothering to investigate further' ('Three texts', 35–9). Each argument has merit; neither can be proved.

Nevertheless, the possibility exists that the scene was deliberately withheld from publication in Qa, and there has been much speculation about why that might have been so. Most of it centres on the presence of a long passage in which the King and Warwick recollect events that led to King Richard's abdication (57–92): since the question of legitimate succession and the possibility of rebellion were very much in the air during the last years of Elizabeth's reign, and since she herself is said to have remarked to her archivist William Lambarde in 1601, 'I am Richard II, know ye not that?', Ricardian material of any sort might have been regarded as potentially seditious.[1] If Master of the Revels Edmund Tilney in 1597 found the references to Richard's abdication in 3.1 offensive and therefore censored the scene, or if press licensers censored it in 1600, or if the printer himself, anticipating possible offence, removed the scene pre-emptively, such action could account for its absence.

But there are problems with assuming censorship. First, even though the deposition scene had been suppressed in early Q copies of *Richard II* and was not printed until 1608, there is no evidence that the deposition was not performed onstage at least until 1601 (Chambers, *Shakespeare*, 2.326–7). Furthermore, even without the deposition scene, *R2* vividly dramatizes political content that is only narrated in *2H4*, so one must question why narrated material should be removed from the quarto of *2H4* as potentially seditious when three quartos of *R2*, potently topical even without the deposition scene, had been allowed to be printed.[2] Second, the theory that 3.1 might have been censored is complicated by the fact that four of the remaining eight passages omitted in Q but printed in F also include Ricardian references. If political sensitivities led to the censorship of these potentially offensive passages, why was 3.1 allowed to pass muster and be included in Qb so soon after the printing of Qa?[3] Moreover, why was the whole of 3.1 initially

1 This anecdote has met with scepticism, most recently from Jonathan Bate (256–86), though a thorough appraisal of historical evidence by Jason Scott-Warren restores credibility to the account of Elizabeth's conversation with Lambarde.

2 Richard Dutton argues that 'the most compelling explanation' for why the murder of a king was allowed to be shown while the 'non-inflammatory abdication' scene was censored 'is that the scene specifically shows Richard's abdication being sanctioned by Parliament, suggesting that parliamentary authority might outweigh that of the monarch' ('Licensing', 382–3).

3 G.W. Williams argues that 3.1 preserves Qb's reference to Richard only 'because the leaf containing the reference was misplaced at the time the political cuts were made in the quarto' ('Text', 177).

withheld, when conceivably the offending 36 lines might have been excised and the rest of the scene left intact, as was the case with the four other Ricardian passages? Weis speculates that the scene was temporarily withheld by Shakespeare's company in an act of self-censorship but, when the licensers proved unexpectedly lenient, was quickly reinstated (84). This scenario, however, assumes a process more complicated than the simple misplacement or disregard of a manuscript sheet at the time of initial printing. In the absence of a compelling case for the removal of the scene in anticipation of a censorship that was never exercised, accidental omission appears, though far from a certainty, a more credible explanation.

Apart from its inclusion of 3.1, Qb is not preferable to Qa. In resetting the text as needed to accommodate 3.1 – involving a total of 153 lines, from 2.4.345 (in Qa, '*Host.* No I warrant you.') to 3.2.103–4 (in Qa, '*Sha.* What think you sir Iohn, a good limbd fellow, yong, strong, and of good friends.') – Valentine Simmes's Compositor A, who has been identified as responsible for both issues of Q,[1] introduced 165 variants in accidentals (spelling and punctuation), averaging more than one per line, and eight more substantial variants – four additions of words or phrases, one notation for an exit, two deletions and one transposition.[2] Unless these variants were corrections that resulted from checking Qa against the manuscript (and only in the provision of an exit for Falstaff at 2.4.386 may they be said to improve Qa), they provide incontrovertible evidence of compositorial inaccuracy and also suggest how frequently this compositor may have erred in his reading of the manuscript on which the text for Qa was based (Humphreys, xii, n.1). Using the ratio of eight substantive variants per 153 lines, I calculate that the compositor would have introduced 157 substantive

1   See W. Ferguson, 19–29, and Williams, 'Text', 173–4.
2   The most thorough analysis of the compositorial resetting of Q is provided by Berger & Williams, 'Variants'.

variants in a Q text of 3,000 lines – and this if he was setting from print, as he most probably did with the text surrounding the cancel. When he worked from manuscript, however, as he did in setting Qa, the compositor's rate of error is likely to have been much higher. G.W. Williams estimates that Compositor A was 'probably responsible for introducing nearly two hundred corruptions by varying from his copy' ('Text', 174), and this is a conservative estimate. Thus, while the logic of compositorial typesetting makes Qa a more reliable text than Qb because it is one step closer to the manuscript, an editor seeking to produce a reliable text must be alert to how fraught with error Qa may be as well.

THE FOLIO

The eight long passages contained exclusively in F bear all the hallmarks of Shakespearean authorship. The decision of which text, Q or F, has greater authority may therefore hinge on whether one concludes that these passages were originally in the copy-text for Q but cut before its printing or, alternatively, that they were added later as authorial revisions. Examination of the eight passages traditionally divides them into two groups (cf. Weis, 85–7): four involve political material recapitulating events dramatized in *Richard II* that are now lamented by the rebels who participated in them; the other four are less explicable cuts possibly made for theatrical purposes, to reduce the burden of actors who were doubling roles or to shorten the text for performance. The division of the two groups is as follows:

Political:

(*a*) 1.1.189–209   Morton argues that since the Archbishop claims power from God and 'enlarge[s] his rising with the blood / Of fair King Richard', his religious insurrection should succeed where Hotspur's failed;

(*b*) 1.3.85–108   The Archbishop comments on the fickleness of the mob who first overthrew King Richard and now, 'enamoured on his grave', have been swayed to overthrow King Henry as well. Although he will use the mob to achieve his goal, he laments the inconstancy of the political process by which insurrection is achieved;

(*c*) 4.1.55–79   The Archbishop compares the current 'burning fever' to the 'disease' that caused the death of Richard, vowing to 'purge' the kingdom with the articles of grievance that he has thus far been prevented from presenting to Henry or, barring that, with arms;

(*d*) 4.1.103–39   Westmorland and Mowbray argue about the aborted duel between Bolingbroke and Mowbray's father that precipitated the rebellion against Richard.

Theatrical:

(*e*) 1.1.166–79   Morton admonishes Northumberland to restrain his grief over the death of Hotspur, reminding him that he knew the risks of rebellion before he sanctioned it;

(*f*) 1.3.21–4   Lord Bardolph warns against proceeding to battle without reinforcement by Northumberland;

(*g*) 1.3.36–55   In a long and strained architectural analogy, Lord Bardolph compares rebellion to the building of a house;

(*h*) 2.3.23–45   Lady Percy delivers a heroic elegy on her husband, the aim of which is to persuade Northumberland not to desecrate Hotspur's memory by lending aid to the Archbishop when he failed to do so for his own son.

Is there evidence that any of these lines were once included in Q or in the manuscript upon which Q was based? Indeed, such evidence is provided in some cases by the fact that the verse lines in the surrounding text of Q are rendered metrically complete only by inclusion of the excised passage. The omission of passage *b*, for instance, leaves a metrically incomplete line for Hastings at 1.3.85, the omission of passage *d* leaves

Mowbray with an incomplete line at 4.1.103, and the omission of passage *h* leaves Northumberland with an incomplete line at 2.3.45. In other cases, meaning is obscured or images rendered unintelligible by the omission of the passage. The lines surrounding passage *a* make no sense without the missing lines: there is no explanation of what Morton 'hear[s] for certain' and 'dare[s] speak' (1.1.188), and Northumberland's 'I knew of this before' (210) has no antecedent. The excision of passage *e* means that Bardolph's 'this loss' (1.1.180) likewise has no antecedent. The excision of passage *f* involves a 'Till' clause whose omission makes unclear the Archbishop's response that 'It was young Hotspur's cause' (1.3.26), for 'It' has no antecedent. Similarly, the excision of passage *h*, in which Lady Percy remonstrates with her father-in-law for forsaking Hotspur, leaves little motivation for Northumberland's reply, 'you do draw my spirits from me / With new lamenting ancient oversights' (2.3.46–7). More significantly, the omission of passage *c* all but eviscerates the Archbishop's justification for rebellion, and the omission of passage *d* leaves Westmorland's 'But this is mere digression from my purpose' (4.1.140) without a referent, for he has said nothing prior to this line.

In all but one instance, therefore, the omission of F-only passages from Q obscures either the metrics or the meaning of surrounding lines in Q. Even the remaining passage of twenty lines (*g*) precedes a speech (56–62) in which Lord Bardolph continues the architectural analogy begun in those lines, and the final line of the omitted passage ends with the conjunctive 'or else' (55), suggesting that it once was contiguous with what follows. One may therefore confidently conclude that at least seven of the passages, and probably all eight, were once a part of the manuscript which served as the copy for Q.

On closer inspection, furthermore, the familiar scholarly distinction between the passages cut for political reasons and those cut for more practical theatrical purposes appears to break down, for all eight passages occur in scenes with the rebels – a total of 168 out of 621 F lines in the affected scenes, or 27% of the total – suggesting that at some point there was a concerted effort to de-emphasize scenes involving the conspiracy. All the cuts, therefore, may have been politically motivated. But why? Omission of the four passages containing references to Richard has typically been ascribed to censorship, though sensitivity to Ricardian material had not prevented the continued performance of *Richard II* as late as 1601 nor the printing of 3.1, with its numerous references to Richard, in Qb of *Part Two*. One could postulate that the printer of *Part Two*, who may have withheld 3.1 pre-emptively as likely to offend authorities, did the same with the other Ricardian passages, and that when they were found not to be offensive, decided that it would be too much trouble for the compositor to reinstate them along with 3.1 in the rush to publish Qb. But this would pile conjecture upon conjecture.

Alternatively, Weis hypothesizes that the reason these passages may have failed to pass muster with the licensers is not that they mention Richard, but that they dramatize the involvement of the Archbishop of York in a treasonous rebellion.[1] This anti-episcopal emphasis might have proved distasteful to the correctors of the press who licensed printed material on behalf of the Privy Council, the Bishop of London, the Archbishop of Canterbury and the Lord Chamberlain. It might therefore have provided reason enough to prompt the shortening of rebel scenes; for despite the fact that not all of the omitted passages involve the Archbishop (though the omission of *b* and *c* dramatically reduces his role), they cumulatively serve to de-emphasize the Prelate's Rebellion, and their excision would therefore have been predicated on reasons different from the temporary withholding of 3.1.

---

1   Weis, 85–6, cites Clare, 68, who argues that the fact that 'the rebellion gains respectability from the leadership of a righteous Archbishop would have been an immediate reason for the censor's intervention'.

The date at which cuts were made may be significant, for if censorship did in fact occur, some have speculated that it was motivated in part by the attempt in 1600 of a Franciscan monk to foment rebellion in Ireland with the gift of six thousand pounds from Spain and the promise of further Spanish military aid.[1] Scenes in *Part Two* that dramatize an archbishop plotting against an established monarch under the guise of religion thus may have cut dangerously close to the bone, reminding authorities of the recent situation in which a bishop colluded with Irish chieftains to rise up against Elizabeth in the name of the Roman Church. But there are problems with this theory. First, as Cyndia Susan Clegg observes, there is no evidence that the Bishop of Dublin was actually fomenting rebellion ('Liberty', 474–5). Further, there is far greater likelihood that playtexts were subject to scrutiny by the Master of the Revels before their performance (in this case 1597) than that they were censored by press licensers at the time of their publication.

The immediate situation in 1600 was hardly dire enough to have warranted seeing a threat in the excised passages: typically licensers of print censored only material that had a direct and explicit bearing on the crown. The books censored during this time did not offend through analogy and innuendo: they actually libelled government officials, challenged the monarch's authority in matters political, ecclesiastical and parliamentary, or championed successors to the monarch (Clegg, 'Liberty', 477).[2] Moreover, the threat of rebellion by Catholics had been

---

1   This conjecture was first made by Alfred Hart (191), reinforced by Humphreys (lxxi) and subsequently taken up by Jowett and Taylor ('Three texts', 41–2).

2   Clegg's caveat is instructive: 'Furthermore, given that the kinds of books that were actually censored did not merely *refer* to political matters but libeled government officials (either at home or abroad), denied the ruling monarch's ecclesiastical or political authority or the authority of Parliament, or advocated successors to the monarch, it seems unwise to credit the press censors with eliminating even sensitive topical allusions unless all other possibilities have been ruled out' ('Liberty', 477). Clegg surveys Elizabethan press censorship more fully in *Press Censorship*: see especially her discussion of the 1599 Bishops' Ban, 198–217.

bruited for years – it had become the obsession of Lord Burleigh – and would have been felt just as potently in 1597 as in 1600. Thus there is no more reason to think that the particular situation of the Dublin bishop would have provoked censorship of the Q text before its publication than that the political climate three years earlier would have caused the Master of the Revels to insist on those cuts prior to performance. In 1597, furthermore, the representation of the Prelate's Rebellion as a broadly popular response to abuses of power might have been found even more objectionable because it potentially invoked an analogous injustice, inflated prices for corn paid by the poor caused by landowners' hoarding it for profit – conditions similar to those that Dutton reports led to rioting in London in 1593 and 1595 and consequently to the censorship of *Sir Thomas More* (*Mastering*, 84–6; also Clegg, 'Liberty', 476–7). Thus, if censorship was involved at all in the cutting of the Q text, one might more reasonably assume that cuts were made by the Master of the Revels (or, pre-emptively, by the company itself) before the play's first performance in 1597 than that they were made at the time of its publication three years later.

But what of the possibility that in 1600, the Earl of Essex's displeasure over his treatment by the Queen in the conduct of the Irish wars might have led to suppression of the Ricardian passages in *Part Two* as covert references to the current situation? Conceivably, passages about sedition heretofore ignored were suddenly found to be inflammatory.[1] Furthermore, the passage in which Lady Percy glorifies Hotspur (*h*) – identifiable as an Essex figure in his misguided heroism – may have been deemed potentially offensive: the Essex association would explain the removal of a passage which, apart from

1 Dutton speculates that by 1600, the younger Henry Cobham, son of the deceased Lord Chamberlain and 'brother-in-law of Robert Cecil, and so by definition an opponent of the Earl of Essex', may have detected 'uncomfortable political connotations' involving Essex in the play and therefore intervened in its publication (*Mastering*, 109–10).

shortening a boy actor's role, is otherwise inexplicable. It might also have prompted the excision of passage *e*, in which Morton discusses the likelihood that Hotspur might 'drop' because 'he walked o'er perils', 'his forward spirit . . . lift[ing] him where most trade of danger ranged'. The shadowy figure of Essex may lurk in these excised passages more substantially than has previously been recognized. Nevertheless, as Clegg reminds us, Essex was not yet in royal disfavour when Q was printed in 1600 ('Liberty', 475). It is tempting to read back into the text what occurred afterwards – the abortive rebellion of February1601 – and assume that Essex was already at odds with the Queen, but such retrospection is historically suspect. The available evidence refutes such an assumption. Censorship thus remains an unproven and highly speculative reason for cuts to have been made in the Q text.

An alternative hypothesis, first advanced by Pope and recently taken up by Jowett and Taylor, is that 3.1 and most – though not all – of the other eight passages were not deleted from but added to the text that had served as copy for Q in an effort to shore up the historical material in *Part Two* and to bind the play more closely to those histories that had preceded it. In other words, these additions were the result of Shakespeare's reworking of material before it was transcribed in a fair copy. In the late twentieth century, interest in this hypothesis sprang from two critical impulses: a determination to view the history plays as a cycle (see pp. 11, 31–3), and a belief that variant texts of the same play often provide evidence of authorial revision. Jowett and Taylor argue that 3.1 and six of the eight passages (all but *b* and *c*, which they claim were censored and whose excision they acknowledge damages surrounding text) may be

> convincingly explained as additions made in the Folio text. . . . Shakespeare seems to have begun to expand the historical matter of the play, and in particular the links with the events he had dramatized in *Richard II*

and *1 Henry IV*, whilst still working on the foul papers. He evidently continued this process of expansion and consolidation, perhaps shortly afterwards when preparing or by adding to the fair copy which was to serve as the prompt-book, a direct or indirect transcript of which must accordingly have eventually served as the printer's copy for F.

(*TxC*, 351)[1]

The influence of the cycle mentality on textual editing finds its fullest expression in a study of Shakespearean revision by Grace Iopollo, who, writing five years after publication of the Oxford *Complete Works*, asserts that the purpose of Shakespeare's additions was for characters to 'recall events already presented in the early plays in order to provide a sense of dramatic and theatrical unity and continuity among all four of the plays . . . perhaps in anticipation of performing the four plays together in repertory'. The additions thus constitute 'Shakespeare's deliberate attempt to provide a type of unified structure and cross-referencing' among them (Iopollo, 130).

Eloquent though this pitch for authorial revision is, it ignores the evidence detailed above that the six passages thought to have been added to F could not have been mere afterthoughts, because their omission from Q makes mincemeat of the surrounding text metrically, or logically, or both. On the contrary, it makes more sense to argue that these passages, including 3.1, may have been omitted to shorten the play for performance by removing historical material deemed unnecessary for audiences already familiar with the earlier plays or for their understanding the present action. In a recent study of the length of printed

---

1 For a full account of the Oxford editors' argument, see Jowett & Taylor, 'Three texts'.

texts vs. manuscript playbooks used for performance, Lukas Erne, concurring with Gurr that many plays would have been too long to perform as published, argues that what has come down to us are literary texts prepared for a readership, and playwrights would have expected their plays to be considerably cut in the playhouse.[1] Evidence of playbooks surviving from this period suggests that a play of 2,500 lines would have taken two and a half hours to perform. Nevertheless, although few plays may have required audiences to stand for longer than that, no evidence exists that plays had to be this short in order to be performed.[2] At 3,350 lines, the Folio text of *Part Two* is one of the longest plays in the canon, third only to *Hamlet* and *Richard III*. Cutting 3.1 and the eight passages found exclusively in F would have reduced the play by a little more than 10% to the length of Qa, which has exactly 3,000 lines.[3]

Were all these passages cut simply to shorten the play for performance? None of them is necessary to advance the plot; on the contrary, they have in common the quality of literary or historical embellishment. The expanded metaphor of building a house, the panegyric to the fallen Hotspur, the King's meditation on sleep – such passages read well as literature but do nothing to further the stage action. Other of the omitted passages, largely narrative, foreground historical continuities between Richard II and Henry IV and thereby emphasize the cyclical nature of the plays, but they would be expendable if *Part Two*

---

1 In ch. 6, 'Why size matters', Erne discusses the relationship between the length of Shakespeare's plays and what we know about the length of performances in London's theatres. He argues that information about how much of a play was performed can best be gleaned not from printed texts but from extant dramatic manuscripts (155–97).

2 The belief that there was any upper limit on how long a performance could be has been ably challenged by David Klein, Michael Hirrel and Steven Urkowitz.

3 Making these cuts alone, however, would not have been sufficient to reduce the text to Erne's idea of an acceptable playing time. He speculates that although manuscript playbooks contained some cuts, actors' parts probably contained even more made during rehearsals (187).

were performed as an independent play. They thicken for readers the political contexts in which history may be understood, but they do little to further the action. Cumulatively, these cuts also reduce the playing time allotted to the play's chronicle history and especially to the rebellion. No cuts, on the other hand, were made in scenes of comedy. As a result, those involving Falstaff must have become more prominent in performance, in recognition perhaps of what had proved most popular with audiences at *Part One*, and the play's balance between history and comedy would have tipped in favour of the latter, especially, as noted earlier, in the juxtaposition of 2.4 and 3.2 which allowed Falstaff to dominate the middle of the play. It is possible, then, to regard the elimination of 3.1 and the eight F-only passages as a preliminary attempt to reduce the length of the play to something more manageable for performance. The copy-text for Qa probably contained these passages marked for deletion: such cuts are consistent with those made in surviving manuscript playbooks for the purpose of shortening a text for performance. The copy-text for F would presumably have contained these passages without marks for deletion.

F as a literary text

The printer's copy for F seems not to have been a playbook, but rather 'a highly sophisticated literary manuscript . . . in which the scribe systematically imposed his own orthography, and was liable to tidy up any feature of his copy, whether compositional or theatrical, which struck him as irregular' (Jowett, 275). By modern editorial standards, therefore, F would seem to be a cleaner and more consistent text on which to base an edition. The inclusion of the eight passages missing from Q suggests its origins in an authorial manuscript, but other corrections of errors possibly introduced by the Q compositor also recommend it. 'Basingstoke', for example, replaces the obviously erroneous 'Billingsgate' in Q as the place where the King spends the night on his return to London (2.1.168); 'Sure-card' is offered as a witty substitution for the colloquial 'Soccard' as Falstaff misremembers Silence's name (3.2.86); 'Samforth' is corrected to 'Stamford' as the location of the fair mentioned by Justice Shallow (3.2.38); and 'Hunkly' is corrected to 'Hinckley' as the fair mentioned by Davy (5.1.23). Among the numerous substitutions and transpositions offered in F, then, some are clearly superior to Q. Others, however, are less warranted, especially when they involve the normalization of pronunciations that would be appropriately idiomatic for the speaker. It defeats the humour of regional dialect when, for example, 'Whitson' is offered as a substitution for Mistress Quickly's 'Wheeson' (2.1.88), or 'Lombard' for her 'Lumbert' (27); or when indications of Shallow's Gloucestershire pronunciations 'Cotsole man' (3.2.21) and 'Dooble' (40) are changed to 'Cot-sal-man' and 'Double'.

F nevertheless provides a consistency and regularity lacking in Q in some significant ways. First, stage directions, which in Q had been sporadic but sometimes revealingly descriptive, have been shorn of description. Gone are Rumour's being '*painted full of tongues*' (Ind.0), Lord Bardolph's entering '*at one doore*' at 1.1.0, the enigmatic entrance for Falstaff '*alone, with his page bearing his sword and buckler*' at 1.2.0, the detail of the King's entering '*in his night-gowne alone*' at 3.1.0, and the identification of place, '*within the forrest of Gaultree*', at 4.1.0. Indeed, all Q stage directions other than those involving entrances and exits have been systematically eliminated. Furthermore, entrances and exits that were either neglected or seemingly misplaced in Q have been more systematically, though by no means completely, accounted for in F. Following the Induction, the text requires the stage to be cleared seventeen times: F provides sixteen of those exits, Q only six. F also provides an entrance for the Porter at 1.1.0 and a Servant for the Chief Justice at 1.2.55; clarifies that '*Bardolph and his Boy*', not '*Bardolfes boy*', enter at 2.4.109; provides a Page for the King at 3.1.0; adds an entrance for Collevile at 4.2.0; and inserts numerous directions throughout for characters whose entrances and exits go unmarked in Q.

F also clears up uncertainties in Q's permissive stage directions and revises the surrounding text accordingly. The indeterminate '*an Officer or two*' who enter with the Hostess at 2.1.0 are listed by their names, '*Fang, and Snare*', in F (though with a variant on the Q spelling '*Phang*'); the '*with other*' at 2.2.0 is gone; the '*Drawer or two*' who open 2.4 are fixed as two in F, shorn of the names Q gives them as the scene progresses (Francis and Will), and their speech attributions sorted out, with two lines excised to clarify that a third drawer does not enter (see 2.4.0.1–2n.); the number of grooms who open 5.5 – no longer '*strewers of rushes*' as in Q – is similarly fixed at two, and a line deleted; the vague '*and one with him*' who accompanies Bardolph at 3.2.54 is identified as '*his Boy*' in F; and a permissive '*and the rest*' who enter with Prince John and Westmorland at 4.2.23 is cut. F also eliminates the ghost characters who populate Q – those for whom an entrance is listed but who do not speak: '*Fauconbridge*' at 1.3.0, '*sir Iohn Russel*' at 2.2.0, '*sir Iohn Blunt*' at 3.1.31 and 5.2.41 (though Blunt needs to enter with Prince John as one of '*the rest*' at 4.2.23, since he is told to guard Collevile at 73), '*Bardolfe*' at 4.1.0 and '*Kent*' at 4.3.0. F also eliminates a line at Q 1.1.161 that is assigned to an otherwise mute character named '*sir Iohn Vmfreuile*' (see 1.1.161 SPn.).

Finally, F regularizes names in stage directions and speech prefixes in Q. Unlike Q's widely varying designation of characters in speech prefixes (see pp. 434–5), F's are terse and relatively uniform: Northumberland is '*Nor*[*th.*]', the Lord Chief Justice is '[*Ch.*] *Iu*[*st*].', Harry is '*P. Hen.*' / '*Pr.*' / '*Prin*[*ce*]', and his brothers are, without variation, '*Ioh*[*n*], '*Glo*[*u*].' and '*Cla*[*r*].'. Shallow is '*Shal*[*low*]' throughout,

Silence is uniformly '*Sil.*' and the boy is '*Pag[e]*'. Those whose speech prefixes F regularizes most rigorously, however, are comic characters: Falstaff, who in Q had seven different designations, is always '*Fal.*' / '*Falst.*' / '*Falstaffe*'; Mistess Quickly, who had six, is exclusively '*Host[esse]*'; and Doll Tearsheet, who had eight, is exclusively '*Dol.*'. F also corrects Q's misattribution, to Shallow, of the speech in which Falstaff ridicules Shallow (3.2.299–331).

This correction of stage directions and regularizing of names has traditionally been thought to provide evidence that the scribal copy used for F was based in part on a playbook used for performance. But as I discussed earlier, surviving manuscript playbooks do not show the attention to detail or the concern with regularity and uniformity that was believed by earlier editors to be the hallmarks of 'promptbooks'. Rather, their stage directions and speech prefixes are typically more haphazard than was assumed they should be, their annotations less complete and more permissive, and ghost characters more often present. Uniformity and consistency, therefore, were never characteristic of playbooks (Werstine, *Manuscripts*, 193–4). Theatrical personnel did not need such help. Readers, however, would have benefited from it; and the scribal interventions apparent in the copy-text for F suggest that it may have been edited with readership in mind.

Two further sources of evidence help to demonstrate that a theatrical playbook did not serve as the copy-text from which the scribe preparing the F text worked. First, the massed entrances at 3.2.0, 4.1.0 and 5.3.0 which list characters who do not appear until later in the scene are probably scribal in origin. Some recent editors have claimed that these entrances originated in notes intended to make sure that actors were ready when called, but this is an anachronistic view of what playhouse personnel did. As Eleanor Prosser argues, these massed entrances may more plausibly be explained as the expedient of a scribe unfamiliar with the demands of a playscript: they were literary devices rather than signs of theatrical practice.[1] Certainly the entrance of the recruits as a group at the opening of 3.2 would diminish the comic effect of their individual appearances as they are called by Shallow later in the scene. Similarly, it makes no sense for Collevile to be listed at the opening of 4.1 when his entrance with Falstaff 351 lines later is also noted in F, nor for Pistol to be listed at the opening of 5.3 when he arrives with news of King Henry's death half way through the scene. The inclusion of Silence at the opening of 5.1, when he plays no part in that scene, may also have sprung from a scribe's impulse to anticipate all characters who he felt should be present.

Second, Q contains stage directions lacking in F that may have been indicative of theatrical practice. Among them are the final '*Exeunt*' for the rebel leaders at 1.3.110; the inclusion of '*and his men*' with the Lord Chief Justice when he enters at 2.1.59; an '*exit hostesse and sergeant*' at 2.1.164; the necessary inclusion of '*and boy*' with Bardolph when he enters at 2.2.66; the indication that '*Peyto knockes at doore*' at 2.4.356; the provision of an '*Exeunt*' for Falstaff, Shallow and Silence at 3.2.219 and, for their return, '*Enter Falstaffe and the Iustices*', at 241; an '*Exit Westmorland*' at 4.1.182; and an indication that a royal procession begins the final scene – '*Trumpets sound, and the King, and his traine passe ouer the stage*' – at 5.5.4.[2]

---

1 Prosser makes this argument convincingly in her study of the roles of scribe and compositor in the F text (19–50). Jowett, making a case for a 'prompt-book text' incorporating Shakespeare's revisions as the source of F, takes issue with some of Prosser's findings in 'Cuts', *passim*. Taylor, in ''Swounds', also takes on Prosser to confirm Jowett, claiming that F may 'derive from a transcript of a late, expurgated prompt-book' (69).

2 Prosser posits a theatrical justification of the royal procession passing twice over the stage (48), but Jowett counters that the Third Strewer's statement that the procession will come *from* the coronation (5.5.3–4), anticipating its arrival at 38, makes its entering twice 'bewildering' – and so, Jowett concludes, F sorts out the 'staging problem' in a manner 'characteristic of a prompt-book' ('Cuts', 284–5) by omitting both the first procession and, since there is now no reason for the strewers

Unless one assumes that a scribe edited out these stage directions from his copy-text, the evidence of a playbook provenance for F remains negligible.

The scribe did, however, heavily sanitize the text. The wholesale elimination of profanity in F has convinced previous editors that its copy-text dates from after the 'Acte to restraine Abuses of Players' was passed by Parliament in 1606 to outlaw profanity on the stage. Gary Taylor argues that such expurgation would have applied only to theatrical performance, not to printing, thus reinforcing his speculation that the copy-text for F was made by consulting a playbook that post-dated 1606.[1] Yet the elimination of profanity in F is not wholly consistent with provisions of the Act, which, as Chambers notes, 'was of very limited application' (*Shakespeare*, 1.238): the Act focused exclusively on 'Abuse of the Holy Name of God' and forebade anyone 'jestingly or prophanely [to] speake or use the holy Name of God or of Christ Jesus, or of the Holy Ghoste or of the Trinitie [in] any Stage play Interlude Shewe Maygame or Pageant'.[2] F eliminates oaths found in Q 134 times – most blatant among them, 'God' or 'God's light' or 'By God's liggens' (62 instances), 'Lord' (10), 'By the mass' (7) and 'Jesu' (4) – sometimes substituting 'Heauen', but often not. Yet anomalies exist. As Werstine observes, 'God has not completely disappeared from F.' Still present are the Hostess's reference

to hurry, the Third Strewer's command to 'dispatch' (4). I would argue, however, that there is no problem to sort out, for the trumpets sound twice: first (4) signalling that the King and his party are on their way to Westminster Abbey, and after some time (37) signalling that the coronation is over and that they are returning. It is therefore likely that Shakespeare intended both processions to occur.

1   In ''Swounds', Taylor concludes that 'with the probable exception of the omission of "zounds" in three plays set from annotated quarto copy, all of the Folio expurgation of profanity can be attributed to theatrical practice ... profanity [having] been outlawed from public performances, not private manuscripts or printed texts' (64).

2   3 Jac I, c. 21. *Statutes of the Realm*, IV, p. 1097. See also Chambers, *Elizabethan*, 4.338.

to 'God's officers' (2.1.50), the Chief Justice's wry comment to Falstaff, 'the Lord lighten thee' (2.1.192) and the Hostess's greeting to the Prince, 'the Lord preserve thy grace' (2.4.294). These surviving profanities, he notes, mark a difference between F and those dramatic manuscripts that show evidence of having passed through the hands of the Master of the Revels after passage of the Act in 1606; and although the Revels Office's censorship of profanity was neither as consistent nor thorough as was once thought, the extent of the surviving profanities in F makes it anomalous.[1]

There are other anomalies. 'Marry', for instance, a mildly profane reference to the Virgin Mary, is cut twice but kept once (3.2.123) and is even introduced as a substitution for Q's 'joy', which was probably a corruption of 'Jesu '(2.4.49). Likewise, 'the devil' is both cut (2.4.1) and kept (2.4.339); 'damned' slips through unscathed (2.4.140); and most inconsistently, 'by heauen', an oath that often in F substitutes for Q's 'God', is itself twice cut (3.2.61–2 and 77). Furthermore, F frequently eliminates mild oaths and phrases that were not censored by the Master of the Revels until the 1620s: 'faith', 'ifaith' and 'in good faith' are cut twenty-one times, though 'in faith' is allowed to stand at 3.2.216–17; 'troth', 'by my troth' and 'in truth' are cut or given substitutions eight times but allowed to stand six; 'upon my soul' is twice replaced by 'upon my life'; Falstaff's 'Blessed are they' is replaced by 'Happie are they' (5.3.137); 'as the psalmist saith' is cut; and such innocuous oaths as 'by're Lady', 'by this hand' and 'by this light' are all expunged as well. Thus only a portion of the profanities cut from or replaced in F fall under the list of those proscribed by the Act; the others were cut at the discretion of someone else.

In an essay on Q2 of *Othello*, Barbara Mowat argues persuasively that scribal intervention can more easily explain such expurgations than the provisions of the Act of 1606. She

---

1 See Werstine, in Folger edn, 288–9, and *Manuscripts*, 326–7.

cites Greg's argument that 'a literary tradition of expurgation' early in the seventeenth century, reflecting a social and political climate that increasingly frowned on profane or blasphemous language, may have led scribes to purge texts 'of expressive irreverence'[1] while transcribing them for readers or preparing them for print. As evidence, she offers Edward Dering's abridgement of the quartos of *Part One* and *Part Two* for a private performance *c.* 1622 (see pp. 480–2), in which the expurgation of irreverent passages was similar to that found in F, even though, as G.W. Williams and Blakemore Evans point out, 'Dering need not in a private performance have feared the application of the Act of 1606'.[2] It is not unreasonable, then, to conclude that other language too, though not profane, might have been deemed offensive and therefore expurgated either by the company in an act of self-censorship or by a scribe such as Ralph Crane, whose discomfort with 'sensual explicitness' and 'fastidiousness' in eliminating 'even very mild oaths' reflected 'either his own misgivings or his assumption about those of the intended recipient of the text' (Dutton, *Censorship*, 157). F has been purged of a number of scatological passages of the sort that might offend the sensibility of a reader but would scarcely have offended playgoers at a public theatre. Two of the omissions are substantial: in one, the Prince invokes God to bawdily disparage Poins's begetting of bastard children (2.2.23–7); in the other, Falstaff mocks Shallow's lechery and consorting with whores when he was a student at Clement's Inn (3.2.310–17). Doll's language is especially ripe in vulgarities such as 'A pox damn you' (2.4.40) which are blotted in F, as are several lines of Falstaffian *double entendre* such as 'No more, Pistol; I would not have you go off here. Discharge yourself of our company, Pistol' (2.4.136–7).

---

1   In 'Q2 *Othello*' (97), Mowat quotes first from Greg, *First Folio*, 152, and then from Taylor, ''Swounds', 77.

2   Mowat, Q2 *Othello*, 101–2, citing the Williams and Evans facsimile edition of Dering, viii.

Other evidence of scribal intervention occurs in the correction of grammar and the substitution of words; in the fleshing out of contractions and the general formalizing of colloquialisms, archaisms and solecisms; and in the altered spelling of names. F boasts hundreds of changes of this sort, all of them recorded in the textual notes. There are fifty-five corrections or clarifications of Q grammar, some warranted, some not. Several are made to provide a missing verb or to ensure subject–verb agreement, as in 'For his divisions . . . Are [Q And] in three heads' at 1.3.70–1; 'There are [Q is] many complaints' at 5.1.38; 'when beards wagge [Q wags] all' at 5.3.34; 'How ill white hairs become [Q becomes]' at 5.5.47; and numerous changes from 'hath' to 'has', 'doth' to 'does' and vice versa. Others correct a verb tense, as in the alteration of the Page's 'calls' to 'call'd' at 2.2.77 or Hastings's report that 'they took their course [Q take their courses]' at 4.1.331 to ensure consistency with surrounding verbs; 'When you were more endeer'd [Q endeere]' at 2.3.11; 'I saw [Q see] him' at 3.2.29; and 'a soldier is better accommodated [Q accommodate]' at 3.2.66–7. F occasionally adds or alters a word to clarify Q's phrasing, as in the addition of 'hath' at 1.2.171; the change of 'slender' to the comparative 'slenderer' at 1.2.144; the provision of a direct object 'them' for Q's 'Diseases make' at 2.4.43; the addition of 'his' before Q's 'apparel' at 3.2.144; and the provision of the verb 'is' to make a clause of the Q fragment 'Other, less fine in carat, more precious' at 4.3.291.

Some of these changes seem simply pedantic and would have run counter to the idiomatic, at times archaic speech expected of characters in this play. F replaces a few of Q's archaisms with modern words or spellings: 'bond' for 'band', 'eare' for 'yeere', 'before' for 'afore', 'others' for 'other', and, frequently, 'if' for 'and'.[1] Among other changes are 'who' to

---

1 As Kastan observes in *Book*, the 1623 Folio and the three that followed it introduced and developed the principle of modernizing Shakespeare's text (82).

'whom' (1.1.28) and 'Whom' to 'Which' (4.3.237), 'whom' being an acceptable alternative to 'which' in the sixteenth century but less so in the early seventeenth; the turning into infinitives of the verbs 'smell' (1.2.156) and 'conceal' (5.3.111) to ensure that Falstaff speak in rhetorical parallelisms; and the emendation of Warwick's 'Of he' to 'Of him' (5.2.16). In so far as a number of these changes destroy the colloquial humour of some of the play's most original language, they are unforgivable. Take, for instance, F's turning the Hostess's comic protests 'Thou wot, wot thou? Thou wot, wot ta?' into the formal 'Thou wilt not? Thou wilt not?' (2.1.55–6); its spoiling a prize Quicklyism in 'desire me to be no more so familiarity' by insisting that she say 'be no more familiar' (98); or its correction of her malapropian term for the Beadle, 'atomy', to 'Anatomy' (5.4.28). Such changes suggest that F was prepared by someone intent on decorum at the expense of any fidelity to the colloquial speech that is so vital to the play in performance.

In an analogous spirit of pedantry, F duly expands the various forms of contractions found in Q. Apart from the comic characters' use of the colloquial ''a', which F invariably translates as 'he', contractions of two or more words are most common in Q, numbering at least eighty. Most typically, F expands Q's ''tis' to 'it is', 'Ile' to 'I will', 'heele' to 'he will', 'theres' to 'there is', 'too't' to 'to it', 'an't' to 'if it', and the like. Often such expansions result in regularizing the speech of more idiosyncratic characters, so that the Hostess's colloquial 'an 'twere' becomes the more formal 'if it were'; her 't'other', 'the other'; the Page's 'A' calls me enow' becomes the more grammatical 'He call'd me euen now'; Pistol's insistent 'giues [give us] some sack' becomes the more polite 'giue me'; Falstaff's 'thou't' is expanded to 'thou wilt', and his 'he'd 'a' to 'he would haue'. F also tends to print the full spelling of Q's one-word contractions, such as 'neuer' for 'nere', 'taken' for 'tane', 'Victuallers' for 'vitlars' and 'Sherife' for 'shrieve'.

The scribe who prepared the manuscript on which F was based also appears to have completed with his own words incomplete verse lines and otherwise fixed metrical irregularities found in Q. A brief survey of Act 4 in F reveals the extent of such scribal intervention. In the first scene, for example, Prince John's admonition to the rebels, 'look to taste the due / Meet for rebellion' – the second line a hemistich which allows a dramatic pause after John's judgement – was rounded out to make a complete iambic line with 'and such Acts as yours' (4.1.344–5); yet earlier, the word 'talking' in John's castigation of the Archbishop as 'an iron man talking' in Q (4.1.236) was expunged, apparently for making the line hypermetrical. In 4.3, 'Canst thou tell that?' was added to 52 to turn a hemistich into a regular verse line; 'and will breake out' was added to 120 and 'how fares your Grace?' to the second half of 180 for the same reason. To accommodate the change of 'tolling' to 'culling' in 205, a direct object is provided at the opening of the next line, 'The vertuous Sweetes', thus requiring a re-lineation of 206–9.

Finally, F includes a peculiarly large number of round brackets which set it apart from Q and therefore would not seem to be traceable to a common source. Taylor has analysed the portion of the play set by Compositor A – just short of twelve pages – and discovered in it 136 pairs of round brackets, only twenty of which coincide with brackets in Q.[1] This compositor's work on previous plays, including *Part One*, suggests that he followed his copy closely with regard to round brackets. Taylor thus concludes that these brackets originated not with the F compositor, but in the copy from which he worked. All of this evidence suggests the intervention of a scribe who, with habits similar to those of Ralph Crane, if not Crane himself, sought to correct what he perceived to be

---

1   See Appendix 1, 'The printer's copy for Folio *2 Henry IV*', in Taylor & Jowett, 245–7. Prior to Taylor, Alice Walker noted 'the abundance of some 260 parentheses in the F text of the play' as opposed to only 40 in Q (*Textual*, 107).

imperfect copy for F and to impose his own sense of decorum on it. The problem confronting an editor, then, is what to make of a Folio text which, with its inclusion of eight passages omitted from Q, seems to be based on a copy-text of some authority, yet also bears unmistakable marks of scribal contamination that render it unreliable.

Was F indebted to Q?

The relationship of F to Q makes the choice of text even more problematic. Some of the alterations, corrections and clarifications detailed above – unless one attributes all of them to a scribe – suggest that F originated in a source text different from that used for Q and, further, cast in doubt whether the scribe who prepared copy for F made any use at all of Q. Conceivably, Q and F derived from entirely different copy. Nevertheless, a few errors or idiosyncrasies in Q, some of which may have resulted from compositorial error, are repeated in F and thus, according to some editors, offer evidence that the manuscript for F was based at least in part on Q or, at the extreme, may have been a heavily annotated copy of Q itself.[1] Those who espouse a connection between Q and F argue that some errors shared by the two are too coincidental to be accounted for in any other way. For instance, a few words common to Q and F – 'hole' instead of 'hold' at Ind.35, 'inuincible' instead of 'invisible' at 3.2.312 and 'rage' instead of 'rags' at 4.1.34 – are all seen as evidence that F borrowed from Q. But this supposition holds only if one regards the QF words as erroneous; and, as I argue in the commentary, a good case can be made for 'hole', 'inuincible' and 'rage' as defensible word choices. Therefore, their appearance in F could be accounted for by their presence in Shakespeare's holograph and

---

1 A. Walker makes a case for Q as the most probable copy-text for F, based on their shared features, common errors, and typographical similarities (*Textual*, 94–120).

any subsequent copies made from it, not necessarily by their presence in Q alone.

Similarly, it is believed that F shares with Q the common misattributions of 3.2.150 to Shallow instead of Falstaff and of 5.5.17 and 19 to Pistol instead of Shallow; but again, as I argue in the commentary, the attribution of these lines in Q and F is perfectly defensible and could have come from any copies derived from Shakespeare's holograph. Other evidence of F's connection to Q may seem more compelling: an intriguing absence of single lines of verse following 4.1.92 and 94 common to corrected copies of Qa and F (see 4.1.93, 95n.), the erroneous use of 'imagine' rather than imagined at 4.1.247 and the idiosyncratic spellings of the words 'downy' and 'down' as 'dowlny' (Q), 'dowlney' (F) and 'dowlne' (QF) at 4.3.163–4. Unless one is willing to posit that the idiosyncrasies of Shakespeare's holograph were replicated in the source manuscript for F without going through Q, these shared deviations, few though they are, suggest that the scribe may have consulted Q in preparing the text for F.

On the other hand, striking differences in spelling and other deviations may indicate that Q was not a source for the manuscript on which F was based. Variations in the spelling of proper names suggest that the F scribe misread manu-script copy rather than Q, which, as print, would have been much easier to decipher: for instance, 'Dombledon' for Q's 'Dommelton' at 1.2.30, 'Dombe' for 'Dumbe' at 2.4.88, 'Bare' for 'Barnes' at 3.2.20 and 'Amurah' for 'Amurath' twice at 5.2.48. Even more striking, at 5.3.102 the name Cophetua, printed as 'Couetua' in Q, appears in F as 'Couitha': F's variant bears the unmistakable signs of a scribal misreading of manuscript, with substitutions of *i* for *e* and *th* for *tu* graphically easy to make. Likewise, at 4.3.308 F prints the word 'ioyne' for Q's 'win': the difference may be most logically explained by the F scribe's misreading of 'winne' in a manuscript and suggests that he was not working from Q (Humphreys, lxxviii).

Other substitutions of words in F suggest an independent source because they are inferior to Q's: 'them' for 'men' (Ind.8), 'head' for 'hard' (1.1.36), 'Speake' for 'Spoke' and 'aduenture' for 'a venter' (1.1.59), 'tucke' for 'tickle' (2.1.59), 'pernitious' for 'virtuous' (2.2.72), 'heart-deere' for 'hearts deere' (2.3.12), 'wee' for 'one' (2.4.28) and 'huisht with bussing Night, flyes' for 'husht with buzzing night-flies' (3.1.11). Such substitutions are unlikely to have been made by a scribe conflating Q with a manuscript because, in Humphreys's words, 'they look wrong, unnecessary, or odd' (lxxviii). Rather, they seem to provide evidence that the copy-text for F was prepared independent of Q.

On balance, the evidence that copy for F was made independent of consultation with Q outweighs evidence of its dependence on it. Nevertheless, coincidence ruled out, F shares just enough idiosyncrasies and errors with Q to hint that the scribe may have consulted Q as a secondary source. The fact that copies of Q were likely to have been widely available – more Q copies of *Part Two* have survived than for any other Shakespeare play – makes it reasonable to assume that the scribe would have had access to one. I would suggest, therefore, though without certainty, that the scribe who prepared the manuscript for F did so by collating Q with a literary transcription of the play, such as the one I have speculated might have been prepared at the insistence of Edmund Tilney in 1597 (see pp. 140–2), which included those passages not found in Q and many of the significant variants listed above.

The printing of F

Differences between Q and F are compounded by the history of the printing of the Folio text by William Jaggard. There was a delay in printing the two parts of *Henry IV*, perhaps because Matthew Law, the bookseller who held the rights to *Richard II* and *Henry IV, Part One*, 'made difficulties over the use of his copies' until he and Jaggard 'came to terms' (Greg, *Publishing*,

89*)*, or perhaps because scribal copy for *Part Two* was not yet ready. In any case, plays in the Folio were typically allocated no more than two quires, or 24 pages (a normal quire having three sheets folded in half and then stitched together to make 6 leaves or 12 pages); and certainly the two *Henry IV* plays, among the longest in the canon, should have been allocated at least that much space. The plays printed before them, *King John* and *Richard II*, filled three quires (a, b, c), with 9 pages of *Richard II* encroaching on quire d. Had the *Henry IV* plays been ready for printing when *Richard II* was finished, they might have been allocated the remainder of quire d and an additional four quires. Instead, however, compositors decided to set *Henry V* first; and in a serious miscalculation, they began casting-off at quire h, leaving just three quires (e, f, g) plus the 3 remaining pages of quire d – a total of only 39 pages – for the two parts of *Henry IV* (Prosser, 74). Realizing that this space was woefully inadequate, the printer apparently decided to insert an extra quire (gg) between g and h so that the *Henry IV* plays would now share a total of 51 pages. Assuming this to be a sufficient allocation, the compositors were 'overly generous' in their setting of *Part One* (Weis, 92), which runs to 26 pages, leaving just 25 for *Part Two*. Yet at 3,350 lines, *Part Two* is the longer of the two plays by 170 lines.

Why would the compositors have made this error in judgement? If the scribal copy of *Part Two* was not yet available when they began casting-off for *Part One*, they may have calculated its length by counting the lines in Q instead, which, with so many passages deleted, has 267 fewer lines than F, and concluded that 25 pages would be ample for the printing. But when they began casting-off the scribal copy and realized that its greater length posed an almost insurmountable problem, their solution was to find any way possible to cram the text into the limited space remaining. In her magisterial study of the printing of the Folio text of *Part Two*, Prosser examines the process by which one of its two compositors, conventionally labelled Compositor B,[1] worked assiduously to compress text typographically by condensing, abbreviating or omitting words, and even by eliminating entire lines in order to squeeze the scribal copy into 25 pages – in effect becoming an editor himself.

Close scrutiny of just one page (g2^r) set by Compositor B, equivalent to 1.2.76–230 in the present edition, will reveal the extent of his ingenuity in solving the problem of having too much text to set per page.[2] With very few exceptions, an F page has 66 lines per column. Verse lines, of course, cannot easily be juggled or crowded together; but this page consists entirely of prose, which is more susceptible to manipulation. Compositor B took full advantage of his options to crowd prose into the least space possible. Two speeches, both in the second column, could be compressed by using legitimate typographical means: in one, at 154–5, he avoided an additional line by tightening the space around letters and by using a turn-up for the word 'Wolfe'; in the other, at 157–8, he avoided putting 'out' on a second line by shortening the Lord Justice's speech prefix to '*Iu.*', eliminating spaces that should follow the speech prefix and the question mark after 'What', and neglecting a period at the end. His other means of compression were more radical. In the first column, he altered 'an ague' to 'age' (99) and cut the repetition of 'in you' (100) in order to end the speech without running on to another line. Shortly thereafter (110), he cut 'you' after 'I pray' and turned up the second 'you' (111) to keep the

---

1 Almost invariably, two compositors were assigned to each play. Compositor B, who textual scholars agree set case y of *Part Two*, was given the task of compressing the text while setting the first half of quire g. A. Walker was the first to identify Compositor A as responsible for setting case x, an identification with which Charlton Hinman concurred (xviii). Although Taylor (*TxC*, 148) subsequently made a case that B's partner on *Part Two* was in fact a new compositor (J), Blayney (xxxvi) has, like Walker, identified him as Compositor A.

2 All of the examples in this and the following paragraphs are drawn from Prosser, 51–121.

The ſecond Part of King Henry the Fourth. 77

on any ſide but one, it is worſe ſhame to begge, then to be on the worſt ſide, were it worſe then the name of Rebellion can tell how to make it.

Ser. You miſtake me Sir.

Fal. Why ſir? Did I ſay you were an honeſt man? Setting my Knight-hood, and my Souldierſhip aſide, I had lyed in my throat, if I had ſaid ſo.

Ser. I pray you (Sir) then ſet your Knighthood and your Souldier-ſhip aſide, and giue mee leaue to tell you, you lye in your throat, if you ſay I am any other then an honeſt man.

Fal. I giue thee leaue to tell me ſo? I lay a-ſide that which growes to me: If thou get'ſt any leaue of me, hang me: if thou tak'ſt leaue, thou wer't better be hang'd: you Hunt-counter, bence: Auant.

Ser. Sir, my Lord would ſpeake with you.

Iuſt. Sir *John Falſtaffe*, a word with you.

Fal. My good Lord: giue your Lordſhip good time of the day. I am glad to ſee your Lordſhip abroad: I heard ſay your Lordſhip was ſicke. I hope your Lordſhip goes abroad by aduiſe. Your Lordſhip (though not clean paſt your youth) hath yet ſome ſmack of age in you: ſome relliſh of the ſaltneſſe of Time, and I moſt humbly beſeech your Lordſhip, to haue a reuerend care of your health.

Iuſt. Sir *Iohn*, I ſent you before your Expedition, to Shrewsburie.

Fal. If it pleaſe your Lordſhip, I heare his Maieſtie is return'd with ſome diſcomfort from Wales.

Iuſt. I talke not of his Maieſty: you would not come when I ſent for you?

Fal. And I heare moreouer, his Highneſſe is falne into this ſame whorſon Apoplexie.   (you.

Iuſt. Well, heauen mend him. I pray let me ſpeak with

Fal. This Apoplexie is (as I take it) a kind of Lethargie, a ſleeping of the blood, a horſon Tingling.

Iuſt. What tell you me of it? be it as it is.

Fal. It hath it originall from much greeſe; from ſtudy and perturbation of the braine. I haue read the cauſe of his effects in *Galen*. It is a kinde of deafeneſſe.

Iuſt. I thinke you are falne into the diſeaſe: For you heare not what I ſay to you.

Fal. Very well (my Lord) very well: rather an't pleaſe you) it is the diſeaſe of not Liſtning, the malady of not Marking, that I am troubled withall.

Iuſt. To puniſh you by the heeles, would amend the attention of your eares, & I care not if I be your Phyſitian

Fal. I am as poore as *Iob*, my Lord; but not ſo Patient: your Lordſhip may miniſter the Potion of impriſonment to me, in reſpect of Pouertie: but how I ſhould bee your Patient, to follow your preſcriptions, the wiſe may make ſome dram of a ſcruple, or indeede, a ſcruple it ſelfe.

Iuſt. I ſent for you (when there were matters againſt you for your life) to come ſpeake with me.

Fal. As I was then aduiſed by my learned Councel, in the lawes of this Land-ſeruice, I did not come.

Iuſt. Wel, the truth is (ſir *Iohn*) you liue in great infamy

Fal. He that buckles him in my belt, cãnot liue in leſſe.

Iuſt. Your Meanes is very ſlender, and your waſt great.

Fal. I would it were otherwiſe: I would my Meanes were greater, and my waſte ſlenderer.

Iuſt. You haue miſled the youthfull Prince.

Fal. The yong Prince hath miſled mee. I am the Fellow with the great belly, and he my Dogge.

Iuſt. Well, I am loth to gall a new-heal'd wound: your daies ſeruice at Shrewsbury, hath a little gilded ouer your Nights exploit on Gads-hill. You may thanke th'

vnquiet time, for your quiet o're-poſting that Action.

Fal. My Lord?   (Wolfe.

Iuſt. But ſince all is wel, keep it ſo: wake not a ſleeping

Fal. To wake a Wolfe, is as bad as to ſmell a Fox.

Iu. What? you are as a candle, the better part burnt out

Fal. A Waſſell-Candle, my Lord; all Tallow: if I did ſay of wax, my growth would approue the truth.

Iuſt. There is not a white haire on your face, but ſhold haue his effect of grauity.

Fal. His effect of grauy, grauy, grauy.

Iuſt. You follow the yong Prince vp and downe, like his euill Angell.

Fal. Not ſo (my Lord) your ill Angell is light: but I hope, he that lookes vpon mee, will take mee without, weighing: and yet, in ſome reſpects I grant, I cannot go: I cannot tell. Vertue is of ſo little regard in theſe Coſtormongers, that true valor is turn'd Beare-heard. Pregnancie is made a Tapſter, and hath his quicke wit waſted in giuing Recknings: all the other gifts appertinent to man (as the malice of this Age ſhapes them) are not wooth a Gooſeberry. You that are old, conſider not the capacities of vs that are yong: you meaſure the heat of our Liuers, with the bitterneſs of your gals: & we that are in the vaward of our youth, I muſt confeſſe, are wagges too.

Iuſt. Do you ſet downe your name in the ſcrowle of youth, that are written downe old, with all the Characters of age? Haue you not a moiſt eye? a dry hand? a yellow cheeke? a white beard? a decreaſing lege? an increaſing belly? Is not your voice broken? your winde ſhort? your wit ſingle? and euery part about you blaſted, with Antiquity? and wil you cal your ſelfe yong? Fy, fy, fy, fir *Iohn*.

Fal. My Lord, I was borne with a white head, & ſomething a round belly. For my voice, I haue loſt it with halowing and ſinging of Anthemes. To approue my youth farther, I will not: the truth is, I am onely olde in iudgement and vnderſtandings: and he that will caper with mee for a thouſand Markes, let him lend me the mony, & haue at him. For the boxe of th'eare that the Prince gaue you, he gaue it like a rude Prince, and you rooke it like a ſenſible Lord. I haue checkt him for it, and the yong Lion repents: Marry not in aſhes and ſacke-cloath, but in new Silke, and old Sacke.

Iuſt. Wel, heauen ſend the Prince a better companion.

Fal. Heauen ſend the Companion a better Prince: I cannot rid my hands of him.

Iuſt. Well, the King hath ſeuer'd you and Prince *Harry*, I heare you are going with Lord *Iohn* of Lancaſter, againſt the Archbiſhop, and the Earle of Northumberland

Fal. Yes, I thanke your pretty ſweet wit for it: but looke you pray, (all you that kiſſe my Ladie Peace, at home) that our Armies ioyn not in a hot day: for iſ I take but two ſhirts out with me, and I meane not to ſweat extraordinarily: if it bee a hot day, iſ I brandiſh any thing but my Bottle, would I might neuer ſpit white againe: There is not a daungerous Action can peepe out his head, but I am thruſt vpon it. Well, I cannot laſt euer.

Iuſt. Well, be honeſt, be honeſt, and heauen bleſſe your Expedition.

Fal. Will your Lordſhip lend mee a thouſand pound, to furniſh mee forth?

Iuſt. Not a peny, not a peny: you are too impatient to beare croſſes. Fare you well. Commend mee to my Coſin Weſtmerland.

Fal. If I do, fillop me with a three-man-Beetle. A man can no more ſeparate Age and Couetouſneſſe, then he can part yong limbes and letchery: but the Gowt galles the

g 2   enz,

24   Sig. g2ʳ from the 1623 Folio

text on one line. In the following speech (112–14), he deleted seven words, 'an't please your lordship, a kind of' to keep the speech to only two lines. He achieved a similar compression by replacing Q's 'doe become' with 'be' at 125; more awkwardly, by replacing Q's 'himselfe' with 'him' at 139; and by altering Q's 'meanes are' to 'Meanes is' and then cutting 'is' after 'waste' at 141–2.

In the second column, Compositor B resorted to even more draconian measures to save space. By cutting the word 'times' following Q's 'costar-mongers' (170), he altered the line's meaning; but that cut, in addition to the omission of 'doe' at 176, allowed him to shorten the speech by one line. Similarly, his cutting of Q's 'your chinne double' and 'yet' at 184–6, along with short spellings of 'wil' and 'cal' and the elimination of spaces after two question marks and between the thrice repeated 'Fy's, enabled him to avoid running the speech onto an additional line. He then 'slashed the equivalent of approximately three-quarters of a Folio type-line' (Prosser, 84) by omitting Falstaff's claim in Q that he was born 'about three of the clock in the afternoone' (187–8). At that point, mid-way down the second column and apparently concerned that his efforts to compress the text had not yet yielded a sufficient number of lines, he decided to blot, just ten lines from the bottom of g2^r, a large portion of the speech in which Falstaff protests being sent to the wars: 'but it was alway yet . . . perpetual motion' (213–19). Cumulatively, then, Compositor B managed to reduce the number of lines that had been allotted to g2^r by seventeen or eighteen. He performed similar surgery on g3 and, though to a lesser degree, on g1^v and g2^v, clearly assuming that 'by cramping the text at every available opportunity', he 'could complete *2 Henry IV* in the twenty-five pages available' (Prosser, 90).

At some point during the process, it must have become clear to the printer that despite Compositor B's best efforts, the text of *Part Two* would not fit into the space remaining. Thus it was decided to add one more sheet – four more pages – to quire gg, and compositors suddenly found themselves with space to fill. The printing could now be more leisurely, and compression yielded to expansion. But this solution posed its own problem, for there was no way in which the yet-to-be-set text could be expanded to fill the 16 pages of gg. Allowing the Epilogue a page to itself (gg8) and using the final page to list characters' names (gg8ᵛ) were ready, if unusual, expedients. But more needed to be done, so Compositor B 'now exercised the same resourcefulness in expanding the text that he had shown in compressing it' (Prosser, 93). An examination of one page, gg5ᵛ, equivalent to 4.3.359 to 5.2.8 in the present edition, will illustrate the methods he used to stretch the text by at least seventeen lines more than it would have required in a normal printing.

One standard compositorial technique for expanding copy was to have single lines run over to a second line. In one case, at the end of the first column, he used wide spacing between words to force the final syllable of 'knowledge' onto the next line (5.1.39–40). Elsewhere he spelled out speech prefixes, usually abbreviated, in full – '*Shallow*' (5.1.34) and '*Warwick*' (5.2.1) – and used thick spaces to have the text run over onto another line. In Falstaff's soliloquy about Justice Shallow, not only does Compositor B spell out the speech prefix, '*Falstaffe*' instead of '*Fal.*'; he also expands his customary abbreviation 'M.' five times, not only to 'Master' but to the longer forms 'Maister' and 'Mayster', in order to justify an additional line for the speech. He does something similar at the end of 5.1, where he twice expands 'M.' to 'Master' in order to lengthen Falstaff's line at 86–7, thereby requiring a separate line for '*Exeunt*'.

Another common device used to expand copy was to divide one verse line into two. Compositor B made frequent use of it, usually dividing the opening line of a speech at a strong caesura, as at the King's 'Laud be to heaven: / Euen there my life must end' (4.3.363), but also dividing lines more arbitrarily, as at Warwick's 'Exceeding well: his Cares / Are now, all ended' (5.2.3). He was particularly adept at dividing lines of prose so that the division seemed logical, often at a transitional point, as in four of Shallow's speeches: for example, when his repeated refusal to excuse Sir John from spending the night is followed by 'Why *Dauie*' on a new line (5.1.4–6; compare 24, 28, 57). If such lines occasionally look like verse, in some instances he prints them as if they actually were verse, capitalizing the first letter of each new line, as in Davy's 'Yes Sir. / Here is now the Smithes note, for Shooing, / And Plough-Irons' (17–18; compare 36–7 and 50–3). By employing such sleight-of-hand divisions alone, Compositor B used nine additional lines of type on gg5^v.[1]

But he had other techniques for expansion as well. The scribe who prepared copy for F omitted formal titles in his stage directions, but Compositor B occasionally inserted them in order to extend the stage direction to another line, as at the opening of 5.2: '*Enter the Earle of Warwicke and the Lord / Chiefe Justice.*' If such additions are innocuous, his expansion of lines with words of his own is not. Three times on this page, he added words that have been widely adopted by editors. In one instance, his addition of the phrase 'the other day' between 'the Sacke he lost' and 'at *Hinckley* Fayre' forces 'Fayre?' onto a new line (5.1.23). Shortly thereafter, his expansion of Davy's appealing the case of William Visor with the words 'a very litle' before 'credite', and the repetition of 'your Worship' in place of 'you' in the next line, caused the final syllable of 'Countenanc'd' to be given its own line (47–9). In these ways, Compositor B altered the scribal text he was charged with reproducing to

---

1 Humphreys, lxxvii, n. 4, lists the prose passages in Q that have been divided into short, irregular lines in F, though he attributes their division to the F scribe, not to the compositor. They are: 2.1.182–3; 2.2.153–5, 157–9, 162–3; 3.2.143, 148, 153; 4.3.3–4; 5.1.6, 17–18, 24, 28, 36, 50–3, 55–7; 5.3.107, 109.

make it fit the space it was allocated. His practices are often condemned as 'corruptions' (Hinman, xviii), as of course they are; but given the difficult circumstances of printing *Part Two*, 'he had no choice but to tamper with his copy', and he did so with a 'high degree of professional skill' (Prosser, 115).

Expedience and necessity thus may account for significant textual variants between Q and F. Resourceful as they were, the compositors of the F text introduced a new level of error, exacerbating the instability of textual transmission to a far greater degree, apparently, than was the case with Q. Despite evidence that F may have been based in part on an authorial copy more complete than the copy-text for Q, the level of scribal intervention and later compositorial intervention makes the F text ultimately more sophisticated and compromised than Q, which quite probably was based on the playbook used by the Lord Chamberlain's Men in 1597. Q, therefore, despite its shortcomings, is the more reliable text on which to base an edition.

APPENDIX 2

Performing conflated texts of Henry IV

In 1995, BBC television broadcast what it called Shakespeare's
Henry IV in a radical abridgement and conflation of *Part One*
and *Part Two*. Directed by RSC associate John Caird, this was
the BBC's most lavish and ambitious Shakespeare production
since the conclusion of its marathon filming of all the plays ten
years earlier (1978–85), and for a new generation of television
viewers it set a high standard for how Shakespeare's history
plays should be performed.[1] Caird focused his production
on what he imagined to be Prince Henry's long-standing
relationship with Hotspur: the two are glimpsed together as
children witnessing the deposition of Richard II, and their
growing rivalry climaxes at the Battle of Shrewsbury, when the
Prince defeats his former friend, winning his proud titles from
him, and with them, the King's paternal approval.

Caird thus uses *Part One* to provide a structure for the whole,
and most of the material in *Part Two* is jettisoned, both the
historical (the flight of Northumberland to Scotland, the
thwarting of the Prelate's Rebellion at Gaultree) and the non-
historical (most of the scenes at Justice Shallow's farm and
much of Falstaff's comic banter with his tavern cronies).
Instead, Caird ingeniously grafts speeches and snippets of
scenes from *Part Two* onto *Part One* to reinforce themes or to
create ironic counterpoints. For example, Hotspur's farewell to
Lady Percy is preceded by Falstaff's farewell to Doll Tearsheet
(an exchange that now occurs prior to Falstaff's march to

1 To shape his history, Caird, working from a script adapted by Michael Hastings,
   liberally interpolated material from *Richard II*, *Henry V*, *Henry VI, Part 3* and
   Merry Wives, as, for example, when he concludes with Falstaff's death – a borrowing from *Henry V* also used by Orson Welles in *Falstaff*. For brief accounts of this
   Henry IV, see *BFI Screenonline: Henry IV* (1995) and Weis, 76–7.

Shrewsbury); the King's chastising his son in *Part One* is intercut with the Lord Chief Justice's interrogation of Falstaff in *Part Two*; and the King's soliloquy on the unease of wearing a crown is spoken immediately prior to the Gad's Hill robbery, as a kind of meditation on political theft, while other lines spoken by the King later in that scene ('O God, that one might read the book of fate, / And see the revolution of the times', 3.1.45–6) are interpolated as ominous glosses on the play-extempore in which Hal and Falstaff each assume the role of king. Following the rebels' defeat at Shrewsbury, Caird swiftly concludes the royal history with the death of the King, the accession of Henry V and the rejection of Falstaff – the only sequence from *Part Two* preserved without radical alteration.

For audiences who had never seen the two parts of *Henry IV* in the theatre, Caird's montage of disparate but thematically related moments offered a politically coherent interpretation of Henry's reign.[1] Those familiar with the complete texts of the two plays, however, would have been aware of what had been lost; for while the linear narrative of *Part One* was kept intact, *Part Two* was only mined for 'bits', its more episodic structure and un-historical characters sacrificed to the need for clarity and compression. As the reviewer in the *Daily Mail* objected, 'Director John Caird brutally re-ordered *Henry IV*, changing the order of scenes to sharpen up the story line, and more or less abandoned Shakespeare's wider historical perspective to concentrate on the father–son relationship' (30 October 1995).[2]

---

1 H.R. Coursen objects to Caird's use of montage to underscore verbal echoes as 'much more heavy handed' than television can accommodate. Coursen's detailed analysis of various sequences in the production is valuable, even if one discounts his argument that Caird's 'reordered, chopped-up version' ultimately confuses the historical chronology and thematic patterns of the plays (42–52).

2 As was true for many directors before him, Caird's overriding concern in the *Henry IV* plays was 'the way in which they talk about inheritance and father/son relationships': see Lisa Vanoli's interview with Caird, 'Fascinating time spent with Henry', *The Stage* (5 October 1995), 34. See also A. Davies.

The sacrifice of the 'wider historical perspective' offered in *Part Two* has a performance history of its own.

The Dering manuscript

An abridgement prepared by Sir Edward Dering, a Kentish gentleman and antiquarian, for a private performance in 1622 or shortly thereafter – but never finished – suggests that readers and performers have wanted to combine the two parts as one since shortly after Shakespeare's death.[1] The Dering manuscript foregrounds the royal history and the conflict between father and son at the expense of those marginalized characters whose 'unofficial' histories were no doubt seen as digressions from the narrative of the Prince's reformation. Dering's skilful conflation of quarto editions of the two plays – which together total 6,148 lines – to a playable 3,401 lines reflects a popular bias in favour of *Part One*. Of the 2,968 lines in Q5 of *Part One*, which was his source, Dering kept 2,621, or 88%; he omitted only two scenes in their entirety – one involving the carriers in Rochester, the other introducing the Prelate's Rebellion, a plot he eliminated entirely from *Part Two* – and cut portions of other scenes, the longest of which was the exchange in which Lady Percy and Lady Mortimer are asked to sing (3.1.192–271).[2] From *Part Two*, in contrast, Dering kept little more than those scenes involving the Prince or the King, a total of 806 lines, or 25%, of the 3,180 lines in the second issue of the Quarto. Scenes drawn from *Part Two* begin late in

1   See the Williams and Evans facsimile edition (Dering, viii). The back of a scrap of paper containing eight lines of text to be inserted in the King's speech following 1.1.20 includes an apparent cast list, drawn from among Dering's friends and relatives, for a private performance of Fletcher's *The Spanish Curate* at Dering's Surrenden estate. *The Spanish Curate* was licensed to be played in 1622, and Francis Manouch, whose name heads the cast list, moved away from the region in 1624, thus providing the dates within which Dering's performance of *Henry IV* must have been intended to occur.

2   I am indebted to Williams and Evans for their comprehensive review of Dering's use of *Part One* (Dering, viii–ix).

Dering's Act 4 with a truncated version of Northumberland's hearing news of Hotspur's death at Shrewsbury – a direct connection to the scenes from *Part One* that precede it – and continue with Lady Percy's persuasion of Northumberland to fly to Scotland. With the elimination of the Archbishop's plot, Dering used these scenes to put a period to the rebellion that opened the play: news of Northumberland's capture brought to the dying King ensures that rebellion will be given no chance to divert attention from the conclusion of the royal history.

Sandwiched between the two Northumberland scenes is a brief comic squabble over debts between Falstaff and the Hostess extracted from *Part Two* (2.1); otherwise, Falstaff appears only in the rejection scene, in which he is granted a scant four and a half lines. Gone are Falstaff's scenes with the Lord Chief Justice, with Doll Tearsheet and with the Ancient Pistol; gone, the scenes of Falstaff's recruiting soldiers, drinking and reminiscing with Justices Shallow and Silence. Dering allows nothing to impede the conclusion of the main plot: the illness and death of the King (a clever splicing together of 3.1 and 4.3); Prince Harry's accession and reassurance of his brothers (a reduction of 5.2); and, immediately following as part of the same scene, his rejection of Falstaff in a speech that concludes with five rather clumsily interpolated lines wherein the new King vows to 'change our thoughtes for honour and renowne' and set his sights on 'the royalty and crowne of Fraunce' (5.10.77–8).[1]

Dering's conflation thus uses portions of *Part Two* – most of them from Acts 4 and 5 – to provide a swift resolution of the royal narrative dramatized in *Part One*, culminating in the reformation of the Prince of Wales, who has already proved himself in battle at Shrewsbury, as a responsible King. For this

---

1   Hodgdon assesses Dering's conservative abbreviation of the play's final scenes and the function of the Prince's last lines as an anticipation of the 'Chronicle deeds' to be dramatized in *Henry V* (*End*, 168–9).

reformation, it was unnecessary that the Falstaff scenes from *Part Two* be included, for they add nothing to the relationship Prince Henry has had with him: they dramatize a Falstaff who, capitalizing on his 'honours' falsely won at Shrewsbury, presides over a comic world that can no longer include the Prince. Dering's abridgement of the two texts thus offers a coherent dramatic action that some scholars speculate may have been Shakespeare's original design for *Henry IV*, before he realized that he had too much chronicle material to include in one play, or before the character of Falstaff grew out of all compass, prompting him to end his play at Shrewsbury and, as a result, leaving little history to be dramatized in the sequel (See Introduction, p. 12). Given Dering's emphasis on the royal narrative, it is not surprising that less than a quarter of his play is drawn from *Part Two*.

Orson Welles's *Falstaff*

In recent decades there have been frequent attempts to perform *Henry IV* as a conflation of the two parts. As with Dering's abridgement, such attempts have tended to foreground the narrative of Harry's coming of age as a triumph of the state over forces of anarchy, and consequently to suppress those aspects of *Part Two* that would call such ideological certainty into question. The earliest and best known of these conflations is Orson Welles's 1965 film *Falstaff*, released in the US two years later as *Chimes at Midnight*. Based on two short-lived stage adaptations which Welles had attempted in the US in 1938 and Ireland in 1960,[1] it offers a complex portrait of Falstaff, its emphasis falling heavily on both the comic resourcefulness and the inevitable tragedy of a great but mistreated hero, and its ingenious cutting and splicing of the two *Henry IV* plays including more of the social panorama from *Part Two* than

---

1   For discussion of these stage versions, see Hapgood, 39–52. Welles's script has been published as *Chimes at Midnight: Orson Welles, Director*.

Dering allowed. In carefully arranged segments of the tavern scenes, Mistress Quickly, Doll Tearsheet and the Ancient Pistol are all allowed to revel with Falstaff, and Falstaff visits Justice Shallow's farm twice, once to recruit soldiers, and later to bilk Shallow of a thousand pounds. The title itself comes from Falstaff's wry acknowledgement to Justice Shallow, in a moment that opens the film, that their youth has passed: 'We have heard the chimes at midnight, Master Shallow' (3.2.214–15). Age, remembrance and a sense of loss pervade the film and heighten the sympathy one feels for Falstaff.

Nevertheless, although Welles foregrounds his own performance as a huge, genial, cunning and dangerously intelligent Falstaff, the overall dramatic arc of his film is determined primarily by the royal coming-of-age story. All references to the Northumberlands and to the Prelate's Rebellion are expunged following the royal victory at Shrewsbury, and the portion of the film drawn from *Part Two* soon narrows to Harry's emergence as a 'true prince'. Rather than political history, Welles explores the psychology of the father–son triangulation, with Harry craving the affection of a surrogate father, Falstaff, who stands between him and the approval he seeks from the emotionally remote King (elegantly played by John Gielgud), and eventually emerging unscathed by 'the two fathers who threaten to submerge his own unique identity, either through guilty rule or guilded license' (Crowl, 72).

Welles is careful to avoid the back-sliding in Harry's relationship with the King in *Part Two* that often puzzles those who expect narrative consistency with *Part One*, as if the Prince had never redeemed himself on Percy's head and won the confidence of his father. Rather, he shapes their encounters in *Part One* to suggest that the King is unpersuaded by evidence of his son's sincerity: distant and cold at their meeting in 3.3, the King scarcely credits Harry's offer to engage Hotspur in single combat, and his expression of pleasure in his son's heroic resolve, 'A hundred thousand rebels die in this!' (3.2.160), is eliminated. Even more tellingly, Welles omits Harry's rescue of his father from Douglas at Shrewsbury, a rescue which in *Part One* salvages the Prince's 'lost opinion' (5.4.47) and provides irrefutable evidence of his loyalty to the King. Most significantly, in a tactical revision of *Part One* that allows the alienation between the Prince and King to continue into *Part Two*, Falstaff claims to have killed Hotspur while the King is present to hear him. Believing that his son has falsely taken credit for Hotspur's defeat, the King turns his back in disgust, obviating any possibility for protest from Harry.[1] The purpose of such textual manipulation is to postpone the reconciliation of father and son to the King's deathbed scene in *Part Two*; but it also allows Harry to prolong his decision to relinquish Falstaff as a surrogate father.

Harry signals his growing displeasure with Falstaff 'four times during the movie', according to Welles, each instance adding cumulative force to the final rejection.[2] The first time, Harry delivers his 'I know you all' soliloquy so that Falstaff can hear him, thus changing the dynamic between the two men (as the camera reveals in Falstaff's reaction to Harry's words) and anticipating the more explicit threat of banishment in the 'I do, I will' concluding the play-extempore. The third time – notable because it was invented by Welles – occurs at Shrewsbury when, after the King has left in disgust, Falstaff attempts to placate Harry with the false bonhomie of his paean to sherris sack (transposed from 4.2.94–123). The Prince, no longer amused by the corrupt knight who has discredited his rightful claim to chivalric rehabilitation in the eyes of his father, turns his back on Falstaff and walks away, casting aside the

---

1 The device of having the King credit Falstaff, not his son, for Hotspur's defeat was borrowed by Michael Bogdanov twenty years later for his English Shakespeare Company history cycle (see pp. 39–41), denying *Part One* its customary resolution and signalling that a sequel in which the King and Prince would reconcile was still to come.

2 See Hapgood, 50; also Cobos & Rubio, 159.

proffered cup of sack as he goes. Thus, however one is encouraged to regard Welles's film as Falstaff's tragedy, with his stark final banishment and long, solitary exit followed by a poignant account of his death borrowed from *Henry V*,[1] ultimately Falstaff's fate is subsumed in the Prince's coming-of-age story, just as it had been in Dering's abridgement, to clarify the play's focus on royal succession and what has to be sacrificed to maintain the order of state.

John Barton's *When Thou Art King*

John Barton's adaptation of the two *Henry IV* plays, performed by the Royal Shakespeare Company as a Theatregoround production in 1969 and revived in 1970, was tellingly titled *When Thou Art King*.[2] Although it may have been inspired by Welles's film released only four years earlier, it is in spirit much closer to Dering's abridgement, with which Barton may have been familiar. He divided *Henry IV* so that each part was given an act, though the act for *Part One* was significantly longer than that for *Part Two*.[3] Barton's rehearsal notes printed in the programme reveal how deeply indebted he was to Dover Wilson's view of the play as allegorical history:

1   Welles's 'overriding visual and structural emphasis . . . to signal farewell' to Falstaff has achieved iconic status. For the most articulate analysis of that cinematic emphasis, see Crowl, 369–80.

2   The programme for *When Thou Art King* when it was performed at the Roundhouse in London in 1970 explains the rationale for the RSC's Theatregoround productions. Based 'on the principle of the Elizabethan touring company which often used small casts and condensed texts', such productions were bare-bones, with minimalist sets and a heavy use of doubling. Thus they were economically viable to tour to regional theatres, civic halls, schools and universities as well as playing seasons as main house repertoire in Stratford-upon-Avon and London.

3   Each part was given a title: *Part One* was 'The Battle of Shrewsbury', *Part Two*, 'The Rejection of Falstaff'. Eventually Barton added an act for *Henry V* as well, titled 'The Battle of Agincourt'; but in any given performance only two acts were presented, and most often they were the two parts of *Henry IV*, the abridgement of *Henry V* having been drubbed by critics as no more than 'a brief précis . . . with all the best bits in' (B.A. Young, *Financial Times*, 17 July 1969).

485

Henry IV reflects the Morality school: enter at one door the young Prince Hal; at the other, the Reverend Vice Falstaff – the tempted and the tempter. It is a Catholic conflict: to achieve salvation you have to experience and overcome sin. . . . Falstaff embodies every aspect and degree of Vanity. A self-indulgent whoremaster, a thief, a liar, a cutpurse, a cheat, a braggadocio, in love with himself and his own company, immensely and seductively attractive. If Hal can survive such a mountainous attack on the senses, then it is certain that Vanity will one day be outfaced.

(RSC programme, *When Thou Art King*, 1969)

Barton's emphasis fell squarely on Hal's growth to moral maturity. As in the RSC history cycles which Barton himself co-directed with Peter Hall in 1964, he insists that the rejection of Falstaff in *When Thou Art King* is 'clearly provided for throughout'. Indeed, he argues, the rejection itself 'is not so surprising as the moderation of the sentence'; and to underscore the new King's moral maturity, he omits the lines in which the Lord Chief Justice commits Falstaff to the Fleet. 'Justice is done,' Barton comments, 'but this time with humanity.'

To narrow the focus of his play to the royal *Bildungsroman*, Barton significantly curtails the scenes of rebellion in *Part One*, preserving only those portions involving Hotspur and Northumberland, whose father–son tensions parallel those between the King and the Prince. He eliminates Worcester, Glendower, the scene in the Welsh camp and the scene with the Archbishop. He splices together portions of the rebels' scenes at Shrewsbury; eliminates all of the scene in which Worcester confronts the King and the Prince except Falstaff's speech on honour, which is appended to an earlier scene (4.2); and merges the scenes remaining in Act 5 into one seamless denouement, with the deepest cuts coming in the rebels' dialogue. In fact, Barton does not introduce the rebels until the play is well under way. Where, in Shakespeare's text, Northumberland, Worcester and Hotspur confront the King in Act 1, Barton postpones that confrontation until nearly a third of the way into his abridgement of *Part One*. Prior to it, he signals his focus on the conflict between the King and the Prince by having the play open with the King asking a question adapted from *Richard II*, 'Can no one tell me of my wayward son?',[1] that leads to an exchange in which he contrasts his own dishonourable Hal with the heroic Hotspur (adapted from *Part One* 1.1.77–89). In this exchange, however, Barton substitutes for Westmorland the Lord Chief Justice, who reports that the Sheriff has sent Hal and his companions to prison.

Barton then provides evidence of Harry's madcap youth never dramatized by Shakespeare. As he had done brilliantly in his 1963–4 adaptation of the *Henry VI* plays titled *The Wars of the Roses*, for which he drew on various sources to insert pseudo-Shakespearean scenes of his own devising, Barton includes a legendary episode that was dramatized in *The Famous Victories of Henry the Fifth* but to which Shakespeare alludes only fleetingly in *Part Two*. When the Lord Chief Justice has arraigned Bardolph for a crime, the Prince enters the chamber, demands Bardolph's release and, when the Lord Chief Justice refuses, strikes him 'on the cheek' (Shakespeare reports it as a 'box of the ear', 1.2.194), for which he is committed to the Fleet. Following this, in a scene clearly inspired by Harry's play-extempore with Falstaff, Francis the drawer and the newly freed Bardolph re-enact the arraignment in sport, with Francis taking the role of Bardolph and Bardolph, the role of the Lord Chief Justice. This scene establishes a tone of comic anarchy in anticipation of the scene in which Falstaff asks Harry (now released from prison) what will happen 'when thou art king' (*Part One* 1.2.22). In answer to that question,

---

1 Quotations are from the promptbook for *When Thou Art King*, Shakespeare Centre Library, Stratford-upon-Avon. The King's actual line in *R2* is 'Can no man tell me of my unthrifty son?' (5.3.1).

Harry's 'I know you all' soliloquy promises the reformation that, as Barton argues, is prepared for throughout the play.

If, in Barton's abridgement of *Part One*, the northern rebellion is narrowed to a personal rivalry between Harry and Hotspur, rebellion is all but absent from his abridgement of *Part Two*. The scene of Northumberland's receiving news of Hotspur's death is drastically reduced, as is his scene with Lady Percy; and, as in Dering's *Henry IV*, the Prelate's Rebellion is cut entirely: there is no aggrieved Archbishop, no royal double-cross at Gaultree. The effect of this abridgement is to tighten the dramatic focus on the contest between the King and Falstaff for Harry's soul – the son torn between two fathers, rather like an Everyman who is tugged by the forces of good and evil: the one father cold but politically astute, the other warm but morally corrupt.

Barton keeps enough material from the early scenes of *Part Two* to foreground Falstaff as the abstract of all sins. He cleverly splices together portions of the scenes in which Falstaff tries to borrow money from the Hostess and then from the Lord Chief Justice (whose role continues from the first act), and he leaves intact most of the long tavern scene in which Falstaff consorts with Doll Tearsheet and the Ancient Pistol. But the scenes at Justice Shallow's farm in Gloucestershire are eliminated, and with them, a more genially rounded portrait of Falstaff. Instead, Barton turns his gaze on the King's illness and his final reconciliation with the Prince. In a conflation that harks back to Betterton's (see pp. 19–21), Barton merges 3.1 – the King's soliloquy on sleep and subsequent musings on the state of the kingdom – with 4.3, in which the King asks, 'Where is the Prince, my son?' (an adaptation of "Where is the Prince your brother?" at 4.3.13). The question is asked of the Lord Chief Justice, for Barton, intent on keeping his cast to a minimum, has eliminated the King's other sons, Clarence and Gloucester, and chosen to move quickly to the King's falling into a swoon, the entry of the Prince and his exit with the crown. Some of the longer speeches in the tense confrontation of father and son are pared down, but the scene itself provides an emotional climax for the play. It marks Harry's ultimate choice to accept his father's mantle and to abjure his former life.

Barton compresses the final scenes to build up the significance of Harry's last encounter with Falstaff. Much of the ancillary material in Act 5 of *Part Two* is jettisoned. Falstaff, presumably on his way north following the Battle of Shrewsbury, says to Bardolph 'we must a dozen miles tonight' (adapted from 3.2.290), then delivers a composite soliloquy that begins by paraphrasing the speech in which, in Shakespeare's original, he mocks the pretensions of Justice Shallow, but whose object of ridicule now is Bardolph, from whom he vows to 'devise matter to keep the Prince in continual laughter' (from 5.1.76–8). This speech segues into Falstaff's unfavourable comparison of Prince John with Prince Harry (from 4.2.85–123), at which point Pistol enters with news of the King's death and Falstaff proceeds to brag that the laws of England are at his commandment (an adaptation of 5.3.83–141 which now excludes Shallow). In an ironic juxtaposition, Barton moves directly to a compression of two scenes: the first, in which the new King rewards the Lord Chief Justice for honourable service to his father; the second, in which he banishes Falstaff, the decisive event towards which the whole play, according to Barton, has tended.

While critics generally praised the 'coherence and drive' that Barton's adaptation gave to the saga of 'Hal's relationship with Falstaff and his education in the art of kingship' (Michael Billington, *The Times*, 4 November 1970), they also regretted the price that had to be paid to achieve such coherence. 'We need to see the circumstances, the concerns of society from which the Prince appears to escape', complained Nicholas de Jongh (*Guardian*, 4 November 1970): in particular, he lamented the simplification of political history and cultural contexts – 'the internal dissensions, the complex of dynastic disputes and the spectrum of life' – from which Harry would emerge as a popular but astute leader. This loss was most keenly felt in the abridgement of *Part Two*, which, more than *Part One*, offers a 'panoramic vision of English society: thus we lose both the mellow comedy of Shallow and Silence and, at the other end of the scale, a crucial incident such as Prince John's betrayal of his pardon to the northern rebels. The latter is particularly significant since without it, we never see in action the kind of treacherous political pragmatism that is no part of Hal's concept of kingship' (de Jongh). What Barton sacrifices in conceiving *When Thou Art King* as Hal's Morality play, therefore, is the subtle balance Shakespeare provides between humane governance and political expedience, between chronicle history and cultural memory.

Dakin Matthews's *Henry IV*

This tradition of sacrificing the peculiar merits of *Part Two* as social history to the interests of a coherent coming-of-age story was followed by American actor and playwright Dakin Matthews in his popular adaptation of the two *Henry IV* plays. Matthews's 'compilation', as he calls it, was first workshopped at the Juilliard School in New York in 1972, just two years after the run of Barton's *When Thou Art King*. It was performed at the Goodman Theatre in Chicago in 1974; revised and performed again by the California Actors Theatre in 1980; further revised for performance by the Denver Center Theatre Company in 1990; re-adapted and lengthened for the 1995 season at the Old Globe in San Diego, where it was directed by Jack O'Brien; and reworked into its final form for the successful Lincoln Center production in 2003, directed by O'Brien and starring Kevin Kline as Falstaff. Since its 100 sold-out performances at Lincoln Center, Matthews's adaptation has achieved a popularity unprecedented among recent adaptations of Shakespeare and played at numerous regional theatres throughout the US.

Like the Dering manuscript and subsequent conflations of the *Henry IV* plays, Matthews's adaptation draws more heavily from *Part One*. He divides the play into three acts – the first two compressing material from *Part One*, the third and shortest telescoping events from the final two acts of *Part Two*. With a direct debt to Welles, whose Prince signals displeasure with Falstaff at four key moments in the film, Matthews explains that he has structured his adaptation to foreground the increasingly strained relationship between Prince Harry and Falstaff, pointing the way to Henry's rejection of Falstaff at the end of *Part Two* and thus, inevitably, focusing on the royal *Bildungsroman*:

> The three-act structure is mounted on the triple rejection of Falstaff, each rejection more serious and more painful for the Prince. The first occurs in jest – at the end of the extempore play in the first major tavern scene; it is the climactic moment of my Act One. The second, an intensely personal leave-taking, occurs on the battlefield of Shrewsbury, when the Prince discovers the body of Falstaff lying next to Hotspur's corpse; this farewell to an (apparently) dead comrade is the climax of my Act Two. The third rejection occurs right after the coronation, and is public, painful, and final. This is the climactic moment of my Act Three.[1]

The first and third of these rejections, of course, are in the Shakespearean text. Matthews is disingenuous about the second, however. When he alludes to the Prince's 'farewell' to an apparently dead Falstaff, he doesn't use the word 'rejection': the reason, I think, is that he wants to avoid drawing attention to lines he himself wrote for this scene in which Harry actually *does* reject Falstaff. In Shakespeare's text, when Falstaff comes back to life carrying with him the corpse of Hotspur, Harry's generous sanctioning of his behaviour is the last he speaks to Falstaff in *Part One*: 'Come, bring your luggage nobly on your

---

1   Matthews, from the introductory essay to his adaptation, 7–8.

back. / For my part, if a lie may do thee grace, / I'll gild it with the happiest terms I have' (5.4.156–8). Matthews keeps these lines, but then adds an exchange in which the Prince, in exasperation, turns his back on Falstaff, as he does in *Chimes at Midnight* (76):

> FALSTAFF. Well, Hal – and shall we to the west together, to baste the devil Welshman with his own leeks?
>
> PRINCE HENRY. No. No, 'twere best to part; go then with my brother John; for heaven 't witness, I have no care to fight with thee. Farewell.

These pseudo-Shakespearean lines explain Falstaff's appearance at Gaultree with Prince John's army in the final act and thus serve a function required by the conflation. But in them, Matthews also chooses to fabricate a repudiation of Falstaff unwarranted by the text of *Part One*, in which the Prince's final words *grace* Falstaff's lies. Matthews thus works against the Shakespearean text to achieve the structural balance and thematic coherence he desires.

Like previous adapters, then, Matthews acknowledges that his primary intention is to 'tell of the transition of power from father to son' in which 'Hal is the real focus of the narrative' and for which *Part Two* is important largely because 'it ties up all the loose ends left dangling from the first play' (5). Yet Matthews also admits that in abridging the plays, he was loath to relinquish 'that handful of magnificent scenes from *Part Two*' (7) – scenes not essential to the political plot – in which, for example, Lady Percy eulogizes Hotspur, Falstaff confronts the Lord Chief Justice and extols the virtues of alcohol, and Falstaff recruits soldiers in Gloucestershire. 'All these would pass unseen and unheard into oblivion', Matthews insists (7), had he not chosen to keep them, though in abbreviated form. However laudable his preservationist impulse may be, he does not preserve the scenes as Shakespeare wrote them. Instead, he picks and chooses parts of scenes – though less artfully than Welles did – so that the resulting text plays like a 'greatest moments from *Henry IV*', fattening Falstaff's role while reducing the characters who surround him to mere caricatures. Mistress Quickly, Doll Tearsheet, Bardolph, the Ancient Pistol and Justices Shallow and Silence, who in the full text of *Part Two* create a rich alternative world to that of the court, are robbed of life – and most of their lines – in Matthews's adaptation.

Matthews grafts some of the best material from the first three acts of *Part Two* onto scenes in *Part One*. To the lively tavern scene early in Matthews's second act (taken from *Part One* 3.3) – on the eve of the march to Shrewsbury – he transfers highlights from the long tavern scene in *Part Two* (2.4). Falstaff's banter with Pistol and Bardolph, his being overheard and called to account by the Prince and Poins disguised as drawers, and his affectionate farewell to Doll are all interpolations from the later play. Mistress Quickly's comic complaint about Falstaff's promise to marry her is interpolated from an earlier scene in *Part Two* (2.1). By grafting this material onto the tavern scene from *Part One*, Matthews argues that he saves colourful characters and unmatchable dialogue that would otherwise have been sacrificed. Yet the effect is not, as it is in the full text of *Part Two*, to dramatize the stories of marginalized people who had no voice in the recording of 'official' history. Instead, the interpolations succeed only in beefing up the role of Falstaff as a great comic adversary for Harry, much as Orson Welles foregrounded Falstaff by diminishing the roles of everyone around him.

The same thing happens two scenes later when Matthews, like Welles, preserves another scene from *Part Two*: that in which Falstaff arrives at the Gloucestershire farm of Justice Shallow to recruit soldiers. To a degree, his decision to relocate this scene to serve as a prelude to the Battle of Shrewsbury makes sense, for by doing so he is quite possibly returning the scene to the position it may have occupied in an early draft of

Part One, whereas Falstaff's stopping to recruit soldiers in Gloucestershire on his way to Yorkshire makes no geographical sense (see pp. 12–13). Matthews thus may have had some justification for preserving and transposing the recruitment scene, yet he ransacked it in much the same way he ransacked the tavern scene in *Part Two* – for good bits to flesh out Falstaff's role. He radically reduces the conversation between Shallow and Silence about country life and Shallow's years at the Inns of Court, and the rag-tag recruits from whom Falstaff must choose – each brilliantly individualized by Shakespeare – are seen but not heard.

In sum, the scene is shorn of the details of quotidian life which help to imprint the Gloucestershire idyll so indelibly on the memory. Instead, Matthews moves quickly to Falstaff's acceptance of bribes from the two recruits who can afford to buy out their service (bribes here, as in *Chimes at Midnight*, only reported by Bardolph) and to his settling for the least likely recruits instead ('food for powder', *Part One* 4.2.64–5). Moreover, as a coda to this action, when Shallow and the others have exited, Falstaff delivers a portion of the soliloquy from *Part One* in which he confesses that he has misused the King's press, something Matthews has just dramatized: first he shows, then he tells. Although there is little logic in this redundancy, Matthews clearly wants the play to be about Falstaff, and that he succeeded in making it so is amply evident in the enthusiastic critical response to Kevin Kline's performance at Lincoln Center. Yet he also wants to contain Falstaff's anarchic energies within the bounds of the narrative of the Prince's reformation. In a sense, then, the fattening of Falstaff's role at the expense of everyone else's makes him a more formidable influence on Harry, and this heightens the significance of Harry's repeated rejection of him – the structural premise of the whole adaptation.

Matthews's conflation of the two parts of *Henry IV*, then, is consistent with the conception that emerged more than a half-century ago of these plays as part of a grand history cycle.

Ideologically conservative, it is a text bent on foregrounding the royal narrative and suppressing those other narratives – of the tavern low-lifes, the country justices and recruits – that have the potential to subvert the 'official' version of events. Today, when staging *Part Two* as a counter to *Part One* – as a study of political opportunism and how history is constructed by those in power – could have a cautionary influence on audiences who have grown cynical about government, Matthews's adaptation has the effect (as Harry has on those former companions who, by his order, wind up in the Fleet) of silencing the voices of opposition in *Part Two*.

An African American *H4*

Voices of opposition, however, have been ringingly heard in more recent – and more daring – conflations of *Henry IV*. In these versions, a play about white male power and privilege has been appropriated by actors traditionally sidelined in its performance history – women and people of colour in particular – whose casting in the roles of English nobility brings an unusual cultural immediacy to the play. A film called simply *H4*, produced by Giovanni Zelko and actor Harry Lennix, who plays the King, and directed by Paul Quinn, refashions the plays to foreground dynastic power struggles within an urban African American community. Completed in 2013, the film has been shown at various colleges and independent film festivals in the US and at professional Shakespeare conferences in the US and the UK, but has not yet been released commercially or made available on DVD.

H4 foregrounds political rivalries – and gang warfare – between different black groups in contemporary Los Angeles: the Welsh and Scots become immigrant Haitians and Jamaicans who fight the native-born African Americans (the English) for territory. The script, adapted by Shakespeare scholar Ayanna Thompson, substitutes local place names and black cultural references for those in the play. Lords become Brothers and

Sisters (five men's roles are re-gendered as women: Northumberland, Mowbray, the Lord Chief Justice and the King's two youngest sons); King Richard is murdered when he returns from his Cuban (not Irish) expedition; and dialogue is peppered with references to neighbourhoods in Los Angeles. The rebels meet at Willowbrook (Wales); Coleville is 'of Burbank' ('the Dale'); the Prince dines with his companions at Cranshaw (Eastcheap); he assures his siblings that 'This is Inglewood, not Guantanamo' ('the English, not the Turkish court'); and most tellingly, his title is Prince of Watts, not Wales.

Though pared down, the script is nonetheless coherent. It begins with the ambush of the previous 'king' (Richard) who is lured into an alley, brutally beaten and killed by young Henry and his gang. As a Chicago critic observes, the dying Richard 'with a parting shot . . . sends a point of his crown into Henry's eye', a 'metaphor for the blind ambition of the usurper',[1] but also an injury which causes Henry to wear a black eye-patch when, twenty years later, he appears as a troubled middle-aged King whose political wars have not ended. As in previous conflations of the two plays, *H4* primarily follows the structure of *Part One*, with brief scenes from *Part Two* – Falstaff and Doll discussing age (2.4) followed by the King's soliloquy on sleep and his conversation with Warwick (3.1) – tucked between the final meeting of the rebels before Shrewsbury and the Battle of Shrewsbury itself, here played out as a war with switchblades and baseball bats in what appears to be an abandoned warehouse. The royal victory is followed in quick succession by the rebels' plotting with the Archbishop (here, 'of New York'), their defeat by treachery, the King's death and finally Harry's accession.

Interestingly, although almost all the major roles are played by black actors, Falstaff is white. There is little explanation

---

1 Marilyn Ferdinand, reviewing *H4* for the Chicago International Film Festival (CIFF) on 17 October 2013, at http://www.ferdyonfilms.com/2013/ciff-2013-h4-2014/19767/.

why a fat but articulate derelict like him would hang out at a black inner-city bar, nor why the Prince would find him so attractive, though it is possible, in a stretch of the imagination, to see Falstaff as representing an 'American consumerist culture . . . that keeps black men down with the hefty weight of centuries of white oppression' (Ferdinand). But if this is what the filmmakers had in mind, little is made of it. Little is made, too, of the robbery at Gad's Hill, which passes almost unnoticed, and Falstaff's banter with Hal is severely curtailed. Furthermore, Falstaff does not even sound American. As played by Scottish actor Angus Macfadyen, he speaks his lines – apart from his 'performance' of the King during the play-extempore, when he channels Marlon Brando's Vito Corleone – with a posh trans-Atlantic accent in sharp contrast to the black 'street' accents used by the other denizens of the Boar's Head. In other words, Macfadyen's Falstaff is less a presiding deity than an odd-man-out in this culture of African American drop-outs.

Even more interestingly, the film uses an alienation device that blends filmic realism with theatrical artifice. It begins with graphic violence in the streets of LA, and all the scenes written in prose – in the bar, at the robbery, even at the 'Shrewsbury' warehouse – are filmed on location, with footage of police in riot gear interspersed among them. But once such realism is established outside the 'court' and the King begins his opening speech, 'So shaken as we are', the political scenes are filmed on a stage – bare except for the occasional prop (a desk, a piano) – so that the formality of the verse is matched by the deliberate artifice of the setting. On this stage, before a black curtain, the King quarrels with the rebel leaders; on this stage, behind a nineteenth-century red tableau curtain, Hotspur hears of his mother Northumberland's flight to Jamaica; on this stage, the Prince vows to his father that he will reform; and on this stage, the Prince's rescue of his father and his combat with Hotspur are played out with swords and medieval bludgeons.

The transformation of Prince Harry (Amad Jackson) from scapegrace to King is marked by this aesthetic shift from filmic realism to theatrical artifice. At the Boar's Head, he speaks very much like an urban black youth, his accent suggesting the depth of his rebellion against his well-spoken father; and the script provides just enough 'American' substitutions to reinforce this rejection of his 'courtly' education. In the play-extempore scene, for example, just after Falstaff, speaking as the King, warns the Prince that there is such a thing as 'bullshit' (for 'pitch') and the Lord Chief Justice is announced, the Prince instructs Falstaff, 'Hide thee behind my ass' ('the arras'). Such American vulgarities wrench Shakespeare's script into the present day. Remarkably, then, once Hal has been called to account by his father in a scene filmed on the stage of an empty theatre, his accent shifts abruptly to received pronunciation. Especially at the King's deathbed, he delivers blank verse with a precision and an emotional delicacy that mark how far he has come from the Boar's Head. In the theatre, it seems, any miracle is possible.

At his coronation procession, filmed in an ornate civic building, the new King reveals the public persona of a born politician. His skill is tested when Falstaff, having wrapped himself in an American flag for the occasion, sings his line 'God save thy grace, King Hal' (5.5.39) to the melody of 'My country, 'tis of thee', which of course was adapted from 'God Save the King', a brilliant irony that draws attention to the central paradox of using a play about feudal struggles in medieval England to comment on black political culture in contemporary America. But perhaps not only the political culture of black America; for as the camera cuts to the new King standing alone onstage, in a spotlight, delivering as public address lines imported from 5.2 that in the text he speaks only to a few assembled nobles, promising 'To mock the expectation of the world' and to 'choose such limbs of noble counsel / That the great body of our state may go / In equal rank with the best-governed nation' (125–36), the film moves beyond the realm

25   Prince Henry (Amad Jackson) at the bedside of the King (Harry Lennix) in *H4*, a film of the *Henry IV* plays directed by Paul Quinn and completed in 2013

of dynastic warfare in Los Angeles to invoke a moving image of a young Barack Obama.

Phyllida Lloyd's all-female *Henry IV*

The all-female *Henry IV* at London's Donmar Warehouse tells another story. Directed by Phyllida Lloyd, whose all-female *Julius Caesar* provoked controversy when it opened at the same venue in 2012, this *Henry* used the framing device of a women's prison in which the inmates perform the play as a kind of therapeutic release. The subject of 'prison Shakespeare' has been in vogue for some time, with claims that performing Shakespeare can be both morally enlightening and psychologically empowering for inmates who feel alienated from the society that locked them up.[1] And so it is with the women who

1   The therapeutic value of having prisoners perform Shakespeare has been promoted for at least two decades. A 2005 American film, *Shakespeare Behind Bars*, documents the work of a non-profit organization of the same name which has been in existence since 1995, and whose mission is to offer 'theatrical encounters with personal and social issues to incarcerated and post-incarcerated adults and juveniles,

perform *Henry IV* – fourteen in all, from diverse backgrounds and of different races – women who, like the men in the play, have established power relations which Lloyd occasionally foregrounds. The society they have formed in prison gives a special resonance to relationships that develop in the *Henry* play they perform; and as they are assigned their parts by the dour, solitary but authoritative woman who will play the King – Harriet Walter with short-cropped hair and a crown made of beer cans – it becomes clear to the audience that the real empowerment for these women will come from their being able to act as men and to identify with the characters they play. The actresses are not cross-dressing. Rather, in their prison jumpsuits, they are playing women who are then asked to assume the roles of men in a play-within-a-play. This metatheatrical device makes the audience aware of the impact that playing Shakespeare is having on the 'real' women in the prison as well as on the actresses who are getting to act Shakespearean roles usually denied them. As one critic observes, 'There's an exhilaration that comes with watching a gifted cast of women tear into the male preserve of these texts' (Matt Wolf, *New York Times*, 22 October 2014).

As with earlier abridgements, this is very much the story of Hal, played by a tall, powerfully built prisoner (Clare Dunne) who speaks with an Irish accent. The play opens with the first tavern scene in *Part One*, in which Hal is snorting a line of coke with Falstaff, who gets it from Poins, the dealer. In this Eastcheap tavern, cocaine, not sack, is the drug of choice. The prisoner assigned the role of Hal is told at the outset that she is to be released in three weeks; thus she is aware throughout that

allowing them to develop life skills that will ensure their successful reintegration into society' (www.shakespearebehindbars.org). For her production, Lloyd collaborated with Clean Break, a British theatre company that works with women affected by the criminal justice system. The therapeutic value of performing Shakespeare in prisons has also been taken up by academics such as Jean Trounstine, Amy Scott-Douglass and Laura Bates.

she is only 'pretending to be one of the "lads", biding her time as much as doing time'; and her determination to be rid of the prisoner who plays Falstaff – the feeder of her drug habit – 'is thus likely to release terrible passions in both the inner and outer plays' (Paul Taylor, *Independent*, 10 October 2014).

Falstaff's fear of losing Hal's loyalty creates a tug of war between them that spills over to the prison. The prisoner 'Falstaff' often breaks character in the manner of a club comic and has to be admonished for it: 'Take it seriously!' barks the 'King' at one point. At a particularly sensitive moment, when Hal has just assured his father 'I shall hereafter, my

26   Prince Henry (Clare Dunne) trying on a crown made of beer cans, in the Donmar Warehouse production of *Henry IV* directed by Phyllida Lloyd, 2014

thrice-gracious lord, / Be more myself' (*Part One* 3.2.92–3), he is interrupted by a loud fart emitted by Falstaff from behind a curtain. When the curtain is thrust aside and 'Falstaff' revealed, the prisoners playing the Prince and King protest that she is not a part of the scene. At such moments the audience is yanked out of the fiction and into the 'real' world of power dynamics within the prison. This Falstaff does not want Hal to leave him behind and, as a performer, has the power to call attention to the fictional nature of Hal's promised reformation.

The actress who plays Falstaff (Ashley McGuire) turns in a raucously vulgar performance that bravely draws attention to her gender. A 'corpulent, cockney and comically delightful' middle-aged woman (Dominic Cavendish, *Telegraph*, 10 October 2014), she is dressed in a vest, or 'muscle shirt' as it is called in the US, which unabashedly displays her rolls of flesh: her Falstaff is the real thing, not a thin man in a fat suit. She dares the audience to look at her unadorned body. Like a gangster, she also dares to bully her fellow prisoners with a 'flash of Kray-style menace' (Simon Edge, *Daily Express*, 11 October 2014). In the tavern scene (*Part One* 2.4), for instance, she physically intimidates the prisoner playing the Hostess, who, as the only Muslim in the cast, seems particularly vulnerable to 'Falstaff's' abuse – a victim of the kind of racism rampant among prison populations. And so, when the newly crowned King Harry banishes Falstaff, the prisoner King is in fact using the play to chasten the prison bully, who 'doesn't deal well with the rejection of her character and has to be carried out in plastic handcuffs wailing' (Edge).

The cutting of the text is particularly severe in this production. The only scenes from *Part Two* that remain are that of the King's death, played with devastating emotional commitment by Harriet Walter, and the rejection of Falstaff. The play ends with the new King's uttering the opening lines of his father's speech in *Part One*, an indication that he – or the prisoner who plays him, 'wan with care' after years of incarceration – is anxious to put civil brawls behind him (her) but uncertain that he (she) can. Apart from the final twenty minutes, the play is shaped by events in *Part One*, with particular focus on the combat between Hal and Hotspur, which is staged as a vicious boxing match between the physically imposing Hal and the wiry, 'muscular, tigerish Hotspur' who has been training with a punching bag in a gym (Andrzej Lukowski, *Time Out*, 10 October 2014). Indeed, Hotspur leads all the rebels in a strenuous work-out session before battle; and in a wryly humorous piece of staging, his observation that 'The King hath many marching in his coats' (*Part One* 5.3.25) is realized when those prisoners boxing in the King's name don papier mâché masks bearing the imprint of Dame Harriet Walter's face.

Behind their masks, however, the diversity of the prisoners is made authentic by the diversity of the acting pool. While the King and the Prince are played by white actors, the rebels – Hotspur, Mortimer and Worcester – are black, and Northumberland, Asian. Rebellion thus wears a dark face, and the performance seems to be making a statement about racial tensions within the prison population as well. But regional and ethnic accents reveal another form of diversity: socio-economic. While the King speaks in an enigmatically posh accent that lapses occasionally into the New York tones of a Robert DeNiro gangster, Hal speaks with an Ulster brogue, Falstaff with a Cockney swagger and Kate Percy – a large woman who comically overwhelms her slightly built husband – with a working-class Glaswegian accent. The prisoners and the actors who play them thus represent the different races, ethnic histories and types of poverty and oppression to be found in the UK today. The *Henry IV* plays themselves, of course, are about building a nation in all its sixteenth-century diversity – English, Scots, Irish, Welsh; but as Susannah Clapp observes, 'In this abridged version you hear few disquisitions about the state of the nation. Instead, the state is embodied onstage' (*Observer*, 11 October 2014).

27 Soldiers in the royal army preparing for battle, wearing boxing gloves and masks of the King (Harriet Walter), in the Donmar Warehouse production of *Henry IV* directed by Phyllida Lloyd, 2014

For the past fifty years, performances of the conflated texts of *Henry IV* have foregrounded the evolution of Hal from scapegrace prince to king with an economy scarcely possible when both parts are performed in their entirety. One consequence of this compression of the plays to provide a consistent narrative focus, however, has been to suppress those other narratives – those of the tavern low-lifes, the country justices and recruits – that give *Part Two* its special character and have the power to subvert the 'official' version of events dramatized in the political plot. Nevertheless, recent productions of the conflated texts have revealed new potentials for *Henry IV* to speak with surprising urgency to contemporary social and political concerns. The Donmar's all-female production set in a women's prison and the African American film set in gangland Los Angeles, by culturally reinventing the *Henry IV* plays, have given to Shakespeare's Plantagenet history new life and purpose.

APPENDIX 3

Casting the play

Shakespeare's plays typically have far larger casts than plays written in later centuries. *Henry IV, Part Two* has one of the largest, with fifty speaking roles, including Rumour and the Epilogue which bookend the play. In addition to two mute characters, a full production requires supernumeraries – court attendants, servants, soldiers, a captain and musicians – in non-speaking roles. It is unlikely that even a prosperous theatre company such as the Lord Chamberlain's Men could have afforded to hire a separate actor for each role, so just as occurs today in performances by Shakespeare theatres around the world, doubling roles was no doubt a necessity.[1] Companies in Shakespeare's London would have had ready access to a large pool of journeyman actors; thus doubling may not have been quite so demanding on actors as it would have been when these companies toured the provinces with a smaller troupe, and when an individual actor may have had to play several roles during a performance.

There is no way of knowing whether doubling occurred only among those actors who played secondary roles, or whether those in primary roles also assumed doubling duty when necessary. If they did not – and today's star-system encourages us to believe that a major actor would never have been asked to double in a minor role – then a company would have had to be flush with actors even when it toured, unless plays were cut

---

1 As evidence of doubling as a common practice in Elizabethan theatre, Kastan (*1H4*, 354) cites an account in Chambers (*Elizabethan*, 2.364) that a Swiss visitor to London in 1599 reported attending a performance of *Julius Caesar* at the Globe in which forty roles were played by 'approximately fifteen actors'. Presumably a company on tour would have had even fewer.

substantially; and in *Part Two*, which has many roles that might qualify as major, the acting troupe would have had to be unrealistically large. It is reasonable to surmise, then, that even principal actors would on occasion have doubled in minor roles. A number of actors might have played as many as six or eight different roles, so long as they had time to change from one costume to another, with a single garment (a jerkin, a cloak, a hat) often sufficient to signal the entry of a new character. No doubt audiences then as now were adept at suspending disbelief.

Scholars who have recently explored the practices of casting Elizabethan plays have arrived at different solutions for the casting of *Part Two*. T.J. King, in a thorough review of the casting needs of both Q and F texts, concludes that for Q, '[t]welve actors can play twenty principal male roles; four boys play four principal female roles and the Epilogue', and a further 'eight men' are required to 'play twenty-four minor speaking parts and twenty mutes', for a total of twenty-four actors. The needs of the F text are similar, he reasons: twelve principal actors and four boys, though a company could make do with only 'six men' to play 'twenty-two small speaking parts and four mutes', for a total of twenty-two actors (*Casting*, 85–6 and Tables 51, 52). In either case, while such a sizable cast might have been possible in London, it certainly would not have been feasible on a provincial tour. David Bradley's view is a bit less expansive. Arguing that the Lord Chamberlain's company had 'a settled composition of sixteen men' throughout the 1590s, he suggests that this number, however 'uncompromising', might have been insufficient to meet the needs of *Part Two*; and in addition, he lists six boys as requisite to round out the cast, for a total of at least twenty-two actors (Bradley, 234). John Jowett demonstrates greater sensitivity to the economics of theatre in his casting chart for the Folio *Part Two*, showing how a cast of ten principal actors, one hired man, and three boys – a total of fourteen – could, with frequent doubling, have performed the full text, though he neglects to assign actors to the roles of the five Gloucestershire recruits ('Cuts', 295).

In the following doubling chart, I attempt to show how a company of only nine men and three boys could perform the play in its entirety. Possible only through extensive doubling, this scheme would require all the principal players but Falstaff to shoulder additional roles. On occasion I have attempted to have an actor's doubled roles resonate in interesting ways, as, for example, when the actor playing the King doubles as the Lord Chief Justice, or when the actor playing Prince John doubles as two officers, Snare and the Beadle, who arrest followers of his brother Harry. In Shakespeare's theatre, furthermore, boy actors could readily switch genders, moving effortlessly from women's roles to those of young men; so it makes sense for the two boys playing the Hostess and Doll, Lady Northumberland and Lady Percy, also to double as the King's two youngest sons, Humphrey and Thomas.

Theatre companies today usually avoid plays with large casts owing to budgetary constraints, unless the number of actors can be significantly reduced by cutting the text or doubling roles. While the amount of doubling my chart suggests requires some quick costume changes and may not be ideal, it would nevertheless allow the play to be performed by a pool of only twelve actors without cuts. The only speaking role not included on the chart is that of the Third Strewer, who has one line at the opening of 5.5, a scene that requires all twelve actors to be present on stage. This line could easily be assigned to the First Strewer. Alternatively, since Falstaff's Page is present but mute in the scene, the boy actor could play a Strewer instead, and the Page never be missed.

DOUBLING CHART

#	Role	Ind	1.1	1.2	1.3	2.1	2.2	2.3	2.4	3.1	3.2	4.1	4.2	4.3	5.1	5.2	5.3	5.4	5.5	Epi
1	Falstaff			x		x			x		x		x	x	x		x		x	x
2	King Henry									x				x						
	Lord Ch. Justice			x		x										x			x	
	Sir John Blunt*												x							
	2 Beadle *																	x		
3	Prince Henry						x		x							x			x	
	Mowbray				x							x								
4	Northumberland		x					x												
	Justice Shallow										x				x		x			
	Westmorland											x	x	x						
	Peto					x			x											
5	Gower					x														
	Archbishop				x							x								
	Justice Silence										x						x			
	Morton		x																	
	Servant to Ch. J.			x																
	Drawer								x											
6	2 Strewer																		x	
	Bardolph					x	x		x		x		x		x		x			x
	Rumour	x																		x
	Travers		x																	
7	Poins						x		x											
	Prince John											x	x	x			x			x
	Snare					x														
	Shadow										x									

508

	Character																			
	Porter	×																		
	1 Beadle																			
8	Pistol															×		×	
	Warwick	×		×					×	×	×	×	×	×		
	Lord Bardolph	×	×												
	Mouldy			×											
	Collevile					×							
	Hastings		×	×		×						
9	Fang		×										
	Francis			×								
	Surrey*			×							
	Bullcalf				×						
	Harcourt						×				
	Davy							×	×		
	1 Strewer									×	
10	Page to Falstaff	×	×	×	×		×		×	×			×	×	×	×	
11	Hostess		×	×									
	Lady Northumb.		×								
	Page to King*			×						×	
	Feeble			×							
	Humphrey						×				
12	Doll Tearsheet	×	×					×	×		×	
	Lady Percy								×		
	Wart		×	×							
	Thomas	×	×	×	×	×	×	×	×	×	×	×

* non-speaking role

Other non-speaking roles (Attendants, Servants, Musicians, a Captain and Soldiers), while not necessary to a performance, may be played by actors as available.

ABBREVIATIONS AND REFERENCES

Quotations from and references to Shakespeare plays other than *2 Henry IV* are from individual volumes of The Arden Shakespeare, Third Series, when available; from The Arden Shakespeare, Second Series, when not. Biblical quotations are from the Bishops' Bible (1568) except when the Geneva Bible (1560) is indicated. In all references, the place of publication is London unless otherwise noted. Abbreviations of parts of speech are those used in the *OED* (2nd edn).

ABBREVIATIONS

ABBREVIATIONS USED IN NOTES

*	precedes commentary notes involving readings altered from the quarto edition of 1600 (Qa) on which this edition is based
( )	enclosing a reading in the textual notes indicates original spelling; enclosing an editor's or scholar's name indicates a conjectural reading
corr	corrected state
conj.	conjecture
dir.	directed by
ed., eds	editor, edited by, editors
edn	edition
F	First Folio
$^{F, F}$	superscripts encasing material adopted from the First Folio
n.	(in cross-references) commentary note
n.d.	no date
n.s.	new series
om.	omitted in
opp.	opposite
Qa	1600 Quarto, first issue
Qb	1600 Quarto, second issue
rev.	revised (by)
rpt.	reprinted in
SD	stage direction
sig.	signature
SP	speech prefix

subst.	substantially
this edn	reading adopted for the first time in this edition
TLN	through line numbering
t.n.	textual note
trans.	translated by
uncorr	uncorrected state
var.	variant

WORKS BY AND PARTLY BY SHAKESPEARE

AC	*Antony and Cleopatra*
AW	*All's Well That Ends Well*
AYL	*As You Like It*
CE	*The Comedy of Errors*
Cor	*Coriolanus*
Cym	*Cymbeline*
DF	*Double Falsehood*
E3	*King Edward III*
Ham	*Hamlet*
1H4	*King Henry IV, Part 1*
2H4	*King Henry IV, Part 2*
H5	*King Henry V*
1H6	*King Henry VI, Part 1*
2H6	*King Henry VI, Part 2*
3H6	*King Henry VI, Part 3*
H8	*King Henry VIII*
JC	*Julius Caesar*
KJ	*King John*
KL	*King Lear*
LC	*A Lover's Complaint*
LLL	*Love's Labour's Lost*
Luc	*The Rape of Lucrece*
MA	*Much Ado About Nothing*
Mac	*Macbeth*
MM	*Measure for Measure*
MND	*A Midsummer Night's Dream*
MV	*The Merchant of Venice*
MW	*The Merry Wives of Windsor*
Oth	*Othello*
Per	*Pericles*
PP	*The Passionate Pilgrim*
PT	*The Phoenix and Turtle*
R2	*King Richard II*
R3	*King Richard III*

RJ	*Romeo and Juliet*
Son	*Sonnets*
STM	*Sir Thomas More*
TC	*Troilus and Cressida*
Tem	*The Tempest*
TGV	*The Two Gentlemen of Verona*
Tim	*Timon of Athens*
Tit	*Titus Andronicus*
TN	*Twelfth Night*
TNK	*The Two Noble Kinsmen*
TS	*The Taming of the Shrew*
VA	*Venus and Adonis*
WT	*The Winter's Tale*

REFERENCES

EDITIONS OF SHAKESPEARE COLLATED

Alexander	*William Shakespeare: The Complete Works*, ed. Peter Alexander (1951)
Ard	*The Arden Shakespeare: Complete Works*, ed. Richard Proudfoot, Ann Thompson and David Scott Kastan, rev. edn (2001)
Ard¹	*The Second Part of King Henry the Fourth*, ed. R.P. Cowl (1923)
Ard²	*The Second Part of King Henry IV*, ed. A.R. Humphreys (1966)
Bate & Rasmussen	*William Shakespeare: Complete Works*, Royal Shakespeare Company Edition, ed. Jonathan Bate and Eric Rasmussen (2006)
Bell	*Bell's Edition of Shakespeare's Plays, as they are performed at the Theatres Royal in London*, 9 vols (1773–4)
Berger	*The Second Part of King Henry the Fourth* (1600), ed. Thomas L. Berger, MSR (Oxford, 1990)
Betterton	*The Sequel of Henry the Fourth: With the Humours of Sir John Falstaffe, and Justice Shallow*, Alter'd from *Shakespear*, by the late Mr. [Thomas] Betterton (1721; facsimile 1969)
Bevington	*The Complete Works of Shakespeare*, 6th edn, ed. David Bevington (New York, 2009)
Blayney	*The First Folio of Shakespeare: The Norton Facsimile*, ed. Charlton Hinman (1968); 2nd edn, ed. Peter W.M. Blayney (New York, 1996)

Boswell–Malone	*The Plays and Poems of William Shakespeare*, ed. James Boswell, with a 'Life of the Poet' by Edmond Malone, 21 vols (1821)
Bullen	*The Works of William Shakespeare*, ed. A.H. Bullen *et al.*, 10 vols (Stratford-upon-Avon, 1904)
Cam	*The Complete Works of William Shakespeare*, ed. William George Clark, John Glover and William Aldis Wright, 9 vols (Cambridge, 1863–6)
Cam[1]	*The Second Part of the History of Henry IV*, ed. J. Dover Wilson (Cambridge, 1946)
Cam[2]	*The Second Part of King Henry IV*, ed. Giorgio Melchiori (Cambridge, 1989)
Capell	*Comedies, Histories, and Tragedies*, ed. Edward Capell, 10 vols (1767–8)
Chester	*The Second Part of King Henry the Fourth*, ed. Allan Chester, Pelican Shakespeare (Baltimore, Md, 1957)
Collier	*The Works of Shakespeare,* ed. J.P. Collier, 8 vols (1842–4)
Collier[2]	*Works*, ed. J.P. Collier, 2nd edn, 6 vols (1858)
Collier[3]	*Works*, ed. J.P. Collier, 3rd edn, 8 vols (1876–8)
Craig	*The Complete Works of William Shakespeare*, ed. W.J. Craig (Oxford, 1892)
Davison	*The Second Part of King Henry the Fourth,* ed. P.H. Davison, New Penguin Shakespeare (Harmondsworth, 1977)
Delius	*Shakespeares Werke*, ed. Nicolaus Delius, 7 vols (1857)
Dering	*The History of King Henry the Fourth, as Revised by Sir Edward Dering, Bart.*, facsimile ed. George Walton Williams and Gwynne Blakemore Evans (Charlottesville, Va., 1974)
Dyce	*The Works of William Shakespeare*, ed. Alexander Dyce, 6 vols (1857)
Dyce[2]	*Works*, ed. Alexander Dyce, 2nd edn, 9 vols (1864–7)
F1	*Comedies, Histories and Tragedies*, The First Folio (1623)
F2	*Comedies, Histories and Tragedies*, The Second Folio (1632)
F3	*Comedies, Histories and Tragedies*, The Third Folio (1663)
F4	*Comedies, Histories and Tragedies*, The Fourth Folio (1685)
Folger	*Henry IV, Part 2*, ed. Barbara A. Mowat and Paul Werstine, New Folger Library Shakespeare (New York, 1999)

Furnivall	*The Works of William Shakespeare*, ed. Nicholas Delius, with an introduction by F.J. Furnivall, The Leopold Shakespeare (1877)
Furnivall, 1909	*The Second Part of Henrie the Fourth*, ed. F.J. Furnivall, with an introduction by F.W. Clarke, The Old Spelling Shakespeare (New York, 1909)
Globe	*The Complete Works of William Shakespeare*, ed. William George Clark and William Aldis Wright, The Globe Edition (New York, 1864)
Hanmer	*The Works of Shakespear*, ed. Thomas Hanmer, 6 vols (Oxford, 1743–4)
Hanmer²	*Works*, ed. Thomas Hanmer, 2nd edn, 6 vols (Oxford, 1770–1)
Hemingway	*The Second Part of Henry the Fourth*, ed. Samuel Burdett Hemingway (New Haven, Conn., 1921)
Herford	*The Works of Shakespeare*, ed. C.H. Herford, The Eversley Shakespeare, 10 vols (1899)
Holland	*Henry IV, Part Two*, ed. Norman N. Holland, Signet Classic Shakespeare (New York, 1965)
Hudson	*The Harvard Shakespeare*, ed. Henry Norman Hudson, 20 vols (Boston, Mass., 1880)
Humphreys	*see* Ard²
Johnson	*The Plays of William Shakespeare*, ed. Samuel Johnson, 8 vols (1765)
Keightley	*The Plays of Shakespeare*, ed. Thomas Keightley, 6 vols (1864)
Kemble	*King Henry IV, The Second Part*, rev. J.P. Kemble after *Bell's Edition* (1804)
Kittredge	*The Complete Works of Shakespeare*, ed. George Lyman Kittredge (Boston, Mass., 1936)
McEachern	*The Second Part of King Henry the Fourth*, ed. Claire McEachern, Pelican Shakespeare (New York, 2000)
Macready	William Macready, *Henry IV, The Second Part*, The Coronation Production (1821); facsimile, ed. Peter Davison (1971)
Malone	*The Plays and Poems of William Shakespeare*, ed. Edmond Malone, 10 vols (1790)
Malone, *Suppl.*	Edmond Malone, *Supplement to the Edition of Shakespeare's Plays Published in 1778*, 2 vols (1780)
Melchiori	*see* Cam²
Neilson	*The Complete Dramatic and Poetic Works of William Shakespeare*, ed. W.A. Neilson (Boston, Mass., 1906)

Norton	*The Norton Shakespeare*, ed. Stephen Greenblatt *et al.* (New York, 1997)
Oxf	*The Complete Works of Shakespeare*, ed. Stanley Wells and Gary Taylor (Oxford, 1986)
Oxf[1]	*Henry IV, Part 2*, ed. René Weis (Oxford, 1998)
Pope	*The Works of Shakespear*, ed. Alexander Pope, 6 vols (1723–5)
Qa	*The Second part of Henrie the fourth* (1600), first issue of the Quarto
Qb	*The Second part of Henrie the fourth* (1600), second issue of the Quarto
Rann	*Dramatic Works of William Shakespeare*, ed. Joseph Rann, 6 vols, vol. 3 (Oxford, 1789)
Ridley	*Henry IV, Second Part*, ed. M.R. Ridley, New Temple Shakespeare (1934)
Riv	*The Riverside Shakespeare*, ed. G. Blakemore Evans (Boston, Mass., 1974)
Rowe	*The Works of Mr William Shakespear*, ed. Nicholas Rowe, 6 vols (1709)
Rowe[3]	*Works*, ed. Nicholas Rowe, 3rd edn, 8 vols (1714)
Shaaber [, Variorum]	*The Second Part of Henry the Fourth*, ed. Matthias A. Shaaber, The New Variorum Shakespeare (Philadelphia, Pa., 1940)
Singer[1]	*The Dramatic Works of William Shakespeare*, ed. Samuel W. Singer, 10 vols (Chiswick, 1826)
Singer[2]	*Works*, ed. Samuel W. Singer, 2nd edn, 10 vols (1856)
Sisson	*William Shakespeare: The Complete Works*, ed. C.J. Sisson (1954)
Staunton	*The Plays of Shakespeare*, ed. Howard Staunton, 3 vols (1858–60)
Steevens	*The Plays of William Shakespeare*, ed. Samuel Johnson and George Steevens, 2nd edn, 10 vols (1773)
Steevens[3]	*The Plays of William Shakespeare*, ed. Samuel Johnson and George Steevens, 3rd edn, 10 vols (1778)
Steevens[4]	*Plays*, ed. Samuel Johnson, George Steevens and Isaac Reed, 4th edn, 15 vols (1793)
Theobald	*The Works of Shakespeare*, ed. Lewis Theobald, with notes by William Warburton, 7 vols (1733)
Theobald[2]	*Works*, ed. Lewis Theobald, 2nd edn, 8 vols (1740)
Thirlby	Styan Thirlby, contributor to Theobald's edition of Shakespeare's *Works* (1733)

Var '03	*The Plays of William Shakespeare*, ed. Isaac Reed, based on Steevens's 1793 edn, 21 vols, The First Variorum (1803)
Warburton	*The Works of Shakespear*, ed. William Warburton, 8 vols (1747)
Weis	*see* Oxf¹
White, R.G.	*The Works of William Shakespeare*, ed. R.G. White, 12 vols (1859)
Winstanley	*Henry IV, Part 2*, ed. L. Winstanley (New York, 1918)

OTHER WORKS CITED OR CONSULTED

Abbott	E.A. Abbott, *A Shakespearean Grammar*, 3rd edn (1870)
Acts	*Acts of the Privy Council of England*, n.s. XXIV A.D. 1592–3, ed. J.R. Dasent, CB (PRO 1901; rpt. Liechtenstein, 1974)
Addenbrooke	David Addenbrooke, *The Royal Shakespeare Company: The Peter Hall Years* (1974)
Ainger	Alfred Ainger, *Lectures and Essays*, 2 vols (1905)
An exposition	*An exposition of certaine . . . Termes of the Lawes* (1598)
Ariosto	Ludovico Ariosto, *Orlando furioso in English heroical verse*, trans. John Harington (1591)
Baldo	Jonathan Baldo, *Memory in Shakespeare's Histories: Stages of Forgetting in Early Modern England* (2012)
Baldwin	Thomas Whitfield Baldwin, *The Organization and Personnel of the Shakespearean Company* (New York, 1961)
Bale	John Bale, *A brefe Chronycle concernynge the Examinacyon and death of the blessed Martyr of Christ Syr Johan Oldecastell the Lorde Cobham* (1544)
Barber	C.L. Barber, *Shakespeare's Festive Comedies* (Princeton, NJ, 1959)
Barbour	John Barbour, *The Bruce*, ed. W.W. Skeat (EETS, 1870)
Baret	John Baret, *An Alvearie or Triple Dictionarie in English, Latin, and French* (1574)
Barish	Jonas A. Barish, 'The turning away of Prince Hal', *SSt*, 1 (1965), 9–17
Barret	Robert Barret, *Theorike and Practike of Moderne Warres* (1598)
Barton, A.	Anne Barton, *The Names of Comedy* (Toronto, 1990)
Barton, J.	*When Thou Art King*, adapted by John Barton, promptbook (1969)

Bate	Jonathan Bate, *Soul of the Age* (2008)
Bates	Laura Bates, *Shakespeare Saved My Life: Ten Years in Solitary with the Bard* (Naperville, Ill., 2013)
Beauman	Sally Beauman, *The Royal Shakespeare Company: A History of Ten Decades* (Oxford, 1982)
Beaumont & Fletcher	*The Dramatic Works in the Beaumont and Fletcher Canon*, ed. Fredson Bowers *et al.*, 10 vols (Cambridge, 1966–96)
Berger, H.	Harry Berger, Jr, 'On the continuity of the *Henriad*: a critique of some literary and theatrical approaches', in Ivo Kamps (ed.), *Shakespeare Left and Right* (1991), 225–40
Berger & Williams, 'Variants'	Thomas L. Berger and George Walton Williams, 'Variants in the Quarto of Shakespeare's *2 Henry IV*', *The Library*, 6.3 (1981), 109–18
Berger & Williams, 'Notes'	Thomas L. Berger and George Walton Williams, 'Notes on Shakespeare's *Henry V*', *Analytical & Enumerative Bibliography*, 12.3–4 (2001), 264–87
Bevington, *Tudor*	David Bevington, *Tudor Drama and Politics* (Cambridge, Mass., 1968)
Bishops' Bible	*The Holy Bible . . . Authorised and Appointed to be read in Churches* (1568)
Bland	D.S. Bland, 'Justice Shallow's "Hem, Boys!"', *N&Q*, n.s. 25 (1978), 132
Blayney, *Folio*	Peter W.M. Blayney, *The First Folio of Shakespeare*, Folger Library exhibition catalogue (Washington, DC, 1991)
Bogdanov & Pennington	Michael Bogdanov and Michael Pennington, *The English Shakespeare Company: The Story of 'The Wars of the Roses' 1986–1989* (1990)
Booth	Stephen Booth, 'Shakespeare in the San Francisco Bay area', *SQ*, 29.2 (1978), 267–78
Bowers	Fredson Bowers, *On Editing Shakespeare* (Charlottesville, 1966)
Boym	Svetlana Boym, *The Future of Nostalgia* (New York, 2001)
Bradley, A.C.	A.C. Bradley, 'The rejection of Falstaff' (1902), *Oxford Lectures on Poetry* (1909), 247–75
Bradley, D.	David Bradley, *From Text to Performance in the Elizabethan Theatre: Preparing the Play for the Stage* (Cambridge, 1992)
Bragg	Melvyn Bragg, *Rich: The Life of Richard Burton* (1988)
Bright	Timothy Bright, *Treatise of Melancholy* (1586)

Bristol	Michael D. Bristol, *Carnival and Theater: Plebeian Culture and the Structure of Authority in Renaissance England* (1985)
Brome	Richard Brome, *A Jovial Crew*, ed. Tiffany Stern, Arden Early Modern Drama (2014)
Brooke	C.F. Tucker Brooke, *The Shakespeare Apocrypha* (Oxford, 1918)
Bulloch	John Bulloch, *Studies on the Text of Shakespeare* (1878)
Bullough	*Narrative and Dramatic Sources of Shakespeare*, ed. Geoffrey Bullough, 8 vols (1957–75)
Bulman, 'Autonomy'	James C. Bulman, 'The autonomy of *Henry IV, Part Two*', in Barbara Mujica (ed.), *Shakespeare and the Spanish Comedia* (Lewisburg, Pa., 2014), 239–50
Bulman, 'Bawdy'	James C. Bulman, ' "To gain the language, 'tis needful that the most immodest word be looked upon and learnt": editing the bawdy in *Henry IV, Part Two*', in Randall Martin and Katherine Scheil (eds), *Shakespeare/ Adaptation/Modern Drama* (Toronto, 2011), 145–65
Bulman, *Henry IV*	James C. Bulman, '*Henry IV, Parts 1* and *2*', in Hattaway, *Companion* (Cambridge, 2002), 158–76
Bulman, 'Performing'	James C. Bulman, 'Performing the conflated text of *Henry IV*: the fortunes of *Part Two*', *SS 63* (2010), 89–101
Bulman, 'Timon'	James C. Bulman, 'The date and production of "Timon" reconsidered', *SS 27* (1974), 111–28
Caesar	*Caesar's War Commentaries*, trans. John Warrington (New York, 1958)
Cahill, *Breach*	Patricia A. Cahill, *Unto the Breach: Martial Formations, Historical Trauma, and the Early Modern Stage* (Oxford, 2008)
Cahill, 'Nation'	Patricia A. Cahill, 'Nation formation and the English history plays', in Dutton & Howard, 70–93
Campbell	Lily Bess Campbell, *Shakespeare's 'Histories': Mirrors of Elizabethan Policy* (San Marino, Calif., 1947)
Capell, *Notes*	Edward Capell, *Notes and Various Readings to Shakespeare, Part the first* (1774)
Case	John Case, *Sphaera Ciuitatis* (1588)
Castiglione	Baldassare Castiglione, *The Courtier*, trans. Thomas Hoby (1561)
Caxton	William Caxton, *Brut Chronicle* (1482)
Certain Sermons	*Certain Sermons or Homilies appointed by the Queenes Maiestie* (1574)

Chambers, *Elizabethan*	E.K. Chambers, *The Elizabethan Stage*, 4 vols (Oxford, 1923; corr. edn, 1951)
Chambers, 'Gleanings'	E.K. Chambers, 'Elizabethan stage gleanings', *RES*, 1 (1925), 76–7
Chambers, *Shakespeare*	E.K. Chambers, *William Shakespeare: A Study of Facts and Problems*, 2 vols (Oxford, 1930)
Chapman, *Achilles*	George Chapman, *Achilles Shield Translated as the other seuen Books of Homer, out of his eighteenth booke of Iliades* (1598)
Chapman, *Plays*	George Chapman, *The Plays of George Chapman: The Comedies*, ed. Allan Holaday (Urbana, Ill., 1970)
Chettle	Henry Chettle, *Kinde-Heartes Dreame* (1592)
Child	Francis James Child, *The English and Scottish Popular Ballads*, 10 vols (Boston, Mass., 1882–98; rpt. 5 vols, 2003)
Clare	Janet Clare, *'Art made tongue-tied by authority': Elizabethan and Jacobean Dramatic Censorship* (Manchester, 1990)
Clark	Peter Clark, *The English Alehouse: A Social History, 1200–1830* (1983)
Clegg, 'Liberty'	Cyndia Susan Clegg, 'Liberty, license, and authority: press censorship and Shakespeare', in Kastan, *Companion*, 464–85
Clegg, *Press*	Cyndia Susan Clegg, *Press Censorship in Elizabethan England* (Cambridge, 1997)
Clowes	W. Clowes, *The Cure of . . . Lues Venerea* (1596)
Cobos & Rubio	Juan Cobos and Miguel Rubio, 'Welles and Falstaff', *Sight and Sound*, 35 (1966), 159
Cogan	Thomas Cogan, *Haven of Health* (1584)
Collinson	Patrick Collinson, 'Merry England on the ropes: the contested culture of the early modern English town', in Simon Ditchfield (ed.), *Christianity and Community in the West* (Aldershot, 2001), 131–47
Cooper	Roberta Krensky Cooper, *The American Shakespeare Theatre: Stratford, 1955–1985* (Washington, DC, 1986)
Corbin & Sedge	*The Oldcastle Controversy: Sir John Oldcastle, Part 1* [and] *The Famous Victories of Henry V*, ed. Peter Corbin and Douglas Sedge (Manchester, 1991)
Cosbie	Arnold Cosbie, *The Manner of the Death and Execution of Arnold Cosbie, for Murthering the Lord Boorke* (1591)

Coursen	H.R. Coursen, *Shakespeare in Space: Recent Shakespeare Productions on Screen* (New York, 2002)
Crane	Mary Thomas Crane, 'The Shakespearean tetralogy', *SQ*, 36.3 (1985), 282–99
Cressy	David Cressy, *Bonfires and Bells: National Memory and the Protestant Calendar in Elizabethan and Stuart England* (Berkeley, Calif., 1989)
Crewe, 'Critical'	Jonathan Crewe, '*Henry IV, Part 2*: a critical history', in Dutton & Howard, 432–50
Crewe, 'Reforming'	Jonathan Crewe, 'Reforming Prince Hal: the sovereign inheritor in *2 Henry IV*', *RD*, n.s. 21 (1990), 225–42
Crowl	Samuel Crowl, 'The long goodbye: Welles and Falstaff', *SQ*, 31.3 (1980), 369–80
CW	see Daniel, *CW*
Daniel, *CW*	Samuel Daniel, *The First Fowre Bookes of the Ciuile Wars between the two Houses of Lancaster and Yorke* (1595)
Daniel, *Works*	Samuel Daniel, *The Complete Works*, ed. A.B. Grosart, 5 vols (1885–6; rpt. New York, 1963)
Daoust	Yvette Daoust, *Roger Planchon, Director and Playwright* (Cambridge, 1980)
David, 'History'	Richard David, 'Shakespeare's history plays: epic or drama', *SS 6* (1953), 129–39
David, *Shakespeare*	Richard David, *Shakespeare in the Theatre* (Cambridge, 1978)
Davies, A.	Anthony Davies, 'Falstaff's shadow', in Sarah Hatchuel and Nathalie Vienne-Guerrin (eds), *Shakespeare on Screen: The Henriad* (Rouen, 2008), 99–117
Davies, R.	R.R. Davies, *The Revolt of Owain Glyn Dwr* (Oxford, 1995)
Davies, T.	Thomas Davies, *Dramatic Miscellanies*, 3 vols (1784)
de Grazia & Wells	Margreta de Grazia and Stanley Wells (eds), *The Cambridge Companion to Shakespeare* (Cambridge, 2001)
Dekker, *Dramatic*	Thomas Dekker, *The Dramatic Works of Thomas Dekker*, ed. Fredson Bowers, 4 vols (Cambridge, 1953–61)
Dekker, *Non-Dramatic*	Thomas Dekker, *The Non-Dramatic Works of Thomas Dekker*, ed. Alexander B. Grosart, 5 vols (1884–6)
Deloney	Thomas Deloney, *Garland of Good Will* (1586)
De Loque	Bertrand De Loque, *Discourse of Warre and Single Combat*, trans. J. Eliot (1591)

Demetz	Peter Demetz, 'The elm and the vine: notes toward the history of a marriage topos', *PMLA*, 73.5 (1958), 521–32
Dent	R.W. Dent, *Shakespeare's Proverbial Language: An Index* (Berkeley, Calif., 1981)
de Somogyi	Nick de Somogyi, *Shakespeare's Theatre of War* (Aldershot, 1998)
Dodsley	Robert Dodsley, *A Select Collection of Old English Plays* (1744), 4th edn, ed. W. Carew Hazlitt, 15 vols (1874–6)
Dollimore	Jonathan Dollimore, *Radical Tragedy: Religion, Ideology and Power in the Drama of Shakespeare and his Contemporaries* (Chicago, Ill., 1984)
Dollimore & Sinfield	Jonathan Dollimore and Alan Sinfield (eds), *Political Shakespeare: Essays in Cultural Materialism* (Ithaca, NY, 1985)
Drakakis	John Drakakis (ed.), *Alternative Shakespeares* (1985)
Drayton	Michael Drayton, *Poly-Olbion* (1612)
Dryden	John Dryden, 'An Essay of Dramatick Poesie' (1668), in *The Dramatick Works of John Dryden*, vol. 1 (1717)
DSK	David Scott Kastan, personal correspondence
Duffin	Ross W. Duffin, *Shakespeare's Songbook* (New York, 2004)
Dutton, *Censorship*	Richard Dutton, *Licensing, Censorship and Authorship in Early Modern England* (Houndmills, 2000)
Dutton, 'Licensing'	Richard Dutton, 'Licensing and censorship', in Kastan, *Companion*, 377–91
Dutton, *Mastering*	Richard Dutton, *Mastering the Revels: The Regulation and Censorship of English Renaissance Drama* (Basingstoke, 1991)
Dutton & Howard	Richard Dutton and Jean E. Howard (eds), *A Companion to Shakespeare's Works*, vol. 2, *The Histories* (Oxford, 2003)
Dyson	Humphry Dyson, *A Booke Containing all such Proclamations as were published during the Raigne of the late Queene Elizabeth* (1618)
Earle	John Earle, *Microcosmographie* (1628)
Edelman	*The Stukeley Plays*, ed. Charles Edelman (Manchester, 2005)
EETS	Early English Text Society
Eliot	John Eliot, *Ortho-epia Gallica, Eliots Fruits for the French* (1593)

Ellis-Fermor	Una Ellis-Fermor, *The Frontiers of Drama* (1945)
ELR	*English Literary Renaissance*
Elyot	Thomas Elyot, *The Boke Named the Gouernour* (1531)
Erne	Lukas Erne, *Shakespeare as Literary Dramatist* (Cambridge, 2003; 2nd edn, 2013)
Fabyan	Robert Fabyan, *The New Chronicles of England and of France* (1516)
Famous Victories	*The Famous Victories of Henry V* (1598), in Corbin & Sedge
Fehrenbach	Robert J. Fehrenbach, 'When Lord Cobham and Edmund Tilney "were att odds": Oldcastle, Falstaff, and the date of *1 Henry IV*', *SSt*, 18 (1986), 87–101
Ferguson, A.	Arthur B. Ferguson, *The Chivalric Tradition in Renaissance England* (Washington DC, 1986)
Ferguson, W.	W. Craig Ferguson, 'The compositors of *Henry IV, Part 2, Much Ado About Nothing, The Shoemakers' Holiday*, and *The First Part of the Contention*', *SB*, 13 (1960), 19–29
Feuillerat	Albert Feuillerat, *Documents relating to the revels at court in the time of King Edward VI and Queen Mary* (Louvain, 1914)
Florio	John Florio, *A World of Wordes, or Most Copious Dictionary in Italian and English* (1598; enlarged edn, 1611)
Forker, *R2*	Shakespeare, *King Richard II*, ed. Charles R. Forker, The Arden Shakespeare, Third Series (2002)
Forker, 'Soul'	Charles R. Forker, 'The state of the soul and the soul of the state: reconciliation in the two parts of Shakespeare's *Henry IV*', in Roger Dahood and Peter E. Medine (eds), *Studies in Medieval and Renaissance History* (New York, 2007), 289–313
Fortescue	J.W. Fortescue, 'The army: military service and equipment', in Sidney Lee and C.T. Onions (eds), *Shakespeare's England: An Account of the Life and Manners of his Age*, 2 vols (Oxford, 1916)
Fox	Adam Fox, *Oral and Literate Culture in England 1500–1700* (Oxford, 2000)
Foxe	John Foxe, *Actes and Monuments of these Latter and Perillous Dayes* (1563)
Garber	Marjorie Garber, *Shakespeare After All* (New York, 2004)
Geneva Bible	*The Bible and Holy Scriptvres Conteyned in the Olde and Newe Testament* (Geneva, 1560)

Gerard	John Gerard, *The Herball, or Generall Historie of Plantes* (1597)
Gibson	James M. Gibson, 'Shakespeare and the Cobham controversy: the Oldcastle/Falstaff and Brooke/Broome Revisions', *Medieval and Renaissance Drama in England*, 25 (2012), 94–132
Goldberg	Jonathan Goldberg, *Sodometries: Renaissance Texts, Modern Sexualities* (Stanford, Calif., 1992)
Gowing, *Dangers*	Laura Gowing, *Domestic Dangers: Women, Words, and Sex in Early Modern London* (Oxford, 1996)
Gowing, 'Gender'	Laura Gowing, 'Gender and the language of insult in early modern London', *History Workshop*, 35 (1993)
Grady	Hugh Grady, 'Falstaff: subjectivity between the carnival and the aesthetic', *MLR*, 96.3 (2001), 609–23
Green	William Green, *Shakespeare's 'Merry Wives of Windsor'* (Princeton, NJ, 1962)
Greenblatt	Stephen Greenblatt, 'Invisible bullets: Renaissance authority and its subversion, *Henry IV* and *Henry V*', in Dollimore & Sinfield, 18–47
Greene	*Life and Complete Works in Prose and Verse of Robert Greene*, ed. Alexander B. Grosart, 14 vols (1881–3)
Greg, *First Folio*	W.W. Greg, *The Shakespeare First Folio: Its Bibliographical and Textual History* (Oxford, 1955)
Greg, *Publishing*	W.W. Greg, *Some Aspects and Problems of London Publishing between 1550 and 1650* (Oxford, 1956)
Grene	Nicholas Grene, *Shakespeare's Serial History Plays* (Cambridge, 2002)
Gurr	Andrew Gurr, *The Shakespearean Stage, 1574–1642*, 3rd edn (Cambridge, 1992)
GWW	George Walton Williams, personal correspondence
Hall	Edward Hall, *The Vnion of the Two Noble and Illustre Families of Lancastre and Yorke* (1548)
Hapgood	Robert Hapgood, '*Chimes at Midnight* from stage to screen: the art of adaptation', *SS 39* (1987), 39–52
Harrison	William Harrison, *The Description of England* (1577), ed. Frederick J. Furnivall, New Shakspere Society (1876)
Hart	Alfred Hart, *Shakespeare and the Homilies* (Melbourne, 1934)
Hattaway, *Companion*	*The Cambridge Companion to Shakespeare's History Plays*, ed. Michael Hattaway (Cambridge, 2002)
Hattaway, 'Dating'	Michael Hattaway, 'Dating *As You Like It,* epilogues and prayers, and the problems of "As the dial hand tells o'er" ', *SQ*, 60.2 (2009), 154–67

Hattaway, 'Falstaff' Michael Hattaway, 'Superfluous Falstaff: morality and structure', in Pierre Kapitaniak and Jean-Michel Déprats (eds), *Shakespeare et l'excès* (Société Française Shakespeare, 2007), 75–87

Hawes Stephen Hawes, *Pastime of Pleasure* (1509) (EETS, vol. 173)

Hawkins Sherman H. Hawkins, '*Henry IV*: the structural problem revisited', *SQ*, 33.3 (1982), 278–301

Hazlitt, *Characters* William Hazlitt, *Characters of Shakespear's Plays* (1817); rpt. in *Hazlitt's Criticism of Shakespeare: A Selection*, ed. R.S. White (Lampeter, 1996)

Hazlitt, *Lectures* William Hazlitt, *Lectures on the English Comic Writers* (1819) (rpt. Oxford, 1920)

Heath Benjamin Heath, *A Revisal of Shakespeare's Text* (1765)

Helgerson Richard Helgerson, *Forms of Nationhood: The Elizabethan Writing of England* (Chicago, Ill., 1992)

Heywood *Dramatic Works of Thomas Heywood*, ed. R.H. Shepherd, 6 vols (1874)

Hillman Richard Hillman, '"Not Amurath an Amurath succeeds": playing doubles in Shakespeare's Henriad', *ELR*, 21 (1991), 161–89

Hinman Charlton Hinman, *The First Folio of Shakespeare. The Norton Facsimile* (New York, 1968)

Hirrel Michael Hirrel, 'Duration of performances and lengths of plays: how shall we beguile the lazy time?', *SQ*, 61.2 (2010), 159–82

Hist. Mss. *Historical Manuscripts Commission*, vols 4 and 5 (1892)

Hodgdon, *End* Barbara Hodgdon, *The End Crowns All: Closure and Contradiction in Shakespeare's History* (Princeton, NJ, 1991)

Hodgdon, *First Part* Barbara Hodgdon, *The First Part of King Henry the Fourth: Texts and Contexts* (Boston, Mass., 1997)

Hodgdon, *Part Two* Barbara Hodgdon, *Henry IV, Part Two*, Shakespeare in Performance Series (Manchester, 1993)

Hogan Charles Beecher Hogan, *Shakespeare in the Theatre 1701–1800: A Record of Performances in London*, 2 vols (Oxford, 1952–7)

Holderness, 'Carnival' Graham Holderness, '"Henry IV": carnival and history', in Graham Holderness (ed.), *Shakespeare's History Plays: Richard II to Henry V* (1992), 151–64

Holderness, *History* Graham Holderness, *Shakespeare's History* (Dublin, 1985)

Holinshed	Raphael Holinshed, *The Chronicles of England, Scotland, and Ireland*, 3 vols, 2nd edn (1587)
Honigmann	E.A.J. Honigmann, 'Sir John Oldcastle: Shakespeare's martyr', in John W. Mahon and Thomas A. Pendleton (eds), *Fanned and Winnowed Opinions: Shakespearean Essays Presented to Harold Jenkins* (1987), 118–32
Hope	Jonathan Hope, *Shakespeare's Grammar* (2003)
Hotson	Leslie Hotson, *Shakespeare versus Shallow* (1931)
Howard & Rackin	Jean E. Howard and Phyllis Rackin, *Engendering a Nation: A Feminist Account of Shakespeare's English Histories* (1997)
Hulme	Hilda M. Hulme, *Explorations in Shakespeare's Language: Some Problems of Lexical Meaning in the Dramatic Text* (1962)
Humphreys, *1H4*	*King Henry IV, Part 1*, ed. A.R. Humphreys, The Arden Shakespeare, Second Series (1960)
Hunt	Maurice Hunt, *Shakespeare's Religious Allusiveness: Its Play and Tolerance* (Aldershot, 2004)
Hunter	G.K. Hunter, '*Henry IV* and the Elizabethan two-part play', *RES*, n.s. 5 (1954), 236–48
Huntley	Richard Webster Huntley, *A Glossary of the Cotswold (Gloucestershire) Dialect* (1868)
Hutson	Lorna Hutson, 'Not the King's two bodies: reading the "body politic" in Shakespeare's *Henry IV, Parts 1 and 2*', in Victoria Kahn and Lorna Hutson (eds), *Rhetoric and Law in Early Modern Europe* (New Haven, Conn., 2001), 166–98
Hutton	Ronald Hutton, *The Rise and Fall of Merry England: The Ritual Year 1400–1700* (Oxford, 1994)
Iopollo	Grace Iopollo, *Revising Shakespeare* (Cambridge, Mass., 1991)
James	*The Poems Etc., of Richard James, B.D.*, ed. Alexander B. Grosart (1880)
Jenkins	Harold Jenkins, *The Structural Problem in Shakespeare's 'Henry the Fourth'* (1956); rpt. in Ernst Honigmann (ed.), *Structural Problems in Shakespeare: Lectures and Essays by Harold Jenkins* (2001), 3–22
Jensen	Phebe Jensen, *Religion and Revelry in Shakespeare's Festive World* (Cambridge, 2008)
JH	Jonathan Hope, personal correspondence
Johnson, *Crowne*	Richard Johnson, *Crowne Garland of Goulden Roses* (1612)
Johnson, *Notes*	Samuel Johnson, *Notes to Shakespeare*, vol. 2, *Histories*, ed. Arthur Sherbo (Los Angeles, Calif., 1957)

Johnson, *Shakespeare*	*Selections from Johnson on Shakespeare*, ed. Bertrand H. Bronson with Jean M. O'Meara (New Haven, Conn., 1986)
Jonson	*Ben Jonson*, ed. C.H. Herford and Percy and Evelyn Simpson, 11 vols (Oxford, 1925–52)
Jorgensen, 'Dastardly'	Paul A. Jorgensen, 'The "dastardly treachery" of Prince John of Lancaster', *PMLA*, 76 (December 1961), 488–92
Jorgensen, 'Rank'	Paul A. Jorgensen, 'Military rank in Shakespeare', *Huntington Library Quarterly*, 14.1 (1950), 17–41
Jorgensen, *World*	Paul A. Jorgensen, *Shakespeare's Military World* (Berkeley, Calif., 1956)
Jowett	John Jowett, 'Cuts and casting: author and book-keeper in the Folio text of "2 Henry IV"', *AUMLA* (*Journal of the Australasian Universities Languages and Literature Association*), 72 (1989), 275–95
Jowett & Taylor	John Jowett and Gary Taylor, 'The three texts of *2 Henry IV*', *SB*, 40 (1987), 31–50
Kastan, *1H4*	Shakespeare, *King Henry IV, Part 1*, ed. David Scott Kastan, The Arden Shakespeare, Third Series (2002)
Kastan, *Book*	David Scott Kastan, *Shakespeare and the Book* (Cambridge, 2001)
Kastan, *Companion*	David Scott Kastan (ed.), *A Companion to Shakespeare* (Oxford, 1999)
Kastan, 'English'	David Scott Kastan, 'Shakespeare and English history', in de Grazia & Wells, 167–82
Kastan, 'Oldcastle'	David Scott Kastan, 'Killed with hard opinions: Oldcastle, Falstaff, and the reformed text of *1 Henry IV*', in Laurie E. Maguire and Thomas L. Berger (eds), *Textual Formations and Reformations* (Newark, Del., 1998), 211–27
Kaul	Mythily Kaul, 'Greene, Harvey, Nashe and the "making" of Falstaff', in R.W. Desai (ed.), *Shakespeare the Man: New Decipherings* (Madison, NJ, 2014), 67–84
Kerrigan	John Kerrigan, '*Henry IV* and the death of Old Double', *Essays in Criticism*, 40.1 (1990), 24–53
King	T.J. King, *Casting Shakespeare's Plays: London Actors and their Roles, 1590–1642* (Cambridge, 1992)
Klein	David Klein, 'Time allotted for an Elizabethan performance', *SQ*, 18.4 (1967), 434–8
Knowles	Ronald Knowles (ed.), *Shakespeare and Carnival: After Bakhtin* (1998)

Kott	Jan Kott, *Shakespeare Our Contemporary* (1965)
Kyd	Thomas Kyd, *The Spanish Tragedy*, ed. Philip Edwards (1959)
Kyng	*Kyng Alisaunder* (EETS, Orig. ser. 227)
Laroque	François Laroque, 'Shakespeare's "battle of carnival and Lent": the Falstaff scenes reconsidered (*1 & 2 Henry IV*)', in Knowles, 83–96
Lee	Sidney Lee, *A Life of William Shakespeare* (1908)
Leiter	Samuel L. Leiter *et al.* (eds), *Shakespeare Around the Globe: A Guide to Notable Postwar Revivals* (New York, 1986)
Lever, 'French'	J.W. Lever, 'Shakespeare's French fruits', *SSt*, 6 (1953), 79–90
Lever, *Measure*	*Measure for Measure*, ed. J.W. Lever, The Arden Shakespeare, Second Series (1965)
Levine	Nina Levine, 'Extending credit in the *Henry IV* Plays', *SQ*, 51.4 (2000), 404–31
Liebler	Naomi Conn Liebler, ' "And is Old Double dead?": nation and nostalgia in *Henry IV, Part 2*', *SS 63* (2010), 78–88
Lindley, *Music*	David Lindley, *Shakespeare and Music* (2006)
Lindley, 'Sneak'	David Lindley, 'Who played Sneak?', unpublished paper
Linthicum	M. Channing Linthicum, *Costume in the Drama of Shakespeare and his Contemporaries* (Oxford, 1936)
Livio	Tito Livio, *Vita Henrici Quinti* (1437)
Lloyd	Lodowick Lloyd, *Stratagems of Jerusalem* (1602)
Long, J.	John H. Long, *Shakespeare's Use of Music: The Histories and Tragedies* (Gainesville, Fla., 1971)
Long, 'Perspective'	William B. Long, 'Perspective on provenance: the context of varying speech-heads', in George Walton Williams (ed.), *Shakespeare's Speech-Headings: Speaking the Speech in Shakespeare's Play* (Newark, Del., 1997), 21–44
Long, 'Precious'	William B. Long, ' "Precious few": English manuscript playbooks', in Kastan, *Companion*, 414–33
Long, 'Stage'	William B. Long, 'Stage-directions: a misinterpreted factor in determining textual provenance', in *TEXT* 2 (1985), 121–37
Lucan	Lucan, *Pharsalia: Dramatic Episodes of the Civil War*, trans. Robert Graves (West Drayton, 1956)
Lyly	John Lyly, *Euphues: The Anatomy of Wit* and *Euphues and His England*, ed. Leah Scragg (Manchester, 2003)

McCabe	Richard A. McCabe, 'Elizabethan satire and the Bishops' Ban of 1599', *YES*, 11 (1981), 188–93
McFarlane	K.B. McFarlane, *Lancastrian Kings and Lollard Knights* (Oxford, 1972)
McGee	C.E. McGee, '*2 Henry IV*: the last Tudor royal entry', in J.C. Gray (ed.), *Mirror up to Shakespeare* (Toronto, 1984), 149–58
McKeen	David McKeen, *A Memory of Honour: The Life of William Brooke, Lord Cobham*, 2 vols (Salzburg, 1986)
McKerrow	R.B. McKerrow, 'A suggestion regarding Shakespeare's manuscripts', *RES*, 11 (1935), 253–75
McMillin	Scott McMillin, *Henry IV, Part One*, Shakespeare in Performance Series (Manchester, 1991)
McMullan	*1 Henry IV*, ed. Gordon McMullan, Norton Critical Edition (New York, 2003)
Madden	D.H. Madden, *The Diary of Master William Silence* (1897)
Mahood, *Bit Parts*	M.M. Mahood, *Bit Parts in Shakespeare's Plays* (Cambridge, 1992)
Mahood, *Wordplay*	M.M. Mahood, *Shakespeare's Wordplay* (1957)
Malory	Sir Thomas Malory, *Le Morte D'Arthur* (1485)
Marcham	*The King's Office of the Revels 1610–1622*, ed. Frank Marcham (1925)
Marcus	Leah S. Marcus, *Puzzling Shakespeare: Local Reading and its Discontents* (Berkeley, Calif., 1988)
Marlowe	Christopher Marlowe, *Tamburlaine the Great*, ed. J.S. Cunningham, The Revels Plays (Manchester, 1981)
Marston	*The Plays of John Marston*, ed. H.H. Wood, 3 vols (Edinburgh, 1934–9)
Martin, R.	Randall Martin, 'Catholic Ephesians in *Henry IV, Part Two*', *N&Q*, 49.2 (2002), 225–6
Massinger	*The Plays and Poems of Philip Massinger*, ed. Philip Edwards and Colin Gibson, 5 vols (1976)
Matthews	*William Shakespeare's Henry IV*, adapted for Lincoln Center Theater by Dakin Matthews (North Hollywood, 2003)
Maxwell	J.C. Maxwell, '2 Henry IV, II.iv.91 ff.', *MLR*, 42 (1947), 485 (York, 2003)
Merlin	Bella Merlin, *With the Rogue's Company: 'Henry IV' at the National Theatre* (2005)
Middleton	*The Works of Thomas Middleton*, ed. A.H. Bullen, 8 vols (1885); and: *Thomas Middleton, The Collected Works*, ed. Gary Taylor and John Lavagnino (Oxford, 2007)

MLR	*Modern Language Review*
Montagu	Elizabeth Montagu, *An Essay on the Writings and Genius of Shakespeare* (1769)
Moorman	F.W. Moorman, 'Shakespeare's history-plays and Daniel's *Civile Wars*', *Shakespeare Jahrbuch*, 40 (1904), 69–83
More	*The Complete Works of St. Thomas More*, ed. Anthony S.G. Edwards *et al.*, vol. 1 (New Haven, Conn., 1997)
Morgann, *Criticism*	Maurice Morgann, *Shakespearian Criticism*, ed. Daniel A. Fineman (Oxford, 1972)
Morgann, *Falstaff*	Maurice Morgann, *An essay on the dramatic character of Sir John Falstaff* (1777)
Morris	Corbyn Morris, *An Essay Towards Fixing the True Standards of Wit, Humour, Raillery, Satire, and Ridicule* (1744)
Mowat, 'Q2 *Othello*'	Barbara A. Mowat, 'Q2 *Othello* and the 1606 "Acte to restraine Abuses of Players"', in Christa Jansohn and Bobo Plachta (eds), *Varianten – Variants – Variantes* (Tübingen, 2005), 91–106
Mowat, 'Reproduction'	Barbara A. Mowat, 'The reproduction of Shakespeare's texts', in de Grazia & Wells, 13–29
MSR	Malone Society Reprints
Mullaney	Steven Mullaney, *The Place of the Stage: License, Play, and Power in Renaissance England* (Chicago, Ill., 1988)
Munday	Anthony Munday, *John a Kent and John a Cumber*, ed. Arthur E. Pennell (New York, 1980)
Nashe, *Pierce*	Thomas Nashe, *Pierce Pennilesse* (1592)
Nashe, *Works*	*The Works of Thomas Nashe*, ed. Ronald B. McKerrow, 5 vols (1904–10); rpt. with supplemental notes by F.P. Wilson (Oxford, 1958)
N&Q	*Notes and Queries*
Neale	J.E. Neale, *Elizabeth I and Her Parliaments 1584–1601*, 2 vols (New York, 1966)
Norwood	Janice Norwood, 'A reference guide to performances of Shakespeare's plays in nineteenth century London', in Gail Marshall (ed.), *Shakespeare in the Nineteenth Century* (Cambridge, 2012), 348–415
Odell	George C.D. Odell, *Shakespeare from Betterton to Irving*, 2 vols (1920; rpt. New York, 1963)
OED	*Oxford English Dictionary*, 2nd edn, prepared by J.A. Simpson and E.S.C. Weiner (Oxford, 1989)
1 Oldcastle	Michael Drayton, Richard Hathway, Antony Munday and Robert Wilson, *The Oldcastle Controversy: Sir*

	John Oldcastle, Part 1 [and] *The Famous Victories of Henry V*, in Corbin & Sedge
Onions	C.T. Onions, *A Shakespeare Glossary* (1911), rev. Robert D. Eagleson (Oxford, 1986)
Orford	Peter Robert Orford, 'Rewriting History: Exploring the Individuality of Shakespeare's History Plays', PhD thesis, University of Birmingham (2006)
Ornstein	Robert Ornstein, *A Kingdom for a State: The Achievement of Shakespeare's History Plays* (Cambridge, Mass., 1972)
Otterbourne	Thomas Otterbourne, *Duo rerum Anglicarum scriptores veteres, Thomas Otterbourne et Joh. Whethamstede* (*c.* 1408), ed. Thomas Hearne (1732)
Ovid, *Heroides*	Ovid, *Heroides*, ed. and trans. Harold Isbell (Harmondsworth, 1990)
Ovid, *Met.*	*The Metamorphoses*, trans. Horace Gregory (New York, 1958)
Paradise Lost	John Milton, *Paradise Lost*, in *The Complete Poetry and Essential Prose of John Milton*, ed. William Kerrigan, John Rumrich and Stephen M. Fallon (New York, 2007)
Parker	Patricia Parker, *Literary Fat Ladies: Rhetoric, Gender, Property* (1987)
Partridge	Eric Partridge, *Shakespeare's Bawdy* (1947)
Patterson	Annabel Patterson, *Reading Holinshed's Chronicles* (Chicago, Ill., 1994)
Pechter	Edward Pechter, *What Was Shakespeare? Renaissance Plays and Changing Critical Practice* (Ithaca, NY, 1995)
Peele, *Alcazar*	George Peele, *The Battle of Alcazar*, in *The Stukeley Plays*, ed. Charles Edelman (Manchester, 2005)
Peele, *Works*	*The Life and Works of George Peele*, ed. Charles T. Prouty *et al.*, 3 vols (New Haven, Conn., 1961–70)
Pendleton	Thomas A. Pendleton, '"This is not the man": on calling Falstaff Falstaff', *Analytical & Enumerative Bibliography*, n.s. 4 (1990), 59–71
Plutarch	*The Lives of the Noble Grecians and Romans*, trans. Thomas North as *Plutarch's Lives*, 10 vols (1579; rpt. 1595)
Pollard, *Pirates*	A.W. Pollard, *Shakespeare's Fight with the Pirates* (1917; 2nd edn Cambridge, 1937)
Pollard, *Shakespeare*	A.W. Pollard, *Shakespeare Folios and Quartos* (1909)

Pollard, 'Variant'	A.W. Pollard, 'Variant settings in *2 Henry IV*', *TLS*, 21 October 1920, 680
Poole, 'Puritanism'	Kristen Poole, 'Facing Puritanism: Falstaff, Martin Marprelate, and the grotesque Puritan', in Knowles, 97–122
Poole, *Religion*	Kristen Poole, *Radical Religion from Shakespeare to Milton: Figures of Nonconformity in Early Modern England* (Cambridge, 2000)
Poole, 'Saints'	Kristen Poole, 'Saints alive! Falstaff, Martin Marprelate, and the staging of Puritanism', *SQ*, 46.1 (1995), 47–75
Potter	Lois Potter, 'The second tetralogy: performance as interpretation', in Dutton & Howard, 287–307
Prior	Moody E. Prior, 'Comic theory and the rejection of Falstaff', *SSt*, 9 (1976), 159–71
Proctor	Thomas Proctor, *Of the Knowledge and Conducte of Warres* (1578)
Prosser	Eleanor Prosser, *Shakespeare's Anonymous Editors: Scribe and Compositor in the Folio Text of '2 Henry IV'* (Stanford, Calif., 1981)
Pugliatti	Paola Pugliatti, *Shakespeare the Historian* (1996)
Puttenham	George Puttenham, *The Arte of English Poesie* (1589)
Rackin	Phyllis Rackin, *Stages of History: Shakespeare's English Chronicles* (Ithaca, NY, 1990)
RD	*Renaissance Drama*
Redmayne	Robert Redmayne, *Vita Henrici Quinti* (*c.* 1540)
Reese	M.M. Reese, *The Cease of Majesty: A Study of Shakespeare's History Plays* (New York, 1961)
RES	*Review of English Studies*
Rhodes	Neil Rhodes, 'Shakespearean grotesque: the Falstaff plays', in Georgia Brown (ed.), *Thomas Nashe* (Surrey, 2011), 47–93
Ribner	Irving Ribner, *The English History Play in the Age of Shakespeare* (Princeton, NJ, 1957)
Riche, *Path-Way*	Barnabe Riche, *Path-Way to Military Practise* (1587)
Riche, *Souldiers*	Barnabe Riche, *Souldiers Wishe to Britons Welfare* (1604)
Ritson	*Robin Hood: A Collection of All the Ancient Poems, Songs, and Ballads*, ed. Joseph Ritson, 2 vols (1795; rpt. 1832)
Robson	Simon Robson, *Choise of Change* (1585)
RP	Richard Proudfoot, personal correspondence
RSC	Royal Shakespeare Company

Sackville	Thomas Sackville, 'Complaint of Henry, Duke of Buckingham', in *The Mirror for Magistrates* (1563)
Sandys	*The Sermons of Edwin Sandys*, ed. J. Ayre (Cambridge, 1841)
Sarlos	Robert K. Sarlos, 'Dingelstedt's celebration of the tercentenary: Shakespeare's histories as a cycle', *Theatre Survey*, 5 (1964), 117–31
SB	*Studies in Bibliography*
Schlegel	August Wilhelm Schlegel, *Vorlesungen über dramatische Kunst und Literatur* (1808), trans. John Black and rev. Alexander Morrison as *A Course of Lectures on Dramatic Art and Literature* (1846)
Scott-Douglass	Amy Scott-Douglass, *Shakespeare Inside: The Bard Behind Bars* (New York, 2007)
Scott-Warren	Jason Scott-Warren, 'Was Elizabeth I Richard II?: the authenticity of Lambarde's "Conversation"', *RES*, 64 (2013) 208–30
Scoufos	Alice-Lyle Scoufos, *Shakespeare's Typological Satire: A Study of the Falstaff–Oldcastle Problem* (Athens, Ohio, 1979)
Shaaber, 'Unity'	Matthias A. Shaaber, 'The unity of *Henry IV*', in James G. McManaway *et al.* (eds), *Joseph Quincy Adams Memorial Studies* (Washington, DC, 1948), 217–27
Shaheen, *Biblical*	Naseeb Shaheen, *Biblical References in Shakespeare's Plays* (Newark, Del., 1999)
Shaheen, *History*	Naseeb Shaheen, *Biblical References in Shakespeare's History Plays* (Newark, Del., 1989)
Shapiro	James Shapiro, *1599: A Year in the Life of William Shakespeare* (New York, 2005)
Sharpe	Will Sharpe, 'A geography of history: considering the roles of place and distance within politics and 'history' in *2 Henry IV*', unpublished paper (2011)
Shaughnessy	Robert Shaughnessy, 'Falstaff's belly: pathos, prosthetics and performance', *SS 63* (2010), 63–77
Sidney	*The Complete Works of Sir Philip Sidney*, 3 vols, ed. Albert Feuillerat (Cambridge, 1912–23)
Sir Thomas More	Anthony Munday and Henry Chettle *et al.*, *Sir Thomas More*, ed. John Jowett, The Arden Shakespeare, Third Series (2011)
Sisson, *Readings*	C.J. Sisson, *New Readings in Shakespeare*, 2 vols (Cambridge, 1956)
Skinner	Quentin Skinner, *Reason and Rhetoric in the Philosophy of Hobbes* (Cambridge, 1996)

Smidt	Kristian Smidt, *Unconformities in Shakespeare's History Plays* (1982)
Smith, H.	Henry Smith, *Sermons* (1609)
Smith, J.	John Hazel Smith, 'The cancel in the Quarto of *2 Henry IV* revisited', *SQ*, 15.3 (1964), 173–8
Smith, T.	Sir Thomas Smith, *De Republica Anglorum* (1583)
Smythe	Sir John Smythe, *Instructions . . . and Orders Mylitarie* (1596)
Soliman	Thomas Kyd (?), *Soliman and Perseda*, ed. Lukas Erne, MSR (Oxford, 2014)
Speaight	Robert Speaight, *Shakespeare on the Stage: An Illustrated History of Shakespearian Performance* (1973)
SQ	*Shakespeare Quarterly*
SS	*Shakespeare Survey*
SSt	*Shakespeare Studies*
Stern	Tiffany Stern, 'Epilogues, prayers after plays, and Shakespeare's *2 Henry IV*', *Theatre Notebook*, 64.3 (2010), 122–9
Stone	Lawrence Stone, *The Crisis of the Aristocracy 1558–1641* (Oxford, 1965)
Stow, *Annales*	John Stow, *Annales, or a general Chronicle of England* (1592)
Stow, *Survey*	John Stow, *A Survey of London* (1598), ed. Charles Lethbridge Kingsford, 2 vols (Oxford, 1908)
Streitberger	W.R. Streitberger, 'A letter from Edmund Tilney to Sir William More', *Surrey Archaeological Collections*, 71 (1977), 225–31
Stubbes	Phillip Stubbes, *The Anatomy of Abuses*, ed. Margaret Jane Kidnie (Tempe, Ariz., 2002)
Sugden	Edward H. Sugden, *A Topographical Dictionary to the Works of Shakespeare* (Manchester, 1925)
Sutcliffe	Matthew Sutcliffe, *The Practice, Proceedings, and Lawes of Armes* (1593)
Taylor, 'Cobham'	Gary Taylor, 'William Shakespeare, Richard James and the house of Cobham', *RES*, n.s. 38.151 (1987), 334–54
Taylor, 'Fortunes'	Gary Taylor, 'The fortunes of Oldcastle', *SS 38* (1985), 85–100
Taylor, ''Swounds'	Gary Taylor, ''Swounds revisited: theatrical, editorial, and literary expurgation', in Taylor & Jowett, 51–106
Taylor & Jowett	Gary Taylor and John Jowett, *Shakespeare Reshaped: 1606–1623* (Oxford, 1993)
Theophrastus	*Theophrastus: Characters*, ed. and trans. James Diggle (Cambridge, 2007)

Thomas	Keith Thomas, *Religion and the Decline of Magic: Studies in Popular Beliefs in Sixteenth and Seventeenth Century England* (1971)
Thorne	Alison Thorne, 'There is a history in all men's lives: reinventing history in *2 Henry IV*', in Dermot Cavanagh, Stuart Hampton-Reeves and Stephen Longstaffe (eds), *Shakespeare's Histories and Counter-Histories* (Manchester, 2006), 49–66
Tiffany	Grace Tiffany, 'Puritanism in comic history: exposing royalty in the Henry plays', *SSt*, 26 (1998), 256–87
Tilley	M.P. Tilley, *A Dictionary of the Proverbs in England in the Sixteenth and Seventeenth Centuries* (Ann Arbor, Mich., 1950)
Tillyard	E.M.W. Tillyard, *Shakespeare's History Plays* (1944)
Timon	*Timon*, ed. J.C. Bulman and J.M. Nosworthy, MSR (Oxford, 1980)
TLS	*Times Literary Supplement*
Tobin	J.J.M. Tobin, 'Another psalm for Falstaff', *N&Q*, 251.3 (2004), 283–4
Traub	Valerie Traub, 'Prince Hal's Falstaff: positioning psychoanalysis and the female reproductive body', *SQ*, 40.4 (1989), 456–74
Trounstine	Jean Trounstine, *Shakespeare Behind Bars: The Power of Drama in a Women's Prison* (New York, 2001)
True Reporte	*The True Reporte of the Service in Britanie Performed lately by the Honourable Knight Sir Iohn Norreys . . . before Guignand* (1591)
Trussler	*The Royal Shakespeare Company, 1982–83*, ed. Simon Trussler (Stratford-upon-Avon, 1983)
Tusser	Thomas Tusser, *A Hundred Good Pointes of Husbandrie* (1557), ed. Dorothy Hartley (1931)
TxC	Stanley Wells and Gary Taylor, with John Jowett and William Montgomery, *William Shakespeare: A Textual Companion* (Oxford, 1987)
Tynan	Kenneth Tynan, *He that Plays the King* (1950)
Tyrwhitt	Thomas Tyrwhitt, *Observations and conjectures upon some passages of Shakespeare* (Oxford, 1766)
Udall	*The Apophthegmes of Erasmus*, trans. Nicholas Udall (1564)
Ulrici	Hermann Ulrici, *Ueber Shakespeare's dramatische kunst* (1839), trans. Alexander Morrison as *Shakespeare's Dramatic Art* (1846)

Upton	John Upton, *Critical Observations on Shakespeare* (1746; 2nd edn, 1748); rpt. in Vickers, *Shakespeare*, vol. 3
Urkowitz	Steven Urkowitz, 'Did Shakespeare's company cut long plays down to two hours playing time?', *Shakespeare Bulletin*, 30.3 (2012), 239–62
Vaughan	Henry H. Vaughan, *New Readings and New Renderings of Shakespeare's Tragedies*, 2 vols (1878–81); 2nd edn, 3 vols (1886)
Vickers, *Artistry*	Brian Vickers, *The Artistry of Shakespeare's Prose* (1968)
Vickers, *Shakespeare*	*Shakespeare, The Critical Heritage*, ed. Brian Vickers, 6 vols (1974–81)
Virgil, *Aen.*	Virgil, *The Aeneid*, trans. W.F. Jackson Knight (1956)
Walker, 'Cancelled'	Alice Walker, 'The cancelled lines in *2 Henry IV*, IV.i.93, 95', *The Library*, 5th series, 6.2 (1951), 115–16
Walker, *Textual*	Alice Walker, *Textual Problems of the First Folio* (Cambridge, 1953)
Walker, W.	William S. Walker, *A Critical Examination of Shakespeare's Text*, 3 vols (1860)
Wallace	Dewey D. Wallace, Jr, 'George Gifford, Puritan propaganda and popular religion in Elizabethan England', *The Sixteenth Century Journal*, 9 (1978), 27–49
Walsham	Alexandra Walsham, *Church Papists: Catholicism, Controversy and Confessional Polemic in Early Modern England* (Woodbridge, NY, 1993)
Walsingham	Thomas Walsingham, *Historia Anglicana* (1418), ed. H.T. Riley, 2 vols (1863)
Webster	John Webster, *The Duchess of Malfi*, ed. John Russell Brown (1964)
Weil	Judith Weil, *Service and Dependency in Shakespeare's Plays* (Cambridge, 2005)
Weil & Weil	*The First Part of King Henry IV*, ed. Herbert Weil and Judith Weil, New Cambridge Shakespeare (Cambridge, 1997)
Weimann	Robert Weimann, *Shakespeare and the Popular Tradition in the Theater* (Baltimore, Md, 1978)
Welles, *Chimes*	Orson Welles, *Chimes at Midnight: Orson Welles, Director*, ed. Bridget Gellert Lyons (New Brunswick, NJ, 1988)
Welles, *Playscripts*	*Orson Welles on Shakespeare: The WPA and Mercury Theatre Playscripts*, ed. Richard France (New York, 1990)

Wells	Stanley Wells (ed.), *Shakespeare in the Theatre: An Anthology of Criticism* (Oxford, 1997)
Werstine, 'Editing"	Paul Werstine, 'Editing Shakespeare and editing without Shakespeare: Wilson, McKerrow, Greg, Bowers, Tanselle, and copy-text editing', *TEXT* 13 (2000), 27–53
Werstine, 'McKerrow's'	Paul Werstine, 'McKerrow's "suggestion" and twentieth-century Shakespeare textual criticism', *RD*, 19 (1988), 149–73; rpt. in. Stephen Orgel and Sean Keilen (eds), *Shakespeare: The Critical Complex* (New York, 1999), 153–77
Werstine, *Manuscripts*	Paul Werstine, *Early Modern Playhouse Manuscripts and the Editing of Shakespeare* (Cambridge, 2012)
Werstine, 'Plays'	Paul Werstine, 'Plays in manuscript', in John D. Cox and David Scott Kastan (eds), *A New History of Early English Drama* (New York, 1997), 481–97
Werstine, 'Post-theory'	Paul Werstine, 'Post-theory problems in Shakespeare editing', *YES*, 29 (1999), 103–111
Werstine, 'Shakespeare'	Paul Werstine, 'Shakespeare more or less: A.W. Pollard and twentieth-century Shakespeare editing', *Florilegium*, 16 (1999), 125–45
West	G. West, 'Scroop's quarrel: a note on *2 Henry IV*, IV.i.88–96', *English Language Notes*, 18.3 (1981), 174–5
Whigham	Frank Whigham, *Seizures of the Will in Early Modern English Drama* (Cambridge, 1996)
White, P.W.	Paul Whitfield White, 'Shakespeare, the Cobhams, and the dynamics of theatrical patronage', in Paul Whitfield White and Suzanne R. Westfall (eds), *Shakespeare and Theatrical Patronage in Early Modern England* (Cambridge, 2002), 64–89
Wiles	David Wiles, *Shakespeare's Clown: Actor and Text in the Elizabethan Playhouse* (Cambridge, 1987)
Williams, *Dictionary*	Gordon Williams, *A Dictionary of Sexual Language and Imagery in Shakespearean and Stuart Literature*, 3 vols (1994)
Williams, *Glossary*	Gordon Williams, *A Glossary of Shakespeare's Sexual Language* (1997)
Williams, *Revolution*	Gordon Williams, *Shakespeare, Sex, and the Print Revolution* (1996)
Williams, 'Second'	George Walton Williams, 'Second thoughts on Falstaff's name', *SQ*, 30.1 (1979), 82–84

Williams, 'Text'	George Walton Williams, 'The text of *2 Henry IV*: facts and problems', *SSt*, 9 (1976), 173–82
Williamson	Audrey Williamson, *Old Vic Drama* (1948)
Wilson, *Dictionary*	F.P. Wilson, *Oxford Dictionary of English Proverbs* (Oxford, 1970)
Wilson, *First Part*	*The First Part of the History of Henry IV*, ed. J. Dover Wilson (Cambridge, 1946)
Wilson, *Fortunes*	John Dover Wilson, *The Fortunes of Falstaff* (Cambridge, 1943)
Wilson, 'Origins'	John Dover Wilson, 'The origins and development of Shakespeare's *Henry IV*', *The Library*, 4th series, 26 (1945), 2–16
Wilson & Pollard	J. Dover Wilson (and A.W. Pollard), 'Shakespeare's hand in the play of "Sir Thomas More" ', *TLS*, 8 May 1919, 251
Winter	William Winter, *Shakespeare on the Stage: Third Series* (New York, 1916)
Woolf, *Reading*	D.R. Woolf, *Reading History in Early Modern England* (Cambridge, 2000)
Woolf, *Social*	Daniel Woolf, *The Social Circulation of the Past: English Historical Culture 1500–1730* (Oxford, 2003)
Worsley & Wilson	T.C. Worsley and J. Dover Wilson, *Shakespeare's Histories at Stratford 1951* (1952)
Woudhuysen	Shakespeare, *Love's Labour's Lost*, ed. H.R. Woudhuysen, The Arden Shakespeare, Third Series (1998)
Wright, *Dictionary*	Joseph Wright, *English Dialect Dictionary*, 6 vols (1898–1905)
Wright, G.	George T. Wright, *Shakespeare's Metrical Art* (Berkeley, Calif., 1988)
Yachnin	Paul Yachnin, 'History, theatricality, and the "structural problem" in the *Henry IV* plays', *Philological Quarterly*, 70 (1991), 163–79; rpt. in *1 Henry IV*, ed. Gordon McMullan, Norton Critical Editions (New York, 2003), 114–28
YES	*Yearbook of English Studies*

INDEX

This index covers references in the Introduction, the Commentary and the Appendices but excludes those in the Textual Notes. The abbreviation 'n.' is used for footnotes in the Introduction and the Appendices but not for Commentary notes. Page numbers in italics indicate figures.